Evaluating Trade and Economic Relations Between India and Southeast Asia

Anita Medhekar
Central Queensland University, Australia

Harpreet Kaur
Central Queensland University, Australia

IGI Global
PUBLISHER of TIMELY KNOWLEDGE

A volume in the Advances in Finance, Accounting, and Economics (AFAE) Book Series

Published in the United States of America by
IGI Global
Business Science Reference (an imprint of IGI Global)
701 E. Chocolate Avenue
Hershey PA, USA 17033
Tel: 717-533-8845
Fax: 717-533-8661
E-mail: cust@igi-global.com
Web site: http://www.igi-global.com

Library of Congress Cataloging-in-Publication Data

Names: Medhekar, Anita, 1962- editor | Kaur, Harpreet, 1960 -editor
Title: Evaluating trade and economic relations between India and Southeast Asia / Anita Medhekar, Harpreet Kaur, editors.
Description: Hershey, PA : Business Science Reference, [2022] | Includes bibliographical references and index. | Summary: "This book investigates the trade and economic linkages between India and Southeast Asia, covering aspects of business, trade and commerce in an attempt to benefit stakeholders to understand the opportunities and challenges while strengthening the cultural ties to each other"-- Provided by publisher.
Identifiers: LCCN 2020018648 (print) | LCCN 2020018649 (ebook) | ISBN 9781799857747 (hardcover) | ISBN 9781799857754 (paperback) | ISBN 9781799857761 (ebook)
Subjects: LCSH: India--Foreign economic relations--Southeast Asia. | Southeast Asia--Foreign economic relations--India. | India--Commerce--Southeast Asia. | Southeast Asia--Commerce--India.
Classification: LCC HF1590.15.S64 E83 2021 (print) | LCC HF1590.15.S64 (ebook) | DDC 337.54059--dc23
LC record available at https://lccn.loc.gov/2020018648
LC ebook record available at https://lccn.loc.gov/2020018649

This book is published in the IGI Global book series Advances in Finance, Accounting, and Economics (AFAE) (ISSN: 2327-5677; eISSN: 2327-5685)

British Cataloguing in Publication Data
A Cataloguing in Publication record for this book is available from the British Library.

For electronic access to this publication, please contact: eresources@igi-global.com.

Advances in Finance, Accounting, and Economics (AFAE) Book Series

Ahmed Driouchi
Al Akhawayn University, Morocco

ISSN:2327-5677
EISSN:2327-5685

Mission

In our changing economic and business environment, it is important to consider the financial changes occurring internationally as well as within individual organizations and business environments. Understanding these changes as well as the factors that influence them is crucial in preparing for our financial future and ensuring economic sustainability and growth.

The **Advances in Finance, Accounting, and Economics (AFAE)** book series aims to publish comprehensive and informative titles in all areas of economics and economic theory, finance, and accounting to assist in advancing the available knowledge and providing for further research development in these dynamic fields.

Coverage

- Interest Rates and Annuities
- Statistical Analysis
- International Trade
- Economic Indices and Quantitative Economic Methods
- Economics of Natural and Environmental Resources
- International Economics
- Applied Finance
- Borrowing and Lending
- Economics of Risks, Uncertainty, Ambiguity, and Insurance
- Field Research

IGI Global is currently accepting manuscripts for publication within this series. To submit a proposal for a volume in this series, please contact our Acquisition Editors at Acquisitions@igi-global.com or visit: http://www.igi-global.com/publish/.

The Advances in Finance, Accounting, and Economics (AFAE) Book Series (ISSN 2327-5677) is published by IGI Global, 701 E. Chocolate Avenue, Hershey, PA 17033-1240, USA, www.igi-global.com. This series is composed of titles available for purchase individually; each title is edited to be contextually exclusive from any other title within the series. For pricing and ordering information please visit http://www.igi-global.com/book-series/advances-finance-accounting-economics/73685. Postmaster: Send all address changes to above address.

Titles in this Series

For a list of additional titles in this series, please visit: http://www.igi-global.com/book-series/advances-finance-accounting-economics/73685

Handbook of Research on Changing World Economic Order in the Post-Pandemic Period
Sushanta Kumar Mahapatra (IBS Hyderabad, The ICFAI Foundation for Higher Education, India) and Vishal Sarin (Lovely Professional University, India)
Business Science Reference • © 2022 • 470pp • H/C (ISBN: 9781799868965) • US $295.00

Handbook of Research on Developing Circular, Digital, and Green Economies in Asia
Patricia Ordóñez de Pablos (The University of Oviedo, Spain)
Business Science Reference • © 2022 • 521pp • H/C (ISBN: 9781799886785) • US $225.00

Handbook of Research on Climate Change and the Sustainable Financial Sector
Odunayo Magret Olarewaju (Durban University of Technology, South Africa) and Idris Olayiwola Ganiyu (University of KwaZulu-Natal, South Africa)
Business Science Reference • © 2021 • 573pp • H/C (ISBN: 9781799879671) • US $295.00

CSR and Management Accounting Challenges in a Time of Global Crises
Ionica Oncioiu (Titu Maiorescu University, Romania)
Business Science Reference • © 2021 • 278pp • H/C (ISBN: 9781799880691) • US $215.00

Impact of Global Issues on International Trade
Ahu Coşkun Özer (Marmara University, Turkey)
Business Science Reference • © 2021 • 291pp • H/C (ISBN: 9781799883142) • US $215.00

Handbook of Research on the Empirical Aspects of Strategic Trade Negotiations and Management
Nuno Crespo (ISCTE – Instituto Universitário de Lisboa, Portugal) and Nadia Simoes (ISCTE – Instituto Universitário de Lisboa, Portugal)
Business Science Reference • © 2021 • 446pp • H/C (ISBN: 9781799875680) • US $265.00

Handbook of Research on Financial Management During Economic Downturn and Recovery
Nuno Miguel Teixeira (Center for Research in Business and Administration, School of Business Sciences, Polytechnic Institute of Setúbal, Portugal) and Inês Lisboa (CARME, School of Management and Technology, Polytechnic of Leiria, Portugal)
Business Science Reference • © 2021 • 566pp • H/C (ISBN: 9781799866435) • US $295.00

IGI Global
PUBLISHER of TIMELY KNOWLEDGE

701 East Chocolate Avenue, Hershey, PA 17033, USA
Tel: 717-533-8845 x100 • Fax: 717-533-8661
E-Mail: cust@igi-global.com • www.igi-global.com

We dedicate this book in the loving memory of our parents:

Shaila Chitnis-Medhekar, Sharad Medhekar, Sudershan Narula, and Late Daljeet S. Narula

Editorial Advisory Board

List of Reviewers

Table of Contents

Detailed Table of Contents

export potential to Brunei, Cambodia, and Thailand amongst Southeast Asian countries.

The chapter analyzes the role of institutions, sources of funding/assistance, and source information in terms of food security and extension policies. The result of the research shows the information on problematic areas in policy implementation with respect to food security and extension policies in terms of poverty reduction. The role of the institution, assistance, and source information are useful in the implementation of other policy sectors in the future, because similar issues or problems may be avoided by taking precautions not to repeat the same mistakes or by applying measures that address the implementation issues. In this way, policy implementation can be carried out effectively, and the outcomes will meet the policy objectives.

In 1992 Narshima Rao launched the Look East Policy to tend towards south-eastern neighbours and also to connect with East Asia. The main goal of the Look East Policy is to increase economic cooperation and strategic defence cooperation to balance the growing Chinese domination over South-East Asia and the sea. In 2014, the Government of India would come up with a new phase of the Look East Policy and announced the Act East Policy that can be considered as the new age of economic development, industrialization, and trade. The Act East Policy and Look East Policy both have some similarity. The chapter analyzes the India-ASEAN trade activities after the formation of ASEAN bloc specifically from 2001 to 2018. To fulfil the objectives of study trade indices, similarity and diversification has been used. The study found that with changing framework of India's foreign policy for ASEAN, trade share of India and ASEAN in the bi-lateral arrangement significantly increased.

The ongoing pandemic has drastically affected the Bay of Bengal countries. Greater cooperation is suggested as these countries are fighting against the common problem and challenge of the coronavirus pandemic. Regional cooperation has become important to overcome the barriers that are mainly pandemic driven which has resulted in an increase in the cost of production and trade in the region. The chapter discusses the benefits that India is likely to get with higher integration with the immediate neighbouring countries with special reference to BIMSTEC region. The Bay of Bengal Initiative for Multi-Sectoral Technical and Economic Cooperation (BIMSTEC) region is a dynamic region with trade as the driver of growth. The region is often overlapped with SAARC regional grouping with almost similar members. BIMSTEC gained its lost recognition in the year 2016, due to its high growth potential to develop sustainably.

The Bay of Bengal Initiative for Multi-Sectoral Technical and Economic Cooperation (BIMSTEC) is a regional cooperation between Bangladesh, India, Sri Lanka, Bhutan, Nepal, Myanmar, and Thailand since the liberalization of these economies. Member countries need to be more proactive for integrated regional cooperative hubs to enhance trade and investment opportunities in health and other sectors of the economy to cope with the pandemic and its impact. The aim of this chapter is to show how BIMSTEC, a regional cooperative body, can be a driver for socio-economic development, inter-regional trade, and investment opportunities for BIMSTEC countries and cope with COVID-19 and its impact. The BIMSTEC area is home to approximately 1.6 billion citizens accounting to 22% of the worlds inhabitants with a joint gross domestic product (GDP) of 2.7 trillion. Unemployment situation of 'new poor' can be tackled through close cooperation among the BIMSTEC nations in an effective manner to achieve 'pareto optimality' through trade and investment among member countries.

This chapter attempts economic analysis of the impact of COVID-19 on the economies of Southeast Asia and India. The impact on tourist footfalls, tourism revenues, national GDPs, and employment will be focused on. The challenges thrown by COVID-19 relating to safety, hygiene, mindshare, and digital tools could help evolve a structurally different tourism landscape in the post-COVID-19 world. Long haul travel may not happen soon, and the countries must develop products incorporating proximity tourism, vaccine tourism, and domestic tourism. Intra-ASEAN travel will have to be developed further to offset the losses caused by the curtailment of long-haul travel. Historical and cultural linkages between Southeast Asia and India should be leveraged to extend Intra-ASEAN travel to the Northeastern States of India. This would create a win-win situation for Southeast Asia as well as India. Targeted investments and subsidies aimed at confidence building of travelers and other stakeholders will go a long way to minimize the economic impact of external shock caused by COVID-19.

India and Thailand have a long-term relationship. Both countries geographically are in extended neighbourhood and share a maritime boundary. Both countries taken together constitute 18.6% of the world's population. They have deep rooted similar history, cultures, philosophies, and religions. They share the same link of Buddhism. Even Hinduism has some reflection on Thai architecture, arts, names of cities, sculpture, dance, drama, and literature. In this chapter, Thailand has been chosen due to physical proximity, cultural, and ideological similarities with India. India and Thailand have celebrated more than 70 years of bilateral diplomatic relationship. In the past two decades, with regular political exchanges of growing trade and investment, India's relationship with Thailand has grown into a comprehensive partnership. India's 'Act East' policy has been complemented by Thailand's 'Act West' policy in bringing the two countries closer. Both countries are important regional partners under BIMSTEC linking Northeastern Indian states with Southeast Asia.

Spiritual tourism is one of the oldest forms of tourism. The purpose of this chapter is to review the key reasons for lack of promotion of investment and economic relations via tourism services related to Buddhist heritage and spiritual tourism circuit and sites to Southeast Asian countries as well as to domestic tourists. Sarnath, in Varanasi, is the hub of Buddhism in India, opened in 2016. There is road, rail, and air connection from Sarnath to various other Buddhist sites. This circuit can be promoted in counties of Southeast Asia and South Asia to spiritual followers of Buddhism as well as 'New Age' Buddhists. Thailand, Japan, and Korea have invested in spiritual infrastructure in Sarnath for their citizens who visit for Buddhist pilgrimage. This chapter identifies the challenges, opportunities, and provides recommendations for the Indian government to provide a business friendly environment and to encourage foreign direct investment for state-of-the-art infrastructure development from Southeast Asian nations around the Buddhist spiritual tourism circuit.

Foreign trade relations are due to the measures of foreign policy adopted and applied by a nation. The Indian foreign policy was majorly West focused and has been substituted with a more nuanced and inclusive policy that promotes the enhancement of security, diplomatic, and trade ties with the Eastern nations. The "Look East" Policy was executed in 1991 and it was substituted as "Act East" in 2014 by Prime Minister Narendra Modi who provided a modern push to the Indian regional diplomacy by concentration on Southeast Asian neighbours. This policy is known as a multi-faceted technique to create strategic connections with numerous individual nations as well as build a lasting relation with Association of Southeast Asian Nations (ASEAN). In this regard, this chapter evaluates the role and responsibility of border states in revitalizing regional socio, cultural, and economic ties with the neighbouring countries. This chapter evaluates how the participation of Northeastern Indian States provides opportunities for New Delhi in ensuring a tremendous regional diplomacy with ASEAN.

Foreword

It is a matter of pride and pleasure for me to write few words for this book being authored by distinguished faculty. *Evaluating Trade and Economic Relations Between India and Southeast Asia* is the requirement of the day keeping in mind the changing geopolitical scenario and increasing interaction between the nations of this region. The foreign policy and diplomacy of a country is the backbone of its economic relations with other countries. The sole objective of the foreign policy is to make maximum friends, minimum enemies or no enemies, to safeguard national interests and to promote economic relations with other countries. While evaluating trade and economic relations of India with the other Southeast Asian countries, this fact cannot be ignored that in International Diplomacy, size matters. The bigger and more powerful a country is, the greater its clout. Simultaneously, much depends on how a small country project itself and interacts with other countries.

This book attempts to cover a vast canvas. There is a strong historical, cultural and trade bonding among the nations of this region and it became all the more important after India's "Look East" to Act East policy and BIMSTEC to promote economic relations. The distinguished authors have attempted to cover all burning topics under fourteen chapters including food security, tourism opportunities, healthcare sector, trading blocs etc. The importance of trade between India and Southeast Asian countries, have been intelligently described and explained through this book. The subject matter is presented in a lucid style so that it could be easily understood even by those who do not have any academic background of Economics.

The international trade plays a very important role in the economic development and sustenance of the nations in this region. The potential markets are not confined to the national frontiers, resulting in, the overseas markets have become the primary markets. COVID-19 continues to besiege developing Asia, but vaccines are changing the nature of pandemic. Quicker rollouts of vaccines, successful containment, and strong global demand are enabling growth in some economies. Many nations in this region are expected to witness positive real GDP growth rates. International trade has been central to economic growth for regions worldwide. The growth begins after the integration of the economy of a nation with global economy. Gradually, the economies of this region are bound to bounce back towards growth trajectory.

The chapters build up the foundations for understanding how the countries work and then explore the key regional issues that concerns the discipline- taking readers from no knowledge to competency. The journey starts by examining and reflecting those international relations is always adapting to events and is therefore never-ending journey of exploring the opportunities for promoting economic relations. This book is designed to capture attention with an engaging narrative that places the reader inside crucial issues so that they can understand how the things work in economic relations among various countries.

The sincere efforts of the authors stand appreciated.

Mahesh Gandhi
Council of International Universities, Germany & Ignited Brains, India & Indus Foundation, USA & The Millennium Schools, India & University of Chicago, USA & Indian Institute of Foreign Trade, India & All India Rail Safety Council, Government of India, India

Foreword

I was really excited to see the planned new book *Evaluating Trade and Economic Relations Between India and Southeast Asia.* It undertakes to examine various aspects of trade and economic relations between the South Asian giant India and the very vibrant and increasingly integrating region Southeast Asia. The book promises to be of great interest and help to a wide range of people, starting from relevant government officials and policy makers to diplomats, from researchers to academics and students, as well as businesses.

The authors have looked at historical, traditional ties between India and Southeast Asia; the very important and long cultural and civilisational interactions morphing into close commercial, economic and strategic ties over the years. They have examined how various policies of these countries reflect the tremendous premium they attach to these relations. India's look East/Act East policies have featured frequently in their discourses. they have sifted through great stores of information and shared relevant selections from them in their papers. While they have provided lot of invaluable raw information, they have also undertaken very useful analyses of issues of comparative advantages enjoyed by certain products from certain countries in some of the other countries.

Some of the authors have looked into the trade and economic ties between India and Southeast Asia in a comprehensive way, while others have looked at specific issues like tourism, food security, health care, access to information, impact of the pandemic and post-pandemic possibilities as well as a general look at the future. Some authors have looked at underpinning significance of the various regional forums like BIMSTEC, SAARC and ASEAN. Some have attempted to look at the challenges and competitive impacts posed by China, the other influential giant in the region. In this context, they have tried to examine the possible role of the QUAD and the Indo-Pacific Strategy.

While the authors try to raise and answer many relevant questions, I feel that this book will be equally important for the questions it may raise in the readers' mind but have not attempted to answer. I have an abiding interest in these questions and issues as I spent over nineteen years of my diplomatic career in this region. I also served as Director, South Asia and Director General, SAARC in my tenures at the Headquarters. Some of the questions and issues that readers of the book will want to look for would be how other countries of South Asia could benefit from India-- Southeast Asia ties? Could they also be included in the relevant supply chains and reap some dividends?

Historically, Indian influencers in Southeast Asia have generally followed the large-scale migration out of India. The migrants carried their culture, including cuisine, dress, language and religion -- not Buddhism alone, but also Hinduism and Islam. How do these ethno-cultural influences impact the trade and economic ties and how they will continue to do so? What impact, if any, does India's Neighbourhood First Policy have on these ties?

China is the largest trading partner of India and many of the ASEAN countries. It happens to be a larger trade partner of all ASEAN countries compared to India. A comparative study could shed interesting light on many of the related issues. The preference of some of the authors to use the QUAD and the Indo-Pacific strategy to contain Chinese influence begs the question as to whether a kind of coexistence and complementarity between the Belt and Road Initiative(BRI) touted by China and the Indo-Pacific Strategy could prove more beneficial to all countries involved and help diffuse the current atmosphere of confrontation and conflict?

I remember, when I was serving as Bangladesh's High Commissioner in Singapore, the Prime Minister of Singapore proudly said that Singapore was aiming to fly high on the two strong and large wings -- China and India. Perhaps, all other countries in South and Southeast Asia could benefit greatly from enhanced cooperation with both the two regional giants.

I wish the book, its authors, and publishers great success. I also wish the readers great and exciting reading. I am sure, many scholars and researchers will be encouraged to follow up on many of the issues raised in the book and many of the unanswered questions that the discourses in the book obviously lead up to.

Ambassador Munshi Faiz Ahmad
Independent Researcher, Bangladesh

Foreword

This book titled *Evaluating Trade and Economic Relations Between India and Southeast Asia* is well-timed and makes a valuable and constructive contribution to the literature, theoretical framework, practical managerial and policy implications pertaining to the economies of South Asia and Southeast Asian Countries, given the changing geo-political environment since the Global Financial Crisis, of 2009-10, and now Global Health Pandemic of COVID -19. The book provides a background to past, present, and future challenges and opportunities in building strong trade and investment economic relationships between India and the Association of Southeast Asian Nations (ASEAN) and Bay of Bengal Initiative for Multi-Sectoral Technical and Economic Cooperation (BIMSTEC) group of nations, to Japan in the far East.

In all the fourteen chapters author have provided innovative recommendations and policy implications to enhance cooperation and connectivity for trade, investment, infrastructure development, food security, health infrastructure, promote tourism and economic relations among India, ASEAN and the BIMSTEC group of countries. In "Look -East Act -East Policy: India and South -East Asian Economic Cooperation", Anita Medhekar & Harpreet Kaur write the sine qua non of the policy, that has commenced in 1990s and renewed in 2016 which has been negated since 1947. In "Indian and ASEAN Trade Relations with Changing Framework of India's Look East Policy", Gurmeet Kaur and Jyotsana Bhangu ascertain that how to foster the economic cooperation and strategic defense cooperation to balance the growing Chinese domination over the Southeast Asia and the Indo-Pacific seas.

Further, in "BIMSTEC – Silver Lining in the Cloud for India During the Pandemic Period", Namita Kapoor and Tavishi Tewary explain how Bay of Bengal Initiative for Multi-Sectoral Technical and Economic Cooperation can integrate the region. Further, as ongoing pandemic has had a dire consequence due to supply chain disruptions on the Bay of Bengal Countries and how regional cooperation has become important to not only achieve the Sustainable Development Goals but also overcome the increased cost of production and encourage international, technological cooperation and trade in region.

In addition to above, in "An Analysis of Tourism Opportunities and Challenges Post COVID -19 between India and Southeast Asia", Munish Duggal and Harpreet Kaur state the impact and challenges thrown by COVID-19 on economies of Southeast Asia and India and adding historical and cultural linkages between Southeast Asia and India. Further, few chapters in the book also critically evaluate, the consolidating the relationship between India and Thailand through tourism because of similar history, cultures, philosophies and religions. In chapter 13 that reads "Japan India Trade Relations: History, Catalysts and Challenges", S. Jobayear Ahmed writes how historic, political, and cultural affiliation between India and Japan led towards positive economic relations and his qualitative approach towards the study also recommends the future course of action for economic development and bilateral relations post- COVID-19.

Having 37 years of experience in higher education, I may say that this book has been drafted very constructively and informatively and the language is very lucid. It is not only useful for the researchers and students of economics, management, and India and Southeast Asian Studies, but also an important tool for students of geo-political, foreign policy, diplomats and international relations. This book can also be an important toolkit for various international business organisations, CEOs, President and Vice President of Multi-National Corporations.

Daniel Jacob Penkar
Sinhgad Institute of Management, Pune, India

Preface

Evaluating Trade and Economic Relations Between India and Southeast Asia sheds light on the trade, economic linkages and their impact on the nations in the past, present, and for the future. Owing to a strong cultural and historical bond, India and Southeast Asia have progressed rapidly. Despite there being political and ideological differences between these two entities, it may not hamper the strong bond, as there are many common shared values among these nations. The history of these nations identifies that the cooperation between them in terms of trade and commerce is not upheld, as per the given potential of these nations. The Indian economy was linked with Southeast Asian countries under the "Look East" policy, which has been re-energized in 2014, under the present Modi government. Now, the "Look East" policy is practically more vibrant than ever before with the motto "Act East." This policy facilitates these countries in emphasizing the importance of better regional connectivity for tourism as well as robust trade, commerce, investment, and building sustainable economic relationships. There is very little understanding of the challenges and opportunities it has posed for the public and private institutions and stakeholders of these policies.

In addition, the Southeast Asian Association along with Bay of Bengal Initiative for Multi-Sectoral Technical and Economic Cooperation (BIMSTEC) has led to a phenomenal growth in terms of imports and exports for these countries and will do so in the post-pandemic period. A free trade area framework established by BIMSTEC, comprising of five South Asian Association of Regional Cooperation (SAARC) countries (Bhutan, Bangladesh, India, Sri Lanka, and Nepal) and two - Thailand and Burma being members of Association of Southeast Asian Nations (ASEAN), are a gateway for Northeastern Indian states, including for other SAARC countries. Aim is to enhance trade, tourism, investment, technical and economic cooperation at multisectoral level between the member countries. Further, the recent Quadrilateral 2020 and September QUAD 2021 meeting of the foreign ministers and leaders from the four democratic countries of Australia, India, Japan, and the USA, with shared values has highlighted the importance of India's Act-East policy to have meaningful dialogue and work together with regional partners to strengthen their economies trade, investment, climate change, produce COVID-19 vaccine, shared cyber security and maritime security concerns for free and open strategy in the Indo-Pacific region to promote peace, stability and sustainable development of the Indo-Pacific countries.

This book is a valuable contribution given the changing geo-political environment pre- and post-pandemic. The 14 chapters study unravel and explore the importance of economic relations between India and Southeast Asian economies, to evaluate whether the win-win strategy works for the strengthening of these countries in terms of both trade relations and political integrity, as well as cooperatively in facing common enemies across international boundaries for cyber, border, and maritime security. Some of the topics covered include food security, tourism opportunities, health care sector, trading blocs, foreign trade, investment, and economic relations between India, BIMSTEC, and Southeast Asian countries. The journey for developing this book has been a long one, where international authors have made a valuable contribution to the body of knowledge and brought forward innovative recommendations and solutions to enhance economic and trade relations between India, Southeast Asian region, and BIMSTEC group of countries.

This book provides relevant theoretical framework and cases in the challenges and opportunities of Act-East policy and benefits from regional groupings of BIMSTEC and ASEAN to enhance relations between India and Southeast Asia that affect trade, investment, and the economy in the 21st century and post-pandemic years, to solve common problems, shares issues and meet the United Nations Sustainable Development Goals. There is a challenge of establishing regional grouping and relationships with appropriate economic strategies for implementing policies for the mutual benefit of India and the Southeast Asian nations, given the changing geo-political environment, security tensions in the South China Seas and the Indo-Pacific region, and the trade and travel restrictions and its impact on the nations during the pandemic period. This book is a valuable reference tool for economists, government officials, policymakers, trade analysts, practitioners, researchers, academicians, and students interested in evaluating economic, trade and investment, opportunities between India and Southeast Asian and BIMSTEC group of nations.

ORGANISATION OF THE BOOK

The following is the brief description of the 14 chapters organised in this book.

Chapter 1 titled "Look-East Act-East Policy: India and South-East Asian Economic Cooperation" introduces the significance of improving relations between India and ASEAN- Southeast Asia, providing a detailed literature review and discussing the importance of "Look-East to Act East" for economic development opportunities for the mutual benefit of the two. In order to reactivate the moribund Look East Policy of the Rao government, the Modi Government of India announced the Act East Policy in 2014, that can be considered as the new age of economic development, industrialization and trade with the Southeast Asian nations going as far East as Japan and Australia. The chapter also evaluates and provides examples of various measures taken by the Indian Government to enhance business, trade and tourism opportunities between India and Southeast Asian countries. Discussions and recommendations along with policy implications of Look-East to Act-East have been highlighted along with opportunities, threats, and challenges. India and Southeast Asian countries share some common traditions. Bilateral and multilateral relationships can be developed and enhanced through Traditions/culture, Trade, Tourism, exchange of Talent and Technological expertise (Five-Ts). The authors also present a conceptual cooperation and security model for achieving economic, both internal, and external security and stability through bilateral and multi-lateral trade agreements (in terms of social, economic, environmental and defence) required to bring stability through bi-lateral and multi-lateral agreements for peace, progress, and prosperity in the region. Final section provides very clear future research directions and conclusions to enhance the knowledge in theory and practice for the economic development of the Northeastern states of India and cooperation with ASEAN for connectivity, commerce, and capacity building for mutual benefit of ASEAN and India.

Chapter 2 titled "Estimating Export Potential of India to Southeast Asian Countries: Panel Gravity Model Approach" estimates the export potential of India with Southeast Asian countries in order to determine new export markets and increase the share of exports in gross domestic product by applying the panel gravity model. This chapter aims to determine the potential Southeast Asian export market for India by comparing the potential export level with the actual exports from India to Southeast Asian countries. The frequency of the variables is annual and belong to the period between 1996 and 2018. On the basis of this analyses, it has been determined that Indian exports to Myanmar, Vietnam, and Singapore are slightly above its export potential. While it exports to Indonesia, Malaysia and the Philippines are far above its export potential. In addition to this, it is determined that India has a high export potential with Brunei, Cambodia, and Thailand amongst Southeast Asian countries. Therefore it is essential to have geographically closer and sustainable export potential markets for Indian goods, to increase its bilateral export potential with Southeast Asian countries.

Chapter 3 titled "The Role of Institutional Assistance and Information Source on Food Security Policy Analysis: An Indonesian Perspective" provides an analysis on the role of institutional sources of funding assistance, information sources in term of food security and extension policy. The findings of the research show that information sources are a problematic area in policy implementation with respect to food security and extension policy in terms of poverty reduction. The role of the institutional assistance and information sources are useful in the implementation of other policy sectors in the future because similar issues or problems may be avoided by taking precautions not to repeat the same mistakes or by applying measures which address the implementation issues. In this way policy implementation can be carried out effectively and the outcomes will meet the policy objectives of food security in Indonesia, which can be applied to India as well.

Chapter 4 titled "Indian and ASEAN Trade Relations with Changing Framework of India's Look East Policy" provides an overview and examines the Look-East policy launched in 1992 by the Rao Government of India, to connect with Southeast Asia, to increase economic and strategic defence cooperation to balance the growing Chinese domination over the Southeast Asia and the Indian Ocean - Bay of Bengal maritime region. The Act East policy attempts to analyse the India-ASEAN trade activities after the formation of ASEAN bloc specifically from 2001 to 2018, to fulfil the objectives of trade and investment opportunities and cooperation for security. This chapter tried to explore India's Look East Policy and Act East Policy in relation to export competitiveness of India and ASEAN countries. By making use of secondary data from the World Bank, Reserve Bank of India (RBI), Asian Development Bank (ADB), United Nation Conference on trade and development (UNCTAD) and United Nation Commodity trade statistic Database from 1992 to 2019, trade indices such as: trade similarity index, diversification index, complementarity index, trade openness and revealed Comparative Advantage (RCA) were developed to analyse different aspects of foreign trade relation of India and ASEAN over a period of time. The study revealed comparative advantage of India for groundnuts, shelled whether or not broken (excluding seed for sowing, roasted or otherwise), light-vessels, fire-floats, floating cranes and other vessels, the navigability of which is the navigability of which is subsidiary to their main function (excluding dredgers, floating or submersible drilling or production platforms; fishing vessels and warships), copper, refined, in the form of cathodes and section of cathodes, frozen shrimps and prawns, even smoked whether in shell or not, include shrimps and prawns in shell, cooked by steaming or by boiling in water (excluding cold-water shrimps and prawns) and frozen, boneless meat of bovine animals having RCA greater than 1. The study also found that with changing framework of India's foreign policy for ASEAN, trade share of India and ASEAN in the bi-lateral arrangement has significantly increased.

Chapter 5 titled "BIMSTEC: A Silver Lining in the Cloud for India During the Pandemic Period" is about enhancing greater cooperation during and post- pandemic period with Southeast Asian countries, to cooperate and combat against the common problem and challenge of the Coronavirus driven social and economic impact on the respective economies and the regions. Therefore, regional cooperation has become important to overcome the barriers which are mainly pandemic driven and resulting in an increase in the cost of production and reduced trade in the region, because of supply chain disruptions. The chapter discusses the benefits that India is likely to get from higher integration with the neighbouring countries, with special reference to Bay of Bengal Initiative for Multi-Sectoral Technical and Economic Cooperation (BIMSTEC) region. The BIMSTEC initiative is a dynamic forum with focus on international trade as the driver of economic growth, with technological cooperation. The BIMSTEC region overlaps with the South Asian Association for Regional Cooperation (SAARC) with 5 member countries from SAARC (Nepal, India, Bhutan, Bangladesh and Sri Lanka) besides Burma and Thailand from Southeast Asia. BIMSTEC gained its lost recognition in the year 2016, resulting from high growth potential to develop sustainably and work together to solve common concerns of BIMSTEC countries to achieve United Nations Sustainable Development Goals.

Chapter 6 titled "The BIMSTEC Free Trade Area: Economic Cooperation, Opportunities, and Challenges" critically discusses the Bay of Bengal Initiative for Multi-Sectoral Technical and Economic Cooperation (BIMSTEC) between Bangladesh, India, Sri Lanka, Bhutan, Nepal, Myanmar, and Thailand since the liberalization of the Indian economy. It is suggested that member countries need to be more proactive for forming integrated regional cooperative hubs to enhance trade and investment opportunities in health and other sectors of the economy, to cope with the pandemic and its impact post-COVID-19. The aim of this chapter is how BIMSTEC, a regional cooperative organisation can be a driver for socio-economic development, inter-regional trade, and investment opportunities for BIMSTEC countries and cope with COVID-19 and its impact? The BIMSTEC region is home to approximately 1.6 billion citizens accounting to 22% of the worlds inhabitants with a joint Gross Domestic Product (GDP) of 2.7 trillion economy. Unemployment situation of 'New Poor' can be tackled, though close cooperation among the BIMSTEC nations in an effective manner to achieve 'Pareto Optimality' through enhancing trade and investment among member countries.

Chapter 7 titled "An Analysis of Tourism Opportunities and Challenges Post COVID-19 Between India and Southeast Asia" provides an economic analysis of the impact of COVID-19 on economies of Southeast Asia and India. The spread of COVID-19 forced countries to announce lockdowns and impose restrictions on movement of people resulting in loss of GDP, employment and almost complete suspension of contact-based services such as travel and tourism. The challenges thrown by COVID-19 relating to safety, hygiene, mindshare & digital tools could help evolve a structurally different tourism landscape in post COVID-19 World. Technical aspects of lockdown and restrictiveness in terms of the Oxford Coronavirus Government Response Tracker (OxCGRT) project, which calculates a Stringency Index and a Containment and Health Index, a composite measure of indicators like testing policy, the extent of contact tracing, requirements to wear face masks, and policies around vaccine rollout are covered in chapter. They suggest that as long-haul, travel may not happen soon, the intra-ASEAN travel will have to be developed further to offset the losses caused by the curtailment of distance travel. This paper suggests that historical and cultural linkages between South-East Asia and India should be leveraged to extend intra-ASEAN travel to North- Eastern States of India. This would create a win-win situation for South-East Asia as well as India. Targeted investments and subsidies aimed at confidence building of travellers and other stakeholders will go a long way to minimize the economic impact of external shock caused by COVID-19. This chapter has immense contemporary value as it analyses the challenges arising out of these lockdowns and restrictions along with responses of the governments. After setting the background by mentioning the macro-economic impact of the COVID-19 on the global economy, it moves on to cover in detail the impact on travel and tourism sectors in India and the South-East Asia. In the process of unravelling the economic impact using quantitative as well as qualitative data, the chapter provides a framework for understanding the challenges and opportunities and how the individual ASEAN countries and India formulated policy responses to these disruptions and challenges.

Chapter 8 titled "Strengthening Bilateral Relationship Between India and Thailand through Tourism" is about enhancing post-pandemic tourism between traditional trading partners, India and Thailand. Both countries not only share a long-term trade relationship but also share maritime boundaries around the Bay of Bengal and the Indian Ocean region. Both countries taken together constitute 18.6% of the world population. They have deep rooted similar history, cultures, philosophies, and religions. They share the same link of spirituality connected with Buddhism and Hinduism. Cities in Thailand are also named after the names of cities from great epic Ramayana and show reflection on Thailand's Buddhist temples, architecture, arts, sculpture, dance, drama, and literature. The authors choose Thailand due to geographical proximity, cultural and ideological similarities with India. India and Thailand have celebrated more than 70 years of bilateral diplomatic relationship. Since nearly for two decades, with regular political exchanges, growing trade and investment, India's relationship with Thailand has grown into a comprehensive partnership. India's 'Act East' policy has been complemented by Thailand's 'Act West' policy in bringing the two countries closer. Both countries are important regional partners under Bay of Bengal Initiative for Multi-Sectoral Technical and Economic Cooperation (BIMSTEC) linking Northeastern Indian states with Southeast Asian countries.

Chapter 9 titled "Promoting Trade and Economic Relations Via Buddhist Spiritual Tourism Circuit Between India and Southeast Asia" is exploring a niche segment of tourism which India can develop and promote to Southeast Asian Countries. Spiritual Tourism is one of the oldest forms of tourism. The purpose of this chapter is to review the key reasons for lack of promotion of investment and economic relations via tourism services related to Indian Buddhist Heritage and Spiritual Tourism Circuit and sites to Southeast Asian Countries as well as to domestic tourists. Sarnath, in Varanasi is the hub of Buddhism in India, opened in 2016. There is road, rail, and air connection from Sarnath to various other Buddhist sites in India. This circuit can be promoted in counties of Southeast Asia and South Asia, to spiritual followers of Buddhism as well as 'New Age' Buddhists. Thailand, Japan, and Korea have invested in spiritual infrastructure in Sarnath for their citizens who visit India for Buddhist pilgrimage. Along with providing literature review on the spiritual tourism and the economic importance of spiritual tourism development and promotion for economic progress, prosperity and peace in regional and global context, the authors introduce the growing significance of Buddhist spiritual tourism circuit in India. Current chapter also explores the key reasons for lack of promotion of investment, and economic relations via tourism services related to Buddhist Heritage and Spiritual Tourism Circuit and sites to Southeast Asian Countries as well as to domestic tourist places. This chapter identifies the challenges and opportunities for sustainable development of Buddhist spiritual tourism circuit and provides recommendations to the Indian government to create business friendly environment to promote trade, travel, tourism and encourage foreign direct investment for state-of-the-art infrastructure development from Southeast Asian nations around the Buddhist spiritual tourism circuit, to enhance economic relationships between India and southeast Asian countries.

Chapter 10 titled "Evaluating the Future Possibilities of the India-ASEAN Economic Relations: A Critical Assessment" links the Foreign Trade Relations to the measures of Foreign Policy adopted and applied by a Nation. The Foreign Policy that was majorly west focused earlier has been substituted by a more nuanced and inclusive policy promoting the enhancement of security, diplomatic and trade ties with the Eastern Nations. In this Section, with the literature review to the initiation of "Look East" Policy, executed in 1991, and its substitution with "Act East Policy" in 2014 by Prime Minister Narendra Modi, which provided a modern push to the India's regional diplomacy by concentrating on neighbours has been discussed. This Policy is known as a multi-pronged and multi-faceted technique to create strategic connections with numerous individual Nations as well as building a lasting relation with Association of Southeast Asian Nations (ASEAN). In this respect, this chapter would evaluate the role and responsibility of border-states in revitalizing regional socio, cultural, and economic ties with the neighbouring states. This paper also discusses as to how the participation of Northeastern States of India, provides opportunities for New Delhi in ensuring a tremendous regional diplomacy with ASEAN countries to foster sustainable international trade relations.

Chapter 11 titled "A Critical Evaluation of India's Look-East to Act-East Policy" critically examines the Look East Policy, launched in 1992 with the objective of economic integration with Southeast Asian countries. After discussing the objectives and differences of both the policies, measures taken were also highlighted. Not only this, but achievement of objectives was also critically evaluated. This would provide an opportunity for growth and transformation of the country because these were the fastest-growing economies. The Indian economy was then opening to the rest of the world. The succession of Look East Policy to Act East Policy in 2014 gave importance to economic cooperation, greater connectivity, and security ties. By departing from the traditional foreign policy imperatives this policy aims to be focussing on the removal of barriers and remoteness of Northeast India. It represents the development model for the far eastern region of India. There has been a sizeable increase in trade and foreign investment opportunities since the launch of the policy with Southeast Asian countries. This policy has helped India strengthen its place amongst its Southeast Asian neighbours and the global economy. In the absence of this policy, the North-eastern states could not have developed much, due to the failure of the trickling down of the benefits of growth from export-oriented and capital-intensive projects. This chapter should be useful for students of International Economics and Development Economics. They will be able to decipher the policy implications for future changes in the policy. This chapter will also interest the researchers of foreign policy and economic relations.

Chapter 12 titled "Compromised Healthcare Sector of India and Other Southeast Asian Countries: Opportunities for Foreign Collaboration" aims to focus on the umpteen challenges in healthcare sector of India which temper the possibility of partnerships with India and the ten South-East Asian Countries. India's public expenditure on healthcare sector is only 1.2% of GDP, and there is an urgent need to prioritize health expenditure due to pandemic. Since the new economic policy reform in 1991, Indian Government has privatized the healthcare sector. In the second wave of COVID-19, public and private hospitals are operating at full capacity with shortages of life-saving medicines, oxygen, ventilators, and vaccines. Lower middle-income groups and homeless poor people are suffering the most. Nations of the world, medical scientific community and pharmaceutical companies put their resources together to discover a vaccine for coronavirus, within a year. To have an effective and sustainable model of doing business in health care it is important to have partnerships and integrating best practices, innovations, for improving and providing equitable and affordable access to healthcare, in a second largest populated country as India.

Chapter 13 titled "Japan-India Trade Relations: History, Catalysts, and Challenges" explores the Japan-India relationship, which is supported by historic, political, and cultural affiliation, which has over many decades usually led towards positive investment, economic and trade relationship between the two nations. Although Japan-India relationship is a few centuries old but surprisingly the statistics of Japan India trade hardly exhibits any mentionable growth, except the recent upward trend in exports to Japan. In fact, India almost failed to capture the near home market even with the growth (about 1% market share) instead of Indian government's efforts to capture greater market share in various aspects. This chapter uses secondary data to qualitatively analyse the objectives of exploring the History, Catalysts, and Impediments of Japan India Trade Relations and recommends the future course of action post-pandemic. The study recommends completion of India's mega projects with Japanese investment, Japan's policy reform, taxation and supportive policy reform, arrangement of social life of the foreigners, zero corruption, forgery and harassment, efficiency, effectiveness, linguistic skill and cultural understanding of human resources and creating opportunity and building organizational capacities between the two countries.

Chapter 14 titled "A Collaborative Study of Foreign Trade and Economic Performance of India with Southeast Asian Countries" discusses critically the Indian economy's state which historically was in distress at the brink of the country's independence since 1947 from the colonial rule and partition. India was fulfilling the development needs of the colonial rulers for 200 years. The state, that should have been responsible for break-through innovations in agriculture and industry, refused to play even a minor role in this regard. On the other hand, during the 20th century, the world was seeing India's accelerated development and expansion in agriculture, industry, improvement in health and growth of Gross Domestic Product for the overall economy. Based on the OECD's Economic Outlook 2021, the Indian economy contracted by 7.7% in 2020 as domestic consumption declined. Despite the COVID-19 related downturn, the OECD has projected India's economy to expand by 9.9% and become the fastest-growing G20 economy of the world. This chapter quantitatively analyses foreign trade of Indian economy with some Asian countries. This research reviews the factors accelerating the development of India's economy, achievement, and obstacles of India's growth of foreign trade and economic performance.

In the past decade the world has experienced global financial crisis, European crisis, and now the global pandemic health emergency for the last 2 years 2020-2021. With COVID-19 driven recessionary impact due to social distancing, travel, and trade restrictions, closing of national and international borders, the economies of the countries have experienced high unemployment rate, negative Gross Domestic Product growth rate and global supply chain disruptions of goods and services. The book is timely and aims to be a leading source of information for having bilateral and multilateral cooperation between India, BIMSTEC and Southeast Asian nations. These nations need to come together to face the future global challenges and cultivate the economic opportunities to find solutions to the shared problems of health crisis due to COVID-19, food security, cyber security, education, climate change, unemployment, infrastructure development, technological innovation, and border and maritime security concerns.

We acknowledge the valuable contributions made by the chapter contributors; without their support the book would not have been completed. Finally, we would like to thank the blind reviewers, Editorial Advisory Board, Maria Rohde - Book Development Coordinator, and the IGI Global Development Team for their regular help and support during the various stages of development of the book.

Anita Medhekar
Central Queensland University, Australia

Harpreet Kaur
Central Queensland University, Australia

Acknowledgment

We appreciate and acknowledge the efforts of everyone towards the development of this book. We wish to sincerely thank all for their invaluable contributions.

We are deeply grateful to all the Authors, to their responses for the call for chapter proposals, revisions involved and chapter submissions for this book on *Evaluating Trade and Economic Relations Between India and Southeast Asia*. Without their valuable contribution we would not have been able to complete this book successfully.

We are also thankful to the blind reviewers of the chapters, who made their contribution by providing invaluable suggestions and feedback, which were implemented by the authors. All the chapter authors made valuable contribution making many revisions to the chapters for presenting their research, and improvements in the process of chapter development.

The work progressed in highly coordinated manner despite the contributors belonging to different parts of the world, in this global pandemic situation.

This work carries, behind it, the encouragement, support and good wishes of many friends and colleagues, though it is difficult to mention their names individually.

We would also like to thank and also acknowledge members of the IGI-Global Publishers' team, Jan Travers Director of Intellectual Property & Contracts for their continuing guidance, coordination, suggestions, and support during the development stage of this book.

Finally, we would like to thank IGI Global publishers for their commitment to international research and publish on current topics impacting the changing geopolitical trade and economic relations .

Anita Medhekar
Central Queensland University, Australia

Harpreet Kaur
Central Queensland University, Australia

Chapter 1
Look-East Act-East Policy:
India and South-East Asian Economic Cooperation

Anita Medhekar
https://orcid.org/0000-0002-6791-4056
Central Queensland University, Australia

Harpreet Kaur
Central Queensland University, Australia

ABSTRACT

The Indian Government's 'Look-East' foreign policy initiative of 1990s and renewed as Act-East in 2016, with countries bordering with the North-Eastern States of India, is a platform to cultivate and strengthen socio-economic and political ties by establishing strategic relationships with the Southeast Asian economies through bi-lateral and multilateral trade, which has been neglected since 1947. The aim of the Act-East policy is to build cultural, commerce, connectivity, and capacity building via trade, tourism, tradition, talent, and technology transfer between North-Eastern India and the Asian neighbours. This chapter critically evaluates measures taken by the Indian Government under this policy to enhance business and trade opportunities with Southeast Asian countries for peace, achieving sustainable development goals, and economic progress.

BACKGROUND

The North-Eastern region of India for decades has remained isolated and underdeveloped since independence, due to successive central governments not having a concrete economic and infrastructure development and security strategy. Hence, it has been cut off from the mainstream Indian economy and is geographically connected by a narrow Siliguri corridor, and land-locked, giving rise to separatist insurgency, illegal migration, supply chain disruptions, and border conflict (Rahmati, Ali, & Kamraju, 2020). There have been old cultural and trade ties between India and South-East Asia for centuries and

DOI: 10.4018/978-1-7998-5774-7.ch001

more so from the British colonial times, when the Indians under the colonial rule as slaves helped British, colonise Malaysia, Burma, Singapore, and Fiji.

In the 21st century, India has emerged as a major nuclear economic power and fifth largest economy in terms of GDP (purchasing power parity) in the world, with second largest population and market following China. The Indian Government's foreign policy initiative of the 1990s 'Look East Policy' (LEP) is to transform the economy by forming economic trade agreements and linkages with countries bordering with the eight North-Eastern states of India. The LEP has been a platform to establish, cultivate, transform, and strengthen socio-economic, trade, tourism, cultural, political and security ties, to form strategic relationships with the ASEAN economies through bi-lateral and multi-lateral trade agreements, which has been neglected since 1962 Indo-China war (Das & Thomas, 2016; Haokip, 2015; Naidu, 2013; Ziipao, 2018).

In 1990's, after the Indian financial and economic crisis, the 'New Economic Policy Reform' initiatives were introduced along with the Look East Policy, by then Prime Minister Narasimha Rao in 1991, to liberalise, privatise and open the economy for foreign investment and trade. The main aim was to provide opportunities for developing the Eastern-States of India and establishing trade, commerce and foreign relationships, economic and defence security cooperation, and engaging with South-Asian countries and the group of ASEAN neighbouring countries. Under the Prime Minister Manmohan Singh, 15 bilateral and multilateral agreements were signed between 2006 to 2011. Further, in 2006, India formed strategic cooperation with the large economies of Brazil, Russia, China, and South Africa (BRICS) on various international platforms such as climate change and world trade organisation (Haokip, 2011, 2015; Ram, 2012; Rana, 2018).

The initial aim in the 1990's of 'Look East Policy' introduced at the end of cold-war, was to engage diplomatically at foreign policy level and cooperate with Association of South-East Asian Nations (ASEAN) countries on economic bilateral relationship, strategic institutional partnerships and play a balancing role with emerging China's encouraging trade and economic development policy, maritime power and influence in the ASEAN region (Banlaoi, 2003; Bajpaee, 2017; Das & Thomas, 2016; Downie, 2015; Goldberg, 2019; Lee, 2015; Nguyen, 2017; Ollapally, 2018; Pant, 2013; Singh, 2018: Yhome, 2015). Further, to exchange expertise on various sectors like agriculture, health, education, fisheries, information technology, energy, transportation, security, and defence, and to enhance and cultivate people-to-people contact for reaping economic benefits from trade, research collaborations, travel and tourism (Naidu, 2013).

"Look East" foreign policy was dormant for over a decade, with no concrete outcome from the various agreements. The Modi BJP-Government in November 2014 at East Asia Summit in Myanmar announced the extension of "Look East Policy" (LEP) to "Act East Policy" (AEP) with the signing of ASEAN Trade-in-Services and Investment, and closer economic and security ties. The revamped AEP was to be proactive and engaging to promote cultural ties, economic cooperation and integration, along with strategic continuous relationship with Indian Eastern States, and establish bilateral and multilateral agreements at regional level with South-East Asian countries and beyond to Japan, South Korea, Australia in the Indo-Pacific to form strategic partnership for economic, political, defence-security of land and sea corridors and social-cultural cooperation to reap potential mutual economic benefits (Ganguly, 2017; Hall, 2016; Lee, 2015; Muni, 2011; Ngaibiakching & Pande, 2020; Nguyen, 2017; Ranjan, 2016; Singh, 2018).

Government's AEP policy is based on four pillars of cooperation- culture, connectivity, commerce, and capacity building (Ministry of External Affairs, 2016). The current BJP government has taken steps to further establish and develop bi-lateral strategic partnership with Singapore, Australia, Indonesia, Japan, Malaysia, Korea, and Vietnam. The government is actively engaging and signing various multi-lateral partnerships such as ASEAN -Regional Forum, East- Asia Summit, Asia Cooperation Dialogue (ACD), Mekong Ganga Cooperation (MGC). Further, for economic trade and development opportunities and to curb the increasing strategic influence and rise of China in South-Asia and South-East Asia (Banlaoi, 2003; Cho & Park, 2013), cooperative agreements are made with the Indian Ocean Rim Association (IORA), India-Pacific Island Cooperation (FIPIC), Bangladesh, Bhutan, and India (BBIN); South Asian Free-Trade Agreement (SAFTA), and Bay of Bengal Initiative for Multi-Sectoral Technical and Economic Cooperation (BIMSTEC). Few of the key projects include India-Myanmar-Thailand Trilateral Highway, Rhi-Tiddim Road, Border Haats/Markets and Kaladan Multi-mode Transit Transport (Ministry of External Affairs, 2016). The 2021 QUAD summit between the four democratic nations USA, Japan, Australia, and India, is a multilateral security framework is an example of strategic cooperation to counterbalance the power of China in the Indo-Pacific region, but also India's Act- East policy for security and vaccination alliance for global pandemic (D'Ambrogio, 2021).

Literature review indicates that publications on business, trade, tourism and economic relations between India and Southeast Asia and Look East Policy is an emerging area of research in context of India, with no empirical findings, but based on historical papers. This conceptual research chapter suggests that Look-East—Act-East Policy of India will bring awareness, connectivity, trade, and tourism development opportunities firstly to the North-eastern States of India, which has been neglected since 1947 independence. Further, it will ast as a catalyst to engage with the bordering neighbouring nations to the East and Southeast Asia, for creating inclusive opportunities for business, bilateral trade, tourism, employment, and sustainable development for their mutual benefit. The aim of this chapter is to: (i) examine and evaluate critically "Look East-Act East" policy of India in providing opportunities for business, trade, tourism and improving economic relations between India and Southeast Asia in achieving sustainable development goals (SDGs).

This chapter is structured as follows. The introductory section of the chapter introduces the importance and significance of improving relations between India and ASEAN- Southeast Asia. Section-2 provides the literature review and discusses the importance of "Look-East to Act-East" policy' that provides economic development opportunities for mutual benefit. Section-3 evaluates and provides examples of various measures taken by the Indian Government to enhance, business, trade and tourism opportunities between India and Southeast Asian countries. Section-4 presents discussions and recommendations for 'Look-East to Act-East' policy implications, opportunities threats and challenges and a conceptual model for achieving internal, economic, and external security and stability through bi and multi-lateral agreements. Final section covers future research directions and conclusions to advance the knowledge in theory and practice for the economic development of the North-Eastern states and cooperation with ASEAN for connectivity, commerce, and capacity building for mutual benefit.

BACKGROUND LITERATURE

Indian financial crisis of 1990's led to the adoption and implementation of new economic policy reforms— liberalisation and privatisation and opening up the economy for international trade and Look East Policy, under the Rao government. As seen from the map in Figure-1 eight (8) North-Eastern states are land-locked, with no access to trade route by sea, are the legacy of the British colonial rule which divided India and left forever with narrow chicken-neck corridors and crocked borders and emerging lifelong border disputes. The four Eastern states share borders with Bangladesh to its East, which is a key partner for maintaining stability in the north-eastern region of India and bridge to South- East Asia and reginal connectivity hub. (Ali, 2018; Shringla, 2018). Map in Figure-1 shows Arunachal Pradesh shares border with Bhutan, China, and Burma. Further, Indian states of Mizoram, Manipur, Nagaland and Arunachala Pradesh share border with China and Burma; and Sikkim with Nepal, Bhutan, and China. Further, Bangladesh and Burma being the only South-East Asian countries, provide the trade corridor to the landlocked North-Eastern Indian states by land and sea, to rest of Southeast Asia.

Figure 1. Map of North-Eastern States of India
Source: Google map

The foreign policy discourse in India is changing, from the Nehruvian non-alignment to economic liberalisation and multi-alignment social logic discourse in the post-cold war era of "international unity in diversity, state sovereignty, enlightened self-interest, non-violence and non-discrimination" (Wojczewski, 2019, p. 185). Since the Modi Government came to power in 2014, it is leaning towards the globalised world with changing geo-political dynamics and leaning towards Indo-Pacific Australian region amidst the global security concerns, as a multi-aligned player in the Central-Asia, South-Asia, and the South- East Asian region to live in peaceful co-existence and cooperation with multilateral partnership agreements with the world, for national security, global health vaccine alliance, and economic development and at the same time asserting Indian autonomy over its geographical territory, with no territorial ambitions over others territory (Bajpaee, 2017; D'Ambrogio, 202; Hall, 2016; Nguyen, 2017; Ranjan, 2016; Wojczewski, 2019).

1. Look East to Act East Policy Initiative

The 'Look-East' foreign policy which was launched in 1990 by the central government in New Delhi, could be interpreted in two ways. First to develop the North-eastern seven states of India and secondly to form diplomatic relations with the Southeast Asian neighbouring countries for bilateral and intra-regional trade, investment, and economic development opportunities. However, in both contexts not much has been done for the last two decades as the eastern region of India is still underdeveloped and lacks infrastructure development and investment in road, rail, airports, seaports, health, education, tourism, industry, and agriculture sectors (Bajpaee, 2017; Lee, 2015; Nguyen, 2017). It is imperative that the eastern states capitals become the future growth cities to establish cross-border relationships for commerce, communication, and capacity building through infrastructure development projects, essential for achieving the SDGs of the eight eastern states of India in particular.

Against this backdrop in 2006, India has signed various bi-lateral and multi-lateral agreements to improve economic relations with the East-Asian neighbours. Such as, 'South Asian Free Trade Agreement' (SAFTA) with neighbouring countries of Bhutan, Bangladesh, Maldives, Nepal, Pakistan and SriLanka. In 2010, India signed free trade agreement with ASEAN countries (AIFTA), and the 'Bay of Bengal Initiatives Multi-Sectoral Technical and Economic Cooperation' (BIMSTEC). In 2009, India's LEP signed a 'Long Term Cooperative Partnership for Peace and Prosperity' with ASEAN countries and India -ASEAN Asian Free Trade agreement and in 2014 partnership with ASEAN was graduated from being economic, political, and socio-cultural to being strategic (Das & Thomas, 2016; Haokip, 2015; Hussain, 2017). Under the Modi Prime Ministership since 2014, the Look-East foreign policy was remained and renewed as Act-East Policy (AEP), which rest on four aims of **(a) Culture, (b) Commerce, (c) Connectivity, and (d) Capacity Building** along with 5-Ts of **(a) Tradition, (b) Talent, (c) Tourism, (d) Trade, and (e) Technology (Ministry of External Affairs, 2016).**

The successor to LEP of the previous government, is the Modi government's AEP, under dynamic geo-political, economic and defence security concerns, has extended and included eastern nations such as Singapore, Japan, South Korea, Indonesia, Malaysia, Vietnam, Pacific Island economies, Australia, and New Zealand. Infrastructure investment by Japan, for increase in commerce, connectivity and capacity building, and defence security ties, is the key to implementing the Act-East-Policy and developing and connecting the North-Eastern state of India by highways, rail and airports, as a gateway to engaging with South-East Asian countries to bring about travel, trade, regional and maritime security and stable economic growth in the region (Chansoria, 2017; Naidu & Yasuyuki, 2019; Ngaibiakching & Pande, 2020; Yhome, 2015). As seen from Figure-2, China is playing a key role with its growing ambitious one-belt and one-road infrastructure investment strategy in North-West Asia, South Asian neighbouring countries of India, and Africa to have access to resources, markets, and the oceans for sea routes in the Arabian sea, the Indian ocean, and the South-China Sea with strategic military presence (Dash, 2018; Lee, 2015; Naidu, 2013). Act-East policy needs Bangladesh, being the hub for regional connectivity between the North-Eastern states of India and the ASEAN under the BIMSTEC grouping.

Figure 2. South-Asia, South-East Asia, Japan, and Australia
Source: Google map

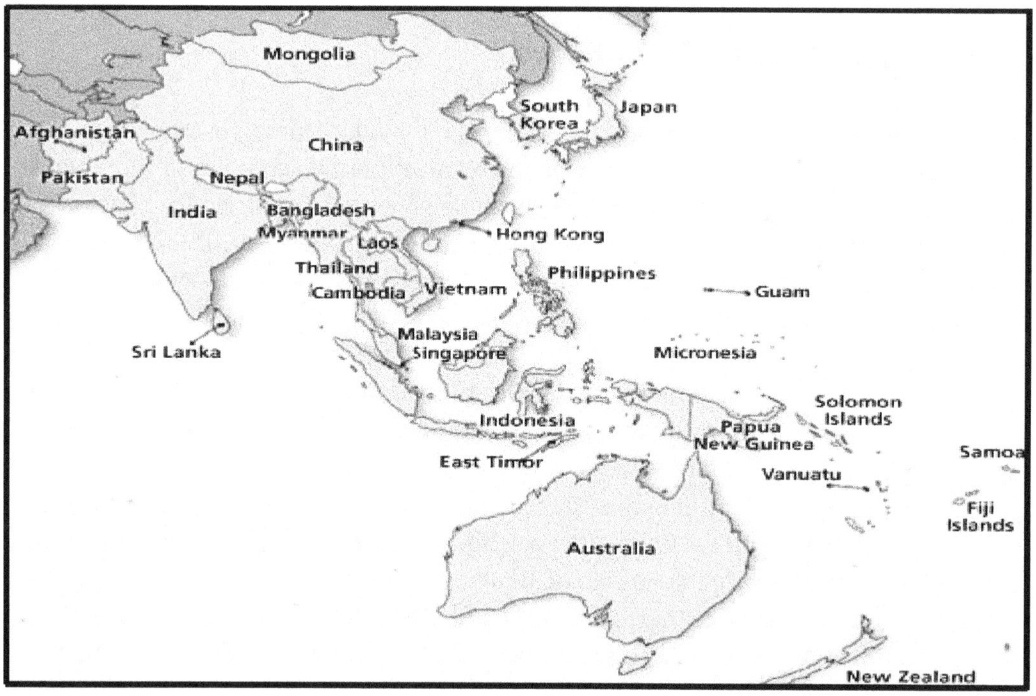

Capacity building can take place with trustworthy and fruitful partnership with countries to support planning and implementation of national infrastructure development, defence and regional security and economic development plans to meet the aims of LEP to which Japan and Singapore are the key countries of foreign direct investment in India, in addition to the growing territorial, defence and maritime ambitions and influence of China in the Indian and the Pacific Ocean region (Banlaoi, 2003; Cho & Park, 2013Chakrabarti, 2014; Dash, 2018; Das & Thomas, 2016; Lee, 2015; Naidu & Yasuyuki, 2019; Tandon, 2016; Yhome, 2015). This trade and economic partnership with ASEAN are possible by investing in developing the eight land-locked North-Eastern States of India (Arunachal Pradesh, Assam, Manipur, Meghalaya, Mizoram, Nagaland, Sikkim, and Tripura) to bring about enhanced socio-cultural, economic, political, regional security and stability of the eastern region (Gogoi, Goswamin, & Borah, 2009; Tandon, 2016).

2. Sustainable Development Goals

India's 12th five-year plan (2012-2017) focussed on achieving "faster, sustainable and more inclusive growth", with various national poverty and rural development programs. (Planning Commission, Govt. of India, 2020). The eight North-Eastern states are the most neglected in meeting the objectives of SDGs as seen from Table -1, which gives an insight into the comparative SDGs performance between states.

Table 1. Performance of Indian States and Union Territories on SDGs

SDGs	1	2	3	4	5	6	7	8	9	10	11	12	13	15	16	Composite
Index score	Aspirant (0-49)				Performer (50-64)				Front Runner (65-99)				Achiever (100)			SDGs
1 Arunachal Pradesh	34	66	50	58	33	88	74	52	31	38	43	67	31	71	62	53
2 Assam	48	39	44	44	33	78	70	62	46	67	40	68	47	90	52	55
3 Manipur	42	69	62	70	34	87	72	27	43	81	28	85	37	100	70	60
4 Meghalaya	68	35	53	55	34	70	52	65	22	76	22	60	36	99	59	54
5 Mizoram	67	75	52	61	37	81	81	42	8	66	33	50	45	75	63	56
6 Nagaland	56	70	29	47	42	75	70	28	23	61	23	100	51	94	84	57
7 Sikkim	65	66	59	58	49	79	97	68	27	64	74	60	38	100	69	65
8 Tripura	70	49	61	55	32	69	56	63	48	45	31	92	37	88	73	58
Andhra Pradesh	69	35	76	52	37	96	86	78	66	68	36	57	70	86	86	67
Bihar	33	26	44	19	40	81	62	64	47	74	50	47	43	54	64	50
Chhattisgarh	49	27	52	52	43	92	56	67	38	60	49	58	29	97	71	56
Goa	53	76	60	71	46	77	95	71	45	19	79	63	41	99	79	65
Gujarat	47	39	67	47	36	92	75	75	88	59	77	33	63	77	86	64
Haryana	47	43	65	68	36	81	77	71	73	54	49	39	34	40	76	57
Himachal Pradesh	60	44	67	81	52	82	64	76	70	78	79	52	61	92	84	69
Jharkhand	28	22	55	42	34	78	50	70	70	64	57	36	27	99	67	53
Karnataka	49	37	72	67	42	88	86	78	40	70	48	72	71	89	75	66
Kerala	64	74	82	74	51	77	70	61	88	75	51	57	58	98	77	70
Madhya Pradesh	40	24	50	54	45	92	62	67	44	68	55	58	47	94	63	58
Maharashtra	47	34	76	65	41	93	82	70	59	70	45	71	50	86	72	64
Odisha	47	34	61	40	35	85	50	59	72	69	51	44	69	99	61	58
Punjab	48	61	71	67	46	74	89	65	69	50	61	35	57	59	83	62
Rajasthan	56	35	58	51	39	76	61	65	38	70	61	30	60	75	76	57
Tamil Nadu	72	48	76	70	40	90	90	74	53	65	51	63	45	91	78	67
Telangana	52	36	66	64	26	84	93	82	61	94	62	58	66	88	77	67
Uttar Pradesh	40	31	34	48	41	94	63	64	63	46	56	62	48	62	69	55
Uttarakhand	64	45	58	66	38	90	78	73	55	59	51	50	59	95	85	64
West Bengal	52	40	70	50	38	83	58	72	68	73	34	57	37	88	73	60
A & N Islands	48	38	65	61	48	85	73	55	13	94	47	69	72	85	65	61
Chandigarh	48	73	54	80	47	100	84	64	74	33	83	77	54	93	89	70
D & N haveli	33	45	57	53	44	91	80	63	100	57	41	65	41	100	80	63
Damn & Diu	58	12	50	43	39	96	81	54	100	80	54	41	46	89	76	61
Delhi	54	56	54	64	27	61	96	60	100	89	63	39	30	82	64	61

Continued on following page

Table 1. Continued

SDGs	1	2	3	4	5	6	7	8	9	10	11	12	13	15	16	Composite
Index score	Aspirant (0-49)				Performer (50-64)				Front Runner (65-99)				Achiever (100)			SDGs
Jammu & Kashmir	58	55	62	54	53	85	76	46	49	47	33	61	59	74	69	59
Lakesha-dweep	56	57	58	62	37	69	43	43	0	93	0	75	100	100	82	63
Puducherry	58	71	71	67	35	86	97	58	86	92	53	43	39	37	94	66
India	50	35	61	58	42	88	70	64	65	64	53	55	60	66	72	60

Source: United Nations SDG India, 2019, p.16 (SDG -14 Life below water not available)

As seen from Table-1, even though India has made some progress in trying to achieve the 17, Sustainable Development Goals (SDGs), of (1) poverty eradication, (2)zero hunger, (3) good health & wellbeing, (4) quality education, (5) gender equality, (6) clean water and sanitation, (7) affordable clean energy (8) work and economic growth, (9) industry, innovation and infrastructure, (10) reduce inequality,(11) sustainable cities and communities, (12) responsible consumption and production, (13) climate action, (14) life below water, (15) life on land, (16) people, justice and strong institutions, (17) partnerships for the goals (UN, 2019). There are significant economic development disparities and inequality in achieving SDGs between the states. Moreover, only three States were placed in the category of Front Runners (with a score in the range 65-99, including both) in 2018 – Himachal Pradesh, Kerala, and Tamil Nadu. In 2019, five more States joined this league – Andhra Pradesh, Telangana, Karnataka, Sikkim, and Goa, taking the total tally to eight (UN-SDG India 2019).

Overall, globally, the composite score for India improved, from 57 in 2018 to 60 in 2019. This indicates that the country overall has progressed forward in its journey towards achieving the SDGs. Five goals drive the positive push – 6 (clean water and sanitation), 7 (affordable and clean energy), 9 (industry, innovation, and infrastructure), 15 (life on land), and 16 (peace, justice, and strong institutions), where India has scored between 65 and 99. Two goals – 2 (zero hunger) and 5 (gender equality) demand special attention, as the overall country score is below 50. Only three States were placed in the category of Front Runners (with a score in the range 65-99, including both) in 2018 – Himachal Pradesh, Kerala, and Tamil Nadu. In 2019, five more States joined this league – Andhra Pradesh, Telangana, Karnataka, Sikkim, and Goa, taking the total tally to eight (SDG India Index & Dashboard 2019-20).

Investment in 17-SDGs in the North-Eastern states is critical for enhancing the effectiveness of income distribution policies and reaping the demographic dividend. Further, incorporation of these much-neglected states in the implementation of SDGs programs and projects. Further, with the current coronavirus pandemic, one needs to see how India will be able to meet these goals and combat poverty, hunger, and health related issues to achieve the SDGs given the global health crisis which is having a negative spill over effect on every sector of the Indian and the global economy.

MAIN FOCUS OF THE CHAPTER

The main aim of this chapter is to critically review the significance of improving relations between India and ASEAN- and the 'Look-East Act-East' policy of the government of India. Further to examine the current and future challenges and opportunities for foreign direct investment (FDI) and economic development opportunities, evaluating the Indian Government's role to enhance, business, trade and tourism opportunities between India and Southeast Asian countries. Finally, propose a conceptual model for achieving internal, economic, external security and stability through bilateral and multi-lateral agreements for cooperation, connectivity, commerce, and capacity building for mutual benefit.

EXAMPLES OF INDIAS LOOK EAST-ACT EAST POLICY

Successful examples of Look East to Act East policy related to trade, tourism and business opportunities, people-to-people contact for exchange of culture, commerce, connectivity, and capacity building are the following, where India has many projects for infrastructure development of rail, road and signed Free Trade agreements with SriLanka, Bangladesh, Singapore, Thailand, Malaysia, South Korea, and Japan.

1. The eight Eastern states of India, share its international eastern border with China (1395km), Bhutan (455km), Bangladesh(1596km), Myanmar (1640) and Nepal (97km). A 22 km long narrow strip of land connects the North-Eastern states of India with the mainland (Gogoi et al., 2009). Visits at diplomatic levels between India and Burma (BIMSTEC) in the last decade have been frequent. India has signed an agreement with Burma over defence training, intelligence sharing in crushing Maoists insurgency movement in the Eastern states of India, including infrastructure development and improving cross- border roads, connecting Calcutta seaport to Sittwe port in Myanmar and highway networks through Burma, connecting India to rest of South East Asia and develop cross-border trade, tourism and markets for exporting tea, fruit, vegetables, herbs to bordering countries and the ASEAN economies.

2. In 2012, Prime Minister Manmohan Singh also signed bilateral infrastructure development and trade agreements with ASEAN countries and Japan (Lee, 2015). India's bi-lateral global partnership with Japan has increased in terms of connectivity and capacity building with technical collaboration and foreign direct investment in Delhi-Metro infrastructure projects, Delhi-Mumbai, Chennai-Bengaluru, and Mumbai-Ahmedabad bullet train and industrial belt project. Further, in 2008 India signed joint declaration of security cooperation with Japan (third country after USA and Australia), for protecting the sea routes from piracy, and Indo-Pacific alliance with Australia for security in the Indian and the pacific oceans (Ranjan, 2016) with increasing China's maritime ambitions and international boundary disputes. Prime Minister Modi's visit in 2015, led to an agreement to transfer defence equipment and technology, joint military research and development projects, training and exercises followed by 2018 'Acquisition and Cross-Servicing Agreement', for enhancing capacities during conflict by exchange of essentials like food, transport, ammunition, fuel, and defence equipment (Naidu & Yasuyuki, 2019).

3. Indian governments engagement with Indonesia, Malaysia, Vietnam, Philippines, and South Korea is increasing at a bilateral level, with the changing landscape of Asian geo-political canvas, with an increasing China's claim over resources and maritime routes in the Indian Ocean, Bay of Bengal, Malacca straight and the South-China Sea. Further, private Indian companies such as Bajaj Auto, Tata, Birla, Jindal steel, banking, textile, and telecommunication sectors have opened branches in Indonesia with increasing cooperation for economic, political, cultural, and joint defence exercises for cooperation in regional security (Pant, 2013).

4. To strengthen cultural ties, telecommunications connectivity and commerce with Northeast Indian state and ASEAN region, continuous efforts are being made through people-to-people cultural contacts, trade, and developing physical infrastructure projects such as airport, road, market, telecommunication, and power supply. The Indian foreign minister Sushma Swaraj stressed the importance of *five Ts-* **a) Tradition, b) Talent, c) Tourism, d) Trade, and e) Technology**, in Act-East Policy (Ministry of External Affairs, 2016; Nguyen, 2017). It is essential to develop friendly relationship with bordering countries, to reap the benefits from 5-Ts, for peace, security, and economic stability in the North-eastern states of India. Some of the major projects include the India-Myanmar-Thailand Trilateral Highway Project which will connect India with Mekong sub-region, Border markets or Haats, and Rhi-Tiddim Road Project and Kaladan Multi-Modal Transit Transport Project. Other projects with Burma to improve trade, travel, cultural ties, and investment include direct flights between Delhi-Bodhgaya-Yangon and bus service between Imphal capital of Manipur to Mandalay (Mishra, 2014). Buddhist rail tourist circuit needs further improvement in terms of international standard of infrastructure facilities, hotels, food courts, shopping malls and medical centres for the comfort of the international tourists.

5. Examples of mutual trust and cooperation between India and Bangladesh are demonstrated in cooperative bi-lateral projects related to water sharing and energy sector security, potential for developing solar and nuclear energy, bus and train services, defence, and security cooperation, which can be transformative and mutually beneficial to both the countries (Ali, 2018; Shringla, 2018). In the energy sector, India is meeting the growing demand for electricity in Bangladesh through its power plant Bheramara–Bahrampur and Tripura–Comilla inter-connection. The visit of Prime Minister Sheikh Hasina in 2017, heralded a golden era with the signing of 36 agreements. Dollar US$13 billion investment agreement was signed to develop energy and power sector along with infrastructure facilities to improve connectivity by bus service, rail and ports to promote trade and travel between India and Bangladesh and connect North-Eastern states with Chittagong port, which will be mutually beneficial and lead to peace, progress and prosperity of millions in Bangladesh and Indian North-Eastern states, and meet the United Nation 17 sustainable development goals with peace, justice and strong institutions and partnerships for growth (Chandiramani, 2019; United Nations, 2019) .

The trans-shipment connectivity projects from West-Bengal Calcutta port to the North-Eastern states of Assam, Arunachal Pradesh, and Tripura via transit facilities in Chittagong port in Bangladesh has saved distance and time. Moreover, road and highway projects for land-locked Bhutan, Nepal, and North-eastern states of India with Bangladesh (BBIN), will encourage people-to-people contacts, improve, and enhance travel, tourism, trade, and business opportunities. Further, 'Kunming Initiative' also known as Bangladesh, China, India, and Myanmar-Economic Corridor (BCIM-EC) will enhance trade and economic development. Furthermore, China's Belt and Road Initiative (BRI) project aims to connect China's landlocked Yunnan province with Bangladesh, North-Eastern state of India, and Myanmar, through networks of roads, rail, air and waterways into Bay of Bengal and the Indian Ocean (Rana, 2018). Furthermore, cooperation in the supply of energy and power by 2021 from India to Bangladesh has progressed with 11,00 MW of power flowing from India to Bangladesh, with major private sector investment from Adani and Reliance Power limited increasing additional power to 2,350 MW, besides clean and green energy options of solar and hydro power (Shringla, 2018).

RECOMMENDATIONS AND DISCUSSION

Critics think that Modi-BJP government has failed to define the real objective of "Act East" policy, which is broadly concerned with external security, economic cooperation and to abolish sub-nationalism in the North-Eastern states of India (Chakrabarti, 2014). The potential economic benefits from this policy have still to be realised, given the strategic Chinese influence and India seen as an emerging power, with dysfunctional relationships and problems with all SAARC neighbouring countries, and its tendency to isolate from external economic and geopolitical factors. On the other hand, India will not be taken seriously by the ASEAN, due to India's non-commitment and sitting on the fence approach, its own relationship with China since 1962 Indo-China war, and the South-Asian Nations is not stable and cooperative since 1947 independence from the British empire (Gaena & Ruohomäki, 2017; Palit, 2016).

It appears that the current Modi-BJP government has missed the opportunity to act like a responsible leader to unite South Asian countries through bi-lateral and multi-lateral trade and show leadership via multi-lateral agreements in South Asian Association of Regional Cooperation (SAARC) to work in a cooperative manner with commitment to peaceful dialogue, economic development, promote, trade, tourism, commerce and joint defence security exercises on land and ocean for progress and prosperity of millions living in South Asian. Simultaneously, India can invest in developing infrastructure facilities in its North-Eastern States and the SAARC region and set an example to the world that it shows commitment to bi-lateral and multi-lateral development projects within the SAARC region besides its differences and can settle age old border disputes through peaceful dialogue and therefore have credibility with its bi-lateral and multi-lateral agreements under the "Act East Policy". As an association, SAARC is dysfunctional with failed talks and agreement at all levels– cultural, commerce, connectivity, capacity building, diplomatic, socio, economic or strategic cooperation to promote economic development, progress, and prosperity thorough cooperative peace dialog for the mutual benefit of all the countries in the SAARC region (Gaena & Ruohomäki, 2017; Haq & Medhekar, 2019).

Given the AEP of the Modi government, the central government needs to deregulate and empower the State and Local governments of the North-Eastern states bordering to make independent decisions with the neighbouring countries of Bangladesh, Bhutan, Burma and China, to play a key role in regional and cross-border foreign policy diplomacy for internal security, border security, economic development and growth of the North-Eastern states, for infrastructure development, education, healthcare facilities, agriculture, eco-tourism and trade encouraging not just government level, but people-to-people and business-business contacts for commerce, connectivity and capacity building, across both side of the border for the mutual benefit of the population of the bordering states.

1. Opportunities

Look East to Act East policy will open numerous opportunities for bilateral trade, capacity building, connectivity, travel and tourism and collaborative partnerships in medical and scientist research, disaster management in case of natural calamities, and medical assistance particularly in solving global coronavirus situation in the SAARC and ASEAN region, where the first self-testing kit for coronavirus has been developed by an Indian scientist from national institute of Virology in Pune, India at an affordable cost of US12$ (Fermina, 2020). The foundation of Indian governments Look East to Act East policy is culture, commerce, connectivity, and capacity building (Lee, 2015; Sundararaman, 2018). The following potential opportunities can mutually benefit India and Southeast Asian economies.

(i) Culture: Collaboration and partnership in the field of education, sports, culture research and development through engagement of artists, sports personalities, students, and scholars in establishing study abroad cultural exchange programs for mutual advantage (Hussain, 2017). Further, it will create travel and tourism opportunities with introduction of e-visa or visa on arrival between India and Southeast Asian economies. Sister city memorandum of understanding could be established, which will encourage visits from scholars, students, artists, and open business opportunities and people-to people contact between the regions.

(ii) Commerce: Indian government is signatory to bilateral and multilateral free-trade agreements with the ASEAN nations, which will provide incentives to integrate with the region given the traditional cultural and trade links. Various multi-lateral agreements have been formed for mutual benefits related to trade, tourism, investment, security, and business opportunities. For example, economic corridor for China's vision of one-belt-one-road consisting of four countries- Bangladesh, China, India, and Myanmar (BCIM). Further, the 'Bay of Bengal Initiative for Multi-Sectoral Technical and Economic Cooperation' (BIMSTEC), between seven (7) member state of - Bangladesh, India, Myanmar, Sri Lanka, Thailand Nepal and Bhutan surrounding the Bay of Bengal. 'South Asian Free Trade Agreement' (SAFTA), and 'Regional Comprehensive Economic Partnership' (REPC) trade agreements between three major economies of China, India and Japan all have potential economic benefits (Goldberg, 2019; Haokip, 2011, 2015; Kshetrimayum & Singh, 2014; Sundararaman, 2018).

(iii) Connectivity: South Asian region with the group of eight SAARC countries is the least connected region in the world (Haq & Medhekar, 2019; Ali, 2018). It is essential to have connectivity through road, rail, airways, and sea including tele-communication internet to connect the local economy with regional, national, and international markets and economies (Haq & Medhekar, 2019; Ziipao, 2018). Therefore, investment in infrastructure is paramount to make sure that all cooperative economic development and trade plans are implemented smoothly for ease of movement of goods and people across-borders within South-Asian SAARC region and Bangladesh in particular, which will further improve connectivity with the ASEAN region in the East. Further, digital connectivity through broadband internet and telecommunications is essential for doing business with the member countries. Developed countries of Japan and Singapore can invest in infrastructure, health, tele-medicine, research, and development sectors of India. Finally, building people-to-people and business-to-business contacts will help to build trust, cooperation for developing trade, travel and investment opportunities at all levels which are mutually beneficial to meet the 17-UN SDGs of millions living below poverty line.

Furthermore, India should develop not just the North-Eastern states of India, but also the Andaman and Nicobar Islands in the Bay of Bengal-Indian Ocean region to its full potential economic and strategic advantage. Under the Look East to Act East Policy, these islands meeting in the Bay-of Bengal and the Indian ocean have no reference and have been neglected. India should first make provision for basic infrastructure, housing, health, education for the first natives/tribal population of the island and preserve their traditional land and culture. These islands can be developed by having state-of-the-art infrastructure facilities and as export free-trade zone hub like Singapore, Hongkong and Dubai. Further, border security and coastal guards including armed force bases with family station, policy and government offices can be established providing a need to develop infrastructure facilities in the Andaman-Nicobar Island chain. It is not too far away in the future, that these islands will be taken over by opportunistic powers, already having greater influence on countries along the coast of the Bay of Bengal, Malacca straight and the Indian Ocean.

(iv) Capacity Building: Exchange of scholars, scholarships, scientists at government-to-government, educational and research institutes and large business houses is essential to collaborate and cooperate for building skills, education, training, technology transfer, and having joint research partnerships in various areas of agriculture, trade, tourism development, power and solar energy, education, health, infrastructure projects, disaster management, joint security and defence exercises, to combat terrorism and sea pirates, establishing markets at the border line-of-control, which will be economically beneficial, creating numerous economic opportunities to achieve the revised 17-SDGs of United Nations adopted in 2015. The SDGs agenda aims to transform the world in the next 15 years under the five pillars of people, planet, prosperity, peace, and partnership. The emphasis of the transformation is based on economic, social, and environmentally sustainable development (UN, 2019).

(v) Economic Zones for Exports: The North-Eastern states can be set up as special economic export processing and manufacturing zone. Export based industries can be established with the help of the government support for small farmers and small and medium enterprises (SMEs) to form cooperatives in the agricultural sector growing high value fruits such as pineapples, lychees, berries, and herbs. Similarly, industrialists and private entrepreneurs can be provided with incentives to set up factories, schools, canned fruit processing plants, tourism facilities, branches of Indian Institute of Technology, and Indian Institute of Management, national level research centres, private hospitals for exports of healthcare services and attracting inbound foreign nationals for tourism, medical and education related services. This will create job opportunities, improve infrastructure facilities, increase domestic and international tourists visiting eastern states, education and training facilities for the local population and improve their standard of living to meet the SDGs of the United Nations. Corporate Social Responsibility (CSR) from the private business houses such as TATA, Birla, and Adani could also go a long way in implementing various development projects, under their CSR programs along the border states of India to benefit the local population.

2. Challenges

Just having high level diplomatic visits, free-trade agreements and policies on paper is not enough unless concrete projects are planned, implemented, and seen to fruition between the countries to address the SDGs for economic transformation, development, stability, peace, and prosperity of the regions. The real challenge is in keeping the focus and implement the economic development projects within the bordering states of North-East, for meeting the four (4) goals of the policy and strengthen the ties with the neighbouring countries of South-East Asia.

The focus of the Indian Central Government since independence along its land borders has been defence/military security, resulting in isolated and underdeveloped western and eastern states bordering villages, and lack of economic security to bring about economic development, growth, connectivity, progress, and prosperity in the bordering villages of India (Haq & Medhekar, 2019). As expressed by De Hoyos (1995) "All of the major conflicts in the region are explosions along the fault lines deliberately left as the legacy of direct British colonial rule." Similarly, in case of the North-Eastern states of India the situation is worse than the western bordering states. Despite its rich bio-diversity, flora, fauna, horticulture, vegetation and natural beauty, where opportunities can be reaped in the 21st century, through international trade and tourism and achieving the aims of LEP – Culture, Commerce, Connectivity and Capacity Building, the North-Eastern states of India have been neglected for 70 years and thus experienced separatist movements due to being underdeveloped, high unemployment, lack of infrastructure and low growth in all aspects of SDGs and macroeconomic indicators.

According to Gogoi et al. (2009) India's North-Eastern region is isolated and underdeveloped due to its remoteness, geographical mountainous terrain, deprived development programs, lack of Indian government's rural development programs regarding health and education, lack of infrastructure investment, and threat from neighbours such as illegal human trafficking, smuggling, law and order, separatist movement, and security issues. For example, Arunachal Pradesh is bordering with China; Assam, Meghalaya, Tripura, and Mizoram bordering with Bangladesh; and Burma bordering with Mizoram, Manipur, Nagaland, and Arunachal Pradesh. Therefore, the economic development, policy and cooperation strategy adopted for these states and bordering countries should be different and examined at a bi-lateral level.

1. The challenge is to first bring about economic development, progress and prosperity in the eight North-Eastern states of India, (Figure-1) so that the capital cities of the these North-Eastern states can act as a business, tourism, manufacturing and export hub and a gateway to connect with the ASEAN group of ten countries, including Japan, Australia and New- Zealand to form partnerships, people-to-people contact and open doors to mutually beneficial economic development, education, employment, healthcare, travel and trade opportunities.
2. Reliable internet and telecommunications, digital connectivity, infrastructure development and joint disaster management expertise is required to mitigate natural calamities such as floods, landslides, and erosion due to heavy rainfall.
3. Challenge of connecting the eight North-Eastern states of India by rail, highways, and air transport with each other, inter-state and intra-regional including with other capital cities of India to the west requires building rail-road transports and air connectivity.
4. Challenge of providing primary healthcare, education, schools, university, clean drinking water supply, sanitation, roads, banking, and postal and tele-communication services in the mountainous regions to bring them in line with rest of Indian states and meet few of the basic 17-SDGs.
5. Lack of electricity supply is a major obstacle to industrial and economic development. Alternative energy such as solar and hydroelectricity could be harnessed for this region given the highest rainfall in Cherrapunji- located on Shillong plateau in Meghalaya state.
6. Government needs to create employment opportunities, in the far eastern mountainous states of India in health, education, tourism, infrastructure development, subsidised housing, and encourage small and medium size industries and service sector.
7. Horticulture industries for commercial reasons can be supported for growing pineapple, lychees, passion fruit and other herbs and aromatic plants used for making perfumes and insect repellent such as chitranella.
8. Management of North-Eastern states border is critical with Burma, Bangladesh and China and settling border disputes once and for all. Joint border fencing with key checkpoints for crossing and security towers should be undertaken along the international boundary, to combat illegal cross-border migration, smuggling of drugs, arms, and human trafficking like the India-Pakistan border. This is essential for maintaining peace and developing the eastern states primary, manufacturing, and service sectors, with special economic zones for processing exports, for effective AEP implementation.
9. The rise of China and its growing economic and military strategic influence in the South China Sea, Indian Ocean region, the Bay-of-Bengal and the Arabian Sea including infrastructure road

projects in Pakistan occupied Kashmir, is critical to this AEP, with the changing geo-political conditions. India is looked upon by the ASEAN countries, Japan, and Australia to play a proactive balancing role, given the territorial claims and dispute of China with many nations in South-East Asia (Lee, 2015; Pant, 2013; Yhome, 2015). India needs to develop its joint defence strategic ties with Indonesia, being closer to the Andaman -Nicobar Islands and the third most populated country in the world.

10. India should first look at neighbouring SAARC countries in South Asia with centuries old strong historical, linguistic, cultural and familial ties and play a credible and key strategic partnership role to bring trust, peace, security, stability, economic progress and prosperity within the SAARC neighbours (Pakistan, SriLanka, Nepal, Bangladesh, Maldives, Afghanistan, and Bhutan), to be able to counter balance the rise of China's defence strategy and debt-trap diplomacy in South Asia and South East Asia (Cho & Park, 2013; Dash, 2018) and the Indian Ocean regions. India needs to be proactive and responsible under the SAARC umbrella and adopt its 4-Cs Culture, Commerce, Connectivity and Capacity Building and 5-Ts strategy of Tradition, Talent, Tourism, Trade, and Technology, for meeting the SDG goals, economic development, peace, and prosperity.

Finally, Hall (2016) mentions that the Modi government's AEP multi-alignment foreign policy is a challenge as the government on one hand wants to maintain equal distance and avoid economic political and military dependence on any of the two powers China and USA. Hall (2016) critiques that due to India's non-aligned policy, no major power came to India's rescue during 1962 Chinese invasion. Further, "…renegotiation of the norms and rules of international relations, there is a risk that multi-alignment might be interpreted, as non-alignment sometimes was, as signalling a lack of commitment on the part of India to interests and ideas that others want to uphold. Countering negative perceptions of multialignment among its many partners may well prove one of the biggest foreign policy challenges Modi's government will have to face" (Hall, 2016, p. 282).

India cannot leave the economic development of its far North-Eastern states to the market forces. Government must play an important role in developing border areas in terms of infrastructure development, tele-communications, road, rail, airways, establish formal market structures small and medium industries, health, education, and other infrastructure facilities and create public sector employment opportunities and provide basic infrastructure facilities to the people in eastern states of India (Gogoi et al., 2009). The piecemeal approach to AEP should first stabilise and strengthen the eight North Eastern states of India, as other states, with government institutions, infrastructure facilities, markets, social, cultural economic, and presence of well-developed and connected bases of the three Indian armed forces and border security and coastal guards. With well-developed bordering states, will the ten ASEAN countries be attracted to economically engage in bilateral trade with India.

The success of AEP with ASEAN and Pacific countries is possible if first these border disputes with China over Arunachal Pradesh is solved. India is the only country sharing borders with China. The QUAD summit is a quadrilateral security cooperation during the pandemic in March 2021, between USA, Japan, Australia, and India, for showing solidarity on Indo-Pacific issues such as providing the global public good as corona-vaccine and counter-balancing the power of China ((D'Ambrogio, 2021). Further, eight (8) North-Eastern states of India need to have well developed socio-economic infrastructure facilities such as transport and communication, well developed markets, political and institutional linkages, road, rail, airports, health, education, and other tourism infrastructure to be ready to do business, trade, and tourism with the immediate bordering nations like Bhutan, Bangladesh, and ASEAN countries. These states have been neglected for too long and the Look East- Act East policies four aims, should first be implemented within the country for its North-Eastern states with, strategic importance bordering with China, Bhutan, Bangladesh, and Burma, rather than looking beyond the international borders.

The four aims of Act-East policy (AEP), Culture, Commerce, Connectivity and Capacity Building- should be first applied to the North-Eastern states of India and SAARC countries. As commented by Rana (2018) "In order to continue its impressive economic growth, India requires a peaceful and stable environment in its neighbourhood. India cannot emerge as a global power if it is unable to attain primacy in its own region" (p. 566). Therefore, India should first establish cooperative partnerships for economic development with SAARC countries and demonstrate successful working of multilateral and bilateral relationships within SAARC as the European and ASEAN region, and within its own country, and develop the bordering states to the Western and the Eastern borders, so that the local population feels that they also have equal access to all the benefits of market, health, education and transport infrastructure as rest of the Indian states. Thereafter, India can look towards South-East Asia and beyond the Pacific borders for security and cooperation via bilateral and multilateral partnerships for socio and economic development, prosperity, and progress.

Figure 3. Proposed Conceptual Model for Cooperation and Security
Source: Developed for this paper

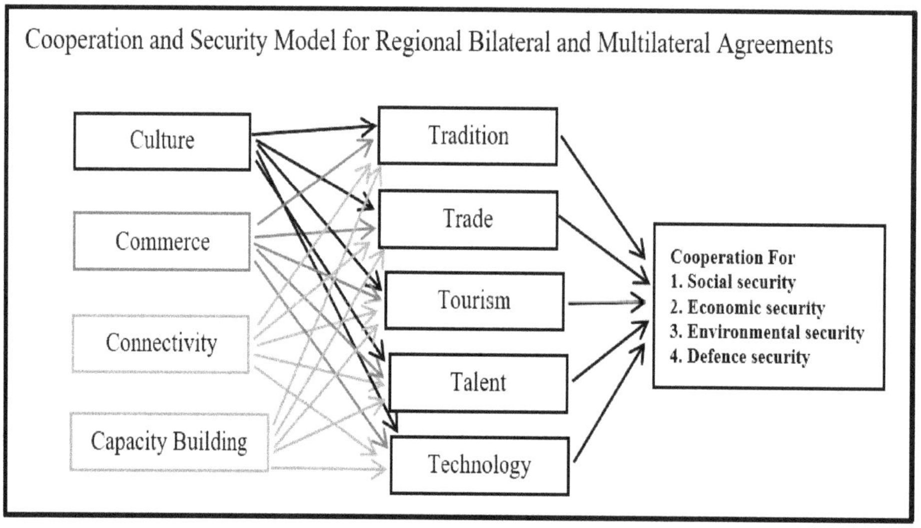

Figure-3 illustrates the proposed conceptual model for cooperation and security in terms of social, economic, environmental and defence, both internal and external required to bring about stability through bi-lateral and multi-lateral agreements for peace, progress, prosperity of the countries. This can be implemented and operationalised at the bilateral and multilateral level by the exchange of Five (5-Ts) Tradition, Trade, Tourism, Talent and Technology between India and the ASEAN Nations.

FUTURE RESEARCH DIRECTIONS

Future empirical research on Look East and Act East Policy since Modi governments policy formulation and implementation in 2014 should examine if all the projects under the policies various bilateral and multilateral agreements have been implemented and its success within the region and cross-border with the neighbouring countries, by testing the conceptual model proposed in Figure-3 for cooperation and security achieving to achieve social, economic and defence security and cooperation, for the mutual benefit, regional security, economic development and growth. Secondly foreign diplomats and officers working in the sector including the businesses dealing with the ASEAN countries, Japan, and Australia, could be interviewed to know the success of costs, benefits and threats of various bilateral and multilateral subregional agreements signed under Act East Policy such as BIMSTEC group of eight countries, and QUAD group of four countries, USA, Japan, Australia, and India to create an enabling and a multilateral cooperative environment for defence security, economic development, and growth of the Asia-pacific and Indo-pacific counties . It is also important to know the opinion of the locals living in these far-Eastern state capitals and in the bordering villages via in-depth interviews as to the benefits, costs, threats of living in these areas from insurgency, rise of Chinese power in eastern states, terrorism activities, illegal migrants, supply-chain disruptions during normal times and also during natural disasters and health emergency, and what they want the local, state and the central government to do to improve their quality of life in terms of border security, peace, economic development, progress and prosperity of the far Eastern region.

CONCLUSION

Act East policy is a positive proactive initiative by the Modi government to build and strengthen India's economic, political, strategic, and cross-border security with neighbouring countries and empower the North-eastern states in cross-border diplomacy for regional security. In the last decade three major powers China, India and Japan have emerged in the Asian region, playing a key role on the international platforms along with Australia. China has economic and military ambitions with border-disputes and regional tensions to control sea routes and islands with ASEAN nations of Malaysia, Philippines, Singapore, South Korea, Indonesia, and Vietnam. India needs to play a balancing act as expected by ASEAN, as there is a need to have cooperation for regional balance of power with regional land and maritime security issues, to tap the untapped economic potential for economic development, peace and progress which is mutually beneficial to all countries.

Act-East policy has many challenges and opportunities to first develop infrastructure and improve connectivity, commerce, and capacity building within the North-eastern states of India and bring progress and prosperity to the North-eastern regions, as well as empower the state to engage with the bordering neighbouring countries such as Bangladesh, Bhutan, Nepal, and Burma for the mutual benefit of the central and the state government along with the neighbouring countries. Further, the North-eastern states, will also be a gateway to improve cross-border relationships through trade, travel and tourism, people-to-people connectivity, and cooperative capacity building for national and economic security, peace, progress, and prosperity in the region. It is first imperative for India to establish its leadership and demonstrate maturity and partnership in tackling SAARC regions age old distrust and conflict with Pakistan since 1947 partition and stop the blame game from both sides, so that ASEAN and Australia can take India's contribution seriously as an emerging and responsible country in providing economic, political and defence security in the region.

In the current COVID-19 global pandemic health emergency and tragedy that is evolving in the second wave, India, and the ASEAN countries to the east, need to focus on investing in health sector and building hospital beds capacity, build more hospitals, diagnostic clinics and oxygen generating plants to avoid such pandemic like situation in the future. India along with SAARC member countries on one hand and the ASEAN, Japan, Australia, and New Zealand, should establish cooperative strategic partnerships for infrastructure and economic development projects, promote cultural, travel and tourism, education and healthcare facilities and have joint security and defence exercises, disaster management and technological transfer, mutual access to markets for the benefit of achieving the SDGs for the population of the countries and the region at large.

REFERENCES

Ali, S. M. (2018). The Current and Future State of India–Bangladesh Relations. *Strategic Analysis*, *42*(5), 529–537. doi:10.1080/09700161.2018.1523079

Bajpaee, C. (2017). Dephasing India's Look East/Act East Policy. *Contemporary Southeast Asia: A Journal of International and Strategic Affairs, 39*(2), 348-372.

Banlaoi, R.C. (2003). Southeast Asian Perspectives on the Rise of China: Regional Security after 9/11. *Parameters*, (Summer).

Chakrabarti, S. (2014). *India Struggling to define its 'Look East' policy looks set to continue*. Available at https://theconversation.com/indias-struggle-to-define-its-look-east-policy-looks-set-to-continue-28104

Chandiramani, J. (2019). Transforming India 2030: Strategies for Sustainable Development Goals. In *International Conference Proceedings*. New Delhi: Capital Publishing Company. Available at https://sse.ac.in/assets/pdf/TransformingIndia2030Completefile.pdf

Chansoria, M. (2017). Japanese investments are instrumental to India's Act East Policy. *Asia Pacific Bulletin, 385*.

Cho, H., & Park, S-H. (2013). The Rise of China and Varying Sentiments in Southeast Asia toward Great Powers. *Strategic Studies Quarterly*, (Summer), 69–92.

D'Ambrogio, E. (2021). The Quad: An emerging multilateral security framework of democracies in the Indo-Pacific region. *European Parliament Research Services*. Available at https://www.europarl.europa.eu/RegData/etudes/BRIE/2021/690513/EPRS_BRI(2021)690513_EN.pdf

Das, G., & Thomas, J. (Eds.). (2016). *Look East to Act East Policy: Implications for India's Northeast*. Routledge. doi:10.4324/9781315657660

Dash, Z. (2018). Economic Security: The Missing Link in India's National Security Architecture. *Strategic Analysis*, *42*(6), 633–639. doi:10.1080/09700161.2018.1557931

de Hoyos, L. (1995). Terrorism in South Asia: London's assault on the nation-state. *Executive Intelligence Review*, *22*(41), 22–41.

Downie, E. (2015). Manipur and India's 'Act East' Policy. *The Diplomat*. Available at https://thediplomat.com/2015/02/manipur-and-indias-act-east-policy/

Femina. (2020). *Meet the Scientist Behind India's First Coronavirus Testing Kit*. https://www.femina.in/trending/achievers/meet-the-scientist-behind-indias-first-coronavirus-testing-kit-152629.html

Gaena, B., & Ruohomäki, O. (2017). *India's 'Look East' – 'Act East' Policy: Hedging as a Foreign Policy Tool*. FIIA, Briefing paper 222. Available at https://www.fiia.fi/en/publication/indias-look-east-act-east-policy

Ganguly, S. (2017). Had Modi truly changed India's foreign Policy? *The Washington Quarterly*, *40*(2), 131–143. doi:10.1080/0163660X.2017.1328929

Gogoi, J. K., Goswamin, H., & Borah, K. C. (2009). *Problems of border areas in NE- India: Implications for the 13th Finance Commission*. Government of India. Available at https://fincomindia.nic.in/writereaddata/html_en_files/oldcommission_html/fincom13/discussion/report14.pdf

Goldberg, J. (2019). What is India's Look East Policy? *ThoughtCo*. Available at https://www.thoughtco.com/look-east-policy-of-india-1435050

Hall, I. (2016). Multialignment and Indian Foreign Policy under Narendra Modi. *The Commonwealth Journal of International Affair*, *105*(3), 271–286. doi:10.1080/00358533.2016.1180760

Haokip, T. (2011). India's Look East Policy: Its evolution and approach. *South Asian Survey*, *18*(2), 239–257. doi:10.1177/0971523113513368

Haokip, T. (2015). India's Look East Policy: Prospects and challenges for Northeast India. *Studies in Indian Politics*, *3*(2), 198–211. doi:10.1177/2321023015601742

Haq, F., & Medhekar, A. (2019). Is Spiritual Tourism a Peace Vehicle for Social Transformation and Economic Prosperity in India and Pakistan? In N. Alexandru-Mircea & M.-O. Nedelea (Eds.), *Marketing Peace for Social Transformation and Global Prosperity* (pp. 189–211). IGI Global Publishing. doi:10.4018/978-1-5225-7464-4.ch010

Hussain, M. (2017). Cultural Foundations of India's Look East Policy: A Critique. *Journal of Southeast Asian Studies*, *5*(3), 147–155.

Kshetrimayum, R. S., & Singh, C. G. (2014). Look East Policy: India's motives and opportunities and threats ahead. *Asian Journal of Research in Business. Economics and Management*, *4*(11), 165–171.

Lee, L. (2015). India as a nation of consequence in Asia: The potential and limitations of India's 'Act East' policy. *The Journal of East Asian Affairs*, *29*(2), 67–104.

Ministry of Eternal Affairs. (2016). *India's Look East Policy*. Available at https://mea.gov.in/lok-sabha.htm?dtl/26554/

Mishra, R. (2014). From Look east to Act East: Transitions in India's Eastward Engagement. *The ASAN Forum*, *8*(1). Available at http://www.theasanforum.org/from-look-east-to-act-east-transitions-in-indias-eastward-engagement/

Muni, S. D. (2011). *India's 'Look East' Policy: The Strategic Dimension*. Institute of South Asian Studies, Working Paper, National University of Singapore.

Naidu, G. V. C. (2013). India and East Asia: The Look East Policy. *Perceptions*, *18*(1), 53–74.

Naidu, G. V. C., & Yasuyuki, I. (2019). India–Japan Defence Ties: Building a Strategic Partnership. *Strategic Analysis*, *43*(1), 13–27. doi:10.1080/09700161.2019.1573556

Ngaibiakching, & Pande, A. (2020). India's Act East Policy and ASEAN: Building a Regional Order Through Partnership in the Indo-Pacific. *International Studies*, *57*(1), 67–78. doi:10.1177/0020881719885526

Nguyen, T. H. (2017). Prospects of ASEAN-India Relations: An Analysis. *European Journal of Social and Human Sciences*, *4*(2), 1–8.

Ollapally, D. M. (2018). How Does India's Look East Policy Look after 25 Years? *Asia Policy*, *13*(2), 146–149. doi:10.1353/asp.2018.0031

Palit, A. (2016). India's Act east Policy and Implications for Southeast Asia. *Southeast Asian Affairs*, 81-92.

Pant, H. V. (2013). China on the horizon: India's Look East Policy gathers momentum. *Orbis*, *57*(3), 453–466. doi:10.1016/j.orbis.2013.05.007

Planning Commission Government of India. (2020). *Twelfth Five Year Plan 2012-2017*. Available at https://niti.gov.in/planningcommission.gov.in/docs/plans/planrel/fiveyr/welcome.html

Rahmati, F., Ali, M. A., & Kamraju, M. (2020). A Study on Strategic Location of Siliguri Corridor and Its Issues. *International Journal of All Research Education and Scientific Methods*, *8*(7), 2–6.

Ram, A. N. (Ed.). (2012). *Two Decades of India's Look East Policy: Partnership for Peace, Progress and Prosperity*. Manohar Publishers & Distributors.

Rana, M. (2018). Transformation of Indo-Bangladesh Relations: From Insecurity to Cooperation in Northeast India. *Strategic Analysis*, *42*(6), 559–577. doi:10.1080/09700161.2018.1559976

Ranjan, V. (2016). Australia and India in Asia: When 'Look West' Meets Act East. *Strategic Analysis*, *40*(5), 425–439. doi:10.1080/09700161.2016.1209906

Shringla, H. V. (2018). India–Bangladesh Relations: An Indian Perspective. *Strategic Analysis*, *42*(5), 524–528. doi:10.1080/09700161.2018.1523080

Singh, A. (2018). *The Nautical Dimension of India's "Act East" Policy Report*. School of International Studies, Nanyang Technological University.

Sundararaman, S. (2018). India–ASEAN Relations: 'Acting' East in the Indo-Pacific. *International Studies*, *54*(1-4), 62–81. doi:10.1177/0020881718787575

Tandon, A. (2016). India's Foreign Policy Priorities and the Emergence of a Modi Doctrine. *Strategic Analysis*, *40*(5), 349–356. doi:10.1080/09700161.2016.1209909

United Nations. (2019). *Sustainable Development Goals and Agenda*. Available at https://www.un.org/sustainabledevelopment/development-agenda/

United Nations SDG India. (2019). *SDG India Index & Dashboard 2019-2020*. Available at https://niti.gov.in/sites/default/files/2019-12/SDG-India-Index-2.0_27-Dec.pdf

Wojczewski, T. (2019). Identity and world order in India's post-Cold War foreign policy discourse. *Third World Quarterly*, *40*(1), 180–198. doi:10.1080/01436597.2018.1552079

Yhome, K. (2015). From "Look East" to "Act East": What it Means for India's Northeast? *Eastern Quarterly*, *11*(1-2), 18–29.

Ziipao, R. R. (2018). Look/Act East Policy, Roads and Market Infrastructure in North-East India. *Strategic Analysis*, *42*(5), 476–489. doi:10.1080/09700161.2018.1523082

ADDITIONAL READING

Das, P. (2018). Security Challenges and the Management of the India–Myanmar Border. *Strategic Analysis*, *42*(6), 578–594. doi:10.1080/09700161.2018.1557932

Hall, I. (2015). Is a 'Modi doctrine' emerging in Indian foreign policy? *Australian Journal of International Affairs*, *69*(3), 247–252. doi:10.1080/10357718.2014.1000263

Joshi, H. (2011). China and India. *Awkward Ascents*, *55*(4), 558–576.

Sajjanhar, A. (2016, May). Taking Stock of India's 'Act East Policy'. *Observer Research Foundation*, (142), 1–6.

Shani, V. (2009). India's foreign policy: Key drivers. *South African Journal of International Affairs*, *14*(2), 21–35. doi:10.1080/10220460709545493

Sikri, R. (2009). India's "Look East" Policy. *Asia-Pacific Review*, *16*(1), 131–145. doi:10.1080/13439000902957624

Singh, R. (2016, June 21). India's act east policy role of defence diplomacy. *South Asia Defence and Strategic Review*, *10*(2), 54.

KEY TERMS AND DEFINITIONS

Bilateral Trade: Bilateral trade is a cross border transaction or commerce that occurs between two countries. Bilateral trade is an agreement between two countries, to promote trade and commerce between them which is mutually beneficial for economic development and stability. It opens markets and eliminates or reduces tariff and non-tariff barriers to trade and agrees not to dump unfairly goods in other country.

Capacity Building: Capacity building is defined as a process of one country helping the other country to solve problems, achieve joint goals, develop human and institutional resources, through training and transfer of technology. This helps to develop and strengthen the abilities, skills, knowledge, research, and development, of its citizens and country, to survive, adapt, thrive, and transform in the dynamic environment with the other from climate change, military dominance, global financial and economic crisis, and threat from pandemic viruses such as SARS and Coronavirus.

Global Health Crisis: Epidemic and a pandemic can be descried as a global health crisis when large number of people die due to human-to-human transmission of a contagious viral disease like Coronavirus- COVID-19. In such a situation, the World Health Organisation declares that countries have to follow health regulations as provided by WHO for the public health safety of the citizens.

Multilateral Trade: Multilateral trade agreement occurs between three or more nations, and they are treated equally, and no one gets a most favoured nation status. The aim is to standardise commerce regulations, encourage exports and imports, reduced tariffs, and quotas between member countries. Multilateral agreements are beneficial to emerging markets developing countries as it makes them more competitive, and trade can be negotiated with more than one country at one time.

Sustainable Development: The Sustainable Development concept was introduced in 1987 by United Nations and is defined as any economic development programs which is capable to manage and utilise scare resources presently to maintain social, economic, and environmental sustainably to meet the needs of the future generations. Principles to achieve human development goals which are sustainable. The universal programs and policies that will lead to achieving United Nations 17-SDGs by 2030 by developed and developing countries. Overall aim of Act-East policies and programs should be to achieve the SDGs through peace, justice, and mutually beneficial partnerships.

Chapter 2
Estimating Export Potential of India to Southeast Asian Countries:
Panel Gravity Model Approach

Ayberk Şeker
https://orcid.org/0000-0001-7750-6286
Bursa Technical University, Turkey

ABSTRACT

It is crucial to estimate the export potential of countries in order to determine new export markets and increase their share of export markets. The chapter aims to determine the potential Southeast Asian export market for India by comparing the potential export level with the actual export from India to Southeast Asian countries. The frequency of the variables is annual and belongs to the period between 1996 and 2018. As a result of the analyses, it has been determined that Indian exports to Myanmar, Vietnam, and Singapore are slightly above its export potential, while its exports to Indonesia, Malaysia, and the Philippines are far above its export potential. In addition to this, it is determined that India has a high export potential to Brunei, Cambodia, and Thailand amongst Southeast Asian countries.

INTRODUCTION

Nowadays, the international trade is the driving force of economic development for countries. In this direction, countries aim to accelerate economic development processes by increasing their trade volumes with each other. It is seen that especially developing and underdeveloped countries tend to create economic cooperation among each other in order to increase their international trade volumes.

Conjunction with the globalization process, the free movement of labor, capital, goods and services between countries has increased and this condition has incremented the volume of international trade. The export volumes of the countries integrated into the global economy increase more and the economic growth levels of the countries raise faster than other countries due to the positive effects arising from

DOI: 10.4018/978-1-7998-5774-7.ch002

the national economy via exports (Dollar, 1992). Together with the integration of underdeveloped and developing countries into the global economy, it is seen that it makes important contributions to the economic development of countries by means of their positive effects of increasing technology investments (Borensztein et al., 1998).

In company with the inception of globalization of the world economy and markets, tendency of countries towards regional economic integration has increased and important economic integrations have been realized in the related process. Although the liberalization of international trade is seen to act in accordance with the principles of the World Trade Organization (WTO), the idea of establishing economic integrations as the main strategy for the expansion of international trade between both developed and underdeveloped countries has come forward (Tumbarello, 2005, p. 3). Almost all of the economic integrations established include socio-economic and political structures as well as countries with many similarities such as cultural formations, geographical proximity and mutual interests.

Trade reforms constituted a part of the extensive programme of structural reforms started in India in the early of 1990s. These reforms have ensured to noticeable changes in the performance of the international trade sector in India (Batra, 2006, p. 327). This change is seen clearly from the increment in trade openness ratio of India according to WTO database. Trade openness ratio raised from 16% a pre-reform ratio (1990) to 40% after the period of reforms (in the 2019). Moreover, India's export share of world exports increased from 0.57% in the 1990 to 2.3% in the 2019. On the other hand, India's trade share in world is still very low and seems underwhelming compared to other Asian countries such as China and Korea. It is clear shown that there is a need to increase India's trade volumes, especially Southeast Asian countries.

In this study, it is aimed to determine the Southeast Asian countries that have the potential export market for India by comparing the potential export levels and real exports. In order to establish the export model between India and Southeast Asian countries, India's exports to Southeast Asian countries, gross domestic product per capita of the countries, distance between India and Southeast Asian countries, average tariff rates of countries, exchange rates of India and Southeast Asian countries, the historical relation between India and Southeast Asian countries, trade openness of Southeast Asian countries and the 2008 global crisis will be used as variables.

The chapter is structured as follows. Background section reviews the literature on trade structure of India and Southeast Asian countries. Next section describes the main focus of the chapter with the statistics. Empirical analysis section presents the econometric model, definitions of variables, data sources and estimation results. Later, export potential of India to Southeast Asian countries are propounded in the solutions and recommendations section. It is aimed to be guided future researchers in future research directions section. Lastly, conclusion section puts forward possible policy implications.

BACKGROUND LITERATURE

Globalization has gained an important impetus in the face of regionalization especially after the Second World War (Sahasrabuddhe, 2012). While South Asia was in a single state structure before the Second World War, many new states emerged after the war and these states were separated culturally, politically and economically. The fusion of various races in the region has brought important diversity to South Asia such as religion, language and culture. Due to the failure of the attempts to establish cooperation between the states, the adverse situation has affected the poor in the region more than other segment of the population. However, the South Asian identity has begun to emerge both within and outside the region with the establishment of the South Asian Regional Cooperation Organization (SAARC) (Rahman & Yaesmin, 2014, p. 20).

In order to facilitate and increase international trade, the complexity caused by excessive documentation and regulations should be avoided as well as following excess procedures should be reduced. Regional collaborations and integrations can facilitate the way to expand markets and create trade opportunities, such as globalization. Regional integrations ensuring political and economic harmony strengthen its members by increasing commercial opportunities. International trade promotion makes the efficiency of regional integrations sustainable in the commercial liberalization process. Trade liberalization promotes integration of national economies effectively and will reduce income and other disparities within and among the countries.

In line with international economic cooperation, commercial relations between India and Association of Southeast Asian Nations (ASEAN) have started to develop under the "Look East Policy" since the 1990s. The complementary economic cooperation between India and ASEAN includes significant mutual gains. Although ASEAN has the population less than half of India, global trade volume of these countries is more than five times that of India. Due to the trade potential of India and ASEAN, the trade volume between India and Southeast Asian countries has increased day by day. After the sectoral dialogue partnership was established between India and ASEAN in 1993, the trade volume between India and ASEAN has increased more than three times and it has created a significant potential for future periods (Madaan, 2004).

The most important issue between India and ASEAN has been agreements on the trade of goods. Although India has participated in trade summits as an ASEAN Dialogue Partner and as a member of the East Asian Summit that convened after both ASEAN summits, it has taken a long time to conclude free trade agreements. At this point, despite the increase in the trade volume of India and ASEAN, it is seen as an important problem that India's level of exports with East Asian countries is less than China. In addition, another problem for India is that imports from ASEAN countries are higher than India's exports to ASEAN (Limaye, 2008).

The trade volume between India and ASEAN has developed more than other countries after the WTO. Trade relations between India and ASEAN countries improved during the period. It is suggested that policy of liberalization and openness of India has served in reinforcement India's trade ties with ASEAN (Ghuman & Madaan, 2009).

It has been revealed that important economic relations can be established between India and ASEAN countries in the fields of maritime, tourism, banking, trade and investment. As a result of the evaluation of these important economic relations between India and ASEAN countries, there is a great need to increase economic cooperation among these countries especially in India's technology exports, banking services and investments (Pradnya, 2009). In this direction, Figure 1 shows the proximity and export potential of India and Southeast Asian countries with each other.

International trade and economic integration are the results of geographical, political and institutional proximity of countries and the openness of their economies to foreign trade, investment and trade participation (Drysdale & Garnaut 1982; Harrigan, 2001; Linnemann, 1966; Tinbergen, 1962). It is stated that rapid integration into the world economy through the liberalization of international trade is the main driving force of economic growth and poverty reduction (van Mulekom et. al, 2006, p. 547).

Figure 1. India and Southeast Asian Countries

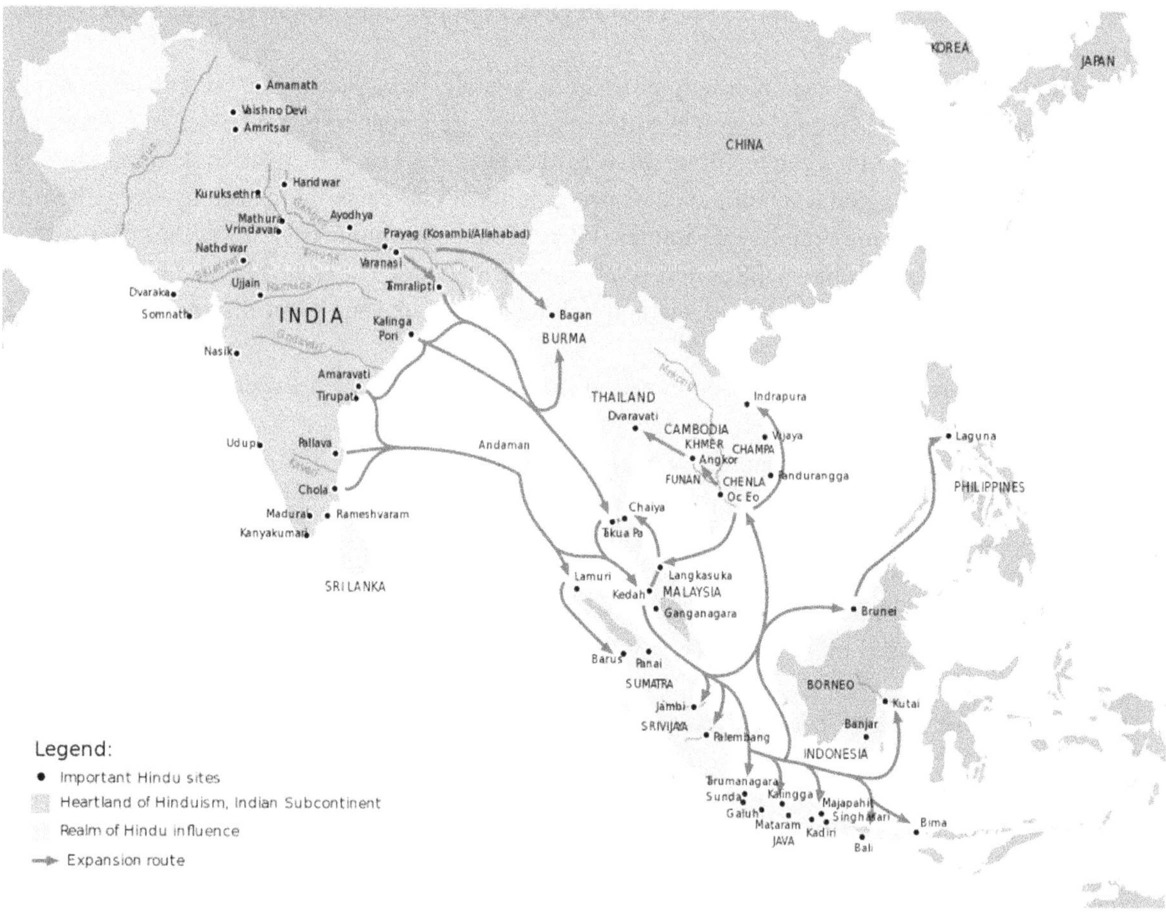

MAIN FOCUS OF THE CHAPTER

It is crucial that developing and least developed countries can accelerate their economic growth. Developing and underdeveloped countries which apply imported substitution policies have been significantly disappointed in the late 1970s, and this situation has led to a reduction in protectionist policies. In addition, the disadvantages of imported-substitution policies and most of the rapidly industrializing countries support the idea of export-based industrialization and development strategy is more successful (Ahmed et al., 2000, p. 591). Inherently, this is consistent with the macroeconomic theory mentioning the importance of exports in the economy (Feder, 1982; Kaldor, 1967; Krueger, 1990; Marin, 1992; Romer, 1989).

Although India experienced a significant economic crisis in 1991, its economy is developing rapidly. The economic crisis has negatively affected the global reliability of the Indian economy. The economic crisis affected the balance of payments and efficiency in the economy adversely and limited the integration of India with the global economy. Due to this economic crisis in 1991, India has started to carry out comprehensive economic reforms. India has become a sectoral dialogue partner with ASEAN in 1992 in the fields of trade, investment, tourism, science and technology, in order to integrate into the global economy. In 1995, India was accepted to ASEAN as a full dialogue partner. As a result of mutual negotiations, a Free Trade Agreement has been signed between India and ASEAN on August 13th, 2009, in Bangkok. Nowadays, when we examine the current economic relations of India with ASEAN, it is seen that it covers a wide range including international commodity trade, service trade, investments, tourism and labor force flows (Acharya & Sharma, 2012, p. 90).

ASEAN countries aim to improve their economic development levels and positions in the world economy. ASEAN countries, which come together to increase the economic development levels of the member countries and enable the countries to participate more actively in the globalization process, target to develop their trade with each other and world. The tariff rates applied by India in international trade (approximately average tariff rate 9%) are quite high compared to international standards. With the AIFTA agreement between ASEAN and India, decreasing these tariff rates gradually is aimed (Veeramani & Saini, 2010, p. 1). Associated with the mutual reduction of tariff rates, international trade volume between India and ASEAN countries has been expected to increase.

Table 1. GDP Per Capita and Economic Growth Rates of India and Southeast Asian Countries (2018)

Countries	GDP Per Capita ($)	Economic Growth (%)
India	2010 $	6,81%
Brunei	31628 $	0,05%
Cambodia	1510 $	7,49%
Indonesia	3893 $	5,17%
Malaysia	11373 $	4,74%
Myanmar	1326 $	6,21%
Philippines	3102 $	6,24%
Singapore	64581 $	3,13%
Thailand	7273 $	4,12%
Viet Nam	2566 $	7,07%

Source: World Bank, data.worldbank.org.

GDP per capita and economic growth rates of India and Southeast Asian Countries are given in Table 1. When India and Southeast Asian countries are analyzed in terms of per capita income, it is seen that Singapore, Brunei and Malaysia have a higher per capita income level than $10000. Considering the economic growth levels of India and South Asian countries, it is revealed that countries show economic growth performance about 5-6%, except Brunei.

Table 2 shows the export and import levels of India and Southeast Asian countries and the shares of international trade in the world. It is seen that the share of Singapore, India, Thailand, Vietnam, Malaysia and Indonesia in the world international trade is higher than other countries. However, the shares of Philippines, Myanmar, Cambodia and Brunei in world trade are below the expected level compared to other countries. Accordingly, it is seen that Singapore, Thailand, Viet Nam, Indonesia and Malaysia could be important export markets for India.

Table 2. Export, Import and World Shares of India and Southeast Asian Countries (2018) (Billion $)

Countries	Export	Export Shares in World	Import	Import Shares in World
India	536	2,14%	642	2,61%
Brunei	7	0,03%	5	0,02%
Cambodia	15	0,06%	15	0,06%
Indonesia	218	0,87%	229	0,93%
Malaysia	246	0,98%	221	0,89%
Myanmar	16	0,07%	21	0,09%
Philippines	104	0,42%	146	0,59%
Singapore	642	2,56%	545	2,21%
Thailand	337	1,34%	285	1,16%
Viet Nam	259	1,03%	251	1,02%

Source: World Bank, data.worldbank.org.

Table 3. India's International Trade with Southeast Asian Countries (Million $)

International Trade	Countries	2016	2017	2018
Export	Brunei	37	48	66
	Cambodia	109	120	179
	Indonesia	3.131	3.762	4.792
	Malaysia	4.188	5.546	6.553
	Myanmar	1.141	1.063	1.242
	Philippines	1.474	1.584	1.745
	Singapore	7.354	11.559	10.450
	Thailand	2.962	3.588	4.386
	Viet Nam	5.957	8.114	6.701
Import	Brunei	461	595	433
	Cambodia	43	47	48
	Indonesia	12.189	16.235	16.045
	Malaysia	8.653	8.901	10.402
	Myanmar	1.084	738	454
	Philippines	475	711	614
	Singapore	6.719	7.235	14.436
	Thailand	5.316	6.456	7.646
	Viet Nam	3.105	4.141	7.223

Source: UN Comtrade Database, comtrade.un.org.

International trade levels of India to Southeast Asian countries are discussed in Table 3. When examining the export and import levels of India to Southeast Asian countries, it is seen that the export and import of India to Singapore, Viet Nam, Malaysia, Indonesia and Thailand is higher the export levels compared to other countries.

Table 4. Export and Import Share of India to Southeast Asian Countries (2018) (Million $)

Countries	Export of India	Share in Total Export of India	Import of India	Share in Total Import of India
Brunei	66	0,01%	433	0,07%
Cambodia	179	0,03%	48	0,01%
Indonesia	4.792	0,89%	16.045	2,49%
Malaysia	6.553	1,22%	10.402	1,62%
Myanmar	1.242	0,23%	454	0,07%
Philippines	1.745	0,33%	614	0,11%
Singapore	10.450	1,95%	14.436	2,25%
Thailand	4.386	0,82%	7.646	1,19%
Viet Nam	6.701	1,25%	7.223	1,12%

Source: UN Comtrade Database, comtrade.un.org.

Table 4 shows the shares of Southeast Asian countries in India's total exports and imports. Examining Table 4, the share of Singapore in India's total exports is highest (1.95%) compared to other Southeast Asian countries. The countries with the highest export share after Singapore are Viet Nam (1.25%), Malaysia (1.22%), Indonesia (0.89%) and Thailand (0.82%). Indonesia has the highest share in total imports of India (2.49%) compared to other Southeast Asian countries. The countries with the highest import share after Indonesia are Singapore (2.25%), Malaysia (1.62%), Thailand (1.19%) and Viet Nam (1.12%) respectively.

When the exports and imports of India to Southeast Asian countries are evaluated, it is very important to determine target countries with international trade potential in terms of creating new markets in global trade, where international competition is rapidly increasing. Accordingly, it is crucial to determine the exports of India to Southeast Asian countries and the levels of potential export to these countries. This paper aims to calculate the potential export volume of India to Southeast Asian countries and to determine the target markets by comparing with the actual export levels.

EMPIRICAL ANALYZES

The aim of this paper is to determine the potential Southeast Asian export market for India by comparing the potential export level with the actual export from India to Southeast Asian countries. In order to create the research model of Indian export to Southeast Asian countries in the study, data on exports of India to Southeast Asian countries, gross domestic product per capita, distance between India and Southeast Asian countries, tariff rates of Southeast Asian countries, exchange rates of India and Southeast

Asian countries, colonial ties between India and Southeast Asian countries, trade openness of Southeast Asian countries are used. Southeast Asian countries included in the analysis are given on Table 10 in the Appendix.

Export potential of India to Southeast Asian countries will be investigated through the panel gravity model within the scope of the study. In this direction, first of all, the variables that have an impact on India's exports to these countries will be analyzed econometrically. The hypotheses to be tested within the scope of the panel gravity model are as follows:

h_1: Gross domestic product per capita of countries have a statistically significant and positive effect on Indian exports to Southeast Asian countries.
h_2: Geographical distance between the two countries have a statistically significant and negative effect on Indian exports to Southeast Asian countries.
h_3: Tariff rates of the countries have a statistically significant and negative effect on Indian exports to Southeast Asian countries.
h_4: The increase in the exchange rate has a statistically significant and positive effect on Indian exports to Southeast Asian countries.
h_5: Colonial ties between the two countries have a statistically significant and positive effect on Indian exports to Southeast Asian countries.
h_6: Trade openness of countries has a statistically significant and positive effect on Indian exports to Southeast Asian countries.
h_7: Economic crisis in 2008 has a statistically significant and negative effect on Indian exports to Southeast Asian countries.

Data on countries' gross domestic product per capita, tariff rates of Southeast Asian countries, exchange rates of India and Southeast Asian countries and trade openness of Southeast Asian countries are obtained from the database of the World Bank. Data of exports of India to Southeast Asian countries are gained from the UN Comtrade Database. In addition, data on countries' distance and colonial ties between India and Southeast Asian countries are acquired from database of Research and Expertise on The World Economy (CEPII). Series used in the paper are annual between 1996 and 2018. The information about the variables used in the study is as follows;

$\ln(exp_{ind})$: Exports of India
$\ln(gdppc_{ind})$: Gross Domestic Product per capita of India
$\ln(gdppc_{sac})$: Gross Domestic Product per capita of Southeast Asian countries
$\ln(lndist)$: Distance between India and Southeast Asian countries
$\ln(tariff_{sac})$: Average tariff rate of Southeast Asian countries
$\ln(exr_{ind})$: Exchange rates of India
$\ln(exr_{sac})$: Exchange rates of Southeast Asian countries
$\ln(colony)$: Colonial ties between India and Southeast Asian countries
$\ln(openness_{sac})$: Trade openness of Southeast Asian countries
$\ln(crisis)$: Economic crisis in 2008

Depending on this information, the panel data model has been created for India and Southeast Asian countries to determine the potential export of India to Southeast Asian countries (1);

$$ln\left(exp_{ind}\right)_{ijt} = \beta_0 + \beta_1 ln\left(gdppc_{ind}\right)_{it} + \beta_2 ln\left(gdppc_{sac}\right)_{jt} + \beta_3 lndist_{ij} + \beta_4 ln\left(tariff_{sac}\right)_{jt}$$
$$+\beta_5 ln\left(exr_{ind}\right)_{it} + \beta_6 ln\left(exr_{sac}\right)_{jt} + \beta_7 colony_{ij} + \beta_8 openness_{ij} + \beta_9 crisis_t + \varepsilon_t \quad (1)$$

Panel Gravity Model Analysis

The main reason for choosing panel data analysis in the study is to make more valid and reliable analysis by evaluating the time and cross-section effects together to create a model for the export of India to Southeast countries. The data set formed as a result of combining the horizontal sectional observations of the units for a certain time period is called panel data. Panel data series consists of "n" number of units and "t" number of observations of these units (Tatoğlu, 2013, p. 2). Panel data analysis provides more consistent and valid estimations in the analyzes as it includes cross-section and time effects.

The gravity model has started to be applied in the international trade literature in the early 1960s. Tinbergen (1962), Pöyhönen (1963) and Linneman (1966) carried out gravity model as the first applications in the international trade literature. Since then, the gravity model has been the most widely used model for estimating international trade flows. While international trade volumes between countries are realized in direct proportion with their economic size and populations, it is stated that the distance between countries will increase commercial costs and will be inversely proportional to distance (Baltagi, 2015, p. 608). Traditional panel gravity model is created as follows (2);

$$T_{ij} = \alpha_0 Y_{i\alpha 1} Y_{i\alpha 2} D_{ij\alpha 3} \quad (2)$$

The gravity model has appeared as a widely used approach to investigate and examine economic variables about international trade flows. A gravity equation is estimated that reveals the determinants of countries' trade flows such us levels of income, population, tariff rates, exchange rates, geographic proximity, historical ties, and cultural similarities (Martinez-Zarzoso, 2003, p. 174). In the literature, gravity model has been constantly employed to estimation of flows of several types such as foreign direct investment, international portfolio investment, especially international merchandise and service trade. Along with the model, export volumes from country i to country j in t time are described by their economic sizes (GDP), populations, and geographical distances.

Theoretical explanations for the use of the gravity model in international trade were very poor until the 1970s. Some theoretical explanations about the gravitational model were propounded with the 1970s. First effort of theoretical explanation of gravity model is realized by Anderson (1979) that investigate the product differentiation via gravity equation. Later, Bergstrand (1985, 1989) also examined the theoretical background of bilateral trade in the papers, whereas it had been employed a differentiated product framework with increasing returns to scale to explain the gravity model by Helpman (1987). However, on the contrary of many researchers remark, the gravity model was used before the 1960s by Ravenstein (1885) and then by Zipf (1946) (Kabir et al., 2017).

The gravity model has traditionally been forecasted via cross-sectional data of countries. However, it is propounded the problem that generation of biased results because of heterogeneity between the countries is not controlled for in an accurate way (Cheng and Tsai, 2008; Cheng & Wall, 2005; Larson et al., 2018; Osabuohien et al., 2019). It has been used panel data, which allows using more general types of heterogeneity in order to reduce the effects of this problem (Westerlund & Wilhelmsson, 2011).

Traditional gravity model employs geographical distance in order to contain the transport costs to the model (Martinez-Zarzoso & Nowak-Lehmann, 2003, p. 297). On the other hand, in the near future Bougheas et al. (1999) demonstrated that transport costs can be represented by public infrastructure as well as by distance. It has been enhanced the gravity model in their article by adding various infrastructure variables (stock of public capital and length of motorway network). Tinbergen's argument is that physical distance is a crude measure of transportation costs relevant foreign countries. Several researchers concentrated on approximations for trade distance between the two trade partners in the preliminary empirical analysis on international trade flows. The most important issue about the distance in the gravity model is how to explain the distance coefficient and whether distance has a linear effect on international trade. Trade costs are directly related to the features of goods, such as fragility, perishability, weight or size. In this regard, trade cost would be country specific, based on country's distance and specialization. Consequently, distance between two countries is substantial for estimation of trade volumes of these countries. Because the increase in the distance between the two countries will increase the trade costs and negatively affect the international trade.

Panel Unit Root Tests

Before panel data analysis, the stationarity of the series should be tested covered by the analysis. In the presence of non-stationary series, spurious regression problem can be occurred, and the analysis results cannot be properly reflected the relationship between the variables. Accordingly, the stationarity of the series will be tested with panel unit root tests at first and then, model estimates regarding the export from India to Southeast Asian countries will be made.

Table 5. Panel Unit Root Test Results

Variables	Im, Pesaran & Shin (2003)		Levin, Lin & Chu (2002)	
	Level		Level	
	C	C+T	C	C+T
$ln(exp_{ind})$	-2.654***	-3.291***	-2.058**	-2.536***
$ln(gdppc_{ind})$	-2.065**	-1.948**	-3.495***	-1.975**
$ln(gdppc_{sac})$	-2.179**	-2.563***	-3.528***	-2.029**
$ln(tariff_{sac})$	-2.709***	-2.906***	-3.973***	-2.413***
$ln(exr_{ind})$	-2.705***	-2.198**	-3.829***	-2.711***
$ln(exrsac)$	-2.766***	-3.284***	-5.237***	-9.566***
openness	-2.399*	-2.765**	-3.033***	-3.118***

Note: "C" stands for constant term, "I + T" represents constant and trend. ***, **, and * indicate significance at 1%, 5% and 10% respectively.

The results of the unit root tests are given in Table 5. According to the results, it has been determined that all series are stationary at their levels, in other words, they do not contain unit roots. Accordingly, it is necessary to start the stage of determining the appropriate estimation model for panel data analysis.

Determination of Panel Data Estimation Model

It is important to determine the appropriate estimation method for the model used in the research within the scope of panel data analysis. In this direction, several tests have been performed on the model within the scope of the study and estimation method is determined, which has effective results. In this context, F Test, Breusch-Pagan Lagrange Multiplier (LM) Test, Score Test, Likelihood Ratio (LR) Test and Hausman Test have been performed on the model.

Pooled model is tested against random effects model via F Test, Breusch-Pagan (1980) LM Test, LR Test and Score Test. h_0 hypothesis of these tests is stated the pooled model gives more effective results than the random effects model. The alternative hypothesis reveals that the random effects model gives more effective results than pooled model.

Table 6. F Test, Breusch-Pagan LM Test, LR Test, Score Test and Hausman Test Results

Tests	F Score	Chibar2(01)	Chi2(1)	Prob>F	Prob>Chibar2	Prob>Chi2	Chi2(7)	Prob>Chi2
F Test	399.4	-	-	0.00	-	-	-	-
LM Test	-	1988.3	-	-	0.00	-	-	-
LR Test	-	521.6	-	-	0.00	-	-	-
Score Test	-	-	6.5e+05	-	-	0.00	-	-
Hausman Test	-	-	-	-	-	-	0.02	1.00

In the pooled model, the assumption is that both constant and slope parameters are fixed according to units and time, in other words, all observations are homogeneous. The pooled model makes estimates under the assumptions that there are no cross-section or time effects, and constant and slope parameters are fixed in the model.

The statistical values and results of the tests performed against the random model of the pooled model are given in Table 6. When the obtained findings are evaluated, h_0 hypothesis, which indicates that the standard errors of unit effects are equal to zero in the research model, can be rejected and the pooled estimation model is not appropriate technique for the analyses. After determining that the classical model is not appreciated, it is tested whether the appropriate estimator is fixed effects or random effects via Hausman Test. According to the result, testing the research model by using a random effects estimator gives more effective results than other estimators.

Assumption Tests in Random Effects Model

The error term of the models used in panel data analysis is accepted to be homoscedastic (constant variance) within and between units. However, it is assumed that there are no periodic and spatial correlations in the error terms of the models (Tatoğlu, 2013, p. 197). It is important to test these assumptions in the random effects model in the subject matter models.

Table 7. Assumption Tests Results

Test	Test Statistics	Prob.
Heteroscedasticity Test Results		
W_0	2.789	0.006
W_{50}	2.431	0.016
W_{10}	2.533	0.012
Autocorrelation Test Results		
Modified Bhargava et al. Durbin-Watson	1.504	* < 2
Baltagi-Wu LBI	1.593	* < 2
LM(lambda=0)	199.57	0.000
LM(Var(u)=0,lambda=0)	1989.39	0.000
Cross-Sectional Correlation		
Pesaran's Test	6.046	0.000
Friedman's Test	60.571	0.000

In the random effects model, heteroscedasticity, autocorrelation and cross-sectional correlation problems can be observed. Panel data analysis assumption tests results are given in Table 7. Accordingly, tests developed by Levene (1960) and Brown and Forsythe (1974) have been carried out to analyze the presence of heteroscedasticity in the random effects model. While Bhargava, Modified Bhargava et al. and Baltagi-Wu LBI tests have been used to analyze the presence of autocorrelation in the model, Pesaran and Friedman tests have been used to analyze the cross-sectional correlation.

Examining the obtained findings in Table 7, the h_0 hypothesis, which states that there is a constant variance, is rejected. Therefore, it has been determined that the estimates made with the random effects model are heteroskedastic. According to results, the h_0 hypothesis, which indicate that there is no first-order autocorrelation for the random effects model, has been rejected by Bhargava et al. (1982) and Baltagi and Wu (1999) tests. Hence, it has been revealed that the model estimated by the random effects model had first-degree autocorrelation. As regards the findings obtained, the h_0 hypothesis that there was no correlation between cross-sections has been rejected as a result of Pesaran (2004) and Friedman (1937) tests, and it has been revealed that there is a cross-sectional correlation in the model.

According to the results of the basic assumptions tests, it has been determined that it is more effective to continue with the panel data analysis with the random effects model and there is a heteroscedasticity, autocorrelation and cross-sectional correlation in the random effects model. Accordingly, consistent results are acquired by using the Parks (1967) and Kmenta (1986) estimator in the random effects model.

Table 8. Parks (1967) and Kmenta (1986) Estimator Results

Dependent Variable: $ln(exp_{ind})$			
Independent Variables	**Coefficients**	**P Value**	
$ln(gdppc_{ind})$	0.755	0.000	
$ln(gdppc_{sac})$	0.786	0.000	
$ln(dist)$	-1.759	0.000	
$ln(tariff_{sac})$	0.009	0.743	
$ln(exr_{ind})$	0.728	0.010	
$ln(exr_{sac})$	0.046	0.025	
colony	-1.885	0.000	
crisis	0.135	0.163	
openness	0.559	0.000	
constant	19.911	0.000	
Wald chi2(9)	700.78	**Prob > chi2**	0.000

In Table 8, the results of Parks (1967) and Kmenta (1986) are given. It was aimed to create a model that measures export potential of India to Southeast Asian countries and analyze factors that affect the exports of India to Southeast Asian countries via gravity model. According to the results, gross domestic product per capita of countries, distance between India and Southeast Asian countries, exchange rates of India and Southeast Asian countries, colonial ties between India and Southeast Asian countries and trade openness of Southeast Asian countries is found statistically significant.

According to results of analyses, h_1, h_2, h_4, h_5 and h_6 hypotheses are rejected. In this direction, it has been revealed that gross domestic product per capita of countries, geographical distance between the two countries, exchange rate, colonial ties between the two countries and trade openness of countries have statistically significant effects on India's exports to Southeast Asian countries. However, h_3 and h_7 hypotheses are not rejected. Accordingly, it has been determined that the tariff rates of the countries and the global economic crisis in 2008 have not statistically significant effect on India's exports to Southeast Asian countries.

SOLUTIONS AND RECOMMENDATIONS

The export potential is calculated by comparing it with the actual export in order to determine whether there is an export potential not used in international trade. Within the scope of the study, the model which is created to determine the potential exports of India with Southeast Asian countries is analyzed and actual and potential export have been calculated. The estimated export potential is compared with the actual export to find out if there is a gap between actual and potential trade.

Export potential is calculated with statistically significant variables in the model as a result of the panel gravity model. Model results are as follows (3):

$$ln\left(exp_{ind}\right)_{ijt} = 19.911 + 0.755 * \ln\left(gdppc_{ind}\right)_{it} + 0.786 * \ln\left(gdppc_{sac}\right)_{jt} - 1.759 * lndist_{ij} + 0.728 * \ln\left(exr_{ind}\right)_{it} + 0.046 * \ln\left(exr_{sac}\right)_{jt} - 1.885 * colony_{ij} + 0.559 * openness_{ij} \quad (3)$$

The export potential is obtained by proportioning the theoretical value of Indian exports to Southeast Asian countries based on the trade equation of India, to the observed export value of India to Southeast Asian countries. The value obtained from the analysis represents the potential export level of India to Southeast Asian countries.

Table 9. Indian Export Potential to Southeast Asian Countries

Year	Brunei	Cambodia	Indonesia	Malaysia	Myanmar	Philippines	Singapore	Thailand	VietNam
1996	19,46	40,63	0,14	0,17	0,48	0,50	0,72	1,00	0,85
1997	52,88	23,44	0,19	0,20	0,48	0,44	0,90	1,24	0,89
1998	31,06	11,89	0,34	0,29	0,90	0,82	1,20	1,20	1,01
1999	89,86	11,15	0,23	0,25	0,88	0,78	1,15	1,00	0,94
2000	47,71	12,92	0,24	0,25	0,76	0,69	1,27	0,99	0,86
2001	66,77	10,82	0,20	0,16	0,46	0,50	0,97	0,87	0,84
2002	34,09	7,65	0,14	0,18	0,39	0,27	0,70	0,78	0,68
2003	37,37	7,47	0,12	0,19	0,56	0,43	0,76	0,95	0,68
2004	44,20	11,52	0,13	0,18	0,42	0,45	0,53	1,02	0,61
2005	60,76	11,14	0,13	0,19	0,48	0,38	0,43	1,01	0,66
2006	7,64	6,39	0,13	0,20	0,58	0,38	0,48	0,98	0,62
2007	44,73	8,41	0,16	0,17	0,64	0,49	0,49	0,98	0,60
2008	27,70	7,87	0,13	0,11	0,63	0,40	0,46	0,95	0,50
2009	17,48	10,07	0,13	0,09	0,94	0,45	0,43	1,12	0,54
2010	25,99	8,48	0,12	0,12	1,23	0,51	0,45	1,21	0,53
2011	0,87	6,78	0,11	0,13	0,75	0,46	0,33	1,14	0,49
2012	25,96	6,66	0,13	0,14	0,99	0,48	0,40	1,05	0,54
2013	22,62	6,37	0,15	0,10	0,84	0,41	0,42	0,94	0,40
2014	20,85	6,57	0,20	0,13	0,85	0,47	0,65	1,21	0,43
2015	22,58	7,62	0,30	0,11	0,87	0,55	0,70	1,35	0,60
2016	18,24	11,88	0,31	0,14	0,70	0,56	0,71	1,55	0,63
2017	15,84	12,30	0,30	0,12	0,91	0,59	0,56	1,49	0,58
2018	13,65	9,26	0,25	0,12	0,88	0,59	0,71	1,39	0,82

Table 9 and Figure 2 (in the Appendix) shows the potential export rate of India to Southeast Asian countries. As a result of the analyze, India has a high export potential to Brunei, Cambodia and Thailand in Southeast Asian countries. However, India exports to Myanmar, Viet Nam and Singapore slightly above its export potential, whereas its exports to Indonesia, Malaysia and Philippines are far above its export potential.

FUTURE RESEARCH DIRECTIONS

Today, the volume of international trade between countries has also increased with the increase in the level of globalization. In this direction, it has become important for countries to develop their commercial relations with their trade partners. The existence of common language, religion and historical ties with each other, the short distances between countries and the customs tariffs discount between countries increase the trade volumes of the countries.

Countries should increment their international trade volumes with the countries of close region in order to exist in international competition. In this direction, it is needed to reduce tariff rates between each other and achieve economic integration in the Southeast Asia. Especially, India should create new trade opportunities and export potential with Myanmar, Viet Nam, Singapore, Indonesia, Malaysia and Philippines, because the trade potential of India has been exceeded to these countries and new trade opportunities need to be created.

In line with the above information and data, it is important to examine in which sectors there are trade opportunities in the academic literature for disclosing the trade potential between India and Southeast Asian countries. Empirical studies will be substantial to ascertain the commercial steps to be taken in order to solve the problems in international trade integration and to realize economic growth expectations. Therefore, the trade policies that should be implemented in order to reduce the tariff rates, stabilizing the exchange rate and eliminate transportation costs should be argued in detail. Because, it has been determined that the distance variable has a significant negative effect in international trade between India and Southeast Asian countries as a result of the analyzes on the trade potential.

CONCLUSION

Increasing the export volume, has an important substantial effects on the economic development and development levels of the countries. Growth of exports is an important issue for India, which has an important economic and trade potential in its economic geography, in order to increase the level of economic development. Accordingly, the exports of India to Southeast Asian countries have been estimated by the gravity model in this study. The paper investigates the export potential of India to Southeast Asian countries in terms of export markets.

As long as countries have effective trade relationships with each other, they are going to have substantial export volume. Therefore, the study contributes to theoretical and empirical literature of international trade by determining the export potential of India to Southeast Asian countries and revealing trade opportunities in terms of countries in this region.

Panel data analysis is performed in order to indicate the export potential of India to Southeast Asian countries in the scope of analyses. As a result of the estimates, gross domestic product per capita of countries, distance between India and Southeast Asian countries, exchange rates of India and Southeast Asian countries, colonial ties between India and Southeast Asian countries and trade openness of

Southeast Asian countries have statistically significant effects on exports of India to Southeast Asian countries as determined.

When the potential exports are compared with the actual exports, it has been determined that India exports to Myanmar, Viet Nam and Singapore slightly above its export potential, while it exports to Indonesia, Malaysia and the Philippines are far above its export potential. In addition, India has a high export potential to Brunei, Cambodia and Thailand in Southeast Asian countries.

The results of the analysis of export potential of India to Southeast Asian countries are shown developing accurate trade policies and incentives to penetrate the export markets of Brunei, Cambodia and Thailand are going to play significant role in increasing the export volume to these countries. In addition, it is concluded that new export incentives and providing the diversification in exports are crucial in order to increase the export volume in Myanmar, Viet Nam, Singapore, Indonesia, Malaysia and the Philippines, which have an export volume exceeding the export potential.

When the results obtained are compared with the findings of Batra (2006), which examines the trade potential of India, it is found that the actual trade to Indonesia, Malaysia and Singapore exceeded the potential trade volume in both studies. In addition, both studies revealed that India has high export potential to Cambodia. However, it is determined that Brunei, whose data could not be obtained by Batra (2006), was an important export market for India, while Myanmar did not have an export potential for India in this study. These results and comparisons reveal the important contributions made to the literature by this study.

Analyzing the export potential and increasing the export volume is an important issue, and it is crucial to carry out more comprehensive studies in order to examine the export potential on sectoral basis and to determine whether the exports of these sectors are stable. Besides, it is important to investigate the effects of countries' trade and travel restrictions on exports of India to Southeast Asian countries due to COVID-19, which emerged in Wuhan, China in 2020, and turned into a global pandemic in a short time. The pandemic process negatively affected international trade, which expanded the production volume and made a net contribution to the gross domestic product. In addition, it is substantial to examine the effects of travel and transportation restrictions imposed by countries on the supply chain in order to establish trade policies for the future.

REFERENCES

Acharya, R., & Sharma, H. (2012). India's trade intensity with ASEAN countries. *Journal of Commerce and Trade*, *7*(1), 90–95.

Ahmed, Q. M., Butt, M. S., Alam, S., & Kazmi, A. A. (2000). Economic growth, export, and external debt causality: The case of Asian countries. *Pakistan Development Review*, *39*(4), 591–608. doi:10.30541/v39i4IIpp.591-608

Anderson, J. E. (1979). A theoretical foundation for the gravity equation. *The American Economic Review*, *69*, 106–116.

Baltagi, B. H. (2015). *The Oxford handbook of panel data*. Oxford University Press. doi:10.1093/oxfordhb/9780199940042.001.0001

Baltagi, B. H., & Wu, P. X. (1999). Unequally spaced panel data regressions with AR(1) disturbances. *Econometric Theory*, *15*(6), 814–823. doi:10.1017/S0266466699156020

Batra, A. (2006). India's global trade potential: The gravity model approach. *Global Economic Review*, *35*(3), 327–361. doi:10.1080/12265080600888090

Bergstrand, J. H. (1985). The gravity equation in international trade: Some microeconomic foundations and empirical evidence. *The Review of Economics and Statistics*, *67*(3), 474–481. doi:10.2307/1925976

Bergstrand, J. H. (1989). The generalized gravity equation, monopolistic competition, and the factor-proportions theory in international trade. *The Review of Economics and Statistics*, *71*(1), 143–153. doi:10.2307/1928061

Bhargava, A., Sosa-Escuderı, W., & Narendranathan, W. (1982). Serial correlation and fixed effects models. *The Review of Economic Studies*, *49*(4), 533–549. doi:10.2307/2297285

Borensztein, E., De Gregorio, J., & Lee, J. (1998). How does foreign direct investment affect economic growth? *Journal of International Economics*, *45*(1), 115–135. doi:10.1016/S0022-1996(97)00033-0

Bougheas, S., Demetriades, P., & Morgenroth, E. (1999). Infrastructure, transport costs and trade. *Journal of International Economics*, *47*(1), 169–189. doi:10.1016/S0022-1996(98)00008-7

Breusch, T., & Pagan, A. (1980). The lanrange multiplier test and its applications to model specification in econometrics. *The Review of Economic Studies*, *47*(1), 239–253. doi:10.2307/2297111

Brown, M. B., & Forsythe, A. B. (1974). The small sample behavior of some statistic which test the equality of several means. *Technometrics*, *16*(1), 129–132. doi:10.1080/00401706.1974.10489158

Cheng, I.-H., & Tsai, Y.-Y. (2008). Estimating the staged effects of regional economic integration on trade volumes. *Applied Economics*, *40*(3), 383–393. doi:10.1080/00036840600606252

Cheng, I.-H., & Wall, H. J. (2005). Controlling heterogeneity in gravity models of trade and integration. *Review - Federal Reserve Bank of St. Louis*, *87*(1), 49–63. doi:10.20955/r.87.49-64

Dollar, D. (1992). Outward-oriented developing economies really do grow more rapidly: Evidence from LCDs. 1976-1985. *Economic Development and Cultural Change*, *40*(3), 523–544. doi:10.1086/451959

Drysdale, P., & Garnaut, R. (1982). Trade intensities and the analysis of bilateral trade flows in a many-country world: A survey. *Hitotsubashi Journal of Economics*, *22*(2), 62–84.

Feder, G. (1982). On export and economic growth. *Journal of Development Economics*, *12*(1-2), 59–73. doi:10.1016/0304-3878(83)90031-7

Friedman, M. (1937). The use of ranks to avoid the assumption of normality implicit in the analysis of variance. *Journal of the American Statistical Association*, *32*(200), 675–701. doi:10.1080/01621459.1937.10503522

Ghuman, R. S., & Madaan, D. K. (2009). India-ASEAN trade relations during post-WTO period. WTO and Asian union, deep and deep publications, 395-406.

Harrigan, J. (2001). *Specialization and the volume of trade: Do the data obey the laws?* National Bureau of Economic Research, NBER Working Papers, 8675.

Helpman, E. (1987). Imperfect competition and international trade: Evidence from fourteen industrial countries. *Journal of the Japanese and International Economies*, *1*(1), 62–81. doi:10.1016/0889-1583(87)90027-X

Im, K. S., Pesaran, M. H., & Shin, Y. (2003). Testing for unit roots in heterogeneous panels. *Journal of Econometrics*, *115*(1), 53–74. doi:10.1016/S0304-4076(03)00092-7

Kabir, M., Salim, R., & Al-Mawali, N. (2017). The gravity model and trade flows: Recent developments in econometric modeling and empirical evidence. *Economic Analysis and Policy*, *56*, 60–71. doi:10.1016/j.eap.2017.08.005

Kaldor, N. (1967). *Strategic factors in economic development*. Cornell University Press.

Kmenta, J. (1986). *Elements of econometrics*. MacMillan.

Krueger, A. O. (1990). Asian trade and growth lessons. *The American Economic Review*, *80*, 108–111.

Larson, J., Baker, J., Latta, G., Ohrel, S., & Wade, C. (2018). Modeling international trade of forest products: Application of PPML to a gravity model of trade. *Forest Products Journal*, *68*(3), 303–316. PMID:32280136

Levene, H. (1960). Robust tests for equality of variances. In I. Olkin, G. Ghurye, W. Hoeffding, W. G. Madow, & H. B. Mann (Eds.), *Contributions to probability and statistics* (pp. 278–292). Stanford University Press.

Levin, A., Lin, F. C., & Chu, S. (2002). Unit root tests in panel data: Asymptotic and finite-sample properties. *Journal of Econometrics*, *108*(1), 1–24. doi:10.1016/S0304-4076(01)00098-7

Limaye, S. (2008). India-Asia Pacific relations: Consolidating friendships and nuclear legitimacy. *Comparative Connections*, 1-22.

Linnemann, H. (1966). *An econometric study of international trade flows*. North Holland Publishing Company.

Madaan, D. K. (2004). India's trade intensity with ASEAN. *The Indian Economic Journal*, *52*(1-2), 142–151.

Marin, D. (1992). Is the export-led growth hypothesis valid for industrialised countries? *The Review of Economics and Statistics*, *74*(4), 678–688. doi:10.2307/2109382

Martinez-Zarzoso, I. (2003). Gravity model: An application to trade between regional blocs. *Atlantic Economic Journal*, *31*(2), 174–187. doi:10.1007/BF02319869

Martinez-Zarzoso, I., & Nowak-Lehmann, F. (2003). Augmented gravity model: An empirical application to Mercosur-European union trade flows. *Journal of Applied Econometrics*, *6*(2), 291–316.

Osabuohien, E. S., Efobi, U. R., Odebiyi, J. T., Fayomi, O. O., & Salami, A. O. (2019). Bilateral trade performance in West Africa: A gravity model estimation. *African Development Review*, *31*(1), 1–14. doi:10.1111/1467-8268.12359

Parks, R. (1967). Efficient estimation of a system of regression equations when disturbances are both serially and contemporaneously correlated. *Journal of the American Statistical Association*, *62*(318), 500–509. doi:10.1080/01621459.1967.10482923

Pesaran, M. H. (2004). *General diagnostic test for cross section dependence in panels.* University of Cambridge, Faculty of Economics, Cambridge Working Papers in Economics, No. 0435.

Pöyhönen, P. (1963). A tentative model for the volume of trade between countries. *Weltwirtschaftliches Archiv*, *90*(1), 93–100.

Pradnya, P. (2009). India-ASEAN economic relations. *Indian Institute of Management, Ahemadabad, Working Paper Series, 108*, 1-24.

Rahman, K. F., & Yaesmin, S. (2014). Regional integration of South Asia through trade facilitation: Challenges and opportunities. *ASA University Review*, *8*(2), 19–38.

Ravenstein, E. G. (1885). The law of migration. *Journal of the Statistical Society of London*, *48*(2), 167–235. doi:10.2307/2979181

Romer, P. (1989). Capital accumulation. In Modern business cycle theory. Press.

Sahasrabuddhe, U. (2012). Regionalization processes in South and Southeast Asia: A comparative study. *The Asian Scholar, 6*.

Tatoğlu, F. Y. (2013). *Panel veri ekonometrisi*. Beta Yayıncılık.

Tinbergen, J. (1962). *Shaping the world economy: Suggestions for an international economic policy*. The Twentieth Century Fund.

Tumbarello, P. (2005). *Regional trade integration and WTO accession: Which is the right sequencing? An application to the CIS*. IMF Working Paper, WP/05/94.

Van Mulekom, L., Axelsson, A., Batungbacal, E. P., Baxter, D., Siregar, R., & De la Torre, I. (2006). Trade and export orientation of fisheries in Southeast Asia: Under-priced export at the expense of domestic food security and local economies. *Ocean and Coastal Management*, *49*(9-10), 546–561. doi:10.1016/j.ocecoaman.2006.06.001

Veeramani, C., & Saini, G. K. (2010). Impact of ASEAN-India FTA on India's plantation commodities: A simulation analysis. *Indira Gandhi Institute of Development Research Working Paper, 4*, 1–20.

Westerlund, J., & Wilhelmsson, F. (2011). Estimating the gravity model without gravity using panel data. *Applied Economics*, *43*(6), 641–649. doi:10.1080/00036840802599784

Zipf, G. K. (1946). The P_1P_2/D hypothesis: On the intercity movement of persons. *American Sociological Review*, *11*(6), 677–686. doi:10.2307/2087063

ADDITIONAL READING

Angles, S., Sundar, A., & Chinnadurai, M. (2011). Impact of globalization on production and export of turmeric in India – an economic analysis. *Agricultural Economics Research Review*, *24*, 301–308.

Beck, K. (2017). Bayesian model averaging and jointness measures: Theoretical framework and application to the gravity model of trade. *Statistics in Transition*, *18*(3), 393–412. doi:10.21307tattrans-2016-077

Greene, W. (2013). *Export potential for U.S. advanced technology goods to India using a gravity model approach*. U.S. International Trade Commission Office of Economics Working Paper, No. 2013-03B.

Jing, S., Zhihui, L., Jinhua, C., & Zhiyao, S. (2020). China's renewable energy trade potential in the "Belt-and-Road" countries: A gravity model analysis. *Renewable Energy*, *161*, 1025–1035. doi:10.1016/j.renene.2020.06.134

Kaur, S., & Nanda, P. (2010). India's export potential to other SAARC countries: A gravity model analysis. *Journal of Global Economics*, *6*(3), 167–184. doi:10.1956/jge.v6i3.59

Kumar, N. R., Singh, B. P., Paul Khurana, S. M., & Pandey, N. K. (2005). Impact of WTO on potato export from India. *Agricultural Economics Research Review*, *18*, 291–304.

Kumar, P., Sahu, N. C., & Ansari, M. A. (2021). Export potential of climate smart goods in India: Evidence from the poisson pseudo maximum likelihood estimator. *The International Trade Journal*, *35*(3), 288–308. doi:10.1080/08853908.2021.1890652

Nanid, S., & Biswas, B. (1991). Export and economic growth in India: Empirical evidence. *The Indian Economic Journal*, *38*(3), 53–59.

Sharma, A., Shanker, C., Tyagi, L. K., Singh, M., & Rao, C. V. (2008). Herbal medicine for market potential in India: An overview. *Academic Journal of Plant Sciences*, *1*(2), 26–36.

Suresh, A., & Mathur, V. C. (2016). Export of agricultural commodities from India: Performance and prospects. *Indian Journal of Agricultural Sciences*, *86*(7), 876–883.

Taneja, N. (2007). *India Pakistan trade possibilities and non-tariff barriers*. Indian Council for Research on International Economic Relations, Working Paper No. 200.

Taneja, N., & Kalita, P. (2011). Most favoured nation: New trade opportunities for India and Pakistan. *Economic and Political Weekly*, *46*(49), 14–17.

Veeramani, C., Aerath, L., & Gupta, P. (2017). Intensive and extensive margins of exports: What can India learn from China? *World Economy*, *41*(5), 1196–1222. doi:10.1111/twec.12592

Yao, X., Yasmeen, R., Li, Y., Hafeez, M., & Padda, I. U. H. (2019). Free trade agreements and environment for sustainable development: A gravity model analysis. *Sustainability*, *11*(3), 1–17. doi:10.3390u11030597

KEY TERMS AND DEFINITIONS

COVID-19: Is a disease caused by a new strain of coronavirus. 'CO' represent for corona, 'VI' for virus, and 'D' for disease. In the past, this disease was mentioned to as '2019 novel coronavirus' or '2019-nCoV'.

Export Potential: Is identified as the export that could be achieved at an optimum export frontier with open and frictionless export possible given the current level of export, transport and institutional technologies or it is the maximum level of export given the current level of determinants of export as well as the least level of restrictions within the economic system.

Gravity Model: Proposes that relative economic size appeals countries to trade with each other whereas greater distances diminished the attraction. Initially, the gravity model was admitted as an empirical one, without any particular basis in trade theory, but the widespread adoption of the gravity model to expound patterns of trade has been observed by economists as an important development on previous theoretical models.

Panel Data Analysis: Is a statistical method, widely used in social science, and econometrics to analyze two-dimensional (typically cross sectional and longitudinal) panel data.

Supply Chain: Is the services essential by the organization to deliver goods or services to the consumer, in basic form. A supply chain is a concentrate on the core activities within our organization necessary to transform raw materials or component parts through to finished products or services.

APPENDIX

Figure 2. Indian Actual and Potential Export to Southeast Asian Countries

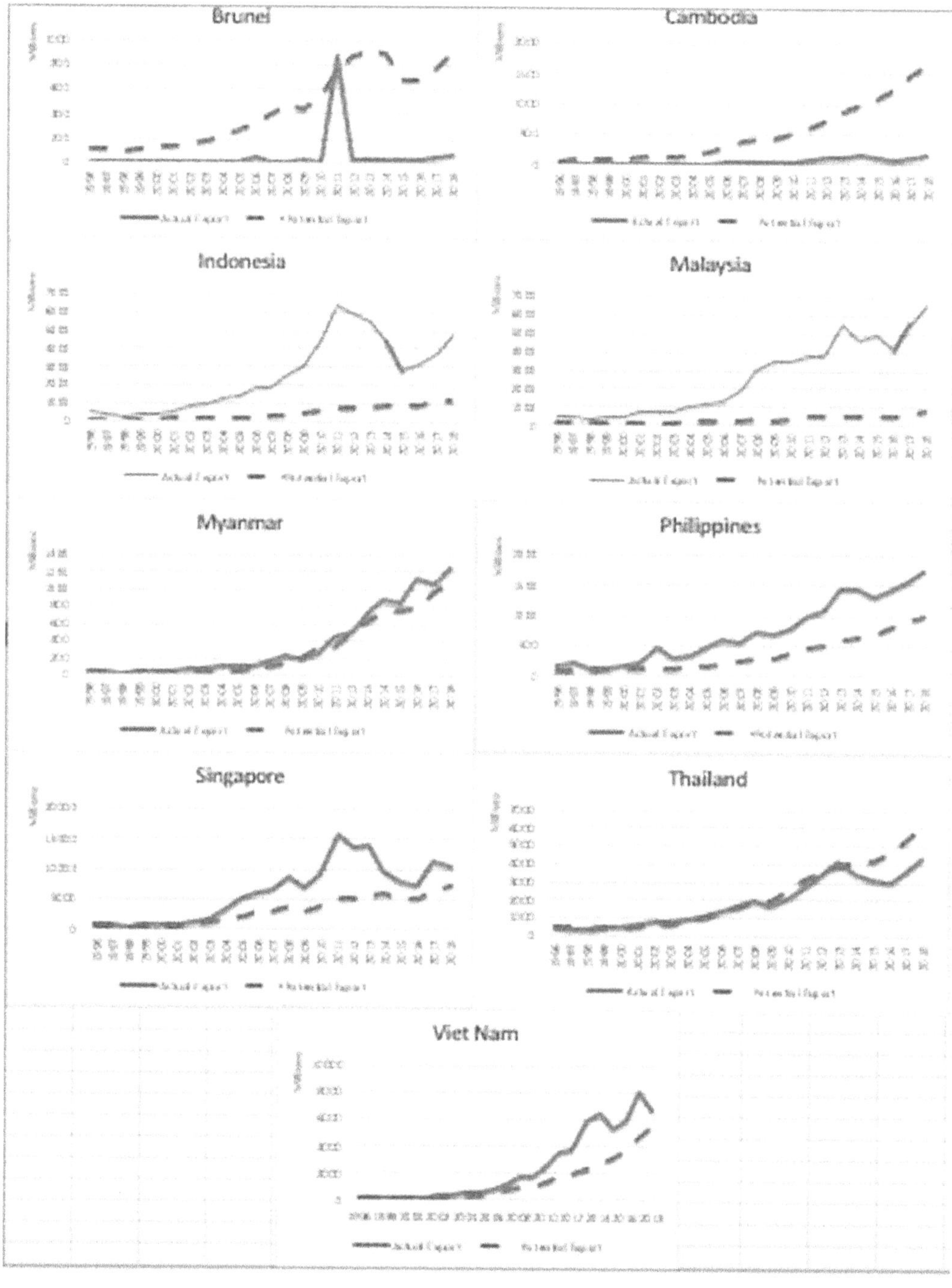

Table 10. Country List

India	Indonesia	Philippines
Brunei	Malaysia	Singapore
Cambodia	Myanmar	Thailand
Vietnam		

Chapter 3
The Role of Institutional Assistance and Information Source on Food Security Policy Analysis:
An Indonesian Perspective

Muhamad Rusliyadi
https://orcid.org/0000-0003-4632-5671
Polytechnic of Agricultural Development Yogyakarta Magelang, Indonesia

ABSTRACT

The chapter analyzes the role of institutions, sources of funding/assistance, and source information in terms of food security and extension policies. The result of the research shows the information on problematic areas in policy implementation with respect to food security and extension policies in terms of poverty reduction. The role of the institution, assistance, and source information are useful in the implementation of other policy sectors in the future, because similar issues or problems may be avoided by taking precautions not to repeat the same mistakes or by applying measures that address the implementation issues. In this way, policy implementation can be carried out effectively, and the outcomes will meet the policy objectives.

INTRODUCTION

The growth in agriculture has been a guiding source of poverty reduction in most developing nations, particularly in the case of rural poverty. The agriculture sector contributes to poverty reduction in terms of employment generation to the poor and supports the development of non-agricultural employment generation in rural fields. Development in agriculture also contributes to a larger supply of food and lower food prices benefiting both rural and urban poor (Grewal et al., 2012).

DOI: 10.4018/978-1-7998-5774-7.ch003

Agricultural development is important in a developing country for achieving industrialization and food security. Farming is the backbone of economic growth in many growing countries, because it provides food security, food self-sufficiency, diversification, and value-added enhancement of competitiveness of exports. Moreover, it increases the wellbeing of farmers and leads directly to poverty reduction.

Indonesia has shifted from an agricultural economy to an industrial one. Nevertheless, the agriculture sector remains a key sector for millions of those who depend directly on agriculture for their livelihood. The agriculture sector has been playing a key role in improving living standards and alleviating poverty. Poverty in rural areas, where most people depend on agriculture for their livelihoods, is one of the immense problems in Indonesia. The poverty level indicates that 16.56% of people in rural areas are poor (CBS, 2010). The increasing numbers of poor people are due to the fact that the bulk of the people cannot satisfy their basic needs and survive at the subsistence level, and therefore ensuring household food security via affordable agricultural workplaces and sustainability scheme policies on the basic demands of the farming sector is vital, especially in terms of food security policy.

According to Darwis and Rusastra (2011), the Food Self-Sufficiency Village Programme (Desa Mandiri Pangan) implemented by community groups was supported by agricultural and non-agricultural capital programmes, as well as by rural financial institutions. It was facilitated by agricultural extension workers and expert consultants. This programme is directed at several other objectives: raising the availability of foodstuffs, growing the family unit entitlement, recovering the efficiency of food supply and access programmes, enhancing the local marketplace availability for selling and buying food products, raising capital and industrial options through the introduction of high-yielding varieties of seeds that agriculture community in rural area can develop to increase income, as well as improving the quality of food consumption handling at the household level, and so forth.

The reasons for choosing the Food Self-sufficiency Village Programme (Desa Mandiri Pangan {DMP}) as the subject of the study are that: 1) The programme has a comprehensives scheme and assistance; 2) The programme has a direct or an indirect beneficial impact on poverty alleviation and food security efforts; 3) This programme is aimed at resolving the existing problems at the grassroots level; 4) It is expected to contribute importantly to rural growth; and, 5) The programme has been implemented in most of Indonesia's provinces.

Active institutions play a very important role in supporting the DMP Programme. There were institutions in the village sites before the introduction of the DMP Programme, such as the village leader, village councils, farmer groups, rice milling units, a village health station unit, a school, a mosque, a church, private lenders, village shops and traders. New institutions introduced by the Programme are affinity groups, food village teams, rice barns and microfinance institutions. In Kedungdowo, the village leader is serving his second elected term. This shows the trust that villagers have for the village head. The relationship of village leader and village council should be harmonious in order to ensure good consultation with the village council, which typically advises and monitors every village activity.

METHOD

This research is focused on the existing food security policy in Indonesia with regard to the DMP Programme that has been implemented since 2006. The methodology used in the study was mainly quantitative, but a qualitative approach was also used to enrich the findings of the quantitative study. Primary data were analysed using Microsoft Excel and Statistical Program for Social Science (SPSS).

Research site in Java island has the largest number of population in Indonesia. It was chosen to represent the research site. Central Java was chosen for this case study because it constitutes 17.0% of the population experiencing poverty (CBS, 2011). Secondly, it has many poor villages when compared to other provinces. Four villages were selected purposively[1].

Two villages from Kebumen Regency, Kedung Dowo Village at Poncowarno District and Selogiri Villlage at Karanggayam District, and the others in Magelang Regency at Madukoro Village Kajoran District and Candirejo Village Borobudur District were selected. These villages have been implementing the programme in varying stages with different characteristics and success rate. (Rusliyadi, et al., 2019)

Data related to the DMP Programme and extension service were collected using unstructured and semi-structured questionnaire. The survey was conducted in four villages, each of which involved 100 samples. Samples were selected using a purposive and clustered sampling technique based on some particular sample criteria. Criteria of the sample chosen were based on farmer characteristics such as rich farmer, poor farmer, farmer leader, the village leader, man and women. The Scoring o the data presented is by author perception and the investigate scoring exercises using replication, cross-check scoring exercises, and interviews. These activities were undertaken with scoring exercises were developed to assess how local people perceived the importance of various environments and resource (Sheil & Liswanti, N 2006).

The purposive sampling technique is a type of non-probability sampling that is most effective when one needs to study a certain cultural domain with knowledgeable experts within. Purposive sampling may also be used with both qualitative and quantitative research techniques. The sample that is selected based on characteristics of a population and the objective of the study. This type of sampling can be very useful in situations when you need to reach a targeted sample quickly, and where sampling for proportionality is not the main concern (Rusliyadi & Libin, 2018)

RESULT AND DISCUSSION

The Role of Institutions, Organizations, Groups and Individuals (Venn Diagram)

The following Venn diagrams show the institutions, organisations, groups and important individuals in each village site. The institution on the Venn diagram is involved directly with villagers in terms of importance activity in the community. The closeness of the relationship between institutions and communities in the group is shown by placing them in the same area. The Venn diagrams also provide information on external and internal factor such us institutions, organisations, groups or individuals linking in the community. The expectation from this diagram is the provision of information on the direct impact of and influential institutions in the community. This tool helps identify and characterise different institutions in terms of impact, cooperation, and link integration in different circumstances in a rural village. The output is the information and provision of relationships between the institutions in terms of delivery of programme activities.

Each Venn diagram shows the importance of institutions in a village community. The assessment of the DMP Programme in this analysis is focused on food security and nutrition issues at household level. The institutional collaboration needs adjustments in measurement, especially closeness relative to other institutions. However, each programme has different target groups or institutions in the community, for example, not all member groups receive allocation of aid from the programme. The cooperation is the key to identifying institutional problems in the community and programme implementation.

The Venn diagrams can be used to discover what formal and informal institutions exist in each village and their relationships and benefits for the local community. The distance between the circles in the diagrams indicates the closeness of their relationship, while their sizes indicate their relative sizes or influence in the community.

Kedungdowo Village

As shown in *Figure 1*, institutions within the village all lie within a larger circle, while outside institutions are shown outside the large circle, with their respective estimated distances from Kedungdowo. The distance here is very important, because the process of assisting a programme will be more effective and efficient when the distance between the donor and recipient policies is not too great so that monitoring and implementation can be maximised. The influence and availability of institutions when needed is determined by the symbiotic relationship between villagers and importance institutions in the village.

Each institution shown is an active institution that plays a role in supporting the DMP Programme. There were institutions in the village before the introduction of the Programme. These were village leaders, village councils, farmer groups, rice milling units, the village health station unit, a school, a mosque, a church, private lenders, village shops or traders. New institutions introduced by the Programme are affinity groups, a food village team, rice barn and microfinance institutions. In Kedungdowo, the village leader is serving his second elected term. This shows that the trust that villagers have in the village head is high. The relationship of village leaders and village councils should be harmonious, since activity in the village needs to be consultative with village councils. Normally the village council gives advice and monitors every activity in the village.

The rice milling unit (RMU) in Kedungdowo is relatively small but useful, because it is not far away for villagers to grind their rice. The RMU is an important institution in the village since its function is like a rice barn or financial institution. The RMU assists villagers by providing farming inputs and store for rice stock. The mechanism involves the villagers being given cash or input in the pre-planting stage and they repay this after harvest in the form of rice or money that is equivalent to the value of inputs provided at the pre-planting stage. It is like a soft loan with low interest, but in some cases the RMU charges double the price of the inputs given to farmers, with the result that the villagers have low earnings. Since the implementation of the DMP Programme in Kedungdowo the introduced rice barns are also providing farmers with micro financing (LKD), which reduces the function of theRMU. The role of the RMU has been taken over by the farmer groups who run the operation of the ricebarn and the LKD. Low interest is an important factor for poor farmers in making a decision to seek a loan, which is handled at the regular meeting of farmer groups. The poor members of society find the rice barn beneficial, especially during periods of food shortages.

The nearest institutions outside the village, such as the district office, the agriculture and forestry office, the military/police outpost and the market are about 7km distant. This is relatively far from the village, which makes coordination less optimal. According to villagers, "a far distance from the district office means lack of information for their development". The centres of district municipalities in general are the centres of economic activity for some villages. The point is that economic development in villages depends on the distance from the village to the district centre. The nearest market is about 7km from the village. It is important to understand that the closer the village is to the market, the more it is developed. The market is, therefore, central to village activity and employment opportunity. The local daily market that provides the basic needs of the rural community is an economic buffer (food security) for surrounding villages to do business. It is related to the previous observation that the availability of a market makes it easier to start or do business.

Figure 1. Venn Diagram for Kedungdowo Village
NB: RMU = Rice Milling Unit, FVT = Food Village Team, FG = Farmer Gorups, AG = Affinity Groups.
Sources: Field work primary data (2013)

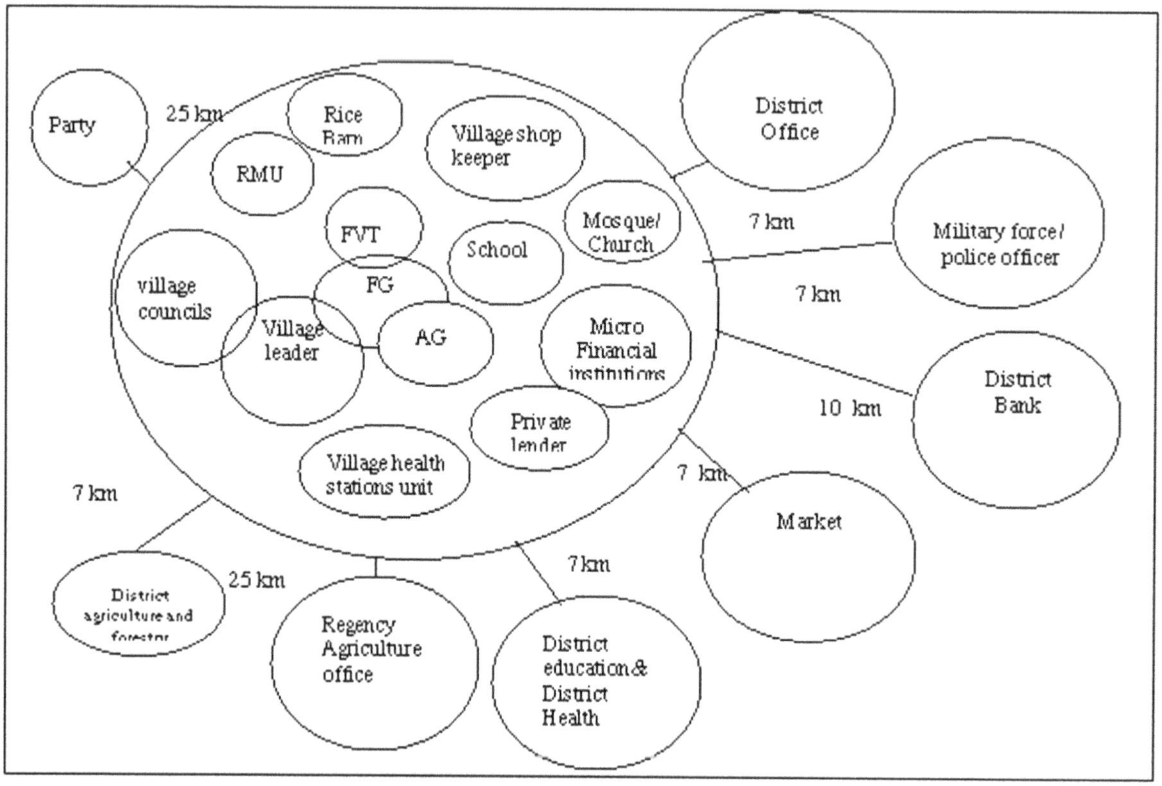

Selogiri Village

Institution/group activity in Selogiri is generally not very dynamic. Village institutions would be involved only if there was a government programme for the village. The village leader has uneasy relations with some community leaders, according to the interviews. This has reduced the effectiveness of existing programmes in the village. Affinity groups as drivers in the DMP Programme are quite active, but the effectiveness level is still below the level of effectiveness in other villages.

Figure 2 describes the general institutional Venn diagram for Selogiri. The distance of the village from the district office is less compared to the situation in Kedungdowo, but the distance to the regency office is considerable – about 35 kilometres. The Affinity Group (AG) formed as a result of the DMP activities consists of four groups of farmers with different business areas of agriculture, livestock, fisheries and cassava cracker manufacturers. Fifty percent of funds are channelled to agricultural groups so that many more farmers are involved in the programme. The village food team (FVT) which consists of representatives of each affinity group holds regular meetings every month attended by the head of the village and the village council. The constraints faced in the implementation of activities and future implementation plans are being worked out together so as to encourage the participation of all levels of society.

Figure 2. Venn Diagram at Selogiri Village
NB: RMU = Rice Milling Unit, FVT = Food Village Team, FG = Farmer Gorups, AG = Affinity Groups.
Sources: Field work primary data (2013)

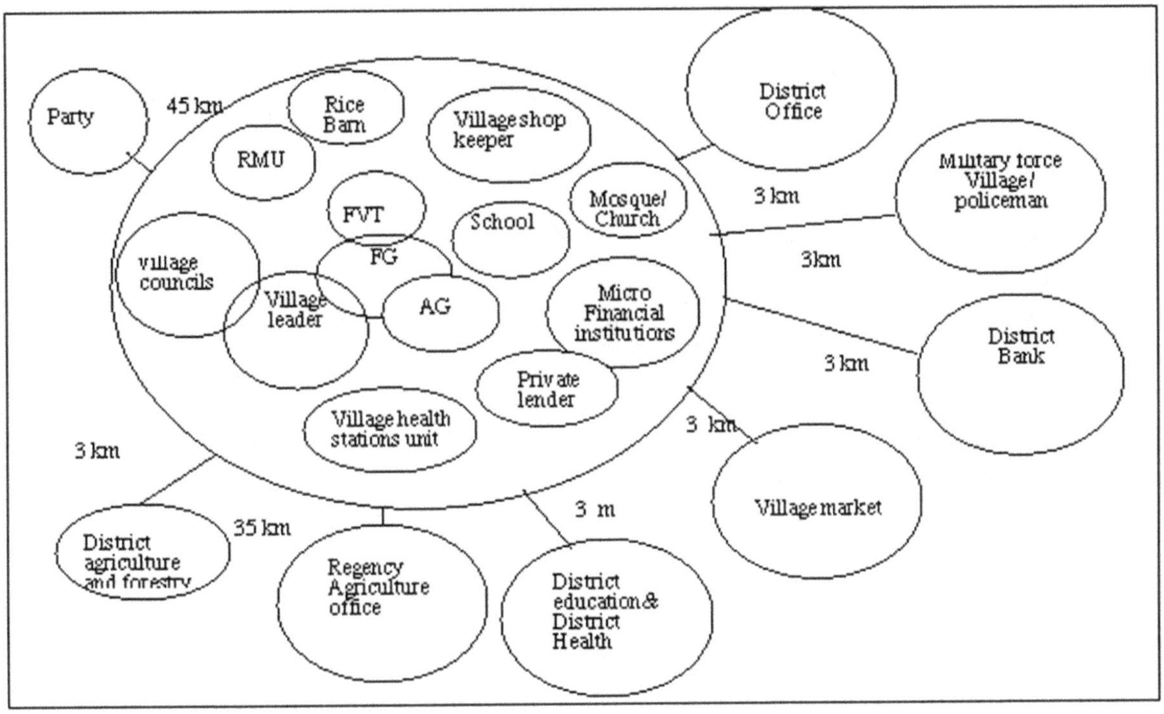

Candirejo Village

The farmer groups in Candirejo are relatively more dynamic than in the other villages. The fundamental difference in the diagram below compared to other villages is, firstly, an absence of rice milling units (RMU) in the village, as farmers grind their rice in a neighbouring village. Secondly, grants are not allocated to the building of rice barns, but are used to purchase livestock in the form of local and *etawa* goats. The allocation of funding is for poor families, which is involved as a farmer group (affinity group). Thirdly, the distance from the village to the district office is 4km. Finally, tourism resources are contributing to the revenue of the village, such as a handicraft store and homestay facilities. Some villagers earn money by selling when local and foreign tourists visit Candirejo.

Figure 3. Venn Diagram for Candirejo Village
NB: RMU = Rice Milling Unit, FVT = Food Village Team, FG = Farmer Groups, AG = Affinity Groups.
Sources: Field work primary data, (2013).

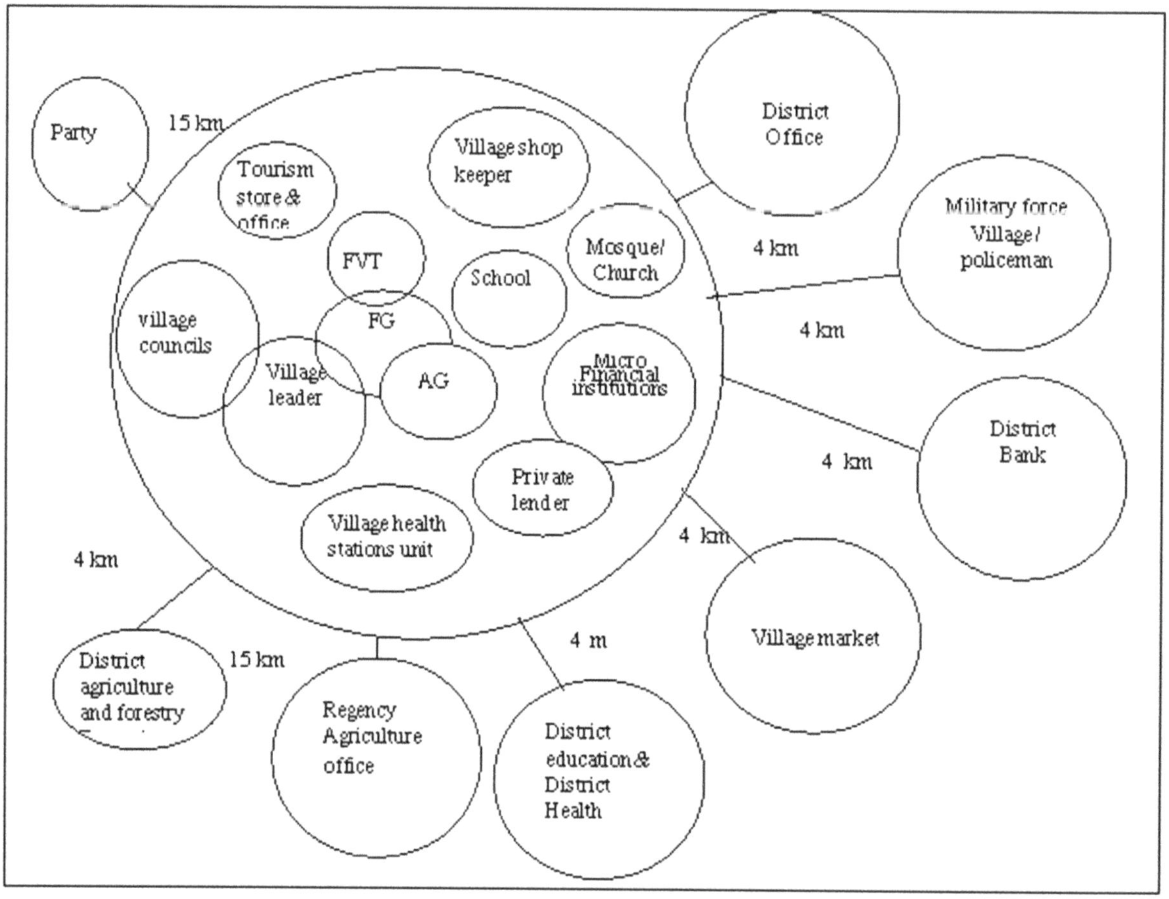

Madukoro Village

Madukoro Village is located on the border between Purworejo Regency and Magelang Regency, relatively far from the centre of the district (about 7km). DMP activities run well as the farming group in this village is much better in terms of their participation. In Madukoro an individual or group has self-motivation initiated by the village leader. High response of the public to a programme makes it easy to introduce and implement it. The important success factor is the efforts of the village/hamlet leader in driving the activity initiated by the DMP Programme. The influence of the hamlet leader in Madukoro is greater than village's head because the village head is relatively young and pays less attention to villagers. The important point of this case is the role of the village head or chief of the hamlet, which is a critical factor in the village's development. Village leaders should have the ability to mobilise the community to be active in most village programmes. Key persons who have great influence in the village have a significant impact on the success of a programme, measured by the highest participation of the community. The policies at village level require effort and involvement from several key persons to achieve implementation impact.

Figure 4. Venn Diagram at Madukoro Village
NB: RMU = Rice Milling Unit, FVT = Food Village Team, FG = Farmer Gorups, AG = Affinity Groups.
Sources: Field work primary data (2013)

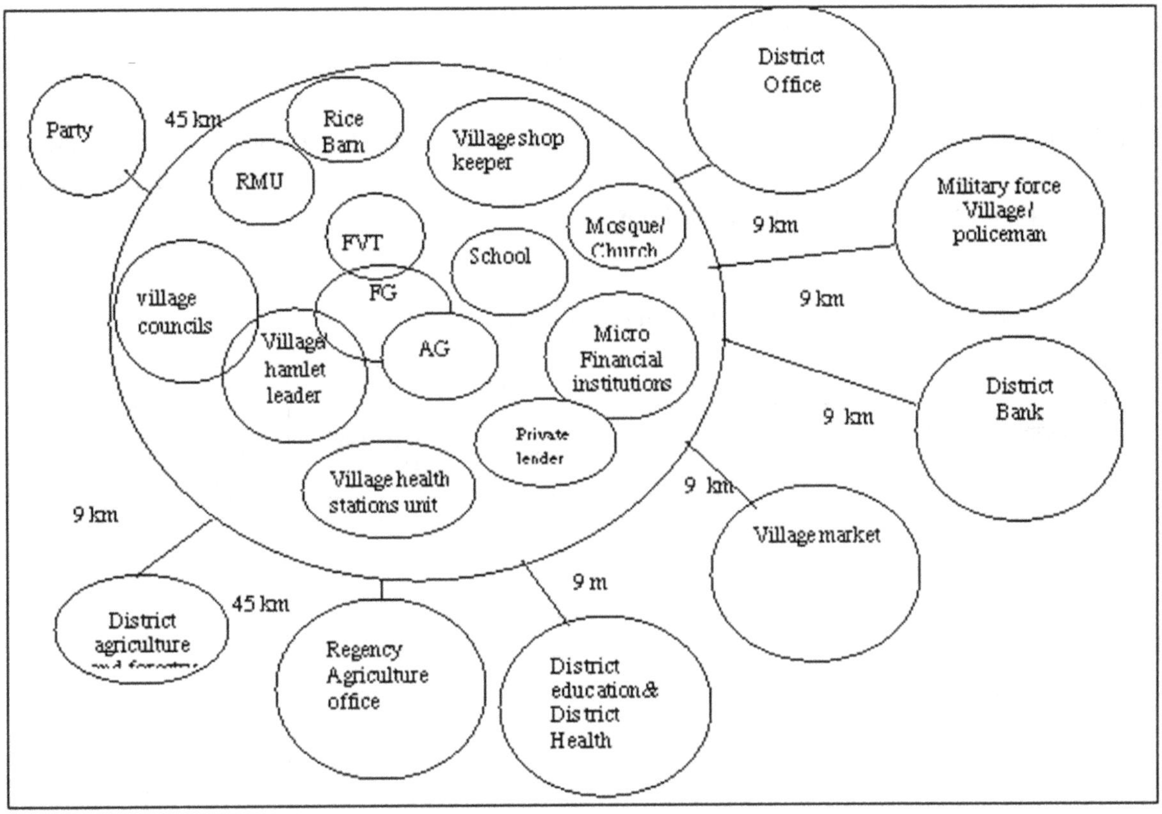

Analysis of the Sources of Information and Assistance

This analysis is the result of focus group discussions (FGD) and randomly surveyed poor households as respondents. Information is a source of knowledge that can be used by farmers to contribute to their income by practical business. To villagers, knowledge is difficult to obtain due to village remoteness. Education alone is not enough for development to take place at village level. Villagers need experience and accurate information. Starting businesses (the opportunity to open/start a business) in the village is difficult because of lack of information and capital. Therefore, information is very helpful for villagers to start a business and information on the latest technologies should also be useful for them to promote business development.

The sources of funding received by the villages are identified and analysed based on perception of the randomly selected villagers. The funding resources are categorised on the basis of where the funding comes from: the State budget (National budget), local budget (Province or Regency budget), International funds, and NGOs. There are four types of assistance made available to the research sites for rural village development: cash funding, physical assistance, aid-type of goods, and types of integrated programmes such as the DMP Programme.

Kedungdowo Village

Based on discussions and analysis of several groups in Kedungdowo (Table 1), villagers receive information from friends, relatives and parents. This shows that verbal information obtained through discussion and conversations is influential. Information obtained through formal schooling is less influential, because it tends to contain theoretical knowledge with little information on practices. Villagers expressed their desire to be continuously trained and exposed to the latest technologies for agriculture, fisheries and husbandry. Extension officers need to be more active at village level in providing information and knowledge-based resources in village workshops.

Table 1. Information Source Scoring of Kedungdowo Village

No.	Information type required	Information Source				
		Media (TV, Newspapers, magazines)	Schools	Extension Officers	Friends, relative, parents	Score
1	Agriculture	3	4	8	9	24
2	Livestock	4	3	7	8	22
3	Fisheries	5	4	7	7	23
4	Forestry	7	3	9	8	27
5	Business opportunity	7	6	6	9	28
6	Markets	8	3	6	8	25
7	Employment	8	4	5	8	25
	Score	42	27	48	57	

NB: Scoring is out of 10; the higher the score, the greater is the information obtained
Sources: Field work primary data (2013)

Funds in Kedungdowo mostly come from the National budget. The majority of the financial resources coming from the central government are distributed through local government. This means that, in the distribution of financial resources, the central government should still consider the local situation by administering a proper allocation of funds. The local government is currently striving to boost revenue by looking to local and foreign investors and persuading them to invest in their areas so that more funding is available for rural development. The local government should be proactive in generating sources of funds through local revenue – *Pendapatan Asli Daerah* (PAD). This point is very important for rural development and the gap between the national and regional budgets can be minimised.

Table 2. Sources of Assistance Scoring of Kedungdowo Village

No.	Type of poverty Assistance	Sources of Assistance				Score
		APBN National Budget	APBD Provinces or Regency Budget	International Funds	NGO	
1	*Bantuan IDT* - National Aid for underdeveloped villages	6	-	-	-	6
2	*Kartu Sehat/Gakin* Health Card	9	-	-	-	9
3	*Raskin* (rice for the poor)	9	-	-	-	9
4	*Bantuan langsung Tunai BLT* - Direct cash assistance	8	-	-	-	8
5	*Desa mandiri pangan (DMP) Programme*	9	-	-	-	9
6	*PAMSIMAS* - Community-Based Water Supply and Sanitation	0	-	8	-	8
7	*Bedah Rumah* - House Renovation Programme	5	7			12
8	Agricultural Extension assistance	8	-	-	-	8
9	*Programme Nasional Pemberdayaan Masyarakat - PNPM Mandiri perdesaan* -National Programme for Community Empowerment - Rural PNPM Mandiri	10	-	-	-	10
	Score	64	7	8		

NB: Scoring is out of 10; the higher the score, the higher its impact
Sources: Field work primary data, (2013).

Selogiri Village

In Selogiri, information obtained from friends, relatives and parents also received high score from respondents. Why are these information sources significant for farmers' farming knowledge? This is because other resources, such as the mass media, are rarely accessed by villagers or they must actively obtain this information, while information from friends, relatives and parents is readily available through daily interactions in the village. Also, this information is free of charge. Villagers might have no time to seek information through the media because of working in the fields.

The sources of financial assistance in Selogiri (Table 4) are almost the same as in Kedungdowo, that is, the majority of financial assistance comes from state funds. The biggest aid funds are derived from the National Programme for Community Empowerment (Rural PNPM Mandiri) at 252 million IDR. These funds were directed to the construction of concrete rural roads with partial support employment comes from the community. Villagers in the group discussions said that the national budget has the greatest impact on physical development in PNPM and the highest score (value of 10: see Table 4) in terms of impact on social development through the Health Card/household health scheme. The agricultural extension programme receives assistance from two fund sources with the same pattern and type but different commodities (wetland rice and upland rice). This programme was initiated by School Field of Integrated Rice Crop Management (*Sekolah Lapang Pengelolaan Tanaman Terpadu* - SLPTT) funded by APBN. The upland rice SLPTT is funded by the Local Budget APBD. The collaboration programme implementation by national and local budgets in the same time but different commodities is possible, but it needs different targets (villagers) and areas (location).

Table 3. Information Source Scoring of Selogiri Village

No.	Information type required	Information Source				
		Media (TV, Newspapers, magazines)	Schools	Extension Officers	Friends, relative, parents	Score
1	Agriculture	2	4	7	8	21
2	Livestock	3	4	8	10	25
3	Fisheries	5	5	6	6	22
4	Forestry	6	4	8	9	27
5	Business opportunity	5	7	5	8	25
6	Markets	7	3	5	7	22
7	Employment	7	3	4	9	23
	Score	35	30	43	57	

NB: Scoring is out of 10; the higher the score, the greater the amount of information obtained
Source: Field work primary data (2013)

Table 4. Sources of Assistance Scoring of Selogiri Village.

No.	Type of poverty Assistance	Sources of Assistance				Score
		APBN National Budget	APBD Provinces or Regency Budget	International Funds	NGO	
1	*Bantuan IDT* - National Aid for underdeveloped villages	5	-	-	-	5
2	*Kartu Sehat/Gakin* Health Card	10	-	-	-	10
3	*Raskin* (rice for the poor)	8	-	-	-	8
4	*Bantuan langsung Tunai BLT* - Direct cash assistance	7	-	-	-	7
5	*Desa mandiri pangan (DMP)* - Food Self-Sufficient village Programme	8	-	-	-	8
6	*PAMSIMAS* - Community-Based Water Supply and Sanitation	0	-	9	-	9
7	*Bedah Rumah* - House Renovation Programme	0	6	-	-	6
8	Agricultural Extension assistance	8	7	-	-	15
9	*Programme Nasional Pemberdayaan Masyarakat - PNPM Mandiri perdesaan* National Programme for Community Empowerment	9	-	-	-	9
	Score	55				

NB: Scoring is out of 10; the higher the score, the higher its impact
Source: Field work primary data (2013).

Candirejo Village

Candirejo is a village which enjoys good access to information. It is a tourist village that often interacts socially and culturally with people from outside the village. The information obtained by villagers is varied and spreads quickly in the village. One example is about business opportunities in other places and success stories become special information for villagers. However, not all villagers have access to the information. It depends on the distance between the village centre where they live and the other villages where their relatives live. The neighbourhood activity in the village is very important, since information resources are mostly transmitted and received from the interactions of people and relatives. Thus the information obtained by villagers is very limited. The important implication from this case is that rural development policy should be focused on providing information through actual practical training in agriculture and business development opportunities, rather than through information provided through various media sources. An additional solution is training on how to get information from reliable resources such as the Internet and news media.

Table 5. Information Source Scoring of CandirejoVillage

No.	Information type required	Information Source				
		Media (TV, Newspapers, magazines)	**Schools**	**Extension Officers**	**Friends, relative, parents**	**Score**
1	Agriculture	4	3	9	10	26
2	Livestock	6	4	8	9	27
3	Fisheries	6	7	9	9	31
4	Forestry	7	3	9	8	27
5	Business opportunity	7	6	6	9	28
6	Markets	7	4	5	9	25
7	Employment	7	6	4	8	25
	Score	40	30	41	52	

NB: Scoring is out of 10; the higher score, the higher the information
Sources: Field work primary data (2013)

The sources of funding assistance in Candirejo can be seen in Table 6. Unlike the previous villages, funds from NGOs are provided. This aid comes in the form of mentoring activities provided near the famous Borobodur Temple in the field of hospitality and tourism. From 2009 until 2011 Candirejo was provided with full assistance by NGOs from Yogyakarta. In 2012 the local government assisted Candirejo through the *Program Nasional Pemberdayaan Masyarakat* - PNPM programme to build infrastructure and support facilities to become a tourist village. The community believes that the tourism programme can contribute significantly to their economy if some villagers take the opportunity to make their homes into guesthouses. In terms of the DMP Programme, its activities are more focused on agriculture development, including introduction of livestock farming packaged with management training, and skills training based on local resource availability. The goal of the Programme is to increase the income of poor families living on the village's border where the impact of tourism is less obvious.

Table 6. Sources of Assistance Scoring of Candirejo Village

No.	Type of poverty Assistance	Sources of Assistance				Score
		APBN National Budget	APBD Provinces or Regency Budget	International Funds	NGO	
1	*Bantuan IDT* - National Aid for underdeveloped villages	7	-	-	-	7
2	*Kartu Sehat/Gakin* Health Card/Gakin scheme	8	-	-	-	8
3	Raskin - Rice for the poor	9	-	-	-	9
4	*Bantuan langsung Tunai BLT* - Direct cash assistance	6	-	-	-	6
5	*Desa mandiri pangan (DMP) Programme* – Food Self-Sufficient village	8	-	-	-	8
6	*PAMSIMAS* - Community-Based Water Supply and Sanitation	0	-	8	-	0
7	*Bedah Rumah* - House Renovation Programme	7	6	-	-	13
8	Agricultural Extension assistance	6	7	-	-	13
9	*PNPM Mandiri perdesaan* - National Programme for Community Empowerment	9	-	-	-	9
10	*Desa Wisata* Tourism Village	9	-	-	8	14
	Score	69	13	8	8	

NB: Scoring is out of 10; the higher score, the higher its impact
Source: Field work primary data (2013)

Madukoro Village

Based on the results of group discussions (Table 7), extension officers have an important role in every activity in the village. The expected function of the extension officers is to successfully disseminate knowledge and information on programme implementation activities. However, the scoring results show that the sources of information are mostly friends, relatives and parents, with total of 63 points, whereas information disseminated by extension officers only scored 57. This means that extension officers need to improve their performance to the expected level, for example, by frequently visit the villages and visiting their friends or relatives so that they know the problems of villagers. In other words, the extension officers need more creativity and innovation in disseminating information. The villagers at Madukoro suggested that the extension activities should not only come from the district level but also from the regency level and even from the provincial level. The extension officers in this case are from various sectors such as agriculture, husbandry, fisheries and even health. In addition, the variety of information from experienced extension officers is very important. The important issue to be borne in mind is the need for information about the villagers to be known deeply by extension officers through observations. Information to be disseminated should include updated technology and knowledge associated with programme implementation.

Table 7. Information Source Scoring of MadukoroVillage

No.	Information type required	Information Source				
		Media (TV, Newspapers, magazines)	**Schools**	**Extension Officers**	**Friends, relative, parents**	**Score**
1	Agriculture	4	4	7	10	25
2	Livestock	5	4	9	9	27
3	Fisheries	6	5	10	9	30
4	Forestry	6	4	8	9	27
5	Business opportunity	8	6	8	8	30
6	Markets	7	4	7	9	27
7	Employment	7	6	8	9	30
	Score	43	33	57	63	

NB: Scoring is out of 10; the higher score, the higher the information
Source: Field work primary data (2013)

Table 8. Sources of Assistance Scoring of Madukoro Village

No.	Type of poverty Assistance	Sources of Assistance				Score
		APBN National Budget	**APBD Provinces or Regency Budget**	**International Funds**	**NGO**	
1	*Bantuan IDT* - National Aid for underdeveloped villages	6	-	-	-	6
2	*Kartu Sehat/Gakin* Health Card/Gakin scheme	10	-	-	-	10
3	Raskin/ rice for the poor	9	-	-	-	9
4	*Bantuan langsung Tunai BLT* - Direct cash assistance	8	-	-	-	8
5	*Desa mandiri pangan (DMP) Programme* – Food Self-Sufficient village	9	10	-	-	19
6	*PAMSIMAS* - Community-Based Water Supply and Sanitation	0	-	7	-	7
7	*Bedah Rumah*/House Renovation Programme	5	6	-	-	13
8	Agricultural Extension assistance	7	7	-	-	14
9	*Programme Nasional Pemberdayaan Masyarakat - PNPM Mandiri perdesaan* National Programme for Community Empowerment	8	-	-	-	8
10	Fishery fishpond programme	8	-	-	-	8
11	*Kawasan Rumah Pangan Lestari (KRPL)* Sustainable Food House zones	8	-	-	-	8
	Score	62	23	7	0	

NB: Scoring is out of 10; the higher score, the higher its impact
Source: Field work primary data (2013).

Madukoro enjoys considerable aid from the government. Many programmes implemented successfully in a village benefit from cooperation by many agencies in implementation and this gives rise to high impact contribution in terms of village development. In the case of Madukoro, the DMP Programme was not implemented in conjunction with other programmes; they were implemented at different times. The point to be learned is that many programmes should be integrated and implemented at the same time so that the impact is more significant.

CONCLUSION AND RECOMMENDATION

The DMP Programme has resulted in the establishment of a microfinancial institution (*Lembaga Keuangan Desa* - LKD) in the village, participated in by farmer groups. However, the funds allocated for the LKD are limited and they cannot cover the needs of all villagers. There remains a lack of capital necessary to start businesses for some farmers. The villagers proposed establishing a farmer cooperative in the village to support 'off-farm' and 'on-farm' activities and to be managed by farmer groups. The aim of the cooperative is to provide the place for savings and loans with low interest rates and to gain profits for the villagers.

On the issue of information sources, analysis shows that the villagers receive information related to the Programme mostly from friends, relatives and parents. Verbal information obtained through discussion and conversations is influential. Information obtained through formal schooling is less influential because it tends to contain theoretical knowledge with little information on practices. Villagers want to be trained and exposed to the latest technologies for agriculture, fisheries and husbandry. Extension officers need to be more active at the village level in provided information and knowledge-based resources.

Analysis on sources of funding shows that villages receive funding mostly from the national budget, implemented through local government. To ensure sustainability in efforts to alleviate poverty central government should continue to consideration the local situation in allocation of funds. The local government is currently striving to boost revenues by looking to local and foreign investors to invest in their villages so that the budget can be increased. The local government should be proactive in generating financial sources through local revenue. In this way the gap between the national and regional budgets can be reduced.

Extension officers play an important role in every activity in the village. Their function is to disseminate knowledge and information on programme implementation. However, that information is mostly obtained from friends, relatives and parents. If extension officers are to play their role they need to frequently visit villages and come to the problems faced. Extension activities should not be only from the district level but also from regency or province level. Information dissemination is more effective if officers are experienced and come from various sectors, such as agriculture, husbandry, fisheries and health. Extension officers need to know villagers' problems through close observation. Information should include up-to-date technology and information in terms of programme implementation.

REFERENCES

Central Bureau of Statistics (CBS). (2010). Indonesia in Number Book. Statistical Yearbook of Indonesia 2010. Badan Pusat Statistik, BPS.

Central Bureau of Statistics (CBS). (2011). Indonesia in Number Book. Statistical Yearbook of Indonesia 2011. Badan Pusat Statistik, BPS.

Darwis, V., & Rusastra, I. W. (2011, June). Optimizing Rural Community Empowerment through Integrating PUAP and Desa Mandiri Pangan Programs. *Agricultural Policy Analysis Journal.*, *9*(2), 125–142.

Gandhi, V. P., & Marsh, R. (2003). Development nd Poverty Reduction: Do Institutions Matter? A Study on the Impact of Local Institutions in Rural India. *The 25th International Conference of Agricultural Economists*.

Grewal, B., Grunfeld, H., & Sheehan, P. (2012). *The contribution of agricultural growth to poverty reduction.* ACIAR Impact Assessment Series Report No. 76. Australian Centre for International Agricultural Research.

Quisumbing, A. R. (2003). Household Decisions, Gender, and Development A Synthesis of Recent Research. Food Policy, 20, 407–423.

Rusliyadi, M., Bin Hj. Mohd. Jamil, A., Maseleno, A., Tri Kumalasari, R., & Othman, M. (2019). Agricultural extension policy, agricultural growth and poverty reduction in Indonesia. *IACSIT International Journal of Engineering and Technology*, *7*(4), 5539–5550. doi:10.14419/ijet.v7i4.13337

Rusliyadi, M., Jamil, A., Mohd, B., & Kumalasar, R. T. (2019). Analysis of household food security policy: Case of food security village programme, Indonesia. *Asian Journal of Agriculture and Rural Development*, *9*(1), 19–32. doi:10.18488/journal.1005/2019.9.1/1005.1.19.32

Rusliyadi, M., & Jamil, A. B. (2020). Participatory Poverty Assessment Effort in Food Security and Extension Policy: Evidence From Indonesia. In V. Erokhin & T. Gao (Eds.), *Handbook of Research on Globalized Agricultural Trade and New Challenges for Food Security* (pp. 481–499). IGI Global. doi:10.4018/978-1-7998-1042-1.ch024

Rusliyadi, M., & Libin, W. (2018). Agriculture development programs for poverty reduction evidences from Indonesia and china - comparative study case. *Asian Journal of Agriculture and Rural Development*, *8*(2), 104–118. doi:10.18488/journal.1005/2018.8.2/1005.2.104.118

Rusliyadi, M., Mohd, H., Jamil, A., & Anshari, M. (2020). Analysis of Food Security Policy by Participatory Poverty Assessment (PPA) Effort: Case in Indonesia. In P. Ordoñez de Pablos, M. Almunawar, & M. Abduh (Eds.), Economics, Business, and Islamic Finance in ASEAN Economics Community (pp. 105-127). Hershey, PA: IGI Global. doi:10.4018/978-1-7998-2257-8.ch006

Sheil, D., & Liswanti, N. (2006). Scoring the importance of tropical forest landscapes with local people: Patterns and insights. *Environmental Management*, *38*(1), 126–136. doi:10.100700267-005-0092-7 PMID:16508796

ENDNOTE

1 Purposive sampling is also known as judgmental, selective, or subjective sampling. Based on the recommendation by the Agricultural and Food Security Agency in Regency Level.

Chapter 4
Indian and ASEAN Trade Relations With the Changing Framework of India's Look East Policy

Gurpreet Kaur
https://orcid.org/0000-0001-9259-2709
Lovely Professional University, India

Jyotsana Bhangu
Lovely Professional University, India

ABSTRACT

In 1992 Narshima Rao launched the Look East Policy to tend towards south-eastern neighbours and also to connect with East Asia. The main goal of the Look East Policy is to increase economic cooperation and strategic defence cooperation to balance the growing Chinese domination over South-East Asia and the sea. In 2014, the Government of India would come up with a new phase of the Look East Policy and announced the Act East Policy that can be considered as the new age of economic development, industrialization, and trade. The Act East Policy and Look East Policy both have some similarity. The chapter analyzes the India-ASEAN trade activities after the formation of ASEAN bloc specifically from 2001 to 2018. To fulfil the objectives of study trade indices, similarity and diversification has been used. The study found that with changing framework of India's foreign policy for ASEAN, trade share of India and ASEAN in the bi-lateral arrangement significantly increased.

INTRODUCTION

From 1950's the economic integration would become a major aspect for economists. It is the process which can remove the restriction on international trade, payments and factor mobility. Integration led to positive outcome for the union of two or more national economies in the form of regional trade ar-

DOI: 10.4018/978-1-7998-5774-7.ch004

rangements. When it comes to the unionism multilateral trade arrangements can also be the part of international trade. Under the WTO (World Trade Organisation) trade barriers remove from all countries which have been its members. These sort of international trade patterns have been a crucial part for world economies to sustain in this globalise world (Carbaugh, 2008). At the global level, since 2008 the GDP and world trade have increased by 26 per cent World GDP (Gross Domestic Product) and the world merchandise trade grew by 2.9 per cent and 3percent respectively in 2018. These trade had been value of $19.67 trillion and China consider as the world leading trader as of 2018. No doubt the world has been divided in to two parts North (Developed Economies) and South (Developing Economies). Various characteristics that have been widen up the gap between these two parts such as share of trade, technology, GDP and other aspects. But the global scenario since 2008 would posturized that in the global trade share developing economies either equally or outperformed when it comes to the participation in world trade has been considered. This would only happen due to existence of regional trade agreements and more preciously South-South trade. This south-south trade estimated around $4.28 trillion in 2018 (World Trade Organization Statistical Review, 2019)

Under this south-south trade the Asian nation would also play the ubiquitous role, because, major Southeast Asian countries, India and China because major Southeast Asian countries and India are known as "Emerging Asia ", with China being a world leaders in international trade. As per the annual growth of emerging Asia would pointed out it is projected to be grow annually of 6.1 per cent during 2019-2023. Where the domestic demand is expected to endorse and the household spending and job market tend towards the reverberating. However, trade can be face detention because of the growing uncertain prospects due to the broadness of tariff measures. But such prospects would not affect the Southeast Asian countries, India and China. Because it is forecasted that Southeast Asian countries, India and China can possess the growth of 5.2 Per cent, 5.9 per cent and 7.3 per cent respectively during 2019-2023. Such consideration would compile the existence of growth in the Asian regions. This keynotes the growth of regional trade arrangements as prosperous in nature. That criterion tends towards the economic integration and cooperation among the Asian nations (Organization for economic cooperation development, 2019).

Economic cooperation and integration would not be entertained if the trade blocks are not there to support the integrity. There are various trade blocs at global level. There are ten major regional trading blocs in the world. Association of South East Asian Nations (ASEAN), APEC (Asia Pacific Economic Cooperation), Brazil Russia India China South Africa (BRICS), European Union (EU), North Africa Free Trade Agreement (NAFTA), Commonwealth of Independent states (CIS), Common Market for Eastern and Southern Africa (COMESA), South Asian Association for Regional Cooperation (SAARC), MERCOSUR and Indian Ocean Rim Association for Regional cooperation(IOR-ARC).

Main concern lies here about the ASEAN - Association of South East Asian Nations is a regional organization made by governments of Indonesia, Malaysia, Philippines, Singapore and Thailand via the Bangkok Deceleration that was signed by the foreign ministers of ASEAN countries on 8th August 1967. This membership further extended to ten member countries. Brunei Darussalam engaged on 8th January 1984, Vietnam on 28 July 1995, Laos and Myanmar on 23 July 1997 as well as Cambodia on 30 April 1999. The main purpose and aim of ASEAN is to accelerate economic growth, social progress and cultural development in the region. It prompts regional peace and stability by aiding respect for justice and rule of law in the relationship among the countries in the region. On January 1992 ASEAN countries signed agreement on the common effective Preferential Tariff scheme- ASEAN free trade area (AFTA). In 1994 ASEAN regional forum (ARF) had been established with aim of adding three broader stages-promotion of confidence building, development of preventive diplomacy and elaboration of approaches to conflicts. Apart from that, on 7th October 2003 there was a deceleration of ASEAN Concord with establishment of ASEAN Economic Community (AEC). This aims to realise of ASEAN vision 2020 with creation of stable prosperous and competitive ASEAN economic region and widen up the economic integration. In 2015 12th ASEAN summit signed the declaration on the acceleration of the establishment of an ASEAN community with major three pillars – political-security community, economic community and socio-cultural community. Overall, all these engagements and framework led to strength the trade and investment relationship with other nations (Ghosh, 2016).

In tend to increase the economic and trade relationship via the regional trade arrangements Indian economy come with foreign policy. In 1992 Narshima Rao launched the Look East Policy (LEP) to lead the southern-eastern neighbours and also to connect with East Asia. Main Goal of LEP is to increase cooperation and strategic defence cooperation to balance the growing Chinese domination over the south-east Asia and South China sea and the Indo-Pacific ocean. In the initial phase of India's Look East Policy this was noticed when India was become its sectoral dialogue partner in 1992 and on 1996 it became its full dialogue partner in the 5th regional forum of ASEAN nations. In 2003 on the second summit of India and ASEAN signed a framework agreement on comprehensive economic cooperation. In 2009 finally the Free Trade Agreement (FTA) was signed between India and ASEAN as the integral part of comprehensive cooperation agreement (CECA). The major requirement would be the "integration" between India and ASEAN. This engagement can be the arc of advantage for India (Ghosh, 2016).

The policy frameworks would quiet up to the mark due to strong integration and cooperation between India and ASEAN would be the result of it. In 2017 trade between India and ASEAN has been rise to 10 per cent to $72 billion. India and Asean accounted for $3 trillion economy and that was highly make both reliable to each other for future integration (Gupta, 2018). This trade relationship would tend to integrate the economy via trade relationship broadly in food, energy, security, infrastructure, human resource development, pharmaceuticals, healthcare and tourism. In the case of capital investment both India and ASEAN can exploit each other. Significantly FTA between India and ASEAN has greater and efficient prospects. This integration would result of development of second phase of LEP. These developments would also be evident because of the present government efforts. Bhartiya Janta Party (BJP) came up with another phase of Look east policy and in 2014 government of India announced the Act East Policy of India in 12th summit of India and ASEAN. This Act East Policy can be considered as the new age of economic development, industrialization and trade. This act east policy and LEP both are having the similarity. Both are focusing on development agenda with its especial focus on strengthening connectivity, infrastructure and people to people contacts and trade. This would indicate due to the establishment of Joint Task force on connectivity initiative to finance physical and digital infrastructure plan between India and ASEAN (Bajpaee, 2017).

Table 1. Key Indicators of India and ASEAN

Basic Indicators	India	ASEAN
AREA (Million km square)	3.28	4.4
Gross Domestic Product (2018) ($ trillion)	2.726	2.9
GDP Per Capita ($ trillion)	2010	4601
Foreign Direct Investment (2018) ($ billions)	43.32	155
Human Development Index (2017)	0.64	0.71
Life Expectation	68.8	74.4
Population (2018) (Billion)	1.3	0.64
Unemployment Rate (per cent)	6	3.2
Fertility Rate	2.2	2.1

Source: World Bank, RBI, ASEAN Key Figures Report, ASEAN Investment Report, UNDP

Table 1 depicts the key indicators of India and ASEAN. This table compares India and ASEAN on the basis of Area, Population, unemployment rate. That is quiet high in India as compare to ASEAN. ASEAN nations come up as a leader in terms of Life expectancy, GDP per capita.

Aim

Majority of studies would not consider the India's look east policy and Act east policy with export competiveness of India and ASEAN. But, this study would consider the look east policy and act east policy of India with its export competitiveness.

Objectives

1. To understand the pattern of trade between India and ASEAN nations.
2. To assess the export competitiveness between India and ASEAN nations.

BACKGROUND

Review of Literature

Haokip (2014) considered the LEP with the aim of developing economic integration and foreign cooperation with ASEAN countries. This study indicated that policy widening up the economic, security and trade linkages between India and ASEAN. It signified positive emergence of LEP on the trade between India and ASEAN. Alam (2015) analysed the bilateral trade between India and ASEAN to check the complementary and competence commodities. The study revealed that trade cooperation between the trading partners had been increased significantly. The study concluded that trade relationship with ASEAN economies lead to greater cooperation as well as regionalize effort of India. Bhattacharyya &

Mandal (2016) revealed that the ASEAN trade deteriorated with its effect on India's Balance of trade. It signified that negative association between the tariff reforms of India and trade potentiality. This study also conceived that till 2012 net surplus would be the favour of India but in 2013 trade had declined due to global slowdown. The study suggested that Free trade agreement between India and ASEAN would tend to surplus if there would be tariff elasticity. Bajpaee (2017) considered LEP as the re-engagement of India with south-east Asia. The study evident that in the first phases through Joint task force LEP's agenda of development, economic integration had been fulfilled between India and ASEAN and in the second phase of LEP the main motive was to acierate the trade with ASEAN. This study presumed that LEP as narrative device of India to establish the linkage with South- East Asia.

Kaur & Sarin (2017) in the study depicted the priority of ASEAN countries for India due to some reason- to decrease the growing dependence of developed economies and to enhance trade relationship. Look east policy is having the goal to increase the trade relationship. This study also compiled that lack of diversification and quality improvement in agriculture export of India to ASEAN were due to stagnant role of Indian government towards the export and such consideration would lead to the positivity of India's look east policy. An analysis of India's Export Competitiveness in context of AIFTA. Sarin (2017) examined that Indian economy had capability to increase the trade with ASEAN without concerning about subsidies. The study explored that due to the Look east policy there would be the increase in the trade competitiveness in some products after the signing the free agreement between India and ASEAN. Chandran and Mukhtar,(2019) in the study used RCA index to found out regionalism efforts in the context of international trade This study propounded that market access to ASEAN nation would no longer helpful for India. Because ASEAN nation would have more trade opportunities rather than India specifically China's dominance in the area of resource based trade. Banik and Kim (2020) investigated the pattern of trade between India and ASEAN. The study used the comparative advantage by country and market comparative advantage. This study revealed that India's exports to ASEAN as far as competitiveness is concerned are not competitive in nature. The reason behind it was government protection measures specifically tariff as well as non -tariff barriers.

Research Gap

Most of the study focused on the trade, investment and economic cooperation between India and ASEAN nations. These studies crucially in sighted the long term trade relationship between India and ASEAN. The previous studies would mainly focus to check the effect of free trade agreement between India and ASEAN nations.

MAIN FOCUS OF THE CHAPTER

Research Methodology

To fulfil the purpose of study secondary data has been used from various authentic data source sites. The data has been collected from the various web sources such as World Bank, Reserve Bank of India (RBI), Asian Development Bank (ADB), United Nation Conference on trade and development (UNCTAD), United Nation Commodity trade statistic Database from 1992 to 2019. To fulfil the objectives of study trade indices such as trade similarity index, diversification index, complementarity index, trade openness and revealed Comparative Advantage (RCA) index has been used.

- **Revealed Comparative Advantage:** This measures the country's export potential. RCA indices would also help the country to process of extend the product as the trade potential as contrary to scenario in which numbers of product can be competitive exports but static in nature. It can also help the country to check the potential trade prospect in future. Countries with higher value of RCA would have better scope in bilateral trade.

$RCA_{ij} = (X_{ij} / X_{it}) \times 100$

(X_{wj} / X_{wt})

Where,

- X_{ij} = Values of country (i's) export of product (j)
- X_{it} = Value of Country (i's) total exports
- X_{wj} = Value of world exports of product (j)
- X_{wt} =Value of world total export

Trade Openness: is measure of economic policy that restricts or invites the trade in the economy. Trade openness index is calculated as ration of arithmetic mean of merchandise exports (x) and imports (m) to GDP (y) (**UNCTAD Handbook of statistics, 2019**).

$TOI_{i,t} = ½ (x_{i,t} + m_{i,t})$

$y_{i,t}$

Where, i designated to country
t tends to time period

- **Export Diversification Index:** refers whether the structure of export by a product of given country or country group differs from world pattern. It is one of highly important indicator for developing countries. Because, there are many developing countries that are mostly dependent on the primary commodities for export earnings. For such matters un-stabilization of prices led to serious shock in terms of trade. Diversification into new primary export products consider as the positive development and strong development effects associated with diversification in to manufacturing goods **(World Bank,2020).** Export diversification index defined as:

$DX_j = (\text{sum } |h_{ij} - x_{ij}|)\ 1$

Where h_{ij} is the share of commodity (i) in the total export of country (j)

x_{ij} is the share of good (i) in the global export of country (j)

- **Import Diversification Index:** refers whether the structure of export by a product of given country or country group differs from world pattern **(World Bank,2020).**

$DX_j = (\text{sum } |h_{ij} - x_{ij}|)\ 2$

Where h_{ij} is the share of commodity (i) in the total import of country (j)
x_{ij} is the share of good (i) in the global import of country (j)

- **Trade Intensity:** is used to find out whether the value of trade between two countries is either greater or smaller would expect as per its important in world trade. It can be define as the share of one country's export going to partner divided by its share of world exports going to its partner **(World Bank,2020).** It can be find as:

$T_{ij} = (x_{ij} / X_{it})_{\times 100}$

(x_{wj} / X_{wt})

Where, x_{ij} value of country (i)'s exports to country (j)
x_{wj} is the value of country (i)'s world export to country (j)
X_{it} is country (i)'s total exports
X_{wt} is country (i)'s total world exports

- **Export Intensity Index:** is calculated as

$X_{ij} = (X_{ij} / X_i)_{\times 100}$

$M_j / (M_g - M_i)$

Where, $\mathbf{X_{ij}}$ = Export of country (i) to (j)
$\mathbf{X_i}$= Global exports of country (i)
$\mathbf{M_j}$= Global imports of country (j)
$\mathbf{M_g}$= Total global import
$\mathbf{M_i}$= Global imports of country (i)
$\mathbf{M_j}$= Global imports of country (j)

- **Import Intensity Index:** is calculated as

$M_{ij} = (M_{ij} / M_j)_{\times 100}$

$X_j / (X_g - X_i)$

Where, $\mathbf{M_{ij}}$ = Imports of country (i) to(j)
$\mathbf{M_j}$ = Global imports of country (j)
$\mathbf{X_i}$= Global exports of country (i)
$\mathbf{X_g}$= Total Global exports
$\mathbf{X_j}$= Global exports of country (j)

- **Trade Complementarity Index:** measures how well the structures of export pattern of one country matches with the import pattern of another. This defines whether the trade profiles are become more or less compatible. Its value lie between 0and 100. It calculates as:

$TC_{ij} = 100(1 - sum(|M_{ik} - X_{ij}| / 2)$

Where, $\mathbf{M_{ik}}$ =share of good (i) in all imports of country (k)
$\mathbf{X_{ij}}$ = Share of good (i) in the global exports of country (j)

India and ASEAN Trade at World-wide level

The trade pattern between India and ASEAN has evident various developments and with the phase of time, various changes have been evident in the trade relation. Table2 depicts the percentage share of India and ASEAN in world trade from 2001 to 2018.

It is evident from the above table that India's percentage share of imports from the world had been significant increases till 2012. Further, it would follow the downward trend until 2017. There is a good context as per as India's import declining is considered. Overall, the percentage increases in imports were more than that of exports. India was highly oil-dependent country. Crucially, machinery goods, electronics and organic chemicals imports had been increased. This would lead to an increase in the imports side of the Indian economy in the integration of trade proportion. It can be considered from the following table1 that the exports to the world from India had increased during this tenure from 0.71 to 1.67 percentages. Whereas, the percentage share of export of ASEAN to World is higher than that of imports. That would portray the Strength of Aggregation of south-east Asia i.e., ASEAN. It is also evident that Exports share of ASEAN were 0.21 times more than that of imports share of ASEAN. Because ASEAN nations have been emerge as the economic power house. It is one of the manufacturing hubs, a growing hub for consumer demand and trade specialised region in the world. In the context of macroeconomic stability, it would rather provide more contribution to the nation's growth. ASEAN economy faced less volatility in the economic growth for the nations.

Table 2. Trade share of India and ASEAN in world (in per cent)

Years	Percentage of imports by India (World)	Percentage of exports by India (World)	Percentage of imports by ASEAN (World)	Percentage of exports by ASEAN (World)
2001	0.8	0.71	5.34	6.25
2002	0.87	0.77	5.49	6.24
2003	0.94	0.79	5.18	6.26
2004	1.05	0.83	5.33	6.23
2005	1.32	0.97	5.47	6.29
2006	1.45	1.01	5.41	6.38
2007	1.55	1.05	5.35	6.18
2008	1.93	1.13	5.73	6.14
2009	2.11	1.43	5.73	6.51
2010	2.28	1.46	6.22	6.98
2011	2.52	1.66	6.31	6.9
2012	2.64	1.57	6.6	6.84
2013	2.46	1.78	6.65	6.78
2014	2.43	1.68	6.57	6.86
2015	2.36	1.61	6.65	7.13
2016	2.22	1.63	6.77	7.22
2017	2.49	1.68	7.13	7.53
2018	2.58	1.67	7.31	7.51

Source: Author's Development based on United Nation commodity trade statistics database

Table3.elaborates the Trade share of India and ASEAN in its respective imports and exports. It is crystal clear from the table that the ASEAN nation had major chunk of share in its import as well as export. Indian economy had very less share in its import and export respectively. Before going further here there are so many developments that India-ASEAN relation had been enjoying. India's free trade agreement with ASEAN nation would give the new development in the context for economic integration between India and ASEAN. It can be evident that ASEAN would get more benefit from free trade agreement. Because of the availability of trade spot these nation would start trading with each other. Main crux that had been get out from that India's look east strategy and free trade agreement would help ASEAN and India trade relationship positively. Most of the benefit would lead to ASEAN nation as aggregation as compared to Indian nation. The new version of India's Look East policy i.e., Act East policy pertains towards the joint venture and collaboration between India and ASEAN that would help India and ASEAN to grow and sustain in terms of trade and collaboration.

Table 3. Trade share of India and ASEAN (in per cent)

Years	ASEAN share in India's Import	ASEAN share in India's Export	India's share in ASEAN import	India's share in ASEAN Export
2001	8.57	7.55	1.05	1.56
2002	8.36	8.98	1.11	1.55
2003	9.23	8.54	1.11	1.75
2004	8.63	9.94	1.42	1.89
2005	7.54	10.24	1.46	2.25
2006	9.14	10.2	1.59	2.48
2007	9.61	9.47	1.79	2.97
2008	8.45	10.68	2.13	3.19
2009	8.99	10.12	1.93	3.24
2010	8.46	10.41	2.08	3.51
2011	8.72	11.44	2.44	3.67
2012	8.74	11.15	2.25	3.6
2013	9.07	11.25	2.06	3.29
2014	9.67	9.85	1.95	3.37
2015	10.62	9.99	1.78	3.46
2016	10.71	10.13	1.91	3.26
2017	10.2	11.97	2.23	3.43
2018	11.27	11.16	2.14	3.5

Source: Author's Development based on United Nation commodity trade statistics database

Diversification of Export and Import

This section of the study confines the diversification of India and ASEAN export and imports from 2001 to 2018. In this section export diversification and import diversification has discussed separately and trend with the phase of time has defined.

Fig 1 depicts the Export Diversification of India and ASEAN from 2001-2018. It is perceptible from the trend of export diversification that ASEAN nations have more export diversification than India. The export diversification of ASEAN was stagnant during this tenure and revolves around 0.6 to 0.65. The study found that Effect of institutional strength, competitiveness, growth in domestic investment, financial sector development, natural resource curse and macroeconomic efficiency has contributed to the positive association the high export diversification of ASEAN. This retaining and highly diverse export of ASEAN would precise due to Foreign Direct Investment attraction by the ASEAN nation. Although in the context of Indian economy Government of India highly pertains towards the export diversification strategy to boost India's exports and scope. The study found that lowering export diversification of India was due to lack of adequate finance and knowledge, high transaction cost and risk and MSME sector faced such hurdles that further impacts the efforts to change the direction of export diversification in India.

Figure 1. Export Diversification of India and ASEAN
Source: Author's Development based on United Nation commodity trade statistics database

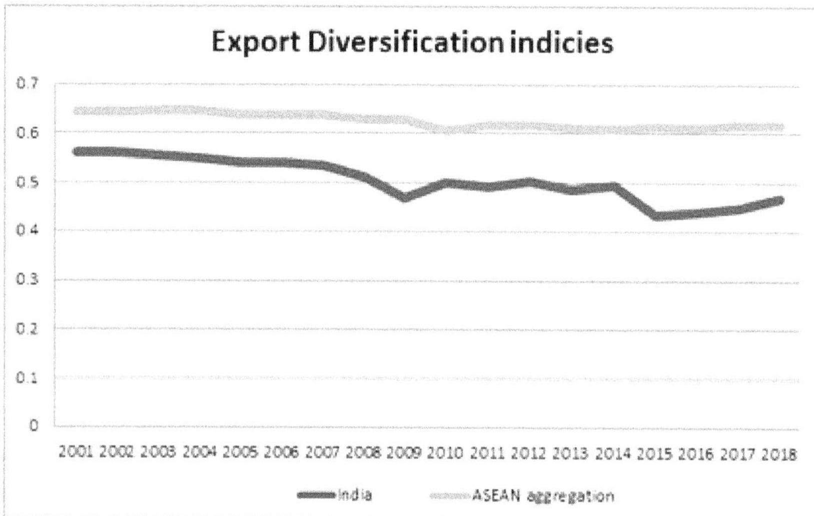

Figure 2. Import Diversification of India and ASEAN
Source: Author's Development based on United Nation commodity trade statistics database

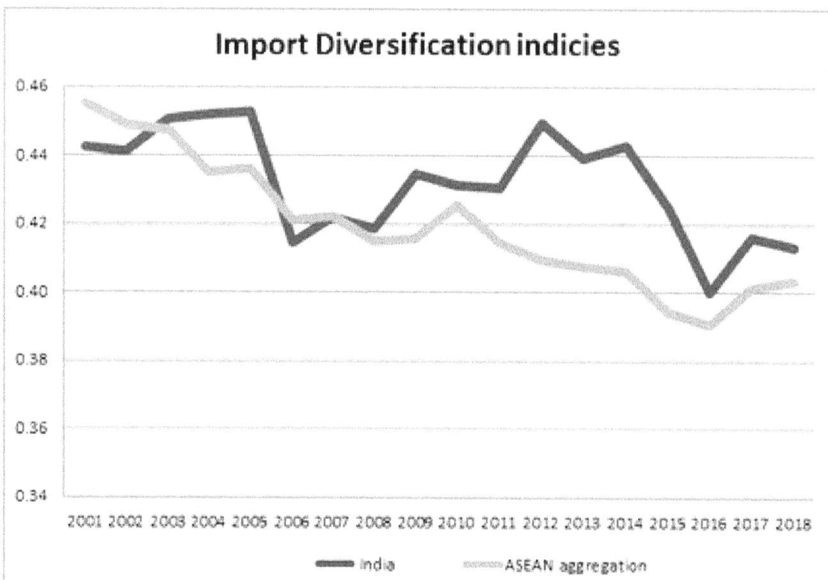

Figure 2 depicts the Import Diversification of India and ASEAN from 2001-2018.Visible from the trend that there has been fluctuation evident in the import diversification of India and ASEAN. Earlier the import diversification of ASEAN has more than that of India from 2001-2003 and after that India led to the import diversification as contrary to ASEAN. The import diversification ranges from 0.46 to

0.40 during this tenure. The study found that short- run and long-run causalities evident from India and ASEAN imports. That further pertain the financial integration and imports diversification in the trade relation. Apart from that Asia region evident the development and move towards the growth and all these factors contributed to the growing demand for new development products which demands the newly developed products. This overall trend defines the slight decrease in the import diversification for both India and ASEAN and Intra trade led to more diversification in the context of imports.

Trade Openness

Table 4. Trade Openness of India and ASEAN

Years	India	ASEAN
2001	13.81	75.42
2002	14.49	70.94
2003	15.03	70.37
2004	17.29	76.87
2005	21.24	75.72
2006	23.17	72.95
2007	22.72	69.77
2008	28.22	70.69
2009	23.41	58.24
2010	24.64	59.38
2011	27.95	61.18
2012	29.02	60.67
2013	28.07	60.39
2014	26.59	60.63
2015	22.40	57.22
2016	20.71	54.06
2017	21.28	56.86
2018	22.46	59.32
Overall(2000-18)	**22.36**	**65.04**
Phase-I(2001-09)	**19.93**	**71.22**
Phase-II (2009-18)	**24.65**	**58.79**

Source: Author's Development based on United Nation commodity trade statistics database

Trade openness of the country confines the measure of economic policy that restricts or invites the trade in the economy. Further, Table 4 elaborated the Trade openness of India and ASEAN from 2001 to 2018. Here the data has been segregated into two phases. Trade openness defines in terms of the average of import and export to GDP for India and ASEAN nation. Trade openness of ASEAN economies had been decreased than that of growth between these two phases. In the context of the Indian economy, it was two times increased. The trade openness for Indian economy was high than that of the second phase. This was entirely due to liberal and good economic policy adopted by India. Especially due to foreign trade policy of India that worked under the umbrella of India's EXIM policy whose main motive is to fraternise: developing export potential, stimulate foreign trade, creation of favourable Balance of trade positions and improving export performance. Under such policies: India's Look East Policy is specially focused by India to improve the trade Performa with South-East nation. Whereas in the second phase the trade openness of the ASEAN nation was very low as contrary to the first phase and on the average, it is 65.04 which was less than that of 2001.The prominent Reason behind it was Common Elimination Preferential Tariff- ASEAN Free Trade Area (CEPT-AFTA) scheme under which the 99 per cent product for Intra trade had been drop down the tariff range to 0-5 per cent. But as such no tariff policy introduced for the non-members of the ASEAN. In crux, in terms of trade openness for import and export for both India has been showing an increasing trend and this was entirely due to liberal policy framework adopted by India and ASEAN. Overall the trade openness of ASEAN nation than that of India that is 59.32 and 22.46 per cent.in this case the trade openness average moves opposite as per the phases is concerned. This section prevails the trade openness of India and ASEAN with the context of its openness for the economic integration and regional blocs unity. This would clearly confine that since 2012 the level of trade openness had been drop drastically but still in the second phase growth was higher in the case of India and lesser in the context of ASEAN. Now, in the further part of the study direction of trade has been discussed as per the trade hotspot for India and ASEAN concerned.

Trade Intensity

Trade intensity is found out whether the value of trade between the two countries is either greater or smaller would expect as per its importance in world trade. It can be defined as the share of one country's export going to partner divided by its share of world exports going to its partner.

Table 5 defines the Trade Intensity of India with ASEAN during 2001 -18. Here India's trade intensity with ASEAN nation has been evident the significant growth. Let's firstly starts with the export intensity, from 2002 the export intensity of India with ASEAN nation has significantly increase till 2008 and afterwards the consistent drop has been emerged it drops from maximum 185 to 148.8 the difference was quite high and move towards the picture of 2001. The reason behind it was the pattern of high import as contrary to low exports by India. That led to drastic changes in the pattern of trade. Whereas in the case of import intensity there has been continuous growth evident till 2007 and further it started to decline till 2015. In 2015 and 2018 the trade intensity of India with ASEAN has been evident high phase. Another reason for sudden distraction could be the global recession of 2008 that would lead to sudden slow- down of trade in the Asian region. In the context of the overall trade intensity, it was consecutively followed the pattern of import and export intensity. The highest trade intensity would evident in 2007 and this highest intensity would face in the pre-global recession when the Asia region evident the higher pace of growth due to its liberalizing policies. But when it comes to the overall change it was positive if the value of 2001 and 2018 compared. The value more than 100 for the trade intensity, export intensity and import intensity would find the positive prospects of trade between India and ASEAN and it move towards the trade integration between these two due to the growing trade flows and intensity. It promotes the importance of growing trade relationship between them. Now, the trade complementarity between India and ASEAN has been discussed.

Table 5. Trade Intensity of India with ASEAN during 2001 -18

Years	Trade Intensity	Export Intensity	Import Intensity
2001	139.86	140.2	136.15
2002	147.66	162.25	132.96
2003	156.1	165.31	146.2
2004	159.37	184.48	137.44
2005	147.48	184.63	118.78
2006	162.36	185.61	141.71
2007	165.76	174.05	153.88
2008	156.21	182.84	136.08
2009	154.3	172.86	136.01
2010	139.71	163.56	119.49
2011	148.28	176.66	124.24
2012	143.35	164.38	125.73
2013	148.76	165.05	131.46
2014	145.08	146.27	138.54
2015	150.5	146.67	146.61
2016	149.52	146.17	145.8
2017	148.77	163.62	133.1
2018	151.51	148.8	147.43

Source: Author's Development based on United Nation commodity trade statistics database

Trade Complementarity

It measures how well the structure of an export pattern of one country matches the import pattern of another. This defines whether the trade profiles become more or less compatible and it generally confines the complementarity. The value of the trade complementarity lies from 0 to 100. Figure 4 explains the trade complementarity of India and ASEAN from 2001 to 2018. Generally, the 0.4 point drops in the trade complementarity of India with ASEAN. The value of trade complementarity as 100 define that composition of needed imports of ASEAN nation would perfectly match with exports of India. This trade complementarity measures the common features between the export profile of India and import profile of ASEAN

In 2001 the trade complementarity was 99.7 which was high close to the 100 and determined as the perfect combination for trade tie-ups. And further, the drop of some points has been evident, and it reached 99.3 which was also closely related to 100. This overall trend of trade complementarity of India with ASEAN evident the positive development whether no doubt the drop had been evident but it was very minimal. If it was rapidly declined then it would be the problem for India.

But right now it works as the positive and fruitful development for the Indian economy. In the crux composition of needed imports of ASEAN nation would perfectly match with exports of India. This defines the strategic and integration of trade ties up. This would more prevail towards the intra-region integration. This would only possible due to the strengthened policy adopted by India whether it is Look

East or Act East. The trade complementarity is more or less skewed in the favour for both the nation and the policy-driven context would confine the importance of growing trade compatibility.

Figure 3. Trade Complementarity of India with ASEAN
Source: Author's Development based on United Nation commodity trade statistics database

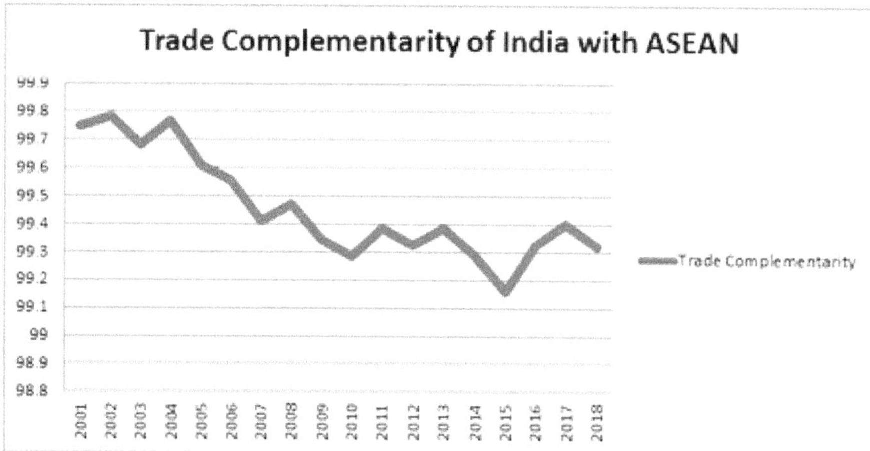

India's Export Competitiveness with ASEAN Nations

This revealed comparative advantage of India's export with ASEAN nations has been discussed. This RCA index has been calculated from 2001 to 2018 and Harmonised System HS-6 digit commodities have been taken. For this study RCA index from 2001 to 2014 has been taken as per the tenure of India's Look East Policy. For Act east policy RCA Index from 2015 to 2018 has been taken. In order to compare the Export competitiveness in the India's Look East Policy changing framework. This revealed the top ten commodities revealed comparative advantage as well as a disadvantage with help of index value. If the RCA value is greater than one than the exported that product from India to ASEAN has revealed comparative advantage for that commodity export and if less than it would have revealed comparative disadvantage.

Table 6 depicts the RCA Index of top ten commodities average value from 2001 to 2014.Basically,India's Look East policy has been changed with Act east policy from 2014 onwards. For that matter, the RCA index from 2001 to 2014 has been discussed. Diamonds, worked, but not mounted or set (excluding industrial diamonds), Oil cake and other solid residues, whether or not ground or in form of pellets, resulting from the extraction of soya-bean oil, Frozen, boneless meat of bovine animals, Record media for sound or image reproducing phenomena, incl. matrices and master for the production of records (excluding gramophone records, discs for laser reading systems, magnetic tapes, cards incorporating a magnetic stripe) have RCA index value is greater than one this would portray the Revealed Comparative advantage in the export of these commodities to ASEAN. Frozen, boneless meat of bovine animals with HS-code 020230 has a greater advantage due to its higher index value of 3.74 and highest among the top commodities. Whereas, in the case of Part and accessories of automatic data-processing machines or for other machines of heading (0.06), Aluminium, not alloyed, unwrought (0.66), Cane or beet sugar and chemically pure sucrose, in solid form (excluding cane and beet sugar containing added flavouring or colouring and raw sugar) (0.51), Polypropylene, in primary forms (0.51) and Commodities not elsewhere specified (0.06) possess the revealed comparative disadvantage as per the average RCA index value from 2001 to 2014. This can be evident that Commodities not elsewhere specified (0.06) and Part and accessories of automatic data-processing machines or for other machines of heading (0.06) possess the greater disadvantageous for trade with ASEAN nations.

Table 6. Revealed Comparative Advantage of India's Export with ASEAN (Average from 2001-2014)

HS Code	HS Product Classification	Average of RCA value (2001-2014)
710239	Diamonds, worked, but not mounted or set (excluding industrial diamonds)	1.06
230400	Oil cake and other solid residues, whether or not ground or in form of pellets, resulting from the extraction of soya-bean oil	2.73
847330	Part and accessories of automatic data-processing machines or for other machines of heading	0.06
999999	Commodities not elsewhere specified	0.06
020230	Frozen, boneless meat of bovine animals	3.74
170199	Cane or beet sugar and chemically pure sucrose, in solid form (excluding cane and beet sugar containing added flavouring or colouring and raw sugar)	0.51
852499	Record media for sound or image reproducing phenomena, incl. matrices and master for the production of records (excluding gramophone records, discs for laser reading systems, magnetic tapes, cards incorporating a magnetic stripe)	1.23
760110	Aluminium, not alloyed, unwrought	0.66
100190	Wheat and meslin (excluding durum wheat)	0.86
390210	Polypropylene, in primary forms	0.51

Source: Author's Development based on United Nation commodity trade statistics database

Table 7 depicts the RCA Index of top ten commodities average value from 2015 to 2018. This table focused on the Act East Policy period RCA index value. It can be clearly evident from the table that Frozen, boneless meat of bovine animals, Light-vessels, fire-floats, floating cranes and other vessels, the navigability of which is the navigability of which is subsidiary to their main function (excluding dredgers, floating or submersible drilling or production platforms; fishing vessels and warships, Frozen shrimps and prawns, even smoked whether in shell or not, include shrimps and prawns in shell, cooked by steaming or by boiling in water (excluding cold-water shrimps and prawns, Copper, refined, in the form of cathodes and section of cathodes and Groundnuts, shelled whether or not broken (excluding seed for sowing, roasted or otherwise) commodities has RCA index value greater than one. This possesses the revealed comparative advantage of India's export commodities to ASEAN nations. Although commodities with RCA index less than one were Light oils and preparations, of petroleum or bituminous minerals which greater than equal 90 per cent by volume, Medium oils and preparations, of petroleum or bituminous minerals, not containing biodiesel, n.e.s, Commodities not elsewhere specified, Diamonds, worked, but not mounted or set (excluding industrial diamonds) and Floating or submersible drilling or production platforms.

This can be observed from Table 6 and Table 7 that under India's Look East policy as well as Act East policy have common top commodities were Diamonds, worked, but not mounted or set (excluding industrial diamonds), Commodities not elsewhere specified and Frozen, boneless meat of bovine animals. Furthermore, Diamonds, worked, but not mounted or set (excluding industrial diamonds) with HS code (710239) RCA index value decreased from 1.06 to o.12. Under the tenure of Act East Policy Diamonds, worked, but not mounted or set (excluding industrial diamonds) said to be revealed comparative disadvantage. Also in the context of and Frozen, boneless meat of bovine animals RCA index has been decreased from 3.74 to 1.96 and still the India's export competitiveness advantage lies in this commodity. Groundnuts, shelled whether or not broken (excluding seed for sowing, roasted or with HS code 120242 emerged as the new top commodity for the export. The RCA index value was quiet high in the case of Groundnuts, shelled whether or not broken (excluding seed for sowing, roasted and have better scope for trade prospects.

Table 7. Revealed Comparative Advantage of India's Export with ASEAN (Average 2015-2018)

HS Code	HS Product Classification	Average RCA value (2015-18)
020230	Frozen, boneless meat of bovine animals	1.96
271012	Light oils and preparations, of petroleum or bituminous minerals which greater than equal 90 per cent by volume	0.66
271019	Medium oils and preparations, of petroleum or bituminous minerals, not containing biodiesel, n.e.s	0.7
999999	Commodities not elsewhere specified	0.02
710239	Diamonds, worked, but not mounted or set (excluding industrial diamonds)	0.12
890590	Light-vessels, fire-floats, floating cranes and other vessels, the navigability of which is the navigability of which is subsidiary to their main function (excluding dredgers, floating or submersible drilling or production platforms; fishing vessels and warships)	4.18
890520	Floating or submersible drilling or production platforms	0.73
030617	Frozen shrimps and prawns, even smoked whether in shell or not, include shrimps and prawns in shell, cooked by steaming or by boiling in water (excluding cold-water shrimps and prawns)	2.23
740311	Copper, refined, in the form of cathodes and section of cathodes	4.03
120242	Groundnuts, shelled whether or not broken (excluding seed for sowing, roasted or otherwise)	22.63

Source: Author's Development based on United Nation commodity trade statistics database

Findings

The trade pattern between India and ASEAN has evident various developments and with the phase of time, various changes have been evident in the trade relation and data is taken from 2001 to 2018. It is evident from the above table that India's percentage share of imports from the world had been significant increases till 2012. Further, it would follow the downward trend until 2017. There is a good context as per as India's import declining is considered. Overall, the percentage increases in imports were more than that of exports. The percentage share of export of ASEAN to World is higher than that of imports.

That would portray the strength of aggregation of south-east Asia i.e., ASEAN. It is also evident that Exports share of ASEAN was 0.21 times more than that of imports share of ASEAN. Moreover, ASEAN nation had major chunk of share in its imports as well as exports. Indian economy had very less share in its imports and exports respectively.

Trade Index has been check to determine the trade relationship between India and ASEAN. From the trade index's study able to get the major outcomes under the India Look East policy as well as Act East Policy since 2001. Diversification Index of Export and Import outcomes define that effect of institutional strength, competitiveness, growth in domestic investment, financial sector development, natural resource curse and macroeconomic efficiency has contributed to the positive association the high export diversification of ASEAN. Lowering export diversification of India was due to lack of adequate finance and knowledge, high transaction cost and risk and MSME sector faced such hurdles that further impacts the efforts to change the direction of export diversification in India. Short- run and long-run causalities evident from trade structure of India and ASEAN imports. That further pertain the financial integration and imports diversification in the trade relation. Apart from that Asia region evident the development and move towards the growth and all these factors contributed to the growing demand for new development products which demand the newly developed products. This overall trend defines the slight decrease in the import diversification for both India and ASEAN and Intra trade led to more diversification in the context of imports.

Trade openness for import and export for both India has been showing an increasing trend and this was entirely due to liberal policy framework adopted by India and ASEAN. Overall the trade openness of ASEAN nation than that of India that is 59.32 and 22.46 per cent. In this case the trade openness average moves opposite as per the phases is concerned. This section prevails the trade openness of India and ASEAN with the context of its openness for the economic integration and regional blocs unity. This would clearly confine that since 2012 the level of trade openness had been drop drastically but still in the second phase growth was higher in the case of India and lesser in the context of ASEAN.

Moreover, trade intensity of India and ASEAN considered: The value more than 100 for the trade intensity, export intensity and import intensity would find the positive prospects of trade between India and ASEAN and it move towards the trade integration between these two due to the growing trade flows and intensity. It promotes the importance of growing trade relationship between them.

Trade Complementarity of India and ASEAN propounded that: composition of needed imports of ASEAN nation would perfectly match with exports of India. This defines the strategic and integration of trade ties up. This would more prevail towards the intra-region integration. This would only possible due to the strengthened policy adopted by India whether it is Look East or Act East. The trade complementarity is more or less skewed in the favour for both the nation and the policy-driven context would confine the importance of growing trade compatibility.

For India's Look East Policy tenure Commodities with RCA >1 and as per technological classification major commodities come under resource based manufacturers commodities. For Act East Policy tenure, It can be also observed the RCA index value greater than one in the case of resource based and medium- high technology manufacturer's commodities as per technology classification as well as India export to ASEAN nation was put forth.

Policy Implication

There has been following Policy Implications has been given in the context of India and ASEAN for future prospects:

1. India and ASEAN have strong trade relationship but as far as trade balance is considered. India has negative trade balance with ASEAN. India should expand the trade with ASEAN nations specifically with emerging countries in the ASEAN nations.
2. India's exports to ASEAN economies are majorly in the form of Resource Based and Medium level Manufacturers. No doubt High Technology Manufacturers commodities have been exported but base of such trade is less. There should be more focus to reluctant with High technology manufacturer's trade in order to boost the trade base.
3. India and ASEAN relationship would become more strength full if the collaboration in terms of road connectivity has been done as well as regionalism would get benefit out of it.
4. India's Economic growth would not significantly impact to boost the trade. For that matter Indian Economy should focus on the efficient allocation of growth patterns for the trade pattern so that trade creation prompted and South-South Cooperation would boost up. India and ASEAN nations would enjoy the benefit out of that.
5. India and ASEAN nation has huge trade intensity and complementarity. In terms of trade potentiality export competitiveness lies in the India's resources based and medium manufacturer's commodities. India should expand the foreign policy i.e., Act East Policy by compelling it with India's Make in India Initiative to boost the regional trade prospects.

CONCLUSION

In nutshell, India and ASEAN would able to strengthen the relationship by the foreign policy adopted by the Indian government. The role of India's look east policy would not deniable it would more helpful to integrate the nation with positive gratitude and have a better scope as Act east policy of India. India's Look East Policy is specially focused by India to improve the trade Performa with South-East nation India's Look East Policy would help the India and ASEAN economic integration and multilateralism. India and ASEAN trade has been crucially started when it becomes its first sector dialogue partner. India's Look East Policy gives the direction for the future prospects of trade and free trade agreement i.e., AIFTA would make the trade easier. The Various studies revealed that trade cooperation, complementariness' between the trading partners had been increased significantly ASEAN India free trade agreement (AIFTA) would enhance the economic cooperation between these two emerging nations. Various study suggested that strong political, economic and integration needed for future ties up with ASEAN and that Free trade agreement between India and ASEAN would tend to surplus if there would be tariff elasticity or remove the tariff barriers.

Bi-lateral trade between India and ASEAN has better scope as per the Trade intensity and trade complementarity is concerned. Both of these indicators possess the positive development of trade integration and growing tie ups. All of but indeed is stability and boost from India side to widen up the trade. In terms of Benefit ASEAN is still leader but necessary is enjoy the fruit by both of them. The benefit of trade openness and export diversification should use as the base to strength the relationship and achieved the growth in terms of trade and development.

India's RCA index values prevail the comparison of top commodities during the India's Look East Policy and Act East Policy tenure. The RCA index and top-notched commodity emerged under Act East Policy would be Groundnuts, shelled whether or not broken (excluding seed for sowing, roasted due to its RCA index of 22.63. Apart from this Frozen shrimps and prawns, even smoked whether in shell or not, include shrimps and prawns in shell, cooked by steaming or by boiling in water (excluding cold-water shrimps and prawns) and Light-vessels, fire-floats, floating cranes and other vessels, the navigability of which is the navigability of which is subsidiary to their main function (excluding dredgers, floating or submersible drilling or production platforms; fishing vessels and warships) also emerged as the newly exported commodities and advantageous too in nature.

That further again reframes in the umbrella of Act East Policy of India. When it comes to trade export and imports are growing significantly with some drastic up and downs. No doubt Act east policy pertain towards the joint venture and collaboration between India and ASEAN that would definitely help India and ASEAN to grow and sustain in terms of trade and collaboration

THE WAY FORWARD

This chapter focused on trade relationship between India and ASEAN countries. For economic development trade play a vital role but there are another factors such as foreign direct investment, migration, government policies, and foreign institutional investment etc. also significant role. In future studies, researches can focus on these factors to analyse the growth of trade as well as economic development.

REFERENCES

Alam. (2015). Indo-Asean Trade relation: An Analysis. *Journal of International Economics*, *6*(1), 73-106.

Bajpaee, C. (2017). Dephasing India's Look East/Act East Policy. *Contemporary Southeast Asia*, *39*(3), 348–372. doi:10.1355/cs39-2d

Banik, N., & Kim, M. (2020). India-ASEAN Trade Relations: Examining the trends and Identifying the Potential. *Global Business Review*. Retrieved from https://sci-hub.tf/10.1177/0972150920953546

Bhattacharyya, R., & Mandal, A. (2016). India-ASEAN free trade agreement: An ex post evaluation. *Journal of Policy Modeling*, *38*(32), 340–352. doi:10.1016/j.jpolmod.2016.02.001

Bhowmik, D. (2019). Impact of Indo-ASEAN import on ASEAN trade and financial integration. *Empirical Economic Review*, *2*(1), 1–34. doi:10.29145/eer/21/020101

Carbaugh. (2008). *International Economics* (11th ed.). New Delhi: Cengage Learning India Pvt Ltd.

Chandran, S., & Mukhtar, J. (2019). Indo-ASEAN Trade Relation: Understanding the advantage sector for India by using Balassa's RCA Index. *Journal of Emerging Technologies and Innovative Research*, *6*(6), 633–640.

Ghosh. (2016). *International relation* (3rd ed.). Delhi: Phi learning Publisher Pvt Ltd.

Haokip, T. (2014). India's Look East Policy: Its Evolution and Approach. *Sage Journals*, *18*(2), 239–257.

Kaur, N., & Sarin, V. (2017). Comparative advantage and competitiveness of Indian agricultural products exports to ASEAN in context of India's Look East Policy. *International Journal of Agricultural and Statistics Sciences*, *1*(1), 159–167.

Pant, H. V., & Deb, A. (2017). *India-ASEAN Partnership at 25.* ORF Issue Brief No.189. https://www.orfonline.org/wp-content/uploads/2017/07/ORF_ Issue_Brief_189_India-ASEAN.pdf

Rao, B. (2003). Looking East: Retrospect and Prospects. *Economic and Political Weekly*, *38*(41), 4317–4318.

Sarin, V. (2017). An analysis of India's Export Competitiveness in context of AIFTA. *International Journal of Commerce and Management*, *11*(2), 32–56.

ADDITIONAL READING

Indian Today. (2016). India's Import Report: A look at India's top 8 imports. *India Today.* https://www.indiatoday.in/education-today/gk-current-affairs/story/india-imports-343823-2016-09-29

PHD Research Bureau. (2015). India's Exports Diversification-CrissCross Outcomes. http://phdcci.in/live_backup/image/data/Research%20Bureau2014/ Economic%20Developments/paper/Exports%20Diversification.pdf

Chapter 5
BIMSTEC:
Silver Lining in the Cloud for India During the Pandemic Period

Namita Kapoor
https://orcid.org/0000-0001-9661-1700
Amity University, India

Tavishi Tewary
https://orcid.org/0000-0001-9414-5320
Jaipuria Institute of Management, Noida, India

Annanya Mohanty
Daedal Research, New Delhi, India

ABSTRACT

The ongoing pandemic has drastically affected the Bay of Bengal countries. Greater cooperation is suggested as these countries are fighting against the common problem and challenge of the coronavirus pandemic. Regional cooperation has become important to overcome the barriers that are mainly pandemic driven which has resulted in an increase in the cost of production and trade in the region. The chapter discusses the benefits that India is likely to get with higher integration with the immediate neighbouring countries with special reference to BIMSTEC region. The Bay of Bengal Initiative for Multi-Sectoral Technical and Economic Cooperation (BIMSTEC) region is a dynamic region with trade as the driver of growth. The region is often overlapped with SAARC regional grouping with almost similar members. BIMSTEC gained its lost recognition in the year 2016, due to its high growth potential to develop sustainably.

INTRODUCTION

The Bay of Bengal Initiative for Multi-Sectoral Technical and Economic Cooperation (BIMSTEC) is a dynamic region with high growth potential to expand sustainably and also having the possibility of growth

DOI: 10.4018/978-1-7998-5774-7.ch005

convergence between member countries (Elangovan, 2019; Towhid & Kiyoto, 2019). Self-propelled growth impulses put these economies on a high growth trajectory. The region is a conglomeration of forceful economies from both South Asia and Southeast Asia. During the period of recession, the BIMSTEC region is one of the most resilient regions of the world with very high economic growth performance. The region has been greatly influenced by the strategy of globalization and has been switching between the strategies of Export-Led Growth (ELG) and Domestic Demand Led Growth (DDLG) from time to time to maintain high growth over time irrespective of the global trade regimes of buoyancy or recession in place. With gradual structural change happening in the region, many regional economies are in the process of becoming industrialized or in the process of 'catching up' industrialization. The convergence of high growth in the region has given a new identity to the region.

BIMSTEC is a sub-regional trading arrangement, comprising seven member nations from the contiguous regions of South Asia and Southeast Asia. From the total of seven members, five of them are from the South Asian region such as Bangladesh, Bhutan, India, Nepal, and Sri Lanka, and the rest two countries are from South East Asia namely Myanmar and Thailand. The regional grouping was established in 1997 with five economies of the South and South-East Asian regions and the grouping was further expanded with the inclusion of Bhutan and Nepal in 2004. The progress in the grouping was slow in the first two decades of its inception but suddenly caught the limelight of the global economy in 2016 with India's robust initiative to foster the region's performance. After the Uri attack in October 2016 (at an Indian military base), India decided to revive BIMSTEC, which was maintaining a low profile for a long period despite having a secretariat in Dhaka and negotiating for a Free Trade Agreement (FTA) among member countries (Padmaja, 2017). After the BRICS Summit in Goa, the Indian Prime Minister held an awareness meeting with BIMSTEC leaders to refocus on the relevance of the grouping. BIMSTEC countries were in agreement with New Delhi's call to boycott the SAARC summit held in November 2016 in Islamabad.

The revival of BIMSTEC came at a time when SAARC cooperation reaches its lowest point on account of the growing standoff between India and Pakistan on the issue of military intervention in 2016. As progress in the SAARC region was almost a standstill over some time, as an alternative regional forum, BIMSTEC emerged as a new regional platform to discuss the regional integration process to enhance regional economic welfare (Rahman & Kim, 2015). BIMSTEC is a vibrant region having large synergies between countries to cooperate for mutual gains in diverse sectors. As regional economies are endowed with self-propelled growth potentials, coming together of these regional economies could take the region on a high growth trajectory.

In various ministerial meetings, BIMSTEC leaders agreed to cooperate in seven key areas including those of trade, investment, logistics, energy, etc. among others. There were broad agreements between member countries in principle to take advantage of the continuity of the regional economies by developing transport infrastructure across borders and adopting suitable regional Agreements to spur economic activities in the region. These trade and investment facilitating measures can promote intra-regional trade (IRT) to grow fast. As such IRT of BIMSTEC has posted a better performance vis-à-vis SAARC during the past decade (Ain & Shah, 2019; Kaur, Sarin & Dhami, 2016). Trade cooperation combined with investment may add more strength to present economic activities within the region. As the region is a combination of littoral and landlocked economies, a cost-effective transportation system is a major impediment for trade within the region. With multi-modal transport facilities, the region can overcome connectivity issues to a large extent (Rahman, 2014). Similarly, trade facilitation is an important issue in the region and new initiatives are in place to overcome such impediments linked to regional trade. For dealing with these problems, a comprehensive regional initiative for evolving a Free Trade Agreement (FTA) was initiated in 2004 and a successful conclusion of this effort is very much on the card (Hossain, 2013; Wijayasiri, 2016). For achieving fast progress in the region, economies have to build a consensus on targeted measures to implement commonly agreed policies.

Rapid liberalization has been underway in several economies to facilitate their integration with the global economy. During the period of global buoyancy of the 2000s, the economy of the BIMSTEC region initiated dialogues with neighbouring countries such as ASEAN and China to strengthen their economic ties in trade and investment. Several studies have indicated that the region has large synergies to cooperate with Japan (Asher & Sen, 2006; Banik and

Bhaumik, 2005; Bhattacharya & Bhattacharyay, 2007; Chotani, 2018; Dey, 2006; Gilbert, 2008; Wijayasiri & De Mel, 2008). The process of liberalization started at different phases in these economies. As a member of ASEAN, Thailand began to implement liberalization policies in the early 1980s, while other South Asian countries began to revoke trade restrictions in the 1990s. However, Sri Lanka (a south Asian country) had its trade liberalization in the 1980s (Wijayasiri & De Mel, 2008). The region is gradually picking up to perform exceedingly well in certain sectors including GVC, automobiles, and machinery sectors, apart from their traditional stronghold in the primary sector.

BIMSTEC's trade between regional economies was 6 percent in the last 10 years, which is slightly higher than SAARC for the corresponding period which was at 5 percent. The growth momentum in trade is growing fast in BIMSTEC (Bhattacharya & Bhattacharyay, 2006). However, the Intra-Regional Trade ratio of the region is laying low as compared to several dynamic regional groupings such as ASEAN, the Pacific Alliance, etc. The reason for the low level of IRT ratio in BIMSTEC is discussed at length in several studies (Kaur, Dutta, & Saini 2020; Kaur & Sarin and Dhami, 2016).

Macroeconomic Dimensions of the Region

While the world is still under pressure of ongoing pandemic and also double-dip recession, the possibility of global recovery is in doubt as the growth prospects of the global economy have moved southwards rapidly since 2018. Series of developments in the global economy such as feeble growth prospects in developed countries, unexpected Brexit, the Sino-US trade war, etc. hurt the growth prospects of the global economy (IMF, 2021). The adverse impact of these incidences is largely reflected in the macro-economic profile of the world economy.

The IMF (2021) shows that the world economy grew by 4% in 2017, fell to 3.6% in 2018, and further to 3.3% in 2019. As growth prospects of the world economy continued to decline, many economies have seen declines in their economic activities as a result of various reasons and these factors vary from one country to another (Pattanaik, 2020). Among major emerging economies, growth prospects were affected for example in India was due to the surge of Non- Performing Assets (NPAs) by the banks, tight credit policies of China, increasing global inequalities, and sporadic instances of trade-related tensions, etc. among others. The World Economic Outlook (IMF, 2021) projected that the rebound of the world economy is likely to occur in 2021 with a foretold growth rate of 5.4 percent. It suggests that the present situation of the global economy is subdued and is worse than what was observed in 2008 after the sub-prime financial crisis (Diebold, 2020).

Table 1. Growth performance of BIMSTEC and Other Regional Groupings (in %)

Year	BIMSTEC	ASEAN	SAARC	BBIN	IORA	GCC
2003	7.5	5.6	7.5	7.0	5.5	9.0
2004	7.5	6.2	7.5	7.7	5.7	8.5
2005	7.1	5.6	7.7	7.7	5.1	5.7
2006	7.0	5.8	7.7	7.9	5.7	6.5
2007	7.2	6.6	7.4	7.1	5.8	4.0
2008	3.2	4.1	3.2	3.3	3.3	5.8
2009	6.4	2.1	7.2	7.6	2.8	-1.8
2010	8.1	7.2	7.6	7.6	5.9	4.6
2011	4.6	4.8	4.8	5.2	4.1	8.5
2012	5.7	5.8	5.5	5.5	3.9	5.1
2013	5.8	4.8	5.7	6.3	4.3	3.4
2014	6.3	4.6	6.9	6.9	4.6	3.5
2015	7.1	4.5	7.4	7.8	4.2	4.0
2016	7.4	4.5	7.2	8.1	5.5	2.4
2017	6.5	5.0	6.4	7.0	4.7	0.2
2018	5.9	4.9	6.1	5.9	4.2	1.8
2019	4.8	4.2	4.7	5.2	3.4	0.5

Source: Author's estimation based on World Development Indicators, World Bank, Online access on March 1, 2021

The BIMSTEC region has been a fast-growing region compared to several neighbouring regional groupings as Shown in Table 1. In terms of the size of the real GDP of the region in comparison with South Asia, we got very interesting results. The growth performances of BIMSTEC, SAARC, and BBIN were somewhat comparable during the buoyancy (2003-07) and it was in the range of 7.1 percent to 7.4 percent in 2007. Between 2006 and 2007, GCC declined very sharply from 6.5 percent to 4.0 percent, which was unprecedented due to the decline in the global demand for hydrocarbon. In the first phase of the recession during 2008-13, the growth profile of the BIMSTEC region declined which was not different from that of the rest of the world but it bounces back from the sub-prime financial crisis with a high GDP growth rate of 8.1 percent in 2010.

Among other adjoining territorial groupings, IORA and ASEAN had experienced a steady but low level of growth performance in the first phase of the global recession. It is suggested that physical capital or investment is one of the major drivers of economic growth in the region (Rahman and Rizvi, 2018). The gross capital formation of the region was falling gradually since the 1970s and has continued the same ever since. However, GDP rose consistently since the early 2010s (Intal Jr, 2017). It may be inferred that as compared to other regional groupings, BIMSTEC countries performed relatively outstanding during the 2nd phase of the recession (Elangovan, 2019). Experiences of oil-exporting countries in West Asia indicate that the growth performance of GCC was declining gradually. Mahadi, Becek, and Chian (2011) suggested that the overdependence of these countries on oil and fluctuations in oil prices ever since 2014 culminated in the operation of the 'Dutch Disease' in these economies leading to straining their economies.

According to World Economic Outlook (IMF 2021), the GCC nations are expected to experience a 6 percentage points drop in GDP due to the volatile situation in the oil market where oil demand had been impacted following pandemic-driven lockdown in several major oil-importing countries.

Table 2.

Year	BIMSTEC						SAARC					
	Exports of goods and services Ratio	FDI, net inflows Ratio	GFCF Ratio	Gross capital formation Ratio	Imports of goods and services Ratio	Trade Ratio	Exports of goods and services Ratio	FDI, net inflows Ratio	GFCF Ratio	Gross capital formation Ratio	Imports of goods and services Ratio	Trade Ratio
2003	23.3	1.0	26.4	27.5	23.3	46.7	15.1	0.6	26.3	27.5	16.4	31.6
2004	26.2	1.2	28.6	32.7	27.1	53.5	17.3	0.7	28.2	32.8	19.3	36.9
2005	27.7	1.5	30.7	35.0	30.4	58.2	18.8	1.0	30.3	34.7	22.2	41.2
2006	28.8	2.2	31.1	35.0	31.1	60.0	20.3	2.0	31.2	35.7	24.4	45.0
2007	28.3	2.1	32.6	37.1	30.7	59.1	20.0	2.2	32.9	38.0	24.7	44.9
2008	30.8	3.3	32.2	34.8	35.1	66.2	22.4	3.4	32.0	34.8	28.7	51.3
2009	26.4	2.4	31.3	35.4	29.7	56.2	19.5	2.4	31.3	36.6	25.4	45.0
2010	28.5	2.0	30.9	36.6	31.6	60.1	21.1	1.5	30.7	36.8	26.3	47.4
2011	30.2	1.8	32.4	36.7	35.8	66.1	23.1	1.8	31.7	36.4	30.3	53.4
2012	30.4	1.6	31.9	36.1	36.2	66.6	23.0	1.2	31.2	35.6	30.6	53.5
2013	30.7	1.8	30.2	32.7	33.4	64.2	23.8	1.3	29.3	31.9	27.9	51.7
2014	28.8	1.7	29.2	32.4	31.0	59.8	21.8	1.6	28.4	32.2	25.7	47.6
2015	25.9	2.1	28.2	30.7	27.3	53.4	19.0	1.8	27.3	30.5	22.4	41.5
2016	25.3	1.8	27.7	29.1	25.5	51.0	18.3	1.8	27.1	28.9	21.2	39.3
2017	24.8	1.5	27.6	29.9	26.5	51.1	17.8	1.3	27.1	29.6	22.0	39.8
2018	25.4	1.6	28.4	31.0	27.9	53.1	18.9	1.4	27.9	30.7	23.9	42.7
2019	23.0	1.5	26.5	28.9	24.8	47.7	17.9	1.6	26.7	29.3	21.9	39.8

Source: *Author's estimation based on World Development Indicators, World Bank, Online access on March 1, 2021*

As discussed earlier, India preferred to engage more closely with BIMSTEC as a consequence of political instability and security threat received from certain neighboring countries. In this context, it is important to examine the economic divergences between the regional groupings. BIMSTEC and SAARC are often compared as the two regional overlapping regions with a considerable level of economic complementarities. We can say that BIMSTEC is a hybrid regional grouping with the combinations of dynamic economies of SAARC with ASEAN (Bhattacharjee, 2018). Owing to the failures of SAARC, an attempt was made to revive the BIMSTEC grouping, and Table 2 shows how BIMSTEC can be an alternative and vibrant grouping in comparison with SAARC. Similar views are also expressed by other studies (Mohan, 2016; Bhattacharjee, 2018; Singh, 2019; Wapmuk, 2015). It is shown in Table 2 that BIMSTEC outperformed SAARC in various macroeconomic segments including those of Gross Capital Formation, Gross Fixed Capital Formation, exports, imports, FDI, openness, among others.

During various global trade regimes [i.e., Buoyancy (2003-07), 1st phase of recession (2008- 13), and 2nd Phase of recession (2014-19)], the ratio of Gross Fixed Capital Formation (GFCF) and Gross Capital Formation Ratio (GCF Ratio) concerning GDP on average, are somewhat similar for both the regional groupings and in certain cases, BIMSTEC has posted an edge over the SAARC region. In the last 15 years, changing growth dynamics of the region can be observed in various trading regimes. The ongoing pandemic and recession have slowed down the growth prospects of the region, but the average growth of the region has not been affected significantly. The growth outlook of the region is an optimist about the V-shaped recovery in 2021 on account of resumption of growth as a result of subsiding of the fury of the pandemic, spur in economic activities in the region and the world economy, removal of trade barriers

across the globe and rejuvenation of supply chain in the world economy. But growth forecast may change in case of resumption of the second and third wave of the pandemic in the region and other parts of the world. The ugly face of the second wave of the pandemic in India has been more pronounced than the earlier one. India resorted to the policy of not going for a complete lockdown of the country and could prevent disruption of the production chain and livelihood security of people along with controlling the rapid spread of the pandemic. The policy has not only supported in maintaining high growth but also improve the overall growth prospects of the BIMSTEC region.

Trade Liberalisation in the BIMSTEC Region

Robust growth and stable macroeconomic dynamics of the region have been the outcome of the emergence of trade as an engine of growth for the region (Rahman & Kim, 2016). The trade sector expanded rapidly during the period of global buoyancy of 2003-07 and slowed down to some extent during the prolonged phase of recession during 2008-20, but the trade sector remained the driving factor for the region. For promoting trade, the regional economies learned to liberalize their trade policy regime in a phased manner and adjusted to various global trade regimes. The prolonged recession over 14 years and the unwarranted spate of the pandemic caused untold misery to the region (Thomas, 2020). However, tariff liberalization in regional economies provided an impetus for the external sector to grow despite the recession in the global economy.

Tariff as Source of Revenue

Trade tax assumes importance in a liberalized economy, particularly in fast-growing emerging economies. Among its key roles in the economy, it gives protection to domestic producers against the onslaught of unabated imports (Cole & Eckel, 2014), offers resistance to unwarranted exports from the country, and generates revenue for the state (Baack & Ray, 1983; Rodrik, 1995). Taxes on exports in developing countries form a very small proportion of their tax revenue, almost non-existent in several countries in BIMSTEC during the last 1½ decades as shown in Table 3. Bhutan is one of such cases where export tax has not been experimented with in the past. Export tax was only enforced during the period of global buoyancy in certain countries in the region such as India, Nepal, and Thailand. During the recession, Nepal continued with the policy of export tax, but the revenue generated from the source diminished regularly. Bangladesh introduced this policy of export tax temporarily in 2012 but almost abandoned it in subsequent years. India and Thailand also dismantled the export tax during the period of recession. With the continuation of the global recessionary trend, certain countries re-imposed/continued with the export tax to evade the possibility of supply disruption at the domestic market due to exports. Such a trend came up particularly in the second phase of recession and some of the countries like Nepal and Sri Lanka adopted such policy stance.

However, the treatment of regional economies with international taxes, particularly export taxes and import tariffs, was different since 2000. In the region, there were three types of tariff regimes that existed, ranging from low to high tariff regimes. Some countries were at the lead in managing a low level of tax collection from such tax on international trade such as Bhutan, Myanmar, and Thailand. While India received a moderate level of tax revenue from this source, others including Bangladesh, Sri Lanka, and Nepal were highly dependent on this source for revenue collection.

Table 3. Structure of Trade Taxes in BIMSTEC Countries

Year	Bangladesh	Bhutan	India	Sri Lanka	Nepal	Thailand	Bangladesh	Bhutan	India	Sri Lanka	Myanmar	Nepal	Thailand
	Taxes on exports (% of tax revenue)						Taxes on international trade (% of revenue)						
2003		0.0			2.0	0.3	25.1	1.7	14.6	14.0	1.2	21.9	9.7
2004		0.0	0.1		1.1	0.4	32.6	1.5	14.9	15.2	3.7	21.9	8.4
2005		0.0	0.1		1.3	0.3	32.4	2.3	14.4	13.7	2.3	19.0	7.4
2006		0.0	0.1	0.0	1.1	0.3	30.9	1.3	15.2	14.6		18.2	6.2
2007	0.0	0.0	0.2	0.0	1.0	0.3	27.1	1.0	14.7	14.2		16.3	5.5
2008		0.0	0.3		0.5	0.0	26.5	0.8	14.1	14.3		17.5	5.3
2009			0.0		0.7	0.0	24.3	1.0	11.4	18.9		16.1	4.6
2010			0.0		0.6	0.0	24.3	0.7	13.5	15.7		16.3	4.5
2011	0.0		0.0		0.2	0.0	24.6	1.0	14.8	16.6		14.5	4.4
2012	0.1		0.0		0.4	0.0	23.4	1.2	14.9	20.3	3.6	15.2	4.9
2013	0.0		0.0		0.2	0.0	20.6	0.9	13.2	16.6	3.1	17.2	4.1
2014	0.0		0.0		0.3	0.0	20.4	3.6	13.0	16.7	3.4	16.8	4.0
2015	0.0		0.0		0.1	0.0	23.7	5.0	12.3	16.7	3.4	16.6	3.6
2016	0.0		0.0	0.2	0.0	0.0	24.5	4.2	10.7	21.5	3.5	15.7	3.4
2017			0.0	0.2	0.0	0.0		4.5	11.1	20.2	3.3	16.0	3.0
2018				0.2		0.0		4.2		17.7			2.9

Source: *World Development Indicators, World Bank, Online data extracted on February 1, 2021*

Though dependence on international trade tax has been different in various regional economies, the global tariff regimes are critical in shaping the level of tax proceeds received from this source. During the period of buoyancy, the share of tax revenue from international trade increased due to the buoyant growth of two-way trade, particularly led by imports. With the onslaught of recession in 2008, the relative size of revenue collection dried up gradually in most of the regional countries due to constraints on their import sector. However, the revival of the international taxes as a source of revenue was noticed in the second phase of recession (i.e., 2008-13), and certain countries witnessed an increased collection of revenue from the sources due to upward revision of their tariff structures to match the global trends of tight tariff regime.

Analysis of Applied & MFN Tariffs

Tariff protection is required to safeguard domestic producers by restricting cheap imports which have the potential to derail domestic production and affect the livelihood of several people. Apart from livelihood security, this has implications for generating income and employment opportunities in the domestic economy. Tariffs and non-tariff barriers are used in protecting domestic producers against imports, but they have their limitations. As a member of the WTO, the Most Favoured Nation (MFN) principle of tariff is conferred to other member countries of the organization. However, some countries provide exemptions to specific target groups over and above the MFN rates, and therefore, applied tariffs are different from MFN tariffs. The pattern of applied tariffs and their relationship with MFN tariffs differ from one country to another. Such divergences are also to be seen among member countries in the BIMSTEC region.

Table 4. Overall Country-wise Simple Average Tariff: Applied and MFN in BIMSTEC

Year	Bangladesh	Bhutan	India	Sri Lanka	Myanmar	Nepal	Thailand	Bangladesh	Bhutan	India	Sri Lanka	Myanmar	Nepal	Thailand
	Tariff rate, applied, simple mean, all products (%)							Tariff rate, most favored nation, simple mean, all products (%)						
2003	19.6		25.6	9.6	4.4	14.9	13.8	19.5		26.9	9.4	5.5	13.7	15.7
2004	18.3	22.2	28.6	10.6	4.3	14.8	11.3	18.4	22.1	29.5	10.4	5.5	13.8	11
2005	15.4	22.2	16.5	11.7	4.3	14.7	10.6	15.3	22.1	19	11.7	5.6	13.8	12
2006	15.2		13.9	11.4	4.2	13.1	10.8	15.3		16.8	11.5	5.6	12.5	12
2007	14.3	11.1	14.7	11.1	4.1	13.1	10.5	14.6	21.9	17.2	11.4	5.6	12.6	10.2
2008	13.8		10	11	3.9	15.1	10.8	14.7		12.8	11.3	5.6	15.4	10.2
2009	14.1		10.3	10.8		12.8	11	14.4		13.1	11.3		12.4	10.2
2010	13.9		8.9	9.8	3.5	13	10.8	14.4		12.5	10.4	5.6	12.3	10.1
2011	13.8		10.6	10	3.3	13.2	11.3	14.4		13.4	10.3	5.6	12.4	10.2
2012	13.5		10.7	9.9	4.8	12.9		14.6		14	10.5	5.6	12.2	
2013	12.9		10.6		4.8	11.8	12	13.9		13.9		5.6	12.2	11.3
2014				9.3		12.7	8.4				9.7		12.2	11.5
2015	12	12.2	9.8	7.9	2.1	12.6	8	13.9	22.3	13.2	8.3	5.6	12.3	11
2016	13		8.9			12.7		13.9		13.7			12.1	
2017			8.9	10.4						13.8	10.3			
2018			9	12.1		12.8				13.8	12.3		13.2	

Source: *World Development Indicators, World Bank, Online data extracted on February 1, 2021*

As a common practice, WTO member country notifies its tariff protection rates which are duly in effect to all member countries of the organization as MFN tariffs as shown in Table 4 for BIMSTEC countries. Various concessions are granted around the MFN tariffs which are applied to various stakeholders in the domestic economy. Tariff concessions or penalties are admissible to MFN rates based on the nature of the product for imports. Therefore, in some countries applied rates are laying above the MFN tariffs, and in several other cases, they lie below the MFN rates. Moreover, applied and MFN rates are also greatly affected by the global trade regimes to control the levels of imports. WTO member countries have the flexibility of changing the magnitude of tariffs within limits which are set by bound tariffs as committed by each member country to the organization.

In the case of several member countries, applied tariffs were lower than MFN tariffs for a considerable number of years in countries like Bangladesh, Bhutan, India, Sri Lanka, Myanmar, and Thailand. Nepal has been observed as the only exception where the overall applied average simple tariff rate was lower than that of the overall MFN simple average tariff rate. The tariff management in developed economies follows a pattern similar to that of Nepal where MFN tariffs are kept at the base level and any derogation from the tariff policy may attract higher tariffs. By following this principle, industrialized countries could maintain a low MFN rate with a high collection rate.

Regarding the direction of movement of average tariff rates, there has been a certain degree of similarity between average applied and average MNF duties. During various trade regimes, regional countries have performed differently though there was some degree of symmetry observed between simple average applied tariff and simple average MFN tariffs. While simple average applied tariff declined for many countries during buoyancy, it increases moderately during the period of recession. Simple average applied rates declined sharply in cases like

Bhutan and India during the period of recession, but the commensurate rise in simple average MFN was not reported in these economies. During the first phase of the recession, the movement of simple average applied tariff was different among regional economies. While Bangladesh, Sri Lanka, and Nepal underwent a declining trend of simple average applied tariffs, India, Myanmar, and Thailand moved in the opposite direction. The second phase of the recession witnessed a more inward-oriented tariff regime in the region.

To sum up, certain broad trends become apparent from the region regarding the movement of tariff rates. The international tax became a major source of revenue for many countries in the BIMSTEC region. Often these policies acted effectively in protecting domestic production against imports and facilitating livelihood security for several people in the domestic economy. Export tax comprised a small portion of total revenue receipt by several regional countries during the period of global buoyancy, but it almost disappeared as a major source of revenue in the second phase of the recession. The simple average rates of applied and MFN tariffs declined during the past 1½ decades with certain degrees of variations except for the period of the second phase of recession. Several regional economies pursued specific tariffs including Thailand, Nepal, and India, but the intensity of the use of specific tariffs declined in the second phase of the recession.

In several countries, peak tariffs are invariably used in the region to protect domestic producers and their livelihood. The magnitude of the use of peak tariff has declined in recent years and India made significant progress in this regard. The regional economies experienced varying levels of average import weighted tariffs which were declining during the last 1½ decades and the primary sector was relatively more protected than the manufacturing sector. The regional economies are on the path of rapid trade liberalization. Reforms in the region are less progressive in the primary sector because agriculture has been the mainstay of the regional economies, and the livelihood security of people is closely associated with the sector. Gradual liberalization in the agricultural sector and the rapid dismantling of trade barriers in the manufacturing sector enabled these economies to integrate with the world economy and has paved the way for achieving high growth, leveraging the trade sector as the engine of growth.

Trade Linkages of BIMSTEC with the World and India

BIMSTEC region is an emergent region in Asia (Yahya, 2005; Batra, 2010) and the pace of its trade integration with the world is largely affected by the prolonged recession and outbreak of Covid-19 in 2020. The region has been having a high degree of compatibility with India in sectors like trade, investment, and Trade in Services (Bhattacharya & Bhattacharyay, 2006). Cooperation in energy trade is also emerging important for the region and India has shown interest in participating in the sector (Banerjee & Dey, 2016 and 2017). Regional cooperation is urgently needed in the region to face the challenge of Industry 4.0 (Bhowmick & Basu, 2020). During the last 1½ decades, India's trade with the region has been growing steadily without any hiccups with the region (Chandran, 2019; De, Joshi, & Amin, 2014). India has also had a trade surplus with the region other than Thailand. The region has chalked out a blueprint to having FTA among the member countries and the proposal is laying with India for ratification (Wijayasiri, 2016). It is apprehended that opening up the Indian market to regional economies may expose the Indian economy to a high-risk area and may become a net trade deficit economy with the region. The extent of additional market access that India is to open up for the regional economies, is a major concern for India. The study attempts to address these trade-related issues involving India in the region.

The existing literature presents that BIMSTEC is one of the fastest-growing regions of the world (RIS, 2016). The region continued to rise during periods of both global buoyancy and recession. The size of the regional grouping to very large in terms of real GDP, savings, investment, and other macroeconomic indicators as compared to several RTAs in Asia. The maintenance of macroeconomic stability with rapid development along with improved social sector development has been the hallmark of the region in recent years.

The regional economies were greatly benefitted by pursuing Export-Led Growth (ELG) during the period of global buoyancy and subsequently switching over to DDLG had enabled the region to be on a high growth path. Taking advantage of fast unilateral liberalization in the region, the regional countries have achieved major strides in expanding their merchandised trade and Trade in Services (TIS) with the region and the world. The region relied on trade in intermediate products for fostering its trade with the regional economies and also with the rest of the world. Regional economies have developed growing interdependence on GVC trade in selected sectors (Rahman and Bari, 2018). For further boosting the sector, there is a need for having an integrated regional approach for trade and investment policy to promote GVC trade within the region.

Taking into account the region's expanding trade sector, it was emerging as a global trading hub for a large number of products. The region has been improving consistently in its global share in trade from 1.95 percent in 2003 to 2.47 percent in 2017. Between 2003 and 2012, the trade share of the BIMSTEC grew linearly with partial disruption for some years, but significant volatility was observed during 2013-18. Therefore, the region witnessed a rise in trade share in the world with a considerable level of volatility. Therefore, regional trade is highly responsive to the global trade regimes. The region has shown increasing participation in intermediate trade through IRT, but GVC is yet to pick up in the regional trade.

Trade is also classified based on its end-use sectors. It is primarily grouped into three broad categories such as primary, intermediate, and final consumption goods. An intermediate segment is one where the sector covers more than half of the global trade every year. The rise of developing countries in international trade is because of intensive trade in this sector. Intermediate trade is further classified into semi-finished products and the global value chain (GVC). Trade-in this sector receives primacy in the global trade, and developing countries are strongly active in this sector. Demand for GVC products is important for the production of final products for global production and export purposes. Final products are further classified into two groups, namely final consumption goods and final capital goods. As emerging countries are largely embarked on industrialization, their import requirements are mostly for intermediate products and final capital goods. Against the backdrop of regional trade, the pattern of intermediate goods in the intra-regional trade of BIMSTEC is examined in Figure 1.

Figure 1. BIMSTEC-Share of Intermediate Products and GVC in total IRT
Source: Author's estimation based on Comtrade, UN Statistical division, online data extracted on February 1, 2021

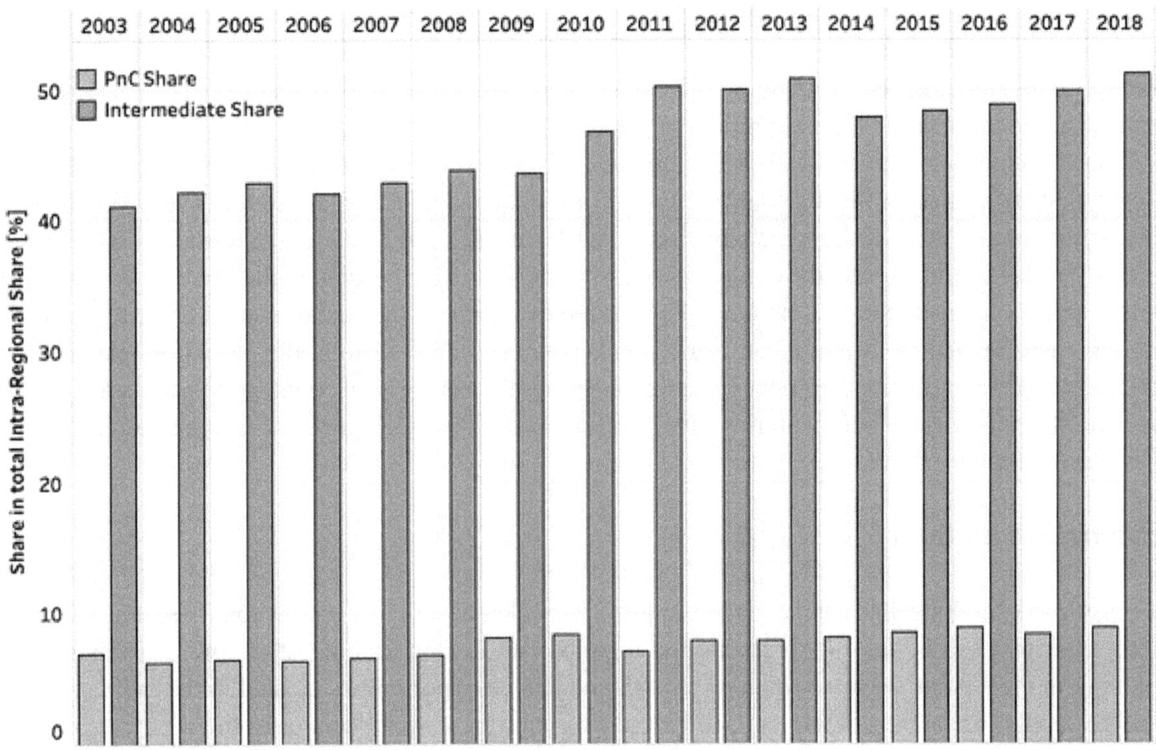

It is shown in Figure 1 that the region trade is extensively engaged in intermediate goods, particularly among regional economies. Share of intermediate in IRT was high and stood over 40 percent during buoyancy. There was an increased share of intermediate products during the recession. The rising share of intermediate goods was highly volatile during the first phase of recession but a steady rise in its share was observed in the second phase of recession. However, the share of the intermediate products in the total IRT exceeded the 50 percent mark in 2018. Contrary to the trend in the intermediate product segment, semi-processed goods took the lion's share in the regional trade. The proportion of parts and components in the total IRT of the region was small and was yet to reach a double-digit mark during 2003-18.

Trade Potential of the Region in India

India is deeply engaged with the regional process since the last decade, and this process is consolidating in the immediate neighbourhood. Despite difficulties in the past, BIMSTEC has picked up steadily in recent years and has taken a major leap in expanding its intra-regional trade to encourage trade cooperation in the region. In this context the role of India is important and its efforts to induct dynamism in the region to stimulate the regional process are warranted.

India's current economic prosperity is largely contingent upon its external sector performance. India's external sector policies have enabled the country to maintain high growth sustainably. Though India's export has increased significantly during the entire period of economic reforms, trade imbalance is becoming a major challenge for the immediate future (Chaudhuri, 2013). This requires fruitful engagement with neighbouring countries to promote trade in the region and also to give a boost to the regional process in the immediate neighbourhood.

Many countries in the region are small and are subject to supply constraints. India has large trade creating opportunities for the regional countries as it has large domestic demand for several products in diversified sectors (Kaur & Gupta, 2020; Saxena & Bhadauriya, 2012; Sharma & Rathore, 2015). Most of the regional countries have the competitiveness to compete in the Indian market but are confronting with supply constraints to meet the large demand requirements of the Indian market. Apart from having large trade potential in the Indian market on account of trade creation, the partial unilateral trade liberalization may generate enormous trade opportunities for the regional countries to access the Indian market. Moreover, BIMSTEC countries have submitted a draft of the Agreement to India for ratification and speedy implementation.

Estimation Method

It is assumed that India has a large market to provide market access to regional countries, but such opportunities may not be fully absorbed by the regional partners on account of supply constraints. For highlighting this point, we are estimating (a) demand-driven opportunities created in the Indian market and (b) supply capabilities of the regional partners to seize these opportunities in India.

Trade opportunities in the Indian market are estimated based on trade opportunities due to the competitiveness of individual regional countries. The FTA draft proposal is with India for some time and India has to take a view in extending a positive nod to the proposal for its effective implementation. India has a slander trade surplus with the region and is apprehending erosion of such marginal trade surplus when India will extend additional market access to other BIMSTEC member countries. In this context, it is important to examine the size of trade potential that the regional economies are having in India for which the latter is much concerned.

In this study, 'trade creation' effects (Viner, 1950) of the regional economies in India are estimated to present their trade potential. By taking the export vector of the exporting country

and the bilateral import vector of India, the export potential of the exporting countries is estimated in India at 6-digit HS, based on UN Comtrade. Since FTA formalities are not completed yet, the present estimation is restricted to 'trade creation' effects to examine the trade potential of regional economies in India. The size of trade potential is expected to rise further with the inclusion of 'trade diversion in the model, particularly in the post-FTA regime. For understanding the trade potential of member countries in India at present, it is estimated at the product level and is presented at the level of the HS Section for each country separately.

Empirical Results

The trade liberalization initiative under FTA would add further to the already existing market in India for the regional partners. The empirical findings indicate that regional countries have large opportunities in the Indian market, but such market openings for many regional countries may not be realized due to supply constraints in these countries. Therefore, the trade potentials in the medium term could be much lower than the overall trade potential existing in the Indian market for individual partner counties.

Table 5. Trade Potentials of BIMSTEC Countries in India **(in Million USD)**

Sec	HS Section	BGD	BTN	LKA	MDV	MMR	NPL	THA
1	Live Animals and Animal Products	7.7	0.0	4.1	0.8	12.2	13.5	24.4
2	Vegetable Products	15.1	23.2	45.5	0.0	178.3	31.4	83.3
3	Animal or Vegetable Fats & Oils	4.0	547.0	4.3	0.0	980.8	9.1	1339.4
4	Prepared Foodstuff, Beverages, etc.	45.6	25.0	98.5	27.9	89.2	53.5	163.8
5	Mineral Products	0.0	1938	53.1	0.0	2093	14.1	261.6
6	Products of Chemicals	383.5	12.9	637.8	0.0	235.6	201.2	2818.2
7	Plastics & Articles thereof	234.1	16.7	546.9	0.0	112.7	69.3	1393.2
8	Raw Hides & Skins, Leather, etc.	104.3	0.0	111.5	0.0	53.5	196.3	142.3
9	Wood & Articles of Wood	0.0	321.1	13.0	0.0	445.3	2.2	164.6
10	Pulp of wood or other Fibers	199.9	12.0	528.0	0.0	2.7	15.7	491.4
11	Textile & Textile Articles	420.8	20.0	164.8	0.7	242.4	401.0	345.9
12	Footwear, Headgear, and Umbrella	22.5	0.4	15.6	0.0	0.2	5.1	34.8
13	Articles of Stone, Plaster, Cement	33.7	0.0	84.6	0.0	25.3	0.2	283.4
14	Natural or cultured pearls, Jewellery	0.0	0.0	5767.6	0.0	0.0	0.0	6001.6
15	Base Metals & Articles of Base Metal	418.0	29.6	1914.9	215	427.0	146.7	3129.4
16	Machinery & Mechanical Appliances	2281	166.0	6267.8	0.0	641.9	330.3	10918
17	Vehicles, Aircraft, and Vessels	437.7	0.0	414.4	0.0	2.8	0.0	1704.5
18	Optical, Photograph & Cinematography	48.9	0.0	630.4	0.0	0.0	0.0	1265.9
19	Arms and Ammunition	0.0	0.0	0.0	0.0	0.0	0.0	0.0
20	Miscellaneous Manufactured Articles	43.3	0.0	87.6	0.0	39.6	62.1	170.1
21	Works of Art Collectors' Pieces	0.0	0.0	0.0	0.0	0.0	0.0	0.0
	Total	4700	3112	17390	244	5583	1551	30736

Source: *Author's estimation based on Comtrade, Trainswits, UN Statistical Division, Online data*
Note: *Estimation of trade potential is based on 'trade creating' effects of Viner (1950)*

Comprehensive economic cooperation of India with the neighbouring countries, particularly with members of BIMSTEC countries, could be beneficial for India by providing access to its domestic market and thereby getting access to a cheap source of imports from these neighbouring countries. The regional countries have export competitiveness in a wide range of products and can substitute several existing suppliers in India. This would enhance global welfare by diverting the source of exports to the most efficient suppliers. The existing trade potential of BIMSTEC countries in India is presented.

The size of trade potentials exiting in the Indian market for the BIMSTEC countries using the trade creation effect is presented in Table 5. Supply capabilities of countries in competitive products vary significantly from one country to another, and therefore level of trade potential in India differs significantly among regional countries. The size of trade potential is visibly large for most of the non-LDCs compared to LDCs in the region. Thailand has the largest stake in the Indian market among the regional partners. From the group of regional LDCs, Myanmar has the largest trade potential among the BIMSTEC partners. While Myanmar has close to 5.5 billion US dollars' trade potential, the similar estimate for other LDCs ranges between over 1.5 billion US dollars to 5.8 billion US dollars per annum.

The trade potential of these neighbouring countries spread over almost all the broad trade sectors of trade in India. As expected, trade potential has been negligible in sectors like handicrafts, arms & ammunition, and several other sectors in agriculture. Regional countries have shown their competence in the exports of both agricultural and manufacturing products. As India is largely dependent on vegetable oils and fats in the agricultural sector, it is, rather, worthwhile to consider competitive regional partners to substitute existing expensive suppliers from the rest of the world to reduce pressure on the sectoral import bill. The partner countries have trade interest in almost all the sectors in India, but some sectors are more critical than others. Some of the prominent sectors for the partner countries in India are chemicals, base metals, plastics, minerals, electric and electronic machinery, etc. among others. It is important to note that market opening by India for the BIMSTEC countries is likely to provide additional market access to the extent of 63 billion US dollars per annum. The size of market access is likely to expand further following the implementation of the FTA. India has to examine the extent to which it can have additional market access to offer to these countries without disturbing its trade balance with the region.

CONCLUSION

Over the past two and half decades of its inception, the BIMSTEC region emerged as a dynamic, high growth, and resilient regional grouping in Asia. The region continued to be dormant for nearly two decades and stole the limelight when India focused its attention on the region in 2016. Irrespective of its history, the contemporary member countries have shown a lot of synergies between themselves to take the region to greater heights. Intra-regional trade of the region has been growing along with its global share over a period.

Unilateral trade liberalization among the regional economies enabled them to become competitive and also helped them in getting integrated with the world economy. Growth prospects of the world economy along with the region went hay way following feeble growth prospects of industrialized economies, Brexit, Sino-US trade war, diminishing role of WTO, conflicting war fronts in several areas, etc. but rebound of the world economy is likely in 2021. Considering the past growth profile of the BIMSTEC region and its macroeconomic fundamentals, the rebound of the region is likely in 2021 along with the world economy. IMF's (2021) forecasting results projected a V-shaped recovery for the region. Broad macroeconomic indicators of the region including real GDP growth, savings ratio, investment ratio, trade performances, openness, the inflow of FDI and remittances, etc. are also supporting the quick recovery of the region in the post-pandemic period.

The high growth trade sector of the region had strong adherence to globalization and most of the regional members resorted to unilateral trade liberalization within the past three decades. These regional countries were successful in arresting unabated imports, protecting domestic producers against dumping, and generating revenue for the exchequer through trade tax instruments. Though the size of revenue was small for large economies, it was vital for some other countries for revenue generation. The region experimented with varieties of instruments under trade taxes including export tax, ad valorem and specific duties, international tariff peaks, etc. during the last 1½ decades. However, tariff regimes in the region were rationalized over a while but it was further tightened up with the continuation of recession and protectionist policies in the global economy.

Trade became the driver of growth for the region despite quick changes in the global trade regimes from buoyancy to recession. Trade regimes had a direct and significant impact on the performances of the external sector of the region. Like other regional trading arrangements and the world economy, the growth performance of the BIMSTEC region followed the same growth sequencing as the world economy. The region experienced steady growth in the share of the region's exports in the world trade during 2003-18 with marginal disruption during the second phase of recession and touched almost 2.5 percent of the global trade in 2017. Similarly, surged intra-regional trade reached close to 6 percent in 2019. The regional economies have shown their increased participation in the intermediate trade within their Intra- Regional Trade, but GVC trade is yet to pick up among these economies. There has been a growing consensus among regional economies to form an FTA in the BIMSTEC region. The results show that regional economies have high trade potential in the Indian market to the extent of 63 billion US dollars per annum. The largest threat is being posted by Thailand where nearly half of the region's trade potential in India is likely to be shared by Thailand alone. Under the

Early Harvest Scheme (EHS), India had already encountered difficulties with the country earlier and India is a bit hesitant to take further risk by joining FTA with the member countries in the BIMSTEC region.

REFERENCES

Ain, Q. U., & Shah, Z. A. (2019). Neo-Regionalism in South Asia: With Reference to the Emergence of BIMSTEC and BBIN. *Research Journal of Social Sciences, 10*(6).

Asher, M., & Sen, R. (2006). *The Role of Japan in BIMSTEC*. Lee Kuan Yew School of Public Policy, National University of Singapore.

Baack, B. D., & Ray, E. J. (1983). The political economy of tariff policy: A case study of the United States. *Explorations in Economic History, 20*(1), 73–93. doi:10.1016/0014-4983(83)90043-8

BanerjeeK.DeyD. (2016). *India and BIMSTEC: A Comparative Study of the Trade Potential of India's Energy Sector Products in BIMSTEC and BIMSTEC 1 Region*. doi:10.2139/ssrn.2874294

Banerjee, K., & Dey, D. (2017). *Trade-in energy services in BCIM, BIMSTEC+ 1, and ASEAN+ 4 regions-potentials and Challenges*. Academic Press.

Banik, A., & Bhaumik, P. K. (2005). *Neighbourhood revisited: Explaining Japanese foreign direct investment in the BIMSTEC region*. CSIRD Discussion Paper: 9/2005. Retrieved from https://www. researchgate. net/profile/Arindam_Banik/publication/253473057_Neighbourhood_Revisited_Explaining_Japanese_Foreign_Direct_Investment_in_the_BIMSTEC_Region/links/546e1edb0cf2b5fc1760 4320.pdf

Batra, A. (2010). Asian economic integration and sub-regionalism: A case study of the BIMSTEC. *International Studies*, *47*(1), 1–25. doi:10.1177/002088171104700101

Bhattacharjee, J. (2018). SAARC vs BIMSTEC: The search for the ideal platform for regional cooperation. *Observer Issue Brief*, *226*, 1–12.

Bhattacharya, S. K., & Bhattacharyay, B. N. (2006). *Prospects of regional cooperation in trade, investment and finance in Asia: an empirical analysis on BIMSTEC countries and Japan*. Academic Press.

Bhattacharya, S. K., & Bhattacharyay, B. N. (2007). An empirical analysis on prospects and challenges of BIMSTEC-Japan trade integration. *Journal of Asian Economics*, *18*(3), 509–536. doi:10.1016/j.asieco.2007.03.001

Bhowmick, S., & Basu, P. (2020). *BIMSTEC and the Fourth Industrial Revolution: The Role of Technology in Regional Development*. Academic Press.

Chandran, B. P. (2019). India BIMSTEC Economic Cooperation: Potential and Prospects. *Indian Journal of Economics and Development*, *15*(4), 489–498. doi:10.5958/2322-0430.2019.00064.7

Chaudhuri, S. (2013). Manufacturing trade deficit and industrial policy in India. *Economic and Political Weekly*, 41–50.

Chotani, V. M. (2018). BIMSTEC and Japan: Exploring Prospects for Renewed Cooperation. *Issue Brief*, 236.

Cole, M. T., & Eckel, C. (2014). *Tariffs Passing Through Retailers: Do Tariffs Actually Protect Domestic Manufacturers?* Academic Press.

De, D., Joshi, R. M., & Amin, U. M. (2014). Impact of BIMSTEC trade agreement on strengthening export performance of Indian firms: An empirical assessment. *International Journal of Business and Globalisation*, *12*(4), 457–470. doi:10.1504/IJBG.2014.062845

DeyD. (2006). *BIMSTEC-Japan: Investment Opportunities and Challenges*. Available at SSRN 905096.

Diebold, F. X. (2020). Real-time real economic activity: Exiting the great recession and entering the pandemic recession (No. w27482). National Bureau of Economic Research.

Elangovan, A. (2019). BIMSTEC, A weak cross-border organization? The growing economies show convergence. г. *Петрозаводск*, *26*, 13.

Gilbert, J. (2008). *BIMSTEC-Japan trade cooperation and poverty in Asia*. Centre for Studies in Asia in International Relations and Development, CSIRD Discussion paper, (9201).

Hossain, S. M. (2013). Impacts of BIMSTEC Free Trade Area: A CGE Analysis. *Journal of Economics and Sustainable Development*, *4*(13), 16–28.

IMF. (2020). *World Economic Outlook*. IMF.

Intal, J. P., & Chen, L. (2017). *ASEAN and member states: Transformation and integration*. Economic Research Institute for ASEAN and East Asia.

Islam, M. S., & Das, R. K. (2014). Bangladesh and BIMSTEC: Performance Evaluation and Development Strategies. *Al-Barkaat Journal of Finance & Management*, *6*(1), 17–25.

Kaur, G., Dutta, K., & Saini, J. (2020). Trade Performance of BIMSTEC Countries since 1997. *Studies in Indian Place Names*, *40*(60), 1105–1115.

Kaur, G., & Gupta, A. (2020). India-BIMSTEC Bilateral Trade Activities: A Gravity Model Approach. In Regional Trade and Development Strategies in the Era of Globalization (pp. 126-145). IGI Global. doi:10.4018/978-1-7998-1730-7.ch007

Kaur, G., Sarin, V., & Dhami, J. K. (2016). Analysis of Intraregional Trade and Investment among India and BIMSTEC: Prospects and Challenges. *International Journal of Social and Economic Research*, *6*(2). Advance online publication. doi:10.5958/2249-6270.2016.00015.5

Mahadi, Y., Becek, K., & Chian, K. W. (2011). The Dutch Disease Hypothesis: Evidence from the Gulf Cooperation Council. *CSPS Strategy and Policy Journal*, *3*, 1–25.

Mohan, N. C. (2016). BIMSTEC: An Idea Whose Time Has Come? *ORF*, (November), 9.

Padmaja, G. (2017). *BIMSTEC: Where India's 'Neighbourhood First'and 'Act East'meet*. National Maritime Foundation.

Pattanaik, S. S. (2020). SAARC COVID-19 Fund: Calibrating a Regional Response to the Pandemic. *Strategic Analysis*, *44*(3), 241–252. doi:10.1080/09700161.2020.1787688

Rahman, M., & Bari, E. (2018). *Research Report 4 Value Chains in BIMSTEC Region Current Status*. Possibilities and Challenges.

Rahman, M. M., & Kim, C. (2015). BIMSTEC Regional Integration: Prospects and Challenges. *Advanced Science and Technology Letters*, *18*, 90–95. doi:10.14257/astl.2015.114.18

Rahman, M. M., & Kim, C. (2016). Prospects for Economic Integration of BIMSTEC: Trade and Investment Scenario. International Journal of u-and e-Service. *Science and Technology*, *9*(4), 235–248.

Rahman, M. S. (2014). *Promoting Transport Connectivity in Southern Asia: A BIMSTEC Perspective*. United Nations Economic and Social Commission for Asia and the Pacific.

Rahman, N., & Rizvi, S. A. (2018). FDI Inflows and Current Account Evidence from BIMSTEC. In *Foreign Direct Investments (FDIs) and Opportunities for Developing Economies in the World Market* (pp. 123–141). IGI Global. doi:10.4018/978-1-5225-3026-8.ch007

RIS. (2016). BIMSTEC: The Road Ahead, Research and information. https://www.ris.org.in/bimstec-road-ahead

Rodrik, D. (1995). Political economy of trade policy. Handbook of International Economics, 3, 1457-1494.

Saxena, S., & Bhadauriya, S. (2012). India and BIMSTEC: An Analysis of India's Trade Performance & Prospects. *Business Analyst: A Refereed Journal of Shri Ram College of Commerce, 33*(1), 103-114.

Sharma, A., & Rathore, C. K. (2015). BIMSTEC and BCIM Initiatives and their Importance for India. *CUTS International*, 1-20.

Singh, K. (2019). India's Regional Cooperation Option: A Comparative Study of BIMSTEC and SAARC. *Political Discourse*, *5*(2), 183–194. doi:10.5958/2582-2691.2019.00006.3

Thomas, C. J. (2020). Revitalising BIMSTEC through Cultural Connectivity from Northeast India. *ORF Issue Brief*, (405).

Towhid, S. K., & Kiyoto, K. (2019). Impact of Trade Openness on Economic Growth: Evidences from BIMSTEC Countries. 社会システム研究, (39), 65-81.

Vinor, J. (1950). *The Customs Union Issue*. Cornegie Endowment for International Peace.

Wapmuk, S. (2015). The Role of India in Regionalism: SAARC, ASEAN, EU, BIMSTEC, IOR-ARC, and MGC: Lessons for Nigeria in the ECOWAS. *IUP Journal of International Relations, 9*(1).

Wijayasiri, J. (2016). Challenges to a BIMSTEC Free Trade Agreement (FTA): A Sri Lankan Perspective. *Cooperative Partnership and Sustainable Development, 101*.

Wijayasiri, J., & De Mel, D. (2008). *BIMSTEC-Japan Cooperation in Trade and Investment: A Sri Lankan Perspective*. Centre for Studies in International Relations and Development (CSIRD) Discussion Paper, 38.

Yahya, F. (2005). BIMSTEC and emerging patterns of Asian regional and interregional cooperation. *Australian Journal of Political Science*, *40*(3), 391–394. doi:10.1080/10361140500203936

Chapter 6
The BIMSTEC Free Trade Area:
Economic Cooperation, Opportunities, and Challenges

Mahboob Muhammad Ali
Dhaka University, Bangladesh

Anita Medhekar
https://orcid.org/0000-0002-6791-4056
Central Queensland University, Australia

ABSTRACT

The Bay of Bengal Initiative for Multi-Sectoral Technical and Economic Cooperation (BIMSTEC) is a regional cooperation between Bangladesh, India, Sri Lanka, Bhutan, Nepal, Myanmar, and Thailand since the liberalization of these economies. Member countries need to be more proactive for integrated regional cooperative hubs to enhance trade and investment opportunities in health and other sectors of the economy to cope with the pandemic and its impact. The aim of this chapter is to show how BIMSTEC, a regional cooperative body, can be a driver for socio-economic development, inter-regional trade, and investment opportunities for BIMSTEC countries and cope with COVID-19 and its impact. The BIMSTEC area is home to approximately 1.6 billion citizens accounting to 22% of the worlds inhabitants with a joint gross domestic product (GDP) of 2.7 trillion. Unemployment situation of 'new poor' can be tackled through close cooperation among the BIMSTEC nations in an effective manner to achieve 'pareto optimality' through trade and investment among member countries.

INTRODUCTION

The changing geo-political environment and increasing ambitions of maritime power by supe-powers in the Indian ocean, Arabian Sea and Bay of Bengal region and more so since COVID-19, it is time for the South Asian Association of Regional Cooperation (SAARC) founded in 1985 and the Bay of Bengal Initiative for Multisectoral Technical and Economic Cooperation (BIMSTEC) which was founded in 1997, includes the seven (7) countries surrounding the Bay of Bengal- Myanmar, Thailand, Bangladesh,

DOI: 10.4018/978-1-7998-5774-7.ch006

India, Bhutan, Nepal and Sri Lanka. Regional grouping of BIMSTEC countries should be proactive and promote regional integration for economic development, trade, growth, political stability and peace (Kaul, 2006; Kelegama, 2001; Kundu, 2014; Schiff & Winters 2003). However, from the very beginning BIMSTEC has neglected investment and sharing resources in the health sector and the education sector, which is actually investing in the human capital – as per the old saying ' healthy mind in a healthy body'. BIMSTEC consists of 21% of world population. It is a bridge between South Asia and Southeast Asian countries, with India's Look-East policy to Thailand's Look- West policy to promote trade, investment and multisectoral cooperation (Bhattacharya & Bhattacharya, 2007; Kundu, 2014). Khan(2012) described that "an ideology of internationalism with special emphasis on socio-economic and political benefits to member states involved in the regional cooperation can usher an era of stability, peace and prosperity for south Asia". Chakravarty(2021) argued that in the strategic and economic domains, the geopolitical order has been impacted adversely by the COVID-19.

World economic scenario is changing and needs different regional cooperative bodies. But BIMSTEC's progress is still very insignificant. Kabir (2015,p.204) argued that "the process of a meaningful economic integration within the bloc should be aimed primarily at policy liberalization, policy reforms and policy coordination amongst member countries." However, still BIMSTEC is not fully activated like ASEAN. Rahman and Grewal (2017) argued that economic engagement and disengagement are part and parcel of political economy and geopolitical concerns. Pandemic situation due to COVID -19 have triggered unprecedented disturbances in production, distribution, consumption, supply chains, tourism, trade, investments, among others (Islam,2021). As such regional integrity is necessity to overcome the aftermath of the COVID19 in the BIMSTEC region. European Union and ASEAN are an example of a successful regional integration for economic development, growth and progress within the region.

According to the Indian Prime Minister Manmohan Singh (2005) regional economic integration should be used as an engine of growth to strengthen their international competitiveness rather than just for promoting trade. Indian current Prime Minister Narendra Modi as reported by The Economic Times (2021) argued that "As a manifestation of our collective will, BIMSTEC has emerged as a promising regional grouping to fulfil the common aspirations of its people and serve the shared interests of the Member States." Problem lies that India has so many multilateral regional bodies as such BIMSTEC is not actually lead by any particular leader of these seven countries though there is a wide scope to develop for the community of these seven countries. Actually, failure of SAARC lead to gear up BIMSTEC but unfortunately with very little progress. Bangladesh Prime Minister Sheikh Hasina (2020) argued that "BIMSTEC forum provides an excellent platform to combat the devastating impact of Covid-I9. We should not leave any stone unturned to utilize this platform in addressing the challenges of the post-Covid-19 era, "still little progress is felt under BIMSTEC to cooperate against fight of COVID-19".

Bay of Bengal is the least integrated region in terms of connectivity and cooperative partnerships for trade, investment and economic development. Besides the 5 South Asian countries, it includes the two Southeast Asian countries – of Thailand and Burma. Japan is second largest trading partner of BIMSTEC countries (Bhattacharya & Bhattacharya, 2007). Since the 24 years from its foundation, besides the annual meetings not much has happened to raise joint resources, strengthen its capabilities and strategic significance: **(i)** To address the economic, maritime security, challenges faced by the countries in the region through BIMSTEC regional institutional cross-border bilateral and multilateral cooperation. **(ii)** China's increasing influence in the region though one-belt-road strategy and maritime power, and **(iii)** Multilateral agreements and connectivity between BIMSTEC countries will keep a check on potential threat from other big countries showing their strategic and maritime power in the region (Das, 2018;

Xavier & Sinha, 2020). Therefore the benefit from transforming the society to the digital economy may outweigh negative impacts and turn threats into opportunities, reduce demand for labor and disguised unemployment and narrow down the scope of creating new employment opportunities in BIMSTEC countries (Ali, 2020). Asian Development Bank (2018, p.32) described that "BIMSTEC could be the organization that links South Asia and Southeast Asia, in transportation terms this wording suggests a dominant east–west orientation, as promoted by India's Look East and Thailand's Look West policies…… the need for promoting intra-regional linkages between all of the BIMSTEC members suggests "Promoting transport connectivity among BIMSTEC Member States" would be a more embracive development theme."

This chapter is structured as follows. The first introductory section of the chapter introduces the growing economic importance and significance of multisectoral technical and economic cooperation such as BIMSTEC. Section two provides the background literature review on overview of BIMSTEC countries, role of BIMSTEC and multisectoral technical and economic cooperation for investment, trade, development, growth, peace, and prosperity, for BIMSRTEC member countries. Section three critically discusses the challenges and provides recommendations or opportunities from BIMSTEC multisectoral agreements. Section four covers practical policy implications followed by future research directions and conclusion, to advance the knowledge in the field multisectoral cooperation as an engine of economic development, growth, trade, investment opportunities, security and prosperity for the member countries. The aim of this paper is how BIMSTEC a regional cooperative body can be a driver for socio-economic development, inter-regional trade, and investment opportunities for BIMSTEC countries and cope with COVID-19 and its impact?

BACKGROUND LITERAURE REVIEW

1. Overview of the BIMSTEC Economies

In order to understand the BIMSTEC multilateral technical cooperation it is important to first get an overview of the BIMSTEC economies and their significance in the Bay of Bengal (BoB), given the SAARC being non-functional, changing geopolitical environment, the rise of China and strategic influence via belt-road initiative. Therefore strategic benefits flowing from enhanced regional integration for economic and political cooperation with trusted and reliable partners for investment, trade, cross-border land and maritime security and peace in the Bay of Bengal and the Indian Ocean region is important in the 21st century. Along with the two Asian countries, Thailand and Myanmar, (Figure-1) five of the SAARC nations are included in BIMSTEC regional integration. This is an which is an alternative regional grouping strongly supported by landlocked, island and small nations within the SAARC region, for supporting cooperative economic development projects, trade, investment, technological exchange, through multilateral and bilateral Free Trade Agreements and liberalization, rail and road links, and promoting stability, security, peace, progress, and prosperity of the region, sharing historical, cultural and economic relationships. Ali (2019-20, p.28) described that "only collaborative effort from the global leaders can diminish the worsening impact of the COVID19 in case of economic, social, and health shocks. As such, all political leaders should take collaborative steps to check health security and preparedness for gravity of the situation after shock period is over."

Figure 1. Map of BIMSTEC Countries
Source: BIMSTEC (2021)

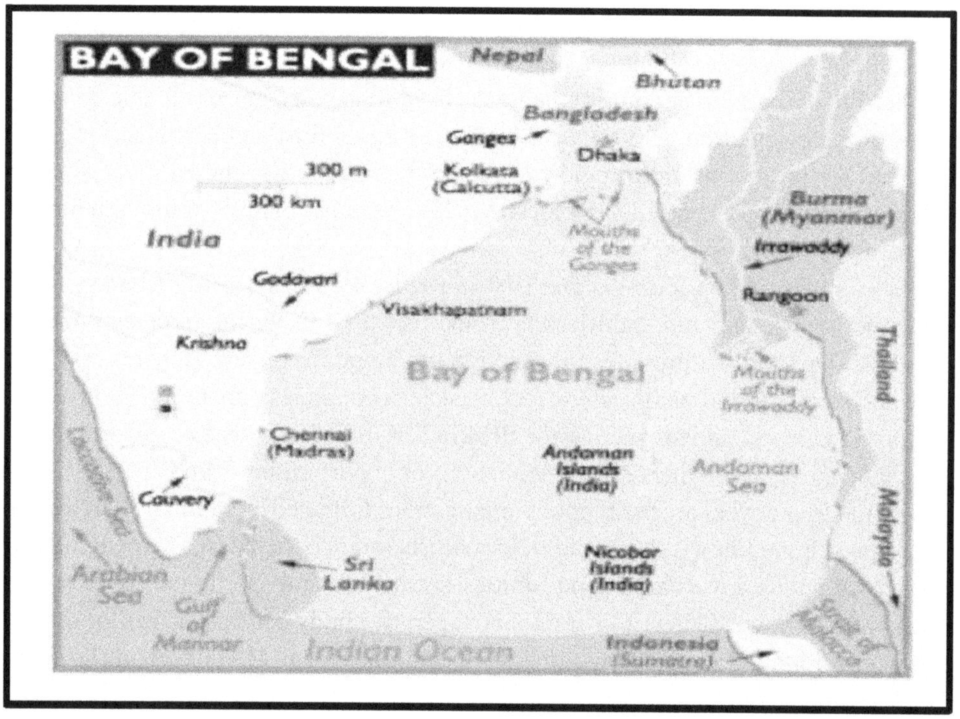

Bhutan: Thimphu is the capital of the Himalayan kingdom of Bhutan and landlocked in the Eastern Himalayas. Bhutan is famous for its philosophy of Gross National Happiness (GNH) Index, which is the foundation of its government's economic development policy. It borders with two powerful and populated countries China in the North and Indian states of Assam, Arunachal Pradesh, Sikkim, and West Bengal. Bhutan is strategically located, and India provides defence security and 80% of its 8 imports are from India. Bangladesh and Nepal are in close proximity with a population of 754,000 thousand and a stable political and macroeconomic environment, hydropower generating capacity, develop agribusiness by investing in downstream value chains, and focusing on GNH index with poverty reduced by 2/3 and improve health, education, gender equality, infrastructure and service provision (World Bank, 2021a).

Bangladesh: Dhaka is the capital of Bangladesh, which was formed in 1971 after partition formerly the part of Pakistan- known as east Pakistan, is the eighth most densely populated country in the world, with 163 million people. It shares land border with India in the west, north and east, Myanmar to southeast, and Bay of Bengal Sea in the south and separated by Siliguri corridor in India from Bhutan and Nepal. Bangladesh is one of the fastest growing economies in the past decade, and has made remarkable progress in reducing poverty, macroeconomic stability and success of ready-made garment (RMG) exports with large number of women employed in this sector. In 2015 it achieved World Bank's lower-middle income status, as poverty declined in 25 years 44% in (1991) to 15% in 2016, based on international poverty line of US$1.90 a day, using 2011 Purchasing Power Parity exchange rate, access to education, health, energy, rural infrastructure and agriculture development (World Bank, 2021b).

India: Delhi is the capital of I*ndia*, country in South Asia. It is the second-most populous country, largest democracy, and the seventh-largest country. India is the world's sixth-largest economy by nominal GDP and the third-largest by purchasing power parity. India shares its border with seven countries- Afghanistan and Pakistan to the North-West, China, Bhutan and Nepal to the North, Myanmar to the far East and Bangladesh to the East. Sri Lanka (from the South-East) and Maldives (from the South-West) are two countries with water borders (World Bank, 2021c). Even though it has emerged as a high-income developing country, it is not able to show its influence as it has many internal problems, and border issues since partition. However, it can show some leadership in successfully functioning of BIMSTEC region with Bangladesh, mutually beneficial to member countries. It has made significant socio-economic progress in agriculture, manufacturing, information technology and other sectors of the economy showing high growth rate of 7 to 8% in the past. However due to COVID-19, trade and travel restrictions its supply chains and businesses have also been negatively impacted.

Myanmar: Nay Pyi Taw is the capital. Myanmar is a Southeast Asian nation of more than 100 ethnic groups, bordering India, Bangladesh, China, Laos, and Thailand. It has a shared colonial history with India and the last Mughal emperor Bahadur Shah Zafar in 1857 was exiled in prison by the British in Burma/Myanmar. It is one of the countries impacted by natural disasters floods, earthquakes, foods, cyclones landslides and droughts (World Bank 2021d).

Nepal: Kathmandu is the capital of Nepal which is a Hindu Himalayan Kingdom and has other religious minorities. Nepal is a landlocked country located in South Asia which is located in the Himalayas, and comprises of the Indo-Gangetic Plain, bordering Tibet of China to the north, and India in West, South and East. Mountain Tourism and its support services are the main sectors of the economy. Since 2017 democratic elections, the decentralized Nepalese government at the local, state and central levels has many challenges to deliver since the economic and devastating impact of the 2016 earthquake such as basic social services, health, education, transportation, tourism and associated infrastructure development in the mountainous regions with the focus on inclusive growth and private sector partnerships (World Bank, 2021e).

Sri Lanka: Historically, Sri Lanka an island economy has a strategic destination along the maritime trade routes to the East for centuries in the Indian Ocean region since the European colonial times. The BIMSTEC has brought about a strategic, economic, trade, and cultural change in the small island economic of Sri Lanka and improved maritime connectivity opportunities surrounded by the Indian Ocean and Arabian sea to its west and Bay of Bengal to the east as a trade route and hub for supply chain transit for cargo ships (Amrith, 2013; Attanayake, 2019). Taking extreme Chinese debt, Sri Lanka is in debt trap nowadays and it is difficult for it to balance the to support the economy during COVID-19 and recover from the debt trap for fiscal sustainability (World Bank, 2021f).

Thailand: Bangkok is the capital of Thailand, which was formerly known as Siam and officially the Kingdom of Thailand, is a country in Southeast Asia. It is located at the centre of the Indochinese Peninsula. It was never colonized by the British, but in return had to give up some land to the empire. Thailand has its development success story and has made remarkable socio-economic progress moving to upper middle-income country with fall in the poverty levels from 65.2% in 1988 to 9.85% in 2018. Thailand shares historical and cultural connections with its bordering nations including India. (World Bank, 2021g).

Table 1. Macro-economic data of BIMSTEC Countries

	Bangladesh	India	Sri Lanka	Nepal	Bhutan	Thailand	Myanmar
GDP annual growth rate	7.9 2018 8.2 2019 5.2 2020	5.4 Jul 19 -24.4 Jul20 1.6 Apr 21	4 Jul 2018 1.1 Jul 2019 -16.3 Jul 2020	6.4 2018 -2.1 2019 4 2020	4.7 2017 3.1 2018 5.5 2019	2.4 Jul 19 -12.1 Jul 20 -2.6 Feb21	6.8 2018 5 2019 2 2020
Inflation %	5.53 2020 5.29 2020 5.26 2021	6.73 July 20 4.59 Dec 20 6.3 May 21	4.2 Jul 2020 3 Jan 2021 5.2 Jun 2021	4.8 Jul20 3.5 Jan 21 3.6 May21	4.55 Apr 20 7.72 Dec 20 9.11 Mar 21	-0.98 Jul 20 -0.34 Jan 21 2.44 May 21	5.24 Apr 20 0.75 Dec 20 1.51 Feb 21
Interest rate %	6.75 2018 6 .0 2019 4.75 2020	6 2019 4.5 2020 4 2021	8 2019 4.50 2020 4.50 2021	6.5 2019 5 2020 5 2021	6 2018 7.4 2019 6.86 2020	1.75 2018 1.5 2019 0.5 2020	10% 2018 10 2019 7 2020
Unemploy-ment %	4.3 2018 4.2 2019 5.3 2020	7.4 Jul 20 9.1 Dec 20 11 May21	4.9 Jul 19 5.4 Jul 20 5.2 Jan 21	2.9 2018 2.8 2019 4.4 2020	3.4 2018 2.7 2019 5 2 020	1 Dec 19 2.1 Jul 20 1.5 Dec 20	0.9% 2018 0.7 2019 1.79 2020
Balance of Trade US$ Billon	-111.6 Ap 20 -181.8 Dec 20 -186 Mar 21	-4830 Jul 20 -1544 Dec 20 -6280 May 21	-208.7 Jul 20 -562.1 Dec20 -889 Apr 21	-120000 Nov 19 - 100000 Apr 20 -80000 Aug 20	-9527 Jul 19 -4795 Jul 20 -5286 Jan 21	3343 Jul 20 -202 Jan 21 800 May 21	-431 Mar20 157 Jul21 68.7 Nov 21
Current Account to GDP	-3.5 2018 -1.7 2019 -1.5 2020	-2.1 2018 -0.9 2019 0.9 2020	2.6 2017 -3.2 2018 -2.2 2019	-0.4 2017 -8.1 2018 -7.6 2019	-18.9 2017 -21.2 2018 -12.2 201 9	5.6 2018 7 2019 4.2 2020	-4.7 2017 -2 2018 -2 2019
Govt. Debt GDP %	28.1 2018 29.6 2019 31.7 2020	68.9 2017 69.8 2018 69.62 2019	79.9 2017 83.7 2018 86.8 2019	26.8 2017 30.4 2018 30.2 2019	110.5 2018 106.6 2019 120.7 2020	41.8 2018 41.1 2019 50.5 2020	40.4 2018 38.8 2019 42.4 2020
Govt. budget Deficit % of GDP	4.8 2018 -4.8 2019 -5.35 2020	-3.42 2018 -4.6 2019 -9.4 2020	-5.5 2018 -5.3 2019 -6.81 2020	-7.1 2017 -10.1 2018 -5.4 2019	-0.3 2018 -2 2019 -6.2 2020	-2.7 2018 -2.4 2019 -1.9 2020	-2.7 2017 -3 2018 -3.5 2019

Source: Trading Economics Data & ADB (2021).

All BIMSTEC countries are severely impacted by COVID-19 pandemic second wave and nationwide lockdowns with fall in growth rates. Various measure has been taken to mitigate and contain the pandemic though lockdowns, masks and isolation. India is worst affected by COVID-19. faced with Table 2 provides the number of corona cases, death, and recovery of BIMSTEC countries relative to their total population of 1.6 billion and individual population in (Worldometer, 2021) which is India (1.38 billion), Bangladesh (230-250 million), Bhutan (0,75 million), Nepal (28.09 million), Sri Lanka (21.8 million), Thailand (69,63 million), and Myanmar (54.8 million) (WHO, 2021).

Table 2. Coronavirus Statistics: BIMSTEC countries

Pandemic June-July 2021	Bangladesh	India	Sri Lanka	Thailand	Myanmar	Nepal	Bhutan
Corona Cases	930042	30458251	262795	270921	161210	642053	2122
Corona Deaths	15065	400312	3157	2141	3478	9179	1
Corona Recovery	816250	29427330	225952	207479	136443	596132	1773
Hospital Beds per/1000*	0.8	0.5	4.2	2.1	1.0	0.3	1.7

Source: Trading Economics from WHO (2021).* Note: from World Bank

2. Role of BIMSTEC: Trade and Investment Led Growth

The Indian governments Look-East to Act-East policy to the land locked eastern states of India and the dysfunctional South Asian Association of Regional Cooperation (SAARC), led to formation of BIMSTEC grouping, where the other South Asian countries to the east wanted to connect with ASEAN group of countries for trade and investment opportunities (Ahmed & Islam, 2019; Brewster, 2014; Kundu, 2014). According to Kelegama (2001), the Bangkok agreement of preferential trading arrangement of 1975, between India, Bangladesh, Sri Lanka, Thailand, Laos, Korea and Myanmar has not produced any concrete results in terms of economic, trade, investment, and security cooperation, mainly due to Thailand, Laos, Republic of Korea, and Myanmar first commitment to ASEAN group. On the other hand BIMSTEC, with trade liberalization of the South Asian economies wanting to have a closer trade relationship with the ASEAN countries, and Thailand wanting to have more trade with the Indian sub-continent, with increasing competition in the ASEAN group. Further, the 1991 Indian and 1997 Asian, financial crisis also slowed down any proactive role played by BIMSTEC nations.

In order to strengthen the Bay of Bengal initiative to advance regional integration Xavier (2018) suggests that **(i)** BIMSTEC should have a liberal multilateral cooperative regional integration between the countries surrounding the Bay of Bengal f to meet common economic and strategic goals. **(ii)** Empower BIMSTEC with sufficient financial and human resources expertise to drive the agenda with shared responsibility. **(iii)** Prioritize continuous and sustainable physical connectivity of people and flow of goods and services through state-of-the-art infrastructure development for encouraging trade, travel and tourism between the member countries and specially the landlocked states of Nepal, Bhutan and Eastern Indian states, with Calcutta (for Nepal and Bhutan) and Bangladesh (Eastern Indian states) as the regional hub for supply chain distribution of goods and services. **(iv)** India being a large country in terms of population, area and GDP, can act as an informal or formal proactive regional leader, and increase investment of resources, regional reforms without compromising the interest and power balance of the other member states. **(v)** Open BIMSTEC to cooperate with Asian Development bank and liberal democratic countries such as Australia, New Zealand, Japan, Canada, and America for dialogue, intra-regional strategic cooperation for security, investment, and trade in goods and services. Table -3 shows the various trade agreements between the BIMSTEC nations.

Bhattacharya and Bhattacharya (2007) empirical study using the gravity model to determine whether the integration of Japan with BIMSTEC as a second largest trading partner, will increase intra-regional trade. The findings conclude that the potential loss of trade for some BIMSTEC member countries will be compensated by gains in other areas of the economy. Such as foreign direct investment, technology transfer, resources transfer, and access to services markets, strengthening the relationships between South Asia ASEAN countries providing a sustainable economic development and growth regional outcome from regional integration for all resulting in meeting some of the United Nations Sustainable Development Goals (UN- SDGs) of poverty reduction, employment, and partnerships (United Nations, 2021).

Southeast Asian countries have adopted the export led growth model now for three decades, such as China, Hongkong, Singapore, Malaysia and Thailand (Shan & Sun, 1998, Titis, 2008). Similarly trade and investment agreements between the small SAARC nations and South Asian Free Trade Area (SAFTA) will reap many socio-economic benefits due to sharing common historical, cultural and geographical proximity (Ahmed, & Islam, 2019). The current dynamic global environment, Globalisation, COVID-19 related trade and travel restrictions and global supply-chain disruptions have highlighted the importance of economic interdependence between countries, bilateral and multilateral trade agreements which should go beyond politics and conflict, with the aim for improving the quality of life of people and meeting the 17- United Nations SDGs for BIMSTEC nations.

Table 3. The Bilateral & Preferential Trade Agreements between the BIMSTEC nations

From	To						
	Bangladesh	**India**	**Sri Lanka**	**Thailand**	**Myanmar**	**Nepal**	**Bhutan**
Bangladesh		BA GSTP SAPTA	SAPTA	BA GSTP SAPTA	BTA	SAPTA	SAPTA
India	BA GSTP SPTA		BA SAPTA ISLBTA	GSTP	BTA	SAPTA BFTA	SAPTA BFTA
Sri Lanka	BA GSTP SAPTA	BA SAPTA ISLBTA		GSTP		SAPTA	SAPTA
Thailand	GSTP	GSTP	GSTP		PTA- ASEAN		
Myanmar	BTA	BTA	BTA	PTA- ASEAN BTA			
Nepal	SAPTA	BFTA	SAPTA				SAPTA
Bhutan	SAPTA	TCT	SAPTA			SAPTA	

Notes: Global System of Trade Preference-GSTP; Bangkok Agreement-BA; Indo-Sri Lanka Bilateral Trade Agreement-ISL-BTA; South-Asian Preferential Trading Arrangement- SAPTA; Free Trade Agreements – FTA; Trade Commerce & Transit -TCT

Source: Kelegama (2001, p.115); BIMSTEC Home Page; Asia Regional Integration Centre

MAIN FOCUS OF THE CHAPTER

The aim of this paper is how BIMSTEC a regional cooperative body can be a driver for socio-economic development, inter-regional trade, and investment opportunities for BIMSTEC countries and cope with COVID-19 and its impact? The research was based on quantitative analysis. Authors found that there was every chance to enhance trade and investment in the regional area so that problems of unemployment, disparity that occurred due to pandemic situation could be tackled and new poor could get benefit of close cooperation in an effective manner. However, leaders of the BIMSTEC countries need to have strong political will so that inter regional cooperation through vertical and horizontal coordination may be established. Friendship among neighbouring countries must be strengthened for which political economy should get importance. Equal opportunities, demographic dividends, and access to financial activities to create employment opportunities for BIMSTEC citizens.

BIMSTEC member countries need to develop harmony, tranquility and be free from religious biased decisions. Geopolitical interest should not hamper among the citizens of these member states and sovereignty and create equal opportunity for fulfillment of basic needs (Ahmed & Islam, 2019). Investment in human capital is the first and foremost area to consider through capacity and capability building through regional cooperation for attaining 17-UN SDGs such as no hunger, poverty, and so on. Promoting, social, economic and vaccine diplomacy is the need of the hour for the BIMSTEC region where the public and private sectors should come together in establishing government to government level pharmaceutical plants and vaccination plants which are affordable and effective by relaxing intellectual property rights for the mutual benefit of the countries and improving the quality of life. Similar cooperative partnerships should be adopted for health, education, infrastructure development, trade and investment opportunities.

METHODOLOGY

This quantitative study uses secondary data sources to analyse the data of BIMSTEC six member countries' Import Expenses with Bangladesh as an example for the period of 2004-05 to 2019-20 to judge the performance of the import efficiencies among the member countries. Similarly the study used standard deviation formula for analyzing the volatility of export receipts of Bangladesh with other six BIMSTEC member countries for the period of 2004-05 to 2019-20 to judge the performance of the export efficiencies among the member countries. Time period of doing entire research work is from January 2021to May 2021 and considering data period of 2004-05 to 2019-20. Standard Deviation (SD) of both imports and exports were determined.

Data Collection: Import Expense data was collected from the Bangladesh Bank (2021a). For export data the study collected Export Income data from Bangladesh Bank (2021b), expressed in local currency Takas.

FINDINGS

Data Analysis From Import Expense

Standard deviation was applied for analyzing the volatility of Import Expenses of Bangladesh with other six BIMSTEC member countries for the period of 2004-05 to 2019-20.

Formula of Standard Deviation is ∂(sigma)= Square Root of Σ(Xi-u)^2/N..................(i)

Here, ∂= Population SD, N = Size of the Population = 96; Xi = Each value of population u = Population means. Table-4 provides results of volatility of import expenses of Bangladesh with other six BIMSTEC nations.

Standard Deviation of price /expense used as a measure of volatility. It is a statistical measure of market volatility, which express how widely prices are dispersed from the average price. Conversely if prices/expenses volatility rises or falls, the SD return high value which indicate high volatility. In this study average population mean is 715792.7292 and SD is 5844423.161, so SD is highly dispersed from the average price or mean, so it indicates the Import Expenses of Bangladesh is highly volatile in nature, and so it is not a good performance indicator in the economy of this region.

Table 4. Volatility of Import Expenses of Bangladesh with six BIMSTEC nations

X1=2004-05=(20050+201449+5283+1246463+1052+6316)=1480613
X2= 2005-06=(19836+216535+7840+1253300+1806+7283)=1506600
X3=2006-07=1889187
X4=2007-08=2806019
X5=2008-09=2455048
X6=2009-10=2764088
X7=2010-11=4186370
X8=2011-12=4567980
X9=2012-13=4515367
X10=2013-14=5425119
X11=2014-15=5149068
X12=2015-16=4882214
X13=2016-17=5596924
X14= 2017-18=8300894
X15=2018-19=7408858
X16=2019-20=5781753
Population Mean (u)= (X1 to X16)/96 = 715792.7292
Σ(Xi-u)^2={(1480613-715792.7292)+(1506600-715792.7292)+(1889187-715792.7292)+(2806019-715792.7292)+…….+(5781753-715792.7292)}^2 =57263418.35 Σ(Xi-u)^2={(1480613-715792.7292)+(1506600-715792.7292)+(1889187-715792.7292)+(2806019-715792.7292)+……+(5781753-715792.7292)}^2 =57263418.35 **Standard Deviation** ∂= SQRT(57263418.35^2/96) SD =5844423.161
Source: Determined by the Authors

Data Analysis From Export Income

Standard deviation formula for analyzing the volatility of Export Receipts of Bangladesh with other six BIMSTEC member countries for the period of 2004-05 to 2019-20 was used. Table -5 provides results of volatility of export income of Bangladesh with other six BIMSTEC nations.

Standard Deviation is a statistic that measures the dispersion of a dataset relative to its mean. Standard Deviation determine market volatility or the spread of asset prices from their average price. When prices move widely, SD is high, meaning an investment will be risky. The speed or degree of changes in prices (in either direction of Import) is called volatility.

- The positive impact of volatility in exports increase is that the potential to make more money quickly due to an increase in export (export income) also increased.
- But the negative impact of high volatility in Export indicates high risk.
- In this research author found high value of SD comparatively to its average mean, which indicate high volatility in export market. As such high volatility in export market diversified economy in various sector, is a positive driver and sign of good economic performance.

Table 5. Volatility of Export income of Bangladesh with six BIMSTEC nations

Y1= 2004-05 = (142730+642494+287949+5975026+290815+531381) = 7870395
Y2 = 2005-06 = 13325088
Y3 =2006-07 = 17098428
Y4 = 2007-08 = 21592979
Y5 = 2008-09 = 22678351
Y6 = 2009-10 = 24132372
Y7 = 2010-11= 38350157
Y8 = 2011-12 = 48202406
Y9 = 2012-13 = 53680661
Y10 = 2013-14 = 37457327
Y11= 2014-15 = 44136976
Y12 = 2015-16 = 57728489
Y13 = 2016-17 = 54336217
Y14 = 2017-18 = 66427310
Y15 = 2018-19 = 88510865
Y16 = 2019-20 = 84039848
Standard Deviation is ∂(sigma) = Square Root of Σ(Yi-u)^2/N ∂ = Population Standard Deviation, N = Size of the Population=96 Yi = Each value of population, u = Population means
Population Mean(u)= (Y1+Y2+Y3+......+Y16)/96 = (7870395+13325088+21592979+......+84039848)/96 = 679567869/96 = 7078831.969
Σ(Yi-u)^2={(7870395-7078831.969) + (13325088-7078831.968)+......+(84039848-7078831.969)}^2 = (566306557.6)^2 Now Standard Deviation of Export Income = SQRT{(566306557.5)^2/96 =57798421(In thousand BDT)
Source: Determined by the authors

DISCUSSION AND RECOMMENDATIONS

The study found that import expenses of Bangladesh is highly volatile in nature, which is not a good performance indicator in the economy of the BIMSTEC region. But the study observed that high volatility in export market diversified economy in various sectors, which is a positive driver and good sign of economic performance. Still BIMSTEC's outcome is not praiseworthy due to ineffective political leadership reality, transformation of energies of reconsidering regional urgencies and permitting BIMSTEC to accomplish its potentials are persisting as necessity of the time, not the extra means to execute. The regeneration of BIMSTEC, in this reverence, might be a healthier option for the Asian integration. May be new member countries as well as inclusion of cooperation in the health and education sector need to be included for strengthening BIMSTEC future survival as a whole. There should be zero tolerance towards anti-social behavior, religious conflicts and terrorism. Entrepreneurial zeal among the member states needs to be based on collaborative effort with inclusive development. Integration among the member states need trust and respect for each-other. One of the member countries has to take responsibility of leadership and rotate the responsibility. Regional supply chain should be properly established with adding value to primary and supportive activities considering inbound and outbound logistics, marketing and proper procurement system. Networking connecting with digitalization system should be made the priority amongst the member countries. Market perfection for which information symmetry is required which may help transparent transactions through financial institutions. Multinational and transnational companies can grow with a higher rate so that income inequality in this regional block can be reduced and employment opportunities can be created. Connectivity and free movement among the member states may be arranged only after all are vaccinated for COVID-19 (vaccination passport) which will ultimately help to enhance trade, foreign direct investment and tourism opportunities. As such political will and commitment from leaders of member states is needed with accountability and inclusiveness.

Though BIMSTEC member countries agreed to establish BIMSTEC Free Trade Area Framework Agreement in order to stimulate trade and investment between members and attract outsiders to trade with and invest in BIMSTEC at a higher level, but still it is not showing effective outcomes. The seven-country forum aimed to achieve its own free trade area by 2017 which has still not been taken off the ground. So far issues pertaining to trade barriers, economic structure, geography, regional development, lack of coordination among financial sector regulators, distinctiveness of BIMSTEC member countries have been addressed only bilaterally, but not in a transnational manner, which have not benefitted the countries. For India, North-eastern landlocked Indian states may find it beneficial for bilateral relationship with Bangladesh but for regional development and gateway to ASEAN countries, much needs to be done in case of developing infrastructure facilities of rail, road and rail in the hilly regions. BIMSTEC member countries should not forgot the rise of China and its policy of one-belt-one-road debt trap for developing countries, to dominate in this BIMSTEC Bay of Bengal and the Indian ocean region for gaining access to trade route and maritime power (Cho & Park 2013). Nealy 2 billion population of the BIMSTEC region will reap the benefits if they form sustainable partnerships between the private and public sectors from demographic dividend by investing in human capital and physical capital and local technological inventions and innovation to achieve the United Nations 17- SDGs (UN, 2021).

India and Bangladesh are a model of good neighborhood partnership focusing on economic development for peace and prosperity for the benefit of the population of the two countries. The agreement to supply gas to Tripura, and the use of the Chattogram and Mongla ports to serve the North-eastern states testify to the goodwill between the two countries. The agreement for a skill development center in Bangladesh to train youth is another example of mutually beneficial efforts. It was correctly pointed out that it is important to address specific problems and respond to Dhaka's call for help on the Rohingya issue. Lack of joint river management and control of floods are vital issues to be discussed between member countries. BIMSTEC University Network can create BIMSTEC Quality Assurance Standard which will help to control overall quality. Framework for Quality Assurance Standard requires a setup as per the guidelines of other BIMSTEC members as well. This will have a better impact on curbing terrorism and also decline of religious extremism. The leaders of BIMSTEC member countries should activate this regional cooperation association without delay and include higher education qualifications framework as a matter of regional cooperation. There will be no dead weight loss, rather there will be Pareto Optimality which will activate social welfare tangency in the Grand Utility Possibility Curve.

BIMSTEC may be stronger as a result of its member countries and proper utilization of its resources. Regional cooperation through BIMSTEC ought to be included in the educational sector where there is immense scope for human capital development. Besides creating white collar labour, blue collar labour may be prepared by universities for which course curricula should be changed by using business process reengineering (Ali, 2020).

At the International Workshop on Need for Changes in the Course Curricula of Business Schools: Positioning & Competency of Business Schools in BIMSTEC Region's education sector. Narendra Modi, Prime Minister of India, envisioned India to be number one under BIMSTEC through regional cooperation steps in the education sector. Like ASEAN University network and ASEAN Quality Assurance, BIMSTEC university network and BIMSTEC Quality Assurance could also be established. Through interchange in teaching - learning system at higher educational institutions among BIMSTEC universities, this could establish a regional benchmark, beneficial for all member countries. Sheikh Hasina, Prime Minister of Bangladesh, and Modi and heads of other member countries emphasised on an educational framework at the Summit, with a hope that through strategic planning, within 10 years, the educational sector of this region would improve. In the changing environment of Myanmar, current regime should come forward to improve their country's political and economic condition gradually turning into democratic regime and try to get regional cooperation to come out of the negative impact of the pandemic situation.

All heads of state should spearhead regional cooperation in education system to build quality human capital by investing in health and education necessary for technological invention and innovation and economic growth for BIMSTEC nations production possibilities frontier to shift outward. There should be a framework not just for teaching, learning, research and extension and consultancy in this region, but it should also be made industry-centric with humanistic values and ethics. Education is a process of continuous improvement which never ends; it rather changes for betterment of the earth and humanity. Political statesmanship role in this geo-political region is needed to lead BIMSTEC for having a better world, quality of life through developing quality educational framework under BIMSTEC. Investment in building human capital has a positive impact on all BIMSTEC nations which needs regional public and private cooperation. To develop a perfect model in the educational arena we can use Public-Private-Foreign (PPF) collaboration. For example, in Bangladesh one can try to establish a branch of Asian Institute of Technology or University of Delhi. For life science or medical education, one can try to set up a branch of Mahidol University, Thailand or Indian Institute of Technology Bombay (IITB). Alternatively set up an independent BIMSTEC research focussed Institute with its branches in capital cities member countries taking in the best quality post graduate students and private sector industry funded research project collaboration with internationally well know BIMSTEC staff.

To have a win-win situation, regional cooperation is very important for which the platform of BIMSTEC can be used especially for the field of higher education. Teacher and student exchanges among different member countries will give better social, psychological, cordial and ethical friendship and value. By expediting the signing of a Free Trade Agreement (FTA), the possibilities of stronger trade and investment ties between the BIMSTEC nations is required to enhance trade and investment opportunities in much need health, education and infrastructure sector; otherwise in the short term, it could replace moribund SAFTA in the region. There is scope between BIMSTEC members, for both land and maritime connectively that can enhance their trade, investment, incomes and welfare of the group of seven countries, of which four are least developed countries –Nepal, Bhutan, Bangladesh and Myanmar.

If the Northeastern part of Indian states manages to nurture stronger links with India's neighboring countries to the East, it will lead to a higher degree of integration with the Eastern Indian states facilitating trade and development as well as attracting foreign direct investment with Bangladesh as the main transit Hub for supply-chains. The possibility of greater connectivity of the Northeast with Myanmar and

Thailand will also be important for a trade route to countries of the ASEAN (Association of Southwest Asian Nations). It will help raise the income of the people in the sub- region as a whole, and also act as a bridge to the rest of Southeast Asia. The underpinning principles of BIMSTEC are sovereign equality, territorial integrity, political independence, non-interference an internal affairs, peaceful coexistence, and mutual benefit, intra- BIMSTEC relations have been mostly harmonious, although Myanmar and Bangladesh are facing a challenge with the issue of the Rohingya refugees (Ali, 2020).

BIMSTEC regions primary objective is to create an enabling environment for rapid economics development through identification and implementation of specific cooperation projects in various sectors of through trade, investment, industry, technology, human resource development, tourism, agriculture, energy, infrastructure development and transportation. Although BIMSTEC has been enforced for more than two decades it has not yet made a significant impact on the business and economic sectors of member countries. It could not organize itself in a cooperative manner as a recognizable force and come forward during natural disasters management, during the price hike for food or COVID mitigation strategies and implementation, and coronavirus vaccine production and distribution to BIMSTEC member countries by India which has a largest pharmaceutical and vaccine production plant in the world, BIMSTEC, thus is unknown as a regional body to the world organizations due to its lack of showing power in the Bay of Bengal- Indian Ocean region and policy impact, whether it is on the education, trade, investment, infrastructure development, or strategic maritime joint military exercises to protect the regions. The biggest challenges that BIMSTEC countries are facing is crossborder terrorism, cross-border refugee and illegal migration issues, rise of China in the Bay-of Bengal-Indian Ocean waters, are serious threats to international peace and security where million in terms of their livelihood are connected to the Bay of Bengal- Indian Ocean region.

The member countries of BIMCTEC have unfortunately not actively engaged and connected with the multilateral organisations to play a strategic role in the Bay of Bengal and the Indian ocean region to benefit from trace, investment and develop strategic land and joint maritime security power in the Bay of Bengal and the Indian ocean region and protect it from other superpowers. Sharing regional resources may strengthen the benefits as now in BIMSTEC member countries due to pandemic situation new poor have been created due to pandemic related unemployment and every chance of 4th industrial revaluation. Ongoing pandemic situation for the last 2 years has shown that how we are lagging behind from the ASEAN member countries in case of beneficial cooperation. Cooperation in hospital management, health and safety, vaccine production and supply are a very big issue. Corruption free medical system in these member countries is required to cope with people selling medicines and oxygen in the black market. A BIMSTEC medical college and hospital which is JCI accredited may be established in each member country under chain hospital system and also continuous research and development process for affordable access to quality healthcare and lifesaving medicines. Regarding production of vaccine a plant of Serum Institute, India it may be established in Bangladesh as per local and foreign cooperation under PPPs model, which may produce anti COVID vaccine and other cost-effective lifesaving drugs for the BIMSTEC member countries to mitigate huge deficit of the vaccine and ensure vaccine as a common public good for each community of the member countries by funding from each member countries in a pro-rata basis. Under the umbrella of BIMSTEC in each country a JCI accredited medical college and hospital under joint venture may be established with JCI accredited. Strong leadership, political will and commitment of these member countries may give a better result.

Challenges and Problems

There are many economic, political, legal, technical and connectivity related challenges for any successful regional integration, given the changing global geo-political environment and since COVID-19 period lock downs, supply chain disruptions, and closing of national and international borders to prevent the spread of virus.

1. *Changing geopolitical environment:* One blet-road initiative projects of China in many developing countries, with good intentions of building infrastructure, has actually led to control of resources, strategic ingratitude's of road, rail and seaports, maritime power for China resulting in debt for the countries.
2. *Internal problems:* BIMSTEC countries are having their own internal issues which need to be resolved to have a beneficial multilateral and bilateral regional relationship. In case of India there is the border issues with Pakistan, religious conflicts within the country, different political views, poverty and population, Rohingya refugees from Thailand crossing borders which has spilled over to Bangladesh and Nepal. Sri Lanka, internal Tamil conflicts and China's control of seaports and airport via one blet-road debt trap.
3. *Myanmar:* India shares 1643 kilometers of land border with Myanmar, which is the gateway to the ASEAN countries. There is a growing Chinese influence in Myanmar, with military rule, threat to democracy, Rohingya refugee issues which has spilled over to India and Bangladesh. This is a concern for peace and stability of Myanmar and the various internal security problems such as lack of democracy, human trafficking, increases poverty, climate change issues, drugs and arms smuggling, within the country needs to be resolved for successful functioning of BIMSTEC.
4. *Trade disruptions from COVID-19:* BIMSTEC regions has experienced like all nations, devastating economic impact on businesses and trade related supply chain disruptions. The challenge is the recovery from COVID-19 and other structural challenges facing the BIMSTEC countries, including diversifying exports between the regions improving urbanization, infrastructure for better supply chain routes in hilly regions.
5. *Addressing vulnerability to climate risk:* For sustainable economic development and meeting the goals of UN-SDGs, BIMSTEC counties have to take small steps to solve this problem as it is usually the vulnerable poor people who suffer the impact of climate change. Multilateral partnerships in natural disaster, sustainable natural resource management, and risk management, and sustainable water and energy resources management
6. *Rohingya Refugee issues:* BIMSTEC countries mainly Bangladesh, India, Thailand and Nepal are facing the problem of influx of Rohingya Refugee's from Myanmar (Chakravarty, 2021). This issue needs to be solved through dialogue to bring a peaceful solution and smooth functioning and success of BIMSTEC multisectoral technical cooperation and economic development programs.
7. *Grass root participatory approach:* BIMSTEC counties should adopt grassroots bottom-up approach to sustainable economic development for meeting the 17 goals of UN-SDGs. With so many political parties of different views and internal corruption can make it difficult to involve the grassroot populations participation to determine what they need, in decision making.
8. *Natural disasters:* BINMSTEC nations are always prone to natural disasters such as earthquakes, cyclone, heavy rain, floods, draught and tsunami. These vagaries of the nature have a devastating impact on the economy and the people quality of life.

9. *Public-Private Partnerships (PPP):* Involving private sector in export-oriented industries, private sector led growth, and infrastructure development and implementing development project under various PPP models Build-Operate-Transfer (BOT) for health, transport, manufacturing services sector, tourism and infrastructure such as road, rail, seaports and airports by the BIMSTEC business groups, to avoid Sri Lanka kind of debt trap and influence of countries who have military and maritime control motives in the Bay of Bengal region.

Besides aforesaid challenges if proper cooperation cannot be built then there is every chance of rise of human trafficking, refugee problem, and rise of terrorism in this region due to ongoing pandemic which is creating new poor.

Policy Implications

BIMSTEC is a driver for regional cooperation for small countries around the Bay of Bengal, as it is a regional alliance of uniting around geographically adjoining South Asian and ASEAN countries, with its headquarters in Bangladesh. In spite of the various initiatives taken in meetings, BIMSTEC is not very much assertive as a regional cooperation body around the Bay of Bengal and Indian Ocean region. BIMSTEC has identified six sectors of focused cooperation. These are: **(i)** trade and investment; **(ii)** technology; **(iii)** transport & communication; **(iv)** energy; **(v)** tourism; **(vi)** fisheries. Even under the focused area they have not considered cooperation in the field of education, science and health sector. These were vital during the pandemic situation. In this contemporary globalization period, countries are interdependent for co-existence. For realizing free market economy, every country is removing tariff and non-tariff barriers by creating regional, bilateral and multisectoral relationship. To overcome the pandemic situation, creation of employment and growth with equity must be motto of these member states which may be arranged with the help of digitization process of cottage, micro and small and medium enterprises by collaborative effort and member states Government can discuss the issue virtually taking utmost care.

Promoting and implementing joint projects and programs is an essence of equality and partnerships to hasten the economic growth and social progress amongst the BIMSTEC member countries. Therefore promoting pro-active collaboration on joint protects on matters of common interest in the medical and health sector, education sector, economic, social, technical, scientific research and development for continuous improvement is needed. The preferential trade agreements and treatment would allow the countries to gain enhanced access in each other's market; the 'enabling clause' provision would provide them the requisite safeguard to protect the sensitive domestic sectors on the other. Moreover, apart from the tariff barriers, it was expected that the trade facilitation measures would significantly lower the level of transaction costs, which currently put a downward pressure on the intra-regional trade volume.

BIMSTEC platform has a huge scope for trade, investment, maritime security and economic development. If it is possible to make BIMSTEC strong, it will ensure high GDP growth rate for the member countries, improving quality of life and meeting the 17-UN-SDGs. But the challenge is that some countries of this alliance are not interested to develop this organization because of their own interest. Investment in human capital has a positive impact on all economies, which needs regional cooperation. To develop a perfect model in the educational arena or health we can use Public-Private-Foreign (PPF) collaboration. To develop a perfect model in the educational arena we can use PPF which means Public-Private-Foreign collaboration. For example, BIMSTEC can set up in Bangladesh a branch of Asian Institute of

Technology or University of Delhi. For Life science or medial education, branch of Mahidol University, Thailand, or Indian Institute of Technology (IIT). Further for the better health management and care of these member states seven chain medical colleges and hospitals which must be JCI accredited may be established with proper research-oriented laboratory and pharmaceuticals in an integrated manner so that access to international benchmarked health facility in each country can be feasible. Incentives can be given to the Scientists so that new class of innovative corporate entrepreneurship can be developed. Therefore, regional cooperation will give BIMSTEC better market access for trade, infrastructure investment, innovative entrepreneurship, to improve human development index and quality of life along with maritime security cooperation in the Bay of Bengal-Indian Ocean region.

FUTURE RESEARCH DIRECTIONS

In the future an in-depth study may be undertaken through both quantitative and qualitative research work for import and export between all the BIMSTEC countries (here as an example only the export-import case of Bangladesh with other BIMSTEC member states was shown). Case studies of each country may be included in the qualitative research with stakeholders' interviews such as government officials, businesses involved in export and import and grassroot population. For quantitative studies, the driving factors for promoting trade, investment and maritime security on the basis of survey and secondary data sources may be done. Studies for BIMSTEC economies may be conducted using forecasting model i.e ARIMA(Autoregressive Integrated Moving Average). This kind of study requires time as well as need huge cost for which research grant from the appropriate authority like World Bank, ADB could be obtained. Another study could look at how BIMSTEC can be expand its vision, mission and focus and include new member country like Indonesia in particular for maritime security, so that Bay of Bengal-Indian Ocean region can remain peaceful, and no country can fall into a debt trap like Sri Lanka.

CONCLUSION

The main aim for BIMSTEC countries is to make sure that there is investment in human capital, health, education, enhanced quality of physical and capital infrastructure, macroeconomic stability, improved business friendly environment to attract foreign direct investment, strengthen fiscal institutions, promote competition, address climate change, land and water resource management challenges, technological innovation for cost-effective local innovative solutions for improving the quality of life of its citizens in the region, with inclusive growth. BIMSTEC goals can be successful if there is political will and commitment by leaders of the member countries for improving the quality of life and security for its population. Connectivity among the member countries need to be improved in all areas, social, economic, trade, investment, and land, air and maritime security. Further due to turbulent situations the countries need the help of establishing vaccine plant especially in Bangladesh so that member countries can get vaccine. The BIMSTEC countries include both developing countries and LDCs and therefore, they are characterized by higher tariff barriers on their imports, vis-à-vis their developed counterparts. It was expected that while on one hand the preferential treatment would allow the countries to gain enhanced access in each other's market; the 'enabling clause' provision would provide them the requisite safeguard to protect the sensitive domestic sectors on the other. Moreover, apart from the tariff barriers, it was expected that the trade facilitation measures would significantly lower the level of transaction costs, which currently put a downward pressure on the intra-regional trade volume. Moreover, member states of like-minded among Asia and beyond need to be increased in the BIMSEC. The regional body as a whole need to revitalize and establishment of BIMSTEC bank among the member states for mutually beneficial joint development projects.

BIMSTEC is an important platform for South Asian countries along the Bay of Bengal region to connect with East Asian neighbours. It is an important platform for regional co-operation for maritime security and has a huge scope for trade, investment in human and physical capital, technological innovation, and numerous economic development opportunities. Vison, mission and focus of BIMSTC need to be restructured and unified effort is required depending on the current turbulent situation, for betterment and attaining pareto optimality for the member countries. But unfortunately, this organization is not in fully functioning position to show its importance in taking concrete steps in implementing joint projects, due to internal issues and weak policy of the member countries.

REFERENCES

Ahmed, B., & Islam, M. T. (2019). Bangladesh-Nepal Trade Relations: Understanding the Influence of Economic Diplomacy. *Jadavpur Journal of International Relations*, *23*(1), 105–119.

Ali, M. M. (2020). Grim situation of the world due to COVID19: Geopolitics under Globalization. *Economic Perspectives*, *3*(1), 24–29.

Ali, M. M. (2020). Digitization of the emerging economy: An exploratory and explanatory case study. *Journal of Governance & Regulation*, *9*(4), 25–36. https://doi.org/10.22495/jgrv9i4art2

Amrith, S. S. (2013). *Crossing the Bay of Bengal: The furies of nature and the fortunes of migrants*. Harvard University Press.

Asia Regional Integration Center. (2021). *Tracking Asian Integration*. Retrieved from https://aric.adb.org/fta/india-bhutan-trade-agreement

Asian Development Bank. (2018). *Updating and Enhancement of the BIMSTEC Transport Infrastructure and Logistics Study*. Final report, July, p.32.

Attanayake, C. (2019). Sri Lankan perspective on the Bay of Bengal. *Journal of the Indian Ocean Region*, *15*(3), 356–362.

Awokuse, T. O. (2008). Trade openness and economic growth: Is growth export-led or import-led? *Applied Economics*, *40*(2), 161–173. doi:10.1080/00036840600749490

Bangladesh Bank. (2021a). *Import Data*. Retrieved from https://www.bb.org.bd/pub/annual/imppayment/imp1920/statable5.pdf

Bangladesh Bank. (2021b). *Export Data*. Retrieved from https://www.bb.org.bd/openpdf.php https://www.bb.org.bd/pub/annual/expreceipt/exp1920/index1920.php

Bhattacharya, S., & Bhattacharya, B. (2007). An empirical analysis on prospects and challenges of BIMSTEC-Japan trade integration. *Journal of Asian Economics*, *18*(3), 509–536.

Brewster, D. (2014). Dividing lines: Evolving mental maps of the Bay of. *Asian Security, 10*(02), 151–167. doi:10.1080/14799855.2014.914499

Brewster, D. (2015). The rise of the Bengal Tigers: The growing strategic importance of the Bay of Bengal. *Journal of Defense Studies, 09*(02), 81–104.

Chakravarty, P. R. (2021, February). COVID-19 and the changing geopolitical order: Changes to BIMSTEC. *Observer Research Foundation. Issue Brief,* (441), 1–10.

Cho, H., & Park, S-H. (2013). The Rise of China and Varying Sentiments in Southeast Asia toward Great Powers. *Strategic Studies Quarterly,* 69-92.

Das, P. (2018). Security Challenges and the Management of the India–Myanmar Border. *Strategic Analysis, 42*(6), 578–594.

Trading Economics. (2021). *Macroeconomic Indicators. Retrieved from Economic Indicators | List by Country.* tradingeconomics.com

Frost, E. L. (2017). *It's time to deepen integration around the Bay of Bengal.* Carnegie India.

Islam, A. M. (2021). Impact of Covid-19 pandemic on global output, employment and prices: An assessment. *Transnational Corporations Review, 13*(2), 189–201.

Kabir, M. (2015, July). Examining trade potential in BIMSTEC: A trade frontier approach. *BIISS Journal, 36*(3), 181–204.

Kaul, M. M. (2006). Regional Groupings: An Overview of BUMSTEC and MGC. *South Asian Survey, 13*(2), 313–322.

Kelegama, S. (2001). Bangkok agreement and BIMSTEC: Crawling regional economic grouping in Asia. *Journal of Asian Economics, 12*(1), 105–121.

Khan, Z. R. (2012). Ideology and internal Dynamics of South Asian Regional cooperation. In Regional Cooperation & Globalization (pp. 31-58). The University Press Limited.

Kumar, S. (2020). Reinvigoration of BIMSTEC and India's Economic, Strategic and Security Concerns. *Millennial Asia, 11*(2), 187–210. doi:10.1177/0976399620925441

Kundu, S. (2014). BIMSTEC at 17: An assessment of its potential. *Indian Quarterly. Journal of International Affairs, 70*(3), 207–224. https://doi.org/10.1177/0974928414535291

Maskorala, R. (2017). Development of Trincomalee Harbor as a Hub for Bay of Bengal region: Building a shipping Hub. In *Trincomalee consultations: Regional Cooperation for economic prosperity and maritime security in the Bay of Bengal* (pp. 72–80). Pathfinder Foundation.

Rahman, M. N., & Grewal, H. S. (2017). Foreign direct investment and international trade in BIMSTEC: Panel causality analysis. *Transnational Corporations Review, 9*(2), 112–121. doi:10.1080/19186444.2017.1326720

Schiff, M., & Winters, A. L. (2003). *Regional Integration and Development.* The World Bank.

Shan, J., & Sun, F. (1998). On The Export-led Growth Hypothesis: The Econometric Evidence from China. *International Journal of Economics and Finance, 1*(1), 341–351.

Shi, X., Yao, L., & Jiang, H. (2019). Regional power connectivity in Southeast Asia: the role of regional cooperation. *Global Energy Interconnection, 2*(1), 444-456.

Singh, M. (2005). *Prime Minister Dr. Manmohan Singh's Haksar Memorial Conference Speech*. Retrieved from http://www.indianembassy.org/press_release/2005/Nov/11.htm

The Economic Times. (2021). *BIMSTEC emerged as a promising regional grouping, says Prime Minister Modi*. Retrieved from https://economictimes.indiatimes.com/news/india/bimstec-emerged-as-a-promising-regional-grouping-says-prime-minister-modi/articleshow/83287601.cms?utm_source=

Dhaka Tribune. (2020, June 5). *23rd BIMSTEC Day: BIMSTEC leaders for joint efforts to combat Covid-19 impact*. Author.

United Nations. (2021). *The 17 Sustainable Development Goals*. Author.

World Bank. (2021a). *Bhutan Economic Profile*. Retrieved from https://www.worldbank.org/en/country/bhutan/overview

World Bank. (2021b). *Bangladesh Economic Profile*. Retrieved from https://www.worldbank.org/en/country/bangladesh/overview

World Bank. (2021c). *India Economic Profile*. Retrieved from https://www.worldbank.org/en/country/india

World Bank. (2021d). *Myanmar Economic Profile*. Retrieved from https://www.worldbank.org/en/country/myanmar/overview

World Bank. (2021e). *Sri Lanka Economic Profile*. Retrieved from https://www.worldbank.org/en/country/srilanka

World Bank. (2021f). *Nepal Economic Profile*. Retrieved from https://www.worldbank.org/en/country/nepal

World Bank. (2021g). *Thailand Economic Profile*. Retrieved from https://www.worldbank.org/en/country/thailand

Xavier, C. (2018). *Bridging The Bay of Bengal: Toward a stronger BIMSTEC*. Carnegie Endowment for International Peace.

Xavier, C., & Sinha, R. (2020). Regional Connectivity and India's BIMSTEC Policy. National Security. *Vivekananda International Foundation, III*(1), 34–51.

Yahya, F. (2005). BIMSTEC and emerging patterns of Asian regional and interregional cooperation. *Australian Journal of Political Science, 40*(3), 391–410. doi:10.1080/10361140500203936

ADDITIONAL READING

Rajapaksa, Y. (2018). *The Odyssey and living legacy of Sieur de La Norelle: The French Lieutenant of the Expedition Escadre de Perse to Ceylon in 1672*. Neptune Publication.

KEY TERMS AND DEFINITIONS

BIMSTEC: This is a regional body comprising of seven member countries along the areas of the Bay of Bengal.

Exports: Goods and services that are produced in Bangladesh such as garments and exported to rest of the world.

Foreign Direct Investment: Foreign direct investment is an investment made by a person, firm or a country in another country. For example, Thailand investing in Bangladesh infrastructure facilities.

Imports: Goods and services produced in other countries that are purchased from rest of the world, by the country's residents, rather than buying goods and services produced domestically.

Multilateral Trade Agreement: When three or more countries are signatories for doing trade with each other for which is agreement are specifying goods and services to be traded, imported, or exported, reduce tariff and non-tariff barriers, with the aim to have free trade agreements between signatory countries.

Regional Integration: Where two or more countries decide to cooperate in order to achieve cross-border trade, investment, peace, economic growth, prosperity, and stability for their economic region. The countries surrounding a region share their resources for economic development, political stability, growth, security, and peace within the region, with a possibility of economic and financial integration with a common institution.

Chapter 7
An Analysis of Tourism Opportunities and Challenges Post COVID-19 Between India and Southeast Asia

Munish Kumar Duggal
https://orcid.org/0000-0003-3588-6940
Independent Researcher, India

Harpreet Kaur
Central Queensland University, Australia

ABSTRACT

This chapter attempts economic analysis of the impact of COVID-19 on the economies of Southeast Asia and India. The impact on tourist footfalls, tourism revenues, national GDPs, and employment will be focused on. The challenges thrown by COVID-19 relating to safety, hygiene, mindshare, and digital tools could help evolve a structurally different tourism landscape in the post-COVID-19 world. Long haul travel may not happen soon, and the countries must develop products incorporating proximity tourism, vaccine tourism, and domestic tourism. Intra-ASEAN travel will have to be developed further to offset the losses caused by the curtailment of long-haul travel. Historical and cultural linkages between Southeast Asia and India should be leveraged to extend Intra-ASEAN travel to the Northeastern States of India. This would create a win-win situation for Southeast Asia as well as India. Targeted investments and subsidies aimed at confidence building of travelers and other stakeholders will go a long way to minimize the economic impact of external shock caused by COVID-19.

INTRODUCTION

The outbreak of the Coronavirus Disease 2019 (COVID-19) was declared a pandemic by the World Health Organization (WHO) on 11 March 2020 (ILO, 2020). Thereafter, COVID-19 spread quickly

DOI: 10.4018/978-1-7998-5774-7.ch007

through areas of China before spreading to other countries in Asia and the Pacific region and ultimately reaching global scale. The global spread of COVID-19 led to many lockdowns and restrictions which while affecting the flow of people across countries challenged the economies in umpteen ways.

Lockdown and restrictiveness is studied in detail by the *Oxford Coronavirus Government Response Tracker* (OxCGRT) project, which calculate a Stringency Index, a composite measure of nine of the response metrics. The nine metrics include: school closures; workplace closures; cancellation of public events; restrictions on public gatherings; closures of public transport; stay-at-home requirements; public information campaigns; restrictions on internal movements; and international travel controls.

The OxCGRT project also calculate a Containment and Health Index, a composite measure of thirteen of the response metrics. This index builds on the Stringency Index, using its nine indicators *plus* testing policy, the extent of contact tracing, requirements to wear face masks/coverings, and policies around vaccine rollout. Table 1 gives an overview of these indices for selected countries. It is clear that in June 2021 India, Vietnam and Philippines had imposed stringent lockdowns compared to Brunei, Thailand and Malaysia.

Table 1. Stringency Index and Containment and Health index

Country	Stringency Index		Containment & Health index	
	22 Jan 20	17 Jun 21	1 Jan 20	17 Jun 21
Brunei	11.11	40.74	3.57	50.71
Cambodia	0	66.2	0	
Indonesia	8.33	68.98	0	71.01
Laos, PDR	0	74.07	0	72.98
Malaysia	11.11	53.7	0	65.6
Myanmar	0	72.22	0	62.38
Philippines	0	71.76	0	73.63
Singapore	19.44	58.33	3.57	73.21
Thailand	0	53.7	0	52.38
Vietnam	0	77.31	0	71.25
India	0	81.94	0	79.92

Source: www.ourworldindiadata.org

This chapter is an attempt to analyze the challenges arising out of these lockdowns and restrictions along with responses of the governments from the viewpoint of impact on travel and tourism sectors in India and the South-East Asia. Given this background, the purpose of this chapter is threefold. First, it aims at pointing out the macro-economic impact of COVID-19 on the global economies. The analysis is mainly based on quantitative data on parameters like GDP, inbound/ outbound tourists, foreign exchange earnings from travel and tourism sectors. Second, it uses both quantitative and qualitative data to provide specific impact of COVID-19 on travel and tourism sectors of South-East Asia and India. To develop an understanding of impact on specific South-East Asian countries, country specific studies incorporating challenges and opportunities are also presented. Third, the chapter provides a detailed analysis of the policy responses to the disruptions and challenges to travel and tourism sectors in each country of South-East Asia, as well as India before arriving at recommendations and areas for future research.

Accordingly, this chapter is structured as follows. (i) Genesis and impact of COVID-19 on the global economies, economies of South-East Asia and India. (ii) the response of the government policies to restore balance between economic development and preventing loss of human lives in individual countries as well as at the level of ASEAN (iii) since COVID-19 is a non- linear event and its trajectory is evolving with emergence of different mutants, the policy prescriptions and recommendations for staying a step ahead of the virus are very important and are also discussed.

BACKGROUND

International Tourism and COVID-19

World destinations received 900 million fewer international tourists between January-October 2020 when compared with the same period of 2019, translating into a loss of US$ 935 billion in export revenues from international tourism. Note that International Tourist Arrivals (ITA) had reached a total of 1.5 billion in 2019 (Economic Survey, 2021).The fall of around 72 per cent in international tourist arrivals over the first ten months of 2020 were primarily due to restrictions on travel, low consumer confidence and a global struggle to contain the COVID-19 virus (Economic Survey, 2021). The fall in international tourist arrivals has carried on into 2021 and UNWTO expects international tourist arrivals to be down about 85 per cent in Q1 2021 over Q1 2020. This also represent a loss of some 180 million international arrivals when compared to pre-pandemic levels (UNWTO, 2021).

The beginning of 2021 instead of bringing relief to the global communities, saw worsening of the pandemic leading to a surge of cases fueled primarily by the emergence of new mutants of COVID-19. This forced most countries to reintroduce not only stricter travel restrictions, including mandatory testing, quarantines but in some cases a complete closure of borders. As a result, by 4th September 2021, the pandemic had affected 220,644,410 persons from 220 countries causing 4.57 million deaths. Apart from this enormous human cost, the pandemic has threatened the prospects of economic development in the World (WHO 2021).

According to World Travel and Tourism Council (WTTC) – a non-profit membership based organization, the travel & tourism sector suffered a loss of almost US$4.5 trillion in 2020, with the contribution to GDP dropping by a staggering 49.1 per cent compared to 2019. These losses are computed based on the actual data of 10.4 per cent contribution of travel and tourism sector to global GDP in 2019 - a share which decreased to 5.5 per cent in 2020 due to pandemic induced restrictions. In terms of employment, an estimated, 62 million jobs were lost in 2020, representing a drop of 18.6 per cent, leaving just 272 million employed across the sector globally, compared to 334 million in 2019 (WTTC, 2021). The threat of job losses persists in post-COVID scenario also as many jobs are currently supported by government welfare schemes and reduced hours, which without a full recovery of the sector could be lost. To arrest the pandemic induced slide in economies, there is an utmost urgency to focus on development of safe vaccines aimed at controlling the ill-effects of evolving variants of the Corona virus disease. Post –COVID scenario could also mean that people will have to learn to live with the Virus.

Currently, there are more than 1200 drugs and vaccines under various stages of development targeting the COVID-19 disease. Major pharmaceutical giants like *Sorrento Therapeutics*, *GlaxoSmithKline*, *and*

Immuno- Precise- Antibodies, Novartis, Roche, Zydus Cadila, Eli Lily, Pfizer and *Grifols* are engaged in the development of these drugs and vaccines. The speed at which these drugs and vaccines are developed, tested and deployed to limit or eliminate the spread effect of the COVID-19 will decide the extent of restoration of travel and tourism sector. This factor will also be the major determinant of the impact of COVID-19 induced decline in travel and tourism sector on the national incomes and employment.

DISCUSSION ON IMPACT OF COVID-19

Inbound Tourism: South-East Asia

Apart from the unique attractiveness of history, culture, and natural landscapes of South-East Asia, low-cost air transport, rising incomes, friendly visa regimes and targeted tourism investments have led to rapidly growing tourism sectors in these countries[1]. The number of visitor arrivals in the region increased significantly, from 37 million in 2005 to nearly 144 million in 2019[2] contributing almost $400 billion to the ASEAN economy in 2019.Pandemic related travel restrictions have led to declines in foreign visitor arrivals in 2020 ranging from about 50 per cent to 80 per cent, reaching nearly 100 per cent in some popular destinations (Mufti and Akhlas 2020).

Most of the inbound tourists in South-East Asia are from China, South Korea and Japan and growth of these economies is likely to affect tourist inflow as well as tourism revenue. As IMF estimates positive growth rates in these economies - China (8.4 per cent), South Korea (3.6 per cent) and Japan (3 per cent) - overall set back to travel and tourism sector in the South-East Asia may be limited (IMF, 2021). However, within the region, Thailand and Malaysia will be relatively more affected by the drop in tourist arrivals[3].

In the gloomy scenario of significant drop in international tourists, intra-ASEAN tourism flows have emerged as an important factor to offset fall in international arrivals. However, Intra-ASEAN tourism flows are unlikely to wipe out completely the losses caused by decline in international tourist flows.

Among various sub sectors of travel and tourism sector, airlines as well as hospitality sub sectors experienced major set- backs. Box 1 sums up the impact on these sub sectors for South-East Asian countries.

Box 1. Impact of Pandemic on the Airlines and hospitality sector

Airlines

- *Cathay Pacific*, the local carrier of Hong Kong having connectivity with almost all South-East Asian countries, was one of the first Asian airlines to ask its staff to take up to three weeks of unpaid leave to reduce costs. More than 25,000 employees, or 75 per cent staff members, complied (Rizzo, 2020).
- Singapore's *Jetstar Asia* also asked staff to take paid and unpaid leave, and also cancelled both annual bonuses and increments.
- *Singapore Airlines* asked its staff to take voluntary or compulsory unpaid leave. As part of Singapore Government's Stabilization and Support Package, 8,000 aviation workers were asked to take part in training initiatives.
- *Malaysia Airlines* offered its 13,000 employees the option of taking three months of unpaid leave (Syed, 2020).
- *PAL*, the Philippines' largest airline, laid off 300 workers in management and administration in February 2020[4].

Hospitality industry

- In Malaysia, 4 per cent of hotel industry workers had been laid off by March 2020, with more workers taking unpaid leave and pay cuts.
- In the tourist-rich Vietnamese city of *Da Nang*, about 23,000 of 35,000 tourism workers were forced to take temporary leave.

Inbound Tourism: India – 2015 to 2019

The tourism sector in India had been performing well with Foreign Tourist Arrivals (FTAs) growing at 14 per cent to reach 10.04 million and Foreign Exchange Earnings (FEEs) growing at 19.1 per cent to touch US$ 27.31 billion in 2017. However, the sector underwent a slowdown in 2018 and 2019 before declining sharply in 2020. The FTAs in 2019 stood at 10.93 million compared to 10.56 million in 2018. The growth rate of FTAs declined from 14 per cent in 2017 to 5.2 per cent in 2018 and further to 3.5 per cent in 2019. Foreign Exchange Earnings (FEEs) from tourism reached US$ 30.06 billion in 2019 compared to US$ 28.59 billion in 2018. The growth rate of FEEs declined from 19.1 per cent in 2017 to 4.7 per cent in 2018 before, picking up slightly to 5.1 per cent in 2019 (Economic Survey, 2021).

Table 2. Selected Indian Tourism Parameters: 2015 to 2019

Parameter	2015	2016	2017	2018	2019
FTAs to India (million)	8.03	8.80	10.04	10.56	10.93
ITAs* to India (million)	13.76	15.03	16.81	17.42	17.91
ITAs around the World (million)	1195	1241	*1333*	*1408*	*1460*
Share of India in World's ITA's (%)	1.15	1.21	1.26	1.24	1.23

* International Tourist Arrivals is the sum of Foreign Tourist Arrivals and NRI arrivals
Source: Economic Survey (Table 7, page 315), Ministry of Finance, Government of India, 2020-21

Table 3. Purpose wise Tourist Arrivals to India: 2019

Country	Tourist Arrivals	Purpose of Travel (%)				
	Numbers	Business *	Tourist **	Medical	Diaspora	Others
Indonesia	50177	19.8	59.2	0.45	3.91	16.63
Malaysia	334579	7.06	63.62	0.09	10.84	18.39
Myanmar	86842	5.45	82.28	4.47	1.11	6.68
Philippines	56393	19.76	30.74	0.55	3.08	45.88
Singapore	190089	14.4	30.17	0.03	17.25	38.15
Thailand	169956	10.17	71.9	0.02	2.12	15.79
Vietnam	33636	12.92	77.33	0.01	1.03	8.7
Others	8868	9.28	62.03	12.62	3.72	12.35
Total SE Asia	930540	10.67	58.29	0.64	8.38	22.02
Total India	10930355	14.69	57.06	6.38	12.67	9.2

*Business &Professional
**Leisure, Holiday, and Recreation
Source: Indian Tourism Statistics (2020), Ministry of Tourism, Government of India

India accounts for 1.23 per cent of world's international tourist arrivals and this share appears to have remained constant in the past four years (Table 2).

Top ten countries contributing to inbound tourists in India are - Bangladesh, USA, UK, Australia, Canada, China, Malaysia, Sri Lanka, Germany and Russia. These countries accounted for 67 per cent of the total foreign tourist arrivals in 2019. Among the foreign tourists, 57.1 per cent visitors visited for leisure, holiday and recreation, 14.7 per cent for business, and 12.7 per cent was Indian diaspora (India Tourism Statistics, 2020) (Table 3).

Mode of transport and gender of visitors from South-East Asia to India for 2019 is in Table 4.

Table 4. Mode of Transport used by Tourists from Southeast Asia-2019

Country	Tourist Arrivals			Mode of Transport (% share)			
	Numbers	Male (%)	Female (%)	Air	Sea	Rail	Road
Indonesia	50177	54	46	95.23	3.01	0.02	1.75
Malaysia	334579	51.2	48.8	98.97	0.59	0	0.44
Myanmar	86842	42.3	57.7	63.76	1.24	0	35
Philippines	56393	45	55	84.88	15.03	0	0.08
Singapore	190089	57	43	99.64	0.14	0	0.21
Thailand	169956	40.4	59.6	84.98	0.69	0	14.34
Vietnam	33636	41.8	58.2	78.81	2.42	0	18.77
Others	8868	55.3	44.7	86.43	0.06	0	13.51
Total	**930540**	**49.1**	**50.9**	**91.36**	**1.64**	**0**	**6.99**

Source: Indian Tourism Statistics (2020), Ministry of Tourism, Government of India

Inbound Tourism: India – Post COVID-19

Based on the data presented in the previous section, it is clear that tourism sector makes a significant contribution to India's GDP and FEE. However, the COVID-19 pandemic has had a debilitating impact on all contact-based services including travel and tourism sector. During H1 2020-21, the services sector contracted by almost 16 per cent (Economic Survey, 2021). Air passenger traffic, rail freight traffic, port traffic, foreign tourist arrivals, and foreign exchange earnings all contracted sharply following the first lockdown in March 2020. Airlines were allowed to resume domestic operations from late May in a calibrated manner. Domestic air passenger traffic has shown a gradual recovery since August, although travel remains muted as compared to 2019. During April to December 2020, the number of domestic passenger traffic was 30.0 million compared to 100.8 million during April to December 2019. During March 2021, all Indian airports taken together handled 161.25 thousand aircraft movements, 17.08 million passengers and 271.20 thousand MT of freight (MOCAA, April 2021). Average daily flights as well passengers have shown sustained rise during June 2021 owing to relaxation in restrictions (Kundu, 2021).

The international traffic reduced from 52.1 million during April-December 2019 to only 55.9 lakhs during April-December 2020[5].

The financial losses of Indian carriers and airports during April-December 2020 is approximately INR 16,000 crore and INR 3,000 crore respectively. The loss in domestic as well as international traffic is also reflected in the FEEs. For example, earnings from tourism declined to US$ 6.16 billion during H1 2020 as compared to US$ 14.19 billion during H1 2019. Later, a massive operation called *Vande Bharat Mission* was launched to repatriate Indians stranded abroad after the breakout of the COVID-19 pandemic and the resultant lockdowns across the world (May 2020)[6]. Under this Mission, the government established *Transport Bubbles* with 27 countries to repatriate its citizens. As of August 2, 2021, travel of over 3.8 million people were facilitated under the *Mission.* Box 2 provides a glimpse of the losses suffered by individual industry players in India.

Box 2. Effect of pandemic on Travel &Tourism sector in India

o Before the pandemic, Delhi airport used to handle 1,500 daily flights but in May 2021 it came down to 325 daily flights. Average daily passenger traffic has also fallen from 1.15 lakh in February 2021 to 30,000 in May 2021.
o The hotel chain *Treebo* implemented a pay cut of its senior management of up to 40 per cent and launched a paid voluntary resignation scheme for its 400 employees.
o The hotel chain *Oyo* cut 5,000 jobs as of April 15, 2021.
o Hyatt regency Mumbai suspended operations on June 7, 2021, due to cash crunch to continue operations and meet the staff salary costs. This happened at a time when, *Maharashtra* state where it is located was relaxing lockdown conditions post second wave (Sarkar, 2021).
o The COVID-ravaged hospitality sector could soon see big M& As with several stressed owners wanting to exit the business by selling assets to big players (Sinha, 2021).
o *Indigo* airline –the largest private carrier in India asked its employees to take leave without pay ranging from 1.5 to 4 days every month (Sarkar, 2021). This was primarily aimed at reducing losses of *Air India* and *Indigo airlines* which are expected to lose around US$ 4.5 billion during FY 2021 and FY 2022.
o *GoFirst* airline announced pay cut of around 16 per cent impacting 800 employees starting May 2021. This will be the second pay cut in the past 2 years (Sarkar, 2021)
o Drop in the air traffic forced *SpiceJet* Airline to adopt the policy of payment to staff as per hours worked and deferment of salary up to 35 per cent (Sarkar, 2021).
o Domestic airline *Spicejet* undeterred by the drop in air traffic focused on cargo movement which made a significant contribution to its financials in FY2021. The airline carried the highest volume of cargo and neutralized a significant proportion of loss of revenue from passenger traffic. *Spicejet* is the only Indian passenger airline that has dedicated freighters in its fleet.
o APP based cab companies- *Ola* and *Uber* too felt the impact of second Corona wave but the impact was lower compared to the first wave. Whereas *Uber* fired 14 per cent of its employees globally, including 600 in India, in May 2020, the same month *Ola* fired a third of its staff (Malik, 2021).

With the ongoing vaccination drive and massive efforts aimed at ramping up medical infrastructure to cope with the third wave of COVID-19, the contact intensive service sectors may show signs of revival from H2 2021-22.

Policy Response: South-East Asia

Not all economies in South-East Asia or India depend on tourism to the same extent. The Tourism Satellite Accounts (OECD 2001, 2008) established a methodology to measure the economic importance of tourism by calculating inbound tourism expenditure as a percentage of GDP.

Thailand and Cambodia have contribution of travel and tourism sector to their national GDP exceeding 10 per cent making them *highly tourism dependent*. Obviously, pandemic induced set back to travel and tourism is expected to give a big shock to economic development in these countries. Malaysia and Singapore, on the other hand, have travel and tourism sector contribution in the range of 5 to 10 per cent and these economies have, therefore, been categorized as *tourism dependent economies*. Laos,

Vietnam and Philippines with contribution in the range of 2.5 per cent to 5 per cent are economies with *major tourism sector* and they are less likely to be adversely affected by the disruption to the travel and tourism sector. Brunei, Myanmar and Indonesia are regarded as economies with *minor tourism* as the contribution of their travel and tourism sector to national GDP is less than 2.5 per cent (ADB, 2020).

The COVID-19 ASEAN Response Fund

Despite differing responses to the challenges posed by COVID-19 to the travel and tourism sector, ASEAN Leaders proactively agreed to establish the COVID-19 ASEAN Response Fund (Fund) to address post-COVID-19 goals of ASEAN countries. The Fund shall serve as a pool of resources to provide support in the detection, control and prevention of COVID-19 transmission and in protecting the safety of medical professionals, healthcare workers, frontline workers, and the wider population of ASEAN Members (ASEAN, 2020).

The Fund aims at procuring necessary medical supplies and equipment which may include test kits/diagnostic tools, personal protective equipment, including medicines and vaccines, other medical supplies and equipment for diagnostic and treatment procedures. The Fund shall also support cooperation in R&D relevant to COVID-19, including research on virology, and other relevant studies, or research relevant to the development of medical treatments and preventive vaccines; technical support in the planning and implementation of containment measures; sharing of best practices; as well as capacity - building of health professionals and frontline workers.

The Fund was established by an initial contribution of 10 per cent from the ASEAN Development Fund. Singapore announced a contribution $100,000 in November 2020. Vietnam donated $5 million worth of health equipment to ASEAN's regional reserves and contributed $100,000 to the Fund. India also announced $1 million aid at the 17th ASEAN-India Summit (Choudhry, 2020).

Having summarized the regional response to COVID-19, in what follows, an attempt is made to provide country-specific insights on policy responses to the challenges posed by "pandemic induced restrictions" to the travel industry.

Policy Response: Indonesia

Indonesia - the largest country in the region has 4.11 million COVID-19 cases (4 September 2021) - the highest number in South-East Asia. Its tourism sector has taken a battering as the country closed its borders to most overseas arrivals starting March 2020. FTAs were down 75 per cent during 2020, with occupancy at star hotels averaging 41 per cent in December, a 20 per cent drop from 2019.

To avoid major setback to economy, the government announced measures to re-stimulate tourism by focusing on ten domestic destinations by making them eligible for financial subsidies under its aid package. The aid package was a combination of tax holiday and cost saving measures. Among other initiatives, the package provided for dedicated funds to subsidize domestic airfares for selected destinations by 30 per cent from March to May 2020. During the same period, jet-fuel prices and airport charges were lowered at selected airports. For six months, the government would subsidize the taxes owed to regional governments by restaurants and hotels located in those ten destinations (ASEAN BRIEFING 2020).

Private hotels in Indonesia proactively introduced a "*pay now, stay later*" system during the pandemic, allowing people to pay room charges in advance at a discounted price for post-COVID-19 stay. This was a novel way of meeting their capital needs and seeking advance commitments of the tourists. The program has been extended until 2022.

It is, thus, clear that alarmed by the forecasts of economic contraction, the policy action by the Indonesian government appears to be away from the lockdown and towards opening of the economy. The government is bucking the global trend of providing vaccines to senior citizens first, and instead opting to vaccinate the younger, working-age population. Despite serious financial crunch, country has already announced free vaccines to all citizens and has taken timely initiatives in securing doses. However, Indonesia faces challenges in terms of terrain, storage, refrigeration, logistics, bureaucratic inertia and corruption. After becoming the first country outside of China to approve the *Sinovac* vaccine, Indonesia began its vaccination program in January 2021. However questions have been raised about the efficacy of Chinese Vaccine –*Sinovac* as more than 350 doctors and medical workers caught COVID-19 despite being vaccinated with *Sinovac*.[7] To assist Indonesia, the World Bank approved a loan of US$500 million to strengthen the preparedness of its health system and support free vaccination program. The World Bank also supported in expanding capacity for patient isolation, increasing the availability of critical care beds, scaling-up testing capacity, and strengthening public risk communications, surveillance and pandemic preparedness (ETHealthWorld, 2021).

Policy Response: Singapore

While Singapore initially managed to contain the virus through widespread testing, contact tracing, and mandatory, well-enforced quarantines, a sharp increase in cases in December 2020 linked to foreign workers' dormitories alerted the government. It has since flattened the curve with the help of an innovative contact tracing mobile app and token system called "trace together" (www.tracetogether.gov.sg). Restrictions over public gatherings were relaxed in a calibrated manner before reopening in end 2020. Meanwhile, the government has permitted economic activities through "green lane" and "travel corridors" with its neighbors for essential and business travel, although a recent global spike in cases has raised questions about timing of such policies.

These "green lane" and "travel corridors" have been opened along with strong policies aimed at providing economic and regulatory incentives to the travel industry. These policies have also focused on confidence-building and providing subsidies. Specifically, the relief package includes tax rebates and financial breaks for businesses and households with a special focus on tourism, aviation, retail, food services and point-to-point transport services. Important tax rebates include: Property tax rebates of 30 per cent for hotels and meeting venues, 15 per cent for international cruise and ferry terminals, 10 per cent for casinos, and 15 per cent for *Changi* Airport which will also get additional rebates on aircraft landing and parking charges, and rental rebates for shops and cargo agents. Taxi drivers and privately-hired drivers receive financial assistance of SG$ 20 per car per day for three months. To build confidence, the government is providing support for professional environmental cleaning and disinfection costs for hotels which provide accommodation for COVID-19 cases. Singapore also created a "*Clean Certification*" system to provide assurance to locals and visitors on cleanliness of tourism venues and facilities implementing rigorous preventive measures.

Among other measures to support the sector, Singapore also waived the license fee for STB-licensed hotels, travel agents, and tourist guides for 2020; reduced by 50 per cent the industry participation fees for STB-led tradeshows; provided salary support of up to 70 per cent of fixed monthly salaries; provided licensed self-employed tourist guides with wage support of $1,000 to assist with living expenses; Thus it is clear that the policy response has been aimed at funding to engage customers and maintain mindshare, providing wage support to the affected workers, organizing online training to up skill the workers for ensuring higher levels of hygiene and deploying tools to accelerate digital transformation.

Policy Response: Thailand

The first confirmed case of Covid-19 outside China was reported on January 13, 2020, in Thailand[8]. COVID-19 cases remained low until March 2020 when the country began to see widespread community spread. Since then, Thailand has done relatively well in combating the coronavirus crisis with quick contact tracing and lockdowns. These measures coupled with a reasonably endowed healthcare system, and practice of mask-wearing explain how Thailand could stand up to the challenges of the pandemic during the first wave in early 2020.

Apart from enforcing lockdown, the government offered 1,000 THB each to 5 million local travelers via a mobile app to buy tour packages to areas outside their home province with the condition of minimum one night stay. The government also launched *"We Travel Together"* program in July 2020 to revive the moribund tourism industry. *Thai* tourists had to pay 60 per cent of normal room rates, with the government subsidizing the rest. The government also covered 40 per cent of the cost of air tickets and allocated 22.4 billion THB for this program in 2020. Hotels added their own discounts to attract more domestic guests despite the extra cost of hygiene.

Given the fact that travel and tourism sector contribute about 20 per cent to its national GDP, major set- backs to travel and tourism could wreak economic havoc on the Thailand economy. Accordingly, the response of the government to protect these sectors and prevent major set- back to its economy was quick as well as comprehensive during both the waves'. The second wave of the coronavirus, which swept through Thailand in mid-December 2020, discouraged people from traveling, and the government / companies were stopped from carrying out promotional events involving crowds. The *Bangkok Metropolitan Administration* decided not to host "Lunar New Year" celebrations and instead spent resources on projects to develop the capacity of entrepreneurs and personnel engaged in tourism. Thailand was hit by a new wave of infections in April 2021 tied to bars and nightlife spots in Bangkok, which had spread to 62 out of 77 provinces. As a result, Thailand lost about $50 billion in tourism revenue in 2020 when foreign arrivals plunged 83 per cent to 6.7 million, from a record 39.9 million in 2019 (Wiriyapong, 2021). The slump was attributed to global travel curbs and tough entry requirements. Phuket was particularly hard hit by job losses and business closures.

A poll in May 2021 a steep rise in *"vaccine hesitancy"* among the Thai public, with the proportion of people willing to take the vaccine falling to 63 percent from 83 percent in January 2021. This drop-off in vaccine confidence appears to largely stem from the perception that the government's handling of the vaccine rollout has been disorganized as well as from a perceived overreliance on *AstraZeneca* and *Sinovac* rather than *Pfizer* and *Moderna*.

"Phuket Sandbox" initiative has been announced from July 1, 2021, which will allow free movement on the island for fully vaccinated tourists, with no self-isolation on arrival. They will be allowed to travel elsewhere in Thailand after 14 days.

The success of "Phuket Sandbox" will decide the trajectory of opening up of tourist hot spots in the region (Wiriyapong, 2021).

Policy Response: Malaysia

Malaysia attracts tourists from its neighbors and allies from the ASEAN region. For 2019 tourism landscape was dominated by Singapore (10,163,882 tourists) followed by Indonesia (3,623,277), China (3,114,257), Thailand (1,884,306), Brunei (1,216,123), India (735,309), South Korea (673,065), Japan (424,694), Philippines (421,908) and Vietnam (400,346). In terms of overall tourist expenditure, the ASEAN region was at top contributing RM 43.72 billion (USD $10.2 billion) in 2019.

The country was implementing '*Visit Truly Asia Malaysia 2020*' campaign to take its foreign tourist numbers to 30 million when it was hit by COVID-19 in early 2020. The lockdown affected tourist flows as well as revenues posing a serious threat to its economic development which, in turn, forced the government to formulate a comprehensive action plan and convert pandemic challenges into opportunities. Malaysia Tourism has short, medium and long-term plans for recovery and revival of tourism.

For short-term recovery plan/quick wins, *Tourism Malaysia* plans to organize public relation activities / social media promotion to boost domestic tourism. It will also intensify the promotion of '*Cuti-Cuti Malaysia*' and '*Malaysia Truly Asia*' campaigns. Individuals are offered income tax relief worth RM1,000 for expenses at registered tourist attractions and accommodations.

Malaysia also approved a range of measures, including a US$ 43 million micro-credit scheme for small businesses in the tourism industry and six-month tax deferment for travel agencies, hotels, airlines and other tourism enterprises starting April 2020. Hotels were also exempted from service tax from March until August 2020 (ASEANBRIEFING, 2020).

In the medium-term, *Tourism Malaysia* plans to engage online collaboration with corporate companies as part of its domestic plan to boost local tourism. This includes launching of several e-travel platforms such as e-Consumer Travel/Trade Fair, e-Malaysia Tourism Travel Bazaar and e-Corporate Travel Bazaar that is targeted for meetings, incentives, conferences and exhibitions (MICE) industry. Cross border tourism with neighboring countries including Singapore, Thailand, Brunei and Indonesia, is also a part of medium-term agenda as they accounted for largest market share in inbound travel of around 68 per cent in 2019.

The long-term strategies include building strategic alliances in smart tourism by optimizing e-marketing and e-promotion via digitalization with active use of big data analytics.

Policy Response: Philippines

With close to 2.04 million *COVID-19 cases, the Philippines* has second highest number of cases in South-East Asia next to Indonesia.[9] In the Philippines, the major airports were closed from March 20, 2020, as part of the Enhanced Community Quarantine (ECQ) which started in the island on 16 March 2020. In other countries, barriers to travel had been imposed in January 2020 adversely impacting the Philippine international tourist arrivals. Domestic tourists, on the other hand, also limited their travel for fear of contracting COVID-19 as well as curtailed availability of transport. As a result of fall in inbound tourism, international tourist receipts in Q1 2020 were estimated to be 36 per cent lower than in Q1 2019. The macro impact of the economic lockdown was reflected in 9.6 percent decline in GDP in 2020 biggest setback to economic development in the South-East Asian region.

In order to assist businesses/ individuals meet the challenges posed by COVID-19, it approved Philippine Economic Stimulus Act (PESA) in June 2020. Under the law, an economic stimulus package amounting to PHP1.3 trillion will be provided in the next four years to fund the COVID-19 testing, wage subsidies, and assistance to MSMEs (Asiaasset, 2020). Under this package, PHP58 bn are given to accredited tourism enterprises for the following programs:

- Interest-free loans or issuance of loan guarantees with terms of up to five years for maintenance and operating expenses
- Credit facilities for upgrading, rehabilitation, or modernization of businesses to be compliant with new health and safety standards
- Marketing and product development promotions
- Grants for education training, and advising of tourism stakeholders for new normal alternative livelihood programs
- Utilization of information technology
- Other relevant programs, including infrastructure to mitigate the economic effects of COVID-19 on the tourism industry

Earlier in 2020, the Philippines government invested $8.5 million in a domestic tourism campaign and reaped benefits (Talavera 2020). However, the detailed outcome of these measures on the revival of travel and tourism sector or on economic development of the country is not yet known.

Policy Response: Brunei

Brunei is a small country with low population, and it shares borders with Malaysia. The country with 3039 COVID-19 cases is a great success story in the region. It has already started opening travel with other countries in South-East Asia. Given the low population density as well as the COVID-19 cases, schools and places of worship were opened in July, followed by businesses and restaurants in end-2020. The success can be attributed to its quick and drastic restrictions on travel, extensive testing, and strict quarantine rules. Brunei appears to be on track to vaccinate 70 percent of its 4, 33000 citizens by end 2021. As travel and tourism constitute a very small proportion of GDP (less than 2 per cent), no special policies have been announced to protect it from the COVID -19 induced travel restrictions.

Policy Response: Cambodia

Cambodia reported 94417 COVID-19 cases and 1937 deaths by September 4, 2021, despite weak health infrastructure and slow policy response. A possible cause of low cases could be low population density and sharing international borders with Vietnam, Laos, and Thailand, all of which controlled the virus relatively well during 2020. In H2 2020, the government implemented plans to revive the economy through calibrated opening up strategies. However, after an outbreak caused by imported cases in late November and fear of possible community spread, the country reverted to movement restrictions. Imported cases rose again in January 2021as migrant workers returned from Thailand due to an outbreak there, which the government quickly addressed. However, a new wave of community transmissions struck in late February 2021 which has not yet peaked (Chorn *et al*, 2021). Lockdowns in April 2021 precipitated a food and inflation crisis. The government has recently turned attention to securing vaccine doses and distribute them free to all citizens.

Policy Response: Laos

Laos, the most rural country in South-East Asia, was also the last to report its first COVID-19 casualty. Laos managed to avoid an outbreak for more than a year, owing in part to its sparse population and location among neighbors who had successfully contained the virus. But the rate of new cases began accelerating in April 2021 taking the case load to 15605 on 4 September 2021. The case load, though small, could severely test the country's underdeveloped healthcare system. In an effort to boost its economy, Laos has already resumed travel with several countries in South-East Asia. First COVID-19 death was reported in Laos on May 9, 2021, over a year into the pandemic.

Policy Response: Myanmar

Myanmar had lowest COVID-19 case load in the region until August 2020. After that, the rate of infections accelerated to reach 409509 cases on 4 September 2021 (Worldometer, 2021). These cases were first detected in the *Rakhine* state and the cases increased later due to national elections on November 8, 2020. The country's underdeveloped healthcare system was over stretched and impeded its ability to cope as new daily case- load reached 1,000 per day. The cash assistance scheme was announced but created controversies over allegations of nepotism and leakages. The military coup in February 2021 is complicating the country's response to COVID-19, as many frontline healthcare workers have joined thousands of citizens to protest against the military rule. Although the government announced continuation of vaccination drive, testing has been suspended, hospital systems have become, and the government has effectively given up on addressing the challenges.

Policy Response: Vietnam

Vietnam has been the region's biggest success story in containment of COVID-19 and minimizing the economic losses. Despite limited resources and a long border with China, Vietnam initially managed to contain the pandemic by halting travel with China early, deploying epidemic control teams to implement a massive test-and-trace regime, and committing to data transparency. Vietnam used lessons learnt from SARS and avian influenza and made timely policy interventions in terms of early action on various fronts including border closures, masking, testing and lockdowns. Vietnam issued national guidelines for Infection Prevention and Control for COVID-19 on February 19, 2020. Life had returned to normal until a second wave spread from the city of *Da Nang* at the end of July. A holistic approach based on engagement with multi-sectoral stakeholders in decision-making processes led to pragmatic policies on quarantines based on possible exposure, rather than symptoms only. With the exception of the *Da Nang* outbreak in August, Vietnam has managed, more or less, to prevent community transmission for a full year while keeping the economy open enough to facilitate a resilient economy with positive GDP growth.

Policy Response: India

In order to minimize the impact of COVID-19 on travel and tourism sector and to keep the sector in sound economic health, the following steps have been undertaken (MOCAB, 2021, MOCAC 2021).

- Domestic air services restarted on 25 May 2020 in a calibrated manner

- Operation of Regional Connectivity Scheme (RCS) - *UDAN (Ude Desh Ka Aam Nagrik)* flights allowed without restrictions
- Established exclusive air-links or Air Bubbles with 27 countries. In addition, international repatriation flights are being operated on many sectors under *"Vande Bharat Mission"*
- Goods and Services Tax (GST) rate reduced to 5 per cent for domestic Maintenance, Repair and Overhaul (MRO) services
- Enabled re-export of leased aircraft in fully or partly knocked-down condition for value realization of serviceable parts
- Encouraged Indian carriers to increase their share in international air cargo traffic
- Adequate care taken to ensure that cargo terminals at airports operated with due safety

Apart from these policies, the government announced Emergency Credit Line Guarantee Scheme (ECLGS) in May 2020 to provide credit guarantees to all MSME sectors affected by COVID- 19. The scheme is extended to cover civil aviation sector and is valid till end- September 2021 or till the INR 3 lakh crore outlay gets exhausted. Airlines and airport operators are expected to benefit through liquidity support amid constrained cash generation ability due to prolonged localized lockdowns. The loan will have 4 year tenure with 12-month moratorium[10]. Under *Atmanirbhar Bharat* package, provident fund contribution of both employer and employee has been reduced to 10 per cent each from existing 12 per cent each for all establishments covered by EPFO up to September 2020. In addition, the government gave relief from various regulatory compliances under Income Tax Act, Companies Act and GST Act for varying periods to ensure business continuity and survival. Earlier, RBI (the Central Bank) extended timelines of moratorium on term loans (MOCAC, 2021).

In addition to measures aimed at enhancing the flow of funds to the sectors facing financial challenges, many other steps have been taken by the Ministry of Tourism[11]. These include (i) evolving operational guidelines for COVID-19 safety and hygiene for hotels, restaurants, tourism service providers to facilitate smooth resumption of business, (ii) extending validity of approval or certifications of hotels and other accommodation units whose project approval were likely to expire, (iii) taking new initiative called SAATHI (System for Assessment, Awareness &Training for Hospitality Industry), for effective implementation of COVID-19 guidelines/SOPs for safe operations of hotels.

The stimulus package for MSME borrowers under ECLGS scheme and other policies mentioned above are expected to provide much-needed liquidity support to tide over the ongoing volatility in the business environment.

RECOMMENDATIONS AND DISCUSSIONS

India Specific

- Given the huge proportion of Indian diaspora constituting about 40 per cent of total inbound international arrivals, Indian tourism policies must facilitate travel of diaspora through strengthening digital platforms and incentivizing travel through tax breaks and subsidies. Thirty million strong Indian diaspora spread in all continents must be used as a "Pull factor" to restore travel and bridge the possible "tourism deficit" in post-COVID-19 scenario.

- Just like "vaccine diplomacy", "medical tourism diplomacy" should find an important place in post COVID-19 recovery strategies. In the Indian context while leisure travellers may not return to Indian places of tourist interest in the short term due to fault-lines in public health infrastructure exposed during the second wave, those waiting for medical treatments abroad especially in African countries could still be attracted to travel to India due to low-cost treatments and proven remote monitoring of already treated patients through the existing digital platforms.
- Indian Industry and trade bodies have suggested setting up of *Permanent Crisis Management Task Forces* to formulate appropriate, cost effective, livelihood-oriented interventions which prepare stakeholders to respond to the challenges posed by COVID-19. While such arrangements already exist, they need to be institutionalized by ensuring representations to all stakeholders including health experts, policy makers and business associations.

RECOMMENDATIONS

- As the COVID-19 virus and its existing variants spread through human-to-human contact, there is a clear trade- off between lockdowns and economic development. Indonesia realized this trade-off early and preferred economic activities by saying no to complete lockdown ensuring smaller GDP shock compared to India which went in for a complete lockdown during the first wave starting March 2020 leading to a huge contraction of 7.3 per cent GDP in FY 20. In the second wave, however, both countries moderated these extreme policies, the positive effects of which will be reaped during FY 2022.
- The multiple policy responses in South-East Asia and India have brought home the centrality of human beings and their livelihoods as the *raison de etre* of economic development and the importance of filling the gaps in provision and delivery of public health in all countries irrespective of their levels of economic development.
- An analysis of the flow of intra-regional tourists in South-East Asia reveals that in 2019, 44.3 million tourists traveled within the ASEAN countries, but COVID-19 caused 36.9 per cent year-over-year decrease in intra-regional travel in 2020 to a low of 27.9 million arrivals. (Global Data, 2021). Despite such decline owing entirely to COVID-19, intra-regional focus on tourism could be a silver lining for the region.
- Intra-regional tourism flows through bilateral / regional travel bubbles can improve tourism activity especially to short-haul destinations which in turn, can protect not only the enterprises but also incomes and jobs of those employed in these sectors. As India already has political, economic and cultural capital with the ASEAN countries, the same should be leveraged to start travel bubble with them.
- Other factors which may promote short-haul travel against long-haul travel in post recovery scenario include fear of travel, COVID fatigue, low propensity to spend caused by incomes loss during the pandemic and uncertainty about safety and hygiene practiced by far off and culturally unrelated countries.
- During periods of low disposable incomes, value of money offered by Low-Cost Carriers (LCCs), makes them better positioned to meet the short haul travel in post recovery scenario. India and

South-East Asia already have good aviation connectivity as more than 13 airlines including LCCs like *Air Asia* and *Malindo Air*, operated on these routes in pre pandemic era and restoration of demand post- COVID-19 appears feasible.

- Trajectory of revival of contact-based services such as tourism will depend on (i) timing and speed of emergence/spread of especially those mutants of COVID-19 which have high transmissibility, or which can cause high human mortality and (ii) the extent of vaccination and the effectiveness of vaccines on the emerging mutants. Besides, the policy message should be to live with the virus with full precautions with masks, hand hygiene.
- In most countries studied in this chapter more than three in four workers in the tourism sector are in informal jobs, leaving them especially vulnerable to the negative impacts of the COVID-19 crisis. Informal sector jobs are characterized by a lack of basic economic and social protection. These workers typically do not have the option to work remotely, and therefore have a heightened risk of infection and job losses. These informal workers must have "dedicated stimulus packages" and policy interventions for ensuring equity as well as sustainable economic activities.
- A large number of non – contact-based services and businesses whose business/production processes could migrate to working from home (WFH) format discovered the potential of digital platforms during lockdowns. The benefits of WFH include: reduction in capital and operational costs resulting in lesser commercial rentals, lesser office expenses and smaller travel costs and savings in travel times of employees. However, WFH modules are likely to depress the demand for long-haul meetings, incentives, conferences and events tourism (OECD 2020). Clearly, the importance of MICE in overall tourism landscape may reduce and tourism revival strategies must incorporate this important structural change.

BEST PRACTICES

- The policy response of Government of Singapore has demonstrated certain good practices in (i) monitoring the movement of quarantined citizens through IT application called "tracing together". Simple to understand idea of introducing "Cleaning Certifications" for the hotels and others providing hospitality services to ensure safety, hygiene and build consumer confidence to restore demand in the battered travel related services needs emulation by others.
- *Spicejet* airline in India, undeterred by the significant declines in passenger traffic seamlessly adapted to the COVID-19 challenges and transformed its business model to handle cargo traffic and making up for the losses from decline in passenger traffic. Learning from best practice of *Spicejet*, another Indian airline – *Indigo* is also thinking of diversifying business to increase its share in the cargo segment. This adaptive and innovative conversion of drop in passenger traffic revenues to cargo traffic windfall gains is not only reducing insolvency risk of these airlines but also protecting livelihoods of their staff.
- Policy frameworks must ensure that during the crisis created by the non- linear events such as COVID-19, corporate entities use their Corporate Social Responsibility (CSR) funds in a coordinated manner to ensure optimum use of resources and lessen the pressure on the public authorities. For example, if the corporates decide to bear full cost of vaccination of their staff, the financial

burden on the public health authorities could be reduced. This awareness among the Corporates is fast emerging in India.

FUTURE RESEARCH DIRECTIONS

- While the immediate response of the ASEAN to set up ASEAN Response Fund is laudable, not much is known about interventions made by the Fund and their outcomes. This must be researched, and any such regional initiatives must be suitably articulated through a communication strategy so that wider community can take advantages and also give suggestions for its fine tuning and possible mid-course corrections.
- *"Vaccine hesitancy"* emanating from lack of education, "message dilution" owing to religious factors, inappropriate political messaging such as in India, Indonesia and the Philippines has adversely affected the universalization of vaccines in the countries which require them the most. Sharp and targeted public awareness campaigns and timely interventions at national and regional levels should be formulated in a cost-effective manner.
- COVID-19 has created perceptions about the "new normal" livelihood patterns which, inter alia, means "living with the virus" and future research must focus on how to make diverse communities adapt to "new normal" in a least disruptive manner.
- Challenges of COVID-19 in terms of COVID fatigue, WFH, decline in disposable incomes owing to wage cuts or job losses leading to low propensity to spend, non- availabilities of many essential commodities, have to be accepted and converted into opportunities.

CONCLUSION

The spread of COVID-19 forced countries to announce lockdowns and impose restrictions on movement of people. As a result travel and tourism eco-system in India and South – East Asia faced serious challenges during most part of 2020 and situation, though improving, is continuing in the second half of 2021.

In the context of travel and tourism flows between India and South-East Asia, it has been empirically established that the extent of inbound tourism from South-East Asia to India is about one-fourth of the outbound tourist traffic from India to South-East Asia. This clearly means that the contribution of Indian tourists to the economies of South-East Asia is much more than the other way around. At the same time, due to historical and cultural factors South-East Asia has fascination for and connections with Indian (including North-Eastern) culture, food and holistic Indian way of healthcare including *Ayurveda* and *Yoga.* Indian policy interventions should try to translate this passion into attracting tourists and visitors. Leveraging of India's strengths such as promoting and deepening cultural links through promotion of *international Buddhist circuit* will also enhance the "soft power" of India.

In order to compensate for the loss of tourists, South-East Asia appears to have a window of opportunity from extending intra-ASEAN travel to selected Indian destinations through the North-East. India, on the other hand, like many other countries can promote domestic tourism which is not only compatible with low disposable incomes and low propensities to spend but also with low confidence to travel long distances. So with suitable positioning and communication strategies, domestic tourism may be easy to revive and could be used to kick start recovery in a post-COVID scenario.

The continuation of COVID-19 for the past 16 months and the fear of more transmissible mutants of COVID-19 is transforming the lives of people to a new "normal" style of health and hygiene oriented living styles based on social distancing. The relative speeds of emergence of new mutants and vaccine deployment, a gradual improvement of the epidemiological situation, continued government support to ensure survival of households and businesses through economic, financial and regulatory measures, a significant improvement in traveler confidence through reduction in COVID-19 fatigue, a major reduction in barriers to travel and monetization of India's cultural capital and its spiritual connect with South-East Asia will be the major drivers of economic and social development in the post COVID- 19 world.

REFERENCES

ADB. (2020). Asian Development Bank. *Policy Brief*, (150), 2–4.

ASEAN. (2020). Retrieved from https://asean.org/storage/53-Finalised-and-APPROVED-TOR_COVID-19-ASEAN-Response-Fund.pdf

ASEANBRIEFING. (2020, March 10). *Indonesia unveils stimulus package to combat Coronavirus*. Retrieved from https://www.aseanbriefing.com/news/indonesia-unveils-stimulus-package-to-combat-coronavirus-impact/

Asiaasset. (2020, April 27). Philippine lawmakers draft 1.3 trillion-peso stimulus bill. *The Journal of Investments and Pensions.*

Balance of Payments and International Investment Position Manual. (2013). In Goods and Services Account. International Monetary Fund.

Boseley, M. (2020, June 4). Trans-Tasman Travel Bubble: Canberra Airport Asks People to Register Interest for New Zealand Flights. *The Guardian.*

Chorn, A., & Stromseth, J. (2021, May 19). *COVID-19 comes to Cambodia*. Brookings. Retrieved from https://www.brookings.edu/blog/order-from-chaos/2021/05/19/covid-19-comes-to-cambodia/

Choudhry, D.R. (2020, Nov. 13). India announces $1 million aid to ASEAN COVID-19 response Fund. *Economic Times.*

De, P. (2015). *ASEAN –INDIA Air Connectivity Report, Round Table on ASEAN-India Air Connectivity.* ASEAN India Centre Research and Information System for (RIS) Developing Countries.

Dey, M. (2021, January 31). Impact of COVID-19 on travel and tourism industry and ways of recovery. *Financial Express.*

Economic Survey. (2021). Department of Economic Affairs, Ministry of Finance, Government of India.

ETHealthworld.com. (2021, June 18). *Indonesia gets $1.3 bln loans from World Bank for Covid response, reforms*. Retrieved from www.health.economictimes.indiatimes.com

Global Data. (2021). Retrieved from https://www.globaldata.com/

International Air Travel Association. (2020, July 28). *Recovery Delayed as International Travel Remains Locked Down*. Press release. Retrieved from https://www.iata.org/en/ pressroom/pr/2020-07-28-02/

International Monetary Fund. (2021). *World Economy Outlook Update, January 2021*. Retrieved from https://www.imf.org/en/Publications/WEO/Issues/2021/01/26/2021-world-economic-outlook-update

KPMG. (2020, April 1). *Potential Impact of COVID-19 on The Indian Economy*. World Bank.

Kundu, R. (2021, June 23). *Tour and travel sector may report up to 40% of pre-Covid revenue in FY22*. The Mint. Retrieved from https://www.livemint.com/news/tour-and-travel-sector-may-report-up-to-40-of-pre-covid-revenue-in-fy22-11624442419668.html

LopezM. L. (2020, Feb. 28). Retrieved from https://cnnphilippines.com/business/2020/2/28/PAL-retrenchment-coronavirus.html

Malik, Y. (2021, June 22). *Business Standard*. Retrieved from https://edition.cnn.com/2021/06/18/asia/vaccinated-indonesian-doctors-covid-19-intl-hnk/index.html

MOCAA. (2021, April). *Ministry of Civil Aviation. Monthly Summary on Civil Aviation*. Retrieved from civilaviation.gov.in/en/publication/monthly-summary

MOCAB. (2021a, March 25). Ministry of Civil Aviation. Government of India. *Lok Sabha*. Unstarred Question 5038 On Effect of COVID-19 on the Aviation sector by D. M. Kathir Anand.

MOCAC. (2021b, March 25). Ministry of Civil Aviation. Government of India. *Lok Sabha*. Unstarred Question 5012 On Effect of COVID-19 on the Aviation sector by Hema Malini

Mufti & Akhlas. (2020). *Supporting Post-COVID-19 Economic Recovery in Southeast Asia*. ADB Brief 175.

NITTA. (2020, Sep. 26). *Myanmar November election overshadowed by COVID-19 surge*. Nikkei Asia. Retrieved from www.asia.nikkei.com

OECD. (2001). *Tourism Satellite Account: Recommended Methodological Framework*. Retrieved from www.oecd.org

OECD. (2008). *Tourism Satellite Account: Recommended Methodological Framework*. Retrieved from www.oecd.org

Rhee, Y. R. (2020, April 15). COVID-19 Pandemic and the Asia-Pacific Region: Lowest Growth since the 1960s. *IMF Blog*. Retrieved from https://blogs.imf.org/2020/04/15/covid-19-pandemic-and-the-asia-pacific-region-lowest-growth-since-the-1960s/

Rizzo, C. (2020, Feb. 6). *Business Insider*. Retrieved from https://www.businessinsider.com/cathay-pacific-employees-3-weeks-unpaid-leave-coronavirus-2020-2?IR

Sarkar, K. (2021, June 8). *CNBC18*. Retrieved from www.cnbc18.com

Shukla, R. (2021, March 22). India emerging as the next best destination for medical tourism post-COVID-19 pandemic. *Financial Express*.

Sinha, S. (2021, June 26). *Some hotels in India up for sale*. TNN.

Suthiphand, C. (1996). ASEAN-India cooperation in trade and tourism: Trends and prospects. *Journal of Asian Economics*, *7*(4). www.sciencedirect.com

Syed, N. (2020, Sep. 6). *Inside Malaysia Aviation Group's employee well-being strategy HRD*. Retrieved from https://www.hcamag.com/asia/specialisation/employee-engagement/inside-malaysia-aviation-groups-employee-well-being-strategy/232350

Talavera, S. (2020, March 10). DOT Pushes through Campaign to encourage more domestic tourists. *Phil Star Global*.

UNWTO. (2020). *World Tourism Barometer*. Retrieved from www.unwto.org

UNWTO. (2021, June 2). *World Tourism Barometer and Statistical Annex*. Retrieved from https://www.unwto.org/news/tourist-numbers-down-83-but-confidence-slowly-rising

Wiriyapong, N. (2021, June 28). All eyes on the sandbox. *The Bangkok Post*.

World Health Organization. (2021). *WHO Coronavirus (COVID-19) Dashboard*. Retrieved from https://covid19.who.int/

World Tourism Organization (UNWTO). (n.d.). *Tourism dashboard*. Retrieved from https://www.unwto.org/unwto-tourismdashboard

World Travel & Tourism Council. (2020, Mar. 23). *COVID-19 Related Policy Shifts Supportive of Travel & Tourism Sector.* Retrieved from www.wttc.org

World Travel and Tourism Council (WTTC). (2021). *Research reveals global Travel & Tourism sector suffered a loss*. Retrieved from https://wttc.org/News-Article/Global-TandT-sector-suffered-a-loss-of-almost-US4-trillion-in-2020

Worldometer. (2021, June 29). Retrieved from https://www.worldometers.info/coronavirus/country/myanmar/

ADDITIONAL READINGS

International Monetary Fund. (2021). World Economy Outlook Update, January 2021. Retrieved from https://www.imf.org/en/Publications/WEO/Issues/2021/01/26/2021-world-economic-outlook-update

KPMG. (2020, April 1). Potential Impact of COVID-19 on The Indian Economy. Retrieved from https://home.kpmg/content/dam/kpmg/in/pdf/2020/04/potential-impact-of-covid-19-on-the-indian-economy.pdf

Malik, Y. (2021, June 22). Business Standard. Retrieved from https://edition.cnn.com/2021/06/18/asia/vaccinated-indonesian-doctors-covid-19-intl-hnk/index.html

UNWTO. (2020). World Tourism Barometer, retrieved from www.unwto.org

World Travel & Tourism Council. (2020, Mar. 23). COVID-19 Related Policy Shifts Supportive of Travel & Tourism Sector, Retrieved from www.wttc.org

KEY TERMS AND DEFINITIONS

Atmanirbhar Bharat: Translates to 'self-reliant India' is a *Hindi* phrase popularized by India in relation to economic development in the country during and after the COVID-19 pandemic. The term is used as an umbrella concept in relation to making India a bigger and more important part of the global economy, pursuing policies that are efficient, competitive and resilient, and being self-sustaining. The '*Atmanirbhar Bharat Abhiyan*' or 'Self-Reliant India Mission' has been used during the announcement of India's COVID–19 pandemic related economic package.

Contact-Based Services: Refer to those economic services which cannot be performed without human contact. The terms are used is the context of lockdowns and restrictions imposed by COVID-19 pandemic.

Transport Bubbles: Are temporary and reciprocal travel arrangements between two countries aimed at restarting commercial passenger services when regular international flights are suspended as a result of the COVID-19 pandemic.

Vande Bharat Mission: Was started to bring back stranded Indians from foreign destinations after suspension of regular international flights due to restrictions imposed to prevent the spread of COVID-19. The Mission is considered to be the world's largest expatriation exercise to bring back stranded Indians from foreign destinations.

ENDNOTES

1 For importance of South-East Asia on the global tourism map and important data see www.adb.org

2 ASEAN Statistics Division, ASEAN Secretariat, 2021

3 Rhee, C. Y. "COVID-19 Pandemic and the Asia-Pacific Region: Lowest growth since the 1960s", IMF Blog, 15 April 2020. For Thailand, 50 per cent decline in tourists in first half of 2020 was projected. Tourism revenues were projected to drop by US$ 1.15 billion in Q1 2020. Singapore expected a 30 per cent drop in tourist arrivals during 2020.

4 M. L. Lopez CNN Philippines, 28 Feb. 2020

5 The decline in numbers is due to suspension of all commercial international flights from March 23, 2020. The ban has been extended till end-August 2021.

6 Till September 2020, *Air India* – the Indian National Carrier operated about 92 per cent of all *Vande Bharat* flights earning about INR 2556 crore.

8 https://edition.cnn.com/2021/06/18/asia/vaccinated-indonesian-doctors-covid-19-intl-hnk/index.html

8 COVID-19 was confirmed to have spread to South-East Asia on 13 January 2020, when a 61-year-old woman from Wuhan in China tested positive in Thailand, making it the first country other than China to report a case

9 The first COVID-19 related death occurred in the Philippine on 2 February, 2020 involving a Chinese man in the Philippines (Wikipedia, The Free Encyclopedia).

10 Federation of Indian Chamber of Commerce and Industry (FICCI) has recommended an increase in repayment tenure of ECLGS to 8 years. It has also suggested that tourism be included in the *Concurrent list* of the Constitution so that both the Centre as well as the States can frame policies for its growth (Millennium Post, June 24, 2021).

11 The details of the steps taken by the Ministry of Tourism, to overcome the crisis in the tourism sector are based on reply of *Rajya Sabha* Question 2397 answered on 16.03.2021 *Rajya Sabha* stands for Upper House of India's Parliament

Chapter 8
Strengthening the Bilateral Relationship Between India and Thailand Through Tourism

Harpreet Kaur
Central Queensland University, Australia

Ayasha Siddika
Australian Institute of Higher Education, Australia

ABSTRACT

India and Thailand have a long-term relationship. Both countries geographically are in extended neighbourhood and share a maritime boundary. Both countries taken together constitute 18.6% of the world's population. They have deep rooted similar history, cultures, philosophies, and religions. They share the same link of Buddhism. Even Hinduism has some reflection on Thai architecture, arts, names of cities, sculpture, dance, drama, and literature. In this chapter, Thailand has been chosen due to physical proximity, cultural, and ideological similarities with India. India and Thailand have celebrated more than 70 years of bilateral diplomatic relationship. In the past two decades, with regular political exchanges of growing trade and investment, India's relationship with Thailand has grown into a comprehensive partnership. India's 'Act East' policy has been complemented by Thailand's 'Act West' policy in bringing the two countries closer. Both countries are important regional partners under BIMSTEC linking Northeastern Indian states with Southeast Asia.

INTRODUCTION

India has been associated with Thailand historically in many ways - by missionaries, trade, sea route and commerce (Rodbamrung, 2021). India and Thailand, both countries taken together constitute 18.6% of the world population (Worldometer, 2021). They have deep rooted similar history, cultures, philosophies, and religious beliefs based on Hinduism and Buddhism. Hinduism also has some reflection on Thai architecture, arts, sculpture, dance, drama, and literature. The Thai language has influence from Pali

DOI: 10.4018/978-1-7998-5774-7.ch008

and Sanskrit languages (Brief on India - Thailand Relations, 2018). In this chapter, Thailand has been chosen due to physical proximity, cultural and ideological similarities with India. India and Thailand have celebrated more than 70 years of bilateral diplomatic relationship. In the past more than two decades, with regular political exchanges, growing trade and investment, India's relationship with Thailand has grown into a comprehensive partnership. India's 'Act East' policy has been complemented by Thailand's 'Act West' policy in bringing the two countries closer.

Both countries are important regional partners linking South and Southeast Asia. They cooperate closely in the ASEAN, East Asia Summit (EAS) and BIMSTEC groupings as Mekong Ganga Cooperation (MGC), Asia Cooperation Dialogue (ACD) and Indian Ocean Rim Association (IORA). The India-ASEAN Agreement on Trade in Goods was implemented in January 2010 and the India-ASEAN FTA in Services and Investments was signed in September 2014 and came into force in July 2015 (Brief on India-Thailand Relations, 2018). Of course, relations between India and Thailand are not new. Religious, cultural, linguistic, mythological and trade links have been coexisting for more than two millennia (Sajjanhar, 2017). This chapter has analysed different types of tourism sector of the two countries and identified how tourism has been contributing to their respective economies. Recommendations have been provided on the prospect of two countries potential areas to improve their economies by strengthening bilateral relationship.

India introduced 'Look East Policy' in 1991, though it was confined to Southeast Asia only, but it brought important changes at the national and international level. Look East policy was implemented with the purpose of rebuilding its economic relations with Southeast Asia to diversify trade away from its main trading partners in North America and Europe (Pande, 2020, p. 69). The Act East Policy (AEP) introduced in November 2014 by the Prime Minister Modi included within its ambit a wider geographical area (extending up to the Pacific Island countries, and within India, greater attention to hitherto neglected North-eastern India which border ASEAN's Myanmar). This multi-faceted policy incorporated different other aspects such as, greater engagement in all spheres, defence cooperation, promotion of infrastructure and development of North-eastern States. Several new initiatives were taken, and earlier projects were sought to be put on a fast track.

Given this, the objective of this chapter is to understand the prospects of enhancing different branches of tourism between India and Thailand. A Literature review has been done on publications on business, trade, tourism and economic relations between India and Thailand that identifies the potentiality of economic growth from bilateral relationship of the two countries. Analysis has been done on no empirical findings but based on historical papers. It will act as a catalyst to strengthen relationship of two countries. Development of this sector will not only stimulate activities in the tourism sector but will also influence other directly or indirectly related sectors. Finally, this will result in the growth of both the economies and improvement in GDP.

The aim of this chapter is to examine and evaluate the prospect of tourism in economic growth of India and Thailand. This chapter is structured as follows. The introductory part introduces the background of two countries Look East Policy and Look Act Policy, Export/Tourism as an Engine of growth, Literature review and Economics benefits and opportunities from Tourism, Challenges facing Tourism industry in two countries, finally relevant recommendation has been provided that would strengthen the relationship of these two countries in terms of economic growth.

BACKGROUND

Look East to Act East Policy

The emergence of economic liberalisation on the global landscape opened new opportunities for various underdeveloped countries as well to coordinate and interact with economically and technologically advanced countries. ASEAN for long followed export-oriented growth strategy by simultaneously pursuing twin objectives of deepening regional integration efforts and carrying out multilateral trade liberalization with the rest of the world (Alam,2015). Southeast Asia's geographical proximity, historical cultural connectivity, and the economic and technological advancement of these nations attracted India towards these countries.

The interaction between these countries was not new but the politico-economic and sociocultural ties between India and East Asia especially Southeast Asia goes back to the pre-Christian era. This was dominated by mercantile links and the spread of Hinduism and Buddhism in the region (Pande, 2020). Despite this proximity, India remained still disconnected from East Asia throughout the cold war period due to the cold war politics (Jindal, 2014).

But after following the most important developments over the past three decades world over, of opening the boundaries for trade, India adopted "Look East Policy'' under the Prime Ministership of P.V. Narasimha Rao in 1991, to establish relations with Southeast Asian Nations which became an integral and prominent part of India's foreign policy and a big strategic design.

The newly emerged 'Look-East policy' was implemented with the purpose of rebuilding its economic relations with Southeast Asia to diversify trade away from its main trading partners in North America and Europe (Pande, 2020, p. 69). The policy aimed to strengthen economic and cultural ties with the countries of the region and with ASEAN. India was embraced as a sectoral partner of ASEAN in 1992, as a dialogue partner in 1995 and as a summit partner in 2002 (Jha & Salim, 2015).

On the economic front India initiated cooperation in trade and investment, science, technology, and tourism (Jindal, 2014). Even Saint-Mezard (2003) acknowledged the 'Look East Policy' initiative of several ASEAN countries as India's partners for promoting trade and investment.

This phase, which began in 2003, extends the coverage of the Look East policy from Australia to East Asia, with Association of Southeast Asian Nations (ASEAN) as its core. The new phase thus marks a shift in focus from trade to wider economic and security cooperation, political partnerships, physical connectivity through road and rail links (Haokip, 2011). The India-ASEAN Free Trade Agreement (IAFTA) was signed on 13 August 2009 in Bangkok. The agreement covers trade in goods between India and the ASEAN members that came into effect on 1 January 2010.

The policy has been described as going through various phases, with an accelerated pace and process of interaction in moving from one phase to the next, marked by a broadening and deepening of India's interaction with the region. This has culminated in the most recent "phase" under the government of Prime Minister Narendra Modi, which has rebranded the policy as "Act East" to signify a more proactive and action-oriented approach towards the region (Bajpaee, 2017).

Introduction of India's 'Act East' policy, an expansion of the existing policy, included deeper security cooperation and defence partnerships as well. In fact, these two policies are the two phases of the same coin of India's policy towards the Asia Pacific region. 'The primary goals behind the Act East policy are both to promote India's economic growth and development and respond to China's rise and expanding influence in the region' (Mazumdar,2021).

This has resulted in a "renewed energy, vigour, and planning in India's engagement with the rest of the world" as it becomes a more "confident, articulate, rising power, willing to claim its place on the global high table and able to discharge its responsibilities", as noted in the Ministry of External Affairs (MEA, 2016).

Replacing "Look" with "Act" implied that India would be taking a more pro-active and action-oriented approach towards the region with a "priority on security, connectivity and regional integration" (MEA, 2015). India's 'Act East' policy has been complemented by Thailand's 'Act West' policy in bringing the two countries closer (MEA, 2019).

India and Thailand celebrated 70th anniversary of their bilateral relationship built on pragmatic cooperation, strategic balancing and accommodation of rival powers and cultural and educational exchanges in 2018. They are in a good relationship since 1947 (Mishra, 2020).

Exports/Tourism as an Engine of Growth

In the globalisation phase, exports form an important source of income and fuel for growth of an economy. A successful export drive stimulates a positive multiplier effect on different sectors of an economy. A study on Zimbabwean economy suggests that trade policies aimed at restoring international competitiveness, for expansion and diversification of export shape the potential of promoting and sustaining economic growth in the medium to long term (Caleb, Mazanai & Netsai, 2014).

Dollar & Kraay (2004) also found a positive relationship between changes in trade volumes and changes in growth rates for 72 developing and 29 rich countries. A study by Eris & Ulasan (2013) of 66 countries examined the strength of causal relationships between trade openness and long-term economic growth and it was found that there exists an indirect and long-term correlation between the two.

Exports in different forms are a big source of economic growth. Tourism, invisible export, holds an important position in its contribution to GDP of any country. At the world level, in 2018, the sector's total contribution to the global economy reached US$8.8 trillion (equating to 10.4% of global GDP) (WTTC, 2019. P 5). Apart from earning foreign exchange tourism industry touches upon different sectors of an economy. Higher foreign exchange earned thus, can be used to import capital equipment which further leads to more domestic investment, employment and consumption, and finally higher growth of an economy (Balaguer & Cantavella-Jorda, 2002). Similar to the Export-Led Growth (ELG) hypothesis, a Tourism-Led Growth (TLG) hypothesis postulates the existence of various arguments for which tourism would become a main determinant of overall long-run economic growth (Tiwari, 2011).

Contribution of travel and tourism to GDP is highest in Philippines (24.6 in 2019) followed by Thailand (21.9 in 2019). Though in India travel and tourism does not have a very high contribution but still its share is 9.1 which has remained stable during 2015-2019.

Tourism, through multifarious linkages, has been playing an important role in the growth of an economy. Through its multiplier effect tourism enhances the growth of all sectors, may it be primary, secondary, or tertiary sectors. It also creates and enhances direct, indirect, and induced employment (Khan et al., 2018). Many developing countries have thus started to regard tourism as an integral part of their economic growth and development strategies since it serves as a source of scarce financial resources, job creation, foreign exchange earnings, and technical assistance (Sinclair, 1998).

Yousuf & Lal (2013) also found that, the tourism sector, which has high inter-industry and cross-country linkages, is well suited to be the leading sector to accelerate regional economic growth and integration. Further, international, and domestic tourism are leading economic activities in the world however due to COVID-19 travel restrictions, this industry has been negatively impacted. The studies of UNWTO shows that tourism volumes and related receipts like GDP, employment and export earnings are expected to move away from the developed countries and towards the less developed countries because of favourable economic, technological, motivational & policy factors (Khan et. al., 2018).

LITERATURE REVIEW

Tourism was described as the activities where people travel and stay in places different from their usual environment for a short time, usually less than a consecutive year. The purpose of this travelling can be leisure, business, or few other activities. Such travelling can be within the country and outside the country (Sharafuddin, 2015).

India and Thailand are the popular tourist destinations in Asia. Both countries have a wide range of places to visit and things to do. The beaches, hill stations, beautiful landscapes, historical monuments, forts, places of religious interests, and many more have made these two countries attractive to the tourists (Phophueksanand, 2017).

Tourism is playing an important role in the GDP of India and Thailand. Hotels, travel agencies, transport including airlines are expanding with the growth of tourism. It is also promoting traditional handicraft business in those countries (Sharma, 2015).

In India tourists are attracted towards historical monuments (Taj Mahal in Agra, Mysore Palace in Mysore, Golden Temple in Amritsar, Bahai Temple in Delhi, Hawa-Mahal in Jaipur a few among many), medical purposes, education, hill stations, beaches, national parks and snake boat race of Kerala, rock climbing, Skiing, Camel safari, Para gliding, Mountaineering, Rafting in white water and Trekking (Arunmozhi & Panneerselvam, 2013).

In Thailand tourists might be going for adventure tourism (caving, trekking, elephant trekking, waterfall abseiling, white-water rafting, mountain biking, snorkelling, sea kayaking, zip lining, sky diving, medical purposes, or education (Sharafuddin, 2015).

Among different types of tourism, medical tourism is growing rapidly and becoming popular in the whole world (Pattharapinyphon, 2019). It consists biomedical procedures, with travel and tourism. Medhekar (cited in Adams et al., 2015; Connell, 2006; Deloitte, 2008; Hofer et al., 2012; Hall, 2015; Turner, 2010, 2011; Veerasoontorn & Beise-Zee, 2010) defined medical traveller or an MT is a patient whose primary motivation is to seek affordable quality of medical treatment/surgery abroad and improve their quality of life.

Various countries in Southeast Asia like India, Thailand, Malaysia, Singapore, etc. are promoting medical tourism aggressively (Kumar, 2011). Among those countries India and Thailand are popular destination for medical tourism. Thailand's best-cost strategy has made medical tourism attractive to many other countries, and India's diversification strategy and cost leadership has made it outstanding in the long-standing market (Ebrahim & Ganguli, 2019).

India's medical service is well known in overseas patients. Low-cost advantage, strong reputation in advanced healthcare sector and diversity of tourist destinations have given India competitive advantage among other countries (Kumar, 2011). India provides a variety of medical services to overseas patients. The country is well known for high-end medical treatment such as cardiovascular surgery, organ transplant, eye surgery, cancer treatment, stem cell, knee replacements and organ replacements (Burns, 2015).

India's reproductive tourism attracts infertile couples from western countries for ovum donation and gestational surrogacy services (Medhekar, 2019).

Indian medical tourism may also include leisure aspect and wellness tourism. Ancient indigenous healthcare traditions are also famous in India that includes Ayurveda, Siddha, Unani, Naturopathy, and Yoga (Kumar, 2011). Medhekar (cited from MTI, 2016) mentioned that India is fifth in the world and second in Asia, in Medical Industry based on destination, and quality of facilities and medical service.

On the other hand, Thailand possesses numerous competitive advantages which provide an upper hand over other neighbouring countries and make the country a leading medical tourism hub in the ASEAN region. The advantages are price benefits, medical expertise, Thai style hospitality, infrastructure, government support and a wide range of tourism products. Thailand is ranked sixth in the world in medical tourism because of lower medical costs and attractive tourist attractions and the trend is growing 14% per year, in line with the growth of the number of international tourists visiting Thailand, which is around 12% per year (Pattharapinyophong, 2019).

Thailand provides various forms of high-end medical service such as cardiac surgery and transplant operation, and has high reputation on providing excellent medical care, doctors are well-trained, other support assistants are also well trained and skilled. Many of physicians have acquired their training and certification from developed nation such as USA, UK, Germany, and Japan. Many public and private sector hospitals in Thailand, in both the public and private sectors, such as Bumrungrad International Hospital, Samitivej Hospital are accredited by the US-based Joint Commission International (JCI) and JCI ensures the standard of this hospital (Pattharapinyophong, 2019). Pattharapinyophong (cited in Joint Commission International, 2016) mentioned that presently are 41 hospitals in Thailand that meet JCI accreditation.

In addition, health care providers targeting medical tourists are well-trained for their foreign language efficiency, especially in English. This is an important consideration for medical tourists from the United States and much of Europe, for whom English is their native language or widely understood second language; hospitals such Samitivej Hospital, Bumrungrad International Hospital and Bangkok Hospital employ translators to serve as a means of effective communication. Bangkok Hospital Phuket provides interpreters in 15 languages and receives about 20,000 international patients a year; while the famous Bumrungrad International hospital in Bangkok claims to employ 109 interpreters; its entire staff speak English (quoted in Pattharapinyophong, 2019).

Coming to 'education tourism', the concept is new from the perspective of literature in the Tourism industry, but the phenomenon has been existing in humanity for a long time. Sharma (2015) mentioned that Education tourism can be for several types that includes ecotourism, heritage tourism, rural/farm tourism, and student exchanges between educational institutions. Education tourism may also be seen as cultural / historical, eco-tourism / nature-based tourism / rural tourism, and study abroad programs, Lifelong Learning (LLL) is "all learning activity undertaken throughout life, with the aim of improving knowledge, skills and competence, within a personal, civic, social and/or employment-related perspective.

India is a popular destination for education for many developed countries along with neighbouring countries. India has been developing its' education sector remarkably. It is reasonable to predict that in future, the country will be one of the largest education hubs in the world. It is well known that India has always been a land of scholars and learners. In ancient times also, India was regarded all over the world for its universities like Taxila, Nalanda, Vikramshila and its scholars (Sheikh, 2017).

Thailand is also a popular destination to education tourism. The sun, sea, and other amusement facilities have been contributing to attract overseas students to the country (Sharafuddin, 2015). Maga and Nicolau (2020) has suggested Thailand, among the ASEAN countries, have sufficient qualities to become an attractive educational tourism destination. Thailand, in accordance with the need of ASEAN and international students, has been developing higher education in teaching international programs, especially at the graduate level in order to have higher education institutions. There were 13,617 foreign students who studied in higher education institutions in Thailand in 2014 in international programs in Thailand in 2014/16 (Jirapornvaree, 2019).

International higher education in Thailand is classified as a degree providing institution where courses and materials are presented in the English language. For International HE programs in Thailand potential students do not need to have the national entrance examination (O-NET/ A-NET). The international HE programs just rely on high school graduation certificates or the equivalent (GED certificate) and/or the SAT or O Level/A-Level scores with an IELTS or TOEFL score as proof of proficiency in English; that makes the country is attractive to neighbour countries (Sharma, 2015).

Heritage tourism also signifies the growth of tourism industry. 'Heritage' is defined according to International Council on Monuments and Sites (ICOMOS) from a general perspective as tangible assets that include natural and cultural environment, encompassing landscape, historic places, and build environment as well as intangible assets such as collection of historical and present cultural practices, knowledge and living experiences.

India is a popular destination of Heritage Tourism in Southeast Asia. People from around the world visit India Heritage tourism as a great means of economic growth and social development, and it is an innovative transformation. It can be a strategy for sustainable economic development (Medhekar & Haq, 2019).

In India apart from 40 cultural world heritage sites including gardens, tombs, caves, forts, religious places and mountain railways, naming a few: Jaipur city, Taj Mahal of Agra, Hill Forts of Rajasthan, the Jantar Mantar of Rajasthan, Red Fort Complex Delhi, a few natural world heritage sites (UNESCO, 2020) which include wildlife parks and wildlife sanctuaries also exist making the country of attraction to the tourists.

Types of tourism will not be complete without the inclusion of spiritual tourism which is comparatively a new concept with an old phenomenon. The concept of Spiritual Tourism has been evolved from the need of people to satisfy their spiritual development and awareness, which sometimes can be linked to the religion, but in many cases beyond that. Spiritual Tourism can be viewed as a phenomenon: when someone visits a specific place outside of his/her usual environment with an intention to fulfil his/her spiritual need, which could be from religious perspective or non-religious, sacred, or experimental in nature, within a Divine context (Farooq, 2012). Religious tourism and pilgrimage both are most of the time included under the same umbrella of spiritual tourism (Phukan et al, 2012).

India is famous for its temples and that is the reason that among the different kinds of tourism in India, pilgrimage tourism is increasing most rapidly. The various places for tourists to visit in India for pilgrimage are Vaishno Devi, Golden temple, Char Dham, and Mathura Vrindavan (Arunmozhi & Panneerselvam, 2013).

UNESCO has listed Ban Chiang Archaeological Site, historic city of Ayutthaya and historic town of Sukhothai and associated historic towns as cultural sites and Dong Phayayen-Khao Yai Forest complex, Kaeng Krachan Forest complex and Thungyai-Huai Kha Khaeng Wildlife Sanctuaries as natural sites of Thailand (UNESCO, 2020).

Thailand is a country with a rich cultural patrimony: a ubiquitous religious architecture because of the secular presence of the Buddhist faith. Thailand's popular sites, Phra That Doi Suthep Temple in Chiang

Mai (North), Wat Phra That Phanom in Nakornphanom (North-eastern), Wat Phra Chettuphon Wimon Mangkhlaram (Wat Pho) (Central), Wat Phra Mahathat Woromaha Vihan in Nakhon Si Thammarat; and Wat Chalong in Phuket (South) attract a good number of tourists (Gaffar, Wetprasit & Setiyorini, 2011).

Many countries raise their culture as the key factor in their tourism pursuits, especially aesthetic or historic countries. Such key factors include not only the way of life, and cultural performances such as cultural dance, but also temples and ancient sites. Moreover, culture has been applied in souvenir designs for tourists such as ancient site models, textile patterns, and several types of decoration (Piboonrungroj & Sangkakorn, 2013). The most important Thai cultural festivals, Loy Krathong and Songkran, are linked to the Indian festivals of Kartik Purnima and Baisakhi. Thais celebrate Loy Krathong on the full moon in November and pay respect to the river by floating the banana leaf cups and asking for forgiveness from the River Goddess Ganges. On Kartik Purnima day people bathe in sacred rivers as the beliefs are that Gods descend of earth and reside in the holy rivers that flow naturally for healthy growth and spiritual grace (Agarwar, 2009-2010). Other important festivals of Thailand: Ghost Festival of Loei Province, Lantern Festival, Chiang Mai, Rocket Festival of Yasothorn Province, Buffalo racing festival, Chonburi, Vegetarian festival, Phuket, Wonderfruit Music and Arts Festival, Chinese New Year, Bangkok, and candle festival on Ubon Ratchathani are famous attractions from both local and foreign tourists.

Tourism sector gets support from different events, which can be clubbed under event tourism. 'Event tourism' is a fast-growing sector where tourists comprise a potential market for events that are pre-planned. Tourism industry has become an important part in the success of those events and is becoming attractive to the overseas market. Such planned events are occasional events and unique because of interactions among the people, and management of that environment. As the events are special and occasional, people enjoy being there. And potential entrepreneurs do not want to miss the opportunity. Event management is an applied field of study and professional practice for planning, designing, and producing the planned events for specific festivals and other celebrations, entertainment, recreation. It also can encompass events of political and state, scientific, sports an arts event; business, and corporate affairs that include meetings, conventions, fairs, and exhibitions, and many private events that include weddings, parties, and any other social events for affinity groups. 16.3% of the tourists to India during 2018 had business and professional visas (Bureau of Immigration). India held major international events such as the Commonwealth Games held in 2010, Meetings, Incentives, Conventions and Exhibitions (MICE) (Subash, 2015, pp11).

Getz (2005) has described Event and tourism in few categories, such as, Cultural festivals, carnivals, commemorations, religious events, summits, royal occasions, political events, VIP visits, art and entertainment, concerts, award ceremonies, meetings, conventions, trade shows, fairs, conferences, seminars, clinics, sports and games, and any other fun. All these events are contributing to attracting tourists.

One of the fastest growing travels is tourism related to sports or exercise, where sport tourism is one of the most extensively studied (Gibson, 1998). Sport event tourism has become an activity that enhances the potential of cities or countries to compete in this globalized world (Kolb, 2017). Weed and Bull (1997) and Yiannakis (2002) describe sports tourism as a leisure activity related to sports, as a goal to exercise or to promote health. Hritz and Ross (2010) said that sports tourism is a journey from one place to another where a sport event is organized, which has become popular among sports-oriented tourists and generating local business benefits.

Wedding tourism is getting momentum in Thailand among other counties in the world. Weddings have been a significant tradition in many cultures for centuries. It is a cause for celebration- to share a couple's new journey with friends, families and relatives and create memories together (Breg, 2013). Destination weddings, on the other hand, are a fairly new concept, but one that has been growing significantly in the past few years (Micallef, 2017). The rise in demand for this niche market has had impact on destinations worldwide (Vidauskaite, 2009). As the wedding tourism industry sees a potential for growth within this market, destinations are being transformed in various ways to attract consumers (Micallef, 2017). Destination wedding occurs when a couple decides to get married outside the zone of their permanent residence. Most of the time, destination weddings are combined with a honeymoon, also termed as 'wedding moon', where couples get married and spend their honeymoon in one location (Micallef, 2017).

There are different reasons for the growth in demand for destination weddings. First, getting married away from home saves money. Second, destination weddings are less stressful. Third, change in consumer preferences are now playing a more important role. Millennials have evolved ideas associated with weddings. With more education and consciousness, millennials tend to have special demands, seeking something different –something that shows their personality (Wall & Mathieson, 2006).

Historically Thailand was one of the world's top honeymoon destinations. Recently the country has become an attractive destination for wedding. Thailand offers a wide range of options to for the couples-to-be, such as themed festival weddings, beach-side or mountain-top weddings, traditional Thai weddings, cultural weddings, and so on. Such tourism promotes other businesses which are related to wedding that includes wedding planning and preparing the ceremony, rings, the bride's dress and groom's suit, hotel accommodation for guests, food, photographer, live band, flower and music arrangement, and honeymoon for the couple. Thailand's physical environment, socio-demographic factors, cost, wedding related product and service, safety and security make the country an attractive wedding tourism destination (Deng, 2012).

As a kind of tourism in India, adventure tourism has recently grown in India. For adventure tourism in India, tourists prefer to go for trekking to places like Ladakh, Sikkim, and Himalaya. Himachal Pradesh and Jammu and Kashmir are popular for the skiing facilities they offer. White-water rafting is also catching on in India and tourists flock to places such as Uttaranchal, Assam, and Arunachal Pradesh for this adrenalin- packed activity. Various kinds of adventure on water, land, and air can be enjoyed in India. The various kinds of adventure tourism in India are Rock climbing, Skiing, Camel safari, Para gliding, Mountaineering, Rafting in white water, Trekking (Arunmozhi & Panneerselvam, 2013).

Wellness tourism is one of the fastest growing forms of international and domestic tourism. Nowadays, the occurrence of working life crises and imbalances in the race for success and less time for leisure can cause stress and depression (D'Amore, 2009; Parmar, 2017). As a result, health and wellness tourism has become a special interest choice among tourists (Bone, 2013; D'Amore, 2009; Kale, 2004; Parmar, 2017; Smith & Kelly; 2006).This form of tourism involves people who travel to a different place to pursue activities that maintain or enhance their personal health and wellness, and who are seeking unique, authentic or location-based experiences. Wellness tourism includes massages, body treatments, facial treatments, exercise facilities & programs, weight loss programs, nutrition programs, pre- and post-operative Spa treatments, and mind/body programs (Arunmozhi & Panneerselvam, 2013).

Economic Benefits and Opportunities From Tourism

Travel and Tourism industry has become the world's largest and fast-growing industry which stimulates the growth of an economy, primarily measured by the enhancement of GDP. It directly contributes to GDP through foreign exchange earnings and indirectly through increase in employment. Tourism is the second largest foreign exchange earner in India and Thailand (Khandare & Phophueksanand, 2017).

It is acting as a big contributor of economic growth and social changes of any economy. It is one of the largest and fastest growing industries in India and Thailand, making it crucial for both countries' economic development. It has been contributing to radical infrastructural development, employment generation, rural development and opening new opportunities. Growth in tourism was driven by a relatively strong global economy, growing middle classes and rapid urbanization in emerging economies, affordable travel, and visa facilitation, as well as technological advances and new business models (UNWTO, 2020).

Tourism sector of Thailand has stimulated 11 percent direct and indirect employment of Thailand's total workforce or 3.42 million people and earning for 79000 million baths for the Thai Government as tax revenue (Khandare & Phophueksanand, 2017). The National Economic and Social Development Council (NESDC, recently renamed from NESDB) stated that in February 2019 that Tourism accounted for 18.4% (or close to one fifth) of the GDP of Thailand (Tourist Project 2020).

In India the share of direct contribution of Travel and Tourism was 10.4% of World GDP in 2019 which declined to 5.5% in 2020 due to ongoing mobility restrictions in the world. The share to Indian GDP was 9.2 percent and 21.9 percent to Thai GDP in 2019. In case of employment at the global level, 1 in 10 jobs belonged to travel and tourism industry supporting 334 million jobs in 2019. Though due to the current epidemic it dropped down to 272 million jobs in 2020.

In 2019 Travel and Tourism directly supported 6.65 percent of total employment in Thailand and 5.15 percent in India (WTTC, 2019).

Employment and investment get stimulus, structure of the economy undergoes a change and foreign exchange earnings increase enhancing the favourable balance of payments. Not only this, but tourism also leads to increase in demand of both primary and secondary sector products along with inbound travel which further results in improved efficiency and growth in different connected sectors.

As such tourism helps the growth of economic, educational, cultural, social, and political sectors (Khan et. al. 2020). In addition to creating direct demand for different products tourism also stimulates indirect demand affecting different sectors of the economy through multiplier process.

Travel and Tourism's Contribution to GDP

The economic contribution of Travel and Tourism can best be captured from its contribution to respective countries' GDP earnings. As the table 1 shows, in Thailand the contribution of Travel and tourism almost doubled in eight years. There has been a regular improvement in the contribution except 2014 when there was a small fall from 32.47 million dollars to 31.51 million dollars. This may be due insecurity of life and curfew being imposed resulting from political disturbance as army took control of the government and suspended the constitution to bring order and enact political reforms in Thailand in May 2014.

In India there has been a steady growth in the contribution of Travel and Tourism to GDP which grew from 59.61 US billion dollars to 98.18 billion dollars.

In terms of percentage the share of Travel and Tourism industry to GDP has been quite strong and it has been regularly on an increase form 15.2 percent in 2011 to 21.9 percent in 2019 except year 2014 which witnessed political instability. But after the restoration of the political atmosphere in Thailand there was a leap jump of 13.14 percent change in 2015 from a negative percent change in the previous year (-3.34 in 2014). So far as the relative share of the Indian Travel and Tourism industry is concerned, it remained more or less the stable with some exceptions. The percentage share was negative too which could not specifically align to any reasons.

Table 1. Travel and Tourism direct contribution to GDP, US$(Billions)

Year	Thailand	India
2011	24.37	59.61
2012	28.26	63.72
2013	32.47	67.77
2014	31.51	72.74
2015	36.66	79.58
2016	39.58	87.17
2017	42.17	91.96
2018	45.45	98.18
2019	-	-

Source: The World Bank

Table 2. Contribution of travel and tourism to GDP (%of GDP)

Year	Thailand		India	
Year	Value	% Change	Value	% Change
2011	15.2	9.07	9.1	-1.82
2012	16.3	7.47	9.2	0.39
2013	18.1	10.88	9.2	0.19
2014	17.5	-3.34	9.2	0.36
2015	19.8	13.14	9.3	0.85
2016	20.6	4.20	9.4	1.10
2017	21.3	3.27	9.3	-0.65
2018	21.6	1.15	9.2	-0.74
2019	21.9	1.44	9.3	1.12

Source: World Data Atlas

Foreign Exchange Earnings and Travel and Tourism

Table 3 shows the foreign exchange earnings from tourism industry. Both the nations showed a consistent increase in foreign exchange earnings over a period of time (2011-2019). The foreign exchange earnings of Thailand increased more than 3 times over this period whereas for India it almost doubled. If one looks at the value, Thai foreign exchange earnings were more than double of India's. This goes in tune with the number of tourists' arrivals.

Though the foreign exchange earnings are almost more than double of India's but the share of tourism receipts to total export earnings in Thailand is almost four times more (20.10% in Thailand and 5.80% in India). This is primarily because Thailand primarily has more dependence on tourists.

Table 3. Foreign Exchange Earnings from Tourism in India and Thailand during 2011-2019

Year	Thailand	India
	US $ Million	US $ Million
2011	25473	17707
2012	31688	17971
2013	39316	18397
2014	36121	19700
2015	42558	21013
2016	46307	22923
2017	53986	27310
2018	58076	28586
2019	62289	30058

Source: Table 2.11.1, India Tourism Statistics 2020, Ministry of Tourism, Govt. of India. (for India), https://www.ceicdata.com/en/indicator/thailand/tourism-revenue (for Thailand)

Table 4. Iinternational tourism receipts (% of total exports) India and Thailand during 2011-2019

Year	Thailand %	India %
2011	11.76	-
2012	12.61	4.13
2013	14.80	4.07
2014	13.80	4.27
2015	16.52	5.01
2016	17.48	5.37
2017	18.73	5.70
2018	18.68	5.43
2019	20.10	5.80

Source: The World Bank

As it is clear from the table 4, though share of Indian tourism as a percentage of total exports is around 6% but for Thailand it occupies 1/5th of the share.

Tourism and Employment

Tourism industry contributing to GDP and foreign exchange also directly and indirectly employs large number of skilled and unskilled people. Employment increases for travel agencies, modes of transportation, hospitality sector, hotels, food industries, handicraft sectors etc.

Table 5. Travel and Tourism Direct Contribution to Employment, %

	India (%)	Thailand (%)
2011	5.01	4.70
2012	4.97	5.61
2013	4.95	6.36
2014	4.98	5.27
2015	4.98	5.94
2016	5.01	6.11
2017	5.04	6.22
2018	5.09	6.42
2019	5.12	6.65*

*Projected
Source: The World Bank

Share of employment in India for trade and tourism industry declined from 2012 during the period for consideration. It did start improving from 2016 onwards but it was quite small. Thailand's share of employment in this industry increased from 4.70% in 2011 to 6.36 in 2013, but which declined again in 2014 due to political disturbances. Next year it showed a continuous improvement. In India, the contribution of travel and tourism to employment as a per cent of GDP has been increasing at a minimal rate though the percent change has turned from negative to positive (-0.35% to 0.41%) with regular fluctuations.

The contribution of travel and tourism to employment as a per cent of GDP in Thailand has been increasing steadily. Its contribution increased from 11.3% in 2011 to 16.2% in 2019.

Table 6. Thailand & India's contribution of travel and tourism to employment (% of GDP)

Year	Thailand		India	
Year	Value	% Change	Value	% Change
2011	11.3	-1.50	7.9	1.25
2012	13.0	15.18	7.9	-0.35
2013	14.7	13.53	7.9	-0.21
2014	12.9	-12.87	7.9	0.81
2015	14.6	13.85	7.9	-0.13
2016	15.2	3.72	8.0	0.48
2017	15.6	2.90	8.0	0.89
2018	15.9	1.71	8.1	0.65
2019	16.2	1.80	8.1	0.41

Source: World Travel and Tourism Council

As such one can conclude that all these economic benefits from tourism may originate from holiday tourism, educational tourism, medical tourism or destination wedding tourism but each type of tourism will affect GDP, foreign exchange earnings and employment in different sectors. Thailand became among the top five destinations of inbound medical tourism spending globally, according to the latest research by the World Travel & Tourism Council (WTTC). 2018 witnessed US$ 600 million earned by Thailand ranking second in the world and India with US$ 450 million holding 6th position (Thaiger, 2020). The main reasons behind this domination are low cost, good quality treatment and developed tourism industry.

Challenges Facing Tourism Industry in India and Thailand

Despite strong growth travel and tourism industry still faces various challenges. Infrastructural development, government policy, unskilled workforce issues, education in hospitality and tourism, proper strategies, crisis management, marketing are a few existing challenges. Inadequate airline capacity, especially during the peak tourist season, low maintained or badly maintained airports, flight delay and cancellations, bad experience in flight and airport are nightmare for tourists (Yogesh Hole, 2019). Being a part of service industry hospitality and tourism face additional challenges related to skilled human resource. Service industry characteristics include intangibility, inseparability, heterogeneity, inseparability of production and consumption. Hence there is a high degree of interaction happens between service provider and the customer. So high skill is required to deal with such customers. Increasing competition levels and complexity over the time are few other big challenges in Hospitality industry (Felix & Bello, 2019).

In India the tourism sector is facing challenges such as lack of good quality tourism infrastructure, global concerns regarding health and safety of tourists, disparate passenger/road tax structures across various states and shortfall of adequately trained and skilled manpower (Subash, 2015).

In Thailand employees of tourism industry pick up their jobs not according to their tastes. Most students choose a tourism major without passion for the career or a good understanding of the expectations and work nature of the tourism and hospitality industry (Jotikasthira et al., 2016). As such many employees of the tourism industry are linked without giving the best service.

Tourists while visiting a country, look at different aspects such as cost, security, service, environment, hospitality, health etc. On the health front, there is a significant need for improvement in ensuring sound health of tourists in India especially considering the low rank of 109 for India in terms of health and hygiene standards as compared for 140 world economies (Subash, 2015). In terms of Overall Global Health Security Index of 2019, Thailand ranks 6 with a score of 73.2 whereas India's rank is 57 with quite a smaller score of 46.5 (GHSI, 2019).

As per the World Economic Forum's Travel and Tourism Competitiveness Report 2013 for 140 world economies, India's air transport infrastructure, ground transport infrastructure and tourism infrastructure have been ranked 39, 42 and 95 respectively indicating considerable scope for improvement (Subash,2015).

Security and counter terrorism are still critical issues in these two countries under consideration. Both countries have concerns regarding combat terrorism, maritime piracy, arms trafficking and natural and man-made disasters (Mishra, 2020). Other neighbouring countries are playing obstacle roles in building strong relationship in between India and Thailand. India's relationship with US and rivalry with China taking a big stake in building the bondage with Thailand. Thailand in many cases plays balancing role between India and China (Mishra, 2020).

Few additional issues like air pollution, environmental pollution, safety of tourists through local transportation, hotel, and delivery of good health related services to the tourists are subject to consideration in improving tourism (Kittisak Jermsittiparsert, 2019). Language is another barrier in tourism sector in Thailand. Rarely people speak and understand English in Thailand. Though there are many attractive places in Thailand for overseas tourists, foreign people face a big challenge in communicating while they must speak to people in using transportation, shops, and hotels.

As tourism directly and indirectly promotes infrastructure, increases consumption; it increases carbon emission in that society (Kittisak Jermsittiparsert, 2019). India and Thailand are developing countries without having proper sustainable planning for maintaining environment balance, which is a big challenge for both.

Governments do not have adequate policy to protect the heritage. Some news from BBC in 2018 says that The Taj Mahal is one of the world's leading tourist attractions which draws 70000 people each day is under threat of being deteriorated. Government is not taking proper measure to protect its' quality. This tomb built in while marble is turning into yellow, brown, and green. Lots of pollution and dust and insects are causing damage (BBC News, 2018).

Economic cooperation is the main driver in relationship of India and Thailand. However, security and counter terrorism still is critical between these two countries. Both countries have concerns regarding combat terrorism, maritime piracy, arms trafficking and natural and man-made disasters (Mishra, 2020). Currently major Indian companies in Thailand include Tata group – Tata Motors (Thailand), Tata Steel Thailand and Tata Consultancy Services, The Aditya Birla Group, Mahindra Satyam, Ranbaxy, Dabur, Lupin, NIIT, Kirloskar Brothers Ltd, Punj Lloyd Group, Polyplex (Thailand) Public Co. Ltd, Precious Shipping PCL and Usha Siam Steel Industries PCL. Leading Thai companies in the fields of Agro-processing, construction, automotive, engineering and banking have active and growing business presence in India (MEA, 2019).

CONCLUSION AND IMPLICATIONS (INCLUDING FUTURE RESEARCH DIRECTIONS)

Though several plans and programmes have already been devised for tackling different challenges in both the countries, successful implementation would be critical to accelerate growth. The employees should be given regular training so that they are in tune with the dynamic changes of the industry. It was suggested in the work of Whamsley (2012) that tourism and hospitality educators should segment students to differentiate their intellectual and behavioral development as needed according to the demand of the hospitality and tourism workforce (quoted in Jotikasthira et al., 2015). Flex.et.al., (2019) also emphasised on developing human resource skills tom improve the tourism and hospitality industry.

A special care should be given to stimulate human resource development. There are many universities and institutions in Thailand that offer degrees in Hotel and Tourism Management and training courses for guides using specific languages such as Russian, Korean, Chinese, Japanese, Spanish, Burmese, Bahasa Indonesian, and Vietnamese. German and French are also used by guides. English is the international language used with many tourists from Southeast Asia, South Asia, and western countries (Srichampa, 2015).

Already in Thailand some programs are designed to develop students in both tourism and hospitality; some others simply develop students for the employment market or for specific segments in the tourism and hospitality sector including culinary arts, aviation services, MICE (Meeting, Incentive Travel, Convention, and Exhibition), spa, and special themes in tourism, particularly sustainable tourism, and creative tourism (Jotikasthira et al., 2015).

The study established that financial resources and time are two major constraints in training of individuals who are already employed in the tourism and hospitality sector. Most institutions are reluctant to release financial resources and their employees for long-term training because they consider such a move as a loss. Hence the respondents recommended that tertiary institutions should consider introducing block release and/or distance learning programmes. This flexible approach, according to the respondents, will allow businesses to release their employees to attend relevant courses as it will be cost effective, and the employees will not be out of work for so long that businesses can be negatively impacted. As per a study by the Indian Ministry of Tourism, only 50 per cent of the employees are employed in the key functional areas. In addition, proper selection of hotel management students, increased focus on grooming and communication skills, on the job training, courses in foreign languages and standardization and monitoring of curricula in private institutions may be required (Subash, 2015).

There should be an improvement in infrastructural facilities such as good quality with reasonable price hotel rooms, easy exchange conversion facility, good quality roads, rail network, availability of tourist vehicles and more information centres in each locality.

On the security front India and Thailand signed an extradition treaty, which is a part of negotiation on external affairs in between these two countries. This bilateral treaty works as a legal framework for protecting the countries against individuals who are involved in terrorism, economic and transnational crimes. Both countries also share a Mutual Legal Assistance Treaty, signed in 2004. Thailand and India are becoming closer on coordination against counterterrorism. Since 2016, the Government of two countries agreed to work together in combating terrorism (Mishra, 2020). In addition to this as various Indian State Governments have established Tourist Police Task Force for ensuring safety and security for tourists, more should be established where these are not. Provision of translators too should be made so that people coming from and going to remote places between these two countries can also enjoy the spirit of tourism.

For the promotion of tourism among these two countries Event specific tours for both domestic and international tourists should be developed. These events may be based on innovative themes of sports, food, fruits, handicrafts, culture and traditions, villages, festivals etc. Special discounts should be offered to repeat travellers in the form of customised packages. There should be increased stakeholder participation involving the government, private sector, and the community at large. These can be developed either as 'products' such as religious, dance, wellness, adventure, nature, rural or agriculture tourisms or as 'experiences' such as the Rama trail planned in Gujarat, or the Spice Route Tourism planned in Kerala (Subash, 2015).

To fully realise the potential of this medical tourism industry, governments MTm policy and accrediting bodies should aim to improve quality of private hospitals, country infrastructure, safety, security, and address all regulatory, legal, and ethical concerns, to get value from MTm with positive healthcare outcomes and make it an attractive destination and a memorable experience for the MT/patients. Finally, the dynamic nature of the healthcare trade policies of host and source countries, and the changing nature of host-country's medical and country infrastructure, economic and political conditions, exchange-rate fluctuations, MTm regulations, hospital branding, destination's attractiveness, and the current negative impact of coronavirus pandemic related travel restrictions and public health concerns, could affect the generalisation of results in future studies (Medhekar, 2020).

Along with medical tourism, if sport activities can be integrated, the tourism industry will stimulate the overall development of the economies of both the nations.

Coming to the tourism related to weddings, it is unarguable that destination weddings can give an economy a big boost. It increases the employment rate and can open new opportunities for both the destination and the people in the host country.

It is very important to update tourism and hospitality work standards as per the changes of external factors. On the job training should be a regular feature of this industry. Student exchanges between educational institutions should be encouraged.

In the current Covid scenario the world level tourism demand has considerably gone down. Flights to most of the countries are stagnant. Both the countries should capture an opportunity to develop more tourist relations among each other. As it could be found that both the countries are strong competitors for medical tourism, these should concentrate in those areas where they can act as complements to each other. Though wellness tourism is achieving the same purpose in both the countries but differences in these can be captured to stimulate tourist activities. Thai tourists can come to India and Indian tourists can go to Thailand. Some wellness training programmes can also be organised based on exchange programme. To encourage tourism from and to not so popular areas, special translators should be organised.

The exchange programs can be used for different types of education, in whichever India or Thailand is good. Special rural area visits can be organised. Meetings/ conferences can be conducted. Once tourism gets momentum it will put different sectors into motion.

More research is required to locate the areas where both the countries can stimulate tourism between the two.

REFERENCES

Adam, K., Snyder, J., Crooks, V., & Johnston, R. (2015). Tourism discourse and medical tourists' motivations to travel. *Tourism Review*, *70*(2), 85–96. doi:10.1108/TR-04-2014-0015

Agarwar, R. (2009-2010). Water Festivals of Thailand. *Silpakorn University International Journal, 9-10*, 7-18. Available at https://citeseerx.ist.psu.edu/viewdoc/download?doi=10.1.1.942.6524&rep–rep1&type=pdf

Alam, M. I. (2015, January-June). Indo-Asean Trade Relation: An Analysis. *Journal of International Economics*, *6*(1), 73–106. http://web.b.ebscohost.com/ehost/pdfviewer/pdfviewer?vid=1&sid=8890abb2-9424-4cde-997f-0746a37baa3d%40sessionmgr103

Arunmozhi, T., & Panneerselvam, A. (2013). Types of Tourism in India. *International Journal of Current Research and Academic Review*, *1*(1), 84–88.

Ashton, A. S. (2018, November 2). Spiritual retreat tourism development in the Asia Pacific region: investigating the impact of tourist satisfaction and intention to revisit: a Chiang Mai, Thailand case study. *Asia Pacific Journal of Tourism Research*, *23*(11), 1098–1114. Advance online publication. doi:10.1080/10941665.2018.1526198

Bajpaee, C. (2017). Dephasing India's 'Look East'/ 'Act East' policy. *Contemporary Southeast Asia*, *39*(2), 348–372. doi:10.1355/cs39-2d

Balaguer, J., & Cantavella-Jordá, M. (2002). Tourism as a Long-run Economic Growth Factor: The Spanish Case. *Applied Economics*, *34*(7), 877–884. doi:10.1080/00036840110058923

BBC News. (2018 July 11). *India Government is 'failing' to protect Taj Mahal.* Available at https://www.bbc.com/news/world-asia-india-44763867

Bhagwati, J., & Srinivasan, T. (1979). Trade Policy and Development. In R. Dornbunsch & J. Frenkel (Eds.), *International Economic Policy: Theory and Evidence* (pp. 1–35). Johns Hopkins University Press.

Bone, K. (2013). Spiritual Retreat Tourism in New Zealand. *Tourism Recreation Research, 38*(3), 295–309. doi:10.1080/02508281.2013.11081755

Breg, J. (2013). *Now and Forever: Growth, Impacts and Future Evolution of Wedding Tourism* [Research paper]. University of Guelph.

Brief on India-Thailand Relations. (2018, Dec.). Available at https://mea.gov.in/Portal/ForeignRelation/Thailand_Brief_Dec_2018.pdf

Burns, R. (2015). Medical tourism opportunities and challenges: Illustration from US-India trade. *International Journal of Healthcare Management, 8*(1), 15–26. doi:10.1179/2047971914Y.0000000091

Caleb, G., Mazanai, M., & Dhoro, N. L. (2014, September). Relationship between International Trade and Economic Growth: A Cointegration Analysis for Zimbabwe. *Mediterranean Journal of Social Sciences, 5*(20), 621–627. doi:10.5901/mjss.2014.v5n20p621

D'Amore, L. (2009). Peace through Tourism: The Birthing of a New Socio-Economic Order. *Journal of Business Ethics, 89*(4), 559–568. doi:10.100710551-010-0407-3

Deng, C. (2012). *Key Factors of Wedding Tourism in Bangkok, Thailand.* The Assumption University Library. Available at: https://repository.au.edu/bitstream/handle/6623004553/2557/AU-Thesis-Fulltext-222439.pdf?sequence=1

Dollar, D., & Kraay, A. (2004). Trade, Growth and Poverty. *Economic Journal (London), 114*(493), F22–F49. doi:10.1111/j.0013-0133.2004.00186.x

Eris, M., & Ulaşan, B. (2013, July). Trade openness and economic growth: Bayesian model averaging estimate of cross-country growth regressions. *Economic Modelling, 33*, 867–883. doi:10.1016/j.econmod.2013.05.014

Farooq, M. A. (2012). Development of Spiritual Tourism Circuits: The Case. *GSTF Journal on Business Review (GBR),* 212 – 218.

Felix, G., & Bello, G. K. (2019). Skills gaps and training needs in the tourism sector in Malawi. *African Journal of Hospitality, Tourism and Leisure*, 1–18.

Gaffar, V., Wetprasit, P., Setiyorini, D., & Puspito, H. (2011). *Comparative Study of Tourist Characteristics on Cultural Heritage Tourism Sites: Survey on Tourist in Indonesia and Thailand Heritage Sites*. Available at https://www.researchgate.net/publication/294682211_COMPARATIVE_STUDY_OF_TOURIST_CHARACTERISTICS_ON_CULTURAL_HERITAGE_TOURISM_SITES_SURVEY_ON_TOURIST_IN_INDONESIA_AND_THAILAND_HERITAGE_SITES/citation/download doi:10.13140/RG.2.1.1605.3525

Getz, D. (2007). Event tourism: Definition, evolution, and research. *Tourism Management*, 403–428.

GHSI. (2019). Validation analysis of Global Health Security Index (GHSI) scores 2019. BMJ Global Health, 5.

Gibson, H. J. (1998). Sport Tourism: A critical analysis of research. *Sport Management Review*, *1*(1), 45–76. doi:10.1016/S1441-3523(98)70099-3

Haokip, T. (2011). India's Look East Policy: Its Evolution and Approach. *South Asian Survey*, *18*(2), 239–257. doi:10.1177/0971523113513368

Hritz, N., & Ross, C. (2010). The Perceived Impacts of Sport Tourism: An Urban Host Community Perspective. *Journal of Sport Management*, *24*(2), 119–138. doi:10.1123/jsm.24.2.119

Husain, A. & Ganguli, S. (2019). A Comparative analysis of medical tourism competitiveness of India, Thailand and Singapore. Tourism: An International Interdisciplinary Journal, 67(2).

Jha, S.N. & Salim, M. (2015, March). India's economic relations and trade with ASEAN: An analysis. *Aweshkar Research Journal, 19*(1), 39-54.

Jindal, N. (2014). *India and ASEAN*. Available at http://politicosse.in/uploads/Politico_2014_Vol-2_No-22.pdf#page=109

Jirapornvaree, A. M. (2019). Factors Influencing ASEAN and International Students of Higher Education Programs in Thailand. *Asian Social Science*, 67–81.

Jotikasthira, N., Phakdeephirot, N., & Teeranoot, S. (2016). Thai Tourism and Hospitality Education: Current Conditions and Strategic Directions. *Rangsit Journal of Educational Studies, 3*(2).

Kale, S. (2004). Spirituality, religion, and globalization. *Journal of Macromarketing*, *24*(2), 92–107. doi:10.1177/0276146704269296

Kelly, C. (2010). Analysing Wellness Tourism Provision: A Retreat Operators' Study. *Journal of Hospitality and Tourism Management*, *17*(1), 108–116. doi:10.1375/jhtm.17.1.108

Khan, A., Bibi, S., Lorenzo, A., Lyu, J., & Babar, Z. U. (2020). Tourism and Development in Developing Ecomnomies: A Policy Implication Prspective. *Sustainability*, *12*(4), 1618. doi:10.3390u12041618

Khandare, V., & Phophueksanand, N. (2017, Jul-Sep). Economics of Tourism Development: A comparative Study of India and Thailand. *Kaav International Journal of Economics, Commerce & Business Management, 4*(3), 656-665.

Kittisak Jermsittiparsert, T.C. (2019). Behavior of Tourism Industry under the Situation of Environmental Threats and Carbon Emission: Time Series Analysis from Thailand. *International Journal of Energy Economics and Policy,* 366 – 372.

Kolb, B. (2017). *Tourism Marketing for Cities and Towns. Using Social Media and Branding to Attract Tourists* (2nd ed.). Routledge. doi:10.4324/9781315543413

Kumar, J., & Hussian, K. (2016). Factors affecting medical tourism destination selection: A Malaysian perspective. *International Interdisciplinary Business-Economics Advancement Journal, 1*(1), 1-10. https://www.doi.org/10.5038/2640-6489.1.1.1000

Maga, A. A., & Nicolau, P. E. (2020). Conceptualizing Educational Tourism and the Education Tourism Potential (evidence from ASEAN countries). Advances in Economics, Business and Management Research, 39.

Majumdar, A. (2021, May). From "Look East" to "Act East": India's Evolving Engagement with the Asia-Pacific Region. *Asian Affairs, 52*(2).

Medhekar, A., & Haq, F. (2019). *Challenges for Innovative Transformation in Heritage Tourism Development in India and Pakistan*. IGI Global.

Medhekar, A., & Wong, H. Y. (2020). Medical travellers' perspective on factors affecting medical tourism to India. *Asia Pacific Journal of Tourism Research, 25*(12), 1295–1310. doi:10.1080/10941665.2020.1837893

Medhekar, A., Wong, H. Y., & Hall, J. E. (2019, February). Factors influencing inbound medical travel to India. *Journal of Health Organization and Management, 33*(2), 155–172. doi:10.1108/JHOM-08-2018-0234 PMID:30950309

Micallef, H. (2017). *Indian weddings in Malta: Impacts and Perspective*. Available at https://www.theseus.fi/handle/10024/133358

Ministry of External Affairs (MEA). (2014-15). *Annual Report*. Available at http://www.mea.gov.in/Uploads/PublicationDocs/25009_External_Affairs_2014-2015__English_.pdf

Ministry of External Affairs (MEA). (2015-16). *Annual Report*. Available at https://www.mea.gov.in/Uploads/PublicationDocs/26525_26525_External_Affairs_English_AR_2015-16_Final_compressed.pdf

Ministry of External Affairs (MEA). (2018-19). *Annual Report*. Available at http://www.mea.gov.in/Uploads/PublicationDocs/31719_MEA_AR18_19.pdf

Mishra, M. S. (2020). India–Thailand Security Cooperation: Strengthening the Indo-Pacific Resolve. *Journal of Asian Security and International Affairs*.

News, B. (2018), July 11). *India Government is 'failing' to protect Taj Mahal*. Retrieved from bbc.com.new:https://www.bbc.com/news/world-asia-india-44763867

Nicolau, A. A. (2020). Education or Recreation: And enquiry into the motives of European Educational Tourists in Thailand (The case of Phuket). *Journal of EU Business School*, 8 - 20.

Pande, A. (2020). India's Act East Policy and ASEAN: Building a Regional Order through Partnership in the Indo-Pacific. *International Studies, 57*(1), 67–78. doi:10.1177/0020881719885526

Parmar, SM. (2017). Wellness tourism: Review and Growth. *PARIPEX- Indian Journal of Research, 5*(9), 33-35.

Phophueksanand, V. K. (2017). Economics of Tourism Development: A Comparative Study of India and Thailand. *KAAV International Journal of Economics*, 656 - 665.

Phukan, H., Rahman, Z., & Devdutt, P. (2012). Emergence of Spiritual Tourism in India. *International Journal of Marketing and Technology*, 2(4), 300–317.

Piboonrungroj, P., & Sangkakorn, K. (2013). *Tourism Logistics Management: A Case of Cultural Creative Tourism in Thailand.* Conference Paper on 'World Conference on Hospitality, Tourism and Event Research'. Available at https://www.researchgate.net/publication/260001134_TOURISM_LOGISTICS_MANAGEMENT_A_CASE_OF_CULTURAL_CREATIVE_TOURISM_IN_THAILAND

Rodbamrung, P. W. (202, July 29). *India – Thailand Relations: And Cultural Links in Soft Power Policy.* Available at https://so04.tci-thaijo.org/index.php/mgsj/article/view/201768/140880

Saint-Mezard, I. (2003). The Look East Policy: An Economic Perspective. In F. Grare & A. Mattoo (Eds.), *Beyond the Rhetoric: The Economics of India's Look East Policy* (pp. 21–43). Manohar.

SajjanharA. (2017, September 15). *ORF.* Available at https://www.orfonline.org/expert-speak/india-thailand-relations-a-70-year-partnership/

Schedneck, C. B. (2020). *Buddhist Tourism in Asia.* University of Hawai'i Press.

Sharafuddin, M.A. (2015). Types of Tourism in Thailand. *e-Review of Tourism Research (eTTR)*, 210–219.

Sharma, A. (2015). Educational Tourism: Strategy for Sustainable Tourism Development with reference of Hadauti and Shekhawati Regions of Rajasthan, India. *Journal of Business Economics and Information Technology*, 1-12.

Sheikh, Y. A. (2017). Higher Education in India: Challenges and Opportunities. *Journal of Education and Practice*, *8*(1). https://files.eric.ed.gov/fulltext/EJ1131773.pdf

Sinclair, M. T. (1998). Tourism and economic development: A survey. *The Journal of Development Studies*, *34*(5), 1–51. doi:10.1080/00220389808422535

Smith, M., & Kelley, C. (2006). Wellness Tourism. *Tourism Recreation Research*, *31*(1), 1–4. doi:10.1080/02508281.2006.11081241

Srichampa, S. (2015). Globalisation and the Language Situation in Thailand. *Journal of Language and Linguistics.* Available at https://www.researchgate.net/profile/Sophana-Srichampa/publication/284148708_Globalisation_and_the_Language_Situation_in_Thailand/links/564c576e08aeab8ed5e877d8/Globalisation-and-the-Language-Situation-in-Thailand.pdf

Subash, T. (2015, Dec.). Tourism in India: Potentials, Challenges and Opportunities. *International Journal of Research and Analytical Reviews, 2*(4).

Sumarniasih, M.A. (2019). Role of Tourism in Economy of Bali and Indonesia. *Journal of Tourism and Hospitality Management,* 34 – 54.

The World Bank. (n.d.). Available at https://tcdata360.worldbank.org/indicators/tot.direct.emp?country=IND&indicator=24644&countries=THA&viz=line_chart&years=1995,2028

Tiwari, A. K. (2011, June). Tourism, Exports and FDI as a Means of Growth: Evidence from four Asian Countries. *The Romanian Economic Journal, 14*(40).

Tourist Project. (2020). *Proceedings of the TOURIST 2nd Cross-Border Conference "Sustainable tourism development: Lessons learned for South East Asian countries"*. Available at https://www.researchgate.net/profile/Nirundon-Tapachai/publication/350978728_2nd_TOURIST_Conference_-_Sustainable_Tourism_-_Shaping_a_Better_Future_20-21_July_2020_Bangkok_Thailand/links/607dd187881fa114b414b241/2nd-TOURIST-Conference-Sustainable-Tourism-Shaping-a-Better-Future-20-21-July-2020-Bangkok-Thailand.pdf#page=387

UNESCO. (2020). *Properties inscribed on the World Heritage List*. Available at http://whc.unesco.org/en/statesparties/IN

UNWTO. (2020). *International Tourism Highlights 2020 Edition*. Available at https://www.e-unwto.org/doi/pdf/10.18111/9789284422456

Vidauskaite, R. (2009). *Destination branding through wedding tourism: The case of the Caribbean* [Master thesis]. University of Ljubljana, EMTM Universities.

Wall, G., & Mathieson, A. (2006). *Tourism: Change, Impact and Opportunities*. Pearson Education Limited.

Weed, M., & Bull, C. (2014, November). Influences on Sport-Tourism Relations in Britain: The Effects of Government Policy. *Tourism Recreation Research, 22*(2), 5–12. Advance online publication. doi:10.1080/02508281.1997.11014796

World Data Atlas. (n.d.). Available at https://knoema.com/atlas/topics/Tourism/Travel-and-Tourism-Total-Contribution-to-GDP/Contribution-of-travel-and-tourism-to-GDP-percent-of-GDP

World Travel & Tourism Council. (2019). *Travel & Tourism: Global Economic Impact & Trends*. Available at https://ambassade-ethiopie.fr/onewebmedia/Tourism-WTTC-Global-Economic-Impact-Trends-2019.pdf

Worldometer. (2021). *Countries in the world by population*. Available at https://www.worldometers.info/world-population/population-by-country/

Yogesh Hole, E. B. (2019). Challenges and solutions to the development of the tourism and hospitality industry in India. *African Journal of Hospitality, Tourism and Leisure*, 1–11.

Yousuf, A., & Lal, R. (2013, Sep.). The Impact of ASEAN on Tourism. *International Journal of Networking & Parallel Computing, 2*(3).

ADDITIONAL READING

Amoah, V., & Baum, T. (1997). Tourism education: Policy versus practice. *International Journal of Contemporary Hospitality Management, 9*(1), 5–12. doi:10.1108/09596119710157531

Bandyopadhyay, R., Morais, D. D., & Chick, G. (2008). Religion and identity in India's heritage tourism. *Annals of Tourism Research, 35*(3), 790–808. doi:10.1016/j.annals.2008.06.004

Bansal, S. P. (2006). Tourism Education in India: A Qualitative and Quantitative Analysis. In D. S. Bharadwaj, K. K. Kamra, & M. Chaudhary (Eds.), *Tourism Education – An Emerging Essential* (pp. 63–84). Kanishka Publishers.

Geary, D. (2008). Destination enlightenment: Branding Buddhism and spiritual tourism in Bodhgaya, Bihar. *Anthropology Today*, *24*(3), 11–14. doi:10.1111/j.1467-8322.2008.00584.x

Tourism Thailand. (n.d.). *Activities*. Retrieved from https://www.tourismthailand.org/See-and-Do/Activities/

KEY TERMS AND DEFINITIONS

Bilateral Trade: It is the exchange of goods between two nations to promote trade and investment.

GHSI: GHS Index provides a comprehensive assessment of countries' health security and considers the broader context for biological risks within each country, including a country's geopolitical considerations and health system and whether it has tested its capacities to contain outbreaks.

Medical Tourism: Travelling within a nation or overseas for medical treatment/surgery to purchase a medical product or healthcare service such as cancer surgery, cosmetic, dental, eye surgery, hip, and knee replacement.

Retreat Tourism: Retreats are usually centres or venues with a pre-prescribed aim of providing a mixture of activities, practices and treatments aimed to balance mind, body, and spirit.

Wellness Tourism: When a person travels within nation or overseas to rejuvenate his/her body, mind and spirit through medicine (traditional medicine) or wellness service.

Chapter 9
Promoting Trade and Economic Relations via Buddhist Spiritual Tourism Circuit Between India and Southeast Asia

Anita Medhekar
https://orcid.org/0000-0002-6791-4056
Central Queensland University, Australia

Farooq M. Haq
https://orcid.org/0000-0002-1620-9226
Canadian University Dubai, UAE

ABSTRACT

Spiritual tourism is one of the oldest forms of tourism. The purpose of this chapter is to review the key reasons for lack of promotion of investment and economic relations via tourism services related to Buddhist heritage and spiritual tourism circuit and sites to Southeast Asian countries as well as to domestic tourists. Sarnath, in Varanasi, is the hub of Buddhism in India, opened in 2016. There is road, rail, and air connection from Sarnath to various other Buddhist sites. This circuit can be promoted in counties of Southeast Asia and South Asia to spiritual followers of Buddhism as well as 'New Age' Buddhists. Thailand, Japan, and Korea have invested in spiritual infrastructure in Sarnath for their citizens who visit for Buddhist pilgrimage. This chapter identifies the challenges, opportunities, and provides recommendations for the Indian government to provide a business friendly environment and to encourage foreign direct investment for state-of-the-art infrastructure development from Southeast Asian nations around the Buddhist spiritual tourism circuit.

DOI: 10.4018/978-1-7998-5774-7.ch009

INTRODUCTION

Spiritual or religious tourism is a niche segment of tourism in general appreciated in the post-secular era since the events of 9-11 (Cohen, 2006; Olsen, 2019). It is one of the oldest forms of tourism or travel for pilgrimage to religious destinations, places of worships, and events (Cohen, 2006; Rinschede, 1992; Vukonic, 1996; Zhang, 2018). Spiritual tourism is a cultural, spiritual, social, and economic, phenomenon related to spiritual places and people (Haq & Medhekar, 2020). It involves people who travel outside their environment within the country or overseas to spiritual or sacred places as pilgrims or spiritual tourists (Das, 2016; Griffin & Raj, 2017). Tourism is the main driver of economic development of a country for job creation and production of goods and services related to particular niche tourism segments such as spiritual tourism- related to different religious, such as Islam, Christianity, Buddhism, Jainism, Hinduism, Zoroastrianism, Judaism, and Sikhism (Das, 2016; Brunn, 2016; Haq & Medhekar, 2014, 2018, & 2020; Olsen, 2019; Rumki & Kushagra, 2018). Spiritual tourists classify themselves in many ways as devotees', 'pilgrims', 'travellers', 'seekers', attending religious conferences, events and festival or 'spiritual adventurers'. "Interestingly, many spiritual tourists have been classified by academic researchers as practicing pilgrimage, religious, special interest, cultural or experiential tourists" (Haq & Jackson, 2009, p.142).

The success of any tourism destination, including spiritual tourism sites, monuments liked with spiritual founders/people such as Buddha, and places can be developed and promoted if the motives and needs of the niche segments of spiritual tourists is identified and looked after by the spiritual tourism goods and service providers at the destination (Finney et al., 2009; Haq & Medhekar, 2020; Shinde et al., 2020; Timothy & Olsen, 2006; Yasuda et al., 2018). Spiritual or religious tourism is motivated by spiritual reasons and can be a visit to a nearby temple, church, or mosque; or for number of days and weeks within the county or across international borders for spiritual/religious purposes to holy cities/ places and holy sites and monuments (Haq & Medhekar, 2018; Zhang, 2018). There is a huge potential to develop, attract foreign direct investment and promote the existing Buddhist spiritual tourism circuit and include other relevant Buddhist heritage sites and monuments in the various northern eastern states of India (Rumki & Kushagra, 2018). However, the niche spiritual tourism segments development is neglected by the central and the state governments and has developed by private sector in a haphazard manner (Bruntz, Schedneck, & Rowe, 2020). According to Centre Bureau for the Promotion of Imports from developing countries (CBI) religious tourism market covers specialised niche products pilgrimage, visiting sacred sites, temples, church mosques, travel with a purpose of worship and mission. These are visited by believers for religious and worship purpose as well as by non-believers for their aesthetic beauty, heritage value, cultural, and architectural importance (CBI, 2021).

The main objective of this chapter is to review the Buddhist spiritual tourism circuit and the reasons for the lack of promotion of trade and investment in tourism services related to Buddhist Heritage and Spiritual Tourism Circuit and sites to Southeast Asian Countries as well as to domestic tourists since it was opened in India (Buddhist Circuit, 2021; International Finance Corporation World Bank {IFC-WB}, 2018). Sarnath, in Varanasi is the hub of Buddhism in India opened in 2016, and there is road, rail and air connection from Sarnath to various other Buddhist sites connected to the Buddhist spiritual circuit (Buddhist Circuit, 2021; Geary, 2008; Phukan, 2015). Until 2016, Central Government of India invested Rupees 132.17 for developing tourism infrastructure under the 'Swadesh Darshan Scheme'. Whereas Uttar Pradesh Government spent Rupees 99.97 crores for developing Buddhist circuit road and rail covering Kushinagar, Srawasti, and Kapilvastu (The Times of India, 2016). Ministry of Indian Railways Government of India and the relevant state governments of Uttar Pradesh and Bihar had initiated the development of Buddhist spiritual tourism circuit by developing railroad infrastructure and online bookings for the tourists (Business Line, 2014; Chakraborty, 2011; Travel Website 2021).

Figure 1. Buddhist Pilgrimage Locations in India
Source: Pinterest (2021)

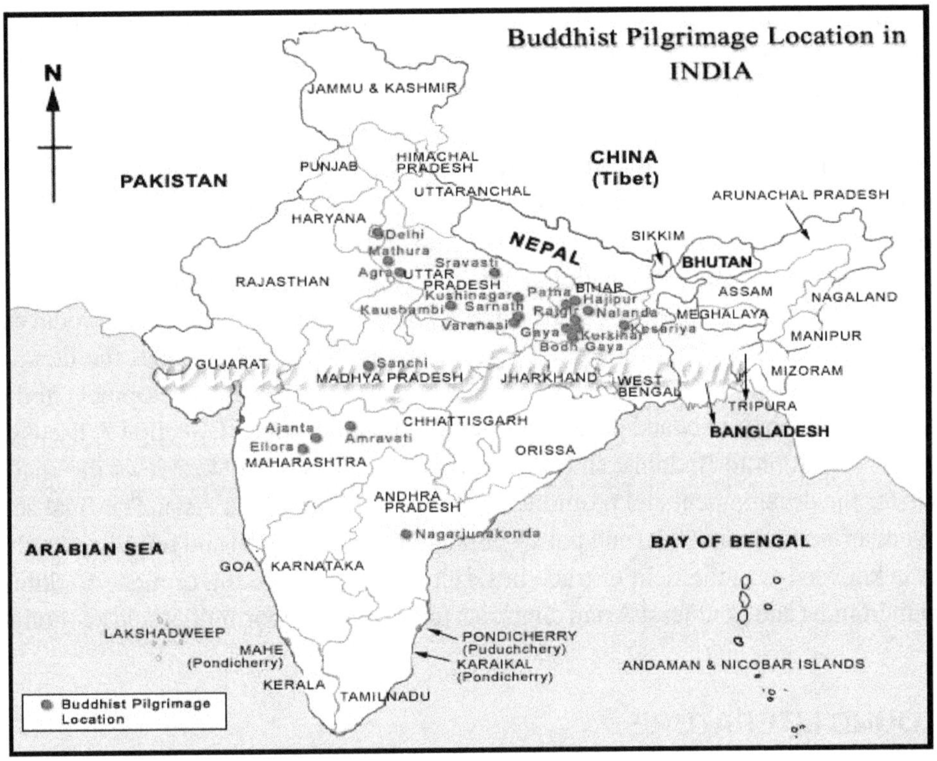

India needs strategic niche spiritual tourism infrastructure development policies and promotional campaigns to attract the right consumers while developing and promoting the Buddhist spiritual circuit as a product and place to Southeast Asian countries under public-private partnerships (PPPs) model for spiritual tourism development and promotion (Haq et al., 2012; International Finance Corporation, 2018). Various stakeholders should form PPPs for Buddhist spiritual tourism development and promotion such as the relevant state and local government authorities, philanthropic organisation, industrialist, travel agents, Indian railways which organises the Buddhist spiritual tourism rail circuit, road transport, and other spiritual tourism service providers in developing and marketing the Indian Buddhist spiritual tourism product and place to the domestic spiritual pilgrims as well as Buddhist Spiritual tourists in Southeast Asian countries (Medhekar & Haq, 2009; Rumki & Kushagra, 2018). Unless data is available from the surveys, in the footsteps of Buddhist trail bookings by road tour and Indian railway trip booking, and visiting sites, it is difficult to estimate in numbers the actual spiritual or religious tourists who travel just for pilgrimage to any religious site, and in case of this paper along the Indian Buddhist circuit, which is a growing segment (International Finance Corporation, 2018; Shinde et al., 2020). According to Yasuda et al. (2018), religious tourism is a growing segment in whole of Asia and in 2011 as per World Religious Tourism Association, 1.70 million religious pilgrims travelled to India alone for spiritual tourism. Figure-1 illustrates the map of Buddhist pilgrimage locations in different states of India.

The Buddhist circuit in India could be signified by the fact that 18 percent of total foreign tourists coming to India in 2011 were originally from Buddhist countries, which indicated a considerable growth compared to overall in-bound tourists (Rumki & Kushagra, 2018). The in-bound tourists from few Buddhist countries like Sri Lanka (4.9 percent), Thailand (1.5 percent), China (2.3 percent), Japan (3.1 percent) and South Korea (1.7 percent) were substantial compared to other countries (Bruntz et al., 2020). Bodhgaya, Sarnath, Rajgir, Nalanda, and Kushinagar, are obviously pulling lots of travellers from Buddhist countries where 70 to 90% foreign tourists come for spiritual or religious reasons associated with Buddhism (Shinde et al., 2020). Among the five Indian cities mentioned above, Sarnath with 29.6% and Rajgir with 31.1% foreign tourists; dominate the market and indicates the available opportunities (International Finance Corporation, 2018). This research is motivated by the research presented by International Finance Corporation (2018), which promises the tourism opportunity by measuring that Indian in-bound tourists from Buddhist nations contain only 0.005 percent of the total Buddhist believers.

This chapter is structured as follows. The first introductory section of the chapter introduces the growing significance of Buddhist spiritual tourism circuit in India. Section 2 provides the literature review on the spiritual tourism and the economic importance of spiritual tourism development and promotion for economic progress, prosperity and peace in regional and global context. Section 3 discusses the case study examples in relation to Buddhist spiritual tourism circuit. Section 4 reviews the challenges and opportunities for the development and promotion in India and South-East Asia. The final section presents recommendations for managerial and policy implications, conclusion and future research directions to advance the knowledge in the field of trade in services sector marketing of niche Buddhist spiritual tourism circuit in India and Southeast Asian countries for business opportunities and economic benefits.

BACKGROUND LITERATURE

Spiritual Tourism

In case of South Asia and Southeast Asian nations, the largest number of spiritual tourists are usually domestic pilgrims who visit spiritual places for annual festivals and regularly for thanksgiving and spiritual reasons besides the internal visitors (Brunn, 2015; Haq & Medhekar, 2014, 2020; Raj & Morpeth, 2007; Yasuda et al., 2018). This study accepts that while Buddhism has directly motivated masses for spiritual tourism, the relevant tourism literature is basically very descriptive. Religious tourists including Buddhists, non-Buddhist and New-Age believers have travelled to holy destinations in various geographical areas, pilgrimage to temples, religious tourist attractions and festivals with Buddhist associations have uncovered the limitation of being inherently descriptive. Three repetitive themes have been observed during the Buddhism related religious and spiritual tourism literature review. Several researchers have written on travel specifically to holy Buddhist sites and the influence of different individuals motivating for such journeys. The primary theme was destination travel and the secondary subject stemmed from the influence of special people related to Buddhism, while lastly were the events and festivals arranged for similar motivations. Furthermore, the activities organised for Buddhist tourists also include visiting temples, organised sessions for prayers/mediation, visiting museums and historic relics, attending religious rituals, souvenir shopping, attending Buddhist festivals, visiting related communities, and attending significant art or music performances. The average stay of international tourists in the Buddhist Circuit is calculated around five to thirteen days, while the package costs on the Buddhist Circuit range from around US$100 per day for budget to $300 for upscale services (International Finance Corporation, 2018).

The experience of religious and spiritual travellers link with their ideals, beliefs and practices, while studies on spiritual tourism have highlighted tactics for tourism marketers targeting travelers from a range of relevant areas motivating researchers for theoretical research and applied research (Buhalis, 2000; Haq & Jackson, 2009; Riege & Perry, 2000; Rinschede, 1992; Yasuda et al., 2018). Analyzing other fundamentals to interpret culture, religion has been persuasive for human beliefs, hence Buddhism as religion is recognized as a foremost factor to study spiritual tourism circuits associated with Buddhism in India (Finney et al., 2009; Raj & Morpeth, 2007).

Spirituality is explained as the heart of religion and a stimulating element that pervades the core structure of religiosity (Mitroff & Denton, 1999; Timothy & Olsen, 2018). Theoretically, spiritual tourism and religious tourism are similar as one of the oldest types of voyages and promise faith to the voyager (Raj & Morpeth, 2007; Rinschede, 1992; Vukonic', 1996). The theoretical margin between spirituality and religion is demonstrated as an acceptance of religion masked as spirituality and spirituality masked as religion (Cohen, 1992; Mitroff & Denton, 1999). The 2017, International Congress on Religious Tourism and Pilgrimage in Portugal, focussed on the potential role of religious tourism and scared places as an instrument for social-economic and cultural development of the destinations linked with sacred places, to which the spiritual tourists are loyal with repeat visits, and so these spiritual places and monuments need to be well managed promoted, preserved, and conserve its authenticity and integrity, as spiritual destinations with effective stakeholders public and private partnerships (UNWTO 2017a).

Spiritual tourism according to Haq and Medhekar (2019) is suggested as a peace vehicle for social transformation and economic prosperity between countries with decades of cross-border disputes such as India and Pakistan. This proposition is further supported by researchers arguing that spiritual tourism is also utilized as a peace building phenomenon between nations by (Akhtar et al., 2019; McIntosh, 2016). The well-known spiritual tourism Buddhist places include: **(i)** Lumbini (in Nepal) –place of birth. **(ii)** Bodhgaya (in Bihar) – where he attained enlightenment under the Bodhi Tree. **(iii)**Sarnath (in Uttar Pradesh) – where he delivered his first sermon. **(iv)** Nalanda and Rajgir (in Bihar) where he lived and taught, and Nalanda became the center of Buddhist learning and teaching. **(v)** Kushinagar (in Uttar Pradesh) – where he died. **(vi)** Kapilavastu (on India Nepal Border) – where Buddha spent his first early years before embarking on the long journey to enlightenment. **(vi)** Vaishali (in Bihar)– Buddha's delivered last sermon. **(vii)** Sravasti (in Uttar Pradesh) – Buddha spent twenty-four rainy seasons here at the Jetavan monastery, built by his disciple Sudatta Anathapindika. **(viii)** Kausambi (in Uttar Pradesh) – Buddha stayed and preached at Kausambi (International Finance Corporation World Bank {IFC-WB}, 2018).

The relationship between Buddhism as a religion and spiritual tourism has gained popularity for researchers as well as Buddhist clergy and followers. Asia is full of places and destinations linked with Buddhism or the historical Buddha as reflected in various tourism circuits, such developments have supported the regeneration of Buddhist places (Shinde et al., 2020). Asia being recognised as number one tourist place, modern practices in travels to Asia recently have appreciated the need for Holy Buddhist sites (Bruntz, Schedneck, & Rowe, 2020). Many Asian government and private agencies are exploring the growing admiration of Buddhism by making holy places such as: mountains, temples, artefacts, and spiritual Buddhist places more tourist-attractive by various techniques including the circuits (International Finance Corporation, 2017). The current tourism atmosphere affected by economic crisis and the breakout of Covid-19; has triggered passion for religious tourism including Buddhist travels re-intellectualising the significances and values of people and places related with Buddhism (Bruntz, et al., 2020; Shinde et al., 2020). A clear example of governments exploiting on broad understanding of Buddhist tourism is the Chinese Mount Wutai that had annual visitors of around a million in 2001 and jumped to three million in 2007.

The conceptual understanding of this chapter is based on considering pilgrimage as the established state of religious tourism with optional spiritual or cultural bundles followed by various services arranged and offered to the travellers (Raj & Morpeth, 2007; Timothy & Olsen, 2018; Vukonic', 1996). Cohen (1992) divided pilgrimage centers into two kinds as the popular and formal pilgrimage. For the popular pilgrimage center, 'the ludic and folksy activities are of greater importance and may even take precedence over the more serious and sublime activities' (Cohen 1992, p. 36). Meanwhile, the formal pilgrimage center is explained travels covering 'the serious and sublime religious activities are primarily emphasized' and 'the pilgrim's principle motive for the journey to such centres is to perform a fundamental religious obligation' (Cohen, 1992, p. 36). Concluding from the aforementioned review, a critical perception that needs recognition for this chapter is that the distinction between spiritual and religious tourism does not portray the main direction of this study, therefore, these two types of tourism associated with Buddhism are going to be considered alike and parallel in theory and business practice of tourism in economics and trade.

Buddhist Spiritual Tourism Development and Promotion in Asia

Literature shows that there is a low level of promotional activity by governments ministry of tourism of Buddhist Spiritual Tourism Circuit in India and overseas, and also lack of awareness among both Indian and foreign tourists about India and other South Asian countries with important Buddhist temples and Ashrams also known as Viharas linked with Buddha as a destination for Buddhist sites, compared to countries such as Burma, Cambodia, Thailand, Vietnam, Japan, and China (Agrawal et al., 2010; Geary, 2008; Haq & Medhekar, 2020; Phukan et al., 2012; Timothy & Olsen, 2006). The key strengths of this Buddhist spiritual tourism circuit (Figure-2) are the well-connected pilgrimage by road, rail, and air, to major capital cities which can service 500 million global Buddhist followers and other spiritual pilgrims, with availability of accommodation and monasteries around Buddhist heritage and spiritual sites (Medhekar & Haq, 2012). However, the safety, availability and quality of spiritual tourism infrastructure management needs regular attention for sustainability of the Buddhist spiritual tourism circuit to cater to the needs and wants of niche domestic and international Buddhist spiritual pilgrims (Chen at al., 2017; Medhekar & Haq,2009; Shinde, 2007). Figure-2 shows that the main Buddhist Circuit Indian Railway Tourist Train sites are located in the Uttar Pradesh and Bihar states, with a side trip by road to Lumbini in Nepal, the birthplace of Buddha (Buddhist Circuit, 2021) .

Empirical research shows that tourism promotes economic development and growth (Leitão & Shahbaz, 2016; Oh, 2005; Sequeira & Maças, 2008; Varghese, 2018). The Indian Economic Strategy 2020-35 clearly states that the Indian government's 2018 *'Swadesh Darshan'* initiative is to attract private sector investment in spiritual tourism and visits by non-resident Indian diaspora (Current Affairs 2018; News India, 2020). This also includes a "national mission for pilgrimage rejuvenation and spiritual augmentation, expanded e-tourist visa facilities, and relaxed coastal land and air regulation" (Varghese, 2018, p.152).

The World Bank (IFC-WB, 2018), report provides a strategic development plan regarding investing in Buddhist Circuit in India through international collaboration with Japan, Thailand, and other countries, in order to preserve the centuries old Buddhist World Heritage Sites such as caves, monasteries, and ashrams. The vision is for goals of developing Buddhist circuit, market positing, branding and promotion, to target markets related to pilgrims, international, and domestic tourists.

Figure 2. The Buddhist Circuit Tourist Train Route Itinerary
Source: Official website Indian Railways (Buddhist Circuit, 2021)

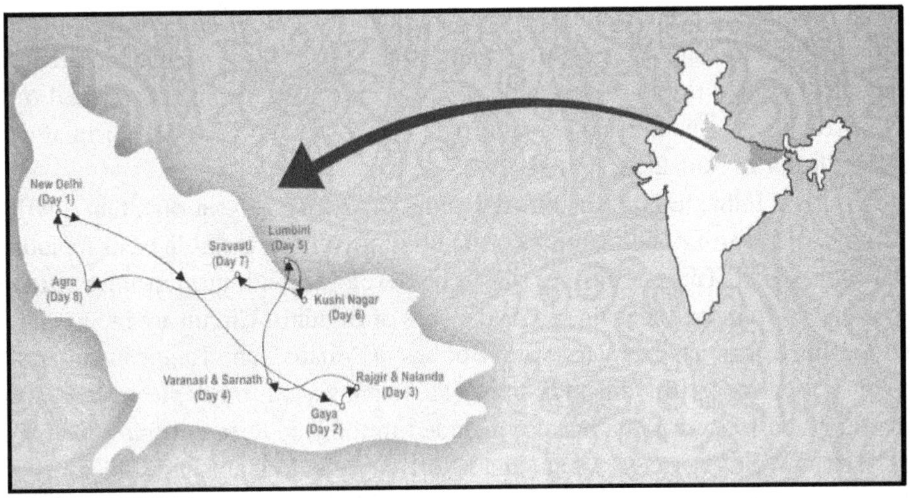

MAIN FOCUS OF THE CHAPTER

The main aim of this chapter is to review the current spiritual development and promotion policy of the government of India and the relevant Indian states where thousands of years old Buddhist heritage such as monasteries and caves are located, considered sacred by the Buddhist spiritual tourists. Further to examine the current and future challenges and opportunities for foreign direct investment (FDI) from Southeast Asian countries to investment in development, promotion, and reciprocal trade and tourism in Buddhist spiritual tourism circuit related goods and services.

According to the United Nations World Tourism Organizations Secretary-General opening address at the world congress on Religion in 2017 at Portugal "Among the many motivations for travelling, visiting cultural or religious sites ranks high on travelers' wish lists. Leveraging the growing interest for religious tourism worldwide is not only beneficial for the tourism sector, but crucial in building cultural dialogue and peace"…. "Religious tourism can also be a powerful instrument for raising awareness regarding the importance of safeguarding one´s heritage and that of humanity and help preserve these important sites for future generations" (UNWTO, 2017b).

CASE OF BUDDHIST SPIRITUAL TOURISM CIRCUIT

'Buddhist Spiritual Tourism Circuit' is in the 'Footsteps of Buddha' and includes all the holy places where Buddha travelled stayed and lived in his place of birth Lumbini now in Nepal (included in the

Buddhist circuit), and in India places of teaching, preaching, enlightenment, achieved Nirvana and rest. They are the spiritual sites and monuments linked with Gautama Buddha, temples, monasteries, of spiritual and religious significance for the global 450 million followers of Buddhism (IFC-WB, 2018) and spiritual people/ visitors. Cohen (2006) was the first spiritual tourism scholar who studied various types and motives of religious or spiritual tourism phenomena and presented two religious/spiritual tourist motives: (i) *formal pilgrimage* indicated the tourist's motives to fulfill religious commitments and rituals like visit to mecca to perform Hajj or Kumbh mela, and (ii) *popular pilgrimage* was identified the non-religious but personal spiritual wellbeing-oriented goals to seek spiritual development. Therefore, 'Buddhist Spiritual Tourism Circuit' is popular amongst the *formal pilgrims* who are the Buddhist followers and scholars of Buddhism, and secondly *popular pilgrimage* includes spiritual /non-Buddhist people who have respect for Buddha and are secular in nature seeking personal spiritual wellbeing and development (Medhekar & Haq, 2012).

Ministry of Tourism India, in 2011 announced under the 12th five-year plan that it will develop 35 tourism circuits by 2016 worth Rs 9,450 crores on a public-private partnership basis including Buddhist circuit (India Today, 2011). This circuits are still to be developed with proport infrastructure facilities and promoted overseas. In India, the main spiritual places of Buddhist Circuit are in Sarnath in Varanasi, Shravasti, and Kushinagar in Uttar Pradesh; and Bodhgaya, Vaishali and Rajgir in Bihar. All these are the main pilgrimage centres for Buddhism in India. There are various other places linked to Buddha in other parts of south and western India but not included in the Buddhist spiritual tourism circuit such as the United Nations World Heritage Ajanta and Ellora caves in Maharashtra. It attracts visitors from India as well as other 30 countries (Buddhist Circuit, 2021; Phukan, 2015). Further Ministry of Tourism India has identified Buddhist ashrams, viharas and stupas in 21 states, to develop and promote interstate Buddhist tourism circuit, to capture the "New-Age" Buddhist tourists from the western countries and traditional markets in Southeast Asia (Current Affairs 2018).

Challenges

There are numerous challenges in protecting, developing infrastructure around centuries old Buddhist spiritual sites and monuments and promoting the Buddhist spiritual tourism circuit similar to other prominent religious monuments from Hinduism, Christianity and Sikhism sites existing in India.

1. **Protecting Heritage Buddhist Spiritual Tourism Sites:** There are centuries old significant heritage Buddhist monuments and temples particularly built along the circuit in the foot-steps of Buddha. Some of these sites have world heritage listing due to which they are protected and preserved. However, around the site there is traffic congestion, air pollution and littering which needs to be removed and surrounded by parks and lawns for peaceful serene environment.
2. **Low quality of Tourism Infrastructure:** There is low quality of tourism related products, services and infrastructure facilities at the site for example poor standards of tourist information booths, tourist accommodation, local transport, lack of quality restaurants, lack of authentic local art/craft shopping facilities, food and water safety, poor hygiene and washroom facilities for domestic and international pilgrims/ tourists.
3. **Health safety and security of tourists:** All domestic or international pilgrims and tourists need to feel safe and secure at all spiritual tourism sites, given the terrorist attacks by fundamental groups. Safety in travel and tourism is considered as terrorist activities similar to September 11 Twin Towers

episode in New York, USA, safety from thefts of personal belongings, and pickpocket. Similarly safety from traffic or adventure tourism accidents, and health related issues, such as failed medical tourism surgery, food poisoning and virus such as SARS and COVID-19 so that there is easy access to healthcare facilities in case of fever, food poisoning, or accident or virus-related fever.

4. **Rail and road infrastructure facilities:** It is essential to improve road and rail infrastructure facilities to provide first class experience to the tourists. Foot path facilities and pedestrian crossing at sites need to be improved and visitor safety should not be compromised.
5. **Lack of employment creation:** Spiritual Tourism sector and Buddhist trail can create job opportunities in areas servicing this segment, such as rail and road transport, hospitality, accommodation, catering services, cleaners, garden maintenance, security, educated and informed tour guides with knowledge of Buddhist heritage, culture, and Buddhist teachings, multilingual tour guides catering to Indian languages as well as foreign languages such as Thai, Japanese, Korean, Vietnamese, Singhalese, and Burmese catering to the overseas spiritual tourists.
6. **Lack of Multilingual tour guides:** Vocational Educational institutions can take the opportunity within their tourism programs to focus on various types of tourism circuits as well as training for multilingual domestic and foreign languages tour guides. There is limited information on Buddhist heritage, history, and stories to interest the local and international pilgrims and the tourists.
7. **Lack of other cultural entertainment**: The spiritual tourism circuits and packaged tours do not provide any other cultural events and entertainment to the visitors for the evening, such as plays on the life of Buddha or local cultural food, music, dance, visit to museums, surrounding villages, hiking in forests, ashram stays for spiritual enhancement, and rural tourism experience for the spiritual tourists.
8. **Lack of involvement of Global Buddhist Organisations**: Given that the Buddhist spiritual tourism circuit includes the footstep trails of Buddha, it is a very important spiritual site for the Buddhist devotees, there is very limited involvement of other Buddhist organisations to invest in the site development and maintenance.
9. **Sustainable development of the Buddhist circuits:** Development of infrastructure facilities and spiritual circuits, tourism sites and markets are always at a cost to the environment, overpopulation, encroaching, conflict of modernity with traditional heritage sites, lack of hygiene, and traffic congestion and pollution around tourism sites, vandalism and destruction of heritage statues and monuments. It is essential that these conflicting goals and challenges are managed in a sustainable manner to meet few of the 17, United Nations Sustainable Development Goals.

Opportunities

All the challenges above can be converted to opportunities for sustainable development, and promotion of Buddhist spiritual tourism circuit.

1. **New Age Buddhist:** Ministry of Tourism India identified centuries old ancient Buddhist monuments in 21 other states and to develop circuits according to the tourism minister "on principles of high tourist value, competitiveness and sustainability in an integrated manner", and promote interstate Buddhist tourism circuit, to "New-Age" Buddhist tourists from the western countries and traditional markets in Southeast Asian consumers. This will not only enrich tourist experience but also create employment opportunities for the locals. Union Ministry of tourism has identified 12

additional circuits- namely: North-East India Circuit, Coastal Circuit, Himalayan Circuit, Krishna Circuit, Desert Circuit, Eco Circuit, Wildlife Circuit, Tribal Circuit, Rural Circuit, Spiritual Circuit, Ramayana Circuit and Heritage (Circuit Current Affairs, 2018). However, the infrastructure development and promotion of these circuits nationally and internally still has to be realised.

2. **Product Development:** To develop the Buddhist spiritual circuit, means to preserve centuries old heritage monuments, parks and environment surrounding the Buddhist monasteries and temples. Further, authentic cultural traditions and activities also need to be preserved with local knowledge, develop new attractions and side trips along the train circuit, to provide authentic product experience to the Buddhist and non-Buddhist visitors with special package (Buddhist Circuit, 2021; Travel Website, 2021). Finally promote new products, tourism services and facilities, local participation, awareness of Buddhist heritage and encourage private sector investment and entrepreneurship to provide quality of spiritual tourism goods and services to the visitors.
3. **Trade and Investment Strategy:** With the growth of market it is important to also attract foreign direct investment business opportunities from countries such as Japan to invest in good quality trains and cabins for the Buddhist circuit, hotels, local transport, airport facilities, restaurants, spiritual wellness resorts and ashrams. Besides develop gardens, hotel infrastructure and other facilities for the organized packaged spiritual tourists as well as independent travellers. A long-term investment and trade strategy is essential for regular development and maintenance of the circuits and related services infrastructure.
4. **Employment Creation:** Development of Buddhist and other circuits will generate employment opportunities for the locals in various sectors related to Buddhist circuit, to cater to the pilgrims and other "New Age" Buddhist needs, beyond the pilgrimage.
5. **Improve Connectivity:** This includes state-of-the-art infrastructure development for improved connectivity for the comfort of the national and international tourists. For example, local road quality, rail, air transport, including internet communication and medical tourism hospital/first-aid facilities. Further, ease of spiritual tourism visa category and immigration at arrival with travel agent representative to receive the pilgrims from arrival to departure.
6. **Human Resource Development:** History department and hotel management school should develop niche tourism related diplomas to train the professional staff required for supporting the Buddhist and other spiritual tourism circuits.
7. **Supply-Chain Operations:** Quality of customer service for the spiritual tourists needs to be improved by developing local supply chains for various tourism services, employment creation and income generating opportunities, through local handicrafts, spiritual souvenirs, holy objects and prayer books, food, culture, hospitality, and transport from arrival to departure for the visitors.
8. **Tapping Underdeveloped markets, branding and packaging:** Branding the Buddhist spiritual tourism circuit, product packaging, promotion/advertising, distribution and sale to unexplored and underdeveloped domestic and overseas markets, travel agents and customers directly through online bookings and as provided by Indian Railways for Buddhist circuit itinerary. Further packaging Buddhist circuit with other Hindu religious circuits for the pilgrimage and Buddhist heritage tourism in other Indian states.
9. **Public-private partnership (PPP) opportunities**: Local and international collaboration for PPP opportunities for funding, trade, investment, product development and promotion. Of spiritual tourism circuit packaged with other heritage tours.

DISCUSSION AND RECOMMENDATIONS

1. **Capacity Building through PPPs:** In order to address the challenge of protecting Buddhist spiritual tourism heritage, capacity building by public and private partnerships (PPPs) projects is the key to bring awareness by involving all stakeholders and the local community, for Buddhist UNESCO world heritage, Buddhist spiritual leaders, government, NGO, philanthropist, archaeology department, educational institutions, universities, architectural firms, academics from various disciplines such as scientist, historians, economist, and sustainable tourism management gurus and artists. Medhekar and Haq (2020) have highlighted the coherence between public and private organizations for the capacity building to enhance spiritual tourism in India and Pakistan. For example the Buddhist world heritage site at Taxila in Pakistan, PPPs were formed between UNESCO, Islamabad government, Comsats Institute of Information Technology and, Hazara University to build capacity and preserve the sites for future generations (UNESCO, 2019). Therefore PPPs for providing a holistic Circuit for Buddhist spiritual tourism between India, Pakistan, Nepal, Sri Lanka, Afghanistan and Bangladesh and Southeast Asian countries governments and Buddhist organizations is essential for promoting a complete Buddhist Spiritual Tourism Circuit.
2. **Promotion and marketing strategies:** The challenge of promotion and marketing to international tourist's heritage and cultural spiritual destinations, is not just about visit to see Buddhist relics from the past. National or international tourists in general also look for facilities and services available to have a positive and satisfying travel experience. These spiritual tourism packages need to promote a Buddhist spiritual tourism circuit brand, and other spiritual and heritage tours packaged with tis circuit, which could be sold by all tour operators, besides direct bookings from the Indian railway sites and specialist Buddhist tour operators, religious organisations, holding exhibitions, online and e-marketing strategies to Buddhist source market countries of Sri Lanka, Bhutan, Thailand, Myanmar, Vietnam, Cambodia, Laos and Tibet.
3. **Employment creation:** Host-communities as stakeholders should be provided with employment opportunities as in all sectors, building, retail, maintenance of the sacred places, tour guides and tour operators to cater to their wellbeing and income opportunities to meet the sustainable development goals of poverty reduction, and employment creation. Constructions of hotels, motel style accommodation, and local secure transport to cater to the needs of spiritual tourists. Local people should be made aware of the potential economic benefits arising from recognizing, developing, preserving centuries old spiritual heritage sites and promotion of all spiritual places, sites and monuments to Southeast Asian countries with large Buddhist following.
4. **Good Safety and security arrangements:** Safety and security of the spiritual tourists at these religious sites, buggies to take older tourists to the temple door, emergency healthcare and first-aid clinic and ambulance facility at the spiritual places and sites, and presence of local police authorities to prevent vandals and terrorism activities, if India wants to attract tourists from Southeast Asia, not just for the Buddhist circuit but also other types of tourism such as heritage, cultural, mountain, beaches and desert.
5. **Hospital and healthcare facility:** The Buddhist spiritual tourism railway circuit should have a medical doctor and nurse on board to cater to the Buddhist trail spiritual tourists in case of any health emergency or sickness faced by visitor on board.

6. **Foreign language tour guides:** It is essential to have foreign language tour guides who are fluent not only in English but also in 1-2 Asian languages Burmese, Thai, Malay, Korean Chinese, and Japanese to cater to overseas spiritual tourists.
7. **Adoption of technology and automation:** Technology has empowered people and it is one of the key drivers of online travel booking available to all visitors whether by air or train, where the potential tourists become their own travel agents. Post OVID-19 the tourism sector will adopt more automated technology for booking, or prerecorded tour guides in different languages with headphone hire at the tourism sites.
8. **Virtual spiritual tourism:** Pandemic will also drive various popular spiritual tourism sites to also adopt innovative 'virtual spiritual tourism tours and views on special events and occasions for an affordable fee. Therefore spiritual tourism sites of major religions need to adopt technology to provide virtual Buddhist spiritual tourism circuit tour, zoom meeting prayers and seminars, with explanation and provide actual 3-D style spiritual experience to the online visitors.
9. **Infrastructure development:** To develop any place or tourism destination, it is important for the government to first develop infrastructure facilities for examples roads, highways, railways and air connectivity, state-of-the-art information and telecommunication technologies, healthcare facilities and education institution, hotels and hospitality accommodation, shopping malls etc., which are the drivers of economics growth and progress linked to tourism. Further, it is also important to provide business friendly environment for attracting private funding from domestic entrepreneurs and foreign direct investment, to drive trade, travel and tourism with South Asian and Southeast Asian neighboring countries.
10. **Public Hygiene and sanitation:** World Health Organisation (WHO, 2020) declared in March 2020 coronavirus as a pandemic -global health emergency, due to being highly contagious. Countries followed the COVID-19 related regulations such as social distancing, imposed travel and travel restrictions, closed state and international borders imposing lockdowns to minimise the spread of the coronavirus. This has made many developing countries with high density of population realize that public health hygiene, access to clean sanitation and washroom facilities and clean environment is so essential to stop the spread of virus in tourist facilities for the locals and visitors alike. It is important that governments at all levels provide clean and green hygienic facilities during all times to maintain public health to attract tourists to spiritual tourism destinations.
11. **Sustainable tourism development:** Finally the key aim for development of any tourism destination in developing country like India or in Southeast Asia should be to meet the few of the identified 17 United Nations Sustainable Development Goals (UN-SDGs). For example in case of Buddhist Spiritual Tourism Circuit development and promotion to southeast Asian countries, the following goals are achievable which aliens also with Buddhist philosophy: Goal-1 No Poverty, Goal-2, No Hunger, Goal-4 Gender Equality, Goal-6: provision of clean water and sanitation, Goal-8 Decent Work and Economics Growth, Goal-9 Industry Innovation and Infrastructure Development, Goal-11 Sustainable Cities and Communities, and Goal-17 Global Partnerships for Sustainable Development (United Nations, 2021). This paper suggests a model for sustainable Socio-Economic Prosperity, and Peace through development of Buddhist Spiritual Tourism Circuit between India, South Asian and Southeast Asian nations, where all the stakeholders of spiritual tourism circuit, need to come together and from a public-private partnerships for planning, development and promotion of the Buddhist circuit.

12. Finally, religion and spirituality are part of everyday life in every society. Marketing and promotion strategy for Buddhist spiritual or religious tourism trails, tours, and festivals in South Asian and to Southeast Asian countries to Buddhist pilgrims and New Age Buddhist followers from the western countries is an important factor for the religious organisations, committees and the governments, as it brings in revenue from spiritual pilgrims and creates employment opportunities, along with keeping culture, tradition, spiritual sites and places functional for future generations. Usually images of spiritual people, saints, holy slogans, spiritual artifacts, temples and spiritual monuments which are internationally recognised are used for marketing and promotions of spiritual tourism sites and ata5trct visitors to sacred places. Spiritual tourism segments as discussed creates many opportunities and benefits for the society and the economy. In the 21st century Spiritual Tourism should be marketed as a driver of peace which is essential for mutual friendship, cooperation, progress and prosperity between nations, as per the core value and teachings of all religions.

Figure-3 provides a model for sustainable economic prosperity and peace through Buddhist spiritual tourism circuit for the people and countries, through public-private partnerships between the stakeholders. The spiritual circuit in figure-2 can be extended to incorporate key places in south India and other neighbouring souths Sian countries where the South Asian railways and specially SriLanka airlines can form partnerships to create new products and more train Buddhist tourism circuits covering other key Buddhist sites for the spiritual tourists.

Figure 3. Sustainable Socio-Economic Prosperity, and Peace through Buddhist Spiritual Tourism Circuit
Source: Developed for this paper

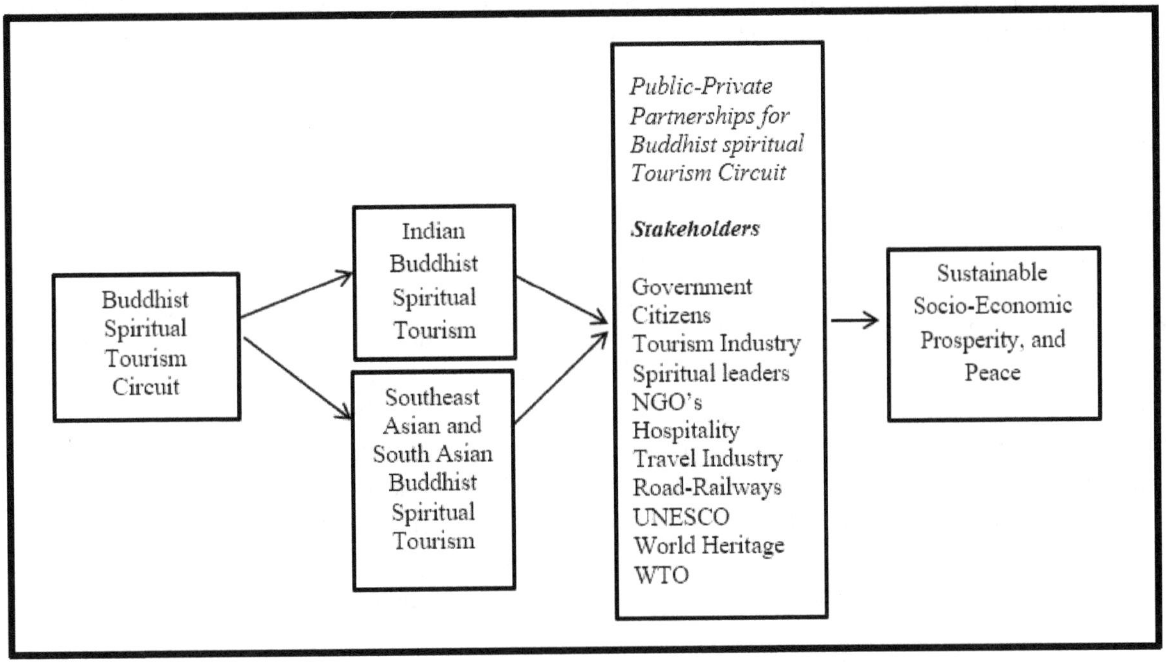

FUTURE RESEARCH DIRECTIONS

India and Southeast Asian countries have religious places and monuments from different religions such as Hinduism, Islam, Christianity, Sikhism, and so the opportunities and potential for development and promotion of different spiritual tourism circuits belonging to other religions can be studied by interviewing the public and private sector stakeholders of these religious places and monuments including the people. Further, the host-communities can be interviewed to explore the direct economic benefits from the development of Buddhist spiritual tourism circuit and also regarding their involvement in terms of grass-root consultancy by the government for the sustainable development of the Buddhist spiritual tourism circuit in order to meet the United Nations sustainable development goals. Further, also in context of Buddha's teaching in today's context which is relevant about promoting international peace, happiness and end to violence, terrorism, and greed by people, businesses, and governments to have a peaceful engagement with all stakeholders for the happiness and wellbeing of all global citizens. Actual spiritual or religious tourists, including budget and high end independent explorers, can be interviewed and surveys to know their perception as a spiritual tourist and if their needs are met at the various locations of Buddhist Spiritual Tourism circuit in terms of **(a)** Buddhist pilgrimage, **(b)** Buddhist ancient heritage, and **(c)** Spiritual enlightenment of body, mind and soul (ashram experience involving meditation, yoga, healthy cooking/eating, de-tox program, self-reflection and minimalist living). Similarly travel agents could be interviewed in terms of marketing and promotion of the Buddhist spiritual tourism circuit in the three categories as a package. Finally, more detailed studies are required to provide a holistic and secular understanding of the various forms and dimensions of spiritual/religious tourism in India, South Asian nations of Pakistan, Sri Lanka, Nepal, Afghanistan and Bangladesh and Southeast Asia. Further, role of government, private sector, religious organisations and in its management and promotion and providing employment and revenue generation opportunities to small and medium businesses to improve their quality of life of people living around the Buddhist pilgrim sites.

CONCLUSION

This chapter reviewed the development and promotion of Indian Buddhist spiritual tourism attracting travellers from Southeast Asian countries. There is a need for a coordinated and management approach with all stakeholders to develop and promote trade and support services, investment opportunities in Buddhist spiritual tourism circuit, which has centuries old collection of Buddhist heritage monuments and temples. These site locations are neglected by the central and state archaeological societies for attracting tourists and providing packaged other sightseeing opportunities along the circuit to enhance visitors experience and provide value. This chapter identified the challenges and opportunities related to Indian Buddhist spiritual tourism. The challenges pinpointed towards lack of protection, safety, infrastructure, disconnection from Buddhist organizations and on-site multilingual services. While opportunities highlight support from the New Age groups, open investment, employment creation, connectivity, and public-private-partnerships. The chapter concludes with recommendations for the Indian government to seek capacity building, provide business friendly environment, health, and safety to for developing, promoting and foreign direct investment from Southeast Asian countries in tourism infrastructure development along the Buddhist spiritual tourism circuit and India's potential of developing Indian domestic and cross-border tourism through spiritual tourism. Realistic recommendations to promote spiritual tourism between India and Southeast Asian nations are provided.

REFERENCES

Agrawal, M., Chaudhary, H., & Tripathi, G. (2010). Enhancing Buddhist tourism in India: An exploratory study. *Worldwide Hospitality and Tourism Themes*, *2*(5), 477–493. doi:10.1108/17554211011090102

Akhtar, M. S., Jathol, I., & Hussain, Q. A. (2019). Peace Building through Religious Tourism in Pakistan: A Case Study of Kartarpur Corridor. *Pakistan Social Science Review*, *3*(2), 204–212. doi:10.35484/pssr.2019(3-II)16

Brunn, S. (Ed.). (2015). *The Changing World Religion Map*. Springer. doi:10.1007/978-94-017-9376-6

Bruntz, C., Schedneck, B., & Rowe, M. (2020). *Buddhist Tourism in Asia*. University of Hawaii Press., doi:10.1515/9780824882822

Buddhist Circuit (2021). *Tourist Train Official Website*. irctcbuddhisttrain.com

Buhalis, D. (2000). Marketing the competitive destination of the future. *Tourism Management*, *21*(1), 97–116. doi:10.1016/S0261-5177(99)00095-3

Business Line. (2014, July 17). Retrieved from https://www.cbi.eu/market-information/tourism/religious-tourism/market-potential

Chakraborty, S. (2011). Developing an Integrated Tourism Circuit in Gar Mandaran Kamarpukur Joyrambati in the State of West Bengal, India. *South Asian Journal of Tourism Heritage*, *4*(1), 144–155.

Chen, L. L., Scott, N., & Benckendorff, P. (2017). Mindful tourist experiences: A Buddhist perspective. *Annals of Tourism Research*, *64*, 1–12. doi:10.1016/j.annals.2017.01.013

Cohen, E. (1992). Pilgrimage centre: Concentric and excentric. *Annals of Tourism Research*, *18*(1), 33–50. doi:10.1016/0160-7383(92)90105-X

Current Affairs (2018). Swadesh darshan Scheme. Retrieved from Government to expand Buddhist tourism circuit to 21 more states. *GK Today*.

Das, A. (2016). The Politics of Pilgrimage Through the Prism of Mass Media. *International Journal of Religious Tourism and Pilgrimage*, *4*(6), 55–66.

Finney, R. Z., Orwig, R. A., & Spake, D. F. (2009). Lotus-eaters, pilgrims, seekers, and accidental tourists: How different travellers consume the sacred and the profane. *Services Marketing Quarterly*, *30*(2), 148–173. doi:10.1080/15332960802619181

Geary, D. (2008). Destination enlightenment: Branding Buddhism and spiritual tourism in Bodhgaya, Bihar. *Anthropology Today*, *24*(3), 11–14. doi:10.1111/j.1467-8322.2008.00584.x

Griffin, K., & Raj, R. (2017). The Importance of Religious Tourism and Pilgrimage: Reflecting on definitions, motives, and data. *International Journal of Religious Tourism and Pilgrimage*, *5*(3), 1–9.

Haq, F., & Jackson, J. (2009). Spiritual Journey to Hajj: Australian and Pakistani Experience and Expectations. *Journal of Management, Spirituality & Religion*, *6*(2), 141–156. doi:10.1080/14766080902815155

Haq, F., & Medhekar, A. (2013). Branding Spiritual Tourism as an Innovation for Peace between India and Pakistan. *International Journal of Social Entrepreneurship and Innovation*, *2*(5), 404-414. doi:10.1504/IJSEI.2013.059312

Haq, F., & Medhekar, A. (2014). *Spiritual tourism between India and Pakistan Business Opportunities and Threats*. Paper presented at Eurasia Business Research Conference, Istanbul, Turkey.

Haq, F., & Medhekar, A. (2018). Economic Effect of Spiritual Tourism in India and Pakistan. In U. Beena & I. Benna (Eds.), *Urbanization and Its Impact on Socio-Economic Growth in Developing Regions* (pp. 66–86). IGI-Global. doi:10.4018/978-1-5225-2659-9.ch004

Haq, F., & Medhekar, A. (2019). Is Spiritual Tourism a Peace Vehicle for Social Transformation and Economic Prosperity in India and Pakistan? In N. Alexandru-Mircea & M.-O. Nedelea (Eds.), *Marketing Peace for Social Transformation and Global Prosperity* (pp. 189–211). IGI-Global. doi:10.4018/978-1-5225-7464-4.ch010

Haq, F., & Medhekar, A. (2020). The Rise of Spiritual Tourism in South Asia as Business Internationalization. *Journal of Management Research*, *7*(1), 52–58.

India Today. (2011). Tourism Ministry to develop 35 tourism circuits by 2016. *India Today*. Retrieved from http://indiatoday.intoday.in/story/tourism-ministry-to-develop-35-tourism-circuits-by-2016/1/164363.html

International Finance Corporation World Bank. (2018). *Investing in Buddhist Circuit*. worldbank.org

Jauhari, J. (2010). How can the visitor experience be enhanced for spiritual and cultural tourism in India? *Worldwide Hospitality and Tourism Themes*, *2*(5), 559–563. doi:10.1108/17554211011090166

Leitão, N. C., & Shahbaz, M. (2016). Economic Growth, Tourism Arrivals and Climate Change. *Bull. Energy Economics*, *4*, 35–43.

McIntosh, I. S. (2016). Xuanzang and Bodhidharma: Pilgrimage and peace-building in Buddhist China and India. *International Journal of Religious Tourism and Pilgrimage,* (6), Article 14.

Medhekar, A., & Haq, F. (2009). Growth of spiritual tourism in India: A public private partnership approach. *International Journal of Business Intelligence & Management*, *1*, 1–12.

Medhekar, A., & Haq, F. (2012). Development of Spiritual Tourism Circuits: The Case of India. *Journal of Global Business Review*, *2*(2), 212–218.

Medhekar, A., & Haq, F. (2020). Capacity Building for Spiritual Heritage Tourism: The Case of India and Pakistan. In S. Srivastava (Ed.), *Capacity Building Through Heritage Tourism an International Perspective*. Apple Academic Press. doi:10.1201/9781003034391-2

Mitroff, I., & Denton, E. E. (1999). *A Spiritual Audit of Corporate America: A Hard Look at Spirituality, Religion, and Values in the Workplace*. Jossey-Bass Inc.

News India. (2020, October 4). *Uttar Pradesh Tourism to develop Kaushambi as part of Buddhist Circuit.* newsd.in

Oh, C.-O. (2005). The contribution of tourism development to economic growth in the Korean economy. *Tourism Management, 26*(1), 39–44. doi:10.1016/j.tourman.2003.09.014

Olsen, D. H. (2019). Review of: Religious Tourism in Asia: Tradition and Change through Case Studies and Narratives, by S. Yasuda, R. Raj & K. Griffin. *International Journal of Religious Tourism and Pilgrimage, 7*(5), 73-75.

Phukan, H., Rahman, Z., & Devdutt, P. (2012). Emergence of Spiritual Tourism in India. *International Journal of Marketing and Technology., 2*(4), 300–317.

Phukan, R.S. (2015). *Buddhist Circuit in India.* mapsofindia.com

Pinterest. (2021). *Buddhist Pilgrimage Locations of India.* Retrieved from https://in.pinterest.com/pin/161003755400282845/

Raj, R., & Morpeth, N. D. (2007). *Religious tourism and pilgrimage festivals management: An international perspective.* CABI Publishers. doi:10.1079/9781845932251.0000

Riege, A. M., & Perry, C. (2000). National marketing strategies in international travel and tourism. *European Journal of Marketing, 34*(11/12), 1290–1305. doi:10.1108/03090560010348452

Rinschede, G. (1992). Forms of religious tourism. *Annals of Tourism Research, 19*(1), 51–67. doi:10.1016/0160-7383(92)90106-Y

Rumki, B., & Kushagra, R. (2018). *Religious tourism: The beginning of a new era with special reference to India.* In S. Yasuda, R. Raj, & K. Griffin (Eds.), *Religious tourism in Asia: Tradition and change through case studies and narratives* (pp. 67–76). CABI Publishers.

Sequeira, T. N., & Maçãs, N. P. (2008). Does tourism influence economic growth? A dynamic panel data approach. *Applied Economics, 40*(18), 2431–2441. doi:10.1080/00036840600949520

Sharpley, R., & Sundaram, P. (2005). Tourism: A Sacred Journey? The Case of Ashram Tourism, India. *International Journal of Tourism Research, 7*(1), 161–171. doi:10.1002/jtr.522

Shinde, K. A. (2007). Visiting Scared Sites in India: Religious Tourism or Pilgrimage? In R. Raj & N. D. Morpeth (Eds.), *Religious Tourism and Pilgrimage Management: An International Perspective* (pp. 170–183). CAB International. doi:10.1079/9781845932251.0184

Shinde, K., Wee, D-S., Fong, L-K., Xiao, H., Kim, Y-H., & Watanabe, T. (2020). *Buddhist tourism in Asia: towards sustainable development.* doi:10.26181/5fd069becb7de

The Times of India. (2016, Oct 4). International Buddhist Conclave 2016 opens in Sarnath. Retrieved from International Buddhist Conclave-2016 opens in Sarnath. *Times of India.*

Timothy, D. J., & Olsen, D. H. (2006). Conclusion: Whither Religious Tourism? In D. J. Timothy & D. H. Olsen (Eds.), *Tourism, Religion & Spiritual Journeys* (pp. 271–278). Routledge. doi:10.4324/9780203001073-29

Timothy, D. J., & Olsen, D. H. (2018). Religious routes, pilgrim trails: Spiritual pathways as tourism resources. In Tourism and Religion: Issues and Implications (pp. 220-235). Channel View Publications.

Tourism India. (2021). *Sarnath Buddhism Pilgrimage - Tourist Attractions in Sarnath*. tourmyindia.com

Travel Website. (2021). *The Train - Buddhist Circuit Tourist Train*. buddhisttrainindia.com

UNESCO. (2019). http:// whc.unesco.org/en/list/1551

United Nations. (2021). *The 17 Sustainable Development Goals*. un.org

UNWTO. (2017a). Retrieved from https://www.unwto.org/archive/europe/event/international-congress-religious-tourism-and-pilgrimage

UNWTO. (2017b). *Tourism can protect and promote religious heritage*. Retrieved from https://www.frh-europe.org/unwto-tourism-can-protect-and-promote-religious-heritage

Varghese, P. (2018). *Indian Economic Strategy 2035*. Department of Foreign Affairs and Trade. Retrieved from https://dfat.gov.au/geo/india/ies/index.html

Vukonic, B. (1996). *Tourism and Religion* (S. Matesic, Trans.). Oxford Pergamon Press.

WHO. (2020). *Coronavirus declared global health emergency by WHO*. Retrieved from https://www.bbc.com/news/world-51318246 https://www.who.int/countries/bgd/

Yasuda, S., Raj, R., & Griffin, K. (Eds.). (2018). *Religious Tourism in Asia: Tradition and Change through Case Studies and Narratives*. CABI International. doi:10.1079/9781786392343.0000

Zhang, J. (2018). To Brand Gandhara, the Ancient Buddhist Centre: Pakistan's potential to develop Buddhist tourism. In S. Yasuda, R. Raj, & K. Griffin (Eds.), *Religious Tourism in Asia: Tradition and Change Through Case Studies and Narratives* (p. 127). CABI Publishers. doi:10.1079/9781786392343.0127

ADDITIONAL READING

Cugini, A. (2021). Religious tourism and Sustainability: From Devotion to Spiritual Experience. Grasso, F., & Sergi, B.S. (Ed.) Tourism in the Mediterranean Se (pp. 55-73). Bingley: Emerald Publishing Limited.

Kumar, A., & Singh, P. (2015). Cultural Heritage Tourism of Ayodhya-Faizabad. *Geographer*, *62*(2), 66–74.

Medhekar, A., & Haq, F. (2012). In the Foot-Steps of Mary MacKillop: The Emergence of Australian Spiritual Tourism Marketing. *Journal of International Business Management & Research*, *3*(7), 114–124.

Qureshi, R. B. (2003). Lineage, Shrine, Qawwali, and Study Circle: Spiritual Kinship in Transnational Sufism. *Religious Studies in Theology*, *22*(1), 63–84. doi:10.1558/rsth.v22i1.63

Shuo, Y. S., Ryan, C., & Liu, G. (2009). Taoism, temples and tourists: The case of Mazu pilgrimage tourism. *Tourism Management*, *30*(4), 581–588. doi:10.1016/j.tourman.2008.08.008

Simone-Charters, M. T., & Boyd, S. W. (2010). Development of Religious Heritage Tourism in Northern Ireland: Opportunities, Benefits and Obstacles. *Tourism (Zagreb)*, *58*(3), 229–257.

Tilson, D. J. (2005). Religious-Spiritual Tourism and Promotional Campaigning: A Church-State Partnership for St. James and Spain. *Journal of Hospitality & Leisure Marketing*, *12*(1-2), 9–40. doi:10.1300/J150v12n01_03

Timothy, D. J. (2011). *Cultural Heritage and Tourism: An Introduction*. Channel View Publications. doi:10.21832/9781845411787

KEY TERMS AND DEFINITIONS

ASEAN: A group of ten countries geographically sharing borders and culture to benefit from bilateral and multilateral trade, travel and investment activities.

Circuit: Circuit includes places which are regularly visit by people. For example, Buddhist circuit includes all the key places that were linked to and visited by Buddha. The Buddhist spiritual pilgrims travel or journey along the Buddhist circuit from his place of birth to where he achieved enlightenment, following the footsteps of Buddha.

Heritage Tourism: Heritage tourism is a niche subset of tourism and relates to visiting centuries old cultural and heritage sites such as spiritual places, forts, monuments, battlegrounds, industrial and geographical sites, and also to experience authentic cultural activities and appreciate the contributions made by our past civilizations.

Millennium Development Goals (MDGs): Millennium Development Goals (MDGs) are the goals adopted in 2000, by the United Nations General Assembly to reduce extreme poverty and set out a series of goals with time-bound targets. These Millennium Development Goals (MDGs) have 8 goals, 21 targets and 60 indicators were to be achieved by the end of 2015. These are nothing but pre-development agenda of sustainable development goals (SDGs).

Multilateral Trade: Multilateral trade agreement occurs between three or more nations, and they are treated equally, and no one gets a most favoured nation status. The aim is to standardize commerce regulations, encourage exports and imports, reduced tariffs and quotas between member countries. Multilateral agreements are beneficial to emerging markets developing countries as it makes them more competitive, and trade can be negotiated with more than one country at one time.

Public-Private Partnerships: It involves cooperation and collaboration between the government and private organizations to plan, develop, and implement projects related to infrastructure, transport, highways, or tourism development that is finance-build-operate-transfer through PPPs.

Spiritual Tourism: Spiritual tourism is about visiting holy and spiritual places of worship belonging to different religions (church, temples, synagogue, and mosques) and gain spiritual experience and enlightenment to improve once wellbeing in terms of body, mind and spirit.

Chapter 10
Evaluating the Future Possibilities of India-ASEAN Economic Relations:
A Critical Assessment

Ezeifekwuaba Tochukwu Benedict
University of Lagos, Nigeria & South America University, USA

ABSTRACT

Foreign trade relations are due to the measures of foreign policy adopted and applied by a nation. The Indian foreign policy was majorly West focused and has been substituted with a more nuanced and inclusive policy that promotes the enhancement of security, diplomatic, and trade ties with the Eastern nations. The "Look East" Policy was executed in 1991 and it was substituted as "Act East" in 2014 by Prime Minister Narendra Modi who provided a modern push to the Indian regional diplomacy by concentration on Southeast Asian neighbours. This policy is known as a multi-faceted technique to create strategic connections with numerous individual nations as well as build a lasting relation with Association of Southeast Asian Nations (ASEAN). In this regard, this chapter evaluates the role and responsibility of border states in revitalizing regional socio, cultural, and economic ties with the neighbouring countries. This chapter evaluates how the participation of Northeastern Indian States provides opportunities for New Delhi in ensuring a tremendous regional diplomacy with ASEAN.

INTRODUCTION

Among the Prominent and significant foreign policy ideology that the India Government has taken and applied in Post Cold War is the Look East Policy (Kalita, 2018). This policy and initiative was applied in the early 1990's against the severe shaking of the economy of India including the immediate end of the Cold War. This Policy or initiative was due to the concerted and joint efforts to extend and widen the strategic alliances with the South East Asian Nations. The Policy was intended to enhance political,

DOI: 10.4018/978-1-7998-5774-7.ch010

economical and strategic links and connections with the Individual Nations including with the Association of the South East Asian Nations (ASEAN) (Kalita, 2018).

The "Look East" Initiative that was inaugurated and allowed in the early 1990s was the part of the motive to re-engage and re-involve with the South East Asia. This Policy has been attributed by majority of the Policy Makers and of the India Scholars as it evolved through numerous "stages" with a process of interaction and accelerated pace in migrating from a phase to another phase; this policy was intended to extend the involvement of India's with the South East Asia Region, the Policy has gone beyond its initial and primary geographical concentration in South East Asia to cover and entail the broader East-Asian and presently Indo-Pacific region that has expanded and widened to its earlier or initial "Economic Interaction" to defense, political and strategic interactions. Currently, this "Look East" Initiative has culminated into modern "phase" under the Prime Minister-ship of Modi Narendra that rebranded and transformed the policy as "Act East" so as to depict a tremendous shift (movement) towards a more action oriented and pro active technique towards the region to promote links and connections in every sphere.

Although, something significant has transformed by the rebranding or repackaging of "Look East" Policy, it is a significant and major question that pertains every scholars and policy makers. One may argue and debate that the different stages of the "Look East" initiative are indepthed in the domestic political rhetoric's rather than foreign policy migrations (shifts) as current government has intended to categorize and distinguish it's foreign policy making from its predecessors. The First and Primary Phase or Stage of the Policy starts with the Congress Government of Prime Minister Rao Narshima; whereas the second stage or phase was linked and connected with the Bhartiya Janta Party (BJP) Prime Minister Vajpayee's Bihari Atal Government in the early 2000's and it continued to remain under the Congress Government of Prime Minister Singh Manmohan in 2004. Lastly, Final Phase of revitalized "Act East" Policy transpired under the Government of Modi Narendra in 2014 (Bajpaee, 2017).

It is essential to emphasize here that the Vaj Payee's Government India articulated the "Neighborhood First" Initiative were the Government aimed to take and apply a more "holistic and integrated" approach and technique to its regional involvements. Since the inception and beginning of this policy, all the Government during this era intended to enhance ties with the Asia-Pacific region since this is the swiftest growing region of the globe to its unparallel development in political, demographic, economic and security terms. Encouraging ties or alliances with the Asian neighbors through Association of the South East Asian Nations (ASEAN) has bridged and widened the gap as well as maximized the connectivity and linkages to wider Asia-Pacific Region. This Paper examines and evaluates how the economic relations or connectivity between ASEAN and India, particularly in the aspect of investments and trade have transformed overtime. However, ASEAN and India share a dynamic connection which goes well or perfectly beyond economics, the easy and simplest migration of services, goods and capital across borders remains the major and utmost concern for both. It is thus essential to evaluate the value chain connectivity between them that enables greater and much economic cooperation or alliance provided adequate or necessary connectivity's. There are less challenges or impediments in regards to Institutional, Physical including People-to-People connectivity which could jeopardize and affect the economic growth of these both regions. These barriers demand urgent consideration by decision and policy makers. Also, this policy depicts a positive development effect and implication on the North Eastern Region (Kalita, 2018)

LITERATURE REVIEW

Maximizing Economic Output and Opportunities for development of trade were said and emphasized to have been limited in the Socialist State steered development model which the Post Independence India adopted. Criticisms emanated from Social Scientists and Economists such as Kohli Atul, for susceptibility of the Indian Nation to influences or effects different powerful and significant lobbies and interests. Neoliberal Theorists glanced at lobbies as a threat and hindrance to governance and democracy. Indian Procedural layers were creating opportunities and privileges to a bloated bureaucracy for indulging in rent seeking attitude and behavior including corruption and socialistic state growth and development ambitions were unwilling to offer and provide reasonable spaces of growth privileges and opportunities needed and required by sectors of the economy. The Size of Private or Sole ownership in Sectors such as connectivity development sector and road construction was small regardless the public demand for faster communication. This was as a result of the capacity and willingness enabling or a better growth in the construction sector as it was limited and restricted by the concentration and focus of public sector investments in major agricultural growth and industrial infrastructure

Unwillingness of the Socialist Development Technique and Model to attain growth aspirations resulted to an ideological or major vacuum in which the socialistic command or demand economic technique was losing or failing credibility and worthiness. The Neoliberal revitalizations in 1990s in India brought about and resulted to Macro-economic transformations to the systems and methods of control on the economy. The reforms were seen as the execution of solutions including the failure and challenges of the developmental state in executing economic and social development objectives and goals.

Reforms as well as adjunct transformation in governance and state structures facilitated and promoted expanding of economic growth benefits. Regulations constricting the activity of the free market were steadily liberalized so that the economy liberalization becomes the National Political Objectives. Private and Sole Involvement in Sectors of the economy of India availed the unveiling to expand and widen diversities in outputs including trade operations.

The Adoption and Application of the Look East Policy in 1991 was an external reflection and depiction of the progressives and successive domestic economic changes and transformations. There was a realization or consciousness that India's becoming a great and major power was indepthed in the leveraging geo-economic foreign policy instruments such as financial lending, investments, economic sanctions, international migrations and investments as well as the development of the economy. With gradual enhancements in relations and connections with South East Asia Countries including the domestic economic growth in the 1980s; Insurgencies transpiring in North East India are more confident or certain of exerting influence in the region through infrastructural developments and also road construction.

"Encouraging and promoting a healthy and an effective external economic environment" prompted the Indian Foreign Policy Modification and change of formulating and preparing the Look East Policy (LEP). The Later 1980s was a period and time of political turbulence in India. Successive Governments came into power without most of the Parliament. By the time, the Congress Party created a relatively stable and effective government in 1991, decline in remittances to India as a result of the Gulf catastrophe and prohibition of Trade with East European Nations that had just emanated from the Communist rule depleted the financial reserves of India. To these were included the domestic financial challenges of populist initiatives including the increasing Non-Productive (Non-Output) expenditure in subsidies and defense. The Economic reforms initiative in India occurring in the background of the Look East Policy (LEP) followed a crisis of balance of payment emanating out of the financial crisis Thus, the reforms period of discovery and knowing the essence of foreign capital in the National economic development as well as the essence of enhancing competitiveness of Indian Products in Foreign Trade. The reforms and changes becomes a progression and direction towards integrating the economy of India with the global economy as foreign investments were invited and welcomed and targets were done for maximizing the export trade of India. In this situation of requiring to secure and ensure the external economic development of India, the emergence of the Asian Tigers and the "Asian Miracle" created and ensured impetus and courage to the foreign policy of India to look to South East Asia as a space of Economic Benefit.

External Initiatives and Policies for the enhancement of trade and particularly in the context of the AEP/LEP have factored and determined the significance of connectivity and linkage infrastructures for trade development and growth. The correlation of economic growth and connectivity development has explained and emphasized political narrativizing of road construction initiatives. The widening of roads is seen and viewed as markers and shakers of economic development. Central Governments and Successive States in India have taken the construction and building of roads as an indicator and measurement of performance of Governments. For instance, in State-Level elections in Bihar in 2015, the Bharatiya Janata Party (BJP) and the Incumbent Janata Dal (United) ran poster campaigns, attacking one another in regards to successes including the alleged embezzlements in road construction initiatives in Bihar.

The Narrative of India rapid and fast economic growth in the Post Liberalization era has seen and witnessed contributions from the road contribution sector. The level of road construction maximized after the economic liberalization. The National Highways Act of 1956 was rectified in 1995, permitting 100 percent Foreign Direct Investment (FDI) in the road construction sector. With the making of this ratification or amendment, Private or Individual Investments began making up for lack of sufficient and adequate state funds or finances in highway maintenance and construction such that the Personal involvement in transport, road construction including connectivity sectors widened. Private Infrastructural Organizations maximized and discovered a conducive atmosphere to growth of the sector. By 2008, Private Involvements in Public-Private Joint road constructions was approximated to have rise up to US $150 billion. But this approximation has been presently surpassed when the currently Instituted Central Planning Body in India called the National Institutions for Transforming India (NITI) Aayog re-approximated aggregate investments into the road construction sector rising at ₹50000000 million or nearly US $730 billion

Connecting Infrastructure and Roads have been crucial and significant in extending and widening of Industry and Trade related economic packages including the notions of welfare to peripheral parts and aspects of the Nations. The Indian Urban Middle Class have gained from the establishing of real estate hubs near to expressways, providing housing amenities, shopping complexes and tourism destinations as well as for rural populations, roads have enhanced access to livelihoods.

In the Periphery Sphere of the Northern Eastern Region of India, as the AEP/LEP has triggered the development of the connectivity (linkage) infrastructure; traders and industrial investors from outside and within the region have welcomed and accepted the pace and stage of Infrastructural development. This comes to be seen and viewed as patronage of businesses and investors for investment summits being held and organized in capital cities of the region. A Summit referred to as "Advantage Assam" held in 2018, Organizations dedicated to investing ₹643,860 million or US $9 Billion in Assam State Governments of the region project bridge and road construction initiative as economic development in the region. The State Governments have been associated in the vision for accelerated and a better economic growth in the region.

It is not solely in India but as well as South East Asia that connectivity constructions and roads have served and acted as an instrument for economic development. Governments in Laos, Indonesia and Thailand have utilized and applied the road constructions for securing and ensuring political regulation in Insurgency affected regions and for attaining economic growth aims and objectives in politically challenging regions. In Northern Thailand, enhancement of laterite roads in the countryside into motorable roads transformed and changed local rural economies. The Motorable roads permitted and allowed women to convey agricultural produce from villages to Chiang Mai City. It was discovered that over a thirty year period when roads were being constructed, the aspirations of villagers modified or changed. The villagers needed better schools in the city, decrease or decline in commuting time to Chiang Mai and Urban employment opportunities.

The application of such a development technique and approach in India makes the AEP/LEP regard infrastructural constructions as a key or tool to economic transformation of the underdeveloped North East Region. With the goals and objectives for the liberalization and reforms of the economy; economic integration with the East and South East Asia Region and sustained economic growth including the development of the North East Axis has been a cornerstone of the AEP/LEP. The Ideology of the Policy pitches the development narrative against the long continuous fights of insurgencies in the axis and delegitimizes violent and fierceful protests against the people and the states. However, insurgencies have not been absolutely abolished. Since 2000, State Security goals and objectives in the region have been accompanied by the State developmental packages for physical connectivity and the building of roads. For instance, in Tripura State, the success and effectiveness of a left front government incumbent in the state until 2018 in transforming and changing a long drawn environment of political violence in the State was characterized to the construction of roads to remote villages and it was also affected or disrupted by violent and dangerous contestations of the armed groups and states in Tripura and to the initiative or ideology of the government in the development of associated and linked basic inter channeled public infrastructures such as community halls, schools and hospitals

In contrast to regional development initiatives in the past, LEP/AEP identified and recognized advantages and benefits for North East India in the building of nearer or closer linkages with ASEAN. It has recognized civilization linkages between South East Asia and North East India as commonness or uniqueness shared and distributed across the regions. The AEP/LEP has made reference, direction and emphasis to the survival of passage routes and traditional trade. Across ASEAN and India, there has been historical evidence and proof of contacts of trade, culture, language, migration and religion between South East Asia and South India for two millennia. Archaeological and Literary sources such as the discovery and unveiling of a port at Kothapatnam in Pradesh Andhra have backed up references to the survival or existence of early and initial trade contacts between places in South East Asia and India. The Soft Power of India in a traditional meaning was stated to have migrated or toured across to South East Asia, carrying the influences or effects of Islamic Culture, Buddhist, Hindu and the Imprinting of a continuity or existence across the regions.

The North East Region was linked to the South East Asian Nations by land instead of sea and thus the region has been emphasized to have more immediate and instant connections and linkages with South East Asia. One of the routes connecting Chindwin and Upper Irrawaddy with a stretch of eastern or upper Assam, that became part and aspect of the Stilwell road during the Second World War is emphasized to have carried or ensured migrating Naga, Shan, and Singpho including other hall tribes across transnational axes. Also, there are references to similarities in lifestyles and food habits of Individuals dwelling places across the region.

Road construction took on a modern dimension after the India. The partition of British India divided or demarcated Bengal into Pakistan and Indian Territories majorly declined and minimized the overland linkage between the territories of India and North East India. Although, despite the political relevance and significance of the developing connectivity, the North East region remain cut off or mapped out from adjoining the territories of India. As a result of the absence of overland communications, industrial output and industrial investment in the region was slack although, the challenge of connectivity was double headed. The unavailability of connectivity stymied industrial development but as well as the lack of connectivity became the motive of Indian development planners to determine shifting and adjusting of Industrial Production units and Developmental Projects outside the region. Thus, the development of the North India became factored and reasoned for the availability or presence of connectivity.

However, the post-independence nation recognized and identified the importance of constructing and ensuring connectivity across its territories, the level and stage of connectivity development to North East India was hesitant and a bit slow. Overland connectivity or linkage across banks of the Brahmaputra River in West Bengal and Assam was solely completed in 1962 with the finishing of the Bridee Construction at Guwahati. The Brahmaputra River moving lengthwise through the territory or boundary of Assam divides the nation. The vastness and extent of the river that makes it one of the largest and biggest rivers in India has traditionally and locally made the construction of bridges across it challenging and it isolated regions of the hill areas and river valley of the North East India. The Challenges of crossing the river delayed and affected land route communication. After Independence, Passengers and Railway Freight migrating to Upper Assam alighted on the Southern Bank of the Brahmaputra located at Guwahati and crossed or migrated the river to re-board trains migrating Westwards to West Bengal and beyond. In 1987, the unveiling of another bridge across the Brahmaputra amalgamated the Bridge at Guwahati in being the solely bridges across the wide river.

The Foreign Policy initiative and strategy of India in the East, adapting to altered or hindered nature of International or foreign economic interactions or communications since the Indian Nation came under the influence or effect of the Neoliberal determination for the market expansion advocates or proposes taking the connectivity and road constructions across foreign borders

The objectives and goals have been ensuring the expansion of foreign trade including exchanges with India's associated or Neighbors in the North East India surroundings –with Myanmar, Bhutan, Nepal, Bangladesh and the ASEAN. For instance, in foreign relations with Bangladesh; India's Neighbor migrated to the North East's South, India has been seeking commercial movement passage through the territories of Bangladesh. The situation and scenarios of connectivity –reopening or unveiling of railway lines, river and land navigational routes that the British had created and ensured during the colonial era through states of the North East Axis and linking West Bengal have been foundational and significant in the present India-Bangladesh Diplomatic connections and relations.

The grant of importance of development of Infrastructural linkages with the North East Regions Foreign Neighbors under the AEP/LEP has been greater and much than Bilateral Foreign Connections ordinarily impressed and permitted on India Foreign Policy. Ensuring of Connectivity and Linkages becomes necessary to reorienting outwards from the traditional ideological backings in Indian Foreign Policy as its Foreign Policy gears and lingers up to take advantage of the expanded and widened economic outputs. As a result of its location at the junction of South East Asia and South Asia Regions, North East India has witnessed the ground and major effect of these policy trends and shifts. The geography of the axis or region comes to be viewed as a gulf between the Sea of the economic opportunities the South East Asian region provides or offers and the expanding economy of India

Since the Look East Policy (LEP) Inauguration, the emphasis on connectivity constructions and roads has come to be seen or viewed in the enhancement of existing and current National Highways linking the North East Region with other parts and areas of India. The Building of Bridge Initiatives upon the Brahmaputra River have almost and nearly come all immediately at the period or time since the unveiling of the Second Bridge across the River in 1987. Regardless of the Four Modern Bridges, the Assam State Government in the North East India has intended to build and construct six more Bridges across the River in 2018

The Bridges which are across the Brahmaputra River are part of an Act East Policy (AEP)/Look East Policy (LEP) –inspired initiative for linking navigable rivers across the axis and its foreign neighbors. With the road development; Networks of Navigable Rivers have emerge as capable and better sites for the redevelopment of the traditional access routes. The Navigable waterways are little or small, shared waterways between Bhutan, North East India, Bangladesh and Myanmar. These Waterways were applied in the colonial and pre-colonial past for drifting down tradable and essential commodities across short distances. Various and of variable volumes including the rivers are also part of the large river systems of the Brahmaputra, the Karnaphuli, the Surma-Barak-Meghna System including the Kaladan Rivers. The Rivers have the benefits and advantages of crossing foreign borders of the regions and thus, are capable or willing of becoming foreign routes.

The Kaladan Multi Modal Transport Initiative is one such riverine and road connection for linking Indian territories in Mizoram to Sittwe Port in Myanmar. River Navigational Routes have amalgamated with buildings and constructing highways to provide trade access to landlocked and remote regions of the North East Region such as Tripura and Mizoram. The Trilateral Highway is a land route initiative intending to amalgamate Moreh in Manipur to Mae Sot in Thailand. India is assisting build roads and bridges for the Kalewa –Tamu – Kalemyo Sector of the Trilateral Highway. An aggregate of 740km of current and present highways in Manipur, Nagaland, Meghalaya and Assam States of North East India linking the towns of Moreh, Imphal, Kohima, Dimapur, Shillong and Dawki have become part of Asian Highways referred to as AH1 and AH2, that elongates all the way from Tokyo in the East End and runs Westwards to Istanbul

Also, the Association of South East Asian Nations (ASEAN) members such as Cambodia, Laos and Vietnam are part of another linkage and connectivity initiative with India since 2014. The Initiative, referred to as the Mekong India Economic Sector (MIEC) has been emphasized to capitalize and emphasize on the potential and essential for shared and distributed ASEAN and India economic as well as for the transit growth of Multilateral Trade through the connectivity and linkage corridors under construction

Other than the foreign connectivity initiatives, there are interconnected and interlinked roads as well as other connectivity expansion initiatives running within the region of the North East India, which seeks and intends to develop feeder trade as well as transit routes to the foreign routes under development. The policy and initiative for maximizing inter sub region linkage has resulted to ordaining and bestowing at least two state institutions in charge for the region – the North Eastern Council (NEC) and the Ministry of Development of North East Region (MDoNER) –with devising schemes and initiatives for the development and enhancement of regional infrastructural linkage

The Ministry of Development of North East Region (MDoNER) initiated a Project referred to as the North East Road Sector Development Scheme in 2015 and obliged the North Eastern Council (NEC) with execution. This Scheme recognizes essential and significant but neglected Inter-State Connectivity and Roads in the North East Area for widening and redevelopment. The Network of Inter State Roads in the North Eastern Council (NEC) has recognized as available for redevelopment aggregate a road and connectivity length of 1665.75km Ministry of Development of North East Region (MDoNER) n.d. in the Financial year of 2016-2017; the North Eastern Council (NEC) allocated and vested nearly 40 percent of its budget to the Communication and Transportation Sector, the highest and greatest among every budgetary sectors (North Eastern Council (NEC) n.d). Through the development of Socio-Politically Backward Areas, Creating Market Access for Agricultural Products and recognizing the importance and essence of State Security Objectives; the State Schemes and Initiatives for Infrastructural Development have as targets and aims the exact vision for the development and growth of the region as the development vision of the AEP/LEP outlines.

The influence and effect of the AEP/LEP has spurred the state as well as maximize connectivity infrastructures rather than road development and construction of the river navigation routes such as airports and railways. Regardless of the condensed location of connectivity and linkages infrastructures in a limited and constrained space of North East India; Distances from established business hubs and industrial sites in Eastern Region of India's from Metropolitan areas and other parts have sought and intended to be covered through the air connectivity development. There are plans and initiatives for developing twelve airports that entails building and constructing of modern airports as well as upgrading and enhancing of current ones across the North East Region that together with the Bigger Airports such as the Imphal and Guwahati Airports envision condensing air/linkage within the areas or regions.

Until Presently, North East India was the sole major region in India to have states that were totally and extremely untouched by the railways lines. Although, Since the time developmental initiative for the region have centered on building and ensuring connectivity and linkage, Projects and Initiatives for the construction of Nine New Railway Lines to link and amalgamate the States of Arunachal Pradesh, Tripura, Manipur and Meghalaya that were previously without rail linkage and connectivity including two projects and initiatives for the conversion and transformation of railway gauge have enhanced rail connectivity within the region. Taking the AEP/LEP Line, State Governments anticipates that enhanced connectivity Infrastructures and roads in the region will block or unveil the North East States Capacity as an emerging and current trade hub or centre of the South East Asia Region

The LEP/AEP has ensured the centrality of developing and enhancing Infrastructural Connectivity as well as linking the roads as well as the connectivity routes in the South East Asia and South Asia in raising and enhancing the North Eastern Region of India to global and worldwide significance. The connectivity development intends to invert the former or previous condition of isolated geographical existence and survival of North East India as well as make it a strategic nodal trade centre in the regions. The vision and mission of the LEP/AEP's for making the region a geographical springboard for rising or uplifting the stakes of India in the geopolitical dynamics of South East Asia and South Asia, thus, has amalgamated foreign policy ambition with the aim and objectives of the economic development for the region.

Historically, the North East Region has trailed and followed behind other parts and areas of India in economic growth and industrial development; this was characterized or featured to a "Step Motherly Treatment" by the Center which resulted to regional political agitations. Natural resources were seen and viewed to be taken away from the region, and, in return, the state made negligible investments in the Industrial Development. In the 1960-1970s, protests occurring in Assam did not reject or revoke the State for neglecting specific and precise societal development demands and desires. For instance, the Assam Movement of 1979-1985, sought apart from the development of cultural capacity, creation of employment opportunities and security of local portfolio or identity. Rather than for freeing and setting free the economy from the clutches of the State, agitation politics in the other parts of the North

East particularly Mizoram, Meghalaya, Manipur as well as Nagaland centered and focused around the demands and needs for cultural security of the societies including recognition

Connectivity, Development of Transport as well as other similar trade infrastructures or the unavailability of it was said or emphasized to have the power and authority to influence in making of the North East India as a Metaphorical overland gap and bridge linking the economic opportunities in South East Asia and India. Through equipping and bestowing the region with infrastructure and industrial development in the form of building connectivity and trade enhancing infrastructure, the LEP/AEP has intended to act on Neoliberal prescriptions for enabling and ensuring of development that have required and enabled states to reduce or decrease controls and regulations on the economy as well as create conditions for the trade growth and industry. The infrastructure focused initiative for the North East Region Development emphasizes that with the establishment and creation of physical connectivity, the market economy will self deliver economic growth in the area or region

However, the Neoliberal route does not concede space for equalizing and equating the presence of economic benefits or opportunities. The poor has been subjected to effects and repercussions of exposure of the economy to volatility in the era of the capital market. Its development paradigm does not have the social agenda of making and ensuring economic growth "pro-poor growth". However, growth in the Neoliberal Paradigm does raise and generates incomes for the poor; the absence or the unavailability of State Intervention maximizes the avenues or means for the wealthy to grow or maximizes their incomes, but the proportionate rise for the poor or needy does not amount or result to much if they start or begin with minimal or very little. The Nature of effects of growth in trade transits and trades, societal reactions in the North East India and the Neoliberal Economic Development Model on People as a result of the reduced and minimized role and responsibility of the State in the Market Outcomes allocations are still being determined and measured.

The inequitable effects of road construction have a bearing on the situation and instance of the North East India. The coming of the LEP/AEP is emphasized to have opened and unveiled the North East Region's Space to insidious agencies of material life. The LEP/AEP has been a criteria and a basis for renewed and a revitalized capital accumulation in the territorial sphere. Regardless of the massive and huge construction of roads as well as other connectivity infrastructure, the North Eastern States on average are the motive for the National Average on the indices of human development. In fact, Present and Current Research Discovers no confirmed and recognized evidence for correlation between social development and road construction

OBJECTIVES OF STUDY

- To examine the objectives and the historical evolution of the Act East and the Look East Policy
- To Study the Programmes and Policies of the India's Government Act East Policy including the strategic transformation that have been brought forth by the execution and the implementation of this initiative and policy
- To understand or comprehend the importance and essence of the North Eastern Region for Act East Policy

METHODOLOGY

For the Purpose and the essence of the Study of "India North East and Act East Policy: Challenges and Opportunities"; a descriptive technique will be adhered. For the research study of this topic, materials have been applied by using the secondary sources.

Current Engagements

The relations or connections between India-ASEAN have transpired and occurred overtime, with India graduating or maximizing from the South East Asian grouping's sectoral Dialogue Partners in 1992 to a Summit Level Partner in 2002. Since then, the both sides have significantly and tremendously involved in promoting security, economic, cultural and political alliance and cooperation. In 2012, during the first ever and primary commemorative and interesting Summit of ASEAN and India, the leaders of all the involved Nations decided to elevate and promote their engagement (involvement) to one of a strategic alliance and partnership

The Year 2017 depicted twenty five years of dialogue partnership between ASEAN and India as well as five years of the Strategic Partnership. India has engaged and participated with ASEAN at both sub regional and regional levels by signing and attesting to the economic cooperation (alliance) agreements with its various members. A Framework agreement in regards to a comprehensive and a well detailed economic cooperation was signed and attested in Bali in October 2003 between ASEAN and India; that was anticipated to eliminate or ban tariff barriers among all of the members as well as finally establishing and ensuring a free trade area in investments, services and goods. This was followed by a final and last agreement on trade in goods signed and attested in Bangkok in 2009 and another on Investment and Services in New Delhi in 2015, but not every barriers or challenges have as yet been prohibited and removed. Bilateral Agreements with different other members such as Malaysia, Singapore and Thailand have also been signed and attested, all of them geared at deepening and promoting the economic integration with the region

Economic Relations: Investments and Trade Linkages

Between 1995 and 2016, trade between ASEAN and India increased at a Compound Average Growth Rate (CAGR) of almost 11.5 percent of total (aggregate) trade of almost US $64.5 billion in 2016, Indian imports from the ASEAN Nations accounted or was responsible for a dominant share of 59 percent, with the exports to the Association of South East Asian Nation (ASEAN) economies accounting for the remaining share. Indian Imports from ASEAN expressed an increased growth of 12.3 percent during this period while the Indian Exports to ASEAN witnessed a Compound Average Growth Rate (CAGR) of 11.4 percent. This entails that the Balance of Trade has favored and benefited the ASEAN member Nations during the reference period.

There are few South East Asian Nations such as Thailand, Malaysia and Singapore that have emerged or thrived as a major and a significant export destination for India. The Major export products to Singapore entail bituminous substances, oil and fuel, floating structures, boats and ships. Indian Imports from Singapore entail Nuclear reactors, organically chemicals, machinery, boilers, mechanical appliances, equipment, electrical machinery, parts and among others. Also, India imports agricultural products from Malaysia. Since there are trade complementary(s) between South East Asian Nations and India in areas such as Minerals, Machineries and Agricultural, among others; trade relations have continued to increase, baring a few or limited periods of East African Crisis such as 1997-1998 including the Global Financial Crisis of 2008-2009.

Although in Investment, India collected almost $13.8 Billion as Foreign Direct Investment (FDI) from the Association of South East African Nation (ASEAN) economies in 2015-2016. The major and main South East Asian Nations investing in India are Thailand, Malaysia and Singapore. Over 99 percent of the total (aggregate) Foreign Direct Investment (FDI) inflows into India emanates from Singapore with other South East Asian Nations responsible for less than a percent. The Singapore-India comprehensive and well detailed economic cooperation agreement has created an impetus to rising partnership and alliance between the two Nations

Conversely, the Indian outflows to Association of South East Asia Nation (ASEAN) Nations documented at US $1.2 Billion in 2015, up from US $0.6 Billion the previous decade Although, outward investments from India have followed and adhered to a downward trajectory after 2012. Even earlier, in 2011; Indian Investment in these Nations declined by US $1.9 Billion. Table 1 indicates the investment flows between ASEAN and India for the period of 2010-2015

Table 1. Investment Flows between ASEAN and India in US $Billion, 2010-2015

	2010	2011	2012	2013	2014	2015
FDI Outflows from ASEAN into India	3.02	1.76	5.29	2.59	6.14	6.97
FDI Inflows from ASEAN from India	3.80	-1.96	6.63	2.10	0.61	1.25

Sources: ASEAN Investment Report, 2016; FDI Statistics of various years from DIPP Website

Note: Foreign Direct Investment (FDI) outflows from ASEAN into India solely entail data or information points for a few and limited South East Asian Nations majorly Indonesia, Philippines, Singapore, Vietnam, Myanmar and Thailand – for others, no data or information is available

In 2015, India accounted and was responsible for solely 1.3 percent of total (aggregate) net inflows into Association of South East Asia Nation (ASEAN). India majorly and vastly invested in the Insurance and Finance Industries and Firms across South East Asia (65 percent), followed by retail and wholesale trade (Nine Percent) including real estate activities (eight percent). Numerous Indian Financial Institutions, such as the Indian Overseas Bank, Bank of Baroda and Andhra Bank have established and formed branches in the ASEAN region. This is vital and significant to integrating and aligning the financial and banking services between the two regions

India – South East Asia Regional Value Chain

Regional Value Chain enhances and promotes economic cooperation and alliance by expanding and widening the market access among countries; Integrating with regional value chains results to benefits such as reduced and minimized cost of trading and manufacturing for the participating and involving Nations. The Benefits or advantages accrue from fragmentation and outsourcing of production (output) in different locations. there are an array of policy measures as well as liberalization of services, capital and goods, trade facilitation, infrastructure quality and competition policy, that promotes and enhance the integration of value chains. Foreign Direct Investment (FDI) flow is a major factor which allows for the economies integration by linking or aligning them to global and regional value chains. At a Business Conclave in Jaipur in February 2017, the Former Indian Industry and Commerce Industry Minister, Sitharaman Nirmala emphasized how textile produces in India could gain by participating or aligning with less developed Nations such as Vietnam, Myanmar, Laos and Cambodia. There is the potential and capacity to create and ensure value chains in textiles between a few ASEAN economies and India as the former import cotton yarn can input used and applied in the production of textiles from India. Creating and ensuring a value chain in fiber is another aspect of possible and necessary alliance between ASEAN and India. Myanmar, for example is open to Foreign Direct Investment (FDI) in the sectors such as agriculture, textiles and garments that are conducive and better to creating and ensuring a value chain between South East Asia and India

The Free Trade in goods agreement signed and attested between ASEAN and India in 2009 has also facilitated and ensured the development of supply chains as well as the production (output) networks in various products such as automobiles and electronics as well as component manufacturing and vehicles

Although, there remain various obstacles to establishing and creating supply chain; such as poor connectivity, non tariff barriers including quality of infrastructure among others

From Look East Policy to Act East Policy

The "Look East Policy" was initiated by the then Prime Minister of India Rao Narasimha (1991-1996) and has thrived during the tenure of the former or past Prime Minister of India Vaj Payee Bihari Atal (1998-2004) subsequently during the time of Singh Manmohan (2000-2014) and lastly under the Prime Minister-ship of Modi Narendra (2014). The Major aim and objectives of this policy were to re-engage and re-involve India's trade concentration with the neighbors as well as to the emerging South East Asian Nations so as to strengthen and enhance the position and stance of India's in this region as well as to avert the dominance of China's from the region. In the present year, the India's relationship and connection with South East Asia has tremendously flourished. Look East Policy of India has three dimension techniques towards the South East Asian Economies that are:

- Firstly, it aims and intentions were to ensure and allow political links or connections including understanding or comprehending with the South East Asian Nations through ASEAN
- Secondly, to enhance or promote the interaction and communication with the South East Nations in regards to Investment and Trade, Technology, Science and Tourism, etc
- Thirdly; to enhance and revitalize the defense links with these Nations (Kalita, 2018)

Connecting India with South East Asian Economies

Key to the task or responsibility of strengthening economic ties between India and the South East Asian Nations is promoting three forms of connectivity: People-to-People, Institutional and Physical.

People-to-People Connectivity

India has a long and a durable history or background of People to People Connectivity with South East Asian Nations mostly with Indonesia, Malaysia and Singapore, which are home to vast populations of the Indian Diaspora. Indians are made up of seven (7) percent of Malaysia's India and Nine (9) percent of

Singapore's Population. India as well as members of the ASEAN jointly coordinate and organize regular and constant exchange initiatives (programmes) for diplomats, farming communities, media personnel and business among others Although, there are certain prohibitions or the bans on the migration of labor and professionals between South East Asia and India. In regards to the agreement on trade in services signed and attested in 2015, ASEAN and India have concurred to liberalize trade in few and limited areas such as Insurance, Finance and Telecommunications Services, while regulating and controlling the migration of Natural Individuals. It is known or said that for the growth of the less developed ASEAN Nations (Myanmar, Cambodia and Laos), Professionals and Skilled Labors are needed. This is an area or aspect where India can play a significant and tremendous role.

Institutional Connectivity

To deepen and promote the connectivity between ASEAN Nations and India, it is important and essential to build and create an effective and a better institutional tie or connectivity by harmonizing investments, trade and financial policies. Physical connectivity (Soft Infrastructure requirements such as telecommunications and transportations) has to be constructed in tandem with proper and necessary institutional settings to attain enhanced cross-regional ties and connectivity

In regards to 2015 report by the Asian Development Bank, there are various opportunities for energy trading between Myanmar and India. Provided with the vast or large natural resources including the hydropower reserves of Myanmar, it becomes a major and significant source of energy for India. Although, a result of the absence of adequate institutional and physical infrastructure between South East Asia and India, energy trading remains underutilized. Moreover, the availability of restrictive regional arrangements and Non Tariff Barriers hinder and disrupt the migration of services and goods. Trade Facilitation measures to minimize the volume of documentation required –and thus the time of transit –are essential and important to enhance economic exchange between South East Asian Nations and India.

Physical/Infrastructural Connectivity

Effective Transport Linkage is essential and vital to India-ASEAN relations. After all, the seamless migration of services and goods across borders is majorly dependent or concentrated on effective and better transportation connections. The reality or fact entails that Infrastructure and Transport impediments occur and thrive between South East Asia and India –as well as poor facilities, missing railway links, poor and damaged quality of roads, lack of customs alliance or cooperation and inadequate port and maritime facilities. All of these have implications or repercussions for any potential and major integration and connection between South East Asia and India. India's North East is essential and important to efforts and motives towards regional connectivity or linkages with ASEAN Nations, provided its strategic locations. Myanmar, for one, shares and uses a land border with India's North East thus creating a bridge between South East Asia and the Indian Markets. Also, enhancing Maritime linkage and connectivity between Myanmar and India is vital and significant to their mutual development and growth. So far, the projects or initiatives that have been carried out by India with Myanmar entail the Kaladan Multimodal Transit Transport Initiative or Project including the Myanmar-India Thailand Trilateral Highway

The Kaladan Multimodal Transit Transport Initiative is the primary and major initiative carried out by India in South East Asia. When finished, this project or initiative will link Kolkata with Sittwe Port in Myanmar, facilitating and ensuring the migration of Cargo across the India-Myanmar Border through the Sea Route. This Project or Initiative will also create an alternative and optional transit route between Myanmar and India's North Eastern Region by creating and forming new road including in Land and Water Linkages Connectivity between them. The Multimodal Trans-Initiative or Project entails different segments, beginning with connecting of Kolkata to Sittwe across the Bay of Bengal and moving on to link Sittwe to the Paletwa town in Myanmar along the Kaladan River. Also, there is plan or an initiative to link Paletwa to the India-Myanmar Border through road that will also be extended and widened to the Lawngtlai Town in Mizoram. Work or Activity on this Project or Initiative is anticipated to be finished by 2020. It is anticipated to revolutionize and modify the transit system for tradable services and goods between Myanmar and India, later extending to the other South East Asian Countries such as Vietnam, Cambodia and others

OPPORTUNITIES AND CHALLENGES

It is essential and important to emphasize the opportunities inherent in this technique as well as to emphasize and state the challenges that will come in its direction. There are three popularly known pillars and foundations which are culture, connectivity and commerce that could provide or cater for various opportunities and benefits to empower the people of the North East India, create hospitable investment climate for the South East Asia Nations, create developmental opportunities, etc. These three pillars have played significant and crucial role in strengthening and enhancing the ties with the South East Asian Nations and in the future need or requirement is to further and also enhance the connectivity or linkages through transport, technology as well as through cultural with the region

In the present decades, India's relations and connectivity with the South East Asian Nations have enhanced tremendously, it has become necessary for the North Eastern Region of India to play the significant and crucial role in overall "Act East" Policy by looking at its geographical proximity and historical socio-cultural with the South East Asian Nations. The Major opportunities that "Act East Policy" could provide for the development of the North Eastern Region in India are as follows:

- Physical Infrastructure and Connectivity that assist in facilitating and ensuring trade
- "Act East" Policy would provide and create opportunity and benefit to the North Eastern Region so as to lure the investors of South East Asia Nations that would invest in various sectors of the development
- North Eastern Region is rich and flourishing in Biodiversity which would be essential and important for the attraction of tourists of the Southern Eastern Nations
- The Northern Eastern Region is well off in regards to Natural Resources, such as spices, oil, coal, limestone and natural gas that provides or caters for opportunity to the North Eastern Region to export their Natural Resources to the South East Asian Nations
- Also, "Act East" Policy provides and creates opportunities to the North Eastern Region to strengthen and enhance its relationship multilaterally or bilaterally with the South East Asia Nations. This aim and objective could be attained through Culture and People to People Contact, Sports, Medicinal and Academic Research (Brahma, September 2018)
- India has an opportunities and privileges to develop and create ties (linkages) with the South Asian Nations since India had civilization and cultural connection with the South Eastern Region.

Maximizing connectivity or linkages between the two multi cultural societies would receive free or less mobility of individuals held centuries or far back

- However, these are varieties of opportunities and benefits for the North Eastern Region for development with the assistant of this dynamic "Act East" Initiative and policy but simultaneously there are different obstacles that come in the path or area of its development. These challenges are emphasized as under:

- There is challenge of insurgency in the North Eastern Region that becomes a hurdle challenges in the path of development. Bearing in mind, Investors do not want to invest in any sector as a result of the state on level of constant and regular insecurity and fear. In such as scenarios, where Individuals always remain in the state of regular fear chances or probabilities of success for any policy or initiative remains very minimal or less
- ASEAN is politically and economically uneven or unequal level playing ground. Both Laos and Vietnam have the Communists Governments; Singapore has a symbolic and significant opposition and a single or sole party political hierarchy and structure; Malaysia having two party democratic structure; Myanmar having the semi democratic political setting, Thailand having Military Rule with the promise and pledge of new or modern constitution; Indonesia has emerging and a new democratic structure; Philippines having a unique and a significant democratic attributes and Brunei having Monarchy (Bhattacharjee, 2016)
- There is lack and absence of infrastructure in the North East Region. Majority of the State roadways or pathways across this region are in deteriorating situation. The North Eastern States totally restricted connectivity or linkages with the rest of India made this policy or initiative unviable.
- The Inabilities or Incapacities of States are another obstacle and hindrance for the effectiveness of this Policy. It is majorly Ministry of Development of North Eastern Region (DONER) and North Eastern Council (NEC) bestowed and vested with unveiling of the North Eastern Nations to South East Asia. Although, functioning of these both agencies is not satisfactory. This absence of coordination between the agencies also deteriorates and worsens the locally or internally generated revenues of the North Eastern Region (Dubey, 2014)
- Also, there is a problem or challenge such as lack and absence of coordination between the Government Parastatals. Security is the major concern or worry of the Northern Eastern Region of India. There is availability of various troops in this region and there are vital and unique legislations such as Armed Forces Special Power Act (AFSPA) that has been enforced and initiated in the North East. North East is the special and unique region where the Ministry of External Affairs (MEA), Ministry of Home Affairs (MHA) and the Ministry of Defense (MOD) control and regulate the every related defense matters.
    - Besides, above emphasized challenges, there are few others obstacles that make the success and the effectiveness of "Act East" Initiative or Policy very tricky. These challenges are as follows:
- The issue or scenario of connectivity or linkages that acts and serves as a major or main challenge in the path of development
- The issue of the South China Sea
- Russia-China Growing and Rising Relationship
- Chinese Diaspora controlling and regulating economy in Singapore, Indonesia and Malaysia
- Regional Security –China's Assertive Responsibility and Role

- India's Lack or Absence of initiatives and ideologies on Investments and Trade in the South East Asian Nations

RECOMMENDATIONS

To make this policy more action-oriented, goal-oriented and dynamic as well as tackle the various challenges, here are the various options that would ensure the effectiveness of this policy

- Economic Development is the most viable sphere or the key aspect where every Nation intends to Succeed. Participation of the Bordering States for the Economic Development of the Nation is inevitable.
- There is the essence to ensure and allow relaxation in visa facilities for the students of the South East Asian Nations. The India Government needs to ensure the best and appropriate infrastructure and educational facilities to the students that comes from these Nations for quality or a better education
- There is the essence to work for the enhancement of regional connections among the Nations of the North East as well as integrating and aligning them with the Policy Concepts/Frameworks.
- There is the need to comprehend comprehensively or appropriately rising equation of the South East Asian Region. Free Trade Agreements such as Regional Comprehensive Partnership, Trans-Pacific Partnership, and Asia Pacific Economic Cooperation are going to play a serious and significant role and responsibility in the near future including how India will benefits or gain from this Free Trade Agreement is essential to assess.
- Also, there is the essence to enhance Social and Cultural links with the South East Asian Nations. Soft Power does not play a serious essential (tremendous) role and responsibility in the formation of perceptions. Sangai Festival of Manipur and Horn Bill Festival of Nagaland have been attracting and luring tourists of the bordering Nations strong social and cultural links, Individual-to-Individual contact with the Neighboring Nations assist in encouraging and ensuring the interest of the concerned and involved Nations
- The Government must seriously and actively develop capacity building and knowledge in the North East
- There is the essence to seriously and actively work on the proposed objectives as well as to discover the reasons why the aims and objectives of the Policy can never be attained
- North East has always been disturbed and greatly deteriorated as a result of insurgency. Major focus and concentration of the Central Governments in this region has been to strengthen and revitalize the security.
- North East must not be a "gateway" or a "pathway" to "Act East" initiative or Policy but rather it must be a convergence point where trade facilitation between ASEAN and the Mainland India would be attainable or possible
- Also, there is the basic need to ensure and allow for active involvement or participation of the bordering Nations in the process of commerce and trade. This will give a new and a modern dynamism to this policy as well as would also assist in enhancing or revitalizing the relations

FUTURE RESEARCH DIRECTIONS

- As India and ASEAN commemorated the 20th Anniversary of Indian –ASEAN relations in December 2012, it would be timely and early to consider and see how the ASEAN-Indian relationship would be qualitatively elevated and enhanced to a higher and maximum level such as strategic partnership
- India enhanced participation in the regional security dialogue as well as connecting ASEAN and India could be vocal and essential points in the future direction of the ASEAN – India Relations. This also needs to be extended to business connectivity. For instance, investment rules and regulations can be made more liberal for companies or firms in India to invest in ASEAN Nation and to apply ASEAN as a launching initiative to reach other parts or jurisdictions of East Asia
- India vibrant participation and involvement in the ASEAN connectivity will benefit not solely ASEAN but as well as India, as it would demonstrate and showcase India's dedication to also integrate itself with South East Asia as well as other parts of East Africa. Economic Linkages could also be explored through India's participation in the execution of the master plan on ASEAN connectivity that not solely covers and entails physical infrastructure connectivity (both maritime and land) but as well as people to people links and institutional connectivity
- India's overriding interest is to preserve and strengthen its strategic independence (autonomy) in a multi polar globe. Therefore, India has indicated its performance for an inclusive, open and loosely structured economy as well as security architecture in the Asia –Pacific where India's role and responsibility would be accepted and welcomed. This coincides with the interest of ASEAN's, as ASEAN ability or willingness to retain its centrality and to leverage its influence and effect on the major powers and authorities would diminish in a geopolitical scenario where power relationship between the US and China, for instance, are majorly defined in the region. Thus, since 1994; ASEAN has initiated and created a process of multilateral security summit which is transparent, inclusive and open of extra regional authorities or powers and that has resulted to the formation of such region mechanisms as the EAS, ADMM + 8, ARF. As well as with APEC (Asia Pacific Economic Cooperation Forum) and also Sub regional functional categorizations such as Mekong-Ganga Corporation, Greater Mekong Basin Cooperation, BIMSTEC, they have created a regional framework for economic and strategic cooperation. Their roles overlap, but they have served ASEAN well as they have provided all the interested and necessary parties an appropriate and essential role (responsibility) to functions in the region
- From the ASEAN point of view, the major consideration is whether India has the commitment and the interest to engage and carry along ASEAN on a long and sustained term basis. This would depend and focus to a vast extent on how both ASEAN and India perceived and view their shared interests in the region. India perceived the essence to engage ASEAN so as to maximize investment and trade flows, to stop or prevent a perceived threat of an Islamic arc disseminating from its western front to the east, and to evaluate the increasing influence of China in ASEAN, especially Myanmar that shares a land border with India. On the ASEAN Perspective, India's rising economic strength, its states (portfolio) as de facto nuclear weapon nation and its preparedness to engage and involve all stakeholders in the ASIA pacific and provide not solely trending economic opportunities for ASEAN but the active participation of India in the region would ensure additional and more driving space for the ASEAN in handling other major powers

- However, shared security and political interests, essential as they are, such as in the ideological affinities and the evolving regional security architecture alone is insufficient or inadequate to sustain a long term relationship. Insufficient as well are common and rampant in the value system such as democracy and pluralism as the ASEAN societies are as diverse as in India. Rather such shared values and interests should serves as the foundation and basis of a long term relationship, solely if they are backed up by efforts to maximize the interdependence and economic stakes as well as public comprehension and political consciousness of the cultural and historical links between the ASEAN Nations and India. A typical instance in the revival or renewal of such links entails the Nalanda University Project. From the 5th Century A.D until its destruction and wreckage during the 12th century, Nalanda was a pre-eminent hub of Buddhist learning and research. The Nalanda University initiative would act to revitalize and renew the historical connections between South East Asia, East and India as well as to reinforce the notions that India is not at the periphery of East Asia but part or aspect of an ancient (traditional) Buddhist globe. Such shared interests and cultures would assist to ensure Corporation. At the practical stage, the Nalanda initiative would assist to attract or lure a foreign investment to develop and modify the infrastructure in the Indian State of Bihar, especially at Buddhist Pilgrimage Sites such as Nalanda, Rajgir and Bodh Gaya. Also, Partnership in the Nalanda initiative would provide numerous spin-offs for Indian/ASEAN co-operation and alliance in the tourism, cultural and educational field.
- In a special and unique address to the Indian Confederation of the Indian Firm on the 12th January 2012, Emeritus Senior Minister Tong.Chok Goh of Singapore demanded for innovative partnership and innovative thinking entailing security settings that would assist contain flash and easy target points in Asia such as the competing claims in the Sea of the South China and also tensions in the Korean Peninsula. Unless there was stability and peace in the region, the sustained growth of Asia was not guaranteed. ESM Goh suggested and emphasized on three ways that India could play a major leadership in the Asia pacific:
- India can contribute to the ASEAN connectivity incentive that strives or intends to integrate the ASEAN region though enhanced, institutional, physical and people to people links. India is already working or performing on an India-Myanmar Thailand Highway as well as its extension to Cambodia and Laos. Also, India is contributing to ICT connectivity and Information Technology such as through the establishment and setting up of e-network for the tele education and tele medicine in Vietnam, Myanmar, Laos and Cambodia
- India and ASEAN needs to redouble their efforts or motives to conclude or finalize the services and investment chapters of the ASEAN-India FTA in 2012, as agreed and concurred to by the Economic Ministers. The FTA is a major building block in the regional economic architecture and would be mutually significant for the businesses and peoples of India and ASEAN
- In the security situation or arena, India being a major participant and stakeholder in the ARF, can provide constructive suggestions or recommendation on how to move or migrate the ARF agenda or initiative forward, an improve practical corporation or alliance in confidence building including preventive democracy.
- These would require or entail a more proactive India, rather than being a "benign actor", in the deliberation in such For a as EAS, ADMM+ and ARF pertaining the economic structure and evolving regional security especially in areas where they are probably to affect or influence the major interests of India such as freedom of navigation and maritime security. India is a major and

key stakeholder as it controls and regulates the sea lanes between the Nicobar and the Andaman Islands in the Indian Ocean.

CONCLUSION

India's "Look East" initiative reconfigured and revitalized as "Act East" initiative has successfully evolved from the last three years. The policy or initiative was initially prepared to create economic bounds with the South East Asian Nations and has gained security, cultural, strategic, social and political discussions in the South East Asian Region. The Nation worked with the aims to make a swifter development of the Nation with the active participation of the North Eastern Nations. The progress of the North Eastern region would result to the populace of the region towards prosperity. Ancient links and Geographical Proximity of the South Eastern Region with the North Eastern Region is the major propeller and shaker of the "Act East" Policy. Also, different critics emphasize that there are different hurdles that act as a stumbling block for the "Act East" Policy. These challenges entails, that is; bureaucratic inertia, absence of coordination at ministerial level, insurgency on the region, lack of investors-friendly legislations, etc. Regardless of varieties of hurdles, still we can emphasize that 'Act East" initiative through North East India is a commendable and significant exercise for the prosperity and the development of the North Eastern Individual. There is a significant demand to adhere to the "bottom up" technique and not the "top down" technique, where North East would decide the contours of the "Act East" initiative and centre would play the role and responsibility of facilitator (Dubey, 2014). Also, North East region requires identifying that it must have leverage on the benefits and opportunities that are available presently. Also, this region must come from the narrative of "isolation" which has kept the region cut and erase off from the benefits and opportunities that are available around it. It is in its interest to provide different forms of support to the undertaken policies. It is quite necessary to evaluate how the Modi Government can reduce the gap between the "Policy Implementation" and the "Policy Formulation" and takes into cognizance the whole local dynamics that will be very essential and significant for the success of "Act East" Policy from the perspective and angle of the North East Region (Yhome, 2015)

Notwithstanding, the numerous promise and allegiances are carried out by stronger or a tighter connectivity between South East Asia and India, there are numerous barriers or impediments which hobble such integration. For one, the delay in completing and finishing infrastructure projects –including highways, seaports, rail and road- as a result to different financial and political challenges has affected the progress and success of economic alliance or cooperation. Bearing in mind its interest in aligning with South East Asia for potential and major benefits or opportunities in different sectors such as gas, energy and agriculture; India has carried out various projects to promote cross regional cooperation and alliance. For example, India invited Myanmar to join and align with the Bay of Bengal Initiative for Multi Sectoral Technical and Economic Cooperation (BIMSTEC) in December 1997, as it has a locational opportunity and benefit which can be leveraged to integrate and align India with South East Asia. It is emphasized and stated that ASEAN and India identify and recognize their shared interests and common challenges as it will assist them promote and encourage cooperation (alliance). Trade in services largely remains safeguarded in ASEAN Member Nations. As India has a comparative benefit and advantage in the services sector, particularly Information Technology (IT) Services, domestic regulations in ASEAN nations requires to be liberalized so as to encourage and trigger cross regional alliance. The impediments of inadequate physical linkages or connectivity (rail and road linkages) as well as with infrastructural bottlenecks (non tariff barriers) requires to be addressed or emphasized to strengthen and enhance the India-ASEAN connectivity and relationship

The ambitious goals of the LEP/AEP's for the North East Region comprise of developing of trade infrastructure and connectivity for seamless transits of commerce between the South East Asia and South Asia Regions. Whereas Traditional Foreign Policy of India was approaching and attaining the North Eastern Region of India though a security vantage, the LEP/AEP "opens up" and unveils, the North East to Investments and Trades which amalgamates geopolitical aims and objectives with the zeal for economic growth expansion. The zeal for economic expansion and trade growth across the South East and South Asia Regions through the Infrastructure Constructions, although, has constituted and comprised a model and technique for the region development which almost concentrates and focuses singularly and majorly in developments of physical infrastructure. Indian engagement and involvement with the ASEAN since the 1990s was to accelerate and promote the modernization and expansion of India Infrastructure in the form of power, ports and roads.

Also, Regional Comprehensive Economic Partnership Agreement is anticipated to enhance investment and trade among all the member nations. This process requires to be expedited. Much progress is envisioned or seen as India-ASEAN connectivity upon the liberalization of the services trade (particularly, migration of natural individuals) including other areas or aspects of essential and common interest.

REFERENCES

Bajpaee, C. (2017). Dephasing India's Look East/Act East. *Contemporary Southeast Asia: A Journal of International and Strategic Affairs, 39*(2), 349.

Bhattacharjee, D. (2016). *India's Act East Policy: Problems and Prospects in North East India*. Indian Council of World Affairs.

Brahma, A. (2018). India's Act East Policy: The North-East States. *International Journal of Innovative Research in Science, 7*(9).

Choudhury, S. (2017). *The Act East Policy and Northeast India: Challenges and Opportunities*. https://www.researchgate.net/publication/320921997

Dubey, R. (2014). *North East India in India's Look East Policy: Constraints and Social Research Foundation*. http://srfaurangabad.org/journals/4thissue/11.pdf

Goyal, & Mukherjee. (2015). *Reinvigorating India's manufacturing sector: Integrating the services value chain with Southeast Asia*. International Growth Centre Blog.

Kalita, S. (2018). India's act east policy and north-east: Challenges and Prospects. *International Journal of Advanced Research and Development, 3*(1).

Pretty, B. (2018). *India-ASEAN Economic connections and relations: Evaluating Future Possibilities*. ORF Issue Brief, Issue No.221.

Rahul,, S.,, & Mark,, G.A. (2004). *India-ASEAN Economic Relations: Future Prospects and Current Status*. Research Gate.

Rao. (2012, July-December). Emerging India's Policy towards Southeast Asia during the Post-Cold War Era. *Area Studies*, *6*(2), 90–109.

Smriti. (2017). India can be reliable and a better source of fibers for ASEAN. *The Pioneer*. https://www.dailypioneer.com/business-and-finance/india-can-be-reliable-source-of-fibres-forasean-smriti-irani.html

Suneja, K. (2017). Create value chains with Countries getting EU, US sops: Government to companies. *Economic Times*. https://economictimes.indiatimes.com/news/economy/policy/create-value-chains-with-nations-getting-us-eu-sops-government-to-companies/articleshow/57382370.cms

Yhome, K. (2015). From "Look East" to "Act East": What it. *Eastern Quarterly*, *2*(1-2), 27. https://www.researchgate.net/publication/311774304

Zulafqar,, A.A. (2009). *North East India and India's Act East Policy: A Critical Review*. Research Gate.

KEY TERMS AND DEFINITIONS

ASEAN: Association of South East Asian Nations (ASEAN) is an economic union consisting of ten member states in the South East Asia that facilitate political, economic, military, security and socio cultural integration and promote intergovernmental corporation between its members and other Nations in Asia.

Economic Development: It entails the creation of wealth from which the community or region benefits are attained or realized.

Economic Growth: It is an increase or rise in the amount of service and goods to be manufactured per head of the population over a particular period of time.

Export: Export in International or Foreign Trade is a good or commodity manufactured in a Nation that is sold into another Nation or a service provided or created in a Nation for a resident or National of another Nation.

Foreign Direct Investment: It is a purchase of an Interest in an Organization by an Investor or a Company located or situated outside its border.

Import: It is the receiving Nation in an export from the sending Nation.

Infrastructure: It is the Basic Organizational and Physical facilities and structures (e.g. roads, hospitals, ICT, library, railways, buildings, power supplies) needed and required for the operation of an enterprise or society. It is a set of fundamental or basics systems and facilities which supports the sustainable functionality of firms and households.

Investment: It is the Item or asset acquired or gotten with the goal or intention of generating appreciation or income.

Look East Policy: It is presently referred to as Act East Policy. It is an India effort to cultivate and ensure extensive strategic and economic relations with the countries of South East Asian to bolster its standing as a counterweight and a regional power to the strategic influence and effect of the People's Republic of China.

Trade: It is the activities of purchasing and selling commodities and services.

Chapter 11
A Critical Evaluation of India's Look-East to Act-East Policy

Shashi Jain
Dev Samaj College for Women, India

Harpreet Kaur
Central Queensland University, Australia

ABSTRACT

The Look-East Policy was launched in 1992 with the objective that economic integration with Southeast Asian countries would provide an opportunity for growth and transformation of the country because these were the fastest-growing economies. The Indian economy was opening up. The Act-East Policy was succeeded by the Look-East Policy in 2014. This policy was to have greater engagement with countries in Southeast Asia. The Act-East Policy gave importance to economic cooperation, greater connectivity, and security ties. By departing from the traditional foreign policy imperatives, this policy focused on removing the barriers and remoteness of Northeast India. It represents the development model of this region. There has been a sizeable increase in trade output with Southeast Asian countries and an increase in foreign investment. This policy has helped India strengthen its place in the global economy. However, northeastern states have not developed much. The poor section of society and the indigenous residents have not gained from export-oriented and capital-intensive projects.

BACKGROUND

A country's economic relations with other countries and foreign trade relations depend on the foreign policy of that country. After Independence, India adopted the foreign policy based on non-alignment as India achieved Independence during the time when the clouds of Cold War were already looming large on the globe, because of which it not only underwent but also experienced the power politics of the Super Powers - USA and USSR. This naturally made India formulate her foreign policy on the lines of non- involvement and non-alignment that became the basic principle of India's foreign policy. The economic model adopted was a middle path between capitalist and socialist economy that is Mixed

DOI: 10.4018/978-1-7998-5774-7.ch011

Economy. However, in 1954, Mahalanobis Model was implemented and it laid emphasis on establishment of Welfare Socialist State in the country (Chaturvedi & Sharma, 2020, pp 882). This economic shift had tilted Indian economy and her foreign policy towards USSR.

After the Chinese attack on India in 1962 and the defeat of India, the Indian government adopted the policy of absolute socialism. India did not pay much attention to Southeast Asian countries because of India's colonial links and western links. The Association of South East Asian countries (ASEAN) was created in 1967 by a group of ten small countries: Brunei, Cambodia, Indonesia, Laos, Malaysia, Myanmar, the Philippines, Singapore, Thailand and Vietnam. Since the region was quite less developed until 1970, it was not considered by India to be an attractive trading and economic partner. Besides, India's own economic policies were insular and protectionist. However, in 1970s East Asian Countries were thriving of open market reforms and liberalization and had started showing signs of rapid advancement. Japan devastated in 1945, due to nuclear attacks, was also emerging as one of the fastest economies of the world. Besides, in 1991, there were significant changes at the national and international fronts. India faced financial crisis in 1991, which coincided with the collapse of the Soviet Union, India's valued economic and strategic partner. These developments compelled the Indian government to have a fresh look at her foreign policy. India also acknowledged the uniqueness and importance of Southeast Asia, which is rich in economic resources and is important from the point of security strategy. These events caused qualitative and structural changes in the foreign policy of India and Southeast Asia. There was dilution of inhibitions from Southeast Asian countries as well and they opened themselves up to develop friendly and warm relations with India. This region thus gained more prominence in the foreign policy of India. With such a background at the national and international level, the Look East Policy was launched in 1992 during the Narasimha Rao's government.

Look East Policy developed gradually and in a pragmatic manner. India needed foreign investment and technology and ASEAN was viewed as a fertile and apt source for it. ASEAN too was attracted by the potential of a more open market. It also was driven by its own strategic compulsions to seek a balance in the region to China's rising power by enhancing its engagement with India. Initiated in 1991, it marked a shift in India's perspective of the world (Haokip, 2011). This was developed and enacted during Narasimha Rao government (1991-1996) and rigorously pursued by the successive governments of Atal Bihari Vajpayee (1998-2004) and Manmohan Singh (2004-2014).

Various researches and publications on different topics discussing the relation between India and Southeast Asia and Look East Policy still show an emerging area of critical research in the context of India though with quite less empirical findings. The aim of this conceptual chapter is to critically evaluate "Look East to Act East" policy of India in providing opportunities for economic, socio cultural cooperation, development of Northeast region and national security issues. It, in a way, tried to incorporate greater engagement in all spheres.

The structure of this chapter starts with the literature review of Look East Policy and Act East Policy followed by the objectives of two. Then difference between the two policies are incorporated. An analysis of measures taken to meet the objectives of the policies has been discussed with critical evaluation. Finally, the future research directions and conclusions have been provided to stimulate the knowledge in theory and practice for the desired growth of Northeastern states and cooperation with ASEAN on different platforms.

LITERATURE REVIEW

India after independence and during the Cold war period did not involve in a direct relationship with the neighboring countries. With the binary division of Cold war geopolitics, India remained non-aligned and inclined towards Soviet Union. It was only in the post-Cold War period, that India stepped on 'Look East' Policy (LEP) in 1992, declared by Narasimha Rao, the then Prime minister of India. Strategic and political compulsions notwithstanding, India's economic interests were of no less importance in determining this shift in the direction for our foreign policy (Sarma and Mehta 2003). Within a few years, of LEP India became a part of various mechanisms of regional cooperation and dialogue with ASEAN nations. India's LEP is aimed at greater economic alignment and an enhanced political role in the dynamic Asia-Pacific Region in general and Southeast Asia in particular (Bragta, 2021). India's LEP yielded rich dividend. India-ASEAN trade increased from about US$10 billion in 2000 to US $70 billion in 2011, accounting for 9 per cent of India's total global trade (Das, 2018).

The Look (Act) East Policy was conceived more as a national policy for promoting trade, technology and investment opportunities. Development of northeastern states was not its primary concern. It is after the initiation of sub regional forums like the Bay of Bengal Initiative for Multi-Sectoral Technical and Economic Cooperation (BIMSTEC), Bangladesh–China–India–Myanmar Forum for Regional Cooperation (BCIM), Mekong– Ganga Cooperation (MGC), etc., that the North East started being projected as a gateway to East and South East Asia (Kakoti, 2020, p. 40).

Barua and Das(2016) exposed that 'in fact, the region (North eastern) had been exposed to international trade on a massive scale during the late-nineteenth century, which continued until the dawn of India's independence, but this has hardly had any impact on the region's economy. Therefore, the real problem of development even today is not really the lack of trading opportunities but the crucial constraints to development faced by the region are the lack of intra-regional and intra-state connectivity and trade, infrastructure, security and governance. The new paradigm of development seems to ignore these constraints by diverting attention to an issue (like connectivity with the outside world) which may have only a marginal impact upon the economy'.

In 2014, under the dynamic leadership of Prime Minister Narendra Modi, the LEP was stepped up to the AEP (Act East Policy). Ever since, AEP has become the part and parcel of geopolitical discourse in India's foreign policy (Saint-Mezard, 2016, 178). The policy that was initially perceived as an economic initiative has added cultural, political and strategic dimensions with the inclusions of established devices for discourse and regional cooperation (Bhure & Malegaonkar, 2019, 21). Further, the AEP should also continue to work on improving India's connectivity with ASEAN, particularly to North-East India via the trilateral highway, the Kaladan project that will connect the ports of Kolkata and Sittwe in Myanmar and the Bay of Bengal Initiative for Multi Sectorial Technical and Economic Cooperation (BIMSTEC), will promote peace and prosperity in the region. Beyond this, linked to ASEAN, India is trying further to strengthen its strategic and economic ties with U.S., Japan, Korea, Australia and China. The important sectors like, technology transfer, civilian nuclear cooperation, defense and innovation are to be given priority by the government's promise of progress, will be renewed (Sajjanhar, 2016). As such, it becomes pertinent to look deeper into the policies critically to provide some suggestions.

Objectives of Look East Policy

Regional Economic Integration: The main objective of the Look East Policy was to increase economic interaction with the East and South East Asia through trade, investment, science technology and tourism. It was realised that these regions had been the fastest growing regions of the world. Japan and the newly industrialising economies of Southeast Asia had been considered as the models of accomplishment for other emerging economies.

Globalisation and Liberalisation: The government of India adopted the policy of reforms, globalisation, and liberalisation in 1991. Under these reforms, Look East Policy sought to forge deeper economic integration with the East and Southeast countries by lowering the trade barriers and by encouraging foreign investment. In fact, Look East Policy (LEP) was an external reflection of the progressive domestic economic transformation of the country. Many bi-lateral, multi-lateral, and Free Trade Agreements were signed with different ASEAN countries. Manmohan Singh, the former Prime Minister conveyed that LEP was a strategic shift in India's vision of the world and India's place in the evolving global economy.

Rapid Economic Growth: It was expected that LEP would bring faster economic development of the country as it would liberalise the economy for ASEAN countries, which were becoming more and more developed. The objective was to access growth opportunities in these countries and to attract foreign investment in the infrastructural sectors to keep pace with the expanding economy.

Development of North-eastern Region: The North- eastern region had lagged behind the other parts of the country in terms of growth and development. The objective of LEP was to equip the region with trade enhancing infrastructure for industrial development by establishing connectivity to Southeast Asian countries. The development of this region was considered important for the overall development of the country as well as for the relationship with other countries. India's LEP correctly identified Northeast region as the gateway to the Southeast and it was one of the major imperatives undertaken by the government at that time.

As such, LEP marked an important breakthrough in India's foreign policy because along with economic liberalisation and moving away from Cold war era policies and activities, India's strategy focused on forging close economic and commercial ties with ASEAN. In pursuance of India's LEP, the dialogue with ASEAN has moved consistently forward from a sectoral-dialogue partner in 1992, membership of the high-profile strategic forum ARF (ASEAN Regional Forum) in 1996, and Indo-ASEAN summits since 2002 (Kesavan, 2020). In 2009, an Indo ASEAN Trade in Goods Agreement (TIGA) was signed. Besides, when there was economic crisis in ASEAN countries in 1997 and it had a deeply negative impact on them e.g. Indonesian capacity declined, Singaporean income was jeopardized, Thailand's economy collapsed and they were in great need for 'stabilising power' via the support of world's economic tycoons such as Japan, China, and India. It was realised that India and ASEAN could mutually help and contribute to the development of both the regions.

Objectives of Act East Policy (AEP)

Greater Engagement in all Spheres: The main objective of the policy was to have greater engagement in all spheres with countries in Southeast Asia as well as with far eastern countries like Japan, South Korea, and countries in the Pacific region like Australia. The Prime Minister of India highlighted 4 C's of AEP; Culture, Commerce, Connectivity and Capacity Building.

Security: Security is an important dimension of India's AEP. With this policy India hopes to deepen its political, economic and security relationships with these countries. India's vision for the region is SAGAR that is security for all and growth for all.

Cultural and Historical ties: Under AEP, the objective is to promote the historical and cultural ties with ASEAN through people-to-people exchange. It has its roots in the broader ideology of' 'Asianism'. As mentioned in the book 'Discovery of India' (Nehru, 2008) the East Asian Countries have cultural and civilization symmetry with India. Both Hinduism and Buddhism spread to these states and for many years co-existed there with mutual respect. In fact, civilization and cultural links date back to thousands of years since the prehistoric times. The region found mention in many classical works such as Ramayana. Hindu religious symbols are very popular in Indonesia. In Cambodia, Thailand, Indonesia and Burma many symbolic remnants of India's influence are clearly visible in their art, culture and civilisation.

Through the centuries, India has been a source of inspiration for art and architecture in countries belonging to the present day ASEAN. Temples of Ankorvat, Pagan, Borobudur and Parambanan bear evidence to the deep penetration of Indian art and architectural forms in Southeast Asia monuments. There are also references to the similarities in food habits and life styles of people inhabiting ASEAN. The cultural relationship between India and Thailand can be traced back through history. Symbols and structure used by the two countries are proof of shared culture and civilisation. The Lion Capital of Ashoka the Great, a Buddhist king who brought Buddhism to Thailand is the national emblem of the country where Hinduism is the religion of the majority of people, while Garuda, a birdlike mythological beast of Hindu tradition is the national emblem of Thailand where the majority is Buddhist. Sanjeev Sanyal (2016) in his book 'The Ocean of Churn' has illustrated Southeast Asia influence on Indian society too. For instance, the Khasis of Meghalaya remain matrilineal to this day (Rathnayake, 2021). In fact, matrilineal customs can also be seen in neighbouring communities that may never have been matrilineal. For instance, in Assamese Hindu wedding, the sindoor (red vermilion) is applied to the forehead of the bride by the mother-in –law at the jurun ceremony that is organised before the wedding (Das, 2020).The Prime Minister Narender Modi tries to invoke these cultural ties whenever he makes a speech to the ASEAN.

Development of North-eastern Region: One of the important objectives of AEP is the development of North-eastern region (NER) because it acts as a gateway to Southeast Asian region, and provides a unique platform to the country to extend its links and ties with the neighbouring countries in the South and Southeast Asia. The NER shares borders with Nepal, Bhutan, China, Myanmar and Bangladesh culminating in a long international border. Myanmar alone is regarded as prime gateway of Northeast to Southeast Asia, which shares a boundary with the states of Arunachal Pradesh, Manipur, Mizoram and Nagaland.

DIFFERENCES IN LEP AND AEP

There are some fundamental differences in both LEP and AEP. LEP was launched at a time when India was in a poor economic state and was in a transition of liberalisation and globalisation. However, when AEP was launched, India was comparatively in a favourable economic position. It was a robust economy. In LEP, the focus was more on boosting trade and investment relations with Southeast Asian countries but AEP has a greater strategic and political angle to the cooperation. Historically, trade was the catalysing factor for India's relations with Southeast Asia, which later was expanded to polity, religion, arts, and literature. AEP laid emphasis on economic cooperation and building infrastructure for greater connectivity, importantly strategic and security ties. Under LEP, economic cooperation was sought basically from ASEAN but under AEP relations were established not only with ASEAN but also with Japan, South Korea, Vietnam, Malaysia and Australia to tackle the changing geopolitical scenario emanating from domination by China. Besides, there was also focus on historical, cultural, linguistic and religious ties through people to people and business to business exchange. More emphasis was laid on the development of NER because it could be the gateway to East Asia and Southeast Asia. Under AEP, there was greater emphasis on defence and security without compromising commerce, culture and connectivity i.e. socio-economic-cultural co-operation.

However, both the policies show two different phases of the foreign policy of the country. India's focus remains on enhancing economic relations with ASEAN via greater infrastructural connectivity and regional development, foreign direct investment and regional security. Though some critics say that these two policies are the two sides of a coin, there is only difference in the nomenclature, and that there is no fundamental difference. In fact, the AEP is more comprehensive and broader. Moreover, it has evolved through various phases with an accelerated pace and process of interactions in moving from one phase to another phase.

The Look East Policy was first intended as an economic strategy to boost India's trade and investment relations with the Southeast Asian region. However, over the years, it not only expanded its geographical reach to include Japan, South Korea and Australia but has also assumed significant strategic and political dimensions. India has now forged strategic partnership with Indonesia, Vietnam, Malaysia, Japan, South Korea and Australia. It has also established close links with countries of BIMSTEC group of countries and the Indian Ocean Rim (IOR). At the Commemorative Summit held in 2012, the Heads of Government recommended establishment of ASEAN-India Centre (AIC) to undertake policy research, advocacy and networking activities and think tanks in India and ASEAN to promote the ASEAN-India Strategic Partnership. AIC has provided inputs to policy makers in India and ASEAN by organising seminars, round tables, workshops, and conferences. AIC provides up-to-date information, data resources, and sustained interaction for promoting ASEAN-India Strategic Partnership. Thus, Look East Policy culminated in to a new phase under the Prime Minister Narendra Modi and was rebranded as Act East Policy and now it includes Indo Pacific region. Thus, India has embarked on a period of radical changes in its foreign and economic policies. Under AEP, the India-Japan strategic partnership has been lifted to a new level, underscoring the importance of Indo –Pacific co-operation. India believed in an Indo-Pacific that is free, open and inclusive and one that is founded upon a cooperative, collaborative rules based order. India has placed the Indo-Pacific at the heart of its engagement with the countries of South, Southeast and East Asia. Gradually, Act East is getting transformed into Act 'Indo-Pacific'. AEP is more pro-active, action-oriented, direct, and vocal about India's interests and concerns than the quieter and subtle Look East Policy (Zulfiqar, 2019).

Under LEP projects, India participated in many supranational organisations like Mekong Ganga Cooperation (MGC) which is an initiative by six countries-India and five ASEAN countries: namely Cambodia, Lao PDR, Myanmar, Thailand, and Vietnam for cooperation in tourism, culture, education, as well as transport and communication. Both the Ganga and Mekong are the Civilisation Rivers and the MGC initiative aimed to facilitate closer contacts among the people inhabiting these two major river basins. The MGC is also indicative of the cultural and commercial linkages among the member countries of the MGC down the centuries. India also participated in The Bay of Bengal Initiative for Multi- Sectoral Technical and Economic Cooperation (BIMSTEC). This aims to create not only an enabling environment for rapid economic development but also accelerate and promote collaboration on matters of common interest in the region. The first India-ASEAN Car Rally was organised in 2004. In proposing, the India ASEAN Car Rally Former Prime Minister Atal Bihari Vajpayee had said it would "draw dramatic attention to our geographical proximity." It started in Guwahati and ended in Indonesia's Botam Island off Singapore. Vajpayee also took the initiative to liberalise air service agreements between India and ASEAN countries.

India became strategic partner in 2012 in the region. India has also been active in regional forums like East Asia Summit (EAS) and ASEAN Regional Forum (ARF). Therefore, Act East policy (AEP) of India succeeded Look East Policy in 2014 by the present government led by the Prime Minister Shri Narender Modi.

Measures Taken

Initiatives to Enhance Connectivity: India views the rise of China as the principal strategic rival and a serious challenge and is forging relations with countries along its periphery to maintain the balance between them. China's rise has also compelled India's outreach to Australia to forge a stronger defence partnership. Japan is the key regional power and shares India's concerns over China's expansion. India is also deepening trade, investment and security ties with the regional power South Korea .Besides, India wants remote Northeast India to connect to Southeast Asia through Myanmar. Various Asian highways and Asian Railway link and natural gas pipe lines have been built .Kaladan Multi model Transport Facility has been created to establish connectivity between Indian ports and Sittwe port in Myanmar. The Mekong Ganga Cooperation and Kenming Initiative have been taken up to boost cooperation in tourism, culture, and education with ASEAN. Mekong has the potential for direct flights between Guwahati-Ho-Ch-Minh City and Imphal-Hanoi. The Indian Myanmar-Thailand Trilateral Highway Project with its extension to Laos and Cambodia has been taken up. A consensus on finalising the proposed protocol of the India-Myanmar-Thailand-Motor Vehicle Agreement (IMT MVA) has been reached. This agreement will have a critical role in realizing seamless movement of passenger, personal and cargo vehicles along roads linking India, Myanmar and Thailand. Once the necessary transit linkages are built, trade and business can flourish through enhanced market access, increased potential for tourism and culture industries, space to mobilise FDI, setting up export-oriented production bases in special economic zones.

PM Modi has announced a line of credit of US$ 1 billion to promote projects that support physical and digital connectivity between India and ASEAN and a Project Development Fund with a corpus of INR 500 crores to develop manufacturing hubs in CLMV countries- Cambodia, Laos, Myanmar and Vietnam at the 13th ASEAN India Summit held in Malaysia in November 2015 (Balasubramanian, 2015). India has also invited the CLMV countries to join the International Solar Chain Alliance and The Resilient Supply Chain Initiative (RSCI) and emphasised that it is focusing on promoting connectivity to boost trade with the region. India also offers to enhance collaboration in the area of Covid-19 vaccine development and distribution.

Economic Cooperation: The economic relationship between India and ASEAN began in 1992 as both the regions recognized each other's trade capabilities (Kapur, 2021). The relationship has since strengthened with India's manufacturing capacity and the rise of ASEAN's services sector exports, namely travel, transport, and business services. The regions have similarities in their levels of economic development because they have rapidly expanding markets and aim to address infrastructural challenges. These similarities offer space for continued and more diversified trade in goods and services as well as business to business engagement between India and ASEAN –tapping into the investment requirements of modernizing industries and consumption trends in each other's markets. Economic engagement in terms of the free movement of goods, services, and capital thus offers mutual benefits for India and ASEAN. This rationale encouraged both the regions to sign the ASEAN- India Free Trade Agreement (AIFTA) in 2009.This trade treaty has certainly boosted bilateral trade.

According to the report by the Ph.D. Chamber of Commerce and Industry, India's merchandise exports to ASEAN increased from US $23 billion in 2010 to US$36 billion in 2018 at a compound annual growth rate (CAGR) of about 5%, while its merchandise imports from the ten member countries increased from US $30 billion in 2010 to US$57 billion in 2018 at a CAGR of about 8%.India's exports to ASEAN were worth US$ 31.49 billion in 2019-20 while its imports from the bloc reached US$ 55.37 billion. In its trade with ASEAN, India has moved to eliminate tariffs on up to 75% of 12000 tariff lines (Kapur, 2021). According to the report from the National Institution for Transforming India (NITI Aayog), this had led to the trade balance worsening in 13 out of 21 sectors. In a report published by Exim Bank of India in January 2018 commemorating 25 years of India's partnership with ASEAN, it was found that India's exports were highly diversified because India has a vast raw material base, large labour market and an increasing manufactured hubs (Kapur, 2021). On the other hand, ASEAN has its own market appeal with its population of large youth cohorts, rising disposable incomes and fast digital economies.

In 2015, the ASEAN –India Trade in Services and Investment Agreement came into force. Key provisions in Services Agreement address transparency, domestic regulations, recognition, and market access, and national treatment, joint committee on services, review, dispute settlement and denial of benefits among others. The Investment Agreement focuses on the protection of investment to ensure fair and equitable treatment for investors, non-discriminatory treatment in expropriation or nationalization and fair treatment. The agreement will also facilitate the movement of Indian service professionals in ASEAN countries.

India's e-commerce sector is on an upward growth trajectory and is projected to be the second largest e-commerce market in the world by 2034. The Indian government allows 100% FDI for B2B e-commerce and 100% under the automatic route for the marketplace e-commerce model (Jaipuria, 2016). COVID 19 has reshaped ASEAN's digital landscape with many governments and businesses being forced to accelerate towards digital economy. The region has over 400 million users, and so its digital landscape presents a unique opportunity for investors. Sectors such as telemedicine, e-commerce, online education, and telecommuting are examples of such scalable digital opportunities. In a move to strengthen economic and commercial partnership in the healthcare sector, India encouraged ASEAN companies to participate in the virtual India-ASEAN Healthcare Expo and Summit held in February 2021. A good deal of ASEAN private investment has also flowed into India in many sectors including construction of ports, highways, food processing, shipping and auto components. Similarly, India's investments in ASEAN have grown considerably in recent years, with Singapore becoming its investment hub.

There is a similar pattern in India's trade with Japan and South Korea. Though India and Japan entered into a Comprehensive Economic Partnership Agreement (CEPA) in 2011, the volume of trade has been decreasing. In 2014-15, trade between the two was US$ 15.71 billion and came down to US$ 14.51 billion in 2015-16. It further declined to US$ 13.60 billion in 2016-17 before it recovered to a record US$ 15.71 billion in 2017-18% (Khan, 2019).

The Prime Minister Modi has shown great interest in acquiring Japanese investment for several infrastructure projects because it is believed that Japan's technological and economic prowess can help accelerate India's development by transforming its infrastructure and manufacturing sectors. In their first summit, meeting in 2014 Modi and Shinzo Abe set the target of doubling Japan's direct investment and the number of Japanese companies in India. Japan agreed to extend US$ 33.5 billion public and private investment in India. This amount would be used to support projects in various sectors including infrastructure, connectivity, transport, smart cities, energy and skill development. PM. Modi decided to set up a number of Japanese industrial townships and electronic parks in India. In turn Shinzo Abe agreed to support 'Make-in India', 'Digital India' and 'Skill India'(Kesavan, 2020).

In India, a special Japan Plus desk has been created at the Ministry of Commerce and Industry to minimise the bureaucratic obstacles in clearing investment projects. The value of Japan's investment jumped from US$ 1.7 billion in 2014 to US$4.7 billion in 2016-17. The cumulative Japanese investment in India from April to December 2016 amounted to US$ 25.2 billion, accounting for 8% of India's total FDI during that period. Japanese investment flowed into several important sectors including automobiles, telecommunications, chemicals and pharmaceuticals. South Korean FDI to India has also been increasing steadily reaching US$ 5.71 billion by the end of 2018(Kesavan, 2020). Korea's presence has become prominent with Hyundai Motors playing a key role. South Korea has virtually taken over India's electronics sector with Samsung and LG playing a prominent role. In fact, they have become a household name in India.

Bangladesh also has land earmarked for development of special 'Indian economic zones' since 2015 (Kathuria, 2017). Bangladesh is India's largest trading partner in the sub-continent with the total bilateral trade between the two nations standing at $9.5 billion in 2019-20 (Mallapur, 2021). India has also been Australia's fifth largest export market and FDI destination, and fifth largest two-way partner. India ranks 10th as the source of imports to Australia (DFAT, 2019).

Socio-Cultural Cooperation: Many measures have been taken and many programmes have been organised to boost People to People interaction with ASEAN such as inviting students to India each year for the Students Exchange Programme, Special Training course for ASEAN diplomats, exchange of Parliamentarians, participation of ASEAN students in the National Children's Science Congress, ASEAN-India Network of Think Tank, ASEAN-India Eminent Persons Lecture Series. The 2nd edition of the ASEAN-India Workshop on Blue Economy was jointly hosted with the Socialist Republic of Vietnam on 18th July 2018. Scholarships in the field of education are given (Mea, 2018). Students from ASEAN countries are offered 1000 Ph.D. fellowships to study in IITs in India (Jaishankar, 2019).

Development of Northeast Region: Development of NER is one of the main objectives of AEP because it acts as a 'gateway' to Southeast Asian Region and it provides a unique platform to the country to extend its ties with the neighbouring countries in the South and Southeast Asia (De, 2019). The region has all the potentialities to develop into India's powerhouse as it has abundant rich sources of energy, natural gas, coal, oil, limestone and other mineral resources. Besides, this region has a potential water resource in the form of river Brahmaputra and its tributaries. This region is also rich in plantation crops, medicinal plants, horticulture products and vegetable spices. This region also provides opportunities for tourism having rare flora and fauna, scenic beauty, unique performing arts and handicrafts (Bhutia, 2020). The NER has been bestowed with a bounty of nature, but it has historically trailed behind other parts of India in industrial development and economic growth. Manipur, Meghalaya, Mizoram and Nagaland demanded recognition and cultural security of the societies.

The infrastructure-centred policy for the development of the Northeast region regards that with the establishment of physical connectivity the market economy will self-deliver economic growth in the region.

The policy has thus presented a 'development model' for the region that is development through establishing physical infrastructure through the forces of market mechanism. Since the time, road construction and other connectivity projects have been taken up in Northeast. Indian government has attempted to make economic environment conducive for industrial investment and growth of trade. The infrastructural development projects have become part of the development agenda along with foreign policy. The policy has shaped the contours of the construction centric development model in Northeast India. The Indian Northeast region has often been understood to be a natural adjunct to Indian neighbourhood policy in the East. The region suffered from a developmental deficit due to remoteness from the industrially advanced parts of India and due to communication and infrastructural lapses in the region. Despite this, after the Indian Independence the region was located within geopolitical security equations in foreign policy priorities. Periodical review of military preparedness against China rather than trade underscored the development of transport and communication in the Northeast.

Trade has expanded because of development of infrastructure and connectivity. There has also been an increase in infrastructural investment in the region and in its international surroundings under the foreign policy objectives.

Railway connectivity has also progressed well in capitals of Northeast region. NER are being connected by rail with the rest of India. Agartala and Silchar are now having broad gauge railway lines and are now connected with other parts of India. Road transport is the dominant mode of transportation. Under Bharatmala Pariyojna about 5300 km long road would be developed for border road and international corridors (The Economic Times, 2019). National Highways and Infrastructure Development Corporation (NHIDCL) has been given the task to complete the construction and maintenance of National Highways in NER. On international projects, road connecting Samdrup Jongkhar (Bhutan) and Guwahati will be upgraded. The Trilateral Highway (TH) between India, Myanmar and Thailand is coming up.

Connectivity through waterways has also witnessed some major changes. Cargo transportation through National Waterway (NW) has been increasing. The various initiatives around water transport provide for a much more flexible system for transport and logistics that can benefit the NER. Heritage tourism along the waterways between the NER and Bangladesh can attract millions of tourists from the region and abroad. Cruise tourism is another opportunity. It is in NER where India's AEP and Japan's 'Open and free Indo-Pacific strategy' converge and both countries are keen to extend their cooperation to the broader Indo-Pacific region. India and Japan are collaborating for projects in Sri Lanka (Kesavan, 2020).

Promoting the use of waterways can lead to greater economic activities along the riverbanks, which will have a positive impact on the local economy and livelihoods. There are three well known pillars ; culture, commerce and connectivity which could provide multiple opportunities to empower the people of NER, create developmental opportunities and create favourable investment climate for Southeast Asian countries. Development of connectivity and physical infrastructure will help increasing the trade, its biodiversity will attract the tourists, rich natural resources will help increase the exports, and better infrastructure will attract the investors from Southeast Asian countries. The relationship between the two regions can be strengthened through people-to-people exchange and through culture, sports, academic and medical research. As a result, the Human Development Index has improved in this region.

We find from the above table that the Human Development Index has been rising in NER showing that the North East States are developing. With goals for reforms and liberalisation of the economy, sustained economic growth and economic integration with the East and Southeast Asia regions, the development of NER has been a cornerstone of the LEP/ACP (Haokip 2011). However, there are still various challenges in the way of development of NER. There is still a problem of insurgency in this region and this does not attract the investors because they are not certain about the safety and security of their investment. This model of development does not provide equal economic opportunities to all people. The poor are vulnerable to effects of exposure of economy to the volatile nature of capital market. This gives more economic opportunities to the rich thereby leading to higher inequality of income, which cause unrest. In this model of development, there is no agenda for 'pro-poor growth'. In spite of the fact that there has been massive construction in NER, the Human Development Index has not been high. Focus on infrastructure building has neglected the social development agenda. In India, the urban middle class has benefitted from the setting up of real estate hubs close to expressways offering amenities, tourism destinations and shopping complexes. For rural population construction of roads have certainly improved access to places of livelihood. However, the local enterprise has not developed and small-scale industries have not flourished. Women in the region are facing many challenges.

Table 1. Human Development Index in North-eastern States

State	1990	1995	2000	2005	2010	2015	2019
Assam	.411	.447	.488	.531	.567	.598	.613
Arunachal Pradesh	.437	.471	.502	.535	.641	.661	.661
Manipur	.495	.526	.559	.598	.681	.694	.697
Meghalaya	.456	.477	.477	.533	.620	.648	.656
Mizoram	.525	.569	.569	.630	.686	.698	.704
Nagaland	.531	.522	.522	.557	.661	.679	.679
Sikkim	.541	.548	.548	.590	.633	.691	.717
Tripura	.447	.531	.531	.561	.608	.643	.658

Source: Compiled by the authors from different Indian National Human Development Reports

The Civil Society Organisations (CSO) protest huge infrastructural investments that it is a new method of facilitating capital-intensive investors to capture economic resources in the region in a renewed manner and take control of systems of production. Protest organisations in Manipur and Meghalaya have opposed projects for extension of railway lines that connectivity might lead to migration of non-indigenous traders and investors and reduce availability of economic opportunities for indigenous people. The tribal inhabitants of the region do not immediately benefit from the new economic opportunities opening up but fear losing the traditionally held rights over lands and resources as these resources are made to fit into private ownership and claimed or taken for public infrastructure construction (Karlsson, 2011). Although the development of infrastructure has increased industrial investment in the region, but it has failed to develop the manufacturing sector. In this way, it had led to extraction of natural resources from the region and thus depletion of rich natural resources of NER. However, the fact remains that NER has many opportunities to take advantage of the cross-market accessibility to Southeast Asia.

NER may consider setting up Special Economic Zones for timber, food processing etc. Industries with potential to serve neighbouring markets and ASEAN need to be identified and promoted in NER (DE, 2019). Besides, harmonisation of custom procedures and other trade facility measures would help facilitate NER trade. In this way, the 'cross border market' would uplift the people of this region from poverty, economic backwardness and would bring prosperity, inculcate entrepreneurial freedom and skills. NCR can exploit their geographical advantage, which will be significant for the whole country in general, and region in particular. To explore land locked NER there is need to develop the inherent of the region by accessing the Southeast Asia countries along with the international route via India Myanmar Thailand Trilateral Highway and its extension to Lao PDR and Cambodia or the Mekong India Economic Corridor (MIEC). These are the inevitable conditions to strengthen the ties with NER which is the central point of the Southeast Asian region. Owing to its geographical proximity with Southeast Asia and its cultural diversity, NER will play an important role in the success of AEP. Besides, it was a great fortune for the people of NER in general and people of Assam in particular, that the great celestial event Pushkar occurred in Brahmaputra in 2019. This encouraged the flow of pilgrims and boosted the tourism activities of not only Guwahati but the whole of NER.

Critical Evaluation

However, it is believed that the introduction and implementation of LEP and AEP have increased the regional and international trade. As the objectives highlighted, these policies were supposed to achieve different goals. To do so it becomes important to critically analyse different aspects.

Issue of China. Under LEP, there has been steadily increasing cooperation on all the fronts with the ASEAN. On the other hand, India has started to figure in the strategic thinking of Southeast Asia (Strachan et al., 2009). Even ASEAN want closer ties with India to balance the influence of China. Singapore played an important role in creating awareness that India has strategic importance in this region because the biggest challenge of the bloc is to develop a unified approach to China, particularly in response to Beijing's claims in the South China Sea, which overlap with claims of several ASEAN members. China knows that India is the only country that could possibly challenge its ascendancy, political hegemony. Australia is also seeking a balance between India, China, as China is Australia's key trading partner, and India is Australia's future growth market for export of resources, tourism, and education. Further, there are tensions between the US and China over trade and border disputes between India and China where China claims to occupy the eastern part of Kashmir and Arunachal Pradesh since the 1962 Sino-India war. China is gaining strategic maritime and military control of the Indian Ocean by investing and building strategic infrastructure projects as the One-Belt-Road initiative, airports and seaports for South Asian countries bordering India. Moreover, China with One-Belt-initiative, military ambitions, maritime power, and disputes over the South China Sea with South Korea, Vietnam and Malacca is looked upon as a global threat with fear and anxiety in Australia, the USA, India, and the ASEAN economies (Medhekar, 2021). On the other hand, China is also aware of the fact that India shares cultural and spiritual ties with Southeast Asia, and this will naturally attract the two regions to come closer. It marked a strategic shift in India's perspective of the world.

Expansion of Defence Ties: India has steadily expanded its defence ties with the East and Southeast Asian countries. India engage with these countries through regional confidence building and cooperation mechanisms like ASEAN Regional Forum (ARF), the Regional Cooperation on Combating Piracy and Armed Robbery against ships in Asia and the Milan exercises that India holds every alternate year. India is bilaterally engaged with the ASEAN countries as well as Japan and South Korea for cooperation in a joint or coordinated way for naval patrolling, fighting piracy and other maritime security threats and military, air, and naval exercises. Maritime security is very necessary in the light of the terrorist attack in Mumbai on 26 November 2008 (Strachan, Kang & Sinha, 2009). Enhanced maritime cooperation with Indonesia, Malaysia, Singapore, and Vietnam has become a focal point. India is also trying to rope in the Philippines to be one of its defence partners, while Manila is considering the acquisition of defence equipment and warships from India.

Achievement of Objectives: The Indian Ministry of External Affairs describes that the objectives of LEP/AEP display three elements of the policy. Firstly, strengthening and exploring different aspects of bilateral relations with the countries of the region. Secondly, enhancing multilateral, sub regional and regional efforts with ASEAN-this is important to having ties with not only ASEAN but also with other dialogue partners and participants through other ASEAN-driven mechanisms and meetings (Das, Das & Paul, 2018). Thirdly, building infrastructure and connectivity with the North-eastern states of India and linking them with the ASEAN region is a key aspect of the Act East Policy. In 2018, the Foreign Minister Sushma Swaraj held a meeting with the Chief Ministers of Northeast States and emphasised on the importance of NER in AEP.

Development of Northeast States: Development of transport, connectivity and other trade related infrastructure or lack of it is said to have a power to influence in making of Northeast India a metaphorical bridge connecting the economic opportunities in India and Southeast Asia. With building of physical infrastructure and institutional infrastructure for communication and linkages, the isolation of these states has been broken. International borders surround the North-eastern Region; thus, it is a launch pad of India to connect with the ASEAN.

Until recently, Northeast India was the only region in India to have states that were completely untouched by railway lines. However, since the time developmental policy for the region has focused on building connectivity, projects for construction of nine new railway lines to connect the states of Meghalaya, Manipur, Tripura, and Arunachal Pradesh that were previously without rail connectivity and two projects for conversion of railway gauge have improved rail connectivity within the region. Taking the LEP/AEP line, state governments expect that improved roads and connectivity infrastructures in the region will unlock the northeastern states' potential as an emerging trade hub of the South East Asia region (Barua, 2020).

Along with creation and development of land trade route from Northeast to the East and Southeast Asian countries, clusters of industries should be built based on the local resources of the region. This has to be accompanied by a parallel boost to agricultural productivity through different steps. Both the state governments and the central government should adopt a proactive role. Infrastructure building in terms of modes of transportation and setting up of industries should be accompanied by social development as well so that the concerned policies are able to witness the desired results of investment. The vast rural masses have to be brought into the process of industrialisation for political viability of trade as a strategy for industrialising the region. For this, utmost importance should be given to raising agricultural productivity in the region with proper flood control measures and other steps. In the absence of a parallel agricultural revolution in the region, trade alone will not be sufficient to bring the region onto a sustained development path.

NER's geographical position, vast land border, rich natural resources and agro-climatic conditions, access to growing ASEAN market and presence of mineral and agro-horticulture resources largely explain as to why NER plays an important role in the AEP. Assam's government has opened a new department called 'Act East Department' and set up a new research centre on Southeast Asia at the Guwahati University. Several industrial parks and clusters, townships, logistics centres have come up in Assam and the rest of Northeast region. Assam has become a favourite investment destination. Some of the companies that have invested in recently are Tata, ITC, Patanjali, Dabur, Spice-Jet, Sun Pharma etc. Many premier hospitals have opened their branches in Guwahati like Apollo, Sankar Netralaya, Fortis and Narayana Health. International hotel chains like TAJ Vivanta, Radisson Blu and Novotel have opened their branches.

Diplomatic Missions: Some countries like Bangladesh and Bhutan have opened their consulates in Guwahati. Singapore has started a skill development centre in Guwahati. Japan-India Act East Forum has been set up to assist the NER to attract Japanese technology and investment, sharing of experiences through skill development, and improvement of connectivity. Japanese packaging technology and expertise may give a big boost to agriculture and horticulture exports from NER and strengthen the supply chain competitiveness. Engaging Japanese private sector companies such as Mitsubishi, NEC Technologies, Toshiba, Sumitomo, Sony and Honda in the Northeast will pave the way towards connecting with larger markets (De, 2019). However, better connectivity with neighbouring countries will provide access to the markets but in NER there is a dearth of skilled labour and enterprise (Bezabaruah & Sarma, 2009). There is still a problem of insurgency specifically in Manipur and Nagaland. Besides, there is a problem of corruption and bureaucratic delays (Nath &Kumar, 2017). In this connection, it is recommended that Bangladesh should be treated as an integral part of AEP because NER is geographically a locked land and must access the rest of India largely via the ''Chicken's Neck'' near Siliguri and it increases the travel time. For example, traders must travel 1,600 km from Agartala in Tripura to Kolkata in West Bengal, via Siliguri. If they travel to the same destination via Bangladesh, they will travel only 600 km and if they take their goods to nearby port of Chittagong in Bangladesh, the distance is only 200 km. This will reduce the cost of transportation resulting in fall of prices of goods and services leading to a strong impact on consumer welfare and fall in poverty (Kathuria, 2017)

Economic Health: After adopting LEP/AEP, the volume of trade with ASEAN, Indo-Pacific and East India has increased. Foreign direct investment has also gone up indicating that there are attractive investment opportunities in India. This investment has helped us fulfil our dream of 'Make in India' and 'Digital India'. The image of India at the international level has improved and it is the third big power after US and China. India is also implementing Quick Impact Projects (QIPs) in Cambodia, Laos, Myanmar, and Vietnam to provide development assistance to grass root level communities in the field of education, water resources and health. Quick Impact Projects are small-scale, low-cost projects that are planned and implemented within a short timeframe (Drishti, 2021). Assistance in the form of medicines and medical supplies was given to ASEAN countries. All these steps show that India has a potential for investment and trade.

Policy Implications

Connectivity in the region particularly in the border areas should be improved. A Northeast branch of NITI (National Institution for Transforming India) Aayog should be set up so that the gap between the Centre and States is bridged. There is a great potential of the ASEAN market for both finished and intermediary goods and services, so it is important that SMEs (Small and Medium Enterprises) should be encouraged in NER and SME FORUM Special Fund should be created.

Development projects earmarked under AEP should be put on a fast track by avoiding cumbersome documentation and bureaucratic procedures. There should be better co-ordination between the office of PMO, Ministry of Finance and Ministry of External Affairs essential in implementing the Act East Projects. EXIM Bank of India should open branches in all Southeast and East Asian countries and the Pacific (De, 2019).

Institutions, which are promised through international declaration or speeches, must be established, like setting up of ASEAN-India Centre (AIC) and ASEAN Studies Centre (ASC). The opening up of Foreign Consulate in NER will facilitate tourism between ASEAN and NER.

The outreach of AEP should be expanded by including Bangladesh and Sri Lanka in AEP because a prosperous Bangladesh offers opportunities for India's Eastern and Northeast States of India. They can also take the advantage of Bangladesh Corridor. There should be focus on BIMSTEC, which is a regional multilateral organisation. It has seven countries as its members, which lie in the littoral and adjacent areas of Bay of Bengal. BIMSTEC not only connects South and Southeast Asia but also the ecologies of the Himalayas and the Bay of Bengal. It mainly aims to create an enabling environment for rapid economic development, accelerate social progress and promote collaboration on matters of common interest in the region.

Thus, LEP/AEP has been one of the signature foreign policy of the Indian government and is a pro-active foreign policy. The movement from LEP to AEP was necessitated by the changing contours of security architecture in the larger context of the Indo-Pacific region. Time is ripe for India to establish a strong partnership with Southeast, East Asia and other Indo-Pacific countries.

CONCLUSION

Finally, it can be concluded that in moving from LEP to AEP, various achievements have been made and many objectives have been fulfilled but much still remains to be attained. Some of the measures, which were on the agenda but could not be implemented and were disrupted due to COVID 19 epidemic. The most affected part is tourism followed by trade. However, India is helping the world with vaccines and medical supplies. During this epidemic too, the security issue cannot be ignored with increasing Chinese presence in South East Asia. Since during this critical hour, the maritime security has emerged as a potential challenge, India has to take a leading role. This time the members should work together to come out of the economic crisis resulting from the minimisation of international trade. India must continue to focus on further strengthening collaborations with ASEAN partners especially for economic revival and sustainability in the coming future.

REFERENCES

Balasubramanian, J. (2015, Nov. 21). *PM Modi Proposes $1 billion line of credit for connectivity with Asean*. Retrieved from https://www.livemint.com/Politics/riD4W4GN503dmSAGwBtZQN/PM-Modi-proposes-1-billion-line-of-credit-for-connectivity.html

Barua, A. & Das, S.K. (2008). Perspectives on Growth and Development in the Northeast: The Look East Policy and Beyond. *Margin-The Journal of Applied Economic Research, 2*(4), 327-350. doi:10.1177/097380100800200401

Barua, T. (2020). The Lok East Policy/ Act East Policy-driven Development Model in Northeast India. *Jadavpur Journal of International Relations, 24*(1), 101-120. Retrieved from https://journals.sagepub.com/doi/pdf/10.1177/0973598420908844

Bezbaruah, M. P., & Sarma, A. (2009, March). Industry in the Development Perspective of North East India. *Dialogue, 10*(3).

Bharadwaj, S. (2019, March 19). In Meghalaya's patriarchy-driven matrilineal society, women turn entrepreneurs for livelihood. *First Post*. Retrieved from https://www.firstpost.com/india/in-meghalayas-patriarchy-driven-matrilineal-society-women-turn-entrepreneurs-for-livelihood-6286081.html

Bhatia, R. (2019). *India's Act Policy: Gains and Prospects*. Retrieved from https://www.gatewayhouse.in

Bhure, R., & Malegaonkar, V. (2019). India's Act East Policy-A Need for Enhancing Connectivity. In P. M. Kamath (Ed.), *Act East Policy of NDA II and Primary Goals: Economic Development, Democracy and National Security* (p. 21). Kalpaz Publications.

Bhutia, S. (2020). Sustainable Tourism for Regional Development in North-East States of India: Trends, Problems and Prospects. *Global Journal of Human-Social Science: B Geography, Geo-Sciences, Environmental Science & Disaster Management, 20*(2). Retrieved from https://globaljournals.org/GJHSS_Volume20/3-Sustainable-Tourism-for-Regional.pdf

Bragta, S. K. (2021, July). Evolving India's Look East to Act East Policy: An Analytical View. *European Online Journal of Natural and Social Sciences, 10*(3), 325-333.

Chaturvedi, A., & Sharma, H. P. (2020, May 20). India's Foreign Policy: A Transformation From 'Look-East' to 'Act-East'. *Journal of Critical Reviews, 7*(11), 882–885.

Choudhury, S. (2017 January). *Northeast India and the Act East Policy: Opportunity & Challenges*. Retrieved https://researchgate.net/publication/320921997

Das, G., Das, S. C., & Paul, U. (2018). Look East Policy: Economic Engagement with ASEAN and East Asian Countries. In G. Das & C. J. Thomas (Eds.), Look East to Act East Policy: Implications for India's northeast. Academic Press.

De, P. (2019, June 1). Act east to act Indo-Pacific: Agenda for the new government. *The Economic Times*. Retrieved from https://economictimes.indiatimes.com/news/defence/act-east-to-act-indo-pacific-agenda-for-the-new-government/articleshow/69591279.cms

De, P. (2019, Oct 16). Act East – North East: Unlocking the Potentials. *The Economic Times*. Retrieved from https://economictimes.indiatimes.com/blogs/et-commentary/act-east-north-east-unlocking-the-potentials/

DFAT. (2019). *Trade and Investment at a Glance*. Australian Government, Department of Foreign Affairs and Trade. Retrieved from https://www.dfat.gov.au/about-us/publications/trade-investment/trade-at-a-glance/trade-investment-at-a-glance-2019/Pages/default#exports

Drishti. (2021). *India's Act East Policy*. Retrieved from https://www.drishtiias.com/daily-updates/daily-news-analysis/india-s-act-east-policy-1

Haokip, T. (2011, September). India's Look East Policy: Its Evolution and Approach. *South Asia Survey, 18*(2), 239-257. Retrieved from https://sas.sagepub.com/content/18/2/239

Jaipuria, T. (2016, Mar. 29). 100% allowed in B2B e-marketplace via automatic route. *Hindustan Times*. Retrieved from https://www.hindustantimes.com/business/100-fdi-allowed-in-b2b-e-marketplace-via-automatic-route-says-govt/story-IXp7ySlpYYvq1RwNhKdZhM.html

Jaishankar, S. (2019 Sep. 25). India: 1000 PhD fellowships to ASEAN students. *The Pie News*. Retrieved from https://thepienews.com/news/india-1000-phd-fellowships-to-asean-students/

Kakoti, D. (2020, Jan.). Look/Act East Policy and Trade Opportunities for North East India: A Review. MSSV Journal of Humanities & Social Sciences, 5(1), 39-48.

Kapur, Y. (2021, Feb. 23). *India-ASEAN Trade and Investment Prospects. India Briefing*. Dezan Shira & Associates. Retrieved from https://www.india-briefing.com/news/india-asean-trade-and-investment-prospects-21779.html/

Kathuria, S. (2017). *Bangladesh Corridor Vital to India's Act East Policy*. The World Bank. Retrieved from https://www.worldbank.org

Kesavan, K. V. (2020, February). *India's 'Act East' Policy and Regional Cooperation*. ORF Special Report # 101. Retrieved from https://www.orfonline.org/wp-content/uploads/2020/02/ORF_SpecialReport_101_India-SouthKorea.pdf#page=7

Khan, S. A. (2019, May). *India-Japan Economic Partnership: Potentials, Promises and Prospects*. Retrieved from https://www.mof.go.jp/pri/international_exchange/visiting_scholar_program/Shamshad2.pdf

Laskar, R. (2013, December). Promoting National Interest through Diplomacy. *Extraordinary and Plenipotentiary Diplomatists.*, *1*(9), 59–60.

Mallapur, C. (2021). *Explained: The flourishing trade ties and friendship between India and Bangladesh*. Retrieved from https://flipboard.com/@moneycontrol/moneycontrol-news-j7nitv49z/explained-the-flourishing-trade-ties-and-friendship-between-india-and-banglades/a-AogOGab9SOe4V1QVCg5zlQ%3Aa%3A3108465186-0f4d7187f3%2Fmoneycontrol.com

Mea.Gov.In. (2018, Aug). *India-ASEAN Relations*. Retrieved from https://mea.gov.in/aseanindia/20-years.htm

Medhekar, A. (2021). Australia-India: Bilateral Trade Opportunities and Challenges. In *Emerging Business and Trade Opportunities between Oceania and Asia* (pp. 57–86). IGI Global Publishing. doi:10.4018/978-1-7998-4126-5

Mukherjee, R. (2020). *East by Southeast: Three challenges for India's 'Act East' policy*. Retrieved from https://www.business-standard.com

Nath, H. K., & Kumar, S. (2017). *India's Act East Policy and the Northeast: A Critical Perspective*. Retrieved from https://researchgate.net

Nehru, J. (2008). *Discovery of India*. Oxford University Press.

Rahul, M. (2020). *Strengthening the Indo-Pacific Order: An Assessment of India's Act East Policy*. Retrieved from https:// issue.com

Rajiv, B. (2019). *India's Act Policy: Gains and Prospects*. Retrieved from https://www.gatewayhouse.in

Rathnayake, Z. (2021, May 30). *Khasis: India's indigenous matrilineal Society*. BBC Travel. Retrieved from https://www.bbc.com/travel/article/20210328-why-some-indians-want-more-mens-rights

Saint-Mezard, I. (2016). India's Act East policy: Strategic Implications for the Indian Ocean. *Journal of the Indian Ocean Region*, *12*(2), 178. doi:10.1080/19480881.2016.1226753

Sajjanhar, A. (2016). *India's Act East Policy: So far and Beyond*. Gateway House-Indian Council on Global Relations. Retrieved from https://www.gatewayhouse.in/indias-act-east-policy-far-beyond/

Sanjaya, B. (2021). *What's going wrong with India's Act East Policy*. Retrieved from https://indianexpress.com

Sarma, A., & Mehta, P. K. (2003). Indo-Asean Trade Prospects: A Study of Trade Complementarity. In F. Grare & A. Mattoo (Eds.), *Beyond the Rhetoric: The Economics of India's Look East Policy*. Manohar Publications.

Sharma, H., & Sharma, R. (2021, Jan 19). Act-East Policy and Future of Northeast India. *The Sentinel*. Retrieved from https://www.sentinelassam.com/editorial/act-east-policy-and-future-of-northeast-india-521374

Strachan, A. L., Kang, H. K., & Sinha, T. (2009, Oct.). *India's Look East Policy: A Critical Assessment. Interview with Amb. Rajiv Sikri*. IPCS Special Report. Retrieved from https://www.files.ethz.ch/isn/108694/SR85-SEARPInterview-Sikri.pdf

Taz, B. (2020). *The Look East Policy/Act East Policy-driven Development Model in Northeast India*. Retrieved from https://journal.sagepub.com

The Economic Times. (2019, June 24). *26,200 km length of economic corridors to be developed under "Bharatmala Pariyojana"*. Retrieved from https://auto.economictimes.indiatimes.com/news/industry/26200-km-length-of-economic-corridors-to-be-developed-under-bharatmala-pariyojana/69928449

Zulfkar, A. (2019, September). India's Act East Policy and North East India. A Critical Review. *International Journal of Research in Social Sciences*, *9*(9). Retrieved from file:///C:/Users/h.kaur/Downloads/IndiasActEastPolicyandNorthEastIndia.pdf

ADDITIONAL READING

Das, G., & Thomas, J. (Eds.). (2016). *Look East to Act East Policy: Implications for India's Northeast*. Routledge. doi:10.4324/9781315657660

Hussain, M. (2017). Cultural Foundations of India's Look East Policy: A Critique. *Journal of Southeast Asian Studies*, *5*(3), 147–155.

Ram, A. N. (Ed.). (2012). *Two Decades of India's Look East Policy: Partnership for Peace, Progress and Prosperity*. Manohar Publishers & Distributors.

Ranjan, V. (2016). Australia and India in Asia: When 'Look West' Meets Act East. *Strategic Analysis*, *40*(5), 425–439. doi:10.1080/09700161.2016.1209906

Sajjanhar, A. (2016, May). Taking Stock of India's 'Act East Policy'. *Observer Research Foundation*, (142), 1–6.

Sikri, R. (2009). India's "Look East" Policy. *Asia-Pacific Review*, *16*(1), 131–145. doi:10.1080/13439000902957624

KEY TERMS AND DEFINITIONS

AEP: Act East Policy.
AIFTA: India Free Trade Agreement.
ARF: ASEAN Regional Forum.
ASC: ASEAN Studies Centre.
BIMSTEC: Bengal Initiative for Multi Sectoral Technical and Economic Cooperation.
HDI: Human Development Index.
LEP: Look East Policy.
MGC: Mekong Ganga Cooperation.
MIEC: Mekong India Economic Corridor.
QIPs: Quick Impact Projects.

Chapter 12
The Compromised Healthcare Sector of India and Other Southeast Asian Countries:
Open Avenues for Foreign Collaboration

Manisha Goswami
GLA University, Mathura, India

ABSTRACT

This chapter aims to focus on the umpteen challenges in the healthcare sector of India which temper the possibility of partnerships with India and the 10 Southeast Asian countries. India's expenditure on the healthcare sector is only 1% of GDP, less than neighboring ASEAN countries. The Indian Government has privatised the healthcare sector. In the second wave of COVID-19, public and private hospitals are operating at full capacity with shortages of life-saving medicines, oxygen, ventilators, and vaccines. Lower middle-income groups and the poor are suffering the most. Nations of the world, medical scientific community, and pharmaceutical companies put their resources together to discover a vaccine for coronavirus within a year. To have an effective and sustainable model of doing business in healthcare, it is important to have partnerships and integrating best practices and innovations for improving and providing equitable and affordable access to healthcare.

INTRODUCTION

Southeast Asian region and India is a profoundly distinct country of varied culture, economic, and social region. From economic powerhouses like Singapore to weaker economies like Cambodia, Laos, and Myanmar, the area is home to many countries. The Association of Southeast Asian Nations (ASEAN) comprises eleven countries: Brunei, Cambodia, Indonesia, Laos, Malaysia, Myanmar, Philippines, Singapore, Thailand, Timor Leste, and Vietnam (United Nation, 2021). The region's overall population is around 625 million (8.58 percent of the global population), with "Indonesia" being the most populous country (representing 40% of Southeast Asia's total population) and "Brunei" being the least populous

DOI: 10.4018/978-1-7998-5774-7.ch012

(United Nation, 2021; Hashim et al., 2012). This chapter focuses on the umpteen challenges in India's healthcare sector, which temper the possibility of association with Southeast Asian Countries.

India and Southeast Asian countries collectively represent 26.28% of the world population, over 1.9 billion people. It accounts for only 4.7% GDP of the world in 2019 after the hit of COVID'19, and it goes down to -3.4% in December 2021. Before the epidemic, Southeast Asia had been experiencing annual growth of around 5% for decades, making it one of the nation's finest regions. It became an enticing economic driver due to a relatively young population fuelling demand and many manufacturing workers. Those advantages are still in play, but first, eliminate COVID-19; wherein India represents 17.7% of the world population. India spends only 1% of its GDP on healthcare (World Health Organization, 2021), much less than the neighbouring nations like Sri Lanka, Bhutan, and Nepal, which are all impoverished in terms of per capita income (Patnaik, 2020).

India has one of the lowest expenditures on healthcare support systems compared to any country. The Indian Government trying to run the country's healthcare sector based on the developed nations' medical support systems like the US has created havoc in the lives of the middle and lower class people in India. India's 32 million residents account for roughly 60% of the global decline in the middle-income tier (those with daily incomes of $10.01-$20) (Pew Research Centre, 2020). Around the same time, the low-income category, which includes those with a daily income of $2 or less, grew by 75 million people, accounting for 60% of the global growth in poverty. Thus, could not afford even the basic healthcare support. Further, healthcare privatization and universal insurance scheme have even made it difficult and costly for US citizens to afford them despite the highest spending of 17.06% on healthcare out of the entire GDP as compared to Cuba (11.74%), Germany (11.25%), France (11.31%) and the UK (9.63%).

Further, growing globalization adds to the misery where individuals' access to health insurance is no longer publicly funded. The private sectors in Singapore, Thailand, and Malaysia have reaped their competitive advantages by clubbing health benefits and treatment for rich foreigners with leisure packages to shoot the demand for those health facilities (Pocock & Phua, 2011). The same is the case in India; a good number of people are visiting for medical treatment from bubble economies such as the United States, the United Kingdom, and Australia. However, the majority of medical tourists who visit India are from Asia and Africa. According to reports, approximately 697,453 international tourists visited India for medical care (Ernst & Young, 2019). India's private medical infrastructure and healthcare support system have received much attention: Kerala, Andhra Pradesh, Maharashtra, and New Delhi. However, medical expenses are quite high for the middle and lower class of people who are in the majority in India, but significantly cheaper for foreigners as they are earning in dollars and spending in rupees (Hashim et al., 2012; Medhekar, 2019; Medhekar et al., 2019).

Additionally, the poor economies, such as the "Philippines" (Reisman, 1996), attributed to a strategy of exporting health professionals to the world and wealthier countries to raise revenue (Chanda. 2002). Even though the monetary benefits of this approach seem to be significant, capital concerns about the negative impact of foreign trade in healthcare and worker mobility on national health systems have surfaced, particularly in terms of worsening gaps among rural and urban societies. Even in Indonesia, healthcare is based on Insurance which creates disparities in providing medical support to people. Hence, Indonesians move to Malaysia for medical support (Meikeng, 2014).

Such disparities further aggravated via global pandemic situation; COVID'19 was first reported on December 19 in the Wuhan of China (World Health Organization, 2021); from there, it crossed all the boundaries and reached every different country from a developed nation to the underdeveloped nations across the globe except 14 countries like North Korea, Turkmenistan, Tuvalu, Tonga, Nauru, Micronesia to name the few (World Health Organization, 2021).

On January 27, 2020, the first instance of the COVID'19 virus was discovered in India. (Andrews et al., 2020). Double mutant COVID-19 entered India in 2021. The WHO named these variants of concern as alpha (B.1.1.7), beta (B.1.351), gamma (P.1), Epsilons (B.1.427 and B.1.429), and delta (B.1.617.2), which was first detected in the UK, South Africa, Brazil, USA and India (Roberts, 2021). India sees a rise in cases of mucormycotic, a rare but dangerous fungal infection. It is called the "black fungus," and it can be deadly; an example of medical negligence, as doctors in India infuse steroids to stop inflammation in COVID patients, contrary to this, increasing blood sugar level another maiming disease called a black fungus. It is also adding to India's growing COVID-19 woes.

Nations of the world and the medical, scientific community, and pharmaceutical companies put their resources together to discover a vaccine for coronavirus within a year. The Serum Institute of India (SII), located in Maharashtra's Pune, produces the CoviShield vaccine, while Bharat Biotech's COVAXIN, The Indian Council of Medical Research (ICMR) - National Institute of Virology collaborated on the development of the COVID-19 vaccine (NIV). Further, India has supplied the vaccine to various Southeast Asian and other countries to combat the ravage of the deadly virus. Despite being the producer of the corona vaccine, India could not manage to fight the corruption rooted at the ground level, which is the reason for the poverty, starvation suffering of Indian citizens. The Indian Government, currently led by Prime Minister Narendra Modi. is substantially taking aggravating measures to improve the nation's sufferings (Varghese, 2018).

Corruption in medical education is also having serious and long-term impact (Nadpara, 2015). Medicine study of the private institution is quite costly in India and inefficient infrastructure of government institution leading medical aspirant to study from private institution than from government institution, pressurizing families to bear costly fees ranging from 20 lakhs to 1 crore (Jolly, 2004; Morrison, 2005) which undesirably compel doctors to charge more money from their patient, fixing commission from chemist and pathologist, that further intensify the situation among pathologist and chemist as they have to pay commission to doctor so they get to indulge into duplicity and other unfair practices (Almuzaini et al., 2013). According to CPI (2020), North Korea, Afghanistan, Cambodia, Bangladesh, Myanmar, Nepal, Laos, Pakistan, Vietnam, Thailand, the Philippines, Sri Lanka, and the Maldives, according to Transparency International, are among the world's most corrupt countries. However, Singapore was ranked seventh in Transparency International's annual list of the least corrupt nations. On the other side, major Asian nations are rated in the lower half of the Corruption Perceptions Index. As a result, establishing effective collaboration in the healthcare industry might be another difficulty. Furthermore, in countries like Cambodia, Bangladesh, Myanmar, Nepal, Laos, Pakistan, Vietnam, Thailand, Philippines, Sri Lanka, Maldives, and even India, the legal framework for combating corruption in the healthcare sector is extremely poor. Corruption in the health sector has serious repercussions for the five aspects of health system performance: availability, reliability, fairness, productivity, and responsiveness of the healthcare system.

Amid coronavirus, where at one side people are struggling for getting oxygen, hospital care unit, ventilators, basic drugs like Remdesivir and diseases diagnosis tools like Chest X-Ray and CT Scan and even crematoriums are not available as the number of deaths are increasing because of depressing healthcare infrastructure and unattended COVID '19 patients on other side people have to find the business of black marketing of essential in such an unprecedented situation. Additionally, the vaccine squandering in India can be largely attributed to low turnout beneficiaries turning up to get vaccinated. Indonesia is the second country in Asia after India to reach this grim milestone.

Therefore, India and Southeast Asian Nations need to understand how to keep the health sector open for effective bilateral and multilateral collaboration. This chapter aims to identify different challenges of collaboration in the healthcare sector and possible measures of overcoming those challenges, which will be mutually beneficial for the safety of 2 billion populations living in Southeast Asia and India. The chapter structure is as follows: The first section provides an overview of India and Southeast Asian nation's current healthcare sector. The second section provides the background literature review on the challenges of the healthcare sector. The third section provides the avenues for possible bilateral and multilateral collaboration in contrast to existing collaboration; collaboration opportunities are also discussed. The last section provides the discussion, future research direction, and conclusion to advance effective collaboration in healthcare among India and Southeast Asian Nations.

LITERATURE REVIEW

Governments throughout the world have long been concerned about their citizens' health. It is not just because of its importance in general human capital creation but also due to the difficulty in leveraging contribution. (Naveed, 2018). The United Nations (UN) recognized health as a right in 1948 (United Nations, 2008). Hence, officials at all branches of administration have a moral duty to strive for health improvement. Thus, many advanced and emerging nations have been tasked with figuring out how to spend in healthcare to promote health (Tangcharoensathien et al., 2015; Zaman & Hossain, 2017). Southeast Asian nations and India have heterogeneous medical support services that are at the profuse level of development. Given the disparities in demographic and epidemiological transition rates and the diversity in culture of the countries among Southeast Asians, it is unsurprising. Regardless of significant progress, Southeast Asia's health systems continue to struggle compared to Western countries (Salmasi et al., 2015).

Insubstantial healthcare has been a worldwide problem that many governments grapple with (Vecchio et al., 2018). The "ASEAN Economic Community" (AEC), which was established in 2015, formed a common market with a population above 625 million people in the "AEC" nations. Thus, facilitating a free flow of goods and services among the member nations. The realm's expeditious economic expansion influences health expenses, as well as the service environment and effectiveness of healthcare provided (Piabuo & Tieguhong, 2017). However, overcrowding in hospitals has been identified as a serious problem in healthcare (Wibulpolprasert et al., 2014).

Overcrowding metrics such as the hospital beds, number of patients for OPD, number of admitted patients in a hospital, the time involved in admission procedure, and the waiting hour are studied to modify healthcare policy (Bond et al., 2007). A hike in demand on healthcare networks leads to a massive crisis of healthcare employees globally.

In India, the catastrophic current wave of coronavirus infections has resulted in a significant increase in mortality and has overburdened the health system. Hospital beds, oxygen, ambulances, medications, and healthcare personnel are all in short supply as the need for healthcare grows. According to analysts, India's private-sector-controlled medicare system is inadequate to cope with such a major catastrophe. India spends extremely little on health compared to other nations with similar levels of wealth and economic growth. Despite being the world's sixth-biggest economy, India spends just 1% of its GDP on health (World Health Organization (WHO), 2021). However, the current Government has promised to increase this to 2.5% of GDP by 2025 (The Economic Times, 2018). Brazil spent 9.5 percent of GDP on health, China and Mexico 5.4 percent, and the United Kingdom 10%. Table 1 indicates India and other Southeast Asian countries' accurate GDP and ranking from lowest to highest (IMF, 2021). Table 1 GDP ranking of India and Southeast Asian Countries.

Table 1. GDP ranking of India and Southeast Asian Countries

World Rank	SEA Country	GDP-PPP
34	Timor-Leste	3,382
47	Cambodia	4,695
67	India	6,461
71	Lao P.D.R.	8,111
75	Philippines	8,452
83	Vietnam	10,869
93	Bhutan	12,060
94	Indonesia	12,222
120	Thailand	18,236
140	Malaysia	27,402
187	Brunei Darussalam	62,371
193	Singapore	97,057

Source: *International Monetary Fund, World Economic Outlook; April 2021*

According to WHO research, 118 countries out of 186 had a serious shortage of 7.2 million competent medical practitioners in 2013 (Yeganeh, 2019). Southeast Asia's average health staff density is 4.3 per 1000 population, compared to 18.9 and 24.8 per 1000 in Europe and the United States of America (US) (WHO, 2021). Unfortunately, this remains true for all Southeast Asia's countries: including Vietnam, Myanmar, Laos, and Cambodia fall short of the WHO's "basic" healthcare requirement (2.28 competent healthcare workers per 1000 population), while "Indonesia" and Thailand narrowly meet it. However, the situation of India is even piteous; the country with a population of 1.3 billion is not having even one doctor per 1000 population as per the record of NSSO is 0.88 doctors per 1000 population and Nurse are 1.77 per 1000 population (NSSO, 2019).

Furthermore, Malaysia and Singapore are exceptions (World Health Organization, 2021). Malaysia has a 30-million-strong culturally diverse society dispersed throughout 13 states and three federal areas. (Index Mundi Malaysia Demographics Profile, 2014) It is a rapidly expanding country, and some Malaysians have embraced new lifestyles, practices, and dietary habits due to urbanization and a thriving economy. Malaysia has a well-developed healthcare system that includes universal health insurance (Peltzer & Pengpid, 2018). However, the Singaporean Government, which once failed in the outbreak of SARS in 2003, now guarantees the best healthcare; even those with low incomes will have access to competent, advance, reasonable, and proven-to-be-effective care. This baseline bundle will vary over time as medical research advances, and the country's economic growth improves its ability to pay.

The commitment to leave no one behind is symbolized by low-cost primary care, sponsored facilities, and the other supportive scheme (Reisman, 2006). After Singapore, Brunei is a developed country with the second-highest Human Development Index among Southeast Asian nations. "Brunei" is ranked fifth in the world in terms of gross domestic output per capita at purchasing power parity, according to the International Monetary Fund (IMF), owing to its oil and gas deposits. It can boast one of the best public healthcare systems in Asia and the world. They have sufficient numbers of doctors and healthcare infrastructure to manage typical situations. Natives have relatively cheap access to public medical services, while expats can acquire them reasonably. Brunei has several clinics and care institutions that employ expats. They have made significant progress in delivering superior medical support by using innovative technologies and free medical treatment. The country's efforts paid off as COVID-19 spread was effectively slowed, and the average life expectancy of the general population was increased.

Additionally, Thailand activated its emergency operations program, launching a society response backed by scientific evidence and guided by collective leadership that prevented a large outbreak. Thailand's health system rapidly responded and implemented strategies to inform and mobilize the society and prevent, detect, treat and trace cases. Village health volunteers, an integral part of the health system, were critical of the national COVID'19 response. Thailand is a country of 69 million people; there are more than one million village volunteers; Samut Sakhon is home to the largest community of Burmese migrant workers in Thailand; migrant health volunteers also become an essential part of stopping the community spread of the deadly virus. Effective collaboration among the public health system, doctors, nurses, village volunteers, and migrant volunteers to make this whole system run effectively (WHO, 2020). These migrant workers are mostly from Cambodia, Myanmar, Lao PDR, and Vietnam, all close neighbours.

However, in India, the Philippines, and Indonesia, the COVID-19 outbreak has intensified the long-term effects of a dysfunctional and inadequate public healthcare system. The country has become an epidemic calamity waiting to happen due to its highly crowded capital, vast social gaps, and inadequate infrastructure. Indian government health spending is among the lowest in the world, averaging US$38 per person per year over the last two decades. An adequate healthcare system is excessively costly and out of reach for many Indians and Filipinos, even in normal periods. Although health spending in the Philippines increased by 10.9 percent (Philippines Statistics Authorities, 2019).

INDIA AND SOUTHEAST ASIAN COUNTRIES HEALTHCARE SYSTEM

Challenges

Untapped Rural Healthcare Sector, Excessive Urbanization

In southeast Asia, nearly half of the population (43%) lives in cities, which is lower than the global average, although there is a wide variance between nations, ranging from 15% in "Cambodia" to 100% in Singapore. The average population density in the region is 133 people per square kilometer, but there are considerable inter-country and intra-country differences. Laos has a population density of 27 people per square kilometer, whereas Singapore has 7022 people per square kilometer. The only two megacities in Southeast Asia, Jakarta, and Manila have significantly greater population densities, with more than 10,000 inhabitants per square kilometer. Despite having comparable population numbers (around 14 million), the increased straddle of Manila and Jakarta make them less congested (ranked 15th and 17th in the world) than Mumbai, Kolkata, and Delhi (ranked 1st, 2nd, and 13th respectively) (UN Population Division, 2021).

Bangkok, Southeast Asia's next largest city, is placed 39th. Despite the region's rapid urbanization being expected to continue, urban economically marginalized populations appear to be less impoverished than anywhere else, with about one-fourth of the population living in extremely pathetic asylums (United Nation, 2021). Three or more of the following essentials of life are not present in a slum family: availability of water, hygiene, stable tenancy, a long-lasting residential construction, and acceptable living space (Leete, 2008; UN-Habitat, 2006). Mainly healthcare services are Rural-urban divide, and the basic healthcare support system is lacking in semi-urban and rural areas. In most nation regions, government health institutions lack key healthcare infrastructure, causing them to be ill-equipped to manage normal demand and forget about catastrophes (Zapata et al., 2020).

India's healthcare system is woefully staffed, both in terms of physicians and allied health personnel. Besides low salaries and depressing working conditions in hospitals, a key reason behind this state is prevailing corruption in India and other southeast Asian developing regions (Gupta et al., 2002; Lewis, 2006; McPake et al., 1999), resulting in the unavailability of a good medical college and adequate training infrastructure (Lim et al., 2010).To bridge the gap, medical and paramedical training institutions must expand significantly. Moreover, growth must be focused in remote communities, where service gaps are the most critical. Though Malaysia's healthcare facilities are better, rural areas are still underserved, as physicians do not want to relocate themselves to remote places at their comfort and convenience (Falcon, 2019). Corruption, violence against medical practitioners, and excessive importance to self-need are the reasons for the imbalanced healthcare infrastructure across India and another Southeast Asian region.

According to the Indian Medical Association, 75% of doctors suffering from bullying at the workplace fear of violence being the 43% prevalent source of anxiety among doctors (Perappadan, 2017). From 2006 to 2017, the number of recorded serious offenses against physicians in India increased, with the largest rates of violence happening in Delhi, Maharashtra, and Uttar Pradesh (Ranjan et al., 2018). Violent behavior is common in the healthcare sector, with rates of 60% worldwide (Schulte et al. 1998; Martino, 2012), and 70 percent of Singapore's hospital employees may have been subjected to violence (Chan et al., 2013; Singapore Medical Association, 2015; Danesh, 2008) With the rising demand for healthcare services, it is more important than ever to recognize and address this issue. Factors contributing to violence against doctors are the absence of quality education in India reservation and political interference in hospital affairs made undeserving people get the seat in medical colleges, resulting in poor quality of emergency care, poor grievance redressal mechanism, poor emergency network, ineffective communication mode among doctors and patient, inefficient management of patient load, ineffective training of healthcare staff (Lim, 2010; Martino, 2012; Schulte et al. 1998).

Unsorted Corruption in Healthcare Sector

Corruption, defined as the "usages, exploitation, or violation" of government role or services for personal benefit (Vian, 2008; Factor et al., 2015), can be perceived or real, financial, or political (Transparency International, 2015) State of corrupt mind adversely impacts the healthcare sector particularly weak and improvised society (Mostert et al., 2012). As per Transparency International's corruption perception index, approximately 1.4 million children die due to medical negligence. Nations with high corruption index are North Korea, Afghanistan, Cambodia, Bangladesh, Myanmar, Nepal, Laos, Pakistan, Vietnam,

Thailand, Philippines, Sri Lanka, and the Maldives. However, Singapore was ranked seventh in Transparency International's annual list of the least corrupt nations. The majority of Asian countries, on the other hand, are ranked in the bottom half of the Corruption Perceptions Index (CPI, 2021). Corruption crops out from inefficient governance (Ciccone et al., 2014). Highly unregulated health industry and a weak regulatory framework have created ideal circumstances for corruption (Brinkerhoff, 2004; Duncan, 2003; Fung et al., 2007; Klitgaard, 1988; Miller et al., 2001; Lewis, 2006; Tella & Savedoff 2001; Ramos, 2003). Irregular and low salaries of healthcare professionals and costly education provoke bribes and controlled supply of essential medical equipment or medicines at the time of crisis (Vian & Burak, 2006).

Corruption further leads to medication error and squandering of medicines, possibly because of fast but unfair and unjustified demographic transition, overpopulation, healthcare professionals shortage, and enormous cultural assortment have pooled to pose significant health challenges for Southeast Asian countries, one of which is the ongoing struggle to identify and reduce medication errors (Hashim et al., 2012). Inadequate ratio of doctors and patient leads to excessive work pressure upon medical professional resulting into sleepless nights, long working hours without intervals, unhygienic environment possibly leads to medication error and corruption at large (Gautam, 2013).

Healthcare Supply Chain Issues

Challenges at the organizational, operational, and environmental level, the medicare supply chain has been particularly sluggish in incorporating sustainable principles (McKone-Sweet et al., 2005). According to the "Economist Intelligence Unit" (EIU), advanced nations spend approximately 10.5 percent of their GDP on healthcare (i.e., "North America" spends 17.4 percent, "Western Europe" spends 10.7%, "Latin America" spends 8.0 percent, "Asia/Australasia" spends 6.6 percent, and "Middle East/Africa" spends 6.4 percent of GDP) (World Healthcare Outlook, 2013). Although India had taken numerous steps toward economic progress in recent decades, boosting its yearly GDP growth rate and lowering poverty. However, in India, little effort has been made to offer essential services such as healthcare. Though, the Governments in India, including Tamil Nadu, Delhi, Haryana, and Rajasthan, have taken steps to refine healthcare and have begun to supply generic medicines free of cost through programs such as "Jan Aushadhi Yojna," "Janani Suraksha Yojna," "Mukhyamantri Nishulk Dava Yojna," and others.

The execution of medicare programs such as the universal access of generic drugs usually suffers difficulties, rendering the medicare supply chain unproductive. Delays in open communication, data accessibility, inappropriate database management, inappropriate purchase, insufficient warehouse, inadequate supply chain management, improper documentation, and lean implementation are some of the noticeable weaknesses of the current government-supported medicare supply chain (Singh et al., 2016). Competitiveness and adaptability can be sharpened through effective lean supply chain (LSC) management. (Moyano-Fuentes et al., 2019). Moreover, lean has a positive impact on the performance of the inbound distribution chain. (Prajogo et al., 2016). For drug safety, pharmaceutical supply chain coordination and inventory management are a must. (Kelle et al., 2012; Uthayakumar & Priyan, 2013).

Unaffordable Medicines

An ineffective supply chain makes drugs unaffordable. However, the Southeast Asia Region is a significant manufacturer and generic pharmaceuticals exporter. India is known as the "world's pharmacy," "exporting to over 170 countries", and Bangladesh, Indonesia, and Thailand have significant local manufacturing. Despite this, India delivered medical supplies to Indonesia, Bangladesh amid COVID'19 (Bhaumik, 2021). Millions of people have benefited during the previous two decades, and not just in impoverished countries. By prescribing Indian generics instead of US-made branded, the US has saved billions of dollars.

Except for countries like Thailand, Bhutan, and Timor-Leste, all Southeast Asian nations spend their money on medications out of their own pockets rather than from public funds. Despite this, most drugs in India, especially critical medicines, remain out of reach for the common Indian. Drug spending accounts for a substantial portion of Indians' healthcare costs and is a major source of financial strain. Consequently, it places considerable financial stress on households: surveys have revealed that medication prices account for "80% of out-of-pocket health expenditures" in "India" and 73% in Myanmar, and only 12.1% in Thailand. The problem of excessive out-of-pocket expenses has driven many middle-class people into poverty. Figure-1 shows the out-of-pocket expense and Doctors per patient.

Figure 1. Out of Pocket Expenses

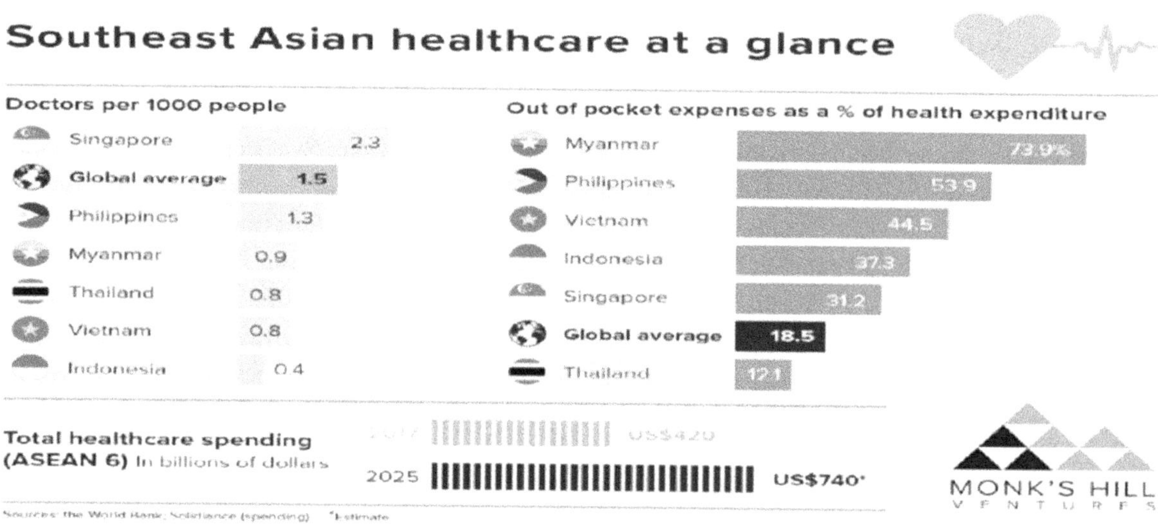

Technology Assault in Healthcare Sector

Frustrated citizens, because of the excessive financial burden upon them of varied taxes and medical expenses out their pockets, have made their anguish towards the system and healthcare service providers. Insensitivity and aggression towards medical professionals. Haug (1973) claimed that the dearth of knowledge and degree of understanding among doctors and the general population had narrowed down substantially, restricting doctors' capacity to retain clinical autonomy. Another rationale might be that growing digitalization and official regulation made professional expertise and opinion more noticeable, as well as more subjects to dispute and examination. The development of the so-called articulated, "information-rich" decisive consumer supplemented this technological attack on medicine's knowledge base since the public and patients no longer trusted their doctors blindly (Nettleton et al., 2005). These emerging issues and prevalent ignorance by the nations' Governments have adversely impacted the citizens' well-being and questioned the bilateral and multilateral relations among different Indian and Southeast Asian regions.

BILATERAL AND MULTILATERAL COOPERATION AND PARTNERSHIP

Bilateral cooperation and partnership can occur among two nations, allowing the tariff-free flow of goods and granting the most favored nation status to such nations in partnership. However, multilateral cooperation and partnership can occur among more than three nations, where the nations agree to reduce and dismantle their tariff and non-tariff barriers (Krugman et al., 2020; Medhekar, 2021). The Bilateral and multilateral agreements between India and other Southeast Asian countries are quite rhetoric; the level of engagement is substantially weak and requires extensive strategic execution of plans chalked out. Figure-2 shows the level of engagement of India with other Southeast Asian countries in terms of connectivity, trade, energy, and security cooperation.

Existing Collaborations

Figure 2. Southeast Asia and India Bilateral Collaboration
Source: *Jonah et al. (2015); RAND Corporation*
NOTE: *Colour encryption - red indicates a low level of involvement; yellow, moderate involvement; and dark green, significant involvement.*

"Nation"	**"Connectivity"**	**"Trade"**	**"Energy"**	**"Security Cooperation"**
"Singapore"				
"Vietnam"				
"Myanmar"				
"Thailand"				
"Malaysia"				
"Indonesia"				
"Philippines"				
"Brunei"				
"Cambodia"				
"Laos"				

Colour encryption - red indicates a low level of involvement; yellow, moderate involvement; and dark green, a significant level of involvement.
Source: **RAND**

Myanmar is the only Southeast Asian country sharing a border with India, and it is the central focus of India for regional connectivity via road, rail, and Indian-financed port facilities. Vietnam is India's longest-standing security partner (Jonah et al., 2015). Thailand, Malaysia, and Indonesia are among the second-tier countries with which "India" has positive and growing economic and security ties, benefit from optimistic and mounting economic and security collaborations. Based on security links, India has the greatest trade with Indonesia and the least with Thailand, but the reverse is true in terms of military exchanges, exercises, and other security metrics; "Malaysia" is in the middle on both economic and security measures (Jonah et al., 2015). The Philippines, Brunei, Cambodia, and Laos are the third-tier countries with which "India" has a limited interaction on all fronts. Although India has no direct conflicts with these countries, they do not play a significant role in Indian security or strategic planning (Jonah et al., 2015). Unfortunately, the existing collaboration is around the economy, security, and political spectrum; however, one of the essential healthcare sectors is still ignored, which should be the focus of the Government at least now begin badly thrashed by the COVID'19 second wave.

Outreach Disparities

Around 123 nations, including the "US", "Germany", "Spain", "South Africa", "Kuwait", "Jordan", "the Dominican Republic", and "Antigua & Barbuda", have received COVID-19-related support from "India". India's involvement and collaboration seem scanty with the ASEAN region. Only three ASEAN member states — Vietnam, Singapore, and Indonesia; currently meet with India to discuss health and economic issues. A Singaporean company has donated 30,000 COVID-19 testing kits to India, while India has promised to send HCQ pills to Malaysia. Philippine government officials, university students, and common citizens have received masks, sanitizers, and medicines from the Indian embassy in Manila.

ECONOMIC BENEFITS FROM COLLABORATION

Being the "Pharmacy for the World," India should develop strong bilateral relations with different Southeast Asian regions; moreover, the indigenous Ayurvedic herb-based medication is quite a powerful source of curing the root disease and boosting the immune system. Indian climatic conditions and soil fertility are sufficiently enough to grow such medicinal herbs naturally. India should increase its scientific research by developing sound research and development labs for scientifically proving its archaic behoof.

Globalization of the Healthcare Sector

With the advent of globalization in the different fields, the healthcare sector shall not remain untouched; eventually, there will be globalization in the healthcare sector as well as no country has all the necessary healthcare resources. "National health systems" examined several remedies to overcome the challenges between 1990 and 2010, including exchanging qualified workforce, caregivers, and surgeons. For example, the United States and the United Kingdom hired a big number of nurses from the Philippines, the Caribbean, and South Africa (Alonso-Garbayo and Maben (2009). Both the home and host countries benefited from such exchanges, as immigrant nurses from the "Philippines" often receive up to nine times more in the UK than they could get at home (Alonso-Garbayo & Maben, 2009). Similarly, many health practitioners and graduates from developing countries such as India, Pakistan, the Philippines, and "English-speaking countries" were employed in the United States. Approximately 25% of American physicians acquired their education in foreign medical schools. Medicare globalization is not limited to the United States and the United Kingdom. More than 50 countries, including Australia, Brazil, Sweden, Malaysia, and the United Arab Emirates, rely on foreign specialists' Global pharmaceutical corporations are following this trend and are continuing to develop new treatments in multiple nations. More medical experiments are being conducted in developing countries like India as they disseminate their research and development activities across the globe (IFC Global Conference, 2005).

Some American hospitals have turned to companies in Australia, Israel, India, Switzerland, and Lebanon to decipher their CT scans quickly to pursue more efficiency and reduced costs. Because the barriers between pharmaceuticals, providers, physicians, biotech, and payers are low, another facet of global convergence in healthcare is the ease in communication and adoption of best practices. Both healthcare providers and recipients are benefitted from increasingly improved technology, allowing for more efficient transmission of information throughout the globe. Medicare globalization is still in its initial phases, but it is proposed to accelerate drastically in the years to come. Globalization of the medicare industry provides an enormous economic potential for multinational firms, but it also poses significant risks to consumers and national medicare systems, such as rising costs, inconsistent or inferior treatment, and unequal access. Thus, pharmaceutical firms' global expansion needs some globally standardized norms and standards.

Better Data and Governance

India's current systems for collecting, processing, and monitoring critical public health and healthcare indicators are ineffective, duplicative, and of dubious quality. Must initiate the collaboration with Singapore, ranked 8th on technological expertise by perception (US, 2021). Such agreements will streamline the demolition of obsolete infrastructures and establish an integrated, strong, and fair health information system. Utilizing recent breakthroughs in data analytics and digital technology, the reliable and timely flow of information across multiple healthcare system levels might dramatically improve preparedness and reactions to any future emergencies.

Technological Diffusion in Healthcare

In many nations worldwide, the adoption of digital technologies in the healthcare industry has accelerated in recent decades. (Laurenza et al., 2018). The "Malaysia Digital Economy Corporation" (MDEC) presented the Cloud-first plan, which intends to stimulate cloud computing adoption in both the business and public sectors (Marston et al., 2011). The province of Tamil Nadu had acquired a transparent, technology-supported system for pharmaceuticals delivery throughout public health institutions. Adequate technological diffusion exposes unfair practices, such as highly disparate pricing for comparable pharmaceutical substances, and combats the selling of counterfeit pharmaceuticals. Furthermore, improving drug procuring and supply regulations for public facilities is essential for ensuring necessary drugs. Bhutan and Sri Lanka, including some of the Indian states (Kerala, Rajasthan, and Tamil Nadu), have rightly executed the "LMIS" to give reliable, real-time information to address the challenges of free vital pharmaceutical crisis and effective management of medicines inventory. Recent data suggests that mobile health can be a boon and provide an alternative to the limits of traditional healthcare delivery (Lee & Han, 2015).

Medical Tourism

Further, with the advent of technological advancement and incorporation of artificial intelligence in developing the precision in healthcare facilities and intensive care unit medical tourism in Southeast Asia will expand exponentially, contribute to the development of the private sector, particularly medical tourism, which is proving to be a valuable commercial prospect. Countries in this region are integrating advanced medical services with a tourism package to leverage their appeal as tourist attractions. Some nations are creating sustainable advantages in service provision based on the organizational structure of their health systems. Thailand has developed a reputation for facial surgery and gender transition procedures, while Singapore draws patients seeking sophisticated therapies such as cardiology, cerebral surgery, and gene therapy. In the years 2006–2007, an estimated 2 million medical tourists visited Singapore, Malaysia, and Thailand, costing these nations approximately US$ 3 billion in treatment expenses. Singapore has a booming health tourism sector and is a medical center of excellence in Southeast Asia.

In the nascent medical tourism business, Government ensures prominent marketing and promotional role. It is a definite trend in Southeast Asia, particularly in Thailand, Singapore, and Malaysia, the primary regional centers for medical tourism have medical tourist visas available and government organizations dedicated to increasing medical tourist inflows (Smith et al., 2009). Indonesian, Philippine, and Vietnamese governments have all showed their interest in entering the medical tourism business because of its possible financial advantages and improved overall population health, such as greater life expectancy and lower child mortality rates (Blouin et al. 2009). Facilitation of foreign direct investment in healthcare infrastructure and medical tourism inflows with associated income can help generate extra resources for healthcare investment. Furthermore, medical tourism can reduce or stop the emigration of healthcare professionals, particularly experts (Hopkins et al., 2010).

RECOMMENDATIONS AND DISCUSSION

Southeast Asian Countries and Indian health systems struggle to ensure that their populations have access to basic health services (Tourism Malaysia, 2010). Malaysian has evolved into a two-tier healthcare system, with private treatments available for those who can manage to pay for and public services available to the remainder of the population (Chee, 2008). The brain drain of Thai public to private health workers has stressed public healthcare services, particularly in rural regions (Pachanee & Wibulpolprasert 2006). Medical tourism's influence on health systems, notably equity of access for foreign and local consumers, is causing significant concern (Turner, 2007). People seek cheaper and higher quality care treatment overseas due to inequities at home, such as low-quality services and the inability to pay. However, "Singapore's" health indices are good, and it is relatively inexpensive at which they were obtained that sets it apart from other high-performing countries. As seen by the city's increased Healthy Life Expectancy, "Singaporeans" are not only living longer, but they are also living healthier lives (HALE). According to the 2013 "Global Burden of Disease" (GBD) survey, "Singaporean" males (females) spend the equivalent of 70.75 (73.35) years of their lives free of disease, which is the second-highest in the world (Murray et al., 2015).

Health policy is not the sole determinant of healthcare results. Circumstances and performance outside the sector also have a significant impact on them. Wealth, hygiene, literacy, and accommodation are all significant determinants. In this sense, Singapore's health policy has benefited substantially from a variety of favourable situations that have aided in improving health. Singapore's GDP per capita was US$430" in 1960, a third of that of "OECD" economies, but it has since risen to approximately US$55,000, more than 50% greater than the OECD average. Households were able to take enhanced care of their well-being as a result of their increased income. Such massive growth becomes possible because of a corruption-free and technologically strong country.

For India and other Southeast Asian countries, combating corruption is inevitable. Corruption Perception Index (2021) reveals that eliminating corruption is critical to improving crisis readiness in a progressively unpredictable environment where calamities frequently occur. In the face of a crisis, governments can use various measures to combat corruption, but controlling corruption is significantly difficult until and unless effective anti-corruption measures are not already in place. Further, increased investment in the health sector, guarantee a steady supply of skilled workers and vital drugs, and gather accurate information on current healthcare outcomes, may help address the shortcomings in the healthcare industry. More funding is also required to increase scientific research capacity throughout the country's various healthcare fields. Stable public funding and the development of a robust cadre of research specialists can help improve readiness and ensure a quick reaction to any catastrophe.

"Thailand" introduced the "Health Insurance Card Scheme" in 2004 for cross-border migrants with low skills (Suphanchaimat, 2017). That creates migrant-friendly services to provide better healthcare to all migrants, regardless of their insurance coverage. The utilization of immigrant volunteer health professionals, portable treatment centers, bilingual signals and bulletin boards, and outreach activities for low-skilled workers are all examples of migrant-friendly services (Tangcharoensathien et al., 2017).

Another very effective project, Migrant Fund (M-Fund), was launched by a private social organization called Dreamlopments for migrant communities residing in Thai–Myanmar border districts such as Mae Sot and Mae Ramat and Phop Phra. Migrant-Fund is a non-profit, charitable, low-cost health insurance program that supports unregistered or economic refugees in the country (Pudpong et al., 2019). These policy initiatives/interventions may increase children's use of health services, resulting in better health outcomes for all children, regardless of insurance status. In addition, the Malaysian model of establishing financial prosperity through modernization and improving quality and accessible basic healthcare services for the poor through Clinic Malaysia; also enabled 24,646 poor individuals to raise their earnings through Citizens Aid Malaysia, and they are constantly improving their corruption perception index, reducing crime, and improving education quality through the back-to-school assistance program and Book Voucher Malaysia, to name a few examples of effective techniques used by Malaysia to address the problem.

Precision in the Healthcare Sector

Medical therapies have always been designed to operate on society based on their study reliability and generalizability; yet treatment outcomes might differ significantly from one person to another. A treatment for one patient may be useless or even hazardous for others. Approximately 30–40% of individuals are prescribed drugs for which the risks exceed the benefits. Thus, the precision medicine field is catching attention and has become a field of interest among many scientists; trying to customize medical treatments to an individual's genetic profile and lifestyle is gaining momentum with digitalization, owing to breakthroughs in genetic cloud technology and analysis. Currently, we are on the cusp of a new era in medicine; with advancements in technology, focused medicine can be developed. Digital screening tests or ancillary technologies will be made available to bring precision in prescribing medicine. However, precision medicine is largely a place in cancer treatment by genomic profiling tests. By the next decade, it is anticipated that 60 percent of patients will benefit from genetic sequencing and data analytics.

Another developing technology that is gaining traction in personalized medicine is 3D printing. 3D printing is booming, with revenues anticipated to reach $35.6 billion by 2024. (Wohlers Report, 2019). Hearing aids, face surgery, customized prosthesis, dental crowns, and surgical implants are all examples where 3D technology has been used in healthcare. Advances in 3D printing are paving the way for new uses in drug development and medical device manufacture. 3D printing is widely used to create highly personalized and adaptive surgical equipment (Krauskopf, 2015). Moreover, 3D technology enables production within hospitals or healthcare facilities, resulting in shorter wait times and lower prices, which will also help the improvised society and the people residing in rural areas.

LIMITATIONS AND FUTURE RESEARCH DIRECTIONS

Some limitations might confine the generalization of the findings. This study was conducted based on information available on WHO, NSSO, and other related extant literature on the healthcare system of India and Southeast Asian nations only. Thus, the study's outcomes can serve as the basis for similar studies in the countries taken for the study. Therefore, future research could emphasize different geographical locations in a broader scope and examine other influencing factors on improving the healthcare system.

Another limitation of this study was that no segregation was done based on public and private hospitals. Therefore, future research may compare the private and public hospitals of India and Southeast Asia region to analyse the difference in the healthcare system. Future research could also use personal medical records to measure the percentage of the compromised healthcare system. Lastly, the individual trust precision and transparency in medical services; therefore, to improve the healthcare support system among Indian and Southeast Asian nations, future research may employ quantitative and qualitative research to triangulate this aspect. Further, as extant literature review supports that healthcare facilities of Singapore, Malaysia, and Thailand are best among other Southeast Asian nations and India. Hence, Future Research should figure out how to incorporate the medical support model of these countries in other Southeast Asian nations and India.

CONCLUSION

The chapter aim at identifying the challenges and opportunities available in the healthcare sector for India and eleven Southeast Asian Nations for effective collaboration. This chapter highlights some major challenges nations facing in building effective collaboration in the healthcare sector. Like medicare, globalization opens an avenue for the exchange of qualified workforce, caregivers, and surgeons, where both the home and host countries benefited from such exchanges and provided the enormous economic potential for multinational firms. Further, in countries like India and Southeast Asian nations other than Singapore, Malaysia, and Thailand, where healthcare facilities are quite advance; needs to develop strong technological expertise like in Singapore to strengthen the infrastructure of the healthcare system, diffusion of technology in healthcare will bring precision in the healthcare services and transparency in the system that helps the developing nations to combat the corruption in Healthcare sector.

COVID-19 demonstrated how corruption impedes emergency response and efforts to assist people who are most in need. It also emphasized the need for government decisions that need to be streamlined. First and foremost, governments of various countries should implement a system that includes complete openness, ownership, fairness, and multi-stakeholder participation in all Covid-19-related programs, plans, and policies. One example is conducting corruption risk studies as part of broader evaluations of health system enhancement and national health planning activities.

Further, prompt publication of outsourcing information ineffective platform and centrally controlled platforms, constructing clear and specific rules and protocols for emergencies and securing their enforcement; "supreme audit institutions" and "anti-corruption agencies" must be autonomous and adequately staffed to be able to function. Specific procedures and technical instruments that allow for authentic monitoring in an emergency must be implemented and deployed whenever needed.

Corruption must be controlled to provide an effective and equitable emergency response, not only to urban areas but also to the countryside; neglect of rural population is one of the major issues of imbalanced growth of nations. Thus, more inclusive societies and stronger resilience for the next global catastrophe are the need of an hour. Countries like Malaysia are growing as they have ensured the basic amenities for all the citizens; the telemedicine project, as an important means of achieving health for all rural Malaysians.

Thus, the compromised health sector must be free from corruption to develop favourable opportunities for collaboration among India and Southeast Asian countries. Thus, employing technology in healthcare not only sharpens the precision level of delivering better healthcare services to the patient; on the other hand, digitization will prove to be more stringent for overcoming corruption. Further, controlled corruption will enhance the percentage of medical tourism a boost economy and image on the global platform. Additionally, the inclusion of advanced technology in medical science opens various avenues for bilateral and multilateral collaboration among Southeast nations and India.

REFERENCES

Almuzaini, T., Choonara, I., & Sammons, H. (2013*). Substandard and counterfeit medicines: A systematic review of the literature*. doi:10.1136/bmjopen-2013-002923

Alonso-Garbayo, Á., & Maben, J. (2009). Internationally recruited nurses from India and the Philippines in the United Kingdom: The decision to emigrate. *Human Resources for Health*, *37*(7), 37. Advance online publication. doi:10.1186/1478-4491-7-37 PMID:19393080

Andrews, M., Areekal, B., Rajesh, K. R., Krishnan, J., Suryakala, R., Krishnan, B., Muraly, C., & Santhosh, P. V. (2020). First confirmed case of COVID-19 infection in India: A case report. *The Indian Journal of Medical Research*, *151*(5), 490–492. doi:10.4103/ijmr.IJMR_2131_20 PMID:32611918

Bhaumik, A. (2021). India resumes helping others with Covid-19 aid to counter China; sends oxygen to Bangladesh, Indonesia. *Deccan Herald*. https://www.deccanherald.com/national/india-resumes-helping-others-with-covid-19-aid-to-counter-china-sends-oxygen-to-bangladesh-indonesia-1012490.html

Blouin, C., Chopra, M., & Hoeven, R. V. (2009). Trade and social determinants of health. *Lancet*, *373*(9662), 502–507. doi:10.1016/S0140-6736(08)61777-8 PMID:19167058

Bond, K., Ospina, M. B., Blitz, S., Afilalo, M., Campbell, S. G., Bullard, M., Innes, G., Holroyd, B., Curry, G., Schull, M., & Rowe, B. (2007). Frequency, determinants, and impact of overcrowding in emergency departments in Canada: A national survey. *Healthcare Quarterly, 10*(4), 32–40. doi:10.12927/hcq.2007.19312 PMID:18019897

Brinkerhoff, D. W. (2004). Accountability and health systems: Toward conceptual clarity and policy relevance. *Health Policy and Planning, 19*(6), 371–379. doi:10.1093/heapol/czh052 PMID:15459162

Chan, A. O. M., Chan, Y. H., & Kee, J. P. C. (2013). Exposure to crises and resiliency of healthcare workers in Singapore. *Occupational Medicine (Oxford, England), 63*(2), 141–144. doi:10.1093/occmed/kqs202 PMID:23223749

Chanda, R. (2002). Trade-in health services. *Bulletin of the World Health Organization, 80*, 158–163. PMID:11953795

Chee, H. L. (2008). Ownership, control, and contention: Challenges for the future of healthcare in Malaysia. *Social Science & Medicine, 66*(10), 2145–2156. doi:10.1016/j.socscimed.2008.01.036 PMID:18329149

Ciccone, D. K., Vian, T., Maurer, L., & Bradley, E. H. (2014). Linking governance mechanisms to health outcomes: A review of the literature in low-and middle-income countries. *Social Science & Medicine, 1*(117), 86–95. doi:10.1016/j.socscimed.2014.07.010 PMID:25054281

CPI. (2020). *Asia Pacific – News*. Transparency.org

Danesh, V. C., Malvey, D., & Fottler, M. D. (2008). Hidden workplace violence: What your nurses may not be telling you. *Healthcare Management (Frederick), 27*(4), 357–363. doi:10.1097/HCM.0b013e31818c810b PMID:19011419

Duncan, F. (2003). *Corruption in the health sector*. USAID Bureau for Europe & Eurasia, Office of Democracy and Governance.

Ernst & Young LLP. (2019). *India: Building the best practices in healthcare services globally*. https://ficci.in/spdocument/23136/FICCI-EY-Report-on-MVT.pdf

Factor, R., & Kang, M. (2015). Corruption and population health outcomes: An analysis of data from 133 countries using structural equation modeling. *International Journal of Public Health, 60*(6), 633–641. doi:10.100700038-015-0687-6 PMID:25994589

Falcon, D. J. (2019). The Healthcare Gap in Rural Malaysia. Lehigh University, 37(6).

Fung, A., Graham, M., & Weil, D. (2007). *Full disclosure: the perils and promise of transparency*. Cambridge University Press. doi:10.1017/CBO9780511510533

Gautam, P. L. (2013). Minimizing medication errors: Moving attention from individual to system. *Journal of Anesthesia, 29*, 293–294. PMID:24106347

Gupta, S., Davoodi, H. R., & Tiongson, E. R. (2002). Corruption and the provision of healthcare and education services. In G. T. Abed & S. Gupta (Eds.), *Governance, corruption, and economic performance* (pp. 245–272). International Monetary Fund.

Hashim, J., Chongsuvivatwong, V., Phua, K. H., Pocock, N., Teng, Y. M., Chhem, R. K., Wilopo, S. A., & Lopez, A. (2012). *Health and Healthcare Systems in Southeast Asia*. United Nations University. https://unu.edu/publications/articles/health-and-healthcare-systems-in-southeast-asia.html

Haug, M. (1937). DE professionalization: An alternative hypothesis for the future. *Sociological Review. Mongraph*, *2*, 195–211.

Hopkins, K., Labonte, R., Runnels, V., & Packer, C. (2010). Medical tourism today: What is the state of existing knowledge? *Journal of Public Health Policy*, *31*(2), 185–198. doi:10.1057/jphp.2010.10 PMID:20535101

IFC Global Conference. (2005). *Investing in private healthcare in emerging markets conference: International Finance Corporation (IFC)*. IFC Global Conference, Washington, DC.

Index Mundi Malaysia Demographics Profile. (2014). Available from: https://www.indexmundi.com/malaysia/demographics

Jolly, P. (2004). *Medical school tuition and young physician indebtedness*. Association of American Medical Colleges.

Kelle, P., Woosley, J., & Schneider, H. (2012). Pharmaceutical supply chain specifics and inventory solutions for a hospital case. *Operations Research for Health Care*, *1*(2-3), 54–63. doi:10.1016/j.orhc.2012.07.001

Klitgaard, R. (1988). *Controlling corruption*. University of California Press. doi:10.1525/9780520911185

Krauskopf, K., Federman, A. D., Kale, M. S., Sigel, K. M., Martynenko, M., O'Conor, R., Wolf, M. S., Leventhal, H., & Wisnivesky, J. P. (2015). Chronic Obstructive Pulmonary Disease Illness and Medication Beliefs are Associated with Medication Adherence. *COPD*, *12*(2), 151–164. doi:10.3109/15412555.2014.922067 PMID:24960306

Krugman, P. R., Obstfeld, M., & Melitz, M. J. (2020). *International Trade Theory and Policy* (11th Global edn). Pearson Education.

Laurenza, E., Quintano, M., Schiavone, F., & Vrontis, D. (2018). The effect of digital technologies adoption in healthcare industry: A case-based analysis. *Business Process Management Journal*, *24*(5), 1124–1144. doi:10.1108/BPMJ-04-2017-0084

Lee, E., & Han, S. (2015). Determinants of adoption of mobile health services. *Online Information Review*, *39*(4), 556–573. doi:10.1108/OIR-01-2015-0007

Leete, R. (2008). Human development and urbanisation. *Ethos*, *2008*(June), 88–97.

Lewis, M. (2006). *Governance and corruption in public healthcare systems*. Working paper number 78. Washington, DC: Center for Global Development.

Lim, J., Bogossian, F., & Ahern, K. (2010). Stress and coping in Singaporean nurses: A literature review. *Nursing & Health Sciences*, *12*(2), 251–258. doi:10.1111/j.1442-2018.2010.00514.x PMID:20602699

Malaysia, T. (2008). *Media info: Health tourism in Malaysia*. Communications and Publicity Division. Retrieved from http:// www.tourism.gov.my/

Marston, S., Li, Z., Bandyopadhyay, S., Zhang, J., & Ghalsasi, A. (2011). Cloud computing-the business perspective. *Decision Support Systems, 51*(1), 176–189. doi:10.1016/j.dss.2010.12.006

Martino, V.D. (2002). *Workplace violence in the health sector - Country case studies Brazil, Bulgaria, Lebanon, Portugal, South Africa, Thailand and an additional Australian study: Synthesis Report*. Academic Press.

McKone-Sweet, K. E., Hamilton, P., & Willis, S. B. (2005). The ailing healthcare supply chain: A prescription for change. *The Journal of Supply Chain Management, 41*(1), 4–17. doi:10.1111/j.1745-493X.2005.tb00180.x

McPake, B., Asiimwe, D., Mwesigye, F., Ofumbi, M., Ortenblad, L., Streefland, P., & Turinde, A. (1999). Informal economic activities of public health workers in Uganda: Implications for quality and accessibility of care. *Social Science & Medicine, 49*(7), 849–865. doi:10.1016/S0277-9536(99)00144-6 PMID:10468391

Medhekar, A. (2019). Emerging Trends of Wellness and Medical Tourism in India. In Global Developments in Healthcare and Medical Tourism. IGI Global. doi:091218-104208

Medhekar, A. (2021). Australia-India: Bilateral Trade Opportunities and Challenges. In *Emerging Business and Trade Opportunities between Oceania and Asia*. IGI Global Publishing. doi:10.4018/978-1-7998-4126-5.ch004

Medhekar, A., Wong, H. Y., & Hall, J. E. (2019). Factors influencing inbound medical travel to India. *Journal of Health Organization and Management, 33*(2), 155–172. doi:10.1108/JHOM-08-2018-0234 PMID:30950309

Meikeng, Y. (2014). Indonesians are the top healthcare tourists to Malaysia. *The Star Online*. Available at: https://www.thestar.com.my/news/nation/2014/11/13/indonesia-top-healthcare-tourists-to-malaysia/#vcjJ50ltdBQsVZgQ.99

Miller, W. L., Grodeland, A. B., & Koshechkina, T. Y. (2001). *A culture of corruption? Coping with Government in post-communist Europe*. Central European University Press.

Morrison, G. (2005). Mortgaging Our Future— The Cost of Medical Education. *The New England Journal of Medicine, 352*(2), 117–119. doi:10.1056/NEJMp048089 PMID:15647572

Mostert, S., Sitaresmi, M. N., Njuguna, F., Beers, E. J. V., & Kaspers, G. J. (2012). Effect of corruption on medical care in low-income countries. *Pediatric Blood & Cancer, 58*(3), 325–326. doi:10.1002/pbc.23408 PMID:22106048

Moyano-Fuentes, J., Bruque-Cámara, S., & Maqueira-Marín, J. M. (2019). Development and validation of a lean supply chain management measurement instrument. *Production Planning and Control, 30*(1), 20–32. doi:10.1080/09537287.2018.1519731

Murray, T., Barber, R. M., Foreman, K. J., Ozgoren, A. A., Abd-Allah, F., Abera, S. F., Aboyans, V., Abraham, J. P., Abubakar, I., Abu-Raddad, L. J., Abu-Rmeileh, N. M., Achoki, T., Ackerman, I. N., Ademi, Z., Adou, A. K., Adsuar, J. C., Afshin, A., Agardh, E. E., Alam, S. S., ... Vos, T. (2015). 'Global, Regional, and National Disability-Adjusted Life Years (DALYs) for 306 Diseases and Injuries and Healthy Life Expectancy (HALE) for 188 Countries, 1990–2013: Quantifying the Epidemiological Transition. *Lancet, 386*(10009), 2145–2191. doi:10.1016/S0140-6736(15)61340-X PMID:26321261

Nadpara, N. (2015). *An Empirical Examination of the effect of corruption on Health Outcomes* [Published doctoral dissertation]. The College of New Jersey.

National Sample Survey Organisation (NSSO). (2019). NSSO, Ministry of Statistics and Programme Implementation. New Delhi: Government of India.

Naveed, M. (2018). *Investment in early childhood health and its implications for human capital accumulation and economic growth* (Doctoral dissertation). Lahore School of Economics.

Nettleton, S., Burrows, R., O'Malley, L., & Watt, I. (2005). The mundane realities of the everyday lay use of the internet for health, and their consequences for media convergence. *Sociology of Health & Illness*, *27*(7), 972–992. Advance online publication. doi:10.1111/j.1467-9566.2005.00466.x PMID:16313525

Pachanee, C., & Wibulpolprasert, S. (2006). Incoherent policies on universal coverage of health insurance and promotion of international trade in health services in Thailand. *Health Policy and Planning*, *21*(4), 310–318. doi:10.1093/heapol/czl017 PMID:16728511

Peltzer, K., & Pengpid, S. (2018). The prevalence and social determinants of hypertension among adults in Indonesia: A cross-sectional population-based national survey. selected African countries. *Health Economics Review*, *7*(1), 23–36. PMID:30229501

Perappadan, B. S. (2017). Majority of doctors in India fear violence, says IMA survey. *The Hindu*. Retrieved from timesofindia.indiatimes.com

Pew Research Centre. (2020). *Pew Research Centre analysis of the World Bank's PovcalNet database*. Author.

Philippines Statistics Authorities. (2019). *Philippine National Health Accounts, Health Spending Grew by 10.9 Percent in 2019.* https://psa.gov.ph/content/health-spending-grew-109-percent-2019

Piabuo, S. M., & Tieguhong, J. C. (2017). *Health expenditure and economic growth-a review of the literature and an analysis between the economic community for Central African States*. CEMAC.

Pocock, N. S., & Phua, K. H. (2011). Medical tourism and policy implications for health systems: A conceptual framework from a comparative study of Thailand, Singapore and Malaysia. *Globalization and Health*, *12*(7), 12. Advance online publication. doi:10.1186/1744-8603-7-12 PMID:21539751

Prajogo, D., Oke, A., & Olhager, J. (2016). Supply chain processes: Linking supply logistics integration, supply performance, lean processes, and competitive performance. *International Journal of Operations & Production Management*, *36*(2), 220–238. doi:10.1108/IJOPM-03-2014-0129

Pudpong, N., Durier, N., Julchoo, S., Sainam, P., Kuttiparambil, B., & Suphanchaimat, R. (2019). Assessment of a Voluntary Non-Profit Health Insurance Scheme for Migrants along the Thai–Myanmar Border: A Case Study of the Migrant Fund in Thailand. *International Journal of Environmental Research and Public Health*, *16*(14), 2581. doi:10.3390/ijerph16142581 PMID:31330995

Ramos, M. (2003). Auditors' responsibility for fraud detection. *Journal of Accountancy*, (January), 28. https://www.aicpa.org/pubs

Ranjan, R. M., Singh, M., Pal, R., Das, J. K., & Gupta, S. (2018). Epidemiology of violence against medical practitioners in a developing country (2006-2017). *Journal of Health Research and Review*, *5*(3), 153. doi:10.4103/jhrr.jhrr_84_17

Reisman, D. (1996). Payment for health in the Philippines. *International Journal of Social Economics, 23*(8), 46–75. doi:10.1108/03068299610122362

Reisman, D. (2006). Payment for health in Singapore. *International Journal of Social Economics, 33*(2), 132–159. doi:10.1108/03068290610642229

Report, C. (2006). *Special focus on corruption and health*. Pluto Press.

Report, W. (2019). *Materials saw record growth*. Retrieved from https://www.3dnatives.com/en/wohlers-report-2019-270320195/#!

Roberts, M. (2021). *What are the India, Brazil, South Africa, and UK variants?* BBC News. Retrieved from https://www.bbc.com/news/health-55659820

Salmasi, S., Khan, T. M., Hong, Y. H., Ming, L. C., & Wong, T. W. (2015). Medication Errors in the Southeast Asian Countries: A Systematic Review. *PLoS One, 10*(9), 136–545. doi:10.1371/journal.pone.0136545 PMID:26340679

Schulte, J., Nolt, J., Williams, R. L., Spinks, C. L., & Hellsten, J. (1998). Violence and threats of violence experienced by public health field-workers. *Journal of the American Medical Association, 280*(5), 439–442. doi:10.1001/jama.280.5.439 PMID:9701079

Singapore Medical Association. (2010). *Violence in the workplace: Survey on the experience of doctors in Singapore*. Retrieved from https://news.sma.org.sg/4211/Violence.pdf

Singh, K., Kumar, R., & Kumar, P. (2016). Strategic issues in pharmaceutical supply chains: A review. *International Journal of Pharmaceutical and Healthcare Marketing, 10*(3), 234–257. doi:10.1108/IJPHM-10-2015-0050

Smith, R., Chanda, R., & Tangcharoensathien, V. (2009). Trade-in health-related services. *Lancet, 373*(9663), 593–601. doi:10.1016/S0140-6736(08)61778-X PMID:19167053

Suphanchaimat, R. (2017). *Health insurance card scheme" for cross-border migrants in Thailand: responses in policy implementation & outcome evaluation* (Doctoral Dissertation). London School of Hygiene & Tropical Medicine.

Tangcharoensathien, V., Mills, A., & Palu, T. (2015). Accelerating health equity: The key role of universal health coverage in the SGDs. *BMC Medicine, 13*(1), 1. doi:10.118612916-015-0342-3 PMID:25925656

Tangcharoensathien, V., Thwin, A., & Patcharanarumol, W. (2017). Implementing health insurance for migrants, Thailand. *Bulletin of the World Health Organization, 95*(2), 146–151. doi:10.2471/BLT.16.179606 PMID:28250516

Tella, R. D., & Savedoff, W. (2001). *Diagnosis corruption: fraud in Latin America's public hospitals*. Inter-American Development Bank.

The Economic Times. (2018). India to increase public health spending. Retrieved from India to increase public health spending to 2.5% of GDP: PM Modi. *The Economic Times*.

Transparency International. (2015). *Bangladesh: overview of corruption and anti-corruption with a focus on the health sector.* Berlin: Transparency International. Retrieved from https://www.u4.no/publications/bangladesh-overviewof-corruption-and-anticorruption-with-a-focus-on-the-health-sector

Turner, L. (2007). First world healthcare at third-world prices: Globalization, bioethics, and medical tourism. *Biosocieties*, *2*(3), 303–325. doi:10.1017/S1745855207005765

UN-Habitat. (2006). *State of the World's Cities: The Millennium Goals and Urban Sustainability*. Earthscan.

UN Population Division World population prospects. (2008). *The revised population database*. https://esa.un.org/unpp/index.asp?panel=2

United Nations. (2008). *The Right to Health. Composition of macro geographical (continental) regions, geographical sub-regions, and selected economic and other groupings*. Fact Sheet-31, UN Statistic Division. Retrieved from http://unstats.un.org/unsd/methods/m49/m49regin.htm#asia

United Nations Department of Economic and Social Affairs. (2012). *World Population Prospects*. Retrieved from https://esa.un.org/wpp/Excel-Data/population.htm

Uthayakumar, R., & Priyan, S. (2013). Pharmaceutical supply chain and inventory management strategies: Optimization for a pharmaceutical company and a hospital. *Operations Research for Health Care*, *2*(3), 52–64.

Varghese, P. (2018). *Indian Economic Strategy 2035*. Department of Foreign Affairs and Trade. Retrieved from https://dfat.gov.au/geo/india/ies/index.html

Vecchio, N., Davies, D., & Rohde, N. (2018). The effect of inadequate access to healthcare services on emergency room visits. A comparison between physical and mental health conditions. *PLoS One*, *13*(8), 202–559. doi:10.1371/journal.pone.0202559 PMID:30138438

Vian, T. (2008). Review of corruption in the health sector: Theory, methods, and interventions. *Health Policy (Amsterdam)*, *23*(2), 83–94. PMID:18281310

Vian, T., & Burak, L. (2006). Beliefs about informal payments in Albania. *Health Policy and Planning*, *21*(5), 392–401. doi:10.1093/heapol/czl022 PMID:16940304

Wibulpolprasert, A., Sittichanbuncha, Y., Sricharoen, P., Borwornsrisuk, S., & Sawanyawisuth, K. (2014). Factors associated with overcrowded emergency rooms in Thailand: A medical school setting. *Emergency Medicine International*, *2014*, 1–4. Advance online publication. doi:10.1155/2014/576259 PMID:25328708

Wibulpolprasert, S., & Pengpaibon, P. (2003). Integrated strategies to tackle the inequitable distribution of doctors in Thailand: Four decades of experience. *Human Resources for Health*, *1*(12), 12. doi:10.1186/1478-4491-1-12 PMID:14641940

World Bank. (2016). *Hospital Beds (per 1,000 people)*. World Health Organization.

World Health Organization. (2021). Retrieved from http://who.int/violence_injury_prevention/violence/activities/workplace/WVsynthesisreport. pdf?ua=1&ua=1

World Healthcare Outlook. (2013). *Economist intelligence unit*. Author.

Yeganeh, H. (2019). An Analysis of Emerging Patterns of Consumption in the Age of Globalization and Digitalization. *FIIB Business Review*, *8*(4), 259–270. Advance online publication. doi:10.1177/2319714519873748

Zaman, S., & Hossain, N. (2017). Universal Health Coverage: A Burning Need for Developing Countries. *Journal of Medical Research and Innovation*, *1*(1), 18–20. doi:10.15419/jmri.41

Zapata, T., Buchan, J., Tangcharoensathien, V., Meliala, A., Karunathilake, I., Tin, N., Nandi, S., Tobgay, T., & Noree, T. (2020). Rural retention strategies in the South-East Asia Region: Evidence to guide effective implementation. *Bulletin of the World Health Organization*, *98*(11), 815–817. doi:10.2471/BLT.19.245662 PMID:33177780

ADDITIONAL READING

Jonah, B., Jennifer, D. P. M., Angel, R., & Bonny, L. (2015). *Look East, Cross Black Waters; India's Interest in Southeast Asia*. RAND Corporation. www.rand.org/t/RR1021

OECD. (2021). *Economic Outlook for Southeast Asia, China and India 2021: Reallocating Resources for Digitalization*. OECD Publishing. doi:10.1787/711629f8-

KEY TERMS AND DEFINITIONS

Bilateral Cooperation: Bilateral Cooperation are the legal agreements between two nations on mutually accepted terms and conditions that facilitate the infrastructural development of the nations involved in the agreement, further increase avenues for economic development also.

Compromised Healthcare: Compromised Healthcare is defined as sub-standard medical services are provided to patients instead of earning extra profit.

Digital Health Technology: Digital Health Technology, also known as m-health/ e-health technology; which enables the effective management of the health record and even supports the quick retrieval of the required information on time supports the accuracy and precision in providing the healthcare services.

Global Public Health Emergency: Global public health emergency is defined as an occurrence of a health emergency at the world level, for example, the situation of a pandemic like Plague, SARS, Ebola, and COVID'19.

Multilateral Cooperation: Multilateral cooperation is the legal agreement between many nations or groups of nations, coming together for increasing the exchange of goods and services among members' nations at liberalized rates.

Technology Assault in Healthcare Sector: It means an excessive availability of information on various platform-related healthcare, making patients rich in information and further developing the so-called articulated patients.

Chapter 13
Japan-India Trade Relations:
History, Catalysts, and Challenges

S. Jobayear Ahmed
Bangladesh Rural Advancement Committee (BRAC), Bangladesh

ABSTRACT

Japanese-Indian relations is supported by historic, political, and cultural affiliation, which usually led towards positive economic relations. Although the Japanese-Indian relationship is a few centuries old, surprisingly, the statistics of trade hardly exhibit any mentionable growth, except the recent upward trend in exports to Japan. In fact, India almost failed to capture the near home market even with the growth (1% market share). Therefore, the chapter is developed based on a qualitative study with the objectives of exploring the history, catalysts, and impediments of Japanese-Indian trade relations and recommends the future course of action. The study recommends completion of India's megaprojects, Japan's policy reform, taxation and supportive reform, arrangement of social life of the foreigners, zero corruption, forgery, and harassment, efficiency, effectiveness, linguistic skill and cultural understanding of human resources, and creating opportunities and building organizational capacities between the two.

INTRODUCTION

Japan has long been neo mercantilist (Smith, 2010) seeking foreign markets' openness while protecting its own, (Lawrence, 1987) through various tariff and non-tariff barriers and standards (Ball, 2010). Japan, symmetric to Ricardo's theory comparative advantages, (Ricardo, 1988), produces high value tech products and imports the low value agricultural products. Krugman & Obstfeld (2010) explained Prisoners' dilemma of Game Theory (Neumann, & Morgenstern, 2007) regarding protectionism and showed that the best outcomes are possible only when both the countries were free. Japan always looks for global business opportunity by pursuing its own principles, utilizing Official Development Assistance (ODA) (Jain, 2017), Infrastructural Development, political and Historical Affiliations, Partnerships and Cultural exchanges as tools for economic and political objectives across the world, taking advantages in cost, taxation, market penetration and distribution. Japan usually looks for Least Developed and developing countries as partners and uses financial affluence and technical competence as tools for supremacy.

DOI: 10.4018/978-1-7998-5774-7.ch013

India is one of the largest economies of the world that Japan has a complementary demographic profile for Japan, Mullen & Arora (2017), cultural and economic bonding and shared sense of togetherness and strong diplomatic relations (Raghuramapatruni & Latha, 2020). The prehistoric relationship since 6 AD has evolved through many upheavals and influenced by many factors like: political values, interests, strategic convergence, geopolitical considerations, Pajon & Mezard (2018). Economic co-operation dominates the mutual relationship, Raghuramapatruni & Latha, (2020) which could reach such stage only after bilateral trade became one of the priorities of India's Look East Policy fifty years after forming the bilateral relations, Reddy, (2014). Although, Shinzo Abe underscored in his book, *Utsukushii kuni e (Towards a Beautiful Country: My Vision for Japan)* (Abe, 2006), that he would not be surprised to observe that if "in another decade, Japan–US and Japan–China ties are overtaken by Japan–India relations" but the trade relationship is dominated by declining/low trade intensity (Raj & Ambrose, 2014) Raghuramapatruni & Latha,(2020)and higher trade potential, Naoki Ono, (2014). Various JETRO publications exhibit Japanese trade and investment preferences for India, although "developing countries provide same resources" Qian et. al., (2008). Kaura suggested to boost the bilateral economic relationship to further strengthen India- Japan ties and India's engagement and the balancing of and vibrancy with all the actors Japan, China and USA (Kaura, 2016) while Singh(2016), attributed the continuous engagement for transforming the bilateral relationship. Joseph & Bera, (2011) identified substantial increase in Japanese FDI which, could cater the FDI requirements of India, Raghuramapatruni, (2012),but need to be diverted into more broad-based market, Atrey, (2014) since Japan invested mostly into the automobile and the electronics sector while Japanese aid facilitated infrastructure development of health, water and sanitation, Choudhury (2017). Enhanced connectivity and understanding could help macro level benefits of the CEPA in terms of trade, investment, and technology flows (Chanda & Tokas, 2020) thereby which could offer several opportunities like: increased cross-border and global market engagements and market entry mechanisms such as strategic alliances, subsidiaries, joint ventures etc. (Ramachandran & Gokila, 2012). Horimoto (Horimoto,2016) believed that, Enhanced and effective Japan-India bilateral relationship is essential against Asian power shift which, will achieve most of their strategic objectives except the guarantee of military assistance in war, Mukherjee, (2018) exemplified by state level reluctance to forming any permanent group like, Democratic security diamond (DSD) (Lee & Lee, 2016). Many researchers found that the relation in Asia Pacific rather than strategic is based on purely economic needs which particularly trade relations have for long been ignored in Japan India bilateral relationship, noticeably through bilateral Trade Balance, Technology Transfer, India's Market Creation and Slow economic revival with the support of Japan. Therefore, it is essential to explore the history, catalysts and constraints of Japan India Trade relation and look for the future scopes and opportunities for cherishing the relationship.

This chapter is structured as follows: After the introduction background literature discusses the history of Japan India Trade relations followed by the chapter objective and the key questions answered throughout the chapter. After that the methods are presented followed by presentation of the main focus of the chapter. The main focus includes an over view of Japan India Trade, Catalysts, Challenges, followed by discussion, future research direction and conclusion.

BACKGROUND

Japan and India have got historic (since 6th AD), economic, trade, diplomatic, strategic, and cultural relations. The legacy of religious, cultural, scholastic relationship (figure 3) and Japan's historic indebtedness to Indian Justice (Justice Radhabinod Pal and the Tokyo Tribunal, n.d.); politics and trade guided the evolution of the relation. British India accounted for 10-15 percent till 1937 and 2-4 percent of Japan's total trade till 1965 (Kojima, 2014) subjected to Japan's Political stance and East Asia Centricity. The economic relationship has been dominated by ODA since 1958 (which was used to impose state level sanctions at times), FDI, trade and number of Japanese companies in India. Japanese ODA helped improve Indian critical infrastructure in: transport, water, energy and forestry & agriculture (Kaura, 2016) while Japan became a key investor in major projects of India (DIPP, 2017). The period 2000-2015 observed a rise in FDI inflow ($18.81 billion), number of companies and ODA Loan(1,934 billion yen from 2003-2013) and additional Investment of 3.5 trillion Yen through Investment Promotion Partnership in: Skill, infrastructure, connectivity, transport, energy, food and water, Urban and Rural Development, river rejuvenation and manufacturing (Kaura, 2016). Besides, China centric risk factors and regional, global politics and disasters; made India an attractive partner to diversify and strengthen economic and political relationships, Raghavan (2013). The Chapter therefore, aims to explore Japan India Trade relation from the perspectives of history, catalysts and challenges and explore the future scopes for the relationship.

OBJECTIVES

The overall objective of the chapter is to know the catalysts and impediments and recommend the future course of action for Japan India Trade Relations. More specifically, the chapter aims at collecting information pertaining to:

- The History of Japan- India Trade Relations
- The Rationale and Catalysts Influencing the growing Trade Relations of Japan and India and
- The Impediments in Furthering the Japan- India Trade Relations

RESEARCH QUESTIONS

The chapter will attempt to answer the following research questions:

- What is the history of Japan- India trade relations?
- What are Catalysts for accelerating the trade relations?
- What are the impediments of furthering the trade relations?

METHODS

The chapter aims to explore both qualitative and quantitative data from various secondary literature, namely: books, journals, reports, statistics, business reports, discussions, and websites affiliated with

Japan, India, ASEAN, Global Organizations like: World Bank, World Trade Organization(WTO), Japan External Trade Organization(JETRO), Academia, Think Tank etc. The data collected and generated have been analyzed using thematic approach, which is recognized as the most common (Guest, 2012, p. 11) and the foundational (Holloway & Todres, 2003) method of analysis of qualitative data. The method emphasized on the content of a text, 'what' is said more than 'how' it is said, the 'told' rather than the 'telling' (Riessman, 2006). The categories and analytical codes have been drawn in alignment with the objectives set. The research questions and conceptual framework had generated an initial start list of analytical codes, which were developed during data analysis. Themes were patterns across data sets that were important to the description of a phenomenon. The themes became the categories for analysis (Fereday & Muir-Cochrane, 2006). Triangulation permitted the search for convergence and divergence in the multiple sources of information gathered in order to develop and confirm (or disconfirm) the analytic themes (Creswell, 2003). The study followed ethical guidelines given by Berg (Berg, 2001) and (Miles & Huberman, 1994) in case of necessity.

MAIN FOCUS OF THE CHAPTER

Japan

Globally, Japan ranks third in gross domestic product (GDP), GDP(PPP) of $4.96 trillion(1% growth rate in 2018), fourth in purchasing power and GDP per Capita (PPP): $43,118 (Japan - Market Overview, 2019). The country ranks third in global import and export, 98th in trade balance and 30th free economy and first in global economic complexity ranking. Currently the country follows Abenomics 2.0 unifying expansive fiscal policy, monetary easing, structural reform, low corporate taxes, increased wages and consumption aiming to boost corporate activities and productivity and drive innovation and trade.

Japan's Demography and Business Prospects

Japan is an aging society (Japan - Market Overview, 2019) with a median age of 47.3 years (Japan: Reaching the Consumer, 2020). The services that would be necessary in Japan are: Pharmaceuticals, Healthcare, Healthcare IT, Biotechnology, Safety products and services, Robotics, Leisure and travel, Educational, Home delivery and financial services. The Japanese are renowned for their brand loyalty due to Quality standards and service expectations, which is subject to recession that compelled them to compromise and popularized the discount or reduction sales, discount stores and own-label products.

Trade: Agreement, Partner and Import and Export

Japan is a major producer, exporter, and importer (fifth) of diversified goods and technologies. Its principal imports include petroleum, liquid natural gas, electrical, industrial, and medical equipment mainly supplied from China, the United States, Australia, South Korea, and Saudi Arabia through various agreements and partnerships. Currently, there have been 18 Partnership or Trade Agreement(FTA) in force (WTO | Regional trade agreements, n.d.) or signed with: Singapore, Mexico, Malaysia, Chile, Thailand, Indonesia, Brunei, ASEAN, Philippines, Switzerland, Viet Nam, India, Peru, Australia, Mongolia, TPP12 (signed), TPP11 and European Union(EU). Japanese import and export in between 2004 and 2018, according to figure 1, shows a growing trend with a positive ratio and usually more than 1. The average annual export was 692488275 thousand USD and the average import was 683037135 thousand USD. Based on the ratio analysis it can be seen that the average ratio of export and import was 1.03.

Figure 1. Japan's Import and Export 2004-2018
Source: Author's Contribution Based on the JETRO Data

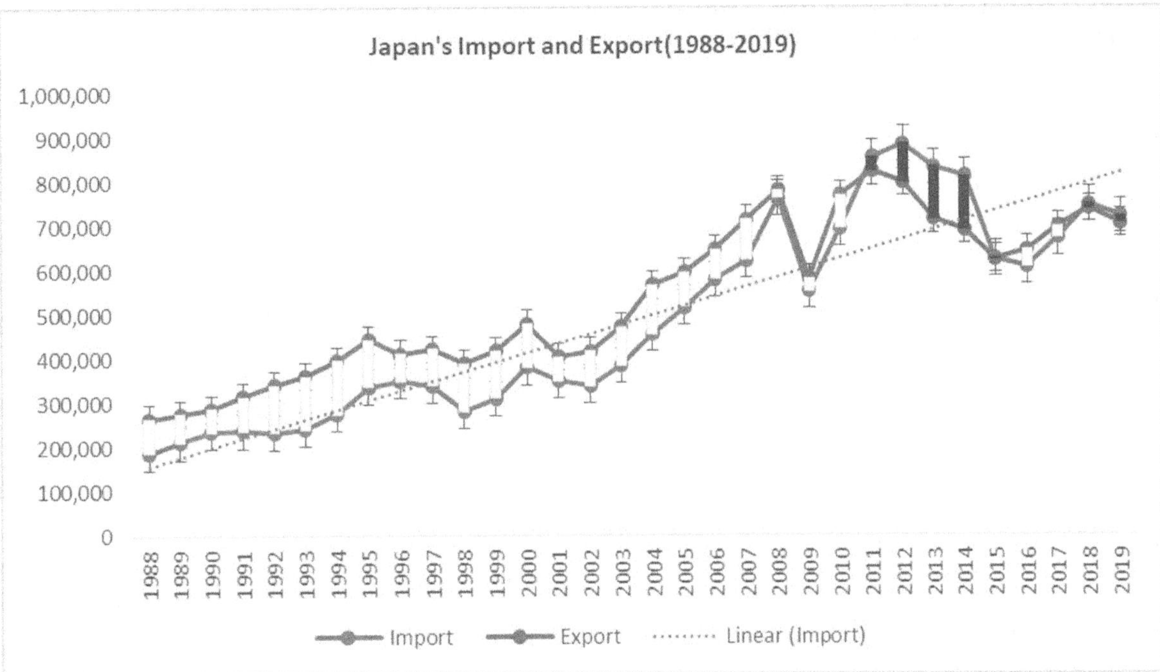

India

India is a densely populated South Asian country with a median age of 28.4(India - median age of the population 1950-2050 | Statista, 2015). The country has a GDP of $2.8 trillion, (5th Globally) (*The RCEP Conundrum: Japan Awaits India's Return*, n.d.), GDP growth rate 6.8%, GDP per capita (US$) 2054.8 USD, Consumer Price Index 180 in 2020 (United Nations, 2021).

India's Trade: Agreement, Partner and Import and Export

India is a major global producer, exporter, and importer of a diverse range of goods and technologies. India (International Trade Administration, 2020) actively engages in regional and bilateral trade negotiations to diversify and expand in export markets while ensuring access to the raw materials, intermediates, and capital goods needed to stimulate value-added domestic manufacturing. Presently, India shares preferential market access and economic cooperation through trade agreements with over 50 other countries. Currently there are 17 trade agreements in force (WTO | Regional trade agreements, n.d.). The major bilateral and regional agreements that India currently has are: Asia Pacific, India ASEAN, Global System of Trade Preferences, South Asia, Sri Lanka, Malaysia, Singapore, Japan, Korea, Bangladesh, China, Lao PDR etc The import and export data of India presents an average export per year of 177652.23 million USD and average import was 262664.97 million USD. Based on the ratio analysis it can be seen that the average ratio of export and import was 1.48. The following figure represents the trend of export and import of Japan in between 1996 and 2021.

Figure 2. India's Import and Export 1996-2021
Source: Author's Contribution Based on the Government of India's Data

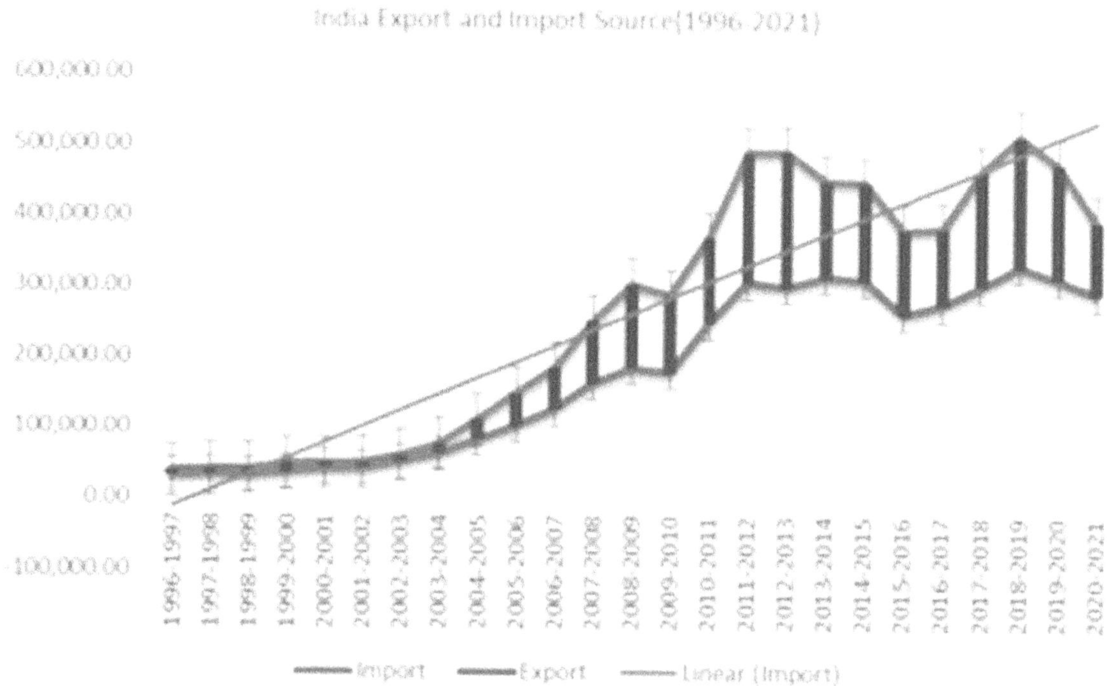

Multitude of Japan India Relations

Although the relationship evolved on necessity but was subjected to multi-faceted circumstantial realities like: politics, culture, policy and diplomacy where trade and economic relation became the main instrument of carrying the relation forward. Trade started with Iron Ore was diversified later and the economic engagement increased with the disbursement of ODA from 1958. A history of friendship and interdependence is likely to develop a very strong economic relation in which the stake holders always stay in a Win-Win situation and support each other in case of need and strive hard to achieve the common pursuits. Japan's bilateral trade with India, totaled US$ 17.63 billion in FY 2018-19. Exports from Japan to India during this period were US$ 12.77 billion and imports were US$ 4.86 billion. The bilateral trade between India and Japan for FY 2019-20 (April - December) totaled to US$ 11.87 billion. India's exports from Japan amounted to US$ 3.94 billion while India's import from Japan amounted to US$

7.93 billion. (Ministry of External Affairs, Government of India, 2020). Therefore the interconnection of various factors with the bilateral trade and economic relation has been shown in, figure 3.

Figure 3. Trajectory of Japan India Relations
Source: Author's Contribution Based on the JETRO Data

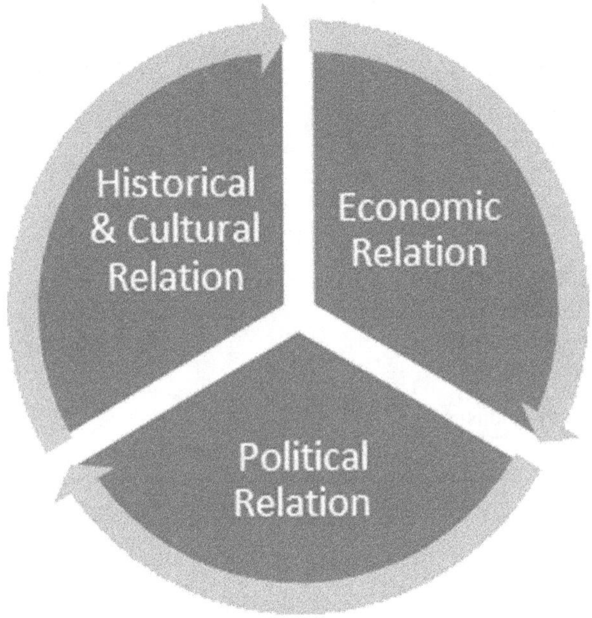

Rostow's Economic Growth Model: Complementarity and Statistics of Japan India Trade

Based on Rostow's Economic Growth Model, Rostow & Rostow, (1990) Japan is at the top: High Mass Consumption while India is still in the third, Take Off Stage. India currently can be featured as fastest-growing middle-class and politically volatility which offered complementarity and risk factor for Japanese

Table 1. Japan India Trade

Japan India Trade, Import and Export:2005-2019										
Year	Total Trade, Yen(Bn)	Japan to India	% of Total Trade	India to Japan, Yen(Bn)	% of Total Trade	Intercountry Trade Gap	Gap % of total Trade	Favourable Situation	Change in Gap	Increase or Decrease
2005	740	388	52.44	352	47.57	36	4.87	Japan	-10	Decrease
2006	990	518	52.33	472	47.68	46	4.65	Japan	10	Increase
2007	1214	723	59.56	491	40.45	232	19.12	Japan	186	Increase
2008	1363	819	60.09	544	39.92	275	20.18	Japan	43	Increase
2009	939	591	62.94	348	37.07	243	25.88	Japan	-32	Decrease
2010	1289	792	61.45	497	38.56	295	22.89	Japan	52	Increase

Figure 4. Rostow's Growth Model
Source: Ministry of Foreign Affairs, Japan (MOFA, 2021)

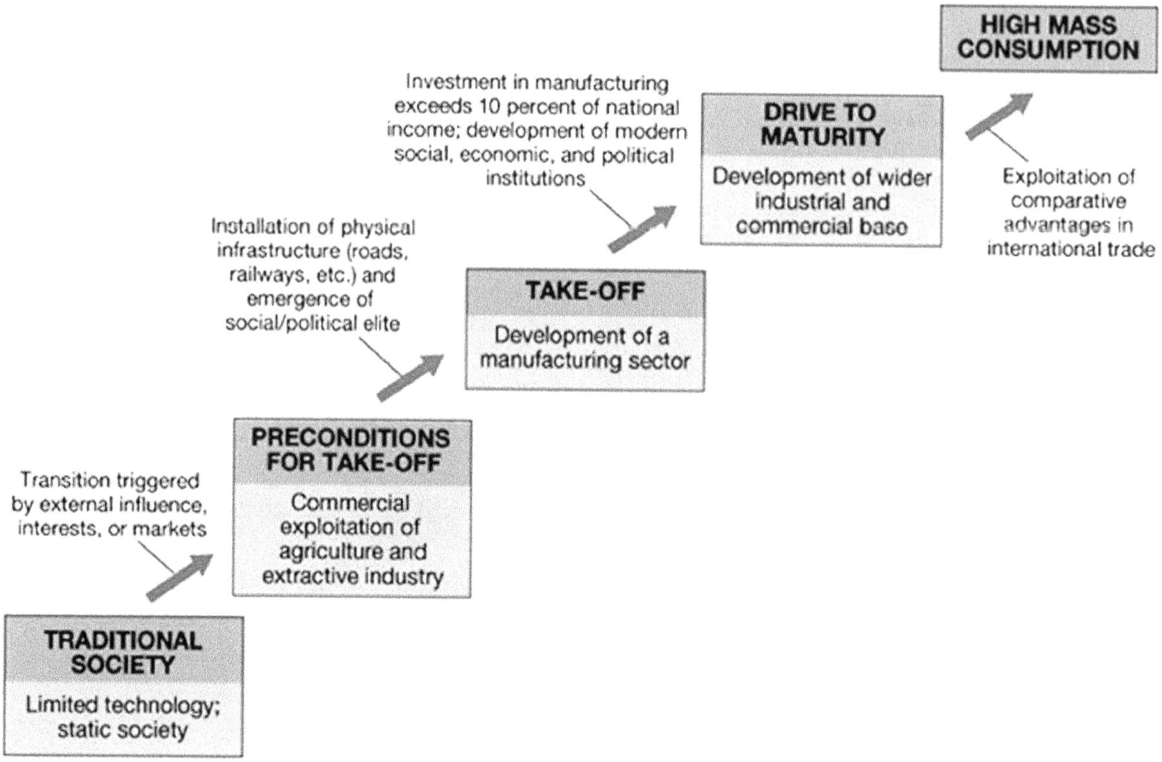

Trade, which with the advent of Japan India Comprehensive Economic Partnership Agreement (CEPA) at the same time resulting varied number and investment pattern of firms across states and volume of inter country trade. Table-1 shows the trade in between the countries observed a steady growth from 2005 to 2019 except 2015 and 2016. It also shows that there have also been a negative trade balance for India.

Traded Goods

Currently, India's primary exports to Japan are: petroleum products, chemicals, elements, compounds, non-metallic mineral ware, fish & fish preparations, metalliferous ores & scrap, clothing & accessories, iron & steel products, textile yarn, fabrics and machinery etc. India's primary imports from Japan are machinery, electrical machinery, iron and steel products, plastic materials, non-ferrous metals, parts of motor vehicles, organic chemicals, manufactures of metals, etc. (Ministry of External Affairs, Government of India, 2020). Figure 5 and Figure 6 represent the trade potential of Indian and Japanese products.

Figure 5. Trade Potential of Indian Goods to Japan

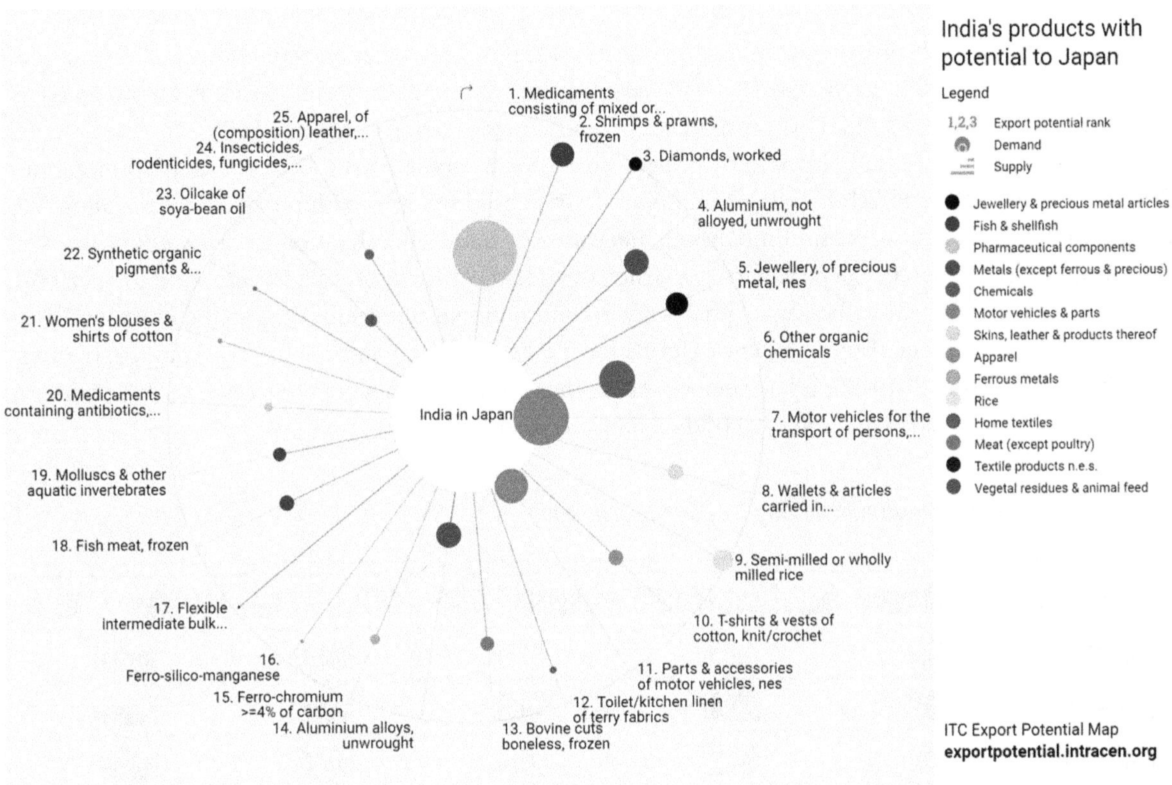

Figure 6. Trade Potential of Indian Goods to Japan
Source: ITC Database

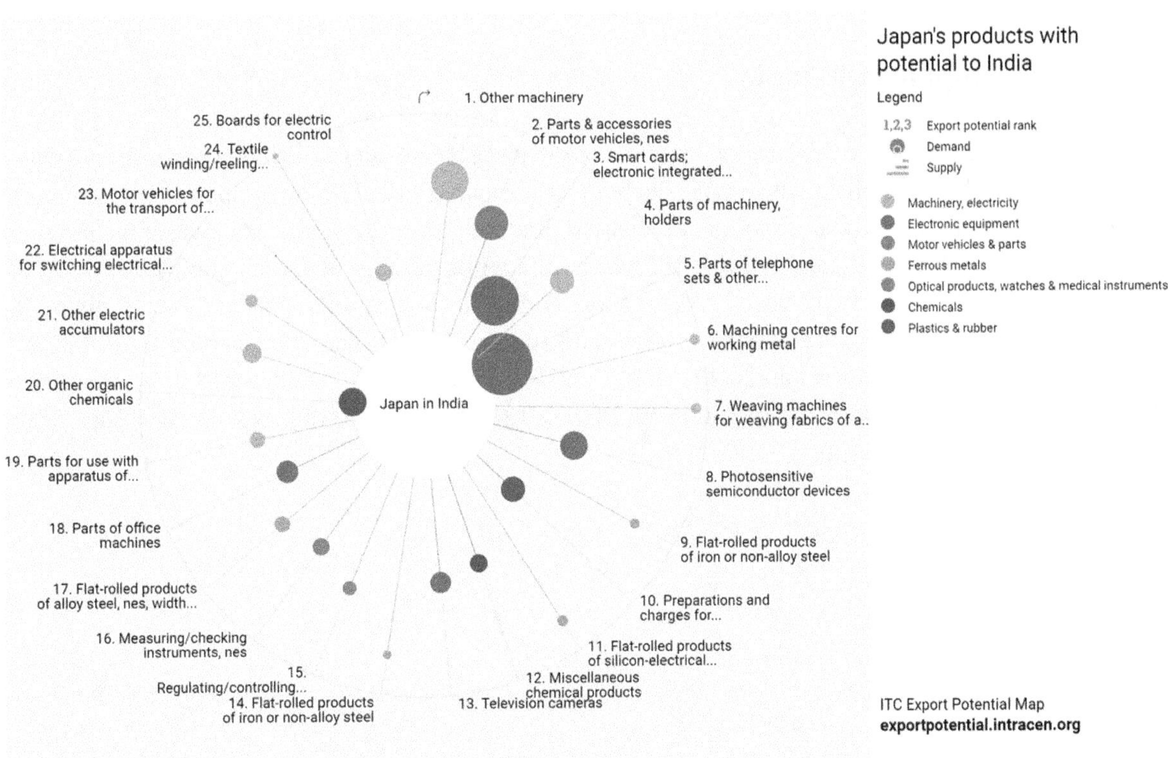

Trade Agreements and their Impact

Economic growth takes place when, liberalization of trade promotes efficiency of allocation of resources to productive uses, exploitation of scale economies, encourages competition, increases factor productivity and increases trade flows, thereby, promoting economic growth, Barro, et. al., (1995). In August 2009 in the culmination of India's 'Look East Policy' an FTA was signed with ASEAN, ratified in August 2011. Between 2010 and 2012, India-ASEAN trade increased by 30% with prospects of reaching $70 billion in 2012. In spite of instituting various measures of trade liberalization in many countries, still there remain some country-specific barriers, which impede the growth of world trade, Kalirajan, (1999). Trade agreements undoubtedly impact positively on international trade subjected to the terms and conditions of the agreement. Table 2 below exhibits the Trade with 10 countries having Trade Agreement with India in the year 2019-20. It has been observed that India has got a negative trade balance with six countries including Japan and the total trade balance is also negative.

Table 2. Trade with Countries having Trade Agreement

FTA/EPA/CEPA	Year of Enforcement	India's Exports FY2019-20	India's Import FY2019-20	Total Trade FY2019-20	Trade Balance FY2019-20
India-Nepal	1999	7160.35	711.61	7871.96	Positive
India-Sri Lanka	2000	3800.91	903.69	4704.6	Positive
India-Afghanistan	2003	997.58	529.84	1527.42	Positive
India-Singapore	2005	8922.66	14746.78	23669.44	Negative

Source: Author, Based on (India's Current Engagements in RTAs, & GOVERNMENT OF INDIA, Ministry of Commerce, 2020)

Japanese Companies in India

JETRO (JETRO, 2021) stated that: the total number of Japanese business establishments in India is 4,948, with a decrease of 74 establishments (1.5% decline) as compared to 5,022 in October 2019. Although the number of Japanese Companies in India increased gradually over the years, in six years the number of companies grew four times and became 1455 from 267 while number of Indian companies working in Japan has surpassed 100. In the year 2020, Japanese companies were established in 19 states out of 28 states and about 99% of the total companies were established in 11 states namely: Haryana 412(28.32%), Maharashtra 250(17.19%), Karnatak220(15.13%), Tamil Nadu200(13.75%), Delhi 145(9.97%), Rajasthan 49(3.37%), Uttar Pradesh 46(3.17%), Gujarat 39(2.69%), Telangana 30(2.07%), West Bengal 26(1.79%) and Andhra Pradesh 18(1.24%).

Table 3. Japanese Companies in India: Number and State wise Distribution

Number of Japanese Companies in India						
Year	**Number of Companies**	**Increase YOY**	**Increase from Base Year**	**YOY Change %**	**% Increase from Base**	**Direction of Change**
2006	267					
2007	362	95	95	35.59	35.59	Increase
2008	550	188	283	51.94	106	Increase
2009	627	77	360	14	134.84	Increase
2010	725	98	458	15.63	171.54	Increase
2011	812	87	545	12	204.12	Increase
2012	926	114	659	14.04	246.82	Increase
[illegible]	[illegible]	[illegible]	[illegible]	[illegible]	[illegible]	[illegible]

Source: The authors Contribution based on Ministry of Foreign Affairs, Japan (MOFA, 2021)

Table 4. Japanese Companies in India: Number and State wise Distribution

Statewise Distribution-Japanese Companies in 2020		
State	**Number of Companies**	**% of Total Number**
Haryana	412	28.32
Maharashtra	250	17.19
Karnataka	220	15.13
Tamil Nadu	200	13.75
Delhi	145	9.97
Rajasthan	49	3.37
Uttar Pradesh	46	3.17
Gujarat	39	2.69
Telangana	30	2.07
West Bengal	26	1.79
Andhra Pradesh	18	1.24
Kerala	9	0.62
Punjab	3	0.21
Jharkhand	2	0.14
Odisha	2	0.14
Madhya Pradesh	1	0.07
Goa	1	0.07
Dedra and Nagar Haveli	1	0.07
Uttarakhand	1	0.07
Total	**1455**	**100**

Source: The authors Contribution based on Ministry of Foreign Affairs, Japan (MOFA, 2021)

Figure 7. Japanese Companies in India: Number and State wise Distribution
Source: The authors Contribution based on Ministry of Foreign Affairs, Japan (MOFA, 2021)

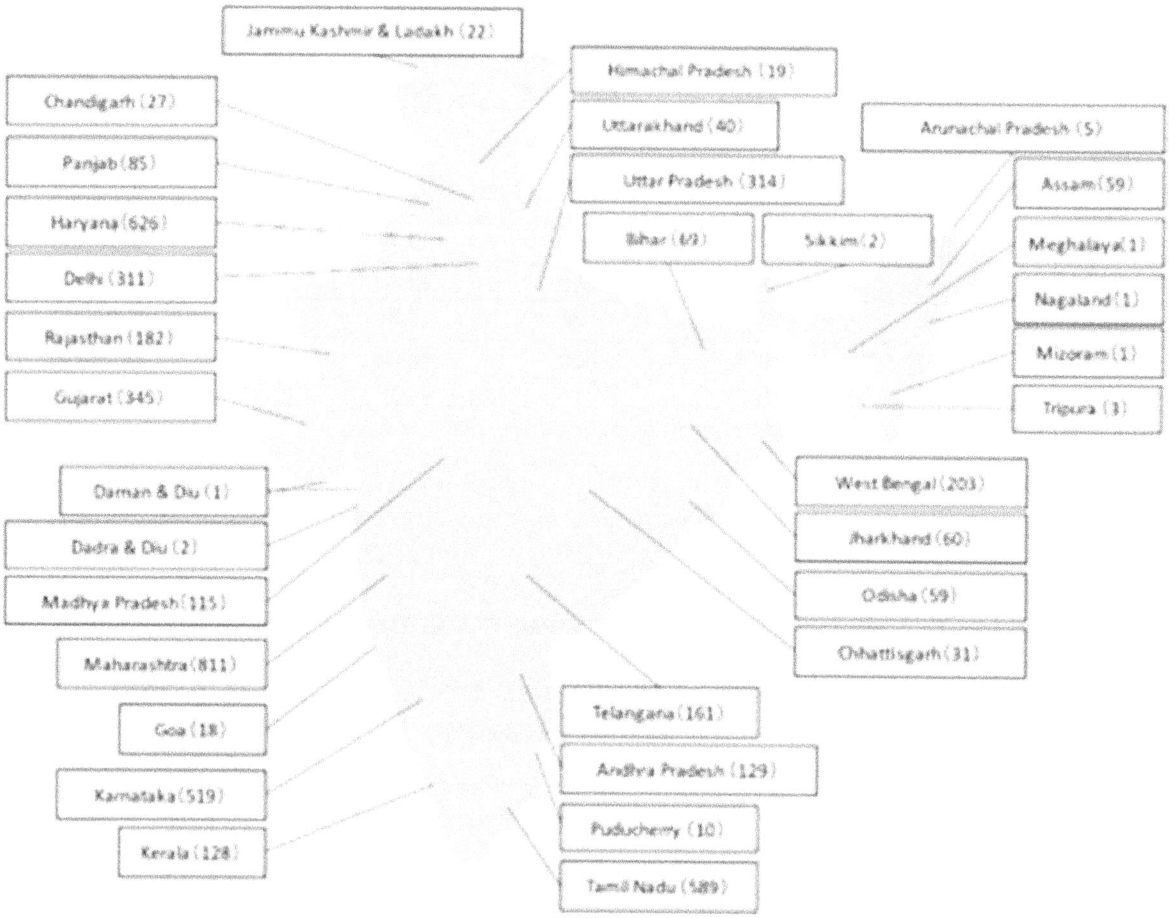

Merger and Acquisition

Scope of expansion, Risk and opportunity diversification, avoidance of competition, Industries and geographical locations, cost of production, acquisition of market share, production facility etc. are a few common causes of Merger and Acquisition. Japanese companies are also increasing in number in India instead of the long held challenges and risk factors like: infrastructure, bureaucracy, lack of information, delay in services, lack of consistent data and different work culture competing with their Korean rivals. Table 5 provides information on the Merger and Acquisition by the Japanese Firms in India.

Figure 8. mM&A in India 2015-2020
Source: (M&A Statistics by Countries - Institute for Mergers, Acquisitions and Alliances (IMAA), 2016) and(Japanese investments in India are poised for a boom, 2021)

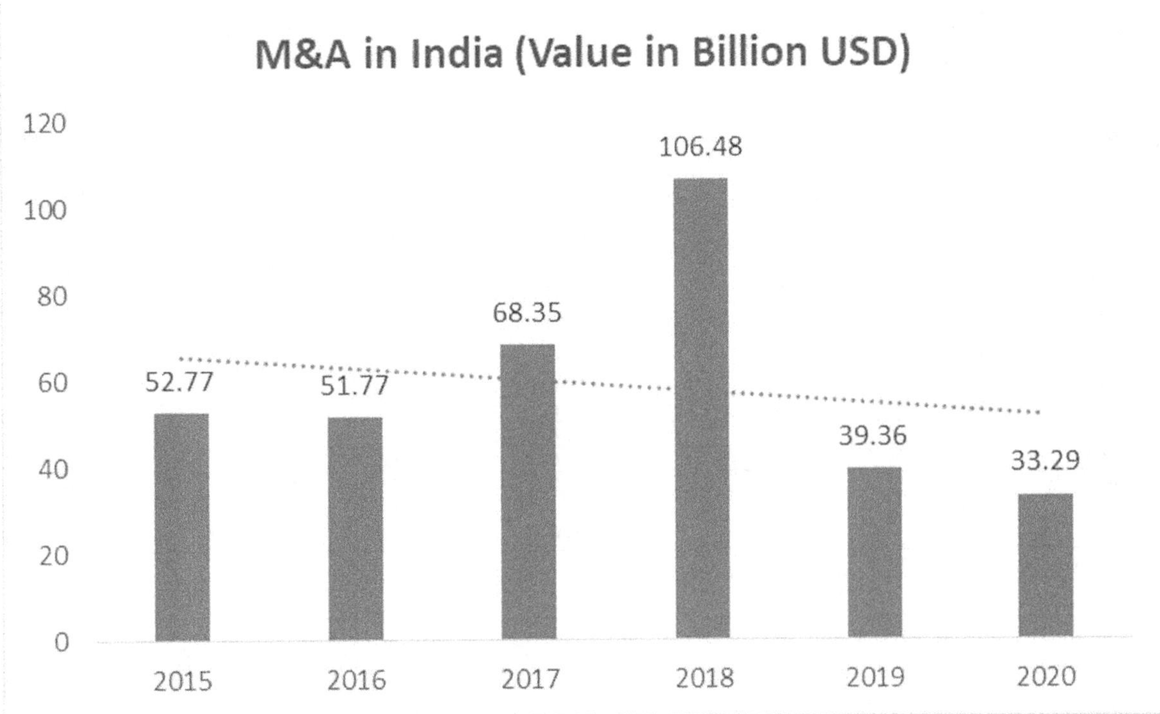

Foreign Direct Investment (FDI)

Cumulatively, from 2000 to 2016 total investment in India have been around US$ 424 billion. During FY 2015-16 and FY 2016-17, Japanese FDI to India increased from US$ 2.61 billion to US$ 4.7 billion,

Table 5. FDI Inflow in India (2000-2016)

FDI Inflow in India (2000-2016)							
Year	FDI ($ million)	Net Change	Net Change from the Base Year	% of Net Change(YOY)	% of Net Change from the Base Year(Base Year)	% of Net Change(YOY)2	% of Net Change from the Base Year(Base Year)3
2000-01	$4,029						
2001-02	$6,130	$2,101	$2,101	52.15	52.15	Increase	Increase
2002-03	$5,035	($1,095)	$1,006	-17.87	24.97	Decrease	Increase
2003-04	$4,322	($713)	$293	-14.17	7.28	Decrease	Increase
2004-05	$6,051	$1,729	$2,022	40.01	50.19	Increase	Increase
2005-06	$8,961	$2,910	$4,932	48.1	122.42	Increase	Increase
2006-07	$22,826	$13,865	$18,797	154.73	466.55	Increase	Increase
2007-08	$34,843	$12,017	$30,814	52.65	764.81	Increase	Increase
2008-09	$41,873	$7,030	$37,844	20.18	939.3	Increase	Increase
2009-10	$37,745	($4,128)	$33,716	-9.86	836.84	Decrease	Increase
2010-11	$34,847	($2,898)	$30,818	7.68	764.01	Decrease	Increase

Source: Ministry of External Affairs, India

Table 6. Investment from Japan to India

Japanese FDI in India(2001-2019)						
Year	Amount of Investment in Yen Billion	Net Change(YOY)	Net Change from the Base Year	% of Change	% Change from the Base Year	Direction of YOY Change
2001	18.4					
2002	18.7	0.3	0.3	1.64	1.64	Increase
2003	14.6	-4.1	-3.8	-21.93	-20.66	Decrease
2004	15	0.4	-3.4	2.74	-18.48	Increase
2005	29.8	14.8	11.4	98.67	61.96	Increase
2006	59.7	29.9	41.3	100.34	224.46	Increase
2007	178.2	118.5	159.8	198.5	868.48	Increase
2008	542.9	364.7	524.5	204.66	2850.55	Increase
2009	344.3	-198.6	325.9	-36.59	1771.2	Decrease
2010	241.1	-103.2	222.7	-29.98	1210.33	Decrease
2011	181	-60.1	162.6	-24.93	883.7	Decrease
2012	223	42	204.6	23.21	1111.96	Increase
2013	210	-13	191.6	-5.83	1041.31	Decrease
2014	282	72	263.6	34.29	1432.61	Increase
2015	369	87	350.6	30.86	1905.44	Increase
2016	564	195	545.6	52.85	2965.22	Increase
2017	357	-207	338.6	-36.71	1840.22	Decrease
2018	387	30	368.6	8.41	2003.27	Increase
2019	624	237	605.6	61.25	3291.31	Increase

Source: Ministry of Foreign Affairs, Japan (MOFA, 2021)

which during FY 2018-19 was US$ 2.96 billion and reached to 3.99 billion for FY 2019-20. (Ministry of External Affairs, Government of India, 2020). Table 5 and 6 provides an overview of FDI inflow to India from the world and Japan respectively.

Recent Collaborations

The recent collaborations of the countries include:

Bilateral and Multilateral Engagement

Besides the bilateral relationship is also complemented by its multilateral engagement through Japan's support of India's acceptance in the East Asia Summit and APEC, Japan's participation in SAARC as an observer and mutual support through supporting each other to the UN Security Council. Besides the relation is also deep rooted through the trilateral engagement of the Indi-Japan and USA in trilateral security dialogues, exercises and the landmark tripartite agreement with Iran and Afghanistan to develop the strategically important Chabahar port in Iran and Japan's investment in the BIG B project of Bangladesh indicates the fostering of a strong relationship among the two countries (Kaura, 2016).

Japanese Projects in India

Japan's projects in India includes mostly infrastructure projects in different states. Figure 9, indicates various undergoing projects financed by JICA in the forms of: Technical Cooperation, Development Study /Technical Cooperation for Development Planning, Loan and Grant Aid. The projects located in Uttar Pradesh, Madhya Pradesh, Bihar, Sikkim, Assam, Meghalaya, Mizoram, Nagaland, Tripura, West Bengal, Jharkhand, Odisha, Andhra Pradesh, Tamil Nadu, Karnataka, Goa, Maharashtra, Gujarat, Rajasthan, Haryana, Himachal Pradesh, Delhi and it's environs, Uttarakhand and All Area/Wide Area Projects. The wide area projects include: Societal Manufacturing, Capacity Development on Highways in Mountainous Regions and Railways, Dedicated Freight Corridor, New and Renewable Energy Development, MSME Energy Saving, PPP Infrastructure Financing and Dairy Development.

Figure 9. Japan's Projects in India
Source: (Activities in India | India | Countries & Regions | JICA, n.d.), 2020

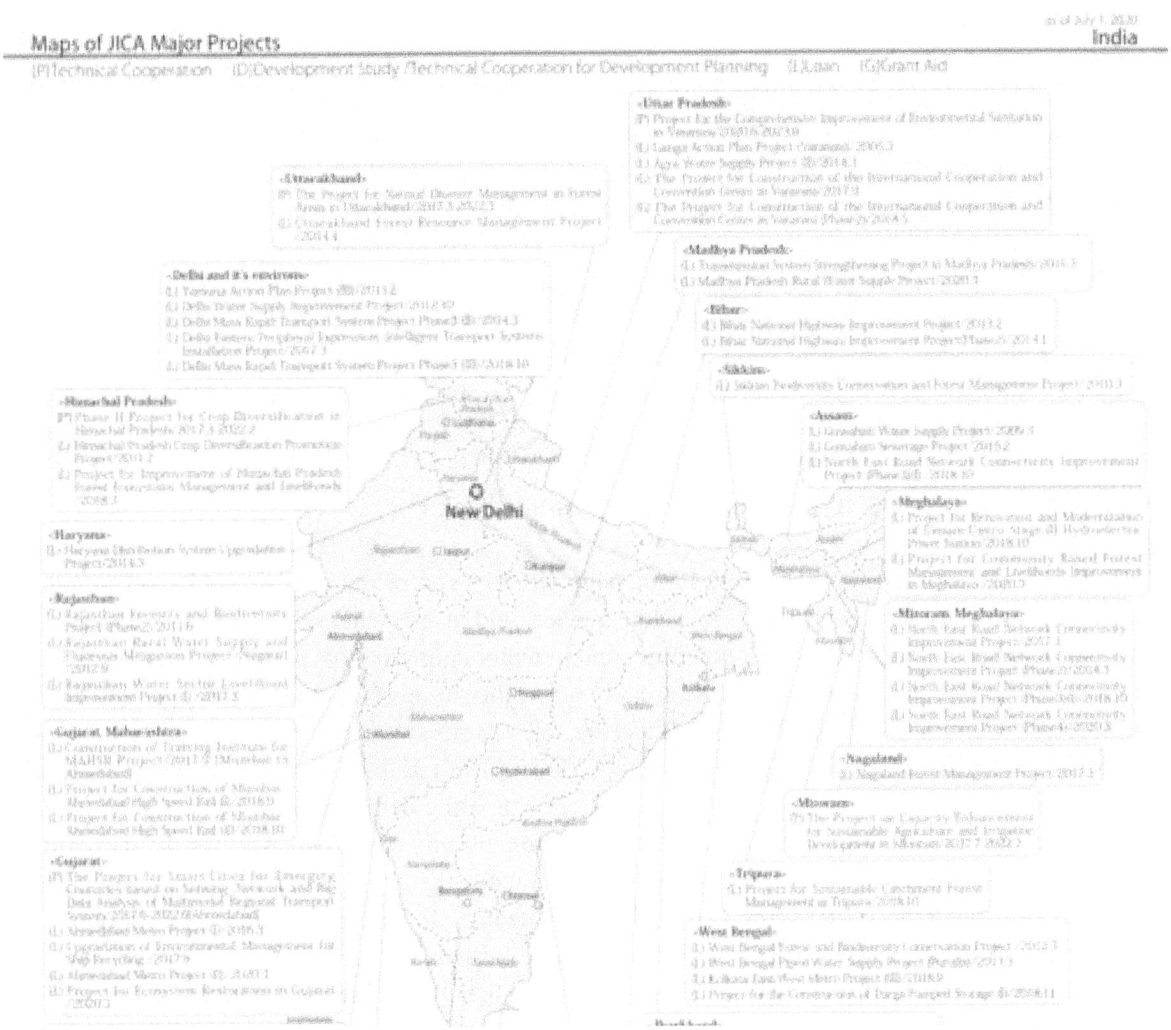

Collaboration and Joint Venture in Research, Human Development and Technology Transfer

India-Japan Digital Partnership (IJDP) and Start-up Hub, the scope of cooperation in S&T/ICT, focusing more on "Digital ICT Technologies", setting up the first Startup Hub in Bangalore by JETRO, Startup-India (under Invest India) and Japan Innovation Network (JIN) signed MOU, cooperation in the field of cyber security, 5G telecommunication infrastructure, and human resource development in ICT sector in third world countries. Besides there have $187 million fund-of-funds programme to invest in Indian Companies working in emerging areas in Science and Technology. MeitY Startup Hub & JETRO signed a partnership agreement to provide a cost free tech. incubation platforms and bringing start-up delegation to Japan for Live Pitching Event with the aim of seeking investors and business partners. The Cabinet Office of Japan and Ministry of Home Affairs of India jointly organized a series of workshops to exchange information on policy and measures and enhance cooperation on disaster risk reduction. Japanese companies have established 12 Japan India Institute of Manufacturing (JIM) in India and 4 Japanese Endowed Courses (JEC) in Indian Engineering Colleges and NSDC completed accreditation of Sending Organizations who will send Technical interns to Japan. Recent Bilateral S&T cooperation initiatives include establishment of three Joint ICT Laboratories in the area of ICT (AI, IoT and Big Data); Initiation of DST-JSPS Researchers Fellowship Programme; MoU for second phase of Indian Beam Line at KEK Tsukuba for advanced materials research Setting up the DBT-AIST Advanced International Laboratory for Advanced Biomedicine (DAILAB) for drug development and therapeutic diseases in India. There are growing links between Japan's Prefectures and States in India through MoUs to cooperate under diverse sectors. Besides there have been significant change in the composition of Indian Community in Japan in recent years with the arrival of a large number of professionals (Ministry of External Affairs, Government of India, 2020).

Regional Comprehensive Economic Partnership (RCEP)

The Regional Comprehensive Economic Partnership (RCEP) comprises a total of 15 member states (Figure 10) who agreed to set new rules on trade, service, and investment and eliminate tariffs on agricultural and industrial products. RCEP does not contain major commitments on labor, the environment, intellectual property, state-owned enterprises, and many other issues (US-ASEAN Business Council | About CPTPP and RCEP, n.d.) while Hinterkoerner, (2020) observed that: China's Dual Circulation Theory could also be applied in RCEP. Horimoto, (2020) suggested that, countries of the Indo-Pacific should share the basic regional principle of multilateralism while democracy should be added as one basic tenet in the FOIP (Chellaney, 2020) and maintain the centrality of the ASEAN (Basu, 2020). Entry into RCEP would increase Japan's GDP and employment while there will be tarrif reduction on certain products both in the import and export. Contrarily, India decided to withdraw from the RCEP due to its limited trade advantage from the RTAs signed (reference: Table 2) and also has got significant amount of trade deficit with the RCEP members (Table 8), although the QUAD partners (who are also in RCEP) wish India to join in the RCEP due to its political, economic, and strategic interests. Apart from missing the Indian companies the chance to join the Asia's economic dynamism driving regional production network (Flake et al., n.d.), India's "Look East" and "Act East" policies might also turn meaningless (*ASEAN's quiet resilience*, 2019). RCEP may also offer incentive to QUAD so long ASEAN members are united on regional geopolitics and restrain from the temptation of market economies (*QUAD vs. RCEP: A Geo-economic Appraisal; By Dr R Srinivasan | C3S India | Chennai Centre for China Studies*, n.d.).

Figure 10. RCEP Members in connection with TPP, CPTPP and ASEAN
Source: Author's Contribution Based on (China, Japan reach breakthrough tariff reduction under RCEP, which products may cost less?, n.d.), GOVERNMENT OF INDIA, Ministry of Commerce, 2020

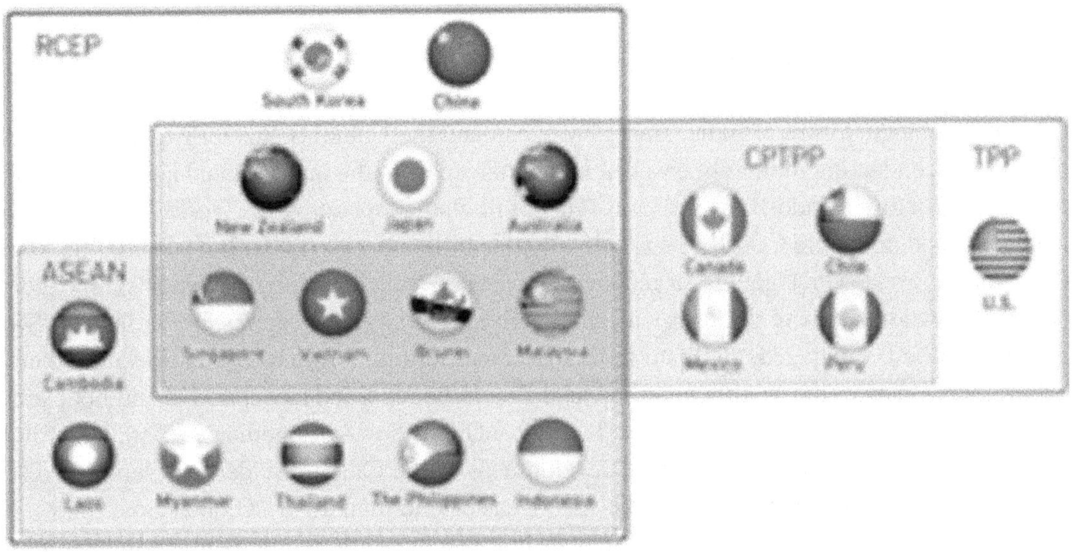

Table 7. India's Trade Balance with the RCEP Countries

RCEP Member Countries	India's Exports FY2019-20	India's Import FY2019-20	Total Trade FY2019-20	Trade Balance FY2019-20
India-Australia	2,952.14	9,782.22	12634.36	**Negative**
India-Brunei	57.62	586.28	643.9	**Negative**
India-Cambodia	188.12	46.69	234.81	Positive
India-China	16,612.75	65,260.75	81873.5	**Negative**
India-Indonesia	4,129.33	15,061.87	19191.2	**Negative**
India-Japan	4,520.25	12434.67	16954.92	**Negative**
India-Lao	25.08	3.09	28.17	Positive
India-Malaysia	6,364.66	9,782.28	16146.94	**Negative**
India-Myanmar	973.89	547.25	1521.14	Positive
India-Newzeland	378.55	521.83	900.38	**Negative**
[illegible]	[illegible]	[illegible]	[illegible]	[illegible]

Asia-Africa Growth Corridor (AAGC)

Asia-Africa Growth Corridor (AAGC) is a joint, participatory, stakeholder co-financed initiative of Japan, India and the African countries where all the stakeholders are equally important. (Panda, 2017). Through its three pillars: synergic vision, investment promotion and joint venture in the third countries the AAGC undoubtedly offers Japan and India a footprint in Africa, supports India to reintegrate East Asia while counterbalancing Chinese influence in the region, Pajon & Mezard (2018).

Quadrilateral Security Dialogue (QUAD)

The Quad is a strategic forum of India, Australia, Japan and the United States for exchanging strategic intelligence and conducting joint military exercises with respect to the international law for a free, open, prosperous and inclusive Indo-Pacific region. They will also cooperate with World Health Organization to develop and distribute COVID-19 vaccines to one billion people in the Indo-Pacific region. The QUAD members invested in Afghanistan and therefore need to reevaluate their priorities. (US withdrawal from Afghanistan deals blow to Quad's security objectives, 2021). Japan aspires for the Japan-US-India triangle to keep the US engaged, facilitate India's rise, and forging a framework enticing to other like-minded partners, Nagao, (n.d.). Although the Quad should be regarded as expansive and not exclusive and should be directed towards a Quad-Plus (Towards a Quad-Plus Arrangement, 2020), but still there is considerable uncertainty about the future development of the Quad provided partners' interest and point of focus. (Expanding Quad to economic sphere easier said than done - Global Times, n.d.). If the QUAD is about the Indo-Pacific therefore without India in the RCEP there is no Indo-Pacific, since the game in East Asia is about economics (Without RCEP, India's Indo-Pacific and North-East Vision Unattainable, n.d.).

Supply Chain Resilience Initiative (SCRI)

The Supply Chain Resilience Initiative is a joint initiative by India, Japan and Australia aimed to enhance supply chain resilience and attain strong, sustainable, balanced and inclusive growth in the Indo-pacific region. The objectives of SCRI are: to attract foreign direct investment, build a mutually complementary relationship among the partner countries and plan to build on the existential supply chain network to reduce their dependence on China (Launch of Supply Chain Resilience Initiative, n.d.) (Mishra, 2021), (QUAD Allies India, Australia & Japan Form A "Supply Chain Shield" Against China's Dominance, 2021). SCRI is likely to enhance Japan India Trade relationship.

Blue Dot Network (BDN)

The Blue Dot Network (BDN) unifies of the USA, Australia and Japan to assist smaller countries in developing internationally certified quality infrastructure to promote investment related transparency. The Blue Dots Network (BDN) actually offers India the opportunity to develop its strategies and be better served by deepening relations with Quad partners (Is Blue Dot Network an alternative to China's BRI?, n.d.). Absence of funding and lack of means to close the global infrastructure are its major set-backs, therefore, Hansbrough,(n.d) suggested it to unify numerous construction and financial vendors to enhance the quality and quantity of global infrastructure investment. Panda, (n.d.), found that India's prospective inclusion in the BDN is a geostrategic necessity which promote alternative global supply chain networks and quality infrastructure in Asia and beyond as well as support to form a "continental connect" through a "Quad Plus" network.

Build Back Better World (B3W) Initiative

Build Back Better World (B3W) is an initiative of G7 states for a values-driven, high-standard, and transparent infrastructure partnership mobilizing private-sector capital in four areas of focus—climate, health and health security, digital technology, and gender equity and equality (The White House, 2021). The initiative has distinct areas of focus; hence, when compared to the BRI, it will share both complementary and competitive equations (Build Back Better World Initiative: A Partnership Against or Beyond China? Manohar Parrikar Institute for Defence Studies and Analyses, n.d.). Since the initiative is taken up by G7 countries wherein the USA and Japan are members and the efforts are dedicated for developing countries where India is a developing country and critical partner for both the USA and Japan therefore it is highly likely for India to be benefitted from the initiative.

Impact of Afghan Crisis

The rise of the Taliban in Afghanistan cast questions and confusions for both Indian(friendship started in 1950, (Chaudhuri & Shende, (2020) and Japanese(friendship began in 1931,P & a, (2021)) investment, security and choices due to risk factors of supply of natural resources, Return on investment and threat from China and Pakistan. India invested USD 3 Billion and developed Human Resources and built roads, dams, power lines, clinics, child care centers, schools, universities and parliament (*What the Taliban takeover of Afghanistan means for India and Pakistan*, 2021). Japan contributed to peace-building, consolidation, and reconstruction providing $6.8 billion assistance (till November 2020) and has pledged to provide $180 million USD annually (P & a, 2021). Therefore, India's examples of boldness beyond the dogma (Kapur, n.d.), necessitate proactive actions since, nertheless the fact of Taliban led Afghanistan, cannot be changed but can be used prudently (Kissinger, 1957) and be vocal to determine essentials for Taliban Government through the UN General Assembly and QUAD summit (Near and present: On the Afghan crisis and India, 2021).

Chabahar Port of Iran

Beyond the economic imperatives of trade and infrastructure, India-Japan cooperation could be a game-changer in the power dynamics of Asia particularly in Chabahar since the countries by the engagement with West Asian states beyond bilateralism, can elevate the level of dialogue and expand strategic cooperation. Japan's participation in the Chabahar port could give India the perfect launch pad for its Indian Ocean ambitions (India-Japan Cooperation on Chabahar Could be a Game-Changer for Asia, n.d.).

The Catalysts of Growth for the Japan-India Trade Relations

The rise of security concern from China, territorial disputes, Japan's vulnerability due to US withdrawal necessitated to forge ties with erstwhile developing but militarily mighty India which was resonated by leadership, foreign policies, complementarity, business attractiveness, cultural affinity, similar aspirations like: UNSC reform, NSG membership, Japan's affluence etc. India's proposition for East Asian Community excluding China and adoption of Look East policies twice and Act East policy (Banerjee & Basu, 2021) to develop strong linkages with the east complemented by Japan's Free and Open Indo Pacific and Revitalization Strategy for using ODA for Economic Infrastructure Financing (Banerjee & Basu, 2021) and resulted into India-Japan Act East Forum in 2017 for developing infrastructure and cultural connectivity projects in India's Northeastern Region (NER) (Ministry of External Affairs, Government of India, 2017). The trade relationship was further fastened by absence of historic dispute or policy issue, Japan's ageism, technological prowess, investible capital, trade diversification, India's rising middle class, demographic dividend, knowledge and services. Besides, a few the 2004 Tsunami in Indonesia, Great Tohuku Earthquake in 2011, severe flooding in Indonesia, possible slowdown of Chinese economy and deficit crisis in Europe necessitated to look for a risk hedge and alternative Choice in the Form of China plus 1 where India became the best Choice. Besides the Collaboration and Joint Venture in Research, Human Development and Technology Transfer, Regional Comprehensive Economic Partnership (RCEP), Asia-Africa Growth Corridor (AAGC), Quadrilateral Security Dialogue (QUAD), Supply Chain Resilience Initiative (SCRI), Blue Dot Network (BDN), Build Back Better World (B3W) Initiative, Impact of Afghan Crisis, Chabahar Port of Iran and Japan's BIG-B and India's BIMSTEC, BBIN and Economic Cooperation centric efforts in Bangladesh have made the countries closer to each other.

Hindrances for the Japan-India Trade Relations

The hindrances of Japan India trade relation entails the followings:

Market Entry

Ease of market entry, market size and diversified demand in Indian market help Japanese Businesses enjoy a lot of advantages while lack of information, market analysis are some disadvantages. On the other hand for the Indian businesses to operate in Japan high standards, higher minimum cost of setting up business, long initial gestation period and slow outcome, limited awareness and contacts limit the potential with Japan also limit the scope of business with Japan.

Japan's Protective Policy

Japan's protectionism for the domestic industries and goods, tariff and non-tariff barriers, higher minimum costs, market entry barriers and the influence of the non-market actors altogether limit the scope of entering the Japanese MARKET. Even if some firms enter or manage to trade with Japan the outcome is so minimal that many businesses end up in dissolution. Japan adopts certain non-tariff barriers to restrain market entry which are shown in table 9, which mentions that Japan adopts a total of 317 non-tariff measures of which the majority are technical measures. Among the technical measures, Sanitary and phytosanitary (SPS) and Technical barriers to trade (TBT) and among the non-technical measures: Price-control measures, including additional taxes and charges are most common.

Table 8. Japan's Non-Tariff Barriers

Technical/Non Technical Measures	UNCTAD Classified Non Tarrif Measures for Import Control	Used By Japan in Import	Number of Measures Adopted By Japan	% of total Measures adopted
Technical Measures	A: Sanitary and phytosanitary (SPS)	Yes	154	48.59
	B: Technical barriers to trade (TBT)	Yes	119	37.54
	C: Pre-shipment inspection and other formalities	Yes	12	3.79
	D: Contingent trade-protective measures	No	0	0
Non Technical Measures	E: Non-automatic licensing, quotas, prohibitions and quantity control measures other than for SPS or TBT reasons	Yes	2	0.64
	F: Price-control measures, including additional taxes and charges	Yes	27	8.52
	G: Finance measures	No	0	0
	H: Measures affecting competition	Yes	3	0.95
	I: Trade-related investment measures	No	0	0
	J: Distribution restrictions	No	0	0
	K: Restrictions on post-sales services	No	0	0
	L: Subsidies	No	0	0
	M: Government procurement restrictions	No	0	0
	N: Intellectual property	No	0	0
	O: Rules of origin	No	0	0
	Total		317	100

Source: Author's Contribution based on open Sources

Setbacks of Japan's Approach to Partnership

Japan is still pursuing the traditional process of bilateral relationship in the form of protectionism, easy and voluminous ODA, FDI, infrastructure development, scholarship to professionals, diplomacy through Japanese studies and's ASEANism or ASEAN centricity sometimes fail to safeguard the best interest of Japan India bilateral relationship particularly by limiting the individual stakeholder's influence and safeguarding of own economy and industry which happened in case of SCRI.

Organizational Capacity, Decision Making and Execution

Opposite to Japan's better organizational capacity, India has a small proportion of management and technical class compared to the huge population and scale of required development and the growth opportunity in the country. In the highly organized Japanese corporate structure, roles and responsibilities are also very fine-grained and hence the culture of consensus-based bottom-up decision-making has also been very effective locally. But the Indian style decisions macro evaluation based top-down faster decision-making but slower execution and balancing with the situational changes.

Homogeneity vs Diversity and Dynamism

Availability of homogeneity driven information in Japan tend Japanese look for too much information and the impossible holistic understanding of diverse and volatile which usually end up in disappointment. On the other hand Indian side gets frustrated with Japanese long decision making process meanwhile, many very worthwhile opportunities are lost.

Predictability vs Volatility

Japan is a highly organized country of precise information and predictability aiding to phenomenal risk reduction and the execution. Contrarily, in India huge diversity and market segmentation make micro level information unavailable and make the averages and aggregates irrelevant. Dynamism and diversity lead to differentiated research outcomes make situations unpredictable for India which force many Japanese Companies to overlook the research and piloting sides of business and ultimately increase their risk while creating own business.

Limited Cultural Exchange and Language Barrier

Limited people, information and cultural Exchange and the language barriers limit the scope of understanding of the culture which also limit the scope of the businesses and lead to differentiated business practices. On the other hand the Japanese reluctance to adopt English as the medium of communication which also limit the scopes of Business.

India's Inadequate Infrastructure and Quality Standards

India has limited critical infrastructure and quality standard for the production system and output quality assurance, therefore, the cost and quality do not match which affect India's bilateral trade. Besides the quality standards are also low which limit their scope to compete with the renowned global brands in Japanese Markets.

DISCUSSION

The rise of China, maritime security challenges in Indian and Pacific Ocean promoted Japan India Bilateral Relationship. Japan always looks for global business opportunity by pursuing its own principles, utilizing Development Assistance, Infrastructural Development, political and Historical Affiliations as tools for taking advantages in cost, taxation, asset transfer and distribution.

Irrespective to the facts and figures, voluminous ODA, FDI, various partnership, bilateral trade, economic, cultural exchange, research and development, joint fund raising or startup ecosystem development, the interests of India is hardly protected. Although the countries are partners in QUAD, SCRI and UNSC reform efforts and are jointly working in Africa, Afghanistan, Bangladesh and Myanmar but the opportunities have not yet been explored sufficiently particularly in trade agreements and trade balance. Besides Japan's protective policy, restraint to market entry in Japan, setbacks of Japan's traditional partnership methods altogether limit the chances of exploring the fullest potential. Besides Japan's too much ASEAN centricity is also a barrier in the bilateral relation because of limiting the influence and interest of individual country. RCEP has predominantly become a 'double edged blade' for India because of the risk of losing market potential and protecting the domestic industries at the same time. On the other hand, India's reluctance has also posed a threat for the QUAD members who won't have a strong justification to remain united for long. Since the relation in Indo Pacific is more economic than strategic and is subjected to volatility and inter-state interdependence where political opponents are commercial allies, there forging a permanent relationship based on rhetoric principles will not sustain long. Besides, although joint effort in countries like: Bangladesh may be supportive but it is important to incorporate the country in QUAD and RCEP and help Bangladesh solve the Rohingya refugee issue with Myanmar for a lasting peace, like mindedness and supportive regionalism.

Challenges

The scope of expanding the trade relationship is curbed by the certain limiting factors described in the subsequent paragraphs:

- Firstly, Japan's trade policy and protectionism to safeguard own interests and the traditional offerings of the so called easy term ODA, Voluminous FDI and market acquisition which if held for long may reduce the interests of the stakeholders.
- Secondly, Japan's too much ASEAN centricity limit the bargaining power and interests of India, which is also a cause of India's unwillingness to join the RCEP.
- Thirdly, Japan's expectation for permanent partnership with the regional powers on the China issue is nearly impossible because of the inter dependence of the countries.
- Fourthly, both the countries invested in Afghanistan(where both are now at stake due to Taliban Occupation), Bangladesh(where public opinion is divided about India or China Question and has disputes with Myanmar on Rohingya issue) are two major challenges since they require long held financial commitments
- Fifthly, The potential domino effects of Afghan crisis through China and Pakistan may limit India's interest in the FOIP and QUAD
- Sixthly, if the efforts like the RCEP, QUAD, QUAD plus, SCRI etc fail to substitute Chinese economic, political and regional influence (particularly for India) in that case the organizations may grow dysfunctional.
- Lastly, Unmet needs of the small regional countries like Bangladesh may sustain the Chinese influence.

OPPORTUNITIES

Japan's management style and application of technology in the larger socioeconomic context has a lot to offer not just to India but to the whole world. Japan's willingness to forge long term relationship with India is an asset. Particularly the case of Afghanistan, Chabahar port of Iran, and Bangladesh issues offer litmus test for the bilateral relations and if well managed in that case can turn out positively for the Japan India construction, logistics and financing companies. The completion of India's mega projects like; DMIC, DFC, industrial townships etc will also have positive outcomes in the relation. Provided that Japan addresses the policy of protectionism and traditional approach of neo mercantilism and India addresses the infrastructural issues, improves product quality, skilled human resources and cultural exchange in that case the businesses may flourish. Business and Economic growth driving regional organizations are also likely to generate positive impact. Therefore it is important both the countries come out of their comfort zones and look at each other more seriously about each other's demonstrated strengths and stability, along with a better understanding of the nature and complexity of business environment and culture.

RECOMMENDATION

The recommendations enlisted here could be helpful for the expansion of the Japan India Trade Relation:

- Completion of India's Mega Projects as Quickly as Possible and enhancing infrastructural support on logistics, backward linkage industry and power supply
- Japan's policy reform on the market entry barriers and adoption of the need based ODA, FDI for India.
- Customizing the traditional Japanese Cultural Diplomacy.
- Growing more openness to mutual interest based non-permanent regionalism
- Policy reform for space, safety, security, social life of the foreigners, VAT, Taxation and Succession Planning, Zero tolerance against corruption, forgery and harassment and relaxed VAT-Tax payment
- Enhancing and sustaining efficiency, effectiveness, linguistic skill of human resources and creating Job, Scope and Opportunity by Partnership, Networking, integration and linkage
- Promotion of wider understanding in between the two cultures and the exchange of knowledge and experiences, building organizational capacities and coming out of comfort zones

FUTURE RESEARCH DIRECTIONS

The study can be applied as a basis of market analysis, demand analysis, for product planning and development, studying regional dynamics for Japan and India. It can also be helpful for Japan's policy reform on the market entry barriers, adoption of the need based ODA, FDI for India, VAT, Taxation and Succession Planning, Zero tolerance against corruption, forgery and harassment and relaxed VAT-Tax payment and enhancing and sustaining efficiency, effectiveness, linguistic skill of human resources and creating Job, Scope and Opportunity by Partnership, Networking, integration and linkage. Besides, it can also be helpful

CONCLUSION

Japan India Trade relationship could not be utilized with fullest potential. Particularly, the interests of India is hardly protected in spite of the growth and changes in the Trade, voluminous ODA, FDI, various partnership, bilateral trade, economic, cultural exchange, research and development. The business and trade relationship in South Asia is not merely trade relation rather is centered on the country specific geopolitical issues like: The rise of China and maritime security challenges in Indian and Pacific Ocean. Therefore, countries like Japan which might be interested to safeguard their vulnerabilities through enhancing various regional engagement like: in QUAD, SCRI, BDN to safeguard national interests and priorities but again they have to consider the requirement of their partners as well. Besides Japan's protective policy, restraint to market entry in Japan, setbacks of Japan's traditional partnership methods, Japan's too much ASEAN centricity also pose certain risk factor for Japan India Trade and Economic Relations. Particularly, pressurizing India to join in the RCEP might backfire because of India's experience with the FTAs and therefore would demand more incentives from Japan. Undoubtedly, the Quality and Compliance standards of Japan is very high, and it is accepted that if a product is successful in Japan, then the product will be successful in any market. But Japan should readjust its focus around mutual interests with India particularly on Afghanistan, Bangladesh and Myanmar due to their investment and rising impact in the region. Particularly, including Bangladesh in QUAD and RCEP will facilitate a sustained Japan India Trade Relation through various complementary regional engagement.

LIMITATIONS OF THE STUDY

The limitation of the study is that it was primarily based on the review of secondary literature and might have been influenced by the subjective judgment of the author.

ACKNOWLEDGMENT

This research received no specific grant from any funding agency in the public, commercial, or not-for-profit sectors. The author is grateful to Department of Japanese Studies and Dhaka School of Economics, University of Dhaka for their guidance, expert opinion and feedback in development of the chapter.

REFERENCES

Abe, S. (2006). *Utsukushii kuni e* [Toward a beautiful nation]. Bungei Shunju.

Activities in India | India | Countries & Regions | JICA. (n.d.). Retrieved September 7, 2021, from https://www.jica.go.jp/india/english/activities/index.html

ANI. (2021, August 18). Afghanistan: Taliban stopped exports, imports from India, says FIEO DG. *Business Standard India*. https://www.business-standard.com/article/news-ani/taliban-stop-exports-imports-from-india-121081801275_1.html

ASEAN's quiet resilience. (2019, December 8). *East Asia Forum*. https://www.eastasiaforum.org/2019/12/08/aseans-quiet-resilience/

Asmussen, C. G. (2014). Strategic factor markets, scale free resources, and economic performance: The impact of product market rivalry. *Strategic Management Journal, 36*(12), 1826–1844. doi:10.1002/smj.2315

Atrey, P. (2014). India-Japan Relations: Economic, Strategic and Security Co-operation. UGC Centre for Southeast Asian & Pacific Studies. D&Dee Publications.

Ayres, A. (2018). *Our time has come: how India is making its place in the world*. Oxford University Press.

Ball, D. A. (2010). *International Business: the challenge of global competition*. McGraw-Hill Higher Education.

Banerjee, S., & Basu, P. (2021, April). India-Japan Partnership in Third Countries: A Study of Bangladesh and Myanmar. *Observer Research Foundation (ORF) Issue Brief*, (460), 3–18.

Barro, R. J., & Sala-i-Martin, X. (1995). *Economic growth*. McGrow-Hill.

Berg, B. (2001). *Qualitative research methods for the social sciences* (4th ed.). Allyn & Bacon.

Build Back Better World Initiative. (n.d.). *A Partnership Against or Beyond China? | Manohar Parrikar Institute for Defence Studies and Analyses*. Retrieved September 3, 2021, from https://idsa.in/issuebrief/build-back-better-world-initiative-jpanda-090821

Chanda, R., & Tokas, K. (2020). *India–Japan Relations in Services & the India–Japan Comprehensive Economic Partnership Agreement*. Academic Press.

Chaudhuri, R., & Shende, S. (2020). *Dealing With the Taliban: India's Strategy in Afghanistan After U.S. Withdrawal*. https://carnegieendowment.org/files/Chaudhuri_Shende_-_Afghanistan.pdf

Chellaney, B. (2020, January 14). Toward an Indo-Pacific concert of democracies. *The Japan Times*. https://www.japantimes.co.jp/opinion/2020/01/14/commentary/japan-commentary/toward-indo-pacific-concert-democracies/#.XrjCI6YVBtU

China, Japan reach breakthrough tariff reduction under RCEP, which products may cost less? (n.d.). https://news.cgtn.com/news/2020-12-01/China-Japan-reach-tariff-reduction-which-products-may-cost-less--VRkd1JKl5S/index.html

Choudhury, S. R. (2017). India–Japan Relations. *International Studies, 54*(1-4), 106–126. doi:10.1177/0020881718791404

Creswell, J. W. (2003). *Research design: Qualitative, quantitative, and mixed methods approaches*. SAGE.

Does Afghanistan Present a New Opportunity for the Quad? (2021, June 17). *Geopolitical Monitor*. https://www.geopoliticalmonitor.com/does-afghanistan-present-a-new-opportunity-for-the-quad/

Eggers, A. J. T. (n.d.). *U.S. Policy in Afghanistan: Changing Strategies, Preserving Gains*. Carnegie Endowment for International Peace. Retrieved August 30, 2021, from https://carnegieendowment.org/2017/05/22/u.s.-policy-in-afghanistan-changing-strategies-preservinggains-pub-70027

Expanding Quad to economic sphere easier said than done - Global Times. (n.d.). Retrieved August 30, 2021, from https://www.globaltimes.cn/page/202105/1223723.shtml

Fereday, J., & Muir-Cochrane, E. (2006). Demonstrating rigor using thematic analysis: A hybrid approach of inductive and deductive coding and theme development. *International Journal of Qualitative Methods*, *5*(1), 80–92. doi:10.1177/160940690600500107

Flake, L., Smith, S., Sambhi, N., Wilson, J., Jaishankar, D., Baruah, D., Lang, D., Padmanabhan, A., & Reddy, M. (n.d.). *Tasks For India's Regional Integration*. https://perthusasia.edu.au/getattachment/Our-Work/Realising-the-Indo-Pacific/PU-24-India-Book-WEB.pdf.aspx?lang=en-AU

Guest, G. (2012). *Applied thematic analysis*. Sage Publications. doi:10.4135/9781483384436

Hansbrough, J. V. (n.d.). *From the blue dot network to the blue dot marketplace: A way to cooperate in strategic*. https://apcss.org/wp-content/uploads/2020/09/11-Hansborough-25thA.pdf

Hinterkoerner, R. (2020, November 17). *QUAD versus RCEP*. Expertise Asia. http://www.expertise-asia.com/2020/11/quad-versus-rcep.html

Holloway, I., & Todres, L. (2003). The status of method: Flexibility, consistency and coherence. *Qualitative Research*, *3*(3), 345–357. doi:10.1177/1468794103033004

Horimoto, T. (2016). *Japan-India Rapprochement and its future issues*. Academic Press.

Horimoto, T. (2020). Indo-Pacific Order and Japan–India Relations in the Midst of COVID-19. *Journal of Asian Economic Integration*, (2), 140–158. Advance online publication. doi:10.1177/2631684620940476

India-Japan Cooperation on Chabahar Could be a Game-Changer for Asia. (n.d.). *The Wire*. Retrieved August 30, 2021, from https://thewire.in/diplomacy/india-japan-cooperation-on-chabahar-could-be-a-game-changer-for-asia

India - median age of the population 1950-2050 | Statista. (2015). https://www.statista.com/statistics/254469/median-age-of-the-population-in-india/

India's Current Engagements in RTAs. (n.d.). *Mcommerce*. Retrieved September 4, 2021, from https://commerce.gov.in/international-trade/trade-agreements/indias-current-engagements-in-rtas/

International Trade Administration. (2020, August 25). *India - Trade Agreements*. Retrieved from International Trade Administration, United States of America: https://www.trade.gov/knowledge-product/india-trade-agreements

Is Blue Dot Network an alternative to China's BRI? (n.d.). *The New Indian Express*. Retrieved September 3, 2021, from https://www.newindianexpress.com/opinions/columns/2021/jun/17/is-blue-dot-network-an-alternative-to-chinas-bri-2317283.html

Japan-US-India Defense Cooperation: Anticipating the US Withdrawal from Afghanistan. (2019, August 19). *The Asan Forum*. https://theasanforum.org/japan-us-india-defense-cooperation-anticipating-the-us-withdrawal-from-afghanistan/

Japanese investments in India are poised for a boom. (2021, January 21). https://www.consultancy.asia/news/3851/japanese-investments-in-india-are-poised-for-a-boom

JETRO. (2021, August 24). *Embassy of Japan.* Retrieved from Government of Japan: file:///D:/ICT-BACKUP/Downloads/2020_co_list_en_pr.pdf

Joseph, M., & Bera, S. (2011). *India-Japan trade and investment relations and their future prospects.* Fore School of Management.

Justice Radhabinod Pal and the Tokyo Tribunal. (n.d.). *The National WWII Museum | New Orleans.* Retrieved September 8, 2021, from https://www.nationalww2museum.org/war/articles/justice-radhabinod-pal-tokyo-war-crimes-trial

Kalirajan, K. (1999). Stochastic varying coefficients gravity model: An application in trade analysis. *Journal of Applied Statistics, 26*(2), 185–193. doi:10.1080/02664769922520

Kapur, M. (n.d.). *A Taliban-led Afghanistan could mean all sorts of problems for India.* Quartz. Retrieved August 30, 2021, from https://qz.com/india/2048396/what-taliban-led-afghanistan-will-mean-for-india/

Kaura, V. (2016). India-Japan Relations and Asia's Emerging Geopolitics. *Indian Journal of Asian Affairs*, 17-35.

Khan, S. (2019). *India-Japan Economic Partnership: Potentials, Promises and Prospects.* https://www.mof.go.jp/pri/international_exchange/visiting_scholar_program/Shamshad2.pdf

Kissinger, H. A. (1957). *Nuclear weapons and foreign policy.* Oxford University Press.

Kojima, M. (2014). The Evolution of Japan-India Economic Relations. In The Rebalance Within Asia: The Evolution of Japan-India Relations (p. 6). Washington, DC: Woodrow Wilson International Centre for Scholars.

Krugman, P. R., & Obstfeld, M. (2010). *International Economics: theory and policy.* Pearson.

Launch of Supply Chain Resilience Initiative. (n.d.). *Drishti IAS.* Retrieved September 3, 2021, from https://www.drishtiias.com/daily-updates/daily-news-analysis/launch-of-supply-chain-resilience-initiative

Lawrence, R. Z., & Krugman, P. (1987). Imports in Japan: Closed Markets or Minds? *Brookings Papers on Economic Activity, 1987*(2), 517. doi:10.2307/2534489

Lee, L., & Lee, J. (2016). Japan-India Cooperation and Abe's Democratic Security Diamond: Possibilities, Limitations and the View from Southeast Asia. *Contemporary Southeast Asia, 38*(2), 284–308. doi:10.1355/cs38-2e

M&A Statistics by Countries - Institute for Mergers, Acquisitions and Alliances (IMAA). (2016). *Institute for Mergers, Acquisitions and Alliances (IMAA).* https://imaa-institute.org/m-and-a-statistics-countries/

Maini, T. S. (2016). *Japan's Effort to Counter China's Silk Road.* The Globalist.

Menon, S. (2016). *Choices: inside the making of India's foreign policy.* Brookings Institution Press.

Miles, M., & Huberman, A. (1994). *An expanded sourcebook: qualitative data analysis.* Sage Publications.

Ministry of External Affairs, Government of India. (2017, December 5). *Launch of India-Japan Act East Forum.* Retrieved from Ministry of External Affairs, Government of India: https://www.mea.gov.in/press-releases.htm?dtl/29154/Launch_of_IndiaJapan_Act_East_Forum

Ministry of External Affairs, Government of India. (2020). *India-Japan_Bilateral_Brief_feb_2020.* Retrieved from Ministry of External Affairs, Government of India: https://mea.gov.in/Portal/Foreign-Relation/India-Japan_Bilateral_Brief_feb_2020.pdf?fbclid=IwAR3MByxRsgiuMZTrflVXFE3ItQx4Wb2Gmhl_2cdmkbzD8kGUN7TJvoVPH7I

Mishra, A. R. (2021, April 27). *India, Japan and Australia unveil supply chain initiative*. Mint. https://www.livemint.com/news/world/india-japan-australia-launch-supply-chain-initiative-to-counter-china-11619532624451.html

MOFA. (2021, August 15). *Region/AsiaPacific/India*. Retrieved from Ministry of Foreign Affairs, Japan: https://www.mofa.go.jp/region/asiapaci/india/index.html

Mukherjee, R. (2018). Japan's strategic outreach to India and the prospects of a Japan–India alliance. *International Affairs, 94*(4), 835–859. doi:10.1093/ia/iiy030

Mullen, R. D., & Arora, K. (2017). *India–Japan brief.* Centre for Policy Research. Retrieved from www.cprindia. org

Nagao, S. (n.d.). *Japan-US-India Defense Cooperation: Anticipating the US Withdrawal from Afghanistan - by Satoru Nagao*. Retrieved September 1, 2021, from https://www.hudson.org/research/15261-japan-us-india-defense-cooperation-anticipating-the-us-withdrawal-from-afghanistan

Near and present: On the Afghan crisis and India. (2021, August 28). *The Hindu*. https://www.thehindu.com/opinion/editorial/near-and-present-the-hindu-editorial-on-the-impact-of-the-afghan-crisis-on-india/article36144643.ece

P, J. (2021, July 25). *Japan's Strategic Choices in Afghanistan | JAPAN Forward*. https://japan-forward.com/asias-next-page-japans-strategic-choices-in-afghanistan/

Pajon, C., & Saint-Mezard, I. (2018). *The Japan-India economic partnership: a politically driven process*. Academic Press.

Panda, J. P. (n.d.). *India, the Blue Dot Network, and the "Quad Plus" Calculus*. Air University (AU). Retrieved August 30, 2021, from https://www.airuniversity.af.edu/JIPA/Display/Article/2278057/india-the-blue-dot-network-and-the-quad-plus-calculus/

Plummer. (2020, November 16). *RCEP: A new trade agreement that will shape global economics and politics*. Brookings. https://www.brookings.edu/blog/order-from-chaos/2020/11/16/rcep-a-new-trade-agreement-that-will-shape-global-economics-and-politics/

Press Release Japanese Business Establishments in India -2020. (n.d.). Retrieved August 29, 2021, from https://www.in.emb-japan.go.jp/PDF/2020_co_list_en_pr.pdf

Qian, G., Li, L., Li, J., & Qian, Z. (2008). Regional diversification and firm performance. *Journal of International Business Studies, 39*(2), 197–214. doi:10.1057/palgrave.jibs.8400346

QUAD Allies India, Australia & Japan Form A "Supply Chain Shield" Against China's Dominance. (2021, April 29). *Latest Asian, Middle-East, EurAsian, Indian News*. https://eurasiantimes.com/quad-allies-india-australia-japan-form-a-supply-chain-shield-against-chinas-dominance/

QUAD vs. RCEP: A Geo-economic Appraisal; By Dr R Srinivasan | C3S India | Chennai Centre for China Studies. (n.d.). Retrieved August 30, 2021, from https://www.c3sindia.org/business-economics/quad-vs-rcep-a-geo-economic-appraisal-by-dr-r-srinivasan/

Quad vs. RCEP: A Resilient Supply Chain, Advantage India? (2021, April 16). *South Asian Voices*. https://southasianvoices.org/quad-vs-rcep-a-resilient-supply-chain-advantage-india/

Raghavan, S. (2013). India as a Regional Power. In W. P. S. Sidhu, P. B. Mehta, & B. Jones (Eds.), *Shaping the Emerging World: India and the Multilateral Order* (p. 64). Brookings Institution Press.

Raghuramapatruni, R., & Latha, D. A. (2020). A study of India's Bilateral Trade with Japan. Humanities & Social Sciences Reviews, 8(4). doi:10.18510/hssr.2020.8435

Raj, P. S., Wing, E., & Ambrose, D. (2014). A brief analysis of India-Japan bilateral trade: A trade intensity approach. *International Journal of Economics, Commerce and Management, 2*(2).

Ramachandran, K. K., & Gokila, R. (2012). International Entrepreneurship—Opportunities and Challenges. In Creativity, Innovation and Entrepreneurship (pp. 21-25). New Delhi, India: Allied Publishers Private Limited.

Reddy, G. J. (Ed.). (2014). *India-Japan Relations: Economic, Strategic and Security Cooperation*. UGC Centre for Southeast Asian & Pacific Studies, Sri Venkateswara University.

Ricardo, D. (1988). *On the principles of political economy, and taxation*. Verlag Wirtschaft Und Finanzen.

Riessman, C. (2006). Narrative analysis. In V. Jupp (Ed.), *The sage dictionary of social research methods* (pp. 186–189). Sage Publications.

Rostow, W. W., & Rostow, W. W. (1990). *The stages of economic growth: A non-communist manifesto*. Cambridge university press.

Schemes | Department for Promotion of Industry and Internal Trade | MoCI | GoI. (2017). http://dipp.nic.in/Schemes/DMIC/

Smith, A. (1776). *An inquiry into the nature and causes of the wealth of nations* (Vol. 1). Cosimo.

The RCEP Conundrum: Japan Awaits India's Return. (n.d.). Retrieved August 30, 2021, from https://thediplomat.com/2021/08/the-rcep-conundrum-japan-awaits-indias-return/

The White House. (2021, June 12). *Fact Sheet: President Biden and G7 Leaders Launch Build Back Better World (B3W) Partnership*. The White House. https://www.whitehouse.gov/briefing-room/statements-releases/2021/06/12/fact-sheet-president-biden-and-g7-leaders-launch-build-back-better-world-b3w-partnership/

Towards a Quad-Plus Arrangement? (2020). *PerthUSAsia*. https://perthusasia.edu.au/our-work/towards-a-quad-plus-arrangement

United Nations. (2021, August 24). *Country profiles*. Retrieved from UN Data: https://data.un.org/default.aspx

US-ASEAN Business Council | About CPTPP and RCEP. (n.d.). *US-ASEAN Business Council*. https://www.usasean.org/regions/tpp/about

Von Neumann & Morgenstern. (2007). *Theory of games and economic behavior*. Princeton University Press.

What the Taliban takeover of Afghanistan means for India and Pakistan. (2021, August 21). *The Economist*. https://www.economist.com/asia/2021/08/21/what-the-taliban-takeover-of-afghanistan-means-for-india-and-pakistan

Without RCEP, India's Indo-Pacific And North-East Vision Unattainable. (n.d.). *Moneycontrol*. Retrieved August 30, 2021, from https://www.moneycontrol.com/news/opinion/without-rcep-indias-indo-pacific-and-north-east-vision-unattainable-7132911.html

WTO | Regional trade agreements. (n.d.). http://rtais.wto.org/UI/publicPreDefRepByCountry.aspx

ADDITIONAL READING

Ahmed, S. (2010). India-Japan FTA in Goods: A Partial and General Equilibrium Analysis. SSRN Electronic Journal. doi:10.2139/ssrn.1708030

Bhattacharya, B. N., & Mukhopadhyay, K. (2015). A comprehensive economic partnership between India and Japan: Impact, prospects and challenges. *Journal of Asian Economics*, *39*, 94–107. doi:10.1016/j.asieco.2015.06.006

Joseph, M., & Bera, S. (2011). *India-Japan trade and investment relations and their future prospects*. Fore School of Management.

Kondo, M. (2012). *Japan-India Economic Relationship: Trends and Prospects*. Research Institute of Economy, Trade and Industry (RIETI).

Masanori, K. (2012). *Japan-India Economic Relationship: Trends and prospects*. Research Institute of Economy, Trade and Industry.

Sato, T. (2012). Economic relations between India and Japan. *Eurasian Geography and Economics*, *53*(4), 457–478. doi:10.2747/1539-7216.53.4.457

KEY TERMS AND DEFINITIONS

Act East Policy: The 'Act East Policy' announced in November, 2014 is and upgrade of the "Look East Policy" and a diplomatic initiative to promote economic, strategic and cultural relations with Southeast Asian countries in the field of connectivity, trade, culture, defence and people-to-people-contact at bilateral, regional and multilateral levels.

ASEAN: The Association of Southeast Asian Nations, or ASEAN, is a group of ten countries of south East Asia, namely: Indonesia, Malaysia, Philippines, Singapore, Thailand, Brunei Darussalam Viet

Nam Lao PDR and Myanmar. It was established in 1967 with four states with a motto of One Vision, One Identity, One Community.

Comprehensive Economic Partnership Agreement (CEPA): The Comprehensive Economic Partnership Agreement was signed in 2011 in between Japan and India with an aim to facilitate trade through tariff reduction for the next ten years but is likely to bring positive impact in Japan India Bilateral Relationship.

Dedicated Freight Corridor (DFC): The Dedicated Freight Corridor (DFC) is the corridor dedicated to carry rail freights at a speed of 100 km/hour through two corridors, the western one in between Haryana and Maharashtra and eastern corridor. The Western Corridor is financed by JICA while the Eastern Corridor is financed by the World Bank and Public Private Partnership (PPP) and the Dedicated Freight Corridor Corporation of India Limited (DFCCIL) oversees the construction of this project.

Delhi Mumbai Industrial Corridor (DMIC): The Delhi Mumbai Industrial Corridor is one of the most prioritized projects of Japan in India. The State sponsored Industrial Development project will cover six state in western India and is estimated to have cost US$ 90 billion that will hopefully double the employment, triple the industrial outputs and quadruple the exports. DMIC development Corporation (DMICDC) works as the Office of Primary Interest (OPI) for the project and coordinates with the Government of Japan on the issue.

Foreign Direct Investment (FDI): A foreign direct investment (FDI) is an investment made by a firm or individual in one country into business interests located in another country. Generally, FDI takes place when an investor establishes foreign business operations or acquires foreign business assets in a foreign company.

Free Trade Agreement (FTA): The Free Trade Agreement is an agreement for tariff free trade with countries. In this system the FTA partners can send their products easily to the partnering country and vice versa. FTA is good for high quality products with minimum price but is not good for the products with premium prices. In this system the richer partner of FTA influences the poorer country by pricing and this system is not conducive for the weaker partner. In case of Japan and India FTA is not helpful India since the economy is poorer.

Japan External Trade Organisation (JETRO): JETRO, or the Japan External Trade Organization, is a government-related organization that works to promote mutual trade and investment between Japan and the rest of the world. Originally established in 1958 to promote Japanese exports abroad, JETRO's core focus in the 21st century has shifted toward promoting foreign direct investment into Japan and helping small to medium size Japanese firms maximize their global export potential.

Look East Policy: Look East policy is an effort to cultivate extensive economic and strategic relations with the nations of Southeast Asia to bolster its standing as a regional power and a counterweight to the strategic influence of the People's Republic of China.

Merger and Acquisition: Mergers and acquisitions (M&A) is a general term that describes the consolidation of companies or assets through various types of financial transactions, including mergers, acquisitions, consolidations, tender offers, purchase of assets, and management acquisitions.

METI: Ministry of Economy, Trade, and Industry (METI) is a ministry of Japan with a mission to develop Japan's economy and industry by focusing on promoting economic vitality in private companies and smoothly advancing external economic relationships, and to secure stable and efficient supply of energy and mineral resources.

ODA: The Official Development Assistance is an arm of the Ministry of Foreign Affairs (Japan) that started in 1954 with the goal of the office is to help developing nations with supplies, civil engineering and other assistance through JICA.

Chapter 14
A Collaborative Study of Foreign Trade and Economic Performance of India With Southeast Asian Countries

Samira Binte-Saif
https://orcid.org/0000-0001-8571-3242
Islami Bank Bangladesh Limited, Bangladesh

ABSTRACT

The Indian economy was in distress at the brink of the country's independence since 1947 from the colonial rule and partition. India was fulfilling the development needs of the colonial rulers. The state that should have been responsible for breakthroughs in agriculture and industry refused to play even a minor role in this regard. On the other hand, during the early 19th century before India's independence, the world was seeing India's accelerated development and expansion in agriculture, industry, health, and the economy. Based on the OECD's Economic Outlook 2021, the Indian economy contracted by 7.7% in 2020 as domestic consumption declined. Despite the COVID-19-related downturn, the OECD has projected India's economy to expand by 9.9% and become the fastest-growing G20 economy of the world. This is a collaborative study of India's economy and foreign trade with some Asian countries. This research reviews the factors accelerating the development of India's economy, achievements, and obstacles of India's growth of foreign trade and economic performance.

INTRODUCTION

India, a South Asian nation, is the seventh-largest country by area, the second-most populous democratic country with over 1.38 billion people of the world. India boasts of an immensely rich cultural heritage including numerous languages, traditions, religions, customs and people. The country holds its uniqueness in its diversity, and hence has adapted itself to international changes with poise and comfort. While the economy has welcomed international companies to invest in it with open arms since liberalization in the

DOI: 10.4018/978-1-7998-5774-7.ch014

1947s, Indians have been prudent and pro-active in adopting global approach, knowledge, and skills in their day-to-day operations. Since the green agriculture revolution and the white milk production revolution in India, the Indian farmers have proudly taken up farming, fishing, advanced agriculture and unique handicrafts as their profession on one hand, while modern industries and professional services sectors are coming up in a big way. India has emerged as the fastest growing major economy in the world and is expected to be one of the top three economic powers in the world over the next 10-15 years, backed by its robust democracy and strong partnerships among with the developed and powerful countries of the world like U.S.A, Russia, Israel, and Saudi- Arab (Puri & Mishra, 2020).

The country is also attracting many global players for strategic investments owing to the presence of vast range of industries, companies, investment avenues and a supportive Government. Large youth population is a strong driver for demand for goods and services and an ample source of manpower for India. **in India during the Colonial Rule**

Though India has progressed far but still there are some problems associated with the development of Indian economy such as unemployment, poor educational standards, poor infrastructure, deterioration in the Balance of Payments, high levels of private debt, increased inequality, large budget and trade deficit and rigid labor laws.

Figure 1. Aim of the chapter

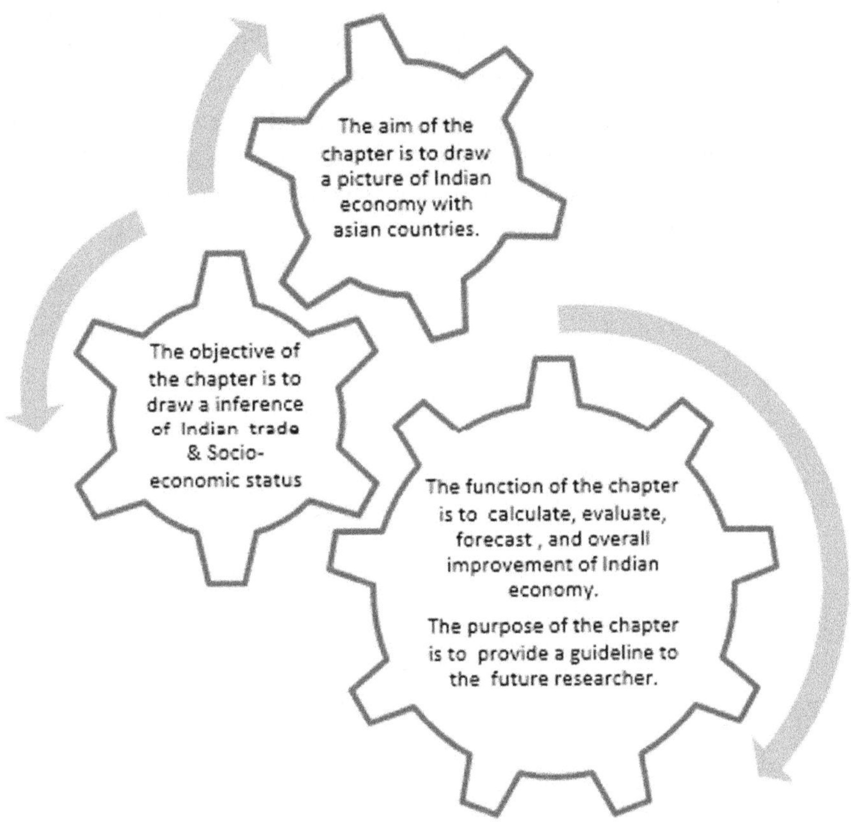

The objective of this chapter is to draw inferences of Indian trade with some Southeast Asian countries – see figure-1. Following the introduction and literature review, methodology, data Analysis, discussion, recommendation, future research directions and conclusion section of the chapter is covered.

LITERATURE REVIEW

The Indian economy is characterized as a middle-income developing market economy in the entire world economy. It is the world's sixth-largest economy by nominal GDP and the third-largest by purchasing power parity (PPP) of the world. Apart from private consumption, India's GDP is also fueled by government spending, investment, and exports. Colonial rulers never made any significant changes for the benefit of the social sector of the country, and this hampered the productive capacity of the Indian economy. During independence, India's literacy was only 17 percent, with a life expectancy of 32.5 years. Therefore, after independence, systematic organization of the economy was a real challenge for the government of that time. The need for delivering growth and development was the urgent need of the political leadership - as the country was riding on the promises and vibes of national fervor. Many important and strategic decisions were taken by 1956 by the Indian government, which are still shaping India's economic journey. At a press conference, Finance Minister Arun Jaitley commented, "*We keep oscillating between the fifth and the sixth largest economy, depending on the dollar rate. As we look at the years ahead, we will be $ 5 tn by 2024 and $ 10 tn by 2030 or 2031" (Sharma, 2019).*

The GDP per capita in India was $ 1963.55 in 2017. The GDP per Capita in India is equivalent to 16% of the world's average, and averaged $ 693.96 from 1960 until 2017. It reached an all - time high of $ 1963.55 in 2017 (Indian Ministry of Finance). The adoption of the New Economic Policy in 1991 saw a landmark shift in the Indian economy, as it ended the mixed economy model and license Raj system - and opened the Indian economy to the rest of the world. The following section (Figure-2) discusses the top performing sectors of the Indian economy.

Figure 2. Indian Economic sectors

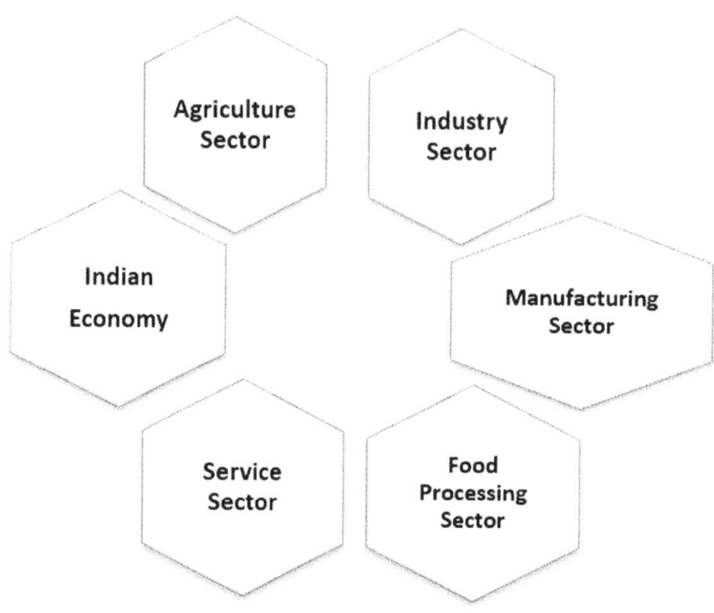

1. Agricultural Sector

One of the most important sectors of the Indian economy is Agriculture and agricultural products. Its share in the GDP of the country has declined and is currently at 14%. However, more than 50% of the total population of the country is still dependent on agriculture directly or indirectly. The Union Budget 2017 - 18 gave high priority to the agricultural sector and aimed to double farmers' incomes by 2022 (Venkat, 2017).

1. Government subsidies to agricultural sector are at an all-time high. Further, cropping patterns have shifted in favor of cash crops such as sugarcane and rubber.
2. Introduction of cooperative farming like – e-choupal makes this sector more productive.
3. Rise of Small Household Goods (SHGs) such as Lijjat Papad, which also accelerate the economic growth of the country.
4. Agricultural land is being brought under industrial and commercial use, thereby straining the remaining agricultural land to produce a large number of crops.
5. Many export sectors have been opened for and depend on agricultural goods.
6. Food processing is emerging as a 'Sunrise Industry' of India now a days.

2. Industry Sector

Another important part of the Indian economy is the industry sector. Changes such as the end of the 'Permit Raj' and opening up of the economy were welcomed in the country with great enthusiasm and optimism.

1. Proliferation of industries, from traditional iron and steel to jute and automobiles, with autonomy in production, marketing and distribution.
2. Reduced red- tapism enhanced industrialization in India.
3. Encouragement to private investments, both domestic as well as FDI for rapid growth.
4. Transfer of technology and benefits of research and development to the advantage of the economy as well as industry.
5. Arrival of investment models such as joint ventures, public-private partnerships, MNCs, start-ups accelerated the growth of industry in India.
6. Private players got an opportunity to enter new business sectors, which were earlier under government monopoly. As a result of these changes, the industrial potential of Indian economy has increased since 1991 (Puri & Misra, 2020).

3. Services Sector

The service sector benefited most from the new economic policy of India, such as Banking, Finance, Business Process Outsourcing - and most importantly IT sector - have seen double - digit growth by few recent years (Puri & Misra, 2020).

1. Indian Information Technology giants such as Infosys, WIPRO(Western India Products) and TCS(Tata Consultancy Services) have made their mark on the global platform.

2. Sixty percent of the GDP's contribution comes from the services sector of India.
3. With its huge demographic dividend potential, India emerged as the Information Technology hub of the world by 1999s.
4. New employment opportunities are being created in this sector as a result percentage of unemployment is reduce.
5. Opening of transportation, tourism, education and medical sectors have led to the growth of service sector competencies of the entire world.

4. Food Processing

Food processing has emerged as a high-growth and high- profit sector and is one of the focus sectors of the *'Make in India'* initiative of Prime Minister Modi, all over the world (Sharma, 2019). The vast availability of raw materials, resources, innovative and skilled manpower, uniqueness in food making, different types and quality of food item, favorable policy measures, and numerous incentives have led India to be considered as a key attractive food market. With a population of 1.3 billion and an average age of 29, as well as a rapidly growing middle - class population that spends a high proportion of their disposable income on food. Therefore, for food processing business, India is a large consumer base country of the world. The total consumption of the food and beverage segment in India is expected to increase from $369 Billion to $1.14 Trillion by 2025. The output of the food processing sector (at market prices) is expected to increase to $958 billion during the same period (Sharma, 2020). India is second to China, in food grains and food crop production in the world. Food making and processing sector has huge potential in India due to increasing urbanization, income levels and a high preference for packaged and processed food both inside and outside of the country (Sharma, 2020).

5. Manufacturing Sector

The manufacturing sector is the second largest contributor to India's GDP after the Services sector. Various government initiatives like Make in India, MUDRA, Sagarmala, Startup India, Freight Corridors, along with a whole - hearted contribution from states have enriched the manufacturing sector, these will also raise the share of the manufacturing sector in the foreseeable future in India (Puri & Mishra, 2020). However, if India's objective is to raise its share of manufacturing in GDP to around 25%, the industry will have to significantly step up its research and development expenditure.

Besides these developments and reforms, it is imperative to bear in mind that in order to tap the highest potential of the Indian economy and ensure good governance, an optimal level of synergy is required between the central and state government. This will not only add strength to Indian cooperative federal structure but will also strengthen India's economy. Initiatives such as Goods and Services Tax (GST), Insolvency and Bankruptcy Code (IBC), Startup India, and Digital India. These, among others, have helped the Indian economy jump 65 ranks (in the last four years) in the World Bank's Ease of Doing Business Report (Sharma, 2020).

These measures cemented India's reputation as one of the few bright spots in an otherwise grim global economy. India is among the fastest growing major economies of the entire world, underpinned by a stable macro - economy with declining inflation and improving fiscal and external balances. Not only that, India was also one of the few economies enacting major 'structural reforms', that have positioned India as a competitive player in the international market in a short time. To make India a $5Trillion economy by 2030, and to achieve consistent 8% growth, NITI Aayog has released a comprehensive document titled, " Strategy for India @ 75". Its main objectives are: **1.** Doubling farmers' incomes in the near future. **2.** Creating an all-India talent pool for the entre and States together - such as the All-India Services. **3.** Providing a major boost to the 'Make in India' campaign. **4.** Achieving 22% tax to GDP ratio by 2023 - up from the current 17%. **5.** Achieving 36% of investment rate by 2023 - up from the current 29% (Sharma, 2020).

Guided by unwavering democratic credentials and strong government leadership, now India is an emerging superpower with a vibrant economic climate of the world. Under Prime Minister Narendra Modi, India's growth rate in the last quarter has been pegged at 7.7%. And with an ever - expanding middle - class base and youth demographic, the opportunity for business has never been better (Sharma, 2020).

India's real gross domestic product (GDP) at current prices stood at Rs. 135.13 lakh crore (US$ 1.82 trillion) in FY21, as per the provisional estimates of annual national income for 2020-21. India is the fourth-largest unicorn base in the world with over 21 unicorns collectively valued at US$ 73.2 billion, as per the Hurun Global Unicorn List. By 2025, India is expected to have ~100 unicorns by 2025 and will create ~1.1 million direct jobs according to the Nasscom-Zinnov report 'Indian Tech Start-up' in order to reduce unemployment. India needs to increase its rate of employment growth and create 90 million non-farm jobs between 2023 and 2030's, for productivity and economic growth according to McKinsey Global Institute. Net employment rate needs to grow by 1.5% per year from 2023 to 2030 to achieve 8-8.5% GDP growth between 2023 and 2030 (Sankhe et al., 2020).

Economic Profile

India's real gross domestic product (GDP) at current prices stood at Rs. 135.13 lakh crore (US$ 1.82 trillion) in FY21, as per the provisional estimates of annual national income for 2020-21 (Table-1) (Department of Economic Affairs of India).

Table 1. Gross Value Added (GVA) Quarterly Estimates

Sectors	Basic Prices 2020-21 at Constant 2011-12 Prices.
Agriculture, forestry & fishing	Rs. 2,040,079 crore (US$ 275.17 billion).
Mining & Quarrying	Rs. 294,644 crore (US$ 39.74 billion).
Manufacturing	Rs. 2,107,068 crore (US$ 284.21 billion).
Electricity, gas, water supply & other utility services	Rs. 306,254 crore (US$ 41.31 billion).
Construction	Rs. 946,396 crore (US$ 127.65 billion).
Trade, hotels, transport, communications & services related to broadcasting	Rs. 2,208,388 crore (US$ 297.88 billion).
Public administration, defence & other services	Rs. 1,677,786 crore (US$ 226.31 billion).
Financial, real estate & professional services	Rs. 2,872,815 crore (US$ 387.50 billion).
Forex Reserves	US$ 605 billion, as of June 4, 2021

Table-1 shows the economic sector of India and basic prices of these sectors. From the table, we see that agriculture, forestry, fishing, real estate, professional service is the most prominent economic sector of India.

Table 2. Foreign Reserves

Criteria	Values
Valuc of Export	India's overall exports between April 2021 and May 2021 were estimated at US$ 98.29 billion.
Export Partners	US, Germany, UAE, China, Japan, Thailand, Indonesia and European Union. India is also tapping newer markets in Africa and Latin America.
Currency (code)	Indian rupee (Rs).
Exchange Rates	Indian rupee per US$: 1 US$ = 72.47 Rs. as of May 28, 2021.
Fiscal Year	April 01 - March 31
Cumulative FDI Equity Inflow	US$ 529.76 billion (from April 2000 to March 2021).

Table-2 shows the export, import values, trade partners , exchange rate, FDI values of India and its overall foreign trade position.

Table 3. Share of the Top Investing Countries and key sectors in FDI Equity Inflow

Country	FDI	Sector	Highest FDI
Mauritius	28%	Services Sector	16%
Singapore	22%	Software & Hardware	13%
US	8%	Telecommunications	7%
Netherlands	7%	Trading	6%
UK	6%	Construction Development	5%
Germany	2%	Automobile	5%
Cyprus	2%	Construction Activities	5%
Cayman Island	2%	Chemicals	3%
UAE	2%	Drugs & Pharmaceuticals	3%
Japan	7%	Hotel & Tourism	3%

Table -3 shows that Mauritius, Singapore, US and UK are the top countries to attract Foreign Direct Investment (FDI) in India. Sector wise FDI, the service sector, computer software and hardware sector, telecommunications sectors are the highest earning sector of the Indian economy. This economic profile of India shows a clear picture of India's sectors wise income, expense and financial strength and weakness.

Recent Indian Economic Developments

With an improvement in the economic scenario, there have been investments across various sectors of the economy. Private Equity - Venture Capital (PE-VC) sector recorded investments worth US$ 20 billion in the first five months of 2021, registering a 2x growth in value compared with the same period in 2020. Some of the important recent developments in Indian economy are as follows: Merchandise exports stood at US$ 62.89 billion between April 2021 and May 2021, while imports touched US$ 84.27 billion. The estimated value of service exports and imports between April 2021 and May 2021 stood at US$ 35.39 billion and US$ 19.86 billion, respectively (IBEF, 2021).

In May 2021, the Manufacturing Purchasing Managers' Index (PMI) in India stood at 50.8. Gross GST collections stood at Rs. 141,384 crore (US$ 19.41 billion) in April 2021. Cumulative FDI equity inflows in India stood at US$ 763.58 billion between April 2000 and March 2021. Foreign Direct Investment (FDI) inflows in India stood at US$ 6.24 billion in April 2021, registering an increase of 38% YoY. India's Index of Industrial Production (IIP) for April 2021 stood at 126.6 against 143.4 for March 2021.Consumer Food Price Index (CFPI) – Combined inflation was 5.01 in May 2021 against 1.96 in April 2021. Consumer Price Index (CPI) – Combined inflation was 6.30 in May 2021 against 4.23 in April 2021. In June 2021, foreign portfolio investors (FPIs) turned net buyers by investing Rs. 12,714 crore (US$ 1.71 billion) into the Indian markets. According to depositories data, between June 1, 2021 and June 25, 2021, FPIs invested Rs. 15,282 crore (US$ 2.06 billion) in equities.

Government Initiatives

The first Union Budget of the third decade of 21st century was presented by Minister for Finance & Corporate Affairs, Ms. Nirmala Sitharaman in the Parliament on February 1, 2020. The budget aimed at energizing the Indian economy through a combination of short-term, medium-term and long-term measures of India (Puri & Misra, 2020). In the Union Budget 2021-22, capital expenditure for FY22 is likely to increase by 34.5% at Rs. 5.5 lakh crore (US$ 75.81 billion) over FY21 (BE) to boost the economy of India. Increased government expenditure is expected to attract private investments, with production-linked incentive scheme providing excellent opportunities to the general public of India. Consistently proactive, graded and measured policy support is anticipated to boost the Indian economy (AILF, 2021).

In May 2021, the government of India s approved the production linked incentive (PLI) scheme for manufacturing advanced chemistry cell (ACC) batteries at an estimated outlay of Rs. 18,100 crore (US$ 2.44 billion); this move is expected to attract domestic and foreign investments worth Rs. 45,000 crore (US$ 6.07 billion). The Union Cabinet approved the production linked incentive (PLI) scheme for white goods (air conditioners and LED lights) with a budgetary outlay of Rs. 6,238 crore (US$ 848.96 million) and the 'National Programme on High Efficiency Solar PV (Photo Voltic) Modules' with an outlay of Rs. 4,500 crores (US$ 612.43 million). In June 2021, the RBI (Reserve Bank of India) announced that the investment limit for FPI (foreign portfolio investors) in the State Development Loans (SDLs) and government securities (G-secs) would persist unaffected at 2% and 6%, respectively, in FY22 (Mint, 2021).

To boost the overall audit quality, transparency and add value to businesses, in April 2021, the RBI issued a notice on new norms to appoint statutory and central auditors for commercial banks, large urban co-operatives and large non-banks and housing finance firms of India. In May 2021, the Government of India has allocated Rs. 2,250 crore (US$ 306.80 million) for development of the horticulture sector in 2021-22, which expand new scope of earning. In November 2020, the Government of India announced

Rs. 2.65 lakh crore (US$ 36 billion) stimulus package to generate job opportunities and provide liquidity support to various sectors of people such as tourism, aviation, construction and housing, entrepreneurship etc. Also, India's cabinet approved the production-linked incentives (PLI) scheme to provide ~Rs. 2 trillion (US$ 27 billion) over five years to create new jobs and boost production level in the economy of India (The Economic Times, 2020).

Numerous foreign companies are setting up their facilities in India on account of various Government initiatives like Make in India and Digital India which expand more scope of earning for the general public of India, Mr. Narendra Modi, Prime Minister of India, launched Make in India initiative with an aim to boost country's manufacturing sector and increase purchasing power of an average Indian consumer than other countries, which would further drive demand and spur development of India, thus benefiting a numerous number of investors. The Government of India, under its Make in India initiative, is trying to boost the contribution made by the manufacturing sector with an aim to take it to 25% of the GDP from the current 17%. Besides, the Government has also come up with Digital India initiative, which focuses on three core components; creation of digital infrastructure, delivering services digitally and to increase the digital literacy.

Some of the recent initiatives and developments undertaken in May and June 2021 by the Indian Government are listed below:

1. RBI Governor, Mr. Shaktikanta Das announced the policy repo rate unchanged at 4%. He also announced various measures including Rs. 15,000 crore (US$ 2.05 billion) liquidity support to contact-intensive sectors such as tourism and hospitality of this country.
2. Finance Ministers of G-7 countries, including the US, the UK, Japan, Italy, Germany, France and Canada, attained a historic contract on taxing multinational firms as per which the minimum global tax rate would be at least 15%. The move is expected to benefit India to increase foreign direct investments in the country as a result the economy of India is becoming stronger.
3. The Indian government signed a US$ 32 million loan with World Bank for improving healthcare services in Mizoram for the general public.
4. The Government of India (GoI) and European Investment Bank (EIB) signed the finance contract for second tranche of EUR 150 million (US$ 182.30 million) for Pune Metro Rail project, which expand and make ease the transportation system of the country.
5. According to an official source, as of June 2021, 29 companies including global electronics manufacturing organizations, such as companies Foxconn, Sanmina SCI, Flex, Jabil Circuit, have registered under the Rs. 12,195 crore (US$ 1.64 billion) production linked incentive scheme for the telecom sector of this country.
6. Union Cabinet has approved the signing of memorandum of understanding (MoU) on migration and mobility partnership between the Government of India, the United Kingdom of Great Britain and Northern Ireland which also open a new door of progress in the economy of India.
7. Minister for Railways and Commerce & Industry and Consumer Affairs, Food & Public Distribution, Mr. Piyush Goyal, launched 'DGFT Trade Facilitation' app to provide instant access to exporters/importers anytime and anywhere in order to make ease the export- import business of the country.
8. Dr. Ahmed Abdul Rahman AlBanna, Ambassador of the UAE to India and Founding Patron of IFIICC, stated that trilateral trade between India, the UAE and Israel is expected to reach US$ 110 billion by 2030.

9. India is expected to attract investment of around US$ 100 billion in developing the oil and gas infrastructure of this country during 2019-23.
10. The Government of India is going to increase public health spending to 2.5% of the GDP by 2025 in order to enhance the health facilities of general public.
11. For implementation of Agriculture Export Policy, Government approved an outlay Rs. 2.068 billion (US$ 29.59 million) for 2019, aimed at doubling farmers income by 2022 all over the country.

As indicated by provisional estimates released by the National Statistical Office (NSO), India posted a V-shaped recovery in the second half of FY21. As per these estimates, India registered an increase of 1.1% in the second half of FY21; this was driven by the gradual and phased unlocking of industrial activities of this country, increased investments and growth in government expenditure. As per the Reserve Bank of India's (RBI) estimates, India's real GDP growth is projected at 9.5% in FY22; this includes 18.5% increase in the first quarter of FY22; 7.9% growth in the second quarter of FY22; 7.2% rise in the third quarter of FY22 and 6.6% growth in the fourth quarter of FY22.

India is focusing on renewable sources to generate energy. It is planning to achieve 40% of its energy from non-fossil sources by 2030, which is currently 30% and have plans to increase its renewable energy capacity from to 175 gigawatts (GW) by 2022. In line with this, in May 2021, India, along with the UK, jointly launched a 'Roadmap 2030' to collaborate and combat climate change by 2030 in order to protect the earth and keep pace with the overall climate change of the world. India is expected to be the third largest consumer economy of the world, as its consumption may triple to US$ 4 trillion by 2025, owing to shift in consumer behavior and expenditure pattern, according to a Boston Consulting Group (BCG) report. It is estimated to surpass USA to become India the second largest economy in terms of purchasing power parity (PPP) by 2040 as per a report by PricewaterhouseCoopers (IBEF, 2021)

India's sugar exports have reached 5.11 million tones so far this year, according to All India Sugar Trade Association (AISTA). Prime Minister Mr. Narendra Modi participated in 'Atmanirbhar Narishakti se Samvad' and interacted with women Self Help Group in order to make the Indian woman safe and financially solvent. The government of India is trying to improve the alignment of education and skills in order to develop a workforce that is future-ready - Union Education Minister. Delhi's Indira Gandhi International Airport (IGIA) has been declared the Best Airport in India and Central Asia. The Chandrayaan-2 has detected the existence of water molecules on the moon was discovered by the Indian scientists. India is one of the top four markets for 5G devices without network support, with 40 million shipments expected by 2021.

Prospects of an economic rebound in South Asia are firming up as growth is set to increase by 7.2 percent in 2021 and 4.4 percent in 2022, climbing from historic lows in 2020 and putting the region on a path to recovery.

But growth is uneven and economic activity well below pre-COVID-19 estimates, as many businesses need to make up for lost revenue and millions of workers, most of them in the informal sector, still reel from job losses, falling incomes, worsening inequalities, and human capital deficits of this country(Puri & Misra, 2020).

This is a well-known fact everyone knows how a Pandemic (Corona-virus Disease- 19) suddenly spread all over the world and changed the complete scenario worldwide economy . The sudden change in the human race has occurred and stopped the wheel of growth and economic development of all countries of the world. Economic development matters very to a great extent if concerned with developing countries like India. Where so many factors get involved in making the nation progressive and competitive with the world's developed economies.

Step towards the lockdown of the nation as the pandemic outbreaks worldwide, was taken by the Govt. of India in the month of March (Mid), 2020 to reduce the spread of COVID-19 through the country. Shutting down the cities, businesses or all the running economic activities have emerged as a break towards developing the economy of India. It, in due course of lockdown, has slowed down and hampered the speed of economic transition of India. Some big industrialized states of India like Gujarat, Maharashtra and Delhi have been converted into the most shattering and devastated in terms of economic contribution. Lockdown is not that easy to be implemented but it has some bitter consequences upon the economy of a country.

India's real GDP showed that GDP braked to its lowest in over six years in 3rd quarter 2019-20, and the outbreak of the COVID-19 posed fresh challenges. Steps taken to contain its spread, such as nationwide restrictions for 21 days and a complete lockdown of states, have brought economic activity to a stand-still and could impact both consumption and investment all over the country. While Indian businesses, barring a few sectors, can possibly insulate themselves from the global supply chain disruption caused by the outbreak due to relatively lower reliance on intermediate imports, their exports to COVID-19 infected nations could take a hit. In sum, the three major contributors to GDP -- private consumption, investment and external trade -- will get adversely affected.

Sectorial Impact of COVID-19 on Indian Economy

1. Apparel and Textile: Production tends to decline by 10 to 12% in the quarter April – June. From a manufacturing perspective, employment would be impacted owing to limited demand in both domestic and international markets.
2. Auto and Auto components: China accounts for 25% of India's automotive parts imports. Trouble in supply of raw material will affect the entire sector General liquidity shortfall in the sector due to NBFC and banking sector situation leading to an impact on sales Indian Association of Tour Operators (IATO) guesstimates the hotel.
3. Aviation and Tourism: Both aviation and travel sector together may suffer loss of about of 85 billion due to travel restrictions imposed on foreign tourists on account of this pandemic, both the sectors, tourism as well as hospitality is watching a potential job loss or around 38 million which directly around 705 of the total workforces of the industry.
4. Building and Construction: Overall pause in the manufacturing sector activity including cement, steel and other building materials affect this sector.
5. Chemical and Petrochemicals: Raw material prices for petrochemicals are falling chiefly driven by crude prices. Additional supply resulting from a price war between Russia and Saudi price. Slowdowns in key downstream industries due to lockdown have a ripple effect on petrochemicals demand, and also for liquid products driven by storage capacity constraints
6. Consumer, retail and internet business: The e-commerce sector will also face the challenges due to COVID-19 and may see a dip in growth. There will be increased pressure on supply chain for deliveries of products and another challenge for Ecommerce companies is that they will need to equip their employees with the appropriate resources to manage operations remotely with little or no disruption.

7. Education and Skilling: Skill institutes in India are training more than 10 million trainees annually– lockdown would decrease the available skilled manpower by 10-15%.
8. Financial Services: Retail financing industry, which was one of the key drivers of credit growth will be impacted for at least two quarters, as the demand for housing assets, consumer goods and working capital financing will get hit due to general slowdown in economic activity from a reporting perspective, banks follow Indian GAAP whilst NBFCs follow Ind-AS. The difference in quantification and reporting of credit costs (Ind-AS is more inflexible) is likely to have a greater impact on the reported results of NBFCs. Globally, the COVID 19 situation has resulted in social engineering scams that are being performed using social media and telecommunication channels.
9. MSME's: A study by the All-India Manufacturers Organization (AIMO) estimates that about a quarter of over 75 million MSMEs in India will face closure if the lockdown due to COVID- 19 goes beyond four weeks and this figure is estimated to touch a whopping 43 per cent if the situation extends beyond eight weeks.
10. Fisheries contribute about 0.9 percent to the GDP. In 2018-19, the total marine fish production was 4.18 million tonnes (GOI, 2020), and the estimated value of marine fish landings during 2018 was estimated at INR 526.36 billion (approx. USD 7.35 billion) at point of first sale and INR 803.20 billion (approx. USD 11.20 billion) at retail market.

According to the latest South Asia Economic Focus, South Asia Vaccinated, the region is set to regain its historical growth rate by 2022. India, which comprises the bulk of the region's economy, is expected to grow more than 10 percent in the fiscal year 2021-22—a substantial upward revision of 4.7 percentage points from January 2021 forecasts. The improved economic outlook reflects South Asian countries' efforts to keep their COVID-19 caseload under control and swiftly roll out vaccine campaigns of India. The Indian Governments' decisions to transition from widespread lockdowns to more targeted interventions, accommodating monetary policies and fiscal stimulation through targeted cash transfers and employment compensation programs—have also propped up recovery of the hampered economy of India. According to Robert Gilpin, "Many critics see International trade as a form of cultural imperialism that must be strictly controlled." India's Exclusive Economic Zone (EEZ) covering 2.02 million sq.km contains diverse and multi-species fish stocks, exploited by multi-gear fisheries, which are mostly concentrated in the coastal areas (<100 m depth) of India. Export Income refers to the net profit derived by a taxpayer from the business of exporting goods and services bur excluding re- exports of a country. Export refers to a product or service produced in one country but sold to a buyer of another country. Exports are one of the oldest forms of economic transfer and occur on a large-scale trade between countries.

"Exporting is cross border sale of domestically grown or produced produce goods" (Cavasgil, 2004). Export earning of a sovereign country that are generated through export goods or service of this native country. Marketing financial services throughout the world is a major source of export earning of any country. An example of export is rice being shipped from China to Bangladesh to be sold in in many countries.

Now ASEAN region is undoubtedly a very dynamic region in Asia and the Pacific. With Indonesia accounting for two-fifth of regional output, value added in South-East Asia (SEA) continues to grow by 5 percent in 2014. According to the World Bank, Singapore and Brunei are the only ASEAN countries that are considered high income countries and have economic stability. Malaysia and Thailand are categorized as upper-middle income economies, while Indonesia, Philippines and Vietnam are considered as lower income economies and have less economic development. Cambodia, Lao PDR and Myanmar, on the other hand are also categorized as low-income country. In spite of progress in reducing poverty, the region still faces development challenges and gaps closely associated with social inequities, natural calamities, geo- politics, terrorism etc. Irregular migration and human trafficking remain significant challenges that will continue to increase in the coming years in Southeast Asia. Migration public health, concerns the governments, particularly the re-emerging infectious disease such as tuberculosis, HIV/AIDS and malaria and now COVID- 19. Natural disasters and conflict in certain areas also pose on-going threats to population and have resulted in the displacement of significant numbers of people to different countries.

However, the growing levels of wealth and the resultant penetration of new technologies in the over all world, means that innovation is necessary if the Red Cross Red Crescent National Societies are to maintain our privileged position within the humanitarian community. In southeast Asia shifting disaster and developmental trends, driven by factors such as climate change, rapid urbanization and weakening social structures, demands more strategic, evidence-based approach to communications and advocacy. This growing focus on the development agenda (Community Safety and Resilience-CSR, National Society Development-NSD, Communication and Advocacy/Humanitarian Diplomacy-HD) in SEA is part of a broader effort in 2014 to re-imagine and reposition the regional delegation in a rapidly changing Red Cross and Red Crescent context. There is a clear need to innovate, adapting their ways of working and communication and understanding better their operating context.

In 2014, the ASEAN region has witnessed widespread natural calamities (Indonesia, Lao and Philippines) and political instability (Cambodia, Myanmar and Thailand), which had greatly impacted some of the development /innovation planned activities of these countries towards the end of the year. The resilience agenda has been structured maximizing health facilities, disaster risk reduction (DRR), NSD, climate risk reduction and increase public health in emergencies as well as other cross-cutting components as defined in the "Resilience House Model" and "Regional Road Map" of Red Cross Red Crescent National Societies of the region of Southeast Asia. The project on building regional capacity and collaboration for community resilience in SEA (Regional Resilience Initiative – RRI, previously named C3R) commenced as a regional project to provide platform for National Societies to explore opportunities in order to build their capacity towards strengthening advocacy/ HD, disaster law and gender and diversity components in National Societies programming, along with technical competencies on DRR, climate change adaptation policy, pandemic preparedness and response preparedness.

Many National Societies and organization in SEA have taken great strides in working with their governments and other key partners to influence the development of laws, rules and regulations for disaster management (DM), risk reduction and response. Given the ongoing activities and momentum with regards to disaster law among National Societies and governments in the Southeast Asia, a dedicated regional disaster law delegate joined the team in the South-East Asia regional delegation (SEARD) in August 2014 to support SEA National Societies in order to build their knowledge and capacity in disaster law and legislative advocacy; to participate in the development or review of DM and related laws (and the associated regulations and guidelines); and in the undertaking of technical assistance projects.

METHODOLOGY

The relationship between India and Southeast Asia in terms of trade, using both quantitative and qualitative data analysis method is applied. The secondary source of data is used in this research. The data from years 2015 to 2019 respectively of India's economy with Southeast Asian countries is taken, to find out the 1) trend of Indian economy, 2) interdependence of Indian economy with Southeast Asian countries, 3) relationship between number of products and export income/ import expense, and the 4) trend analysis of income and expense of Southeast Asia which create an impact of Indian economy. Regression analysis, trend analysis, coefficient of variance, standard deviation analysis, test of hypothesis technique for the data analysis purpose is used.

Regression analysis can be utilized to assess and valuate the strength and trend of Indian economy in terms of export and import relationship between variables and for modeling the future relationship between them. The riskiness of export and import of India between Southeast Asia, was also analyzed using standard deviation and coefficient of variance formula. Hypothesis were tested in order to established or reject a null hypothesis.

Null Hypothesis

1. The export income of India with Brunei comparing with other three countries show a positive economic achievement.
2. The export income of India with Myanmar comparing with other three countries show a positive economic achievement.
3. The export income of India with Indonesia comparing with other three countries shows a positive economic achievement.
4. The export income of India with Philippines comparing with other three countries show a positive economic achievement.

Data Analysis and Results

Export income of India of year 2019.
Now , T- Statistic,

Table 4. WITS Report- year 2019

Export country	Trade(US$ Thousand)
Brunei	56810.18
Myanmar	956900.52
Indonesia	4515383.36
Philippines	1635533.80

$T=(X-u)/\partial/\sqrt{n}$
Population mean= 1791156.965
Standard Deviation (SD)= 1669548.684
The level of significance ∞=0.05 T value greater than +2 or less than -2 is acceptable

Table 5. Hypothesis Testing- Countries trading with India

Criteria	Level of Significance¥=0.05	Null Hypothesis		Reason
Country	Calculated value	Accept	Reject	
Brunei	-2.077623494	Accept/True		Less than -2
Myanmar	-0.999379596		Reject/ False	Greater than -2
Indonesia	3.2634285	Accept/True		Greater than +2
Philippines	-0.186425429		Reject/False	Greater than -2

Here for Brunei the calculated value is less than -2 . The null hypothesis is accepted. So the export income of India with Brunei comparing with other three countries is a positive economic achievement is true.

Here for Myanmar the calculated value is greater than -2 so the null hypothesis is not accepted, so the export income of India with Myanmar comparing with other three countries is a positive economic achievement is not true.

Here for Indonesia the T statistic value is 3.263425 greater than +2 so the null hypothesis is accepted. So the export income of India with Indonesia comparing with other three countries is a positive economic achievement is true.

Here for Philippines the T statistic value is -0.186425429 greater than -2 so the null hypothesis is rejected, so the export income of India with Philippines comparing with other three countries a positive economic achievement is not true.

Coefficient of Variation=1669548.684/1791156.965=0.932105295

Ideally, if the coefficient of variation formula should result in a lower ratio of the standard deviation to mean return, then the better the risk-return trade-off. F-Statistic(Evaluate relationship between export income and import expense of India). The following Table- 6 shows the Export and Import of India in year 2019.

Table 6. Export and import of India-Year 2019

Country	Export (USD Thousand)	Import(USD Thousand)
Brunei	56810.18	581368.78
Myanmar	956900.52	506730.44
Indonesia	4515383.36	15563891.08
Philippine	1635533.80	556912.78
Thailand	4331648.86	7034310.20
Vietnam	5512870.24	7446093.33
Total	17009146.96	31689306.61

(Source: WITS Report- year 2015-2019:

Null Hypothesis: The Export income of India has no effect /impact on Import expense of India among with Brunei, Myanmar. Indonesia, Philippine, Thailand and Vietnam in year 2019. Table-7 shows imports and exports Standard deviation of India with selected Asian countries

Table 7. Exports and imports

Criteria	Value	Criteria	Value
Mean	2834857.827	Mean	5281551.102
Standard Deviation(S.D)	2037929.932	Standard Deviation(S.D)	5487816.147
Variance of Export(∂1^2)	4.98379009*10^12	Variance of Import(∂2^2)	3.613935128*10^13
Coefficient of Variance(C.V) of Export	0.718882588	Coefficient of Variance(C.V) of Import	1.038053877

Now. F- Statistic=∂1^2/∂2^2
=4.98379009*10^12/3.613935128*10^13
=0.137904802

F calculated value is less than table value (5.79). If table value is smaller than the calculated value rejects the null hypothesis and table value is greater than the calculated value accepts the null hypothesis. So the export income of India has no impact on import expense of India among with Brunei, Myanmar. Indonesia, Philippine, Thailand and Vietnam in year 2019 is true. Regression Analysis:(Evaluate the relationship between number of export goods and export income of India)

Table 8. (Source: WITS Report- year 2015-2019)

Year	Number of Export Product (X)	Export Income(Y)
2015	4424	264381
2016	4411	260327
2017	4418	294364
2018	4450	322922
2019	4442	323251
Total	22145	1465245

Table 9.

X	Y	X^2	Y^2	X*Y
4424	264381	19571776	6.989731316*10^10	1169621544
4411	260327	19456921	6.777014693*10^10	1148302397
4418	294364	19518724	8.66501645*10^10	1300500152
4450	322922	19802500	1.042786181*10^11	1437002900
4442	323251	19731364	1.04491209*10^11	1435880942
Total		98081285	4.330874517*10^11	6491307935

Table 10.

Year	Regression Analysis Model (Y=2.128946474*10^10+(-4806767.146*X))
Y2015	24326886.1
Y2016	86814858.99
Y2017	53167488.97
Y2018	-100649059.7
Y2019	-62194922.53

Table- 10 shows that the linear relationship between number of export products and export income of India.

Regression Analysis for Imports evaluate the relationship between number of import products and import expense of India.

Table 11. Number of Products imported & Income

Year	Import Product(X)	Import (Y)
2015	4313	390745
2016	4310	356705
2017	4317	444052
2018	4343	617946
2019	4356	478884
Total	21639	2288332

Table 12.

X	Y	X^2	Y^2	X*Y
4313	390745	18601969	1.52681655*10^11	1685283185
4310	356705	18576100	1.27238457*10^11	1537398550
4317	444052	18636489	1.971821787*10^11	1916972484
4343	617946	18861649	3.818572589*10^11	2683739478
4356	478884	18974736	2.293298855*10^11	2086018704
Total	2288332	93650943	1.088289435*10^12	9909412401

Table 13. linear relationship between number of import goods and import expense of India

Year	Regression Analysis Model Y=2.042155048*10^10+(-4718585.15*X)
Y2015	70292728.05
Y2016	84448483.5
Y2017	51418387.45
Y2018	-71264826.45
Y2019	-132606433.4

Trend analysis of Southeast Asian countries in terms of income and expense of year 2014, 2015, 2016, 2017 and 2018.

Table 14. Trend analysis of Income of Southeast Asian Country

Year (x)	Income(Y)	Deviation(X)=x-2016	X^2	X*Y	Y=a+bX
2014	1623830	-2	4	-3247660	1723442.2
2015	1742763	-1	1	-1742763	1693522.5
2016	1802205	0	0	0	1663602.8
2017	1607206	1	1	1607206	1633683.1
2018	1542010	2	4	3084020	1603763.4
Total	ΣY=8318014		ΣX^2=10	ΣX*Y= -299197	

Source: LSI Southeast Asia Region Annual Report 2014-2018

Now, a=ΣY/n
=1663602.8
b=Σ(X*Y)/ΣX^2
=-29919.7

From the above table the author observes that the trend of income of Southeast Asian countries are decreasing year after year. Which indicate the southeast Asian countries faces a loss in yearly revenue.

Table 15. Trend analysis of expense of Southeast Asian Country (source: ILSI Southeast Asia Region Annual Report 2014. 2015, 2016,2017, 2018 respectively)

Year(x)	Expense(Y)	Deviation(X)=x-2016	X^2	X*Y	Y=a+bX
2014	1544144	2	4	-3088288	1634217.4
2015	1649787	-1	1	-1649787	1554849.7
2016	1687808	0	0	0	1581305.6
2017	1576062	1	1	1576062	1554849.7
2018	1448727	2	4	2897454	1528393.8
Total	ΣY=7906528		ΣX^2=10	Σ X*Y= -264559	

Now, a=ΣY/n =1581305.6; b=Σ(X*Y)/ΣX^2 =-26455.9

From the above table the expense of Southeast Asian countries is also decreasing year by year.

Limitations of this study were: Calculation gives approximate result due to limited availability of secondary-data; All types of data of Indian economy are not available in WITS report; Information of Indian export- import trade is not available in website; Data only for Southeast Asian countries trade with India is not available on the website; ILSI Southeast Asia Region Annual Report has small data regarding income and expense of Southeast Asia.

DISCUSSION AND RECOMMENDATION

India's foreign trade is mainly with various Asian countries facing trade deficit situation since many years. In this research, the author analysis the export income of India from some Southeast Asian countries like Brunei, Myanmar, Indonesia, Philippines, Thailand and Vietnam. T-Statistic formula is used to evaluate the export income performance of India among with four Southeast Asian countries- Brunei, Myanmar, Indonesia and Philippines.

1. Results show that, *Null Hypothesis* is true and accepted for two countries Brunei and India. The T -Statistic shows that the performance of India with Myanmar and Philippines countries is not a good economic achievement. India earns a sound export income from Indonesia and Brunei in year 2019.
2. The *coefficient of variation* allows investors/exporter to determine how much volatility, or risk, is assumed in comparison to the amount of return expected from investments. Ideally, if the coefficient of variation formula should result in a lower ratio of the standard deviation to mean return, then the better the risk-return trade-off. Coefficient of variance is 0.932105295, which is less than

1, which indicate that India has a less risky investment with those four countries Brunei, Myanmar, Indonesia and Philippines.

3. *Standard Deviation* is applied for analysis of export income and import expenses of India with some Southeast Asian countries such as Brunei, Myanmar, Indonesia, Philippines, Thailand and Vietnam. Standard Deviation of price /expense used as a measure of market volatility to express how widely prices are dispersed from the average price/mean value price. Conversely if prices/ expenses swingy wildly up and down, the Standard Deviation return high value which indicate high market volatility.
4. In this study the *average mean of import* is 5281551.102 USD and SD is 5487816.147 (5487816.147-5281551.102= 206265.045). Thus, SD is highly dispersed from the average price or mean, so it indicates the Import Expense of India is volatile in nature, it is not well economic performance indicator in foreign trade. Again the coefficient of variance of import is 1.038053877, which is greater than one, which indicate high risk in investment or higher the risk return trade off.
5. So in *terms of import of India* other countries faces a high risk return trade off, which is not a positive sign of economic activities. For export income Standard Deviation is 2037929.932, and Average Mean is 2834857.827 (2037929.932 -2834857.827=-796927.895) USD. When prices move widely, SD is high, meaning an investment will be risky. Low standard deviation means data are clustered around the mean or average price. In this research author found low value of Standard Deviation comparatively to its average mean *in terms of export*, which indicate less market volatility in export market of India with those Southeast Asian countries. In terms of export high volatility increase export income, the potentiality of make more money quickly is possible if high volatility exists in export market. Again high volatility in export market indicates diversify the economy in various sectors. So, in terms of export less volatility indicate India earn comparatively less income but less risk in performing foreign trade with Southeast Asian countries in year 2019.The coefficient of variance for export is 10.71882588, less than 1, which indicate less risk return trade off, so less riskiness in export market.
6. Further, **F- Statistic** test was used to evaluate the impact of export income on import expense of India and with these six countries (Brunei, Myanmar, Indonesia, Philippines, Thailand and Vietnam. The calculated value is 0.137904802 which is smaller than the F- table value(5.79), table value is greater the calculated value accepts the null hypothesis. So the Export income of India has no effect on Import expense of India among with Brunei, Myanmar, Indonesia, Philippines, Thailand and Vietnam in year 2019 is true. Which means that India has no relation between export and import with those six countries. India performs foreign trade with those six countries both in export and import by different rate. India gets export income from those six countries at a different rate. Again India traded import with those six countries which are not proportionately/linearly related with the export income . The country India imports goods from those countries at a different percentage or rate. So the export income India has no effect of import expense with those six countries in year 2019.
7. The *linearity between the number of export goods/ product and export income* from year 2015 to 2019 is analysed. The *linear relationship* between number of product import and the import expense of India from year 2015-2019. For export goods the author finds that in year 2015- 2017 there is a positive linear relationship exists between the number of export goods and the export income .If the number of export goods/products increase the export income is also increase. But for year 2018 and 2019 there is an inverse relationship found between the number of export products and the export income of India. This happens because tax of products, tariff, and rise in exchange rate

are increase in this year .An appreciation of money such as pounds will lead to export becoming more expensive in those year. So though the number of export product increase in year 2018 and 2019 the export income is decrease in those year.

8. While in year 2015-2017 there is a linear relationship exists between the number of import goods and import expense. If the number of import goods increase the import expense is also increased and vice versa. In year 2018 and 2019 there is an inverse relationship exists between the number of import products and import expense. In this year import expense decrease though number of imported goods increased. This typically indicates economic strength and a sustainable trade surplus or deficit of a country. If exports are growing, but imports have declined significantly, it may indicate that foreign economies are in better shape than the domestic economy of India. This happens change in relative price will decrease import in year 2018 and 2019 of India.
9. The findings from t*rend value of income and expense of Southeast Asian countries* show that the trend value of income of Southeast Asian countries are decreased year by year. Which indicate the South-east Asian countries earning is lower day by day. The source of earning of Southeast Asian countries are Interest Earning, Science Clusters Fund, Conference/Meeting Registrations, General Sponsorship, Publications, other income, RMG income etc. The earning from these sources is decreasing day by day. As a result India considered as a trade partner of southeast Asian country has also earn less revenue/income. From the above calculation the author observes that the expense of Southeast Asian countries is also decreasing year by year.
10. The expense sector of Southeast Asia are Conferences/Meetings, Research, Publications, Administration and Operations. Development and Governance, Science Clusters Activities etc. Southeast Asian countries are lowering their expense in these sectors. Which is not a good sign of development. So India also faces some difficulties, because India performs various activities in terms of research, publications, development, conference, science clusters activities with Southeast Asian countries very interdependently. So lowering the expense of these sector of Southeast Asian countries also make a bad impact of India's economic and research development.

Recommendations

In order to develop trade and economic relationship between India and Southeast Asia:

1. K*nowledge partnership:* Education, training and research underpin their economic and people to people engagement across all sectors of India. So to build a strong knowledge partnership between India and Southeast Asia.
2. *Complementarity*: Target India's economic needs and government priorities where they align with Southeast Asian country's competitive advantages.
3. *Interoperability:* Make their (Indian) market and industries more compatible, harmonies and standards and remove barriers to trade and investment with those southeast Asian countries.
4. *Understanding*: Foster a contemporary and objective mutual understanding of how their industries, government and societies work for the development of the country.
5. *Relationship building:* Invest in long term and workable relationships with the people and institutions of Southeast Asia and also maintain the relationship strongly.

FUTURE RESEARCH DIRECTION

The potential future research for this study can draw policy implications and inference from the data collection method, gain knowledge from the empirical analysis of the Indian economy, to increase exports to neighbouring South Asian countries.

CONCLUSION

Foreign trade plays a vital role in the economy of each country. Foreign trade helps a country to utilize its natural resources and to export its surplus production; it contributes hugely to the GDP of a country. India exports approximately 7500 commodities to about 190 countries, and imports around 6000 commodities from 140 countries. The top 1% of India's companies accounted for 38% of total exports of India. India exports of goods and services as percentage of GDP is 18.41% and imports of goods and services as percentage of GDP is 21.14%.

Foreign trade in India includes all imports and exports to and from India. At the level of Central Government it is administered by the Ministry of Commerce and Industry. Foreign trade accounted for 48.8% of India's GDP in year 2018. According to data from the Ministry of Commerce and Industry, India's overall exports between April 2021 and June 2021 were estimated at US$ 147.64 billion (a 50.24% YoY increase), while overall imports were estimated at US$ 156.58 billion (80.75% YoY increase). So till now India face a trade deficit. India trades with many Asian countries of South Asian regions including China, Japan, Chili, Saudi Arab, United Arab Emirates, Qatar, Jordan. The country mostly depends on imported goods from these Asian countries. To improve the balance of payment and trade the country now focuses on the development of the Industry, Information Technology, Education and Health sectors.

To enable substantial growth in exports from India and import to India to boost the economy of the country and to double the percentage share of global merchandise trade in the next five years the Government of India has taken several initiatives. The Government of India tries to enhance export to Southeast Asia and other countries of the world and reduce the dependency of foreign product, and also encourages its people to use '*Made in India*' products.

REFERENCES

Aljandalia, A. (2016). *Quantitative Analysis and IBM ® SPSS ® Statistic*. Springer International Publishers. doi:10.1007/978-3-319-45528-0

All India Legal Forum. (2021). *Government Initiatives*. Retrieved from https://allindialegalforum.in/2021/06/11/government-initiatives/

BaberH. (2020). Spillover Effect of COVID-19 on the Global Economy. *Transnational Marketing Journal (TMJ), 8*(2), 177-196. https://ssrn.com/abstract=3717456 doi:10.2139/ssrn.3743111

Buckley, P. J. (1992). Problem and development in the core theory of International Business Studies. *Journal of International Business Studies, 21*(4), 657–665. doi:10.1057/palgrave.jibs.8490346

DuBois, F., & Reeb, D. (2000). Ranking the International Business Journals. *Journal of International Business Studies*, *31*(4), 689–704. doi:10.1057/palgrave.jibs.8490929

Goswami, K. (2020). *India's unemployment rate spiked to 23% due to the Covid-19 lockdown*. Retrieved from https://www.indiatoday.in/education-today/latest-studies/story/indiasunemployment-rate-spike-to-23-due-to-covid-19-lockdown-1665581-2020- 04-10

India Brand Equity Foundation. (2021). *About Indian Economy Growth Rate & Statistics*. Retrieved from https://www.ibef.org/economy/indian-economy-overview

India Population. (2020). *Country meters*. Retrieved from https://countrymeters.info/en/India

Jack, R., & Westwood, R. (2006). Postcolonialism of Qualitative Research in International Business. *Management International Review*, *46*(4), 481–501. doi:10.100711575-006-0102-x

Jagannathan, R. (2020). *Modi must not extend lockdown. The economy won't survive on a ventilator for long*. Retrieved from https://theprint.in/opinion/modi-must-not-extend-lockdown-economywontsurvive-on-ventilator-for-long/397757/

Karvanen, J. (2015). Study design on casual models. *Scandinavian Journal of Statistics*, *42*(2), 361–377. doi:10.1111jos.12110

Lu, H., Stratton, C.W. & Tang, Y. (2020). *An outbreak of pneumonia of unknown etiology in Wuhan, China: The mystery and the miracle.* doi:10.1002/jmv.25678

Mint. (2021). *RBA announces FPI investment limits in G-secs and SDLs*. Retrieved from https://www.live-mint.com/industry/banking/rbi-announces-fpi-investment-limits-in-g-secs-and-sdls-11622479759242.html

Puri, V. K., & Misra, S. K. (2020). *Indian Economy (Its Development Experience)*. Himalaya Publishing House.

Rajan, G. (2020). *Raghuram Rajan on how India can get back to work after coronavirus lockdown*. https://scroll.in/article/958281/full-text-raghuram-rajan-on-how-india-cangetback-to-work-after-coronavirus-lockdown

Sankhe. (2020). *India's turning point: An economic agenda to spur growth and jobs*. McKinsey Global Institute. Retrieved from https://www.mckinsey.com/featured-insights/india/indias-turning-point-an-economic-agenda-to-spur-growth-and-jobs

Sardar, T., Nadim, S. S., Rana, S., & Chattopadhyay, J. (2020). Assessment of lockdown effect in some states and overall India: A predictive mathematical study on COVID-19 outbreak. *Chaos, Solitons, and Fractals*, *139*, 110078. doi:10.1016/j.chaos.2020.110078 PMID:32834620

Sharma, A. (2019). *Indian Economy: An Overview*. Retrieved from https://www.investindia.gov.in/team-india-blogs/indian-economy-overview

Stratton, W., & Yi-Wei, T. (2020). An outbreak of pneumonia of unknown etiology in Wuhan, China: The mystery and the miracle. *Medical Virology*, 401-402.

The Economic Times. (2020). *India to spend $27 billion over 5 years to boost manufacturing*. Retrieved from https://auto.economictimes.indiatimes.com/news/industry/india-to-spend-27-billion-over-5-years-to-boost-manufacturing/79171904

Tisdell, C. A., & Roy, K. C. (Eds.). (1998). *An Overview of Tourism in India's Economic Development*. Nova Science Publishers.

Venkat, V. (2017). Will Budget help double farmers' income. *The Hindu*. Retrieved from https://www.thehindu.com/business/agri-business/Will-Budget-help-double-farmers%E2%80%99-income/article17198101.ece

WTTC. (2018). *Travel & Tourism Economic Impact*. Retrieved from https://www. wttc.org/-/media/files/reports/economic-impact-research/regions-2018/world2018.pdf

Zubedi, S. P. (2013). India's new bilateral investment promotion and protection treaty with Nepal: A new trend in state practice. *ICSID Review*, *28*(2), 384–404. doi:10.1093/icsidreviewit027

ADDITIONAL READING

Bandyopadhyay, R., Morais, D., & Chick, G. (2008). Religion and identity in India's heritage tourism. *Annals of Tourism Research*, *35*(3), 790-808. doi:.annals.2008.06.004 doi:10.1016/j

Kujawa, J. (2017). Spiritual tourism as a quest. *Tourism Management Perspectives*, *24*, 193–200. doi:10.1016/j.tmp.2017.07.011

KEY TERMS AND DEFINITIONS

Coefficient of Variation: The coefficient of variation (CV) is a statistical measure of the relative dispersion of data points in a data series around the mean. The coefficient of variation (CV) is a measure of relative variability of data.

Export: Exports are the exchange of goods and services that are produced in one country and sold to buyers in another.

Import: An import is a good or service bought in one country that was produced in another country or state.

India: The word "India" is a Western transliteration of the Sanskrit word "Sindhu", meaning "body of water". It specifically refers to what we know today as the Indus River, though the word could be used for any large body of water. India is a large peninsular region that is usually referred to as a subcontinent and is located in southern Asia south of the Himalayas between the Bay of Bengal and the Arabian Sea.

Regression Analysis: Regression Analysis is a set of statistical methods used in the estimation of relationship between a dependent variable and one or more independent variables of a research/analysis.

Trend Analysis: Trend analysis is a technique used in technical analysis that attempts to predict future value or price movements based on recently observed trend data for specific research.

Compilation of References

Abe, S. (2006). *Utsukushii kuni e* [Toward a beautiful nation]. Bungei Shunju.

Acharya, R., & Sharma, H. (2012). India's trade intensity with ASEAN countries. *Journal of Commerce and Trade*, *7*(1), 90–95.

Activities in India | India | Countries & Regions | JICA. (n.d.). Retrieved September 7, 2021, from https://www.jica.go.jp/india/english/activities/index.html

Adam, K., Snyder, J., Crooks, V., & Johnston, R. (2015). Tourism discourse and medical tourists' motivations to travel. *Tourism Review*, *70*(2), 85–96. doi:10.1108/TR-04-2014-0015

ADB. (2020). Asian Development Bank. *Policy Brief*, (150), 2–4.

Agarwar, R. (2009-2010). Water Festivals of Thailand. *Silpakorn University International Journal, 9-10*, 7-18. Available at https://citeseerx.ist.psu.edu/viewdoc/download?doi=10.1.1.942.6524&rep=rep1&type=pdf

Agrawal, M., Chaudhary, H., & Tripathi, G. (2010). Enhancing Buddhist tourism in India: An exploratory study. *Worldwide Hospitality and Tourism Themes*, *2*(5), 477–493. doi:10.1108/17554211011090102

Ahmed, B., & Islam, M. T. (2019). Bangladesh-Nepal Trade Relations: Understanding the Influence of Economic Diplomacy. *Jadavpur Journal of International Relations*, *23*(1), 105–119.

Ahmed, Q. M., Butt, M. S., Alam, S., & Kazmi, A. A. (2000). Economic growth, export, and external debt causality: The case of Asian countries. *Pakistan Development Review*, *39*(4), 591–608. doi:10.30541/v39i4IIpp.591-608

Ain, Q. U., & Shah, Z. A. (2019). Neo-Regionalism in South Asia: With Reference to the Emergence of BIMSTEC and BBIN. *Research Journal of Social Sciences, 10*(6).

Akhtar, M. S., Jathol, I., & Hussain, Q. A. (2019). Peace Building through Religious Tourism in Pakistan: A Case Study of Kartarpur Corridor. *Pakistan Social Science Review*, *3*(2), 204–212. doi:10.35484/pssr.2019(3-II)16

Alam. (2015). Indo-Asean Trade relation: An Analysis. *Journal of International Economics*, *6*(1), 73-106.

Alam, M. I. (2015, January-June). Indo-Asean Trade Relation: An Analysis. *Journal of International Economics*, *6*(1), 73–106. http://web.b.ebscohost.com/ehost/pdfviewer/pdfviewer?vid=1&sid=8890abb2-9424-4cde-997f-0746a37baa3d%40sessionmgr103

Ali, M. M. (2020). Digitization of the emerging economy: An exploratory and explanatory case study. *Journal of Governance & Regulation*, *9*(4), 25–36. https://doi.org/10.22495/jgrv9i4art2

Ali, M. M. (2020). Grim situation of the world due to COVID19: Geopolitics under Globalization. *Economic Perspectives*, *3*(1), 24–29.

Ali, S. M. (2018). The Current and Future State of India–Bangladesh Relations. *Strategic Analysis*, *42*(5), 529–537. doi:10.1080/09700161.2018.1523079

Aljandalia, A. (2016). *Quantitative Analysis and IBM® SPSS® Statistic*. Springer International Publishers. doi:10.1007/978-3-319-45528-0

All India Legal Forum. (2021). *Government Initiatives*. Retrieved from https://allindialegalforum.in/2021/06/11/government-initiatives/

Almuzaini, T., Choonara, I., & Sammons, H. (2013). *Substandard and counterfeit medicines: A systematic review of the literature*. doi:10.1136/bmjopen-2013-002923

Alonso-Garbayo, Á., & Maben, J. (2009). Internationally recruited nurses from India and the Philippines in the United Kingdom: The decision to emigrate. *Human Resources for Health*, *37*(7), 37. Advance online publication. doi:10.1186/1478-4491-7-37 PMID:19393080

Amrith, S. S. (2013). *Crossing the Bay of Bengal: The furies of nature and the fortunes of migrants*. Harvard University Press.

Anderson, J. E. (1979). A theoretical foundation for the gravity equation. *The American Economic Review*, *69*, 106–116.

Andrews, M., Areekal, B., Rajesh, K. R., Krishnan, J., Suryakala, R., Krishnan, B., Muraly, C., & Santhosh, P. V. (2020). First confirmed case of COVID-19 infection in India: A case report. *The Indian Journal of Medical Research*, *151*(5), 490–492. doi:10.4103/ijmr.IJMR_2131_20 PMID:32611918

ANI. (2021, August 18). Afghanistan: Taliban stopped exports, imports from India, says FIEO DG. *Business Standard India*. https://www.business-standard.com/article/news-ani/taliban-stop-exports-imports-from-india-121081801275_1.html

Arunmozhi, T., & Panneerselvam, A. (2013). Types of Tourism in India. *International Journal of Current Research and Academic Review*, *1*(1), 84–88.

ASEAN. (2020). Retrieved from https://asean.org/storage/53-Finalised-and-APPROVED-TOR_COVID-19-ASEAN-Response-Fund.pdf

ASEAN's quiet resilience. (2019, December 8). *East Asia Forum*. https://www.eastasiaforum.org/2019/12/08/aseans-quiet-resilience/

ASEANBRIEFING. (2020, March 10). *Indonesia unveils stimulus package to combat Coronavirus*. Retrieved from https://www.aseanbriefing.com/news/indonesia-unveils-stimulus-package-to-combat-coronavirus-impact/

Asher, M., & Sen, R. (2006). *The Role of Japan in BIMSTEC*. Lee Kuan Yew School of Public Policy, National University of Singapore.

Ashton, A. S. (2018, November 2). Spiritual retreat tourism development in the Asia Pacific region: investigating the impact of tourist satisfaction and intention to revisit: a Chiang Mai, Thailand case study. *Asia Pacific Journal of Tourism Research*, *23*(11), 1098–1114. Advance online publication. doi:10.1080/10941665.2018.1526198

Asia Regional Integration Center. (2021). *Tracking Asian Integration*. Retrieved from https://aric.adb.org/fta/india-bhutan-trade-agreement

Asiaasset. (2020, April 27). Philippine lawmakers draft 1.3 trillion-peso stimulus bill. *The Journal of Investments and Pensions*.

Asian Development Bank. (2018). *Updating and Enhancement of the BIMSTEC Transport Infrastructure and Logistics Study*. Final report, July, p.32.

Asmussen, C. G. (2014). Strategic factor markets, scale free resources, and economic performance: The impact of product market rivalry. *Strategic Management Journal, 36*(12), 1826–1844. doi:10.1002/smj.2315

Atrey, P. (2014). India-Japan Relations: Economic, Strategic and Security Co-operation. UGC Centre for Southeast Asian & Pacific Studies. D&Dee Publications.

Attanayake, C. (2019). Sri Lankan perspective on the Bay of Bengal. *Journal of the Indian Ocean Region, 15*(3), 356–362.

Awokuse, T. O. (2008). Trade openness and economic growth: Is growth export-led or import-led? *Applied Economics, 40*(2), 161–173. doi:10.1080/00036840600749490

Ayres, A. (2018). *Our time has come: how India is making its place in the world.* Oxford University Press.

Baack, B. D., & Ray, E. J. (1983). The political economy of tariff policy: A case study of the United States. *Explorations in Economic History, 20*(1), 73–93. doi:10.1016/0014-4983(83)90043-8

BaberH. (2020). Spillover Effect of COVID-19 on the Global Economy. *Transnational Marketing Journal (TMJ), 8*(2), 177-196. https://ssrn.com/abstract=3717456 doi:10.2139/ssrn.3743111

Bajpaee, C. (2017). Dephasing India's Look East/Act East. *Contemporary Southeast Asia: A Journal of International and Strategic Affairs, 39*(2), 349.

Bajpaee, C. (2017). Dephasing India's Look East/Act East Policy. *Contemporary Southeast Asia: A Journal of International and Strategic Affairs, 39*(2), 348-372.

Bajpaee, C. (2017). Dephasing India's Look East/Act East Policy. *Contemporary Southeast Asia, 39*(3), 348–372. doi:10.1355/cs39-2d

Balaguer, J., & Cantavella-Jordá, M. (2002). Tourism as a Long-run Economic Growth Factor: The Spanish Case. *Applied Economics, 34*(7), 877–884. doi:10.1080/00036840110058923

Balance of Payments and International Investment Position Manual. (2013). In Goods and Services Account. International Monetary Fund.

Balasubramanian, J. (2015, Nov. 21). *PM Modi Proposes $1 billion line of credit for connectivity with Asean.* Retrieved from https://www.livemint.com/Politics/riD4W4GN503dmSAGwBtZQN/PM-Modi-proposes-1-billion-line-of-credit-for-connectivity.html

Ball, D. A. (2010). *International Business: the challenge of global competition.* McGraw-Hill Higher Education.

Baltagi, B. H. (2015). *The Oxford handbook of panel data.* Oxford University Press. doi:10.1093/oxfordhb/9780199940042.001.0001

Baltagi, B. H., & Wu, P. X. (1999). Unequally spaced panel data regressions with AR(1) disturbances. *Econometric Theory, 15*(6), 814–823. doi:10.1017/S0266466699156020

Banerjee, K., & Dey, D. (2017). *Trade-in energy services in BCIM, BIMSTEC+ 1, and ASEAN+ 4 regions-potentials and Challenges.* Academic Press.

BanerjeeK.DeyD. (2016). *India and BIMSTEC: A Comparative Study of the Trade Potential of India's Energy Sector Products in BIMSTEC and BIMSTEC 1 Region.* doi:10.2139/ssrn.2874294

Banerjee, S., & Basu, P. (2021, April). India-Japan Partnership in Third Countries: A Study of Bangladesh and Myanmar. *Observer Research Foundation (ORF) Issue Brief,* (460), 3–18.

Bangladesh Bank. (2021a). *Import Data.* Retrieved from https://www.bb.org.bd/pub/annual/imppayment/imp1920/statable5.pdf

Bangladesh Bank. (2021b). *Export Data.* Retrieved from https://www.bb.org.bd/openpdf.php https://www.bb.org.bd/pub/annual/expreceipt/exp1920/index1920.php

Banik, A., & Bhaumik, P. K. (2005). *Neighbourhood revisited: Explaining Japanese foreign direct investment in the BIMSTEC region.* CSIRD Discussion Paper: 9/2005. Retrieved from https://www. researchgate. net/profile/Arindam_Banik/publication/253473057_Neighbourhood_Revisited_Explaining_Ja panese_Foreign_Direct_Investment_in_the_BIMSTEC_Region/links/546e1edb0cf2b5fc1760 4320. pdf

Banik, N., & Kim, M. (2020). India-ASEAN Trade Relations: Examining the trends and Identifying the Potential. *Global Business Review.* Retrieved from https://sci-hub.tf/10.1177/0972150920953546

Banlaoi, R.C. (2003). Southeast Asian Perspectives on the Rise of China: Regional Security after 9/11. *Parameters,* (Summer).

Barro, R. J., & Sala-i-Martin, X. (1995). *Economic growth.* McGrow-Hill.

Barua, A. & Das, S.K. (2008). Perspectives on Growth and Development in the Northeast: The Look East Policy and Beyond. *Margin-The Journal of Applied Economic Research, 2*(4), 327-350. doi:10.1177/097380100800200401

Barua, T. (2020). The Lok East Policy/ Act East Policy-driven Development Model in Northeast India. *Jadavpur Journal of International Relations, 24*(1), 101-120. Retrieved from https://journals.sagepub.com/doi/pdf/10.1177/0973598420908844

Batra, A. (2006). India's global trade potential: The gravity model approach. *Global Economic Review, 35*(3), 327–361. doi:10.1080/12265080600888090

Batra, A. (2010). Asian economic integration and sub-regionalism: A case study of the BIMSTEC. *International Studies, 47*(1), 1–25. doi:10.1177/002088171104700101

BBC News. (2018 July 11). *India Government is 'failing' to protect Taj Mahal.* Available at https://www.bbc.com/news/world-asia-india-44763867

Berg, B. (2001). *Qualitative research methods for the social sciences* (4th ed.). Allyn & Bacon.

Bergstrand, J. H. (1985). The gravity equation in international trade: Some microeconomic foundations and empirical evidence. *The Review of Economics and Statistics, 67*(3), 474–481. doi:10.2307/1925976

Bergstrand, J. H. (1989). The generalized gravity equation, monopolistic competition, and the factor-proportions theory in international trade. *The Review of Economics and Statistics, 71*(1), 143–153. doi:10.2307/1928061

Bezbaruah, M. P., & Sarma, A. (2009, March). Industry in the Development Perspective of North East India. *Dialogue, 10*(3).

Bhagwati, J., & Srinivasan, T. (1979). Trade Policy and Development. In R. Dornbunsch & J. Frenkel (Eds.), *International Economic Policy: Theory and Evidence* (pp. 1–35). Johns Hopkins University Press.

Bharadwaj, S. (2019, March 19). In Meghalaya's patriarchy-driven matrilineal society, women turn entrepreneurs for livelihood. *First Post.* Retrieved from https://www.firstpost.com/india/in-meghalayas-patriarchy-driven-matrilineal-society-women-turn-entrepreneurs-for-livelihood-6286081.html

Bhargava, A., Sosa-Escuderı, W., & Narendranathan, W. (1982). Serial correlation and fixed effects models. *The Review of Economic Studies, 49*(4), 533–549. doi:10.2307/2297285

Bhatia, R. (2019). *India's Act Policy: Gains and Prospects*. Retrieved from https://www.gatewayhouse.in

Bhattacharjee, D. (2016). *India's Act East Policy: Problems and Prospects in North East India*. Indian Council of World Affairs.

Bhattacharjee, J. (2018). SAARC vs BIMSTEC: The search for the ideal platform for regional cooperation. *Observer Issue Brief*, *226*, 1–12.

Bhattacharya, S. K., & Bhattacharyay, B. N. (2006). *Prospects of regional cooperation in trade, investment and finance in Asia: an empirical analysis on BIMSTEC countries and Japan*. Academic Press.

Bhattacharya, S. K., & Bhattacharyay, B. N. (2007). An empirical analysis on prospects and challenges of BIMSTEC-Japan trade integration. *Journal of Asian Economics*, *18*(3), 509–536. doi:10.1016/j.asieco.2007.03.001

Bhattacharyya, R., & Mandal, A. (2016). India-ASEAN free trade agreement: An ex post evaluation. *Journal of Policy Modeling*, *38*(32), 340–352. doi:10.1016/j.jpolmod.2016.02.001

Bhaumik, A. (2021). India resumes helping others with Covid-19 aid to counter China; sends oxygen to Bangladesh, Indonesia. *Deccan Herald*. https://www.deccanherald.com/national/india-resumes-helping-others-with-covid-19-aid-to-counter-china-sends-oxygen-to-bangladesh-indonesia-1012490.html

Bhowmick, S., & Basu, P. (2020). *BIMSTEC and the Fourth Industrial Revolution: The Role of Technology in Regional Development*. Academic Press.

Bhowmik, D. (2019). Impact of Indo-ASEAN import on ASEAN trade and financial integration. *Empirical Economic Review*, *2*(1), 1–34. doi:10.29145/eer/21/020101

Bhure, R., & Malegaonkar, V. (2019). India's Act East Policy-A Need for Enhancing Connectivity. In P. M. Kamath (Ed.), *Act East Policy of NDA II and Primary Goals: Economic Development, Democracy and National Security* (p. 21). Kalpaz Publications.

Bhutia, S. (2020). Sustainable Tourism for Regional Development in North-East States of India: Trends, Problems and Prospects. *Global Journal of Human-Social Science: B Geography, Geo-Sciences, Environmental Science & Disaster Management*, *20*(2). Retrieved from https://globaljournals.org/GJHSS_Volume20/3-Sustainable-Tourism-for-Regional.pdf

Blouin, C., Chopra, M., & Hoeven, R. V. (2009). Trade and social determinants of health. *Lancet*, *373*(9662), 502–507. doi:10.1016/S0140-6736(08)61777-8 PMID:19167058

Bond, K., Ospina, M. B., Blitz, S., Afilalo, M., Campbell, S. G., Bullard, M., Innes, G., Holroyd, B., Curry, G., Schull, M., & Rowe, B. (2007). Frequency, determinants, and impact of overcrowding in emergency departments in Canada: A national survey. *Healthcare Quarterly*, *10*(4), 32–40. doi:10.12927/hcq.2007.19312 PMID:18019897

Bone, K. (2013). Spiritual Retreat Tourism in New Zealand. *Tourism Recreation Research*, *38*(3), 295–309. doi:10.1080/02508281.2013.11081755

Borensztein, E., De Gregorio, J., & Lee, J. (1998). How does foreign direct investment affect economic growth? *Journal of International Economics*, *45*(1), 115–135. doi:10.1016/S0022-1996(97)00033-0

Boseley, M. (2020, June 4). Trans-Tasman Travel Bubble: Canberra Airport Asks People to Register Interest for New Zealand Flights. *The Guardian*.

Bougheas, S., Demetriades, P., & Morgenroth, E. (1999). Infrastructure, transport costs and trade. *Journal of International Economics*, *47*(1), 169–189. doi:10.1016/S0022-1996(98)00008-7

Bragta, S. K. (2021, July). Evolving India's Look East to Act East Policy: An Analytical View. *European Online Journal of Natural and Social Sciences, 10*(3), 325-333.

Brahma, A. (2018). India's Act East Policy: The North-East States. *International Journal of Innovative Research in Science, 7*(9).

Breg, J. (2013). *Now and Forever: Growth, Impacts and Future Evolution of Wedding Tourism* [Research paper]. University of Guelph.

Breusch, T., & Pagan, A. (1980). The lanrange multiplier test and its applications to model specification in econometrics. *The Review of Economic Studies*, *47*(1), 239–253. doi:10.2307/2297111

Brewster, D. (2014). Dividing lines: Evolving mental maps of the Bay of. *Asian Security*, *10*(02), 151–167. doi:10.1080/14799855.2014.914499

Brewster, D. (2015). The rise of the Bengal Tigers: The growing strategic importance of the Bay of Bengal. *Journal of Defense Studies*, *09*(02), 81–104.

Brief on India-Thailand Relations. (2018, Dec.). Available at https://mea.gov.in/Portal/ForeignRelation/Thailand_Brief_Dec_2018.pdf

Brinkerhoff, D. W. (2004). Accountability and health systems: Toward conceptual clarity and policy relevance. *Health Policy and Planning*, *19*(6), 371–379. doi:10.1093/heapol/czh052 PMID:15459162

Brown, M. B., & Forsythe, A. B. (1974). The small sample behavior of some statistic which test the equality of several means. *Technometrics*, *16*(1), 129–132. doi:10.1080/00401706.1974.10489158

Brunn, S. (Ed.). (2015). *The Changing World Religion Map*. Springer. doi:10.1007/978-94-017-9376-6

Buckley, P. J. (1992). Problem and development in the core theory of International Business Studies. *Journal of International Business Studies*, *21*(4), 657–665. doi:10.1057/palgrave.jibs.8490346

Buddhist Circuit (2021). *Tourist Train Official Website*. irctcbuddhisttrain.com

Buhalis, D. (2000). Marketing the competitive destination of the future. *Tourism Management*, *21*(1), 97–116. doi:10.1016/S0261-5177(99)00095-3

Build Back Better World Initiative. (n.d.). *A Partnership Against or Beyond China? | Manohar Parrikar Institute for Defence Studies and Analyses*. Retrieved September 3, 2021, from https://idsa.in/issuebrief/build-back-better-world-initiative-jpanda-090821

Burns, R. (2015). Medical tourism opportunities and challenges: Illustration from US-India trade. *International Journal of Healthcare Management*, *8*(1), 15–26. doi:10.1179/2047971914Y.0000000091

Business Line. (2014, July 17). Retrieved from https://www.cbi.eu/market-information/tourism/religious-tourism/market-potential

Caleb, G., Mazanai, M., & Dhoro, N. L. (2014, September). Relationship between International Trade and Economic Growth: A Cointegration Analysis for Zimbabwe. *Mediterranean Journal of Social Sciences*, *5*(20), 621–627. doi:10.5901/mjss.2014.v5n20p621

Carbaugh. (2008). *International Economics* (11th ed.). New Delhi: Cengage Learning India Pvt Ltd.

Central Bureau of Statistics (CBS). (2010). Indonesia in Number Book. Statistical Yearbook of Indonesia 2010. Badan Pusat Statistik, BPS.

Central Bureau of Statistics (CBS). (2011). Indonesia in Number Book. Statistical Yearbook of Indonesia 2011. Badan Pusat Statistik, BPS.

Chakrabarti, S. (2014). *India Struggling to define its 'Look East' policy looks set to continue.* Available at https://theconversation.com/indias-struggle-to-define-its-look-east-policy-looks-set-to-continue-28104

Chakraborty, S. (2011). Developing an Integrated Tourism Circuit in Gar Mandaran Kamarpukur Joyrambati in the State of West Bengal, India. *South Asian Journal of Tourism Heritage*, *4*(1), 144–155.

Chakravarty, P. R. (2021, February). COVID-19 and the changing geopolitical order: Changes to BIMSTEC. *Observer Research Foundation. Issue Brief*, (441), 1–10.

Chan, A. O. M., Chan, Y. H., & Kee, J. P. C. (2013). Exposure to crises and resiliency of healthcare workers in Singapore. *Occupational Medicine (Oxford, England)*, *63*(2), 141–144. doi:10.1093/occmed/kqs202 PMID:23223749

Chanda, R., & Tokas, K. (2020). *India–Japan Relations in Services & the India–Japan Comprehensive Economic Partnership Agreement.* Academic Press.

Chanda, R. (2002). Trade-in health services. *Bulletin of the World Health Organization*, *80*, 158–163. PMID:11953795

Chandiramani, J. (2019). Transforming India 2030: Strategies for Sustainable Development Goals. In *International Conference Proceedings*. New Delhi: Capital Publishing Company. Available at https://sse.ac.in/assets/pdf/TransformingIndia2030Completefile.pdf

Chandran, B. P. (2019). India BIMSTEC Economic Cooperation: Potential and Prospects. *Indian Journal of Economics and Development*, *15*(4), 489–498. doi:10.5958/2322-0430.2019.00064.7

Chandran, S., & Mukhtar, J. (2019). Indo-ASEAN Trade Relation: Understanding the advantage sector for India by using Balassa's RCA Index. *Journal of Emerging Technologies and Innovative Research*, *6*(6), 633–640.

Chansoria, M. (2017). Japanese investments are instrumental to India's Act East Policy. *Asia Pacific Bulletin, 385.*

Chaturvedi, A., & Sharma, H. P. (2020, May 20). India's Foreign Policy: A Transformation From 'Look-East' to 'Act-East'. *Journal of Critical Reviews*, *7*(11), 882–885.

Chaudhuri, R., & Shende, S. (2020). *Dealing With the Taliban: India's Strategy in Afghanistan After U.S. Withdrawal.* https://carnegieendowment.org/files/Chaudhuri_Shende_-_Afghanistan.pdf

Chaudhuri, S. (2013). Manufacturing trade deficit and industrial policy in India. *Economic and Political Weekly*, 41–50.

Chee, H. L. (2008). Ownership, control, and contention: Challenges for the future of healthcare in Malaysia. *Social Science & Medicine*, *66*(10), 2145–2156. doi:10.1016/j.socscimed.2008.01.036 PMID:18329149

Chellaney, B. (2020, January 14). Toward an Indo-Pacific concert of democracies. *The Japan Times*. https://www.japantimes.co.jp/opinion/2020/01/14/commentary/japan-commentary/toward-indo-pacific-concert-democracies/#.XrjCI6YVBtU

Cheng, I.-H., & Tsai, Y.-Y. (2008). Estimating the staged effects of regional economic integration on trade volumes. *Applied Economics*, *40*(3), 383–393. doi:10.1080/00036840600606252

Cheng, I.-H., & Wall, H. J. (2005). Controlling heterogeneity in gravity models of trade and integration. *Review - Federal Reserve Bank of St. Louis*, *87*(1), 49–63. doi:10.20955/r.87.49-64

Chen, L. L., Scott, N., & Benckendorff, P. (2017). Mindful tourist experiences: A Buddhist perspective. *Annals of Tourism Research*, *64*, 1–12. doi:10.1016/j.annals.2017.01.013

China, Japan reach breakthrough tariff reduction under RCEP, which products may cost less? (n.d.). https://news.cgtn.com/news/2020-12-01/China-Japan-reach-tariff-reduction-which-products-may-cost-less--VRkd1JKl5S/index.html

Cho, H., & Park, S-H. (2013). The Rise of China and Varying Sentiments in Southeast Asia toward Great Powers. *Strategic Studies Quarterly,* 69-92.

Cho, H., & Park, S-H. (2013). The Rise of China and Varying Sentiments in Southeast Asia toward Great Powers. *Strategic Studies Quarterly*, (Summer), 69–92.

Chorn, A., & Stromseth, J. (2021, May 19). *COVID-19 comes to Cambodia.* Brookings. Retrieved from https://www.brookings.edu/blog/order-from-chaos/2021/05/19/covid-19-comes-to-cambodia/

Chotani, V. M. (2018). BIMSTEC and Japan: Exploring Prospects for Renewed Cooperation. *Issue Brief*, 236.

Choudhry, D.R. (2020, Nov. 13). India announces $1 million aid to ASEAN COVID-19 response Fund. *Economic Times.*

Choudhury, S. (2017 January). *Northeast India and the Act East Policy: Opportunity & Challenges.* Retrieved https://researchgate.net/publication/320921997

Choudhury, S. (2017). *The Act East Policy and Northeast India: Challenges and Opportunities.* https://www.researchgate.net/publication/320921997

Choudhury, S. R. (2017). India–Japan Relations. *International Studies*, *54*(1-4), 106–126. doi:10.1177/0020881718791404

Ciccone, D. K., Vian, T., Maurer, L., & Bradley, E. H. (2014). Linking governance mechanisms to health outcomes: A review of the literature in low-and middle-income countries. *Social Science & Medicine*, *1*(117), 86–95. doi:10.1016/j.socscimed.2014.07.010 PMID:25054281

Cohen, E. (1992). Pilgrimage centre: Concentric and excentric. *Annals of Tourism Research*, *18*(1), 33–50. doi:10.1016/0160-7383(92)90105-X

Cole, M. T., & Eckel, C. (2014). *Tariffs Passing Through Retailers: Do Tariffs Actually Protect Domestic Manufacturers?* Academic Press.

CPI. (2020). *Asia Pacific – News.* Transparency.org

Creswell, J. W. (2003). *Research design: Qualitative, quantitative, and mixed methods approaches.* SAGE.

Current Affairs (2018). Swadesh darshan Scheme. Retrieved from Government to expand Buddhist tourism circuit to 21 more states. *GK Today.*

D'Ambrogio, E. (2021). The Quad: An emerging multilateral security framework of democracies in the Indo-Pacific region. *European Parliament Research Services.* Available at https://www.europarl.europa.eu/RegData/etudes/BRIE/2021/690513/EPRS_BRI(2021)690513_EN.pdf

D'Amore, L. (2009). Peace through Tourism: The Birthing of a New Socio-Economic Order. *Journal of Business Ethics*, *89*(4), 559–568. doi:10.100710551-010-0407-3

Danesh, V. C., Malvey, D., & Fottler, M. D. (2008). Hidden workplace violence: What your nurses may not be telling you. *Healthcare Management (Frederick)*, *27*(4), 357–363. doi:10.1097/HCM.0b013e31818c810b PMID:19011419

Darwis, V., & Rusastra, I. W. (2011, June). Optimizing Rural Community Empowerment through Integrating PUAP and Desa Mandiri Pangan Programs. *Agricultural Policy Analysis Journal.*, *9*(2), 125–142.

Das, G., Das, S. C., & Paul, U. (2018). Look East Policy: Economic Engagement with ASEAN and East Asian Countries. In G. Das & C. J. Thomas (Eds.), Look East to Act East Policy: Implications for India's northeast. Academic Press.

Das, A. (2016). The Politics of Pilgrimage Through the Prism of Mass Media. *International Journal of Religious Tourism and Pilgrimage, 4*(6), 55–66.

Das, G., & Thomas, J. (Eds.). (2016). *Look East to Act East Policy: Implications for India's Northeast*. Routledge. doi:10.4324/9781315657660

Dash, Z. (2018). Economic Security: The Missing Link in India's National Security Architecture. *Strategic Analysis, 42*(6), 633–639. doi:10.1080/09700161.2018.1557931

Das, P. (2018). Security Challenges and the Management of the India–Myanmar Border. *Strategic Analysis, 42*(6), 578–594.

de Hoyos, L. (1995). Terrorism in South Asia: London's assault on the nation-state. *Executive Intelligence Review, 22*(41), 22–41.

De, P. (2015). *ASEAN –INDIA Air Connectivity Report, Round Table on ASEAN-India Air Connectivity*. ASEAN India Centre Research and Information System for (RIS) Developing Countries.

De, P. (2019, June 1). Act east to act Indo-Pacific: Agenda for the new government. *The Economic Times*. Retrieved from https://economictimes.indiatimes.com/news/defence/act-east-to-act-indo-pacific-agenda-for-the-new-government/articleshow/69591279.cms

De, P. (2019, Oct 16). Act East – North East: Unlocking the Potentials. *The Economic Times*. Retrieved from https://economictimes.indiatimes.com/blogs/et-commentary/act-east-north-east-unlocking-the-potentials/

De, D., Joshi, R. M., & Amin, U. M. (2014). Impact of BIMSTEC trade agreement on strengthening export performance of Indian firms: An empirical assessment. *International Journal of Business and Globalisation, 12*(4), 457–470. doi:10.1504/IJBG.2014.062845

Deng, C. (2012). *Key Factors of Wedding Tourism in Bangkok, Thailand*. The Assumption University Library. Available at: https://repository.au.edu/bitstream/handle/6623004553/2557/AU-Thesis-Fulltext-222439.pdf?sequence=1

Dey, M. (2021, January 31). Impact of COVID-19 on travel and tourism industry and ways of recovery. *Financial Express*.

DeyD. (2006). *BIMSTEC-Japan: Investment Opportunities and Challenges*. Available at SSRN 905096.

DFAT. (2019). *Trade and Investment at a Glance*. Australian Government, Department of Foreign Affairs and Trade. Retrieved from https://www.dfat.gov.au/about-us/publications/trade-investment/trade-at-a-glance/trade-investment-at-a-glance-2019/Pages/default#exports

Dhaka Tribune. (2020, June 5). *23rd BIMSTEC Day: BIMSTEC leaders for joint efforts to combat Covid-19 impact*. Author.

Diebold, F. X. (2020). Real-time real economic activity: Exiting the great recession and entering the pandemic recession (No. w27482). National Bureau of Economic Research.

Does Afghanistan Present a New Opportunity for the Quad? (2021, June 17). *Geopolitical Monitor*. https://www.geopoliticalmonitor.com/does-afghanistan-present-a-new-opportunity-for-the-quad/

Dollar, D. (1992). Outward-oriented developing economies really do grow more rapidly: Evidence from LCDs. 1976-1985. *Economic Development and Cultural Change, 40*(3), 523–544. doi:10.1086/451959

Dollar, D., & Kraay, A. (2004). Trade, Growth and Poverty. *Economic Journal (London), 114*(493), F22–F49. doi:10.1111/j.0013-0133.2004.00186.x

Downie, E. (2015). Manipur and India's 'Act East' Policy. *The Diplomat*. Available at https://thediplomat.com/2015/02/manipur-and-indias-act-east-policy/

Drishti. (2021). *India's Act East Policy*. Retrieved from https://www.drishtiias.com/daily-updates/daily-news-analysis/india-s-act-east-policy-1

Drysdale, P., & Garnaut, R. (1982). Trade intensities and the analysis of bilateral trade flows in a many-country world: A survey. *Hitotsubashi Journal of Economics*, *22*(2), 62–84.

Dubey, R. (2014). *North East India in India's Look East Policy: Constraints and Social Research Foundation*. http://srfaurangabad.org/journals/4thissue/11.pdf

DuBois, F., & Reeb, D. (2000). Ranking the International Business Journals. *Journal of International Business Studies*, *31*(4), 689–704. doi:10.1057/palgrave.jibs.8490929

Duncan, F. (2003). *Corruption in the health sector*. USAID Bureau for Europe & Eurasia, Office of Democracy and Governance.

Economic Survey. (2021). Department of Economic Affairs, Ministry of Finance, Government of India.

Eggers, A. J. T. (n.d.). *U.S. Policy in Afghanistan: Changing Strategies, Preserving Gains*. Carnegie Endowment for International Peace. Retrieved August 30, 2021, from https://carnegieendowment.org/2017/05/22/u.s.-policy-in-afghanistan-changing-strategies-preservinggains-pub-70027

Elangovan, A. (2019). BIMSTEC, A weak cross-border organization? The growing economies show convergence. г. *Петрозаводск*, *26*, 13.

Eris, M., & Ulaşan, B. (2013, July). Trade openness and economic growth: Bayesian model averaging estimate of cross-country growth regressions. *Economic Modelling*, *33*, 867–883. doi:10.1016/j.econmod.2013.05.014

Ernst & Young LLP. (2019). *India: Building the best practices in healthcare services globally*. https://ficci.in/spdocument/23136/FICCI-EY-Report-on-MVT.pdf

ETHealthworld.com. (2021, June 18). *Indonesia gets $1.3 bln loans from World Bank for Covid response, reforms*. Retrieved from www.health.economictimes.indiatimes.com

Expanding Quad to economic sphere easier said than done - Global Times. (n.d.). Retrieved August 30, 2021, from https://www.globaltimes.cn/page/202105/1223723.shtml

Factor, R., & Kang, M. (2015). Corruption and population health outcomes: An analysis of data from 133 countries using structural equation modeling. *International Journal of Public Health*, *60*(6), 633–641. doi:10.100700038-015-0687-6 PMID:25994589

Falcon, D. J. (2019). The Healthcare Gap in Rural Malaysia. Lehigh University, 37(6).

Farooq, M. A. (2012). Development of Spiritual Tourism Circuits: The Case. *GSTF Journal on Business Review (GBR)*, 212 – 218.

Feder, G. (1982). On export and economic growth. *Journal of Development Economics*, *12*(1-2), 59–73. doi:10.1016/0304-3878(83)90031-7

Felix, G., & Bello, G. K. (2019). Skills gaps and training needs in the tourism sector in Malawi. *African Journal of Hospitality, Tourism and Leisure*, 1–18.

Femina. (2020). *Meet the Scientist Behind India's First Coronavirus Testing Kit*. https://www.femina.in/trending/achievers/meet-the-scientist-behind-indias-first-coronavirus-testing-kit-152629.html

Fereday, J., & Muir-Cochrane, E. (2006). Demonstrating rigor using thematic analysis: A hybrid approach of inductive and deductive coding and theme development. *International Journal of Qualitative Methods*, *5*(1), 80–92. doi:10.1177/160940690600500107

Finney, R. Z., Orwig, R. A., & Spake, D. F. (2009). Lotus-eaters, pilgrims, seekers, and accidental tourists: How different travellers consume the sacred and the profane. *Services Marketing Quarterly*, *30*(2), 148–173. doi:10.1080/15332960802619181

Flake, L., Smith, S., Sambhi, N., Wilson, J., Jaishankar, D., Baruah, D., Lang, D., Padmanabhan, A., & Reddy, M. (n.d.). *Tasks For India's Regional Integration.* https://perthusasia.edu.au/getattachment/Our-Work/Realising-the-Indo-Pacific/PU-24-India-Book-WEB.pdf.aspx?lang=en-AU

Friedman, M. (1937). The use of ranks to avoid the assumption of normality implicit in the analysis of variance. *Journal of the American Statistical Association*, *32*(200), 675–701. doi:10.1080/01621459.1937.10503522

Frost, E. L. (2017). *It's time to deepen integration around the Bay of Bengal.* Carnegie India.

Fung, A., Graham, M., & Weil, D. (2007). *Full disclosure: the perils and promise of transparency.* Cambridge University Press. doi:10.1017/CBO9780511510533

Gaena, B., & Ruohomäki, O. (2017). *India's 'Look East' – 'Act East' Policy: Hedging as a Foreign Policy Tool.* FIIA, Briefing paper 222. Available at https://www.fiia.fi/en/publication/indias-look-east-act-east-policy

Gaffar, V., Wetprasit, P., Setiyorini, D., & Puspito, H. (2011). *Comparative Study of Tourist Characteristics on Cultural Heritage Tourism Sites: Survey on Tourist in Indonesia and Thailand Heritage Sites*. Available at https://www.researchgate.net/publication/294682211_COMPARATIVE_STUDY_OF_TOURIST_CHARACTERISTICS_ON_CULTURAL_HERITAGE_TOURISM_SITES_SURVEY_ON_TOURIST_IN_INDONESIA_AND_THAILAND_HERITAGE_SITES/citation/download doi:10.13140/RG.2.1.1605.3525

Gandhi, V. P., & Marsh, R. (2003). Development nd Poverty Reduction: Do Institutions Matter? A Study on the Impact of Local Institutions in Rural India. *The 25th International Conference of Agricultural Economists.*

Ganguly, S. (2017). Had Modi truly changed India's foreign Policy? *The Washington Quarterly*, *40*(2), 131–143. doi:10.1080/0163660X.2017.1328929

Gautam, P. L. (2013). Minimizing medication errors: Moving attention from individual to system. *Journal of Anesthesia*, *29*, 293–294. PMID:24106347

Geary, D. (2008). Destination enlightenment: Branding Buddhism and spiritual tourism in Bodhgaya, Bihar. *Anthropology Today*, *24*(3), 11–14. doi:10.1111/j.1467-8322.2008.00584.x

Getz, D. (2007). Event tourism: Definition, evolution, and research. *Tourism Management*, 403–428.

Ghosh. (2016). *International relation* (3rd ed.). Delhi: Phi learning Publisher Pvt Ltd.

GHSI. (2019). Validation analysis of Global Health Security Index (GHSI) scores 2019. BMJ Global Health, 5.

Ghuman, R. S., & Madaan, D. K. (2009). India-ASEAN trade relations during post-WTO period. WTO and Asian union, deep and deep publications, 395-406.

Gibson, H. J. (1998). Sport Tourism: A critical analysis of research. *Sport Management Review*, *1*(1), 45–76. doi:10.1016/S1441-3523(98)70099-3

Gilbert, J. (2008). *BIMSTEC-Japan trade cooperation and poverty in Asia.* Centre for Studies in Asia in International Relations and Development, CSIRD Discussion paper, (9201).

Global Data. (2021). Retrieved from https://www.globaldata.com/

Gogoi, J. K., Goswamin, H., & Borah, K. C. (2009). *Problems of border areas in NE- India: Implications for the 13th Finance Commission*. Government of India. Available at https://fincomindia.nic.in/writereaddata/html_en_files/oldcommission_html/fincom13/discussion/report14.pdf

Goldberg, J. (2019). What is India's Look East Policy? *ThoughtCo*. Available at https://www.thoughtco.com/look-east-policy-of-india-1435050

Goswami, K. (2020). *India's unemployment rate spiked to 23% due to the Covid-19 lockdown*. Retrieved from https://www.indiatoday.in/education-today/latest-studies/story/indiasunemployment-rate-spike-to-23-due-to-covid-19-lockdown-1665581-2020- 04-10

Goyal, & Mukherjee. (2015). *Reinvigorating India's manufacturing sector: Integrating the services value chain with Southeast Asia*. International Growth Centre Blog.

Grewal, B., Grunfeld, H., & Sheehan, P. (2012). *The contribution of agricultural growth to poverty reduction*. ACIAR Impact Assessment Series Report No. 76. Australian Centre for International Agricultural Research.

Griffin, K., & Raj, R. (2017). The Importance of Religious Tourism and Pilgrimage: Reflecting on definitions, motives, and data. *International Journal of Religious Tourism and Pilgrimage, 5*(3), 1–9.

Guest, G. (2012). *Applied thematic analysis*. Sage Publications. doi:10.4135/9781483384436

Gupta, S., Davoodi, H. R., & Tiongson, E. R. (2002). Corruption and the provision of healthcare and education services. In G. T. Abed & S. Gupta (Eds.), *Governance, corruption, and economic performance* (pp. 245–272). International Monetary Fund.

Hall, I. (2016). Multialignment and Indian Foreign Policy under Narendra Modi. *The Commonwealth Journal of International Affair, 105*(3), 271–286. doi:10.1080/00358533.2016.1180760

Hansbrough, J. V. (n.d.). *From the blue dot network to the blue dot marketplace: A way to cooperate in strategic*. https://apcss.org/wp-content/uploads/2020/09/11-Hansborough-25thA.pdf

Haokip, T. (2011, September). India's Look East Policy: Its Evolution and Approach. *South Asia Survey, 18*(2), 239-257. Retrieved from https://sas.sagepub.com/content/18/2/239

Haokip, T. (2011). India's Look East Policy: Its evolution and approach. *South Asian Survey, 18*(2), 239–257. doi:10.1177/0971523113513368

Haokip, T. (2014). India's Look East Policy: Its Evolution and Approach. *Sage Journals, 18*(2), 239–257.

Haokip, T. (2015). India's Look East Policy: Prospects and challenges for Northeast India. *Studies in Indian Politics, 3*(2), 198–211. doi:10.1177/2321023015601742

Haq, F., & Medhekar, A. (2013). Branding Spiritual Tourism as an Innovation for Peace between India and Pakistan. *International Journal of Social Entrepreneurship and Innovation, 2*(5), 404-414. doi:10.1504/IJSEI.2013.059312

Haq, F., & Medhekar, A. (2014). *Spiritual tourism between India and Pakistan Business Opportunities and Threats*. Paper presented at Eurasia Business Research Conference, Istanbul, Turkey.

Haq, F., & Jackson, J. (2009). Spiritual Journey to Hajj: Australian and Pakistani Experience and Expectations. *Journal of Management, Spirituality & Religion, 6*(2), 141–156. doi:10.1080/14766080902815155

Haq, F., & Medhekar, A. (2018). Economic Effect of Spiritual Tourism in India and Pakistan. In U. Beena & I. Benna (Eds.), *Urbanization and Its Impact on Socio-Economic Growth in Developing Regions* (pp. 66–86). IGI-Global. doi:10.4018/978-1-5225-2659-9.ch004

Haq, F., & Medhekar, A. (2019). Is Spiritual Tourism a Peace Vehicle for Social Transformation and Economic Prosperity in India and Pakistan? In N. Alexandru-Mircea & M.-O. Nedelea (Eds.), *Marketing Peace for Social Transformation and Global Prosperity* (pp. 189–211). IGI Global Publishing. doi:10.4018/978-1-5225-7464-4.ch010

Haq, F., & Medhekar, A. (2020). The Rise of Spiritual Tourism in South Asia as Business Internationalization. *Journal of Management Research*, *7*(1), 52–58.

Harrigan, J. (2001). *Specialization and the volume of trade: Do the data obey the laws?* National Bureau of Economic Research, NBER Working Papers, 8675.

Hashim, J., Chongsuvivatwong, V., Phua, K. H., Pocock, N., Teng, Y. M., Chhem, R. K., Wilopo, S. A., & Lopez, A. (2012). *Health and Healthcare Systems in Southeast Asia*. United Nations University. https://unu.edu/publications/articles/health-and-healthcare-systems-in-southeast-asia.html

Haug, M. (1937). DE professionalization: An alternative hypothesis for the future. *Sociological Review. Mongraph*, *2*, 195–211.

Helpman, E. (1987). Imperfect competition and international trade: Evidence from fourteen industrial countries. *Journal of the Japanese and International Economies*, *1*(1), 62–81. doi:10.1016/0889-1583(87)90027-X

Hinterkoerner, R. (2020, November 17). *QUAD versus RCEP*. Expertise Asia. http://www.expertise-asia.com/2020/11/quad-versus-rcep.html

Holloway, I., & Todres, L. (2003). The status of method: Flexibility, consistency and coherence. *Qualitative Research*, *3*(3), 345–357. doi:10.1177/1468794103033004

Hopkins, K., Labonte, R., Runnels, V., & Packer, C. (2010). Medical tourism today: What is the state of existing knowledge? *Journal of Public Health Policy*, *31*(2), 185–198. doi:10.1057/jphp.2010.10 PMID:20535101

Horimoto, T. (2016). *Japan-India Rapprochement and its future issues*. Academic Press.

Horimoto, T. (2020). Indo-Pacific Order and Japan–India Relations in the Midst of COVID-19. *Journal of Asian Economic Integration*, (2), 140–158. Advance online publication. doi:10.1177/2631684620940476

Hossain, S. M. (2013). Impacts of BIMSTEC Free Trade Area: A CGE Analysis. *Journal of Economics and Sustainable Development*, *4*(13), 16–28.

Hritz, N., & Ross, C. (2010). The Perceived Impacts of Sport Tourism: An Urban Host Community Perspective. *Journal of Sport Management*, *24*(2), 119–138. doi:10.1123/jsm.24.2.119

Husain, A. & Ganguli, S. (2019). A Comparative analysis of medical tourism competitiveness of India, Thailand and Singapore. Tourism: An International Interdisciplinary Journal, 67(2).

Hussain, M. (2017). Cultural Foundations of India's Look East Policy: A Critique. *Journal of Southeast Asian Studies*, *5*(3), 147–155.

IFC Global Conference. (2005). *Investing in private healthcare in emerging markets conference: International Finance Corporation (IFC)*. IFC Global Conference, Washington, DC.

IMF. (2020). *World Economic Outlook*. IMF.

Im, K. S., Pesaran, M. H., & Shin, Y. (2003). Testing for unit roots in heterogeneous panels. *Journal of Econometrics*, *115*(1), 53–74. doi:10.1016/S0304-4076(03)00092-7

Index Mundi Malaysia Demographics Profile. (2014). Available from: https://www.indexmundi.com/malaysia/demographics

India - median age of the population 1950-2050 I Statista. (2015). https://www.statista.com/statistics/254469/median-age-of-the-population-in-india/

India Brand Equity Foundation. (2021). *About Indian Economy Growth Rate & Statistics*. Retrieved from https://www.ibef.org/economy/indian-economy-overview

India Population. (2020). *Country meters*. Retrieved from https://countrymeters.info/en/India

India Today. (2011). Tourism Ministry to develop 35 tourism circuits by 2016. *India Today*. Retrieved from http://indiatoday.intoday.in/story/tourism-ministry-to-develop-35-tourism-circuits-by-2016/1/164363.html

India's Current Engagements in RTAs. (n.d.). *Mcommerce*. Retrieved September 4, 2021, from https://commerce.gov.in/international-trade/trade-agreements/indias-current-engagements-in-rtas/

India-Japan Cooperation on Chabahar Could be a Game-Changer for Asia. (n.d.). *The Wire*. Retrieved August 30, 2021, from https://thewire.in/diplomacy/india-japan-cooperation-on-chabahar-could-be-a-game-changer-for-asia

Intal, J. P., & Chen, L. (2017). *ASEAN and member states: Transformation and integration*. Economic Research Institute for ASEAN and East Asia.

International Air Travel Association. (2020, July 28). *Recovery Delayed as International Travel Remains Locked Down*. Press release. Retrieved from https://www.iata.org/en/ pressroom/pr/2020-07-28-02/

International Finance Corporation World Bank. (2018). *Investing in Buddhist Circuit*. worldbank.org

International Monetary Fund. (2021). *World Economy Outlook Update, January 2021*. Retrieved from https://www.imf.org/en/Publications/WEO/Issues/2021/01/26/2021-world-economic-outlook-update

International Trade Administration. (2020, August 25). *India - Trade Agreements*. Retrieved from International Trade Administration, United States of America: https://www.trade.gov/knowledge-product/india-trade-agreements

Is Blue Dot Network an alternative to China's BRI? (n.d.). *The New Indian Express*. Retrieved September 3, 2021, from https://www.newindianexpress.com/opinions/columns/2021/jun/17/is-blue-dot-network-an-alternative-to-chinas-bri-2317283.html

Islam, A. M. (2021). Impact of Covid-19 pandemic on global output, employment and prices: An assessment. *Transnational Corporations Review*, *13*(2), 189–201.

Islam, M. S., & Das, R. K. (2014). Bangladesh and BIMSTEC: Performance Evaluation and Development Strategies. *Al-Barkaat Journal of Finance & Management*, *6*(1), 17–25.

Jack, R., & Westwood, R. (2006). Postcolonialism of Qualitative Research in International Business. *Management International Review*, *46*(4), 481–501. doi:10.100711575-006-0102-x

Jagannathan, R. (2020). *Modi must not extend lockdown. The economy won't survive on a ventilator for long*. Retrieved from https://theprint.in/opinion/modi-must-not-extend-lockdown-economywontsurvive- on-ventilator-for-long/397757/

Jaipuria, T. (2016, Mar. 29). 100% allowed in B2B e-marketplace via automatic route. *Hindustan Times*. Retrieved from https://www.hindustantimes.com/business/100-fdi-allowed-in-b2b-e-marketplace-via-automatic-route-says-govt/story-IXp7ySlpYYvq1RwNhKdZhM.html

Jaishankar, S. (2019 Sep. 25). India: 1000 PhD fellowships to ASEAN students. *The Pie News*. Retrieved from https://thepienews.com/news/india-1000-phd-fellowships-to-asean-students/

Japanese investments in India are poised for a boom. (2021, January 21). https://www.consultancy.asia/news/3851/japanese-investments-in-india-are-poised-for-a-boom

Japan US India Defense Cooperation: Anticipating the US Withdrawal from Afghanistan. (2019, August 19). *The Asan Forum*. https://theasanforum.org/japan-us-india-defense-cooperation-anticipating-the-us-withdrawal-from-afghanistan/

Jauhari, J. (2010). How can the visitor experience be enhanced for spiritual and cultural tourism in India? *Worldwide Hospitality and Tourism Themes*, *2*(5), 559–563. doi:10.1108/17554211011090166

JETRO. (2021, August 24). *Embassy of Japan*. Retrieved from Government of Japan: file:///D:/ICT-BACKUP/Downloads/2020_co_list_en_pr.pdf

Jha, S.N. & Salim, M. (2015, March). India's economic relations and trade with ASEAN: An analysis. *Aweshkar Research Journal, 19*(1), 39-54.

Jindal, N. (2014). *India and ASEAN*. Available at http://politicosse.in/uploads/Politico_2014_Vol-2_No-22.pdf#page=109

Jirapornvaree, A. M. (2019). Factors Influencing ASEAN and International Students of Higher Education Programs in Thailand. *Asian Social Science*, 67–81.

Jolly, P. (2004). *Medical school tuition and young physician indebtedness*. Association of American Medical Colleges.

Joseph, M., & Bera, S. (2011). *India-Japan trade and investment relations and their future prospects*. Fore School of Management.

Jotikasthira, N., Phakdeephirot, N., & Teeranoot, S. (2016). Thai Tourism and Hospitality Education: Current Conditions and Strategic Directions. *Rangsit Journal of Educational Studies, 3*(2).

Justice Radhabinod Pal and the Tokyo Tribunal. (n.d.). *The National WWII Museum | New Orleans*. Retrieved September 8, 2021, from https://www.nationalww2museum.org/war/articles/justice-radhabinod-pal-tokyo-war-crimes-trial

Kabir, M. (2015, July). Examining trade potential in BIMSTEC: A trade frontier approach. *BIISS Journal*, *36*(3), 181–204.

Kabir, M., Salim, R., & Al-Mawali, N. (2017). The gravity model and trade flows: Recent developments in econometric modeling and empirical evidence. *Economic Analysis and Policy*, *56*, 60–71. doi:10.1016/j.eap.2017.08.005

Kakoti, D. (2020, Jan.). Look/Act East Policy and Trade Opportunities for North East India: A Review. MSSV Journal of Humanities & Social Sciences, 5(1), 39-48.

Kaldor, N. (1967). *Strategic factors in economic development*. Cornell University Press.

Kale, S. (2004). Spirituality, religion, and globalization. *Journal of Macromarketing*, *24*(2), 92–107. doi:10.1177/0276146704269296

Kalirajan, K. (1999). Stochastic varying coefficients gravity model: An application in trade analysis. *Journal of Applied Statistics*, *26*(2), 185–193. doi:10.1080/02664769922520

Kalita, S. (2018). India's act east policy and north-east: Challenges and Prospects. *International Journal of Advanced Research and Development, 3*(1).

Kapur, M. (n.d.). *A Taliban-led Afghanistan could mean all sorts of problems for India*. Quartz. Retrieved August 30, 2021, from https://qz.com/india/2048396/what-taliban-led-afghanistan-will-mean-for-india/

Kapur, Y. (2021, Feb. 23). *India-ASEAN Trade and Investment Prospects. India Briefing*. Dezan Shira & Associates. Retrieved from https://www.india-briefing.com/news/india-asean-trade-and-investment-prospects-21779.html/

Karvanen, J. (2015). Study design on casual models. *Scandinavian Journal of Statistics*, *42*(2), 361–377. doi:10.1111jos.12110

Kathuria, S. (2017). *Bangladesh Corridor Vital to India's Act East Policy*. The World Bank. Retrieved from https://www.worldbank.org

Kaul, M. M. (2006). Regional Groupings: An Overview of BUMSTEC and MGC. *South Asian Survey*, *13*(2), 313–322.

Kaur, G., & Gupta, A. (2020). India-BIMSTEC Bilateral Trade Activities: A Gravity Model Approach. In Regional Trade and Development Strategies in the Era of Globalization (pp. 126-145). IGI Global. doi:10.4018/978-1-7998-1730-7.ch007

Kaura, V. (2016). India-Japan Relations and Asia's Emerging Geopolitics. *Indian Journal of Asian Affairs*, 17-35.

Kaur, G., Dutta, K., & Saini, J. (2020). Trade Performance of BIMSTEC Countries since 1997. *Studies in Indian Place Names*, *40*(60), 1105–1115.

Kaur, G., Sarin, V., & Dhami, J. K. (2016). Analysis of Intraregional Trade and Investment among India and BIMSTEC: Prospects and Challenges. *International Journal of Social and Economic Research*, *6*(2). Advance online publication. doi:10.5958/2249-6270.2016.00015.5

Kaur, N., & Sarin, V. (2017). Comparative advantage and competitiveness of Indian agricultural products exports to ASEAN in context of India's Look East Policy. *International Journal of Agricultural and Statistics Sciences*, *1*(1), 159–167.

Kelegama, S. (2001). Bangkok agreement and BIMSTEC: Crawling regional economic grouping in Asia. *Journal of Asian Economics*, *12*(1), 105–121.

Kelle, P., Woosley, J., & Schneider, H. (2012). Pharmaceutical supply chain specifics and inventory solutions for a hospital case. *Operations Research for Health Care*, *1*(2-3), 54–63. doi:10.1016/j.orhc.2012.07.001

Kelly, C. (2010). Analysing Wellness Tourism Provision: A Retreat Operators' Study. *Journal of Hospitality and Tourism Management*, *17*(1), 108–116. doi:10.1375/jhtm.17.1.108

Kesavan, K. V. (2020, February). *India's 'Act East' Policy and Regional Cooperation*. ORF Special Report # 101. Retrieved from https://www.orfonline.org/wp-content/uploads/2020/02/ORF_SpecialReport_101_India-SouthKorea.pdf#page=7

Khan, S. (2019). *India-Japan Economic Partnership: Potentials, Promises and Prospects*. https://www.mof.go.jp/pri/international_exchange/visiting_scholar_program/Shamshad2.pdf

Khan, S. A. (2019, May). *India-Japan Economic Partnership: Potentials, Promises and Prospects*. Retrieved from https://www.mof.go.jp/pri/international_exchange/visiting_scholar_program/Shamshad2.pdf

Khan, Z. R. (2012). Ideology and internal Dynamics of South Asian Regional cooperation. In Regional Cooperation & Globalization (pp. 31-58). The University Press Limited.

Khan, A., Bibi, S., Lorenzo, A., Lyu, J., & Babar, Z. U. (2020). Tourism and Development in Developing Ecomnomies: A Policy Implication Prspective. *Sustainability*, *12*(4), 1618. doi:10.3390u12041618

Khandare, V., & Phophueksanand, N. (2017, Jul-Sep). Economics of Tourism Development: A comparative Study of India and Thailand. *Kaav International Journal of Economics, Commerce & Business Management, 4*(3), 656-665.

Kissinger, H. A. (1957). *Nuclear weapons and foreign policy*. Oxford University Press.

Kittisak Jermsittiparsert, T.C. (2019). Behavior of Tourism Industry under the Situation of Environmental Threats and Carbon Emission: Time Series Analysis from Thailand. *International Journal of Energy Economics and Policy*, 366 – 372.

Klitgaard, R. (1988). *Controlling corruption*. University of California Press. doi:10.1525/9780520911185

Kmenta, J. (1986). *Elements of econometrics*. MacMillan.

Kojima, M. (2014). The Evolution of Japan-India Economic Relations. In The Rebalance Within Asia: The Evolution of Japan-India Relations (p. 6). Washington, DC: Woodrow Wilson International Centre for Scholars.

Kolb, B. (2017). *Tourism Marketing for Cities and Towns. Using Social Media and Branding to Attract Tourists* (2nd ed.). Routledge. doi:10.4324/9781315543413

KPMG. (2020, April 1). *Potential Impact of COVID-19 on The Indian Economy*. World Bank.

Krauskopf, K., Federman, A. D., Kale, M. S., Sigel, K. M., Martynenko, M., O'Conor, R., Wolf, M. S., Leventhal, H., & Wisnivesky, J. P. (2015). Chronic Obstructive Pulmonary Disease Illness and Medication Beliefs are Associated with Medication Adherence. *COPD*, *12*(2), 151–164. doi:10.3109/15412555.2014.922067 PMID:24960306

Krueger, A. O. (1990). Asian trade and growth lessons. *The American Economic Review*, *80*, 108–111.

Krugman, P. R., & Obstfeld, M. (2010). *International Economics: theory and policy*. Pearson.

Krugman, P. R., Obstfeld, M., & Melitz, M. J. (2020). *International Trade Theory and Policy* (11th Global edn). Pearson Education.

Kshetrimayum, R. S., & Singh, C. G. (2014). Look East Policy: India's motives and opportunities and threats ahead. *Asian Journal of Research in Business. Economics and Management*, *4*(11), 165–171.

Kumar, J., & Hussian, K. (2016). Factors affecting medical tourism destination selection: A Malaysian perspective. *International Interdisciplinary Business-Economics Advancement Journal*, *1*(1), 1-10. https://www.doi.org/10.5038/2640-6489.1.1.1000

Kumar, S. (2020). Reinvigoration of BIMSTEC and India's Economic, Strategic and Security Concerns. *Millennial Asia*, *11*(2), 187–210. doi:10.1177/0976399620925441

Kundu, R. (2021, June 23). *Tour and travel sector may report up to 40% of pre-Covid revenue in FY22*. The Mint. Retrieved from https://www.livemint.com/news/tour-and-travel-sector-may-report-up-to-40-of-pre-covid-revenue-in-fy22-11624442419668.html

Kundu, S. (2014). BIMSTEC at 17: An assessment of its potential. *Indian Quarterly. Journal of International Affairs*, *70*(3), 207–224. https://doi.org/10.1177/0974928414535291

Larson, J., Baker, J., Latta, G., Ohrel, S., & Wade, C. (2018). Modeling international trade of forest products: Application of PPML to a gravity model of trade. *Forest Products Journal*, *68*(3), 303–316. PMID:32280136

Laskar, R. (2013, December). Promoting National Interest through Diplomacy. *Extraordinary and Plenipotentiary Diplomatists.*, *1*(9), 59–60.

Launch of Supply Chain Resilience Initiative. (n.d.). *Drishti IAS*. Retrieved September 3, 2021, from https://www.drishtiias.com/daily-updates/daily-news-analysis/launch-of-supply-chain-resilience-initiative

Laurenza, E., Quintano, M., Schiavone, F., & Vrontis, D. (2018). The effect of digital technologies adoption in healthcare industry: A case-based analysis. *Business Process Management Journal*, *24*(5), 1124–1144. doi:10.1108/BPMJ-04-2017-0084

Lawrence, R. Z., & Krugman, P. (1987). Imports in Japan: Closed Markets or Minds? *Brookings Papers on Economic Activity*, *1987*(2), 517. doi:10.2307/2534489

Lee, E., & Han, S. (2015). Determinants of adoption of mobile health services. *Online Information Review*, *39*(4), 556–573. doi:10.1108/OIR-01-2015-0007

Lee, L. (2015). India as a nation of consequence in Asia: The potential and limitations of India's 'Act East' policy. *The Journal of East Asian Affairs*, *29*(2), 67–104.

Lee, L., & Lee, J. (2016). Japan-India Cooperation and Abe's Democratic Security Diamond: Possibilities, Limitations and the View from Southeast Asia. *Contemporary Southeast Asia*, *38*(2), 284–308. doi:10.1355/cs38-2e

Leete, R. (2008). Human development and urbanisation. *Ethos*, *2008*(June), 88–97.

Leitão, N. C., & Shahbaz, M. (2016). Economic Growth, Tourism Arrivals and Climate Change. *Bull. Energy Economics*, *4*, 35–43.

Levene, H. (1960). Robust tests for equality of variances. In I. Olkin, G. Ghurye, W. Hoeffding, W. G. Madow, & H. B. Mann (Eds.), *Contributions to probability and statistics* (pp. 278–292). Stanford University Press.

Levin, A., Lin, F. C., & Chu, S. (2002). Unit root tests in panel data: Asymptotic and finite-sample properties. *Journal of Econometrics*, *108*(1), 1–24. doi:10.1016/S0304-4076(01)00098-7

Lewis, M. (2006). *Governance and corruption in public healthcare systems*. Working paper number 78. Washington, DC: Center for Global Development.

Limaye, S. (2008). India-Asia Pacific relations: Consolidating friendships and nuclear legitimacy. *Comparative Connections*, 1-22.

Lim, J., Bogossian, F., & Ahern, K. (2010). Stress and coping in Singaporean nurses: A literature review. *Nursing & Health Sciences*, *12*(2), 251–258. doi:10.1111/j.1442-2018.2010.00514.x PMID:20602699

Linnemann, H. (1966). *An econometric study of international trade flows*. North Holland Publishing Company.

LopezM. L. (2020, Feb. 28). Retrieved from https://cnnphilippines.com/business/2020/2/28/PAL-retrenchment-coronavirus.html

Lu, H., Stratton, C.W. & Tang, Y. (2020). *An outbreak of pneumonia of unknown etiology in Wuhan, China: The mystery and the miracle.* doi:10.1002/jmv.25678

M&A Statistics by Countries - Institute for Mergers, Acquisitions and Alliances (IMAA). (2016). *Institute for Mergers, Acquisitions and Alliances (IMAA).* https://imaa-institute.org/m-and-a-statistics-countries/

Madaan, D. K. (2004). India's trade intensity with ASEAN. *The Indian Economic Journal*, *52*(1-2), 142–151.

Maga, A. A., & Nicolau, P. E. (2020). Conceptualizing Educational Tourism and the Education Tourism Potential (evidence from ASEAN countries). Advances in Economics, Business and Management Research, 39.

Mahadi, Y., Becek, K., & Chian, K. W. (2011). The Dutch Disease Hypothesis: Evidence from the Gulf Cooperation Council. *CSPS Strategy and Policy Journal*, *3*, 1–25.

Maini, T. S. (2016). *Japan's Effort to Counter China's Silk Road.* The Globalist.

Majumdar, A. (2021, May). From "Look East" to "Act East": India's Evolving Engagement with the Asia-Pacific Region. *Asian Affairs, 52*(2).

Malaysia, T. (2008). *Media info: Health tourism in Malaysia*. Communications and Publicity Division. Retrieved from http:// www.tourism.gov.my/

Malik, Y. (2021, June 22). *Business Standard*. Retrieved from https://edition.cnn.com/2021/06/18/asia/vaccinated-indonesian-doctors-covid-19-intl-hnk/index.html

Mallapur, C. (2021). *Explained: The flourishing trade ties and friendship between India and Bangladesh*. Retrieved from https://flipboard.com/@moneycontrol/moneycontrol-news-j7nitv49z/explained-the-flourishing-trade-ties-and-friendship-between-india-and-banglades/a-AogOGab9SOe4V1QVCg5zlQ%3Aa%3A3108465186-0f4d7187f3%2Fmoneycontr-ol.com

Marin, D. (1992). Is the export-led growth hypothesis valid for industrialised countries? *The Review of Economics and Statistics*, *74*(4), 678–688. doi:10.2307/2109382

Marston, S., Li, Z., Bandyopadhyay, S., Zhang, J., & Ghalsasi, A. (2011). Cloud computing-the business perspective. *Decision Support Systems*, *51*(1), 176–189. doi:10.1016/j.dss.2010.12.006

Martinez-Zarzoso, I. (2003). Gravity model: An application to trade between regional blocs. *Atlantic Economic Journal*, *31*(2), 174–187. doi:10.1007/BF02319869

Martinez-Zarzoso, I., & Nowak-Lehmann, F. (2003). Augmented gravity model: An empirical application to Mercosur-European union trade flows. *Journal of Applied Econometrics*, *6*(2), 291–316.

Martino, V.D. (2002). *Workplace violence in the health sector - Country case studies Brazil, Bulgaria, Lebanon, Portugal, South Africa, Thailand and an additional Australian study: Synthesis Report*. Academic Press.

Maskorala, R. (2017). Development of Trincomalee Harbor as a Hub for Bay of Bengal region: Building a shipping Hub. In *Trincomalee consultations: Regional Cooperation for economic prosperity and maritime security in the Bay of Bengal* (pp. 72–80). Pathfinder Foundation.

McIntosh, I. S. (2016). Xuanzang and Bodhidharma: Pilgrimage and peace-building in Buddhist China and India. *International Journal of Religious Tourism and Pilgrimage*, (6), Article 14.

McKone-Sweet, K. E., Hamilton, P., & Willis, S. B. (2005). The ailing healthcare supply chain: A prescription for change. *The Journal of Supply Chain Management*, *41*(1), 4–17. doi:10.1111/j.1745-493X.2005.tb00180.x

McPake, B., Asiimwe, D., Mwesigye, F., Ofumbi, M., Ortenblad, L., Streefland, P., & Turinde, A. (1999). Informal economic activities of public health workers in Uganda: Implications for quality and accessibility of care. *Social Science & Medicine*, *49*(7), 849–865. doi:10.1016/S0277-9536(99)00144-6 PMID:10468391

Mea.Gov.In. (2018, Aug). *India-ASEAN Relations*. Retrieved from https://mea.gov.in/aseanindia/20-years.htm

Medhekar, A. (2019). Emerging Trends of Wellness and Medical Tourism in India. In Global Developments in Healthcare and Medical Tourism. IGI Global. doi:091218-104208

Medhekar, A. (2021). Australia-India: Bilateral Trade Opportunities and Challenges. In *Emerging Business and Trade Opportunities between Oceania and Asia* (pp. 57–86). IGI Global Publishing. doi:10.4018/978-1-7998-4126-5

Medhekar, A., & Haq, F. (2009). Growth of spiritual tourism in India: A public private partnership approach. *International Journal of Business Intelligence & Management*, *1*, 1–12.

Medhekar, A., & Haq, F. (2012). Development of Spiritual Tourism Circuits: The Case of India. *Journal of Global Business Review*, *2*(2), 212–218.

Medhekar, A., & Haq, F. (2019). *Challenges for Innovative Transformation in Heritage Tourism Development in India and Pakistan*. IGI Global.

Medhekar, A., & Haq, F. (2020). Capacity Building for Spiritual Heritage Tourism: The Case of India and Pakistan. In S. Srivastava (Ed.), *Capacity Building Through Heritage Tourism an International Perspective*. Apple Academic Press. doi:10.1201/9781003034391-2

Medhekar, A., & Wong, H. Y. (2020). Medical travellers' perspective on factors affecting medical tourism to India. *Asia Pacific Journal of Tourism Research*, *25*(12), 1295–1310. doi:10.1080/10941665.2020.1837893

Medhekar, A., Wong, H. Y., & Hall, J. E. (2019, February). Factors influencing inbound medical travel to India. *Journal of Health Organization and Management*, *33*(2), 155–172. doi:10.1108/JHOM-08-2018-0234 PMID:30950309

Meikeng, Y. (2014). Indonesians are the top healthcare tourists to Malaysia. *The Star Online*. Available at: https://www.thestar.com.my/news/nation/2014/11/13/indonesia-top-healthcare-tourists-to-malaysia/ #vcjJ50ltdBQsVZgQ.99

Menon, S. (2016). *Choices: inside the making of India's foreign policy*. Brookings Institution Press.

Micallef, H. (2017). *Indian weddings in Malta: Impacts and Perspective*. Available at https://www.theseus.fi/handle/10024/133358

Miles, M., & Huberman, A. (1994). *An expanded sourcebook: qualitative data analysis*. Sage Publications.

Miller, W. L., Grodeland, A. B., & Koshechkina, T. Y. (2001). *A culture of corruption? Coping with Government in post-communist Europe*. Central European University Press.

Ministry of Eternal Affairs. (2016). *India's Look East Policy*. Available at https://mea.gov.in/lok-sabha.htm?dtl/26554/

Ministry of External Affairs (MEA). (2014-15). *Annual Report*. Available at http://www.mea.gov.in/Uploads/PublicationDocs/25009_External_Affairs_2014-2015__English_.pdf

Ministry of External Affairs (MEA). (2015-16). *Annual Report*. Available at https://www.mea.gov.in/Uploads/PublicationDocs/26525_26525_External_Affairs_English_AR_2015-16_Final_compressed.pdf

Ministry of External Affairs (MEA). (2018-19). *Annual Report*. Available at http://www.mea.gov.in/Uploads/PublicationDocs/31719_MEA_AR18_19.pdf

Ministry of External Affairs, Government of India. (2017, December 5). *Launch of India-Japan Act East Forum*. Retrieved from Ministry of External Affairs, Government of India: https://www.mea.gov.in/press-releases.htm?dtl/29154/Launch_of_IndiaJapan_Act_East_Forum

Ministry of External Affairs, Government of India. (2020). *India-Japan_Bilateral_Brief_feb_2020*. Retrieved from Ministry of External Affairs, Government of India: https://mea.gov.in/Portal/ForeignRelation/India-Japan_Bilateral_Brief_feb_2020.pdf?fbclid=IwAR3MByxRsgiuMZTrflVXFE3ItQx4Wb2Gmhl_2cdmkbzD8kGUN7TJvoVPH7I

Mint. (2021). *RBA announces FPI investment limits in G-secs and SDLs*. Retrieved from https://www.livemint.com/industry/banking/rbi-announces-fpi-investment-limits-in-g-secs-and-sdls-11622479759242.html

Mishra, A. R. (2021, April 27). *India, Japan and Australia unveil supply chain initiative*. Mint. https://www.livemint.com/news/world/india-japan-australia-launch-supply-chain-initiative-to-counter-china-11619532624451.html

Mishra, M. S. (2020). India–Thailand Security Cooperation: Strengthening the Indo-Pacific Resolve. *Journal of Asian Security and International Affairs*.

Mishra, R. (2014). From Look east to Act East: Transitions in India's Eastward Engagement. *The ASAN Forum, 8*(1). Available at http://www.theasanforum.org/from-look-east-to-act-east-transitions-in-indias-eastward-engagement/

Mitroff, I., & Denton, E. E. (1999). *A Spiritual Audit of Corporate America: A Hard Look at Spirituality, Religion, and Values in the Workplace*. Jossey-Bass Inc.

MOCAA. (2021, April). *Ministry of Civil Aviation. Monthly Summary on Civil Aviation*. Retrieved from civilaviation.gov.in/en/publication/monthly-summary

MOCAB. (2021a, March 25). Ministry of Civil Aviation. Government of India. *Lok Sabha*. Unstarred Question 5038 On Effect of COVID 19 on the Aviation sector by D. M. Kathir Anand.

MOCAC. (2021b, March 25). Ministry of Civil Aviation. Government of India. *Lok Sabha*. Unstarred Question 5012 On Effect of COVID-19 on the Aviation sector by Hema Malini

MOFA. (2021, August 15). *Region/AsiaPacific/India*. Retrieved from Ministry of Foreign Affairs, Japan: https://www.mofa.go.jp/region/asiapaci/india/index.html

Mohan, N. C. (2016). BIMSTEC: An Idea Whose Time Has Come? *ORF*, (November), 9.

Morrison, G. (2005). Mortgaging Our Future— The Cost of Medical Education. *The New England Journal of Medicine, 352*(2), 117–119. doi:10.1056/NEJMp048089 PMID:15647572

Mostert, S., Sitaresmi, M. N., Njuguna, F., Beers, E. J. V., & Kaspers, G. J. (2012). Effect of corruption on medical care in low-income countries. *Pediatric Blood & Cancer, 58*(3), 325–326. doi:10.1002/pbc.23408 PMID:22106048

Moyano-Fuentes, J., Bruque-Cámara, S., & Maqueira-Marín, J. M. (2019). Development and validation of a lean supply chain management measurement instrument. *Production Planning and Control, 30*(1), 20–32. doi:10.1080/09537287.2018.1519731

Mufti & Akhlas. (2020). *Supporting Post-COVID-19 Economic Recovery in Southeast Asia*. ADB Brief 175.

Mukherjee, R. (2020). *East by Southeast: Three challenges for India's 'Act East' policy*. Retrieved from https://www.business-standard.com

Mukherjee, R. (2018). Japan's strategic outreach to India and the prospects of a Japan–India alliance. *International Affairs, 94*(4), 835–859. doi:10.1093/ia/iiy030

Mullen, R. D., & Arora, K. (2017). *India–Japan brief.* Centre for Policy Research. Retrieved from www. cprindia. org

Muni, S. D. (2011). *India's 'Look East' Policy: The Strategic Dimension*. Institute of South Asian Studies, Working Paper, National University of Singapore.

Murray, T., Barber, R. M., Foreman, K. J., Ozgoren, A. A., Abd-Allah, F., Abera, S. F., Aboyans, V., Abraham, J. P., Abubakar, I., Abu-Raddad, L. J., Abu-Rmeileh, N. M., Achoki, T., Ackerman, I. N., Ademi, Z., Adou, A. K., Adsuar, J. C., Afshin, A., Agardh, E. E., Alam, S. S., ... Vos, T. (2015). 'Global, Regional, and National Disability-Adjusted Life Years (DALYs) for 306 Diseases and Injuries and Healthy Life Expectancy (HALE) for 188 Countries, 1990–2013: Quantifying the Epidemiological Transition. *Lancet, 386*(10009), 2145–2191. doi:10.1016/S0140-6736(15)61340-X PMID:26321261

Nadpara, N. (2015). *An Empirical Examination of the effect of corruption on Health Outcomes* [Published doctoral dissertation]. The College of New Jersey.

Nagao, S. (n.d.). *Japan-US-India Defense Cooperation: Anticipating the US Withdrawal from Afghanistan - by Satoru Nagao*. Retrieved September 1, 2021, from https://www.hudson.org/research/15261-japan-us-india-defense-cooperation-anticipating-the-us-withdrawal-from-afghanistan

Naidu, G. V. C. (2013). India and East Asia: The Look East Policy. *Perceptions, 18*(1), 53–74.

Naidu, G. V. C., & Yasuyuki, I. (2019). India–Japan Defence Ties: Building a Strategic Partnership. *Strategic Analysis, 43*(1), 13–27. doi:10.1080/09700161.2019.1573556

Nath, H. K., & Kumar, S. (2017). *India's Act East Policy and the Northeast: A Critical Perspective*. Retrieved from https://researchgate.net

National Sample Survey Organisation (NSSO). (2019). NSSO, Ministry of Statistics and Programme Implementation. New Delhi: Government of India.

Naveed, M. (2018). *Investment in early childhood health and its implications for human capital accumulation and economic growth* (Doctoral dissertation). Lahore School of Economics.

Near and present: On the Afghan crisis and India. (2021, August 28). *The Hindu*. https://www.thehindu.com/opinion/editorial/near-and-present-the-hindu-editorial-on-the-impact-of-the-afghan-crisis-on-india/article36144643.ece

Nehru, J. (2008). *Discovery of India*. Oxford University Press.

Nettleton, S., Burrows, R., O'Malley, L., & Watt, I. (2005). The mundane realities of the everyday lay use of the internet for health, and their consequences for media convergence. *Sociology of Health & Illness, 27*(7), 972–992. Advance online publication. doi:10.1111/j.1467-9566.2005.00466.x PMID:16313525

News India. (2020, October 4). *Uttar Pradesh Tourism to develop Kaushambi as part of Buddhist Circuit*. newsd.in

News, B. (2018), July 11). *India Government is 'failing' to protect Taj Mahal*. Retrieved from bbc.com.new:https://www.bbc.com/news/world-asia-india-44763867

Ngaibiakching, & Pande, A. (2020). India's Act East Policy and ASEAN: Building a Regional Order Through Partnership in the Indo-Pacific. *International Studies, 57*(1), 67–78. doi:10.1177/0020881719885526

Nguyen, T. H. (2017). Prospects of ASEAN-India Relations: An Analysis. *European Journal of Social and Human Sciences, 4*(2), 1–8.

Nicolau, A. A. (2020). Education or Recreation: And enquiry into the motives of European Educational Tourists in Thailand (The case of Phuket). *Journal of EU Business School*, 8 - 20.

NITTA. (2020, Sep. 26). *Myanmar November election overshadowed by COVID-19 surge*. Nikkei Asia. Retrieved from www.asia.nikkei.com

OECD. (2001). *Tourism Satellite Account: Recommended Methodological Framework*. Retrieved from www.oecd.org

OECD. (2008). *Tourism Satellite Account: Recommended Methodological Framework*. Retrieved from www.oecd.org

Oh, C.-O. (2005). The contribution of tourism development to economic growth in the Korean economy. *Tourism Management, 26*(1), 39–44. doi:10.1016/j.tourman.2003.09.014

Ollapally, D. M. (2018). How Does India's Look East Policy Look after 25 Years? *Asia Policy, 13*(2), 146–149. doi:10.1353/asp.2018.0031

Olsen, D. H. (2019). Review of: Religious Tourism in Asia: Tradition and Change through Case Studies and Narratives, by S. Yasuda, R. Raj & K. Griffin. *International Journal of Religious Tourism and Pilgrimage, 7*(5), 73-75.

Osabuohien, E. S., Efobi, U. R., Odebiyi, J. T., Fayomi, O. O., & Salami, A. O. (2019). Bilateral trade performance in West Africa: A gravity model estimation. *African Development Review*, *31*(1), 1–14. doi:10.1111/1467-8268.12359

P, J. (2021, July 25). *Japan's Strategic Choices in Afghanistan | JAPAN Forward*. https://japan-forward.com/asias-next-page-japans-strategic-choices-in-afghanistan/

Pachanee, C., & Wibulpolprasert, S. (2006). Incoherent policies on universal coverage of health insurance and promotion of international trade in health services in Thailand. *Health Policy and Planning*, *21*(4), 310–318. doi:10.1093/heapol/czl017 PMID:16728511

Padmaja, G. (2017). *BIMSTEC: Where India's 'Neighbourhood First'and 'Act East'meet*. National Maritime Foundation.

Pajon, C., & Saint-Mezard, I. (2018). *The Japan-India economic partnership: a politically driven process*. Academic Press.

Palit, A. (2016). India's Act east Policy and Implications for Southeast Asia. *Southeast Asian Affairs*, 81-92.

Panda, J. P. (n.d.). *India, the Blue Dot Network, and the "Quad Plus" Calculus*. Air University (AU). Retrieved August 30, 2021, from https://www.airuniversity.af.edu/JIPA/Display/Article/2278057/india-the-blue-dot-network-and-the-quad-plus-calculus/

Pant, H. V., & Deb, A. (2017). *India-ASEAN Partnership at 25*. ORF Issue Brief No.189. https://www.orfonline.org/wp-content/uploads/2017/07/ORF_ Issue_Brief_189_India-ASEAN.pdf

Pant, H. V. (2013). China on the horizon: India's Look East Policy gathers momentum. *Orbis*, *57*(3), 453–466. doi:10.1016/j.orbis.2013.05.007

Parks, R. (1967). Efficient estimation of a system of regression equations when disturbances are both serially and contemporaneously correlated. *Journal of the American Statistical Association*, *62*(318), 500–509. doi:10.1080/01621459.1967.10482923

Parmar, SM. (2017). Wellness tourism: Review and Growth. *PARIPEX- Indian Journal of Research*, *5*(9), 33-35.

Pattanaik, S. S. (2020). SAARC COVID-19 Fund: Calibrating a Regional Response to the Pandemic. *Strategic Analysis*, *44*(3), 241–252. doi:10.1080/09700161.2020.1787688

Peltzer, K., & Pengpid, S. (2018). The prevalence and social determinants of hypertension among adults in Indonesia: A cross-sectional population-based national survey. selected African countries. *Health Economics Review*, *7*(1), 23–36. PMID:30229501

Perappadan, B. S. (2017). Majority of doctors in India fear violence, says IMA survey. *The Hindu*. Retrieved from timesofindia.indiatimes.com

Pesaran, M. H. (2004). *General diagnostic test for cross section dependence in panels*. University of Cambridge, Faculty of Economics, Cambridge Working Papers in Economics, No. 0435.

Pew Research Centre. (2020). *Pew Research Centre analysis of the World Bank's PovcalNet database*. Author.

Philippines Statistics Authorities. (2019). *Philippine National Health Accounts, Health Spending Grew by 10.9 Percent in 2019*. https://psa.gov.ph/content/health-spending-grew-109-percent-2019

Phophueksanand, V. K. (2017). Economics of Tourism Development: A Comparative Study of India and Thailand. *KAAV International Journal of Economics*, 656 - 665.

Phukan, H., Rahman, Z., & Devdutt, P. (2012). Emergence of Spiritual Tourism in India. *International Journal of Marketing and Technology*, *2*(4), 300–317.

Phukan, R.S. (2015). *Buddhist Circuit in India.* mapsofindia.com

Phukan, H., Rahman, Z., & Devdutt, P. (2012). Emergence of Spiritual Tourism in India. *International Journal of Marketing and Technology.*, *2*(4), 300–317.

Piabuo, S. M., & Tieguhong, J. C. (2017). *Health expenditure and economic growth-a review of the literature and an analysis between the economic community for Central African States*. CEMAC.

Piboonrungroj, P., & Sangkakorn, K. (2013). *Tourism Logistics Management: A Case of Cultural Creative Tourism in Thailand.* Conference Paper on 'World Conference on Hospitality, Tourism and Event Research'. Available at https://www.researchgate.net/publication/260001134_TOURISM_LOGISTICS_MANAGEMENT_A_CASE_OF_CULTURAL_CREATIVE_TOURISM_IN_THAILAND

Pinterest. (2021). *Buddhist Pilgrimage Locations of India.* Retrieved from https://in.pinterest.com/pin/161003755400282845/

Planning Commission Government of India. (2020). *Twelfth Five Year Plan 2012-2017*. Available at https://niti.gov.in/planningcommission.gov.in/docs/plans/planrel/fiveyr/welcome.html

Plummer. (2020, November 16). *RCEP: A new trade agreement that will shape global economics and politics*. Brookings. https://www.brookings.edu/blog/order-from-chaos/2020/11/16/rcep-a-new-trade-agreement-that-will-shape-global-economics-and-politics/

Pocock, N. S., & Phua, K. H. (2011). Medical tourism and policy implications for health systems: A conceptual framework from a comparative study of Thailand, Singapore and Malaysia. *Globalization and Health*, *12*(7), 12. Advance online publication. doi:10.1186/1744-8603-7-12 PMID:21539751

Pöyhönen, P. (1963). A tentative model for the volume of trade between countries. *Weltwirtschaftliches Archiv*, *90*(1), 93–100.

Pradnya, P. (2009). India-ASEAN economic relations. *Indian Institute of Management, Ahemadabad, Working Paper Series, 108*, 1-24.

Prajogo, D., Oke, A., & Olhager, J. (2016). Supply chain processes: Linking supply logistics integration, supply performance, lean processes, and competitive performance. *International Journal of Operations & Production Management*, *36*(2), 220–238. doi:10.1108/IJOPM-03-2014-0129

Press Release Japanese Business Establishments in India -2020. (n.d.). Retrieved August 29, 2021, from https://www.in.emb-japan.go.jp/PDF/2020_co_list_en_pr.pdf

Pretty, B. (2018). *India-ASEAN Economic connections and relations: Evaluating Future Possibilities.* ORF Issue Brief, Issue No.221.

Pudpong, N., Durier, N., Julchoo, S., Sainam, P., Kuttiparambil, B., & Suphanchaimat, R. (2019). Assessment of a Voluntary Non-Profit Health Insurance Scheme for Migrants along the Thai–Myanmar Border: A Case Study of the Migrant Fund in Thailand. *International Journal of Environmental Research and Public Health*, *16*(14), 2581. doi:10.3390/ijerph16142581 PMID:31330995

Puri, V. K., & Misra, S. K. (2020). *Indian Economy (Its Development Experience)*. Himalaya Publishing House.

Qian, G., Li, L., Li, J., & Qian, Z. (2008). Regional diversification and firm performance. *Journal of International Business Studies*, *39*(2), 197–214. doi:10.1057/palgrave.jibs.8400346

QUAD Allies India, Australia & Japan Form A "Supply Chain Shield" Against China's Dominance. (2021, April 29). *Latest Asian, Middle-East, EurAsian, Indian News*. https://eurasiantimes.com/quad-allies-india-australia-japan-form-a-supply-chain-shield-against-chinas-dominance/

QUAD vs. RCEP: A Geo-economic Appraisal; By Dr R Srinivasan | C3S India | Chennai Centre for China Studies. (n.d.). Retrieved August 30, 2021, from https://www.c3sindia.org/business-economics/quad-vs-rcep-a-geo-economic-appraisal-by-dr-r-srinivasan/

Quad vs. RCEP: A Resilient Supply Chain, Advantage India? (2021, April 16). *South Asian Voices*. https://southasianvoices.org/quad-vs-rcep-a-resilient-supply-chain-advantage-india/

Quisumbing, A. R. (2003). Household Decisions, Gender, and Development A Synthesis of Recent Research. Food Policy, 20, 407–423.

Raghavan, S. (2013). India as a Regional Power. In W. P. S. Sidhu, P. B. Mehta, & B. Jones (Eds.), *Shaping the Emerging World: India and the Multilateral Order* (p. 64). Brookings Institution Press.

Raghuramapatruni, R., & Latha, D. A. (2020). A study of India's Bilateral Trade with Japan. Humanities & Social Sciences Reviews, 8(4). doi:10.18510/hssr.2020.8435

Rahman, M. S. (2014). *Promoting Transport Connectivity in Southern Asia: A BIMSTEC Perspective*. United Nations Economic and Social Commission for Asia and the Pacific.

Rahman, K. F., & Yaesmin, S. (2014). Regional integration of South Asia through trade facilitation: Challenges and opportunities. *ASA University Review*, *8*(2), 19–38.

Rahman, M. M., & Kim, C. (2015). BIMSTEC Regional Integration: Prospects and Challenges. *Advanced Science and Technology Letters*, *18*, 90–95. doi:10.14257/astl.2015.114.18

Rahman, M. M., & Kim, C. (2016). Prospects for Economic Integration of BIMSTEC: Trade and Investment Scenario. International Journal of u-and e-Service. *Science and Technology*, *9*(4), 235–248.

Rahman, M. N., & Grewal, H. S. (2017). Foreign direct investment and international trade in BIMSTEC: Panel causality analysis. *Transnational Corporations Review*, *9*(2), 112–121. doi:10.1080/19186444.2017.1326720

Rahman, M., & Bari, E. (2018). *Research Report 4 Value Chains in BIMSTEC Region Current Status*. Possibilities and Challenges.

Rahman, N., & Rizvi, S. A. (2018). FDI Inflows and Current Account Evidence from BIMSTEC. In *Foreign Direct Investments (FDIs) and Opportunities for Developing Economies in the World Market* (pp. 123–141). IGI Global. doi:10.4018/978-1-5225-3026-8.ch007

Rahmati, F., Ali, M. A., & Kamraju, M. (2020). A Study on Strategic Location of Siliguri Corridor and Its Issues. *International Journal of All Research Education and Scientific Methods*, *8*(7), 2–6.

Rahul, M. (2020). *Strengthening the Indo-Pacific Order: An Assessment of India's Act East Policy*. Retrieved from https:// issue.com

Rahul,, S.,, & Mark,, G.A. (2004). *India-ASEAN Economic Relations: Future Prospects and Current Status*. Research Gate.

Raj, P. S., Wing, E., & Ambrose, D. (2014). A brief analysis of India-Japan bilateral trade: A trade intensity approach. *International Journal of Economics, Commerce and Management, 2*(2).

Rajan, G. (2020). *Raghuram Rajan on how India can get back to work after coronavirus lockdown*. https://scroll.in/article/958281/full-text-raghuram-rajan-on-how-india-cangetback-to-work-after-coronavirus-lockdown

Rajiv, B. (2019). *India's Act Policy: Gains and Prospects*. Retrieved from https://www.gatewayhouse.in

Raj, R., & Morpeth, N. D. (2007). *Religious tourism and pilgrimage festivals management: An international perspective*. CABI Publishers. doi:10.1079/9781845932251.0000

Ram, A. N. (Ed.). (2012). *Two Decades of India's Look East Policy: Partnership for Peace, Progress and Prosperity*. Manohar Publishers & Distributors.

Ramachandran, K. K., & Gokila, R. (2012). International Entrepreneurship—Opportunities and Challenges. In Creativity, Innovation and Entrepreneurship (pp. 21-25). New Delhi, India: Allied Publishers Private Limited.

Ramos, M. (2003). Auditors' responsibility for fraud detection. *Journal of Accountancy*, (January), 28. https://www.aicpa.org/pubs

Rana, M. (2018). Transformation of Indo-Bangladesh Relations: From Insecurity to Cooperation in Northeast India. *Strategic Analysis*, *42*(6), 559–577. doi:10.1080/09700161.2018.1559976

Ranjan, R. M., Singh, M., Pal, R., Das, J. K., & Gupta, S. (2018). Epidemiology of violence against medical practitioners in a developing country (2006-2017). *Journal of Health Research and Review*, *5*(3), 153. doi:10.4103/jhrr.jhrr_84_17

Ranjan, V. (2016). Australia and India in Asia: When 'Look West' Meets Act East. *Strategic Analysis*, *40*(5), 425–439. doi:10.1080/09700161.2016.1209906

Rao. (2012, July-December). Emerging India's Policy towards Southeast Asia during the Post-Cold War Era. *Area Studies*, *6*(2), 90–109.

Rao, B. (2003). Looking East: Retrospect and Prospects. *Economic and Political Weekly*, *38*(41), 4317–4318.

Rathnayake, Z. (2021, May 30). *Khasis: India's indigenous matrilineal Society*. BBC Travel. Retrieved from https://www.bbc.com/travel/article/20210328-why-some-indians-want-more-mens-rights

Ravenstein, E. G. (1885). The law of migration. *Journal of the Statistical Society of London*, *48*(2), 167–235. doi:10.2307/2979181

Reddy, G. J. (Ed.). (2014). *India-Japan Relations: Economic, Strategic and Security Cooperation*. UGC Centre for Southeast Asian & Pacific Studies, Sri Venkateswara University.

Reisman, D. (1996). Payment for health in the Philippines. *International Journal of Social Economics*, *23*(8), 46–75. doi:10.1108/03068299610122362

Reisman, D. (2006). Payment for health in Singapore. *International Journal of Social Economics*, *33*(2), 132–159. doi:10.1108/03068290610642229

Report, W. (2019). *Materials saw record growth*. Retrieved from https://www.3dnatives.com/en/wohlers-report-2019-270320195/#!

Report, C. (2006). *Special focus on corruption and health*. Pluto Press.

Rhee, Y. R. (2020, April 15). COVID-19 Pandemic and the Asia-Pacific Region: Lowest Growth since the 1960s. *IMF Blog*. Retrieved from https://blogs.imf.org/2020/04/15/covid-19-pandemic-and-the-asia-pacific-region-lowest-growth-since-the-1960s/

Ricardo, D. (1988). *On the principles of political economy, and taxation*. Verlag Wirtschaft Und Finanzen.

Riege, A. M., & Perry, C. (2000). National marketing strategies in international travel and tourism. *European Journal of Marketing*, *34*(11/12), 1290–1305. doi:10.1108/03090560010348452

Riessman, C. (2006). Narrative analysis. In V. Jupp (Ed.), *The sage dictionary of social research methods* (pp. 186–189). Sage Publications.

Rinschede, G. (1992). Forms of religious tourism. *Annals of Tourism Research, 19*(1), 51–67. doi:10.1016/0160-7383(92)90106-Y

RIS. (2016). BIMSTEC: The Road Ahead, Research and information. https://www.ris.org.in/bimstec-road-ahead

Rizzo, C. (2020, Feb. 6). *Business Insider*. Retrieved from https://www.businessinsider.com/cathay-pacific-employees-3-weeks-unpaid-leave-coronavirus-2020-2?IR

Roberts, M. (2021). *What are the India, Brazil, South Africa, and UK variants?* BBC News. Retrieved from https://www.bbc.com/news/health-55659820

Rodbamrung, P. W. (202, July 29). *India – Thailand Relations: And Cultural Links in Soft Power Policy*. Available at https://so04.tci-thaijo.org/index.php/mgsj/article/view/201768/140880

Rodrik, D. (1995). Political economy of trade policy. Handbook of International Economics, 3, 1457-1494.

Romer, P. (1989). Capital accumulation. In Modern business cycle theory. Press.

Rostow, W. W., & Rostow, W. W. (1990). *The stages of economic growth: A non-communist manifesto*. Cambridge university press.

Rumki, B., & Kushagra, R. (2018). *Religious tourism: The beginning of a new era with special reference to India*. In S. Yasuda, R. Raj, & K. Griffin (Eds.), *Religious tourism in Asia: Tradition and change through case studies and narratives* (pp. 67–76). CABI Publishers.

Rusliyadi, M., Mohd, H., Jamil, A., & Anshari, M. (2020). Analysis of Food Security Policy by Participatory Poverty Assessment (PPA) Effort: Case in Indonesia. In P. Ordoñez de Pablos, M. Almunawar, & M. Abduh (Eds.), Economics, Business, and Islamic Finance in ASEAN Economics Community (pp. 105-127). Hershey, PA: IGI Global. doi:10.4018/978-1-7998-2257-8.ch006

Rusliyadi, M., Bin Hj. Mohd. Jamil, A., Maseleno, A., Tri Kumalasari, R., & Othman, M. (2019). Agricultural extension policy, agricultural growth and poverty reduction in Indonesia. *IACSIT International Journal of Engineering and Technology, 7*(4), 5539–5550. doi:10.14419/ijet.v7i4.13337

Rusliyadi, M., & Jamil, A. B. (2020). Participatory Poverty Assessment Effort in Food Security and Extension Policy: Evidence From Indonesia. In V. Erokhin & T. Gao (Eds.), *Handbook of Research on Globalized Agricultural Trade and New Challenges for Food Security* (pp. 481–499). IGI Global. doi:10.4018/978-1-7998-1042-1.ch024

Rusliyadi, M., Jamil, A., Mohd, B., & Kumalasar, R. T. (2019). Analysis of household food security policy: Case of food security village programme, Indonesia. *Asian Journal of Agriculture and Rural Development, 9*(1), 19–32. doi:10.18488/journal.1005/2019.9.1/1005.1.19.32

Rusliyadi, M., & Libin, W. (2018). Agriculture development programs for poverty reduction evidences from Indonesia and china - comparative study case. *Asian Journal of Agriculture and Rural Development, 8*(2), 104–118. doi:10.18488/journal.1005/2018.8.2/1005.2.104.118

Sahasrabuddhe, U. (2012). Regionalization processes in South and Southeast Asia: A comparative study. *The Asian Scholar, 6.*

Saint-Mezard, I. (2003). The Look East Policy: An Economic Perspective. In F. Grare & A. Mattoo (Eds.), *Beyond the Rhetoric: The Economics of India's Look East Policy* (pp. 21–43). Manohar.

Saint-Mezard, I. (2016). India's Act East policy: Strategic Implications for the Indian Ocean. *Journal of the Indian Ocean Region, 12*(2), 178. doi:10.1080/19480881.2016.1226753

Sajjanhar, A. (2016). *India's Act East Policy: So far and Beyond.* Gateway House-Indian Council on Global Relations. Retrieved from https://www.gatewayhouse.in/indias-act-east-policy-far-beyond/

SajjanharA. (2017, September 15). *ORF.* Available at https://www.orfonline.org/expert-speak/india-thailand-relations-a-70-year-partnership/

Salmasi, S., Khan, T. M., Hong, Y. H., Ming, L. C., & Wong, T. W. (2015). Medication Errors in the Southeast Asian Countries: A Systematic Review. *PLoS One, 10*(9), 136–545. doi:10.1371/journal.pone.0136545 PMID:26340679

Sanjaya, B. (2021). *What's going wrong with India's Act East Policy.* Retrieved from https://indianexpress.com

Sankhe. (2020). *India's turning point: An economic agenda to spur growth and jobs.* McKinsey Global Institute. Retrieved from https://www.mckinsey.com/featured-insights/india/indias-turning-point-an-economic-agenda-to-spur-growth-and-jobs

Sardar, T., Nadim, S. S., Rana, S., & Chattopadhyay, J. (2020). Assessment of lockdown effect in some states and overall India: A predictive mathematical study on COVID-19 outbreak. *Chaos, Solitons, and Fractals, 139,* 110078. doi:10.1016/j.chaos.2020.110078 PMID:32834620

Sarin, V. (2017). An analysis of India's Export Competitiveness in context of AIFTA. *International Journal of Commerce and Management, 11*(2), 32–56.

Sarkar, K. (2021, June 8). *CNBC18.* Retrieved from www.cnbc18.com

Sarma, A., & Mehta, P. K. (2003). Indo-Asean Trade Prospects: A Study of Trade Complementarity. In F. Grare & A. Mattoo (Eds.), *Beyond the Rhetoric: The Economics of India's Look East Policy.* Manohar Publications.

Saxena, S., & Bhadauriya, S. (2012). India and BIMSTEC: An Analysis of India's Trade Performance & Prospects. *Business Analyst: A Refereed Journal of Shri Ram College of Commerce, 33*(1), 103-114.

Schedneck, C. B. (2020). *Buddhist Tourism in Asia.* University of Hawai'i Press.

Schemes | Department for Promotion of Industry and Internal Trade | MoCI | GoI. (2017). http://dipp.nic.in/Schemes/DMIC/

Schiff, M., & Winters, A. L. (2003). *Regional Integration and Development.* The World Bank.

Schulte, J., Nolt, J., Williams, R. L., Spinks, C. L., & Hellsten, J. (1998). Violence and threats of violence experienced by public health field-workers. *Journal of the American Medical Association, 280*(5), 439–442. doi:10.1001/jama.280.5.439 PMID:9701079

Sequeira, T. N., & Maçãs, N. P. (2008). Does tourism influence economic growth? A dynamic panel data approach. *Applied Economics, 40*(18), 2431–2441. doi:10.1080/00036840600949520

Shan, J., & Sun, F. (1998). On The Export-led Growth Hypothesis: The Econometric Evidence from China. *International Journal of Economics and Finance, 1*(1), 341–351.

Sharafuddin, M.A. (2015). Types of Tourism in Thailand. *e-Review of Tourism Research (eTTR),* 210 – 219.

Sharma, A. (2015). Educational Tourism: Strategy for Sustainable Tourism Development with reference of Hadauti and Shekhawati Regions of Rajasthan, India. *Journal of Business Economics and Information Technology,* 1-12.

Sharma, A. (2019). *Indian Economy: An Overview.* Retrieved from https://www.investindia.gov.in/team-india-blogs/indian-economy-overview

Sharma, A., & Rathore, C. K. (2015). BIMSTEC and BCIM Initiatives and their Importance for India. *CUTS International*, 1-20.

Sharma, H., & Sharma, R. (2021, Jan 19). Act-East Policy and Future of Northeast India. *The Sentinel*. Retrieved from https://www.sentinelassam.com/editorial/act-east-policy-and-future-of-northeast-india-521374

Sharpley, R., & Sundaram, P. (2005). Tourism: A Sacred Journey? The Case of Ashram Tourism, India. *International Journal of Tourism Research*, *7*(1), 161–171. doi:10.1002/jtr.522

Sheikh, Y. A. (2017). Higher Education in India: Challenges and Opportunities. *Journal of Education and Practice*, *8*(1). https://files.eric.ed.gov/fulltext/EJ1131773.pdf

Sheil, D., & Liswanti, N. (2006). Scoring the importance of tropical forest landscapes with local people: Patterns and insights. *Environmental Management*, *38*(1), 126–136. doi:10.100700267-005-0092-7 PMID:16508796

Shi, X., Yao, L., & Jiang, H. (2019). Regional power connectivity in Southeast Asia: the role of regional cooperation. *Global Energy Interconnection*, *2*(1), 444-456.

Shinde, K., Wee, D-S., Fong, L-K., Xiao, H., Kim, Y-H., & Watanabe, T. (2020). *Buddhist tourism in Asia: towards sustainable development.* doi:10.26181/5fd069becb7de

Shinde, K. A. (2007). Visiting Scared Sites in India: Religious Tourism or Pilgrimage? In R. Raj & N. D. Morpeth (Eds.), *Religious Tourism and Pilgrimage Management: An International Perspective* (pp. 170–183). CAB International. doi:10.1079/9781845932251.0184

Shringla, H. V. (2018). India–Bangladesh Relations: An Indian Perspective. *Strategic Analysis*, *42*(5), 524–528. doi:10.1080/09700161.2018.1523080

Shukla, R. (2021, March 22). India emerging as the next best destination for medical tourism post-COVID-19 pandemic. *Financial Express*.

Sinclair, M. T. (1998). Tourism and economic development: A survey. *The Journal of Development Studies*, *34*(5), 1–51. doi:10.1080/00220389808422535

Singapore Medical Association. (2010). *Violence in the workplace: Survey on the experience of doctors in Singapore*. Retrieved from https://news.sma.org.sg/4211/Violence.pdf

Singh, M. (2005). *Prime Minister Dr. Manmohan Singh's Haksar Memorial Conference Speech*. Retrieved from http://www.indianembassy.org/press_release/2005/Nov/11.htm

Singh, A. (2018). *The Nautical Dimension of India's "Act East" Policy Report*. School of International Studies, Nanyang Technological University.

Singh, K. (2019). India's Regional Cooperation Option: A Comparative Study of BIMSTEC and SAARC. *Political Discourse*, *5*(2), 183–194. doi:10.5958/2582-2691.2019.00006.3

Singh, K., Kumar, R., & Kumar, P. (2016). Strategic issues in pharmaceutical supply chains: A review. *International Journal of Pharmaceutical and Healthcare Marketing*, *10*(3), 234–257. doi:10.1108/IJPHM-10-2015-0050

Sinha, S. (2021, June 26). *Some hotels in India up for sale*. TNN.

Smith, A. (1776). *An inquiry into the nature and causes of the wealth of nations* (Vol. 1). Cosimo.

Smith, M., & Kelley, C. (2006). Wellness Tourism. *Tourism Recreation Research*, *31*(1), 1–4. doi:10.1080/02508281.2006.11081241

Smith, R., Chanda, R., & Tangcharoensathien, V. (2009). Trade-in health-related services. *Lancet*, *373*(9663), 593–601. doi:10.1016/S0140-6736(08)61778-X PMID:19167053

Smriti. (2017). India can be reliable and a better source of fibers for ASEAN. *The Pioneer*. https://www.dailypioneer.com/business-and-finance/india-can-be-reliable-source-of-fibres-forasean-smriti-irani.html

Srichampa, S. (2015). Globalisation and the Language Situation in Thailand. *Journal of Language and Linguistics*. Available at https://www.researchgate.net/profile/Sophana-Srichampa/publication/284148708_Globalisation_and_the_Language_Situation_in_Thailand/links/564c576e08aeab8ed5e877d8/Globalisation-and-the-Language-Situation-in-Thailand.pdf

Strachan, A. L., Kang, H. K., & Sinha, T. (2009, Oct.). *India's Look East Policy: A Critical Assessment. Interview with Amb. Rajiv Sikri*. IPCS Special Report. Retrieved from https://www.files.ethz.ch/isn/108694/SR85-SEARPInterview-Sikri.pdf

Stratton, W., & Yi-Wei, T. (2020). An outbreak of pneumonia of unknown etiology in Wuhan, China: The mystery and the miracle. *Medical Virology*, 401-402.

Subash, T. (2015, Dec.). Tourism in India: Potentials, Challenges and Opportunities. *International Journal of Research and Analytical Reviews, 2*(4).

Sumarniasih, M.A. (2019). Role of Tourism in Economy of Bali and Indonesia. *Journal of Tourism and Hospitality Management,* 34 – 54.

Sundararaman, S. (2018). India–ASEAN Relations: 'Acting' East in the Indo-Pacific. *International Studies*, *54*(1-4), 62–81. doi:10.1177/0020881718787575

Suneja, K. (2017). Create value chains with Countries getting EU, US sops: Government to companies. *Economic Times*. https://economictimes.indiatimes.com/news/economy/policy/create-value-chains-with-nations-getting-us-eu-sops-government-to-companies/articleshow/57382370.cms

Suphanchaimat, R. (2017). *Health insurance card scheme" for cross-border migrants in Thailand: responses in policy implementation & outcome evaluation* (Doctoral Dissertation). London School of Hygiene & Tropical Medicine.

Suthiphand, C. (1996). ASEAN-India cooperation in trade and tourism: Trends and prospects. *Journal of Asian Economics*, *7*(4). www.sciencedirect.com

Syed, N. (2020, Sep. 6). *Inside Malaysia Aviation Group's employee well-being strategy HRD*. Retrieved from https://www.hcamag.com/asia/specialisation/employee-engagement/inside-malaysia-aviation-groups-employee-well-being-strategy/232350

Talavera, S. (2020, March 10). DOT Pushes through Campaign to encourage more domestic tourists. *Phil Star Global*.

Tandon, A. (2016). India's Foreign Policy Priorities and the Emergence of a Modi Doctrine. *Strategic Analysis*, *40*(5), 349–356. doi:10.1080/09700161.2016.1209909

Tangcharoensathien, V., Mills, A., & Palu, T. (2015). Accelerating health equity: The key role of universal health coverage in the SGDs. *BMC Medicine*, *13*(1), 1. doi:10.118612916-015-0342-3 PMID:25925656

Tangcharoensathien, V., Thwin, A., & Patcharanarumol, W. (2017). Implementing health insurance for migrants, Thailand. *Bulletin of the World Health Organization*, *95*(2), 146–151. doi:10.2471/BLT.16.179606 PMID:28250516

Tatoğlu, F. Y. (2013). *Panel veri ekonometrisi*. Beta Yayıncılık.

Taz, B. (2020). *The Look East Policy/Act East Policy-driven Development Model in Northeast India*. Retrieved from https://journal.sagepub.com

Tella, R. D., & Savedoff, W. (2001). *Diagnosis corruption: fraud in Latin America's public hospitals*. Inter-American Development Bank.

The Economic Times. (2018). India to increase public health spending. Retrieved from India to increase public health spending to 2.5% of GDP: PM Modi. *The Economic Times*.

The Economic Times. (2019, June 24). *26,200 km length of economic corridors to be developed under "Bharatmala Pariyojana"*. Retrieved from https://auto.economictimes.indiatimes.com/news/industry/26200-km-length-of-economic-corridors-to-be-developed-under-bharatmala-pariyojana/69928449

The Economic Times. (2020). *India to spend $27 billion over 5 years to boost manufacturing*. Retrieved from https://auto.economictimes.indiatimes.com/news/industry/india-to-spend-27-billion-over-5-years-to-boost-manufacturing/79171904

The Economic Times. (2021). *BIMSTEC emerged as a promising regional grouping, says Prime Minister Modi*. Retrieved from https://economictimes.indiatimes.com/news/india/bimstec-emerged-as-a-promising-regional-grouping-says-prime-minister-modi/articleshow/83287601.cms?utm_source=

The RCEP Conundrum: Japan Awaits India's Return. (n.d.). Retrieved August 30, 2021, from https://thediplomat.com/2021/08/the-rcep-conundrum-japan-awaits-indias-return/

The Times of India. (2016, Oct 4). International Buddhist Conclave 2016 opens in Sarnath. Retrieved from International Buddhist Conclave-2016 opens in Sarnath. *Times of India*.

The White House. (2021, June 12). *Fact Sheet: President Biden and G7 Leaders Launch Build Back Better World (B3W) Partnership*. The White House. https://www.whitehouse.gov/briefing-room/statements-releases/2021/06/12/fact-sheet-president-biden-and-g7-leaders-launch-build-back-better-world-b3w-partnership/

The World Bank. (n.d.). Available at https://tcdata360.worldbank.org/indicators/tot.direct.emp?country=IND&indicator=24644&countries=THA&viz=line_chart&years=1995,2028

Thomas, C. J. (2020). Revitalising BIMSTEC through Cultural Connectivity from Northeast India. *ORF Issue Brief*, (405).

Timothy, D. J., & Olsen, D. H. (2018). Religious routes, pilgrim trails: Spiritual pathways as tourism resources. In Tourism and Religion: Issues and Implications (pp. 220-235). Channel View Publications.

Timothy, D. J., & Olsen, D. H. (2006). Conclusion: Whither Religious Tourism? In D. J. Timothy & D. H. Olsen (Eds.), *Tourism, Religion & Spiritual Journeys* (pp. 271–278). Routledge. doi:10.4324/9780203001073-29

Tinbergen, J. (1962). *Shaping the world economy: Suggestions for an international economic policy*. The Twentieth Century Fund.

Tisdell, C. A., & Roy, K. C. (Eds.). (1998). *An Overview of Tourism in India's Economic Development*. Nova Science Publishers.

Tiwari, A. K. (2011, June). Tourism, Exports and FDI as a Means of Growth: Evidence from four Asian Countries. *The Romanian Economic Journal, 14*(40).

Tourism India. (2021). *Sarnath Buddhism Pilgrimage - Tourist Attractions in Sarnath*. tourmyindia.com

Tourist Project. (2020). *Proceedings of the TOURIST 2nd Cross-Border Conference "Sustainable tourism development: Lessons learned for South East Asian countries"*. Available at https://www.researchgate.net/profile/Nirundon-Tapachai/publication/350978728_2nd_TOURIST_Conference_-_Sustainable_Tourism_-_Shaping_a_Better_Future_20-21_July_2020_Bangkok_Thailand/links/607dd187881fa114b414b241/2nd-TOURIST-Conference-Sustainable-Tourism-Shaping-a-Better-Future-20-21-July-2020-Bangkok-Thailand.pdf#page=387

Towards a Quad-Plus Arrangement? (2020). *PerthUSAsia.* https://perthusasia.edu.au/our-work/towards-a-quad-plus-arrangement

Towhid, S. K., & Kiyoto, K. (2019). Impact of Trade Openness on Economic Growth: Evidences from BIMSTEC Countries. 社会システム研究, (39), 65-81.

Trading Economics. (2021). *Macroeconomic Indicators. Retrieved from Economic Indicators | List by Country.* trading-economics.com

Transparency International. (2015). *Bangladesh: overview of corruption and anti-corruption with a focus on the health sector.* Berlin: Transparency International. Retrieved from https://www.u4.no/publications/bangladesh-overviewof-corruption-and-anticorruption-with-a-focus-on-the-health-sector

Travel Website. (2021). *The Train - Buddhist Circuit Tourist Train.* buddhisttrainindia.com

Tumbarello, P. (2005). *Regional trade integration and WTO accession: Which is the right sequencing? An application to the CIS.* IMF Working Paper, WP/05/94.

Turner, L. (2007). First world healthcare at third-world prices: Globalization, bioethics, and medical tourism. *Biosocieties, 2*(3), 303–325. doi:10.1017/S1745855207005765

UN Population Division World population prospects. (2008). *The revised population database.* https://esa.un.org/unpp/index.asp?panel=2

UNESCO. (2019). http:// whc.unesco.org/en/list/1551

UNESCO. (2020). *Properties inscribed on the World Heritage List.* Available at http://whc.unesco.org/en/statesparties/IN

UN-Habitat. (2006). *State of the World's Cities: The Millennium Goals and Urban Sustainability.* Earthscan.

United Nations Department of Economic and Social Affairs. (2012). *World Population Prospects.* Retrieved from https://esa.un.org/wpp/Excel-Data/population.htm

United Nations SDG India. (2019). *SDG India Index & Dashboard 2019-2020.* Available at https://niti.gov.in/sites/default/files/2019-12/SDG-India-Index-2.0_27-Dec.pdf

United Nations. (2008). *The Right to Health. Composition of macro geographical (continental) regions, geographical sub-regions, and selected economic and other groupings.* Fact Sheet-31, UN Statistic Division. Retrieved from http://unstats.un.org/unsd/methods/m49/m49regin.htm#asia

United Nations. (2019). *Sustainable Development Goals and Agenda.* Available at https://www.un.org/sustainabledevelopment/development-agenda/

United Nations. (2021). *The 17 Sustainable Development Goals.* Author.

United Nations. (2021). *The 17 Sustainable Development Goals.* un.org

United Nations. (2021, August 24). *Country profiles.* Retrieved from UN Data: https://data.un.org/default.aspx

UNWTO. (2017a). Retrieved from https://www.unwto.org/archive/europe/event/international-congress-religious-tourism-and-pilgrimage

UNWTO. (2017b). *Tourism can protect and promote religious heritage.* Retrieved from https://www.frh-europe.org/unwto-tourism-can-protect-and-promote-religious-heritage

UNWTO. (2020). *International Tourism Highlights 2020 Edition.* Available at https://www.e-unwto.org/doi/pdf/10.18111/9789284422456

UNWTO. (2020). *World Tourism Barometer*. Retrieved from www.unwto.org

UNWTO. (2021, June 2). *World Tourism Barometer and Statistical Annex*. Retrieved from https://www.unwto.org/news/tourist-numbers-down-83-but-confidence-slowly-rising

US-ASEAN Business Council | About CPTPP and RCEP. (n.d.). *US-ASEAN Business Council*. https://www.usasean.org/regions/tpp/about

Uthayakumar, R., & Priyan, S. (2013). Pharmaceutical supply chain and inventory management strategies: Optimization for a pharmaceutical company and a hospital. *Operations Research for Health Care*, *2*(3), 52–64.

Van Mulekom, L., Axelsson, A., Batungbacal, E. P., Baxter, D., Siregar, R., & De la Torre, I. (2006). Trade and export orientation of fisheries in Southeast Asia: Under-priced export at the expense of domestic food security and local economies. *Ocean and Coastal Management*, *49*(9-10), 546–561. doi:10.1016/j.ocecoaman.2006.06.001

Varghese, P. (2018). *Indian Economic Strategy 2035*. Department of Foreign Affairs and Trade. Retrieved from https://dfat.gov.au/geo/india/ies/index.html

Varghese, P. (2018). *Indian Economic Strategy 2035*. Department of Foreign Affairs and Trade. Retrieved from https://dfat.gov.au/geo/india/ies/index.html

Vecchio, N., Davies, D., & Rohde, N. (2018). The effect of inadequate access to healthcare services on emergency room visits. A comparison between physical and mental health conditions. *PLoS One*, *13*(8), 202–559. doi:10.1371/journal.pone.0202559 PMID:30138438

Veeramani, C., & Saini, G. K. (2010). Impact of ASEAN-India FTA on India's plantation commodities: A simulation analysis. *Indira Gandhi Institute of Development Research Working Paper, 4*, 1–20.

Venkat, V. (2017). Will Budget help double farmers' income. *The Hindu*. Retrieved from https://www.thehindu.com/business/agri-business/Will-Budget-help-double-farmers%E2%80%99-income/article17198101.ece

Vian, T. (2008). Review of corruption in the health sector: Theory, methods, and interventions. *Health Policy (Amsterdam)*, *23*(2), 83–94. PMID:18281310

Vian, T., & Burak, L. (2006). Beliefs about informal payments in Albania. *Health Policy and Planning*, *21*(5), 392–401. doi:10.1093/heapol/czl022 PMID:16940304

Vidauskaite, R. (2009). *Destination branding through wedding tourism: The case of the Caribbean* [Master thesis]. University of Ljubljana, EMTM Universities.

Vinor, J. (1950). *The Customs Union Issue*. Cornegie Endowment for International Peace.

Von Neumann & Morgenstern. (2007). *Theory of games and economic behavior*. Princeton University Press.

Vukonic, B. (1996). *Tourism and Religion* (S. Matesic, Trans.). Oxford Pergamon Press.

Wall, G., & Mathieson, A. (2006). *Tourism: Change, Impact and Opportunities*. Pearson Education Limited.

Wapmuk, S. (2015). The Role of India in Regionalism: SAARC, ASEAN, EU, BIMSTEC, IOR-ARC, and MGC: Lessons for Nigeria in the ECOWAS. *IUP Journal of International Relations, 9*(1).

Weed, M., & Bull, C. (2014, November). Influences on Sport-Tourism Relations in Britain: The Effects of Government Policy. *Tourism Recreation Research*, *22*(2), 5–12. Advance online publication. doi:10.1080/02508281.1997.11014796

Westerlund, J., & Wilhelmsson, F. (2011). Estimating the gravity model without gravity using panel data. *Applied Economics, 43*(6), 641–649. doi:10.1080/00036840802599784

What the Taliban takeover of Afghanistan means for India and Pakistan. (2021, August 21). *The Economist.* https://www.economist.com/asia/2021/08/21/what-the-taliban-takeover-of-afghanistan-means-for-india-and-pakistan

WHO. (2020). *Coronavirus declared global health emergency by WHO.* Retrieved from https://www.bbc.com/news/world-51318246 https://www.who.int/countries/bgd/

Wibulpolprasert, A., Sittichanbuncha, Y., Sricharoen, P., Borwornsrisuk, S., & Sawanyawisuth, K. (2014). Factors associated with overcrowded emergency rooms in Thailand: A medical school setting. *Emergency Medicine International, 2014*, 1–4. Advance online publication. doi:10.1155/2014/576259 PMID:25328708

Wibulpolprasert, S., & Pengpaibon, P. (2003). Integrated strategies to tackle the inequitable distribution of doctors in Thailand: Four decades of experience. *Human Resources for Health, 1*(12), 12. doi:10.1186/1478-4491-1-12 PMID:14641940

Wijayasiri, J. (2016). Challenges to a BIMSTEC Free Trade Agreement (FTA): A Sri Lankan Perspective. *Cooperative Partnership and Sustainable Development, 101.*

Wijayasiri, J., & De Mel, D. (2008). *BIMSTEC-Japan Cooperation in Trade and Investment: A Sri Lankan Perspective.* Centre for Studies in International Relations and Development (CSIRD) Discussion Paper, 38.

Wiriyapong, N. (2021, June 28). All eyes on the sandbox. *The Bangkok Post.*

Without RCEP, India's Indo-Pacific And North-East Vision Unattainable. (n.d.). *Moneycontrol.* Retrieved August 30, 2021, from https://www.moneycontrol.com/news/opinion/without-rcep-indias-indo-pacific-and-north-east-vision-unattainable-7132911.html

Wojczewski, T. (2019). Identity and world order in India's post-Cold War foreign policy discourse. *Third World Quarterly, 40*(1), 180–198. doi:10.1080/01436597.2018.1552079

World Bank. (2016). *Hospital Beds (per 1,000 people).* World Health Organization.

World Bank. (2021a). *Bhutan Economic Profile.* Retrieved from https://www.worldbank.org/en/country/bhutan/overview

World Bank. (2021b). *Bangladesh Economic Profile.* Retrieved from https://www.worldbank.org/en/country/bangladesh/overview

World Bank. (2021c). *India Economic Profile.* Retrieved from https://www.worldbank.org/en/country/india

World Bank. (2021d). *Myanmar Economic Profile.* Retrieved from https://www.worldbank.org/en/country/myanmar/overview

World Bank. (2021e). *Sri Lanka Economic Profile.* Retrieved from https://www.worldbank.org/en/country/srilanka

World Bank. (2021f). *Nepal Economic Profile.* Retrieved from https://www.worldbank.org/en/country/nepal

World Bank. (2021g). *Thailand Economic Profile.* Retrieved from https://www.worldbank.org/en/country/thailand

World Data Atlas. (n.d.). Available at https://knoema.com/atlas/topics/Tourism/Travel-and-Tourism-Total-Contribution-to-GDP/Contribution-of-travel-and-tourism-to-GDP-percent-of-GDP

World Health Organization. (2021). Retrieved from http://who.int/violence_ injury_prevention/violence/activities/workplace/WVsynthesisreport. pdf?ua=1&ua=1

World Health Organization. (2021). *WHO Coronavirus (COVID-19) Dashboard.* Retrieved from https://covid19.who.int/

World Healthcare Outlook. (2013). *Economist intelligence unit*. Author.

World Tourism Organization (UNWTO). (n.d.). *Tourism dashboard*. Retrieved from https://www.unwto.org/unwto-tourismdashboard

World Travel & Tourism Council. (2019). *Travel & Tourism: Global Economic Impact & Trends*. Available at https://ambassade-ethiopie.fr/onewebmedia/Tourism-WTTC-Global-Economic-Impact-Trends-2019.pdf

World Travel & Tourism Council. (2020, Mar. 23). *COVID-19 Related Policy Shifts Supportive of Travel & Tourism Sector*. Retrieved from www.wttc.org

World Travel and Tourism Council (WTTC). (2021). *Research reveals global Travel & Tourism sector suffered a loss*. Retrieved from https://wttc.org/News-Article/Global-TandT-sector-suffered-a-loss-of-almost-US4-trillion-in-2020

Worldometer. (2021). *Countries in the world by population*. Available at https://www.worldometers.info/world-population/population-by-country/

Worldometer. (2021, June 29). Retrieved from https://www.worldometers.info/coronavirus/country/myanmar/

WTO | Regional trade agreements. (n.d.). http://rtais.wto.org/UI/publicPreDefRepByCountry.aspx

WTTC. (2018). *Travel & Tourism Economic Impact*. Retrieved from https://www. wttc.org/-/media/files/reports/economic-impact-research/regions-2018/world2018.pdf

Xavier, C. (2018). *Bridging The Bay of Bengal: Toward a stronger BIMSTEC*. Carnegie Endowment for International Peace.

Xavier, C., & Sinha, R. (2020). Regional Connectivity and India's BIMSTEC Policy. National Security. *Vivekananda International Foundation*, *III*(1), 34–51.

Yahya, F. (2005). BIMSTEC and emerging patterns of Asian regional and interregional cooperation. *Australian Journal of Political Science*, *40*(3), 391–394. doi:10.1080/10361140500203936

Yasuda, S., Raj, R., & Griffin, K. (Eds.). (2018). *Religious Tourism in Asia: Tradition and Change through Case Studies and Narratives*. CABI International. doi:10.1079/9781786392343.0000

Yeganeh, H. (2019). An Analysis of Emerging Patterns of Consumption in the Age of Globalization and Digitalization. *FIIB Business Review*, *8*(4), 259–270. Advance online publication. doi:10.1177/2319714519873748

Yhome, K. (2015). From "Look East" to "Act East": What it. *Eastern Quarterly, 2*(1-2), 27. https://www.researchgate.net/publication/311774304

Yhome, K. (2015). From "Look East" to "Act East": What it Means for India's Northeast? *Eastern Quarterly*, *11*(1-2), 18–29.

Yogesh Hole, E. B. (2019). Challenges and solutions to the development of the tourism and hospitality industry in India. *African Journal of Hospitality, Tourism and Leisure*, 1–11.

Yousuf, A., & Lal, R. (2013, Sep.). The Impact of ASEAN on Tourism. *International Journal of Networking & Parallel Computing, 2*(3).

Zaman, S., & Hossain, N. (2017). Universal Health Coverage: A Burning Need for Developing Countries. *Journal of Medical Research and Innovation*, *1*(1), 18–20. doi:10.15419/jmri.41

Zapata, T., Buchan, J., Tangcharoensathien, V., Meliala, A., Karunathilake, I., Tin, N., Nandi, S., Tobgay, T., & Noree, T. (2020). Rural retention strategies in the South-East Asia Region: Evidence to guide effective implementation. *Bulletin of the World Health Organization*, *98*(11), 815–817. doi:10.2471/BLT.19.245662 PMID:33177780

Zhang, J. (2018). To Brand Gandhara, the Ancient Buddhist Centre: Pakistan's potential to develop Buddhist tourism. In S. Yasuda, R. Raj, & K. Griffin (Eds.), *Religious Tourism in Asia: Tradition and Change Through Case Studies and Narratives* (p. 127). CABI Publishers. doi:10.1079/9781786392343.0127

Ziipao, R. R. (2018). Look/Act East Policy, Roads and Market Infrastructure in North-East India. *Strategic Analysis, 42*(5), 476–489. doi:10.1080/09700161.2018.1523082

Zipf, G. K. (1946). The P_1P_2/D hypothesis: On the intercity movement of persons. *American Sociological Review, 11*(6), 677–686. doi:10.2307/2087063

Zubedi, S. P. (2013). India's new bilateral investment promotion and protection treaty with Nepal: A new trend in state practice. *ICSID Review, 28*(2), 384–404. doi:10.1093/icsidreviewit027

Zulafqar,, A.A. (2009). *North East India and India's Act East Policy: A Critical Review*. Research Gate.

Zulfkar, A. (2019, September). India's Act East Policy and North East India. A Critical Review. *International Journal of Research in Social Sciences, 9*(9). Retrieved from file:///C:/Users/h.kaur/Downloads/IndiasActEastPolicyandNorth-EastIndia.pdf

About the Contributors

S. Jobayear Ahmed is a Deputy Manager, Monitoring, Evaluation and Research in BRAC Urban Development Program. He possesses extensive research experience on International Trade, Business Model and Market Development, Financial Inclusion, Public Private Partnership, Human Security and Disaster Risk Reduction. He studied Entrepreneurship Economics, Business, Japanese Studies and Law from Dhaka School of Economics, Institute of Business Administration (IBA) and Department of Japanese Studies in Dhaka University, Bangladesh University of Professionals and Bangladesh Open University. He also studied Japanese Language and Culture in Sophia University, Tokyo, Japan.

Jyotsana Bhangu is post graduate student at Mittal School of Business (#MHRD NIRF India Rank 38; #ACBSP USA, Accredited), Lovely Professional University, Phagwara, Punjab(India). Her expertise areas like International Economics and Development Economics. She has published his research ideas in journals and attended various workshops and conference in area of International Economics and Econometrics. She has published research paper in UGC care List- Our Heritage.

Munish Duggal holds Master's degrees from India and the United Kingdom and Doctorate in Economics from India. He belongs to prestigious Indian Economic Service since 1986 and has occupied key economic positions in the various Economic Ministries of Indian Federal Government Prior to joining Indian Economic Service, he handled teaching assignments for about 3 years. His academic orientation got him various international assignments in the United Nations and UNDP during 1999 to 2004. He worked as a Dean of the Civil Service Academy in Timor Leste. During 34 years of his career, he has travelled extensively to over 25 countries from 6 continents and this wide experience is reflected in his writings and policy prescriptions.

Manisha Goswami is working in GLA University, Mathura in the capacity of Assistant Professor and has been awarded with the best teacher. University Grant Commission of India has also awarded her with Junior Research Fellowship. She has published several papers in national and international journal of repute indexed in SCOPUS and Google Scholar. Her domain of interest are Strategic Human Resources Management like Psychological Contract, Emotional Intelligence, Employer Branding, Employee Engagement, Gig Economy.

Farooq Haq is an Associate Professor and Coordinator for MBA and BBA Programs in Faculty of Management at the Canadian University Dubai. He received his PhD from Charles Darwin University in Australia in 2011. His research interests are in various types of special interest tourism such as spiritual and heritage tourism. He is also among the early researchers of Islamic Marketing, halal branding and marketing of Islamic products and services. He has several publications as journal articles, conference papers and book chapters in his areas of research.

Namita Kapoor is a Professor (Assistant) at Amity University with 22 years of teaching and research experience in Market Research, Mathematical Economics, Managerial Economics and Econometrics. As a facilitator, mentor and coach, she has conducted Faculty Development Programmes in the area of Questionnaire Designing ,Multivariate Analysis, Data Analytics, Business Analytics and many more.

Gurpreet Kaur is currently Assistant Professor at Mittal School of Business (#MHRD NIRF India Rank 38; #ACBSP USA, Accredited), Lovely Professional University, Phagwara, Punjab (India). Dr. Kaur received his PhD degree in Economics, Lovely Professional University, Punjab, India and received UGC research fellowship (ID-MANF-2012-13-SIK-PUN-10414). Have an analytical bent of mind with good experience in analyzing academic data and handling Curriculum Development. Her expertise entails areas like International Economics, regional trade agreements and finance, and Econometric Models. She has published her research ideas in journals, edited book, conference proceedings in the areas of International Economics and finance and econometrics Models. She has presented several papers in International and National level seminars and participated in various workshops and FDP's. She has published 15 research papers in Journals (International and National) and 04 chapters in refereed edited books (Scopus Listed), attended 13 national and international conferences. She is an editor of international book published by IGI Global on Regional trade and developments strategies in the era of globalization. She has guided 7 M.Sc. dissertation students and 7 Ph.D research-scholars.

Annanya Mohanty is working with Daedal-Research is a research and consulting firm specialized in providing research reports and customized business research and analysis. She is a quick learner and has the ability to rapidly achieve organization, assume job responsibilities and adapt to new methods and technologies. She has proven ability to work efficiently in both independent and team environments.

Ayberk Şeker is an Assistant Professor with a demonstrated history of working in the International Trade, International Finance and Internatinoal Logistics at Bursa Technical University. Skilled in Innovation and Technology Management, High-Technology Exports, Economic Integration, International Trade Organizations and Import-Export Management. He did his graduation from Yıldız Technical University, Bachelors Degree in Political Science and International Relations, Istanbul, Turkey; University of Yalova, M.A. and Ph.D in International Trade and Finance, Yalova, Turkey.

Ayasha Siddika is teaching in Higher Education in the discipline of Business for more than twelve years. Educational background includes MBA in HR, Grad. Dip. in Business Administration, M.Com. in Management, B.Com. (hons) in Management. She also completed advanced diploma degrees in Leadership & Management, Communication and Marketing. Prior to teaching, she worked in Business Organisations and managed her own business. Her hobbies are reading philosophy, watching movies & documentaries, and listening to music.

Tavishi Tewary has over 11 years of experience in policy research and trade impact assessment. She has published various research papers in international journals of high repute. She has also conducted FDPs on data Analysis using SPSS. She has academic experience teaching postgraduate business school students for the past 11 years. Currently, she is working as an Assistant Professor in Jaipuria Institute of Management , Uttar Pradesh.

Index

A

B

C

D

E

F

G

H

I

J

L

M

N

O

P

Q

R

S

T

V

W

www.ingramcontent.com/pod-product-compliance
Lightning Source LLC
LaVergne TN
LVHW081250011026
849162LV00006BA/1401